ALTO

Straight Life

Art Pepper

D1274982

Straight Life

The Story of Art Pepper

UPDATED EDITION

by Art and Laurie Pepper

Introduction by Gary Giddins

Discography by Todd Selbert

DA CAPO PRESS

First Da Capo Press edition 1994

This Da Capo Press paperback edition of *Straight Life* is an
unabridged republication of the edition published in New York
in 1979, with the addition of a new introduction by Gary Giddins,
a new afterword by Laurie Pepper, and a new discography by
Todd Selbert. It is reprinted by arrangement with Laurie Pepper.

5 6 7 8 9 10   0201

Published by Da Capo Press, Inc.
A member of the Perseus Books Group

Library of Congress Cataloging in Publication Data

Pepper, Art, 1925–
  Straight life: the story of Art Pepper / by Art and Laurie Pepper;
introduction by Gary Giddins; discography by Todd Selbert.
—Updated ed.
    p.   cm.
  Originally published: New York: Schirmer Books, c1979.
  Discography: p.
  Includes index.
  ISBN 0-306-80558-8 (pbk.)
  1. Pepper, Art, 1925–   . 2. Saxophonists—United States—Biog-
raphy. I. Pepper, Laurie. II. Title.
ML419.P48A3 1994
788.7'3165'092—dc20   93-41700
[B]   CIP

Introduction to the Da Capo edition

ART PEPPER always had a distinctive sound, even back in 1943, when he made his recording debut with a halting solo on a Stan Kenton session: cool on the surface, with a skittish undercurrent that often made the prettiness seem restive. In the nearly forty years he made records, his style became increasingly personal—by turns bitter and timorous, knowing and scared. For a while, when he consciously imitated John Coltrane, his sound became icily strident. That phase didn't last long: the nature of his introspection didn't lend itself to Coltrane's steely embouchure or his effusiveness. At his best, Pepper's solos were shaped by a patient elegance, his phrases sculpted with dynamic logic and an even disposition. He had a miraculous ear for melody notes and a rhythmic sense that was all but imperturbable; he modulated the intensity of his swing to drive home the meaning of his melodies. He could make you laugh at his virtuoso conceits and weep at his unrequited passions.

But juxtaposing *Straight Life,* Pepper's brazen and unvarnished autobiography, with his playing merely points up the perils of reading too much meaning in music. The loveliness, ingenuity, and commitment to craft in his recordings finds few correlatives in the confused, tormented persona that emerges in the book. Indeed, it seems remarkable that the music was possible at all.

The lives of few artists have been told as comprehensively as Art Pepper's—*Straight Life* is almost fanatically confessional, and one of the finest of all jazz autobiographies. I've always regretted that it was originally published by a firm associated with music (Schirmer) and marketed accordingly, because it received insufficient attention from mainstream media. At the time of publication, Pepper was compared with Henry Miller, Jack Kerouac, and Malcolm X. Dan Wakefield, who knows what addiction is and how to write about it, welcomed *Straight Life* as "an honest and wrenching portrayal"; Whitney Balliett credited Pepper with "the ear and memory and interpretive lyricism of a first-rate novelist."

Because *Straight Life* was not written from the perspective of the *former* addict, it is a departure in the genre of tape-recorded accounts of junkie jazz musicians: "That's what I practiced," Pepper writes, "And that's what I still am. And that's what I will die as—a junkie." He makes no attempt to cosmeticize his criminal tendencies or iron out the numerous contradictions. Nor is the reader primed to admire Pepper, who whines, justifies, patronizes, and vilifies. Still, his scrupulous honesty and uncommon powers of observation are admirable, and this is a brave, valuable book. Pepper's narcissism allows him to go overboard occasionally with intimate revelations; yet it also permits him to summon up events with uncanny detail not only in recounting what happened but in recreating his emotional responses.

Art Pepper was born in 1925, in California, to a merchant seaman and his fifteen-year-old wife. He was so sickly his family didn't expect him to survive; when his parents divorced, he was placed in the care of his paternal grandmother—"a dumpy woman, strong, unintelligent. She knew no answers to any problems I might have." He grew up afraid of everything and resentful of his family. When he became a cog in the prison system, he adopted those very characteristics he despised in his grandmother to prove his strength: "I had to be tough. I had to ridicule anything that indicated weakness." His arrests followed his surrender to heroin, which he insists provided the only relief from sexual obsessions that had turned him into an obsessive masturbator, a rapist, a voyeur. In *Straight Life*, he recounts sexual exploits with the relish of a pornographer.

He turned to alcohol and pot to rid himself of anxieties, but nothing worked until a woman band singer cajoled him into a hotel john, taught him to sniff smack, and made a bee-line for his fly. "I finally found peace," he says, and yet it is the peace that passeth liberal understanding: in a minute, he's ranging like a John Wayne reactionary, switching his hero worship from musicians to junkies:

I looked at myself in the mirror and I looked at Sheila [a pseudonym for the singer] and I looked at the few remaining lines of heroin and I took the dollar bill and horned the rest of them down. I said, "This is it. This is the only answer for me. If this is what it takes, then this is what I'm going to do, whatever dues I have to pay. . . . " And I *knew* that I would go to prison and that I wouldn't be weak; I wouldn't be an informer like all the phonies, the no-account, the non-real, the zero people that roam around, the scum that slither out from under rocks, the people that destroyed music, that destroyed this country, that destroyed the world, the rotten, fucking, lousy people that for their own little ends—the black power people, stinking motherfuckers that play on the fact that they're black, and all this fucking shit that happened later on—the rotten, no-account filthy women that have no feeling for anything. . . .

He continues in that vein for a while and concludes, with no trace of irony, "All I can say is, at that moment I saw that I'd found peace of mind."

This is alienation with a trudgeon, a narcissist's ravings. Yet it's a side of a man who in those same years revealed in his music a gentility and generosity of spirit that made him one of the most distinctive and emotive improvisers of his generation. He attempts in his book to justify his indulgences by parading them nakedly, giving and asking for no quarter.

Pepper had already achieved a measure of stardom in the straight world. He'd appeared with Benny Carter's band, and for five years (1946-51), following his stint in the Army, he emerged as the most admired soloist in the Stan Kenton orchestra. Yet he was sinking deeper and deeper into the netherworld. His first marriage broke up, and a second one became a grotesque and vindictive battle between two junkies who tortured each other relentlessly until she informed on him. Then Pepper, who felt more for his long-suffering dog than for his second wife ("The Story of Diane—The Great

Zeeeero"), embarked on a maniacal revenge that was short-circuited, like so much else in his life, by the requirements of his addiction. The music seemed to come last, though it's impossible to suspect that when you hear the fugitive recordings from the early Fifties. In those days, he seems to have chosen as his models Lester Young, Zoot Sims, Charlie Parker, and Lee Konitz—a matrix of hot and cool stylings, girded by fierce rhythms, rich in exquisite harmonies. Still, except for a couple of beguiling Savoy dates and two private sessions with Hampton Hawes, Pepper hardly recorded at all.

Then, in 1956, he started making the rounds as a sideman. He appeared on numerous sessions led by Shorty Rogers, Chet Baker, Marty Paich, Hoagy Carmichael, John Graas, Mel Torme, Barney Kessel, June Christy, Henry Mancini, Andre Previn, Helen Humes, and others. During the same years, 1956 to 1960, he hooked up with Les Koenig's Contemporary Records, and produced a series of masterful albums. Those sessions were a respite, a period of grace. With his lithe, dry-ice sound, he emerged as the sharpest white player in L.A.—a qualitative and racial distinction of profound importance to him. Even in his last years, he wanted nothing less than to be the first white player to loom as "the inspiration for the whole jazz world."

It's astounding to read in *Straight Life* that Art had to be propped up to play on sessions that became epiphanies of the West Coast jazz movement. Pepper's intonation was clear and balmy (on clarinet and tenor as well as alto), but the texts of his solos were shaded with longings. The tensile and deliberated phrasing was a means to a direct and manly emotional expressiveness that was virtually antithetical to the cool posturings of those improvising beach boys who tried to recreate California jazz as fun in the midnight sun. Could he really have been nodding out when those cover photos were taken? He appeared so strong and uncomplicatedly handsome. He recorded his last Contemporary date in November of 1960. Except for a sideman gig eight weeks later, a guest stint with Buddy Rich's orchestra in 1968, and a little-heard featured spot with the Mike Vax Big Band in 1973, Art Pepper disappeared from records and, as far as most people were concerned, from public view for fifteen years.

He had made the big time: San Quentin. Pepper was caught stealing to support his habit, devoting his most creative energies to planning heists, many of which could have been better executed by Laurel and Hardy. (The most satisfying moment of his life, he says, was a successful heist.) The prison sequences in *Straight Life* are among the best I've ever read, vivid and impassioned and stubbornly convinced that the moral life of the yard—where a rapist is treated with contempt, but a gang rape proves a gang's bravery; where a rat is lower than a child molester—is superior to that of the outside. His language and vision superficially resemble that of Gary Gilmore in Mailer's *The Executioner's Song*: both men are proudly homophobic, murderous on the subject of informers, indifferent to the outcome of their crimes, vain, and convinced of their own courage and moral impunity. In San Quentin, Pepper starts thinking "how great it would be to kill someone and really be accepted as a way out guy," but he always, sometimes through the intervention of friends, managed to keep some control; several acquaintances explain it as cowardice. He also turned increasingly racist in jail, a widespread phenomenon that in a particularly lucid moment he traces to the prison system itself. (Paradoxically, this in no way mitigated his conviction that the great jazz players and, indeed, the moral giants of the music were predominantly black.) Upon his release, he spent time in North Beach in San Francisco, seething to kill blacks; he talks about organizing a white vigilante committee "who'd stick up for the white race." Soon enough he returned to heroin to alleviate the hatred over which he had no more control than he did his sexual obsessions.

Finally, at the nadir of his life, he retreated to Synanon. The Sixties were in full gear, and he wore an earring and hit the rock joints with his tenor; but his life was empty and even his mother refused him lodging. The description of life at Synanon is as uncompromising as the jail sequences; he is alternately damning and grateful. The best thing to happen to him there was meeting Laurie, who became his wife, lover, mother, babysitter, manager, editor, and co-author.

Art left Synanon in 1971. Four months later, his father died—a release, Laurie speculates, that may have made it easier for Art to think of himself as a man. He started working as a musician again, playing casuals and clinics, touring colleges, sitting in. But his ambivalence about music remained. In 1977, three events, in Laurie's estimation, forced him to reappraise his gift and his life: In March, he played a concert series in Tokyo with Cal Tjader, and the crowds cheered him as though "he might have been the Beatles"; in June he toured the East Coast for the first time as a leader, playing two dates at the Village Vanguard; in September, he got busted after a car accident that almost killed him. Laurie recalls, "Art discovered then that he couldn't go 'home' again to jail. There was no honor, no welcome there. All his buddies were dead. He was an old man. He wasn't a bigshot. He went through a long spell of depression, aggravated by sobriety and by Les Koenig's death in November. When he went back to Japan with his own band in February of 1978, he'd just about decided to be a musician. Galaxy signed him in September. That did it. That and the publication of *Straight Life*."

Pepper's sudden reappearance in 1975 had been something of a second coming in musical circles. For the next seven years, his frequent recordings and tours, and the publication in 1979 of *Straight Life*, transformed him from a gifted altoist who had made a string of semi-classic albums in the Fifties to a touchstone for the very aesthetics of jazz music. He wasn't merely back; he was back with a vengeance.

What sobered the critics and fans (many of them musicians) about those last years was the aggressiveness of his creativity, a refusal to coast that made every performance a conscientious statement—a "trip," in the prison lingo he favored. If you thought you were going to sit back, sip your whiskey, and drowsily tap your foot, you were in the wrong place. Pepper could draw blood (usually his own), especially on ballads. He was always thinking, thinking, thinking. And he made you think; he reminded you how you came to love this music in the first place.

Armstrong once said, "Jazz is only what you are." Pepper's understanding of that was profound. He had lived a dark, cold life and this was his last stand. He shamelessly set it all out on the table, in writing and in music. He was a drug user, and he put that into his music. He was white in a music in which most of the innovators were black, and he accepted that as a challenge. "It looks to me like life begins at fifty," he wrote, "and I never thought I'd live to see fifty, let alone start a new life at this age." He set up an ambitious agenda for himself (to be the best saxophonist in the world, for starters), and, driven in part by a paranoia that convinced him that everyone wanted him to fail, he found new ways to stretch his endurance. You could hear that in his playing, and it was riveting.

The subject of music is not ignored in *Straight Life*. Pepper discusses his influences at length, his concern with tone, his conviction that a man's music must respect the moral rightness of his life—he gives Miles Davis, John Coltrane, Zoot Sims, Dizzy Gillespie as examples. There's a revealing description of his famous '50s session with Red Garland—I wish there were more of the same—and sharply observed anecdotes about road trips with Kenton, Buddy Rich, and others. His account of a jam session with Sonny Stitt that closes the book is as lyrical a celebration of a bandstand plight as I know of. When he wails like this, Pepper the memoirist isn't too far from Pepper the recording artist.

But it is Laurie Pepper who is responsible for the book's shape and much of its literary texture, and her efforts can hardly be overpraised. Using the standard oral history techniques of modern anthropology, she crafted a brutal montage of voices—relatives, acquaintances, and friends, as well as disingenuous magazine interviews—that amplify and contradict Pepper's steely narrative. She allows Pepper to come through whole, boasting of a crime on one page and declaring absolute innocence on the next. The text is eloquent, witty, and credible. When I reviewed the book for *The Village Voice*, I wrote that Pepper was better than William Burroughs on the subject of drugs and better than Malcolm Braly on prison life, an evaluation that is easier to make today, when neither Burroughs's *Junky* nor Braly's *On the Yard* are as well remembered. But it hardly matters that Laurie Pepper brought the book to life; her ear and editorial instinct turned Art's stories and obsessions into a hellfire narrative. The collaboration was seamless, and every page is wounding and real.

When Art returned to New York in May 1980, he asked me to come by with my copy of *Straight Life* so that he could inscribe it. One of the things he wrote was, "[Thanks] for being so honest in the last article." That was the *Voice* review, in which I had enumerated many of the least appealing aspects of his character, as detailed in his book. He liked people to be polite, but honest. Our first encounter had followed his 1977 debut at the Village Vanguard. I had sat there opening night mesmerized, and then went home to write a reverie in which there were even more egregious puns than the title, "The Whiteness of the Wail." I really didn't know anything about him, except the Contemporary records and some of his own liner comments, and the way he looked and sounded on stage—gaunt and tenuous, compulsively talkative, searing and punchy in his playing—so I was flying by the seat of my pants in speculating about drugs and race and everything else. My essay was more presumptuous than knowledgeable. You can imagine how surprised (and relieved) I was when Laurie called the day it came out in *The Village Voice* and said, "Art wants to meet you. He wants to know how come you know so much about him." It never occurred to me to say: It's all there in his music.

—Gary Giddins

(This introduction incorporates portions of "Art Pepper Talks Straight," from *The Village Voice*, February 18, 1980, and "Endgame," the notes to Art Pepper's *The Complete Galaxy Recordings*, 1989, by permission of the author.)

Gary Giddins, jazz critic for The Village Voice, *is the author of* Riding on a Blue Note, Rhythm-a-Ning, Celebrating Bird, Satchmo, Faces in the Crowd, *and a forthcoming biography of* Bing Crosby.

What is the use of talking and there is no end of talking,
There is no end of things in the heart.

Ezra Pound

For their contributions to this book we wish to thank:

Karolyn April	Jerry Maher
Sarah Bartold	Shelly Manne
Benny Carter	Johnny Martizia
Ann Christos	Don Menza
June Christy	John Noble
Bob Cooper	Millie Noble
Sammy Curtis	Marty Paich
Alan Dean	Thelma Pepper
Hersh Hamel	Marie Randall
John Koenig	Freddy Rivera
Steve Kravitz	Lee Young

Special thanks to Todd Selbert for everything.

Contents

This is a true story, a tape recorded narrative by Art Pepper (and those who've known him) which I have transcribed and edited. In order to avoid embarrassing a number of people, some details have been changed and pseudonyms are occasionally used. Attitudes, intentions, and feelings attributed by Art Pepper to anyone besides himself should be understood by the reader to be Art's impressions, not fact.

—Laurie Pepper

Cast of Characters
(in order of appearance)

Cora Hahn Pepper Noble (Grandma): *Art's paternal grandmother.*
She was responsible for Art's upbringing. Her children were
Arthur Edward Pepper Senior and Richard Pepper (Dicky Boy),
and a stepson, Shorty Noble.

Arthur Edward Pepper (Art Senior, Moses, Daddy, Pop): *Art's
father.* A merchant marine, machinist, fisherman, longshoreman,
union organizer.

Mildred Bartold (Ida Bartold, Mildred Bayard, Millie, Moham):
Art's mother. Art senior's first wife, she married him when she
was fifteen.

Sarah Schecter Bartold: Married Vincent Joseph Bartold and
raised his niece, Ida (Millie), Art's mother.

Thelma Winters Noble Pepper: Married at first to Art Senior's
stepbrother, Shorty, she had three children—John, Bud, and
Edna. Deserted by Shorty, she married Art's father.

John Noble and Mildred (Millie) Moore Noble: Thelma's son and
his wife. Art considered John Noble his cousin.

Johnny Martizia: Introduced Art to improvised music (jazz). He is
still a professional singer and guitarist.

Patti (Madeleine) Moore Pepper: Art's first wife. They were
married in 1943.

Lee Young: Brother of the legendary Lester Young, he has been
active in all aspects of music since childhood and led the band
at the Club Alabam which gave Art his start in jazz. He is now
an executive at Motown Records.

Benny Carter: One of the most respected and prolific figures in jazz. He is a composer, saxophonist, trumpet player, and educator and has written numerous film and television scores. He led a band in 1943 in which Art Pepper played briefly.

Patricia Ellen Pepper: Art's daughter with Patti. She was born in 1945.

Alan Dean: Alan Dean was a pop singer in England during the war years when he met Art. He now lives in Australia, and is still a singer, touring occasionally, as well as a composer, arranger, and producer of television and radio commercials.

Hersh Hamel: Has known Art since the late '40s. He is a bassist living in Los Angeles.

Freddy Rivera: Was one of a group of musicians, which included Art Pepper, who played jam sessions in and around Los Angeles during the late '40s and early '50s. He now teaches at a California college.

June Christy and Bob Cooper: Were "girl singer" and tenor player, respectively, with the Stan Kenton orchestra from the mid to late '40s. Christy is semi-retired although she still sometimes tours and records. Coop is very active in the studios and plays jazz whenever he can.

Sammy Curtis: Was a member of the Stan Kenton orchestra. He prefers that his name and the specifics of his career be withheld.

Shelly Manne: Has been for many years one of the world's finest and most popular jazz drummers. He was a member of the Kenton orchestra during the '50s, ran a nightclub, "Shelly's Manne Hole," in Los Angeles during the '60s and early '70s, has toured extensively with his own groups, has composed scores for television and films, and has been abundantly recorded.

Diane Suriaga Pepper: Art's second wife. They were married in 1957.

John Koenig: Present owner of Contemporary Records and the son of the late Lester Koenig who was Art's mentor and friend, producer of many of Art's finest albums.

Marty Paich: Arranger, composer, pianist. Has recorded in all these capacities under his own name and for numerous popular and jazz artists and has composed scores for television and films.

Steve Kravitz: Reed player, was Art's student in 1960. He is an active studio musician.

Ann Christos: Has been Art's fan and his friend for almost twenty years.

Jerry Maher: Jerry and Art became friends in San Quentin where both were serving sentences.

Marie Randall: The sister of Diane Pepper, Art's second wife.

Christine: Art's lover, 1966–1969.

Don Menza: Was a member of the Buddy Rich band of 1968. He is a composer, plays all saxophones, clarinets and flutes, has toured widely playing jazz, and is a successful studio musician.

Karolyn April: A Synanon alumna and friend.

Laurie LaPan Miller Pepper: Art's third wife. They met in Synanon in 1969, and were married in 1974.

PART 1

1925–1954

1 | Childhood

1925-1939

MY GRANDMOTHER was a strong person. She was a solid German lady. And she never would intentionally have hurt anyone, but she was cold, very cold and unfeeling. She was married at first to my father's father and had two sons, and when he died she remarried. And the man that she married liked her son Richard and didn't like my father whose name was Arthur, the same as mine.

My father's stepfather beat him and just made life hell for him. Richard was the good guy; he was always the bad guy. When he was about ten years old he couldn't stand it anymore, so he left home and went down to San Pedro, down to the docks and wandered around until somebody happened to see him and asked him if he would like to go out on a ship as a cabin boy, and so he did. That was how he started.

He went out on oil tankers and freighters doing odd jobs, working in the scullery, cleaning up, running errands. Because he left home, naturally his schooling was stopped, but he always had a strong desire to learn, so he began studying by himself. He was interested in machinery and mathematics. He studied and kept going to sea and eventually, all on his own, he became a machinist on board ship. He went all over the world. He became a heavy drinker, did everything, tried everything. He lived this life until he was twenty-nine years old, never married, and then one day he came into San Pedro on a ship belonging to the Norton Lilly Line; they'd been out for a long time; he had a lot of money, so he went up to the waterfront to his

3

usual bars. And going into one of them he saw a young girl. She was fifteen years old. Her name was Mildred Bartold.

My mother never knew who her parents were. She remembers an uncle and an aunt who lived in San Gabriel. They were Italian. They seemed to love her but kept sending her away to convents. Finally she couldn't stand the convents anymore, so she ran away, and she ended up in San Pedro, and she met my father.

She was very pretty at the time with that real Italian beauty, black hair, olive skin. My father had gotten to the point where he was thinking about settling down, getting a job on land, and not going to sea anymore. They met, and he balled her, and he felt this obligation, and I guess he cared for her, too, so he married her.

So here she was. She had finally gotten out into the world and all of a sudden she's married to a guy that's been all over, has done all the things she wants to do and is tired of them, and then she finds herself pregnant. She wanted to drink, look pretty, have boyfriends. She was very boisterous, very vociferous. She would get angry and demand things, she wouldn't change, she wouldn't bend. Naturally she didn't want a baby. She did everything she could possibly do to get rid of it, and my father flipped out. That was why he married her. He wanted a child.

She ran into a girl named Betty Ward who was very wild. Betty had two kids, but she was balling everybody and drinking, and she told my mother what to do to get rid of the baby. My mother starved herself and took everything anybody had ever heard of that would make you miscarry, but to no avail. I was born. She lost.

I was born September 1, 1925. I had rickets and jaundice because of the things she'd done. For the first two years of my life the doctors didn't think I would live but when I reached the age of two, miraculously I got well. I got super healthy.

During this period we lived in Watts, and my father continued going to sea. He hated my mother for what she had tried to do. She was going out with this Betty; I don't know what they did. They'd drink. I'd be left alone. The only time I was shown any affection was when my mother was just sloppy drunk, and I could smell her breath. She would slobber all over me.

One time when my father had been at sea for quite a while he came home and found the house locked and me sitting on the front porch, freezing cold and hungry. She was out somewhere. She didn't know he was coming. He was drunk. He broke the door down and took me inside and cooked me some food. She finally came home, drunk, and he cussed her out. We went to bed. I had a little crib in the corner, and my dad wanted to get into bed with me. He didn't want to sleep with her. She kept pulling on him, but he pushed her away and called her names. He started beating her up. He broke her nose. He broke a couple of ribs. Blood poured all over the floor. I remember the next day I was scrubbing up blood, trying to get the blood up for ages.

They'd go to a party and take me and put me in a room where I could hear them. Everybody would be drinking, and it always ended up in a fight. I remember one party we went to. They had put me upstairs to sleep until they were ready to leave. It was cloudy out, and by the time we got there it was night. I looked out the window and became very frightened, and I remember sneaking downstairs because I was afraid to be alone. They were all drinking, and this one guy, Wes—evidently he'd had an argument with his wife. She went into a bathroom that was off the kitchen and she wouldn't come out; there was a glass door on this bathroom, so he broke it with his fist. He cut his arm, and the thing ended up in a big brawl.

My parents always fought. He broke her nose several times. They realized they couldn't have me there. My father's mother was living in Nuevo, near Perris, California, on a little ranch, one of those old farms. They took me out there. I was five. And that was the end of my living with my parents and the beginning of my career with my grandmother. I saw my grandmother, and I saw that there was no warmth, no affection. I was terrified and completely alone. And at that time I realized that no one wanted me. There was no love and I wished I could die.

Nuevo was a country hamlet. Children should enjoy places like that, but I was so preoccupied with the city and with people, with wanting to be loved and trying to find out why other people were loved and I wasn't, that I couldn't stand the country because there was nothing to see. I couldn't find out anything there. Still, to this day, when I'm in the country I feel this loneliness. You come face to face with a reality that's so terrible. This was a little farm out in the wilderness. There was my grandmother and this old guy, her second husband, I think. I don't even remember him he was so inconsequential. And there was the wind blowing.

It was a duty for my grandmother. My father told her he would pay her so much for taking care of me; she would never have to worry—he always worked and she knew he would keep his word. I think she was afraid of him, too, for what she had done to him. For what she had allowed to be done to him when he was a child.

My grandmother was a dumpy woman, strong, unintelligent. She knew no answers to any problems I might have or anything to do with academic type things. She was one of those old-stock peasant women. I never saw her in anything but long cotton stockings and long dresses with layers of underclothing. I never saw her any way but totally clothed. When she went to the bathroom she locked the door with a key. Anything having to do with the body, bodily functions, was nasty and dirty and you had to hide away. I don't know what her feelings were. She never showed them. She had a cat that she gave affection to but none to me. I grew to hate the cat. My grandmother was—she was just nothing. There was no communication. Whenever I tried to share anything at all with her she would say, "Oh, Junior, don't be silly!" Or, "Don't be a baby!" I had a few clothes and a bed, a bed away from her, a bed alone in a room I was scared to death in. I was afraid of the dark.

I was afraid of everything. Clouds scared me: it was as if they were living things that were going to harm me. Lightning and thunder frightened me beyond words. But when it was beautiful and sunny out my feelings were even more horrible because there was nothing in it for me. At least when it was thundering or when there were black clouds I had something I could put my fears and loneliness to and think that I was afraid because of the clouds.

We moved from Nuevo to Los Angeles and then to San Pedro, and during the time of the move to L.A. the old guy disappeared. I guess he died. My parents separated and they came to see me on rare occasions. My mother came when she was drunk. My father always brought money, and every now and then he'd spend the night. When he came I'd want to reach him, try to say something to him to get some affection, but he was so closed off there was no way to get through. I admired him, and I thought of him as being a real man's man. And I really loved him.

My father was trim, real trim. He had a slender, swimmer's body. He had blue eyes, blonde hair. He had a cleft in his chin. He had a halting, faltering voice, but pleasant sounding, and a way about him that commanded respect. He'd been a union organizer and a strike leader on the waterfront, and he had a bearing. People listened to him. I nicknamed him "Moses" because I felt he had that stature, that strength, and soon everybody in the family was calling him that.

My father was tall, he was strong, and I felt he thought I was a sissy or something. I abhorred violence, but in order to try to win his love I'd go to school and purposely start fights. I fought like a madman so I could tell him about it and show him if I had a black eye or a cut lip, so he would like me. And when I got a cut or a scrape in these fights I would continue to press it and break it open so that on whatever day he came it would still be bad. But it seemed like the things he wanted me to do I just couldn't do. Sometimes he'd come when I was eating. My grandmother cooked a lot of vegetables, things I couldn't stand—spinach, cauliflower, beets, parsnips. And he'd come and sit across from me in this little wooden breakfast nook, and my grandmother would tell me to eat this stuff, and I wouldn't eat it, couldn't eat it. He'd say, "Eat it!" My grandmother would say, "Don't be a baby!" He'd say, "Eat it! You gotta eat it to grow up and be strong!" That made me feel like a real weakling, so I'd put it in my mouth and then gag at the table and vomit into my plate. And my dad was able, in one motion, to unbuckle his belt and pull it out of the rungs, and he'd hit me across the table with the belt. It got to the point where I couldn't eat anything at all like that without gagging, and he'd just keep hitting at me and hitting the wooden wall behind me.

My mother was going with some guy named Sandy; he played guitar, one of those cowboy drunkards that runs around and fights. I was going to grammar school and I remember once she came when I was eating lunch in the school yard. She went to the other side of the fence and called me. She was wearing a coat with a fur collar. I was scared because my father had told me, "Don't have anything to do with her! She didn't want you to be born! She tried to kill you! She doesn't love you! *I* love you! I take care of you!" But he didn't *act* like he loved me. I left the yard, and she took me in a car. I said, "I can't go with you." But she took me anyway. She smelled of alcohol and cigarettes and perfume and this fur collar, and she was hugging me and smothering me and crying. She took me to a house and everybody was drunk. I tried to get away, but they wouldn't let me leave. She kept me there all night.

When I was nine or ten my dad took me to a movie in San Pedro: *The Mark of the Vampire*. It was the most horrible thing I'd ever seen. It was fascinating. There was a woman vampire, all in white, flowing white robes, a beautiful gown, and she walked through the night. It was foggy, and it reminded me of the clouds. In the movie, whoever was the victim would be inside a house. The camera looked out a window and there was the vampire: there she would be walking toward the window.

I had a bedroom at the back of my grandmother's house, and my window looked out on the backyard. There was an alley and an empty lot. After this movie, whenever I got ready for bed, I could feel the presence of someone coming to my window. I would envision this woman walking toward me. I started having nightmares. She had a perfect face, but she was so beautiful she was terrifying—white, white skin, and her eyes were black, and she had long, flowing, black hair. She wore a white, nightgownish, wispy thing. Her lips were red and she had two long fangs. Her fingers were long and beautiful, and she held them out in front of her, and she had long nails. Blood dripped from her nails and from her mouth and from the two long fangs. It seemed she sought me out from everyone else. There was no way I could escape her gaze. I'd scream and wake up and run to my grandmother's room and ask her if I could get in bed with her, and she'd say, "Don't be silly! Don't be a baby! Go back to bed!"

This went on and on. I'd have nightmares and wake up screaming. Finally my grandmother told my dad and he took me to a doctor. The doctor gave me some pills to relax me, and it went away. But I kept having the fears. If I went to open a closet door I'd be scared to death. If I went walking at nighttime I'd see things in the bushes.

I'd wander around alone, and it seemed that the wind was always blowing and I was always cold. San Pedro is by the ocean, and we lived right next to Fort MacArthur. Maybe during the First World War there was a lot of action there, but around 1935 it was just a very big place staffed by a few soldiers. It was on a hill, and you could see the ocean all around, and there was a lot of fog and a lot of weeds and trees and brush and old barbed wire, and there was a large area that had been at one time, I think, a big oil field. They had huge oil tanks that went down into the ground very deep, overgrown with weeds. I used to go through the fence and wander around the fort. I'd climb down into these oil things.

Closer to the water they had big guns, disappearing guns, set in cement and steel housings. Every now and then they'd fire them to test them, and they'd raise up out of the ground. But most of the time they were quiet, and I'd sneak around and climb down onto the guns. Down below they had giant railroad guns, cannons, and anti-aircraft guns that they'd practice on; you could feel them going off.

On weekends I'd walk down the hill to a place called Navy Field, where there were four old football fields with old stands. The navy ships docked in the harbor, and the sailors had games, maybe four games going at once. I'd go down alone and sit alone in the stands and watch. Once I was walking under the stands to get out of the wind, and I looked up and saw the people. And the women, when they stood up, you could see under their dresses. That really excited me, so I started doing that, walking around under the stands on purpose to look up the women's dresses.

I built up my own play world. I loved sports, and I'd play I was a boxer or a football player. I even invented a baseball game I could play alone with dice, but boxing was the one I really got carried away with. At that time Joe Louis was coming up as a heavyweight. I would go out in the garage and pretend I was a fighter. I had a little box I sat on. I'd hear an imaginary bell and get up in this old garage and fight, and it was actually as if I was in the ring. Sometimes I'd get hit and fall down and be stunned, and I'd hear the referee counting, and I'd get up at the last minute, and just when everybody thought I was beaten I'd catch my opponent with a left hook. And then I'd have him against the ropes. I'd knock him out, and everybody would scream and throw money into the ring and holler for me, and I'd hold my hands together and wave to the crowd.

I played by myself for a long time and then, much as I hated to be with other kids, because I felt I wasn't like them, they wouldn't like me, I wanted to play sports so bad I overcame that and started playing in empty lots, and I was extremely good at sports. I was good in school, too. My drafting teacher in junior high said I really had a talent, and my father dreamed that one day he'd send me to Cal Tech here or Carnegie Tech back east so I could do something in mathematics or engineering.

My mother's side of the family was very musical. Her aunt and uncle—I think their last name was Bartolomuccio, shortened to Bartold—had five children. They all played musical instruments. The youngest boy was Gabriel Bartold, and as a child he played on the radio, a full-sized trumpet. He'd put it on a table and stand up to it and blow it.

The Bartolds lived in San Gabriel in a big house. In the back they had a lath-house, an eating place with a big round table. I remember going there several times and all the activity in the kitchen with the aunts and I don't know who-all making pasta; they made the most fantastic food imaginable. The men drank their homemade wine and ate and ate and ate, and the children were very attentive to the adults. I was very young, and the only thing I really remember is the daughter who was an opera singer. I remember hearing her sing and how pretty she was. She looked like a little angel, and she sang so beautifully with the operatic soprano voice.

I loved music, and when I passed a music store and saw the horns glittering in the window I'd want to go inside and touch them. It seemed unbelievable to me that anybody could actually play them. Finally I told my dad I just had to have a musical instrument. I wanted to play trumpet like my cousin Gabriel. My dad agreed to get somebody to come out and see what was happening with me. He found this man somewhere, Leroy Parry, who taught saxophone and clarinet, and brought him out to the house. In playing football I had chipped my teeth. Mr. Parry looked at my mouth and said I would never be able to play trumpet well because my teeth weren't strong. He said, "Why don't you play clarinet? You'd be excellent on clarinet. Give it a try." I still wanted to play trumpet, but I figured I'd better take advantage of what I had, so I started lessons on clarinet when I was nine years old.

Mr. Parry didn't play very well, but he was a nice guy, short and plump with a cherubic face, warm, happy-go-lucky. He had sparkling little eyes. You could never imagine him doing anything wrong or nasty or unpleasant. He invited me to his house for dinner a couple of times and I met his wife. She liked me, and they had no children of their own, so she would send me candy that she made. Mr. Parry was like another father to me, and I used to love talking to him. That's what our lessons were. None of them had anything to do with technicalities or the learning of music. It was just talking, having somebody to talk to. And I never had to practice. Just before Mr. Parry came I'd get my clarinet out and run through the lesson from the previous week. He'd think I'd been practicing the whole time. When I did play I played songs. I played what I felt. I didn't want to read anything or play exercises.

My father lived nearby. He was working as a longshoreman, and he lived with a woman named Nellie as man and wife. He never married her. He'd visit us and pay the bills. When it was time for school he'd give my grandmother money to get me a few clothes. He drank all the time, too. He used to get mean sometimes; he'd get loud and talk on and on and recite "The Face on the Barroom Floor" and all kinds of weird things.

After I started playing the clarinet my father would come and take me down to San Pedro to the bars. I've been there lately and the place is all cleaned up, but at that time, down by the waterfront, the whole area was nothing but bars, and there were fishermen, Slavonians, Italians, Germans—almost every nationality known was in those bars. A few had entertainment, a beat strip show, but most of them were just places guys went to hang out and talk. They weren't the kind of bars women would go in or that hustlers were at. They were men's bars, where they'd drink and talk about fishing and the waterfront and driving winches and their problems with management, to talk about the union. They were real tough guys; they were all my dad's friends. He would take me to several different bars, sit me up on the bar, and make me take out my clarinet and play little songs like "Nola" and "Parade of the Wooden Soldiers" and "I Can't Give You Anything but Love," "The Music Goes Round and Round," "Auld Lang Syne." The guys would ask for other songs, and I'd play them, and they'd listen. My father would stand right by me and stare at them and nod his head—like they'd *better* like it or he'd smack 'em in the mouth! And he was a big guy, and he'd be drunk. I got the feeling that they did like it because I was his boy. They liked boys. I was *his* boy: "That's Art's boy. He plays nice music." "Yeah, nice boy. *Play* that thing, boy!" They'd pat me on the back. They'd grab my arm and shake my hand—almost hurt my hand they were so rough: "You just keep it up, boy. You don't want to be like us." I was like their child. All their children. "You keep that up and you won't have to do like we do." And they would have fingers missing, and some guys would have an arm gone. Things would drop on them and they'd lose legs, feet, fingers. I could get away from that and be respectable and not have to get dirty and get hurt and work myself to death. And so they'd drop a dollar bill in my hand or fifty cents or a silver dollar. I'd end up with fifteen, twenty dollars just from these guys, and my dad never took the money from me. He said, "That's yours. You earned that." I always felt scared before I played, but after I did it I was proud and my dad was proud of me.

My grandmother was always talking about Dick, her son, the favorite. According to my dad Dick never helped my grandmother at all, never brought her anything, never gave her any money, but she thought he was just great and went on and on about how good he was and how bad my dad was. My dad supported her. One day my dad came over and there was talk about paying some kind of insurance for her. He felt that Richard should pay part of it. My dad was drinking, and he decided to go over and see Dick—"Dicky Boy" he called him. He just hated him.

Dick was a plain-looking man. He had dull-colored, hazel eyes; he was a dull person, nondescript and withdrawn. But he always felt that he was right. He always considered himself a good person. Maybe he was. My dad had got him a job as a longshoreman and had done nothing but good for him, but he said Dick had never shown any appreciation.

We went over there, me and my dad. We went inside. He started talking to them. Dick's wife's name was Irma, and she was just like him, thin, with no beauty, dull, lightish hair, faded eyes. Everything was faded about both of them. My dad tried to reason with them, tried to find out if they would pay anything. Irma said, "No! She's taking care of your brat: you pay it!" They got into a terrible argument. When they started hollering I got scared; I ran out to the car; but they were getting so crazy I felt something terrible was going to happen so I ran back, grabbed my dad, and tried to pull him out of the house. I got him to the car but he was too insane to drive. I opened the door and pushed him into the passenger side. He had just started teaching me how to drive. Dick ran out of the house with a big hammer, and when my dad saw him coming he tried to get out of the car to get at him, but I started the car up, praying I could get it going, trying to hold on to my dad at the same time. He's screaming out the window at them, and Irma's just screaming on the lawn, and here comes Dick with this hammer. By a miracle I was able to start the car. As Dick saw it moving he threw, and I pulled out just as the hammer hit the window in the back. It hit right where my dad's head would have been and shattered the glass. We got away. I looked over at him and saw that he was cut, there was blood on his face, and he was still raging about what he was going to do to Dick. Then he stopped. I guess he realized what had happened—that I was driving the car and had possibly saved his life or stopped him from killing. He might have killed both of them.

I drove back to my grandmother's house, and she wasn't there. I took him inside. I led him into the house and made him go into the bathroom and sat him down on the toilet and got a washrag. During the ride he had looked at me while I was driving, and I felt that he was seeing me for the first time. And I felt really good that I had done something that was right. I wiped the blood off his face. He wasn't cut bad, and he looked at me, and that was the first time I ever felt I had reached him at all. I felt good about myself and I felt that he loved me.

Right after that my grandmother came home and broke the

spell. He looked at her and realized how she was. I realized how she was. He started raving at her about her Dicky Boy, and I remember cussing her out myself, telling her that her Dicky Boy wouldn't pay a penny, that he'd tried to kill my dad, that I would kill him, that she was an unfeeling, rotten, ungrateful bitch. She flipped out at both of us. She didn't care anything at all about him being cut: "How dare you go over there and bother Richard and his wife?" She kept at him and at him, ranking him and goading him, and finally he grabbed her and started to strangle her. Probably all his life he'd wanted to kill her. She certainly deserved to be killed by him, and I had the feeling of wishing that he *would* kill her, thinking it would maybe free me. She wouldn't be there and something else would have to be done with me. Maybe he would have to take me to live with Nellie, who was warm and nice and feminine and smelled pretty. And so, for this moment, I was hoping he'd kill her, but all of a sudden I realized what would happen to *him*, so I grabbed him, and finally he let her go, and she ran screaming out into the street.

(Sarah Schechter Bartold)*   My husband was born in Italy. I think he said he had four sisters, but maybe there were three. Two were living when I went there many years ago. I couldn't say a word. They brought a chair outside. They didn't invite me in. They were country people, very suspicious.

My husband went to study for the priesthood when he was a young man, but he didn't like the things he saw going on there. He came to this country, and he was a waiter. He also worked in the coal mines. When I met him he was an insurance man. We met back east. I worked daytimes, and then I went with him to all his prospects at night. But I actually never got, out of fifty-eight years with him, more than he told me. And what difference does it make?

I don't remember anything about Ida [Mildred Bartold, Art's mother]. She was seven or eight when she came to us. She was pretty, but she was a terrible little troublemaker right from the beginning. She was a liar, a little liar. But I really don't

* See Cast of Characters on page x, for identification of speakers.

remember why she was sent to live with us. Maybe they felt that she would do better in America. As far as I knew she was one of my husband's sisters' children. She was a little liar, and that's the whole story. A child who fibs can do an awful lot of damage, especially when you have little children of your own. She lied about all sorts of things, about the other children—"This one did that." And they were younger than she was, so I thought it best not to have her around. But why stir up the past and cause her son to have hard feelings about her? She was his mother. Was he her only child? Did he inherit anything when she died? She had nothing to leave? I remember her mostly as a terrible fibber.

(Thelma Winters Noble Pepper) Arthur Senior, "Daddy," was born in Galena, Kansas, and then I think they went to this Missouri mining town. Grandma's [Art's grandmother's] first husband worked in the lead mines. And it was a real sad thing there because her husband, I think his name was Sam Pepper, was a periodic drunkard. Every weekend when he got paid, he'd go to the saloon to cash his check, and then usually there was nothing left. So this one time, they were visiting Sam's sister's family, and this sister's husband and Sam, they both got drunk, and the sister called the police, who took 'em both to jail, and I think they must of give 'em a thirty-day sentence. And while he was in jail, the place where Grandma lived—they evicted her. She had four or five children at that time (one had just died), and there wasn't no place for her to go, so they sent her to the poor farm, she and the children. And she was expecting then. She was carrying her twins. They told her, "You know that you can't keep your children here. They'll have to be put up for adoption." She said no way was she going to let her children be put up for adoption, so she went back to where they had been living. She knew an old man that had a run-down, old chicken house. She asked him if she could move in there, and he told her that if she thought she could make that livable, she could have it, and she did. When Sam come out of jail he didn't look for her. He just stayed away. He just decided to beat it. So that ended that, and that was two months before her twins was born. This all gives you an idea of why Grandma was like she was.

The twins was only three weeks old when she went to work. She and her sister-in-law took in washing together. And the boys—the sister had a boy about Daddy's age—they'd deliver and pick up. I guess this was in 1895. Daddy would have been about nine years old.

When the twins was fifteen months old they got—at that time they called it membranous croup, but now we know that it was diphtheria. So one of 'em died, and they took him away to be buried, and then the second one got so sick it couldn't breathe, so she'd walk it, day and night. Fifteen days apart they died. And this last one, Grandma was so wore out with taking care of them for so long, the neighbors induced her to lay down and take a nap. She washed the dead baby and dressed him and put him on a pillow on her sewing machine. While she was asleep, the authorities came in and took the baby, didn't even wake her up. And that affected her tremendously. When she was here with me and Daddy, dying, she lived that again. One day I heard her crying and I went in there. She was crying just fit to break her heart, and she said, "Oh, why didn't they wake me? Why did they take him away without waking me?" She didn't even get to attend the funeral of that second baby.

After that I think she run a kind of boardinghouse for miners. At that time women couldn't get jobs like they can now. Joe Noble was one of the boarders. Then when Joe started a butcher shop, she helped him in the butcher shop. They decided to get married, and that's when Joe come out here to California. They were married in 1913.

Daddy didn't live with them. When he was growing up he spent most of his time on his uncle's ranch back in the middle west somewhere. Daddy never went to school beyond the fifth grade. Then he went to work. I think he was seventeen when he joined the merchant marine. I don't know when it was that he lost his eye. Every once in a while he got tired of being at sea, and he'd take a stateside job. He was working on a bean huller, and he got a bean hull in his eye. That put it out. You couldn't tell it on him. He was the handsomest man I ever saw. I knew him for years before I knew that eye was no good.

Well, Daddy's stepfather just tolerated him. They didn't have no open quarrels that I know of. When Daddy'd come to port, San Pedro, he'd go to see them, but he never stayed overnight. His home port was San Francisco, so he'd come down here to see his mother and say hello and goodbye. He loved his mother very devotedly, but she didn't care too much for him because she hated anybody that drank to excess and Daddy always drank to excess. Dick was her favorite. He didn't drink at all, and when her other children died, he was the baby. But, anyhow, Dick was a very affectionate, loving person, see, and Daddy wasn't. Daddy was kinda standoffish, like her. Well, Daddy thought when he supported her and took care of her, that showed his love. He didn't do a lot of talkin.' That was the way it was. And I know when she died—Oh, my—he'd sit in that chair there and cry like a baby. He says, "Why couldn't she tell me she loved me? Just once. Why couldn't she tell me she loved me?" All three of 'em: there was Grandma, and Daddy, and Junior; they didn't communicate with each other.

I was married to Shorty—that was Daddy's stepbrother—in 1920; Johnny was born in October of 1921; and it was March of the following year that I first saw Daddy. He'd just come by for a few minutes, said hello to Grandma, and was gone. And the next time he came in port, my second baby, Buddy, was about six months old, so that was two and a half years later. He come up to see Grandma again, but this time he brought Millie [Mildred Bartold, Art's mother] with him. That would be 1924, when they got married. Well, Millie fell in love with my Buddy. He was one of those pink and white babies, all soft and cuddly, you know. She wanted a baby. She didn't figure on Junior [Art] being sickly and hard to take care of.

Millie said she was born back east in New Jersey or New York, and her uncle and his wife, the Bartolds, brought her to California when she was just a little girl. Her real name was Ida. She didn't know her last name. She'd got a lot of sisters and brothers somewhere. Well, they made a regular little doll of her. Her slightest wish—they got it for her, until they had kids of their own. Then her name was mud. Her aunt wasn't very good to her after she had children of her own. She'd accuse Millie of doing something, and if she said she didn't do it, she wasn't allowed nothing to eat until she admitted she did it. Millie said she went three days one time without anything to eat because she knew she hadn't done what she was accused of, but she finally told her aunt she did just to get out from under. Then she ran away from home. She ran away a lot of times, and that's why, I think, the Bartolds finally put her in a convent school. But she ran away from there, too. For a while she was put in a foster home; she was very happy there. But then she met this woman, Mildred Bayard. Millie must have been about fourteen then. This woman wanted Millie to go with her to one of the Harvey Houses out in the desert—I think it was Barstow—as a waitress. I don't know what kind of experience she had out there, but she run away from there, too, and she went down to [San] 'Pedro to be a waitress.

She was looking for the employment office, and she stopped Daddy on the street to ask him where it was, and he said he'd take her there. He did, but the next day he got her a job with somebody he knew that run a restaurant because he was very well known in 'Pedro. So, let's see. The first day she met Daddy. The second he got her a job. And then he asked her how old she was. When she told him she was fifteen, she said he got as white as a sheet. The next day they went up to Los Angeles and got married at some Bible college. She gave her name as Mildred Bayard on the marriage license. And then he brought her home to Grandma.

Daddy thought that if Millie could stay with Grandma while he was sailing—at that time he was sailing between 'Pedro and Seattle on a lumber boat . . . But she didn't get along very good. She was a nice, friendly girl, you know; Italians usually are. And the family wasn't very nice to her, the Noble family. They were very clannish, and they didn't seem to take to her too good. She didn't know what to do with her time, and I think she did things she shouldn't have. Anyhow, after a couple of trips, Daddy decided that that wouldn't do. He'd have to come stateside. That's when he went to work in a machine shop. I was living in Watts then, and I kinda lost track of 'em until Junior was born.

Oh, my! Poor little thing! He had rickets and yellow jaundice when he was born, and he was so skinny that his hands and his feet looked like bird claws. When he was three or four months old! Couldn't get nothing to agree with him. I don't know if she couldn't or if she didn't want to, but Junior was a bottle baby. I don't imagine she had any milk anyway. She didn't eat right. Junior couldn't assimilate cow's milk. They had him to half a dozen different doctors, and they all told 'em the same thing: "He can't live." They took him to Children's Hospital in L.A., and the doctors gave them a formula for barley gruel. It had to be cooked all day, and in that she put Karo syrup and so much dextro-maltose, and that agreed with him. But he was still awfully skinny and they couldn't bathe him in water—he was too weak. The doctor told them that if they bathed him in olive oil, that would nourish him, too. He looked like death warmed over.

Daddy and Millie had lots of fights about Junior not being Daddy's. He was sailing when she got pregnant, and Junior would have either had to be two weeks early or two to three weeks late. And so this Betty Ward, a friend of Millie's, smart-aleck woman that she was, she was there when Junior was born, and she said to the doctor, "Is he a full-term baby?" The doctor said, "Yes, he came right on time." So there was that question. But in time, Daddy realized that Junior had to be his. There were too many features the same. You know them turned up toes that Junior has? And Daddy's arms are shaped, were shaped, here just exactly like Junior's.

But Millie was unfaithful. Might as well say it. I remember when me and Shorty lived in the big house, and she and Daddy lived in the back. Daddy worked swing shift, and she'd go out, and she asked me to listen for Junior in case he woke up. She got home one night just by the skin of her teeth, just soon enough to get her clothes off and jump in bed before Daddy got home. Scared her to death.

This Betty Ward had several children and they were all mean as could be to Junior. They were all older than he, and they would tease him just to hear him holler 'cause he'd make a real big commotion when he was upset about anything. They're the ones that got him afraid of food touching on a plate. Millie and Betty would go tomcattin' somewhere and leave him with these kids. There'd be plenty of food for the kids, but when it come time to eat, they wouldn't let Junior have any. And when they'd finally decide to give him something to eat, they'd put it on his plate so that the food would touch each other and then they'd tell him, better not eat it, that it'd poison him. First time I realized that was one time when Millie and Daddy were separated. He came by with Junior just at mealtime, and I set Junior a place not knowing how he was. I just fixed his plate like I did for my kids, and he set up such a yowl. He says, "You hate me! You want me to die!" And I couldn't figure out what was the matter with him, and he says, "Well the food is *touching!* That'll poison me! I'll die!" And he wouldn't eat nothing either.

Daddy's nickname for Millie was "Peaches" because her complexion was so perfect. She never had to wear makeup. She was a very pretty girl, but she got heavy as soon as she got married. Millie never cared too much for women, but she loved me. We were closer than most sisters. When we were neighbors, Millie'd bring Junior over to me every day. She'd get all her housework done up, her house nice and clean, and then she'd bring Junior over to me and go out tomcattin' and come over and get him just before time to go for Daddy. One time Junior told me—I guess he'd been having a hard time one way or another—"I sure wish you was my mother." That sure made me proud, I'll tell you.

Later on Daddy got a job on the tuna fishing boats. One time they were reported lost at sea, and they were gone for forty days. They had got becalmed on the ocean, out there somewhere. Usually they'd be gone for two weeks, come back for a few days, and go out again. And Millie would leave Junior out in the cold, no supervision, nothing to eat. Daddy come home and found that one time. The landlady lived in the front house, and they lived in the back. So, after that, he made arrangements with her that Junior was to come to her house after school. But I don't think Daddy made many trips after that.

Daddy and Millie fought all the time. They'd have regular knockdown–drag-outs nearly every day. And Junior would get underneath the sink and sit there and scream bloody murder. It's no wonder he grew up the way he did. He never did have a normal childhood. Only with Grandma, and she wasn't affectionate enough. And he was Italian, and so, you know, he needed more affection than other people.

Millie and Daddy separated half a dozen times. It was on-again, off-again. She'd leave every whipstitch. Then, when she found the going too rough, why, she'd come back. And Daddy always took her back because, he said, to his way of thinking a child needed its mother. That was a strong point with him, even though he got to the point where he actually disliked her intensely. Still he thought that she would be better for Junior than somebody else.

There was one time when Daddy and Millie separated—I think Junior was only about nine or ten months old. Oh, well, she left him before that. She left him when Junior was only a few months old. She left the baby with Irma, Dick's wife, and she went home to her aunt (Mrs. Bartold), and the aunt promptly brought her home to Arthur the next day. That's when all this buisness came out that we had never heard of before. The aunt give Daddy a real dressing down. She told him, "When you married Ida," that's what she called her, "When you married Ida you assumed responsibility for her because she was a ward of the court before that. So no matter what she does, she is your responsibility until she's twenty-one years old." Daddy knew he was licked.

There was another time that they were separated for nine months, and Daddy and Junior lived with Grandpa Joe and Grandma in Watts. Grandma took care of him then, and that's when he made the most progress physically. Because he didn't have this upheaval all the time. He was just a little fellow then. He ate regular and had regular hours, and he was a pretty happy baby. Millie'd come to see him once in a while, but Daddy forbid her to take him anyplace. Then after nine months they got back together again. They finally broke up once and for all when Junior was seven. And that's when he went to live with his grandmother permanently.

At that time Grandma had a chicken ranch over here in Nuevo. Grandpa Joe had died, and she had her brother helping her out there. She had traded her house for the ranch. Then she couldn't make the payments on it, so she traded her interest in the ranch for a house on Eighty-third Street in Watts.

Sandy was the man that Millie was going with while Daddy was off fishing, while they were still married. And he didn't like Junior at all. But she went to live with him after she and Daddy separated for good. She used to tell me all kinds of things: when Daddy'd get paid, he did her like he did me, too, later; he'd give her all the money he brought in. So she was buying up pillows and pillow slips and sheets, towels; she was fixin' it all together. Then, when she got what she wanted, she told me, she intended to leave Daddy and go with Sandy. And she kept this stuff at my house.

Well, I knew what her plans was, but I think Betty Ward told Daddy 'cause he knew everything she did. Everything. So, one day, here comes Millie in Sandy's car. She came to get the suitcases with all these towels. And here comes Daddy. Nobody expected him. He looked around until he found the suitcases in my boys' closet, and he took each one of them towels and just ripped it in half, and they had a knockdown–drag-out fight right in my house. Well, that was the last time they were together. When she got back over to Grandma's house, she picked up Grandma's iron and threw it at Daddy and it just missed him. Would have killed him if it didn't. She went to stay with Sandy after that.

Now, Sandy wanted to marry her. Daddy was in the L.A. County Hospital for an operation on his head, some polyps or something. He was always having to have operations. Then, while Daddy was there, Sandy had a stroke and they took him to the hospital, too, same floor. I met Millie at the elevator, you know, and she told me she was hoping that Daddy would die so she'd get Junior. But Sandy wouldn't have Junior; he wouldn't even consider takin' him. Still, she thought if she married Sandy and Daddy died, she'd get Junior. But Sandy died. That was poetic justice for you, I guess. Sandy died right there in the hospital.

Grandma used to tell me how sorry she felt for Junior. Like one day, she told me she found him just sittin'. She thought he was reading a book, but he was just sittin' there, not making a sound, and the tears just rolled down his face. She asked him what was the matter, and he said he wished he had a mother and a father and sisters and brothers like other children had.

Junior was just little when he got interested in music. Mr. Parry was his first teacher, and I'm sure Junior remembers him. He was about nine years old, and they were living in Watts, and Mr. Parry recognized immediately that he was very gifted. In fact, when they moved to 'Pedro, Mr. Parry was so impressed with his talent that he made the trip from L.A. every week to teach him.

Grandma was proud of Junior's talent. Oh my, yes! She'd talk about it, too, to other people. She might not have bragged to him, but to anybody else who would listen she would brag to high heaven about Junior's talent. Because she knew in her mind that he was going to be very rich and famous when he got grown. Junior kind of took the place of the children she lost. But she never was lovey-dovey, even with her own kids.

He could do no wrong, Junior couldn't. She'd get out of patience and angry with him sometimes: he liked to aggravate her; he'd bait her—instead of using a spoon, he'd slurp his soup out of the dish. He'd put his head way down. Hahahaha! And Grandma firmly believed that when he grew up he was going to be an outstanding musician, and she used to tell him, "You're going to be in society. You're going to be in a position where you'll need to know manners!" And I remember him making the statement "I'm going to be such a great musician that it won't make no difference if I have manners or not!"

John and Millie Noble

(John) I can't say why it took place; I was only six or seven. I just went into their house there on May Avenue in Watts to get Art Junior to play. We were always climbing trees. And here were Moses and Moham [Art Senior and Millie, Art's mother] going at it hammer and tongs. They were battin' one another around, calling each other all the names in the book. Art Junior was squalling and a-wailing underneath the sink, and I was afraid to try to run for the front door to get out again, so I just went down on the kitchen floor with him. I was as scared as he was. They were bangin' one another around. She hit him with a pot or pan; some doggone thing clattered down on the floor. Moses had a very explosive temper, and Moham was like a wildcat; she'd fight anything and kinda kept us kids a little bit away.

We called him Moses, Art Senior. Art Junior made up that name. Him and I talked about it. He said, "He's as old as Moses and he's as wise as Moses." And from that time on it was Moses.

He was a self-educated man, very intelligent in quite a few ways because he educated himself in the field of diesel

engineering, and he was a machinist, first-class. He had
fantastic tools, and he was very meticulous. His greatest love,
of course, was the labor movement. He started in Seattle. It was
the IWW, the Wobblies, and he progressed in that field for as
many years as he could until they finally kicked him out of
Washington State, and he became acquainted with Harry
Bridges and became an organizer for him to create the ILWU.

Moses was very one-way about his thinking. He researched
what he was interested in and then that's the way it was in his
mind. I learned a lot from him, and I'm quite certain that
everyone that was around him did. He was a hard person to
forget. You either loved him or you hated him. There was no
middle road.

My next vivid thought about Moses was during the '38
strike, when he had a small Plymouth sedan, and they were
going to go out and get some scabs. And they did a good job at
that time on those people who were trying to break that strike.

He was about six foot tall, and he was lean, and he had
that bad eye, and he had his right thumb cut off, let's see, by
an accident in a machine shop after that '38 strike. He was there
because they were trying to run him off the waterfront. He had
to get off the waterfront there for quite a spell.

(Millie)   What about that rumor about Pancho Villa?

(John)   That wasn't a rumor. That was a fact. Moses and a
friend of his took a boat out from San Pedro, and they were
supposed to be going out fishing. Well, this friend—Moses never
mentioned his name to me—headed due south when they got
out of the harbor, and it wasn't until they were at sea that
Moses learned that they were going to Mexico with a load of
firearms for Pancho Villa's revolution.

There was another occasion in '29 or '30 where Moses had
to leave the country because of his union activities, and he
went to the Philippine Islands and ran a bar in Manila. When
he came back, which was after the big depression had already
set in and settled across the country, he came back with quite a
little bit of money, and he was back commercial fishing again.
He made several trips down to South America. I recall he

brought back tuna fish, and being as the whole family was there—Grandma and Irma and Dick Pepper and us kids—well, he salted up some tuna in a big barrel and he put too much salt in it and it burnt the tuna up to where we couldn't eat it. But he tried. He wanted to do it on his own. And he was always out to help anyone. That was one of his big things. Even if he didn't like you, he'd try to help you. Later in life . . . That probably explains how he was with Moham. My wife could never understand it. We'd go over to their house and here was his wife and his ex-wife sitting knitting on the same couch. The whole family stayed together all these years. That was very important to Moses.

(Millie) Remember that time Moses wanted to buy some property? He was going to have him and Mommy [Thelma] live on the middle of that property. On one corner was going to be Junior and Patti; another corner, Bud [John's brother] and his wife, Aud; us in this corner. He was going to be . . .

(John) He was going to be the patriarch. He wanted to keep us together so we could always be in contact with one another, but there's one thing Moses didn't visualize, I don't believe, and that was such a fast-moving civilization coming up, going faster than he could think.

Grandma Noble was a very, very—hahahaha!—stubborn and hardheaded woman, but you had to love her. Art lived with her, you see, and was under her domination more or less. Grandma had set ideas, same as Moses did, and when she told Art Junior, "I don't want you smoking! I don't want you doing this!" well, she expected to be obeyed, and Art, of course, didn't obey very easily. She was the same way with me, but I loved her very much because she did so much in trying to help me, although I didn't agree with the way she went about it. She tried to make me be industrious, clean living. She was a very good woman. Her ideas about young people probably coincided with mine in this modern day and age.

Grandma and Moses fought hammer and tongs verbally, being both as stubborn and hardheaded as they were. They couldn't come to a meeting of the minds. Grandma didn't like the way Moses was living with some of the women he went around with. Moses was her son and she thought she had some control over him. Moses wouldn't conform at all. He paid her bills, made sure everything was there, furniture, food, but he didn't want her telling him what to do, the same way *he* wanted to tell *other* people what to do. It was a conflict constantly, always a friction.

Moses always admired my mom when she was a young woman. He was in love with her for many years before they finally got married. My dad treated my mom very shabbily. And Moses didn't believe that a man should treat a woman shabbily. He could knock her down and kick her—that's fine—but he had to feed her and give her the necessities of life. With Shorty, he'd go down and work, longshoring, and leave Momma with no money. He'd spend it all in the bars. He wasn't like Moses. He wouldn't take care of the family first and *then* go drink it up. He'd spend all the money down there and come home broke. We didn't have food in the house.

Dad left in 1939, '40, and Mom and Moses got together. He was always quite attracted to her, and he, in her eyes, was a good provider even though he drank and horsed around. He'd been divorced from Moham, oh years and years. In 1942, when I entered the navy, Mom told me he was staying at some hotel in San Francisco, so I went to see him before I shipped out. I woke him up in his hotel room; his gang was workin' up there. We spent one evening and all night together, and he told me, just before I left, he says, "Well, John, I'm gonna go back and marry your mom." And I says, "Well, that's okay with me, Moses. I hope you have a lot of fun."

They started living together, and by the time I came back from the service, Momma could legally get married again. By that time, Moses was in his fifties, and he always treated my mom like a queen because he saw what my dad had done to her and to me, beat me up, threw me out. Moses loved kids, and the old man would beat the poop out of my brother Bud and I. Moses couldn't stand to see children mistreated, beat, and without food. And *he* brought us food, gosh yes! Moses'd come to the house and bring us food and sometimes clothing because my old man would feed us all canned tomatoes and then he'd tell my mom, "Cook me up a steak."

When we were in grammar school, Bud and I used to go

over to where Art lived with Grandma and build little wooden stick airplanes and play on the floor or outside. We flew kites together. Now, everybody called him Junior, and he didn't like it, and I didn't blame him. I always called him Art. And when the other kids wanted to fight or beat him up, he was always protective of his mouth because even when he was a small kid he was playing the horn. Mr. Parry, his teacher, was always warning him about hurting his mouth; he said that was his livelihood to come. So I'd get into arguments with Art, but I never fought with him like Billy Pepper did, and Bud. I'd intercede on the few occasions I was around when it happened, and Art always respected me for that. I think that was more or less the bond between us.

I used to go over, to go swimming or something with Art, and I'd have to wait while he finished his lessons. Art was excited about his music to the extent that when I came over he'd show me a music lesson or passage that Mr. Parry had left him and he'd say, "How does this sound, John?" He'd play it for me. I didn't know one note from another, but I listened and I could see just how enthusiastic he was. The last time I saw Mr. Parry and Art practicing in the living room there, Mr. Parry said, "Art, you keep this up and your name will be in lights all over this whole country." Of course, Art was a little puffed up about that.

We used to talk. I had my mom, who showed a lot of love and protection for us kids; whereas Art, his mother was not there and he had to depend on Grandma and her strictness and Moses and his very vocal—he was very forceful in the way he spoke, especially when he was a young man. Art used to love to get away; we spent a lot of time together just because of that. And he'd often say, "I wish I could just get away from Grandma, from Moses." He talked very little about Moham. Very little. Because, you see, she was too young then to be very maternal toward him. She went her way and let Art Junior go his, and he resented that very much. But he liked my mom real well. Momma was always loving toward him and she petted him, which he didn't have because Grandma Noble wasn't a loving type of person in that respect except to me. She never expressed any affection or love for Art when he was a little boy.

When we got older, we did a lot of drinkin', both of us. We'd go to a drugstore; they didn't demand your identity. We'd buy a pint of Four Roses, take our girls out on a date, and we'd drink it up. Usually, I went back to Grandma's house with Art and slept in the same bedroom there, and we'd get up in the morning and drink up all Grandma's milk outta the icebox because we both had hangovers. We'd guzzle it down. And then we'd go to the beach, Cabrillo Beach. We'd mostly finagle some beer to drink down there. We'd swim, sit out on the rocks.

After the war, and just before the war started, Art took me out on some of his jam sessions that he'd go to on Central Avenue. He'd take me to these clubs, and they were mostly black people that he associated with very closely. They were fine musicians, and they accepted him when he'd come in there because he was that good.

One night Art was playing, and they had this dancer, a mulatto girl—we were drinkin' it up. She came around and danced on these tables, slipped off her garter, threw it up in the air, and I caught it. She said, "You're the one!" I didn't know what to do. I was too young. She got down off the table, stretched the garter out, and put it around my neck. She says, "You have to kiss your way out of that." I was thrilled to pieces, but here were all these people looking on. Especially all these black people. Art was still up there jammin'. I told him about it when he came back to the table, and he says, "Well, you missed your big chance." Oh, lordy! That was before the war. Now, I left in '42 and I didn't see Art again until '46.

———————

2 | Patti

1930–1944

I HAD my first sexual experience I can remember when I was four or five. I was still living with my parents in Watts. They had some friends who lived nearby, Mary and Mike, who had a daughter, Francie, about four years older than me. Francie was slender, she had black hair, she had little bangs cut across and a pretty face, and she had a look about her of real precociousness. She had a devilish look about her, and she was very warm. Hot. She had nice lips, her teeth were real white, a pink tongue, and her cunt was pink and clean. A lot of little girls smell acid or stale, but . . . I remember sometimes we'd be playing together on the front lawn—there would be other kids around—and she would sit on my face in her little bloomers; nobody acted like they noticed anything. She's sitting there, and I'm sniffing her ass and her cunt and her bloomers, and it always smelled real sweet and nice.

My folks used to go out with Mary and Mike and get drunk and leave me with Francie. They'd make a bed on the floor, and we'd go to bed, and she'd want me to kiss her, to kiss her cunt. She'd make me get down there and lick her, and she would do the same thing to me. It was very exciting, and I always imagined, when we got older, that we would really make love like grownups do. Years and years later, when I was divorced from my first wife I ran into Francie, and I wanted to ball her, but she was in love and she wouldn't do it.

In addition to Richard and my father my grandmother had a stepson named Shorty, and Shorty's wife, Thelma, later married my father, but when I was a child she was my aunt and I thought of her children as my cousins. She had two boys a little older than me, John and Bud, and a daughter Edna. One time I remember we were sleeping together, me and John and Bud at my grandmother's house, and my grandmother happened to come in; she might have heard us giggling. She turned on the light, and we had the blankets off and were playing with each other's little peepees. She wigged out at us. She said she was going to tell Thelma that we were evil, she was going to tell my dad, and I said, "Oh, please don't tell dad!" She told us that our peepees were going to grow real long; they were going to grow out of our pants legs and trail after us down the street; and everybody was going to laugh at us and say, "For shame!"

Thelma and Shorty lived near my grandmother so I used to see Thelma a lot. She was sweet and pleasant, and I always wished that she had been my mother because she was very understanding and I could talk to her. Where my mother was harsh Thelma was gentle. I felt I could get her to sympathize with me and baby me.

Thelma had that typically American look, a sweet, clean look about her. She had mousey brown hair and light skin. She had a very trim body, and she was soft, like a little dove or a little doe. She wore cotton housedresses that she made herself. They folded over in front; she'd put a pin there, and you could always see part of her breast. I'd go around and watch her doing the dishes or the laundry and I'd look down her dress. And when I hugged her I would always want to put my head between her breasts.

As I said, my grandmother locked the door when she went to the bathroom and she'd leave the key in the door so you couldn't see through the keyhole. It made the idea of going to the bathroom something that was nasty, that you had to hide. But also, because of the locked door, it seemed to me that it was exciting, really evil, and I became attracted to bathrooms to see what went on in there. I started looking out our windows at night, when the lights went on, and sometimes the woman next door would be in the bathroom. I couldn't see anything, but the idea that she was there excited me. I started walking around at night and looking, when I was walking, if there were lights on in the windows.

At Thelma's house the bathroom had two doors and there

were keyholes but no keys in these doors, so I used to peek at Thelma or at Edna when they were in there and get an erection and play with myself. I would go in the bathroom after they left and play with myself.

By the time I was eleven I was totally preoccupied with sex. Every time a woman bent over or crossed her legs my eyes automatically saw her. It was constant. I never stopped fantasizing. I could virtually strip women naked as they walked by me. And then it wasn't like it is now. They didn't have bookstands or movies. You couldn't find pictures of naked women or people balling. *I* couldn't. The only thing you'd run into was an occasional little funny book. They had little, teeny comic books in those days, about four by six, about Hairsbreadth Harry, Maggie and Jiggs, Terry and the Pirates, all those old cartoon people, Blondie and Dagwood. I don't know if they were made in Mexico, but that's where people got them, and they were drawn just like the funny papers only sexy. People made love. The girls all wore little cotton dresses, and that's what turned me on—the sight of a woman in a dress that was cotton and clinging. I could just imagine what was underneath. In the funny books you buy now sex is ridiculed and used as a tool to rank some political figure or party or to protest, but these were purely sex magazines, and I used to get turned on by them.

I started asking around if there were any girls who . . . I wanted to actually have contact with a woman. I did have this little girlfriend who played the accordian. She was very sweet and nice. I used to carry her accordian home from grammar school and it almost killed me because it was so heavy, but I was afraid to try anything, so I'd just rub my arm against her or something like that. Rub my hand against her ass accidentally.

Some kid I knew in school told me about a girl who would let you see her and play with her. She wasn't pretty or sexy. She was real thin and tall. She had black hair and a bony face with a long, pointed nose, but her eyes had a look about them, oh, she had a real saucy look, and just the idea that she might let me do something! I started pursuing her and talking to her and finally one Saturday we went to the park and she let me look at her cunt and play with it and she played with me until I came. I walked her home, and she invited me to come over and see her where, she said, we could get more comfortable. But I was disappointed because even though it was exciting, and I knew I would be after it all the time, it wasn't the way I wanted it to be.

I started working on Central Avenue in 1941. I'd play at nightclubs and some chick would come in, a black chick or a white chick, and she'd say, "Come on out with me at intermission. I'll make you feel good." Or, "I'll take care of you." I'd be at the Ritz Club, which was very informal; the musicians just sat and played at the tables and a chick would come and sit in the chair next to me and put her hand in my lap and play with me and look at me, saying "Oh, you're sweet. I'd sure love to take you home." She might take my hand and put it on her leg, put it up under her dress. Then we'd go out and get in a car and go to a liquor store and get a jug, and we'd stop someplace. If she lived nearby we'd go to her pad real quick, and she would suck on me until I came or I would fuck her. I enjoyed parts of it, but it wasn't what I imagined when I looked in windows and played with myself and I thought that the *real* experience would always be denied me for some reason.

There was a girl I fell for at San Pedro High, she really moved me, and I thought everything might be different with her. She had long hair that hung over her shoulders, full lips, very light skin, and a nice body, rounded with not overly large, but full breasts, and she had pink nipples that got hard, which always denoted a lot of passion to me in a woman. She had a sexy smell, a clean smell, and she just loved to neck and to touch. I remember one time we were sitting in her dad's car in the alley. She lived in an old wooden house set way back on a big lot. We were playing around and were just about to the point where I was going to fuck her when all of a sudden here comes her dad out of the house with her mother. Her mother was hysterical. Her father screamed, "We're at war!" The Japanese had just bombed Pearl Harbor and a bunch of our battleships were sunk and thousands of Americans killed. Delano Roosevelt was going to declare war.

The war started, and they were having blackouts in San Pedro because of Fort MacArthur and the harbor. The girl left town with her family. I felt that something could have happened with her. I went back to the window peeping, and I ran into some terrible experiences with dogs chasing me, and I thought I was really hung up to be like that. But then one day I ran into Patti in study hall, and the feeling I'd wanted was there. And I changed levels from the way I'd been, preferring fantasizing to the actual act, and I realized that that had been because I didn't care for the girls, that it was the combination of sex and love that made it wonderful. And that's the way it proved out.

Because I was working so much, playing music, my grandmother and I moved to Los Angeles so I could be closer to the jobs, and in 1941 we were living on Seventy-third Street between Towne and San Pedro and I was going, on and off, to Fremont High School.

I had no friends at Fremont. I went because I had to go. I might as well have been on a desert island. But one day in study hall I looked around and saw a girl sitting at one of the desks. I looked and there she was, the most beautiful girl I'd ever seen. I started thinking about her. I'd think about her at night and everything, you know, but she was a "nice girl" and the only kind of girl I could have anything to do with would be a bad girl, a nasty girl. I started sitting behind her in study hall, and one day she turned around and talked to me. She asked some little silly question about math or did I have a pencil. I wasn't able to speak to her. I started sweating. I couldn't look her in the eye. I mumbled something. About a week later, I walked into class a few minutes early and she was there. She said, "I don't feel like studying today." I said, "I don't feel like studying either." It just came out before I realized I was being intimate with her in replying like that. She said, "Why don't we leave and go someplace else?" We got up and walked out.

We left the school. I kept looking at her thinking how beautiful she was. I couldn't believe I was actually with her, and every now and then I'd brush my hand against her arm. Her teeth were white; they sparkled. Her eyes—the whites of them were almost a blue-white. She had dimples and this real innocent face, a kind of bewildered look on her face all the time. She had very light skin, no marks on it, and from the neck down . . . What really moved me was she had a body at fifteen or sixteen that was a woman's body, full breasts, full hips, small waist, and she had a flirty look about her. She was a real flirt but I always thought that was just her way; later I interrogated her about it and she said she was a virgin. That really excited me. She had beautiful breasts and legs and skin and fingers and ears and it was almost more than I could stand. I didn't know why she had asked me to come out there, to leave the class, and I didn't know what to do, so we just walked around and talked and she told me about herself. She said her name was Madeleine Moore but to call her Patti because she didn't like Madeleine. So that was Patti.

She lived about twenty blocks from me. I walked her home, and we talked and talked and talked, and for the first time I began to doubt all the feelings I had about myself. She thought I was wonderful and that I was handsome; I could tell from the way she looked at me, from the way she acted. And she seemed like a nice girl. I was certain she was a nice girl and that she liked me. And it was so different from the night before and what would happen tonight at the Ritz Club or the Club Alabam. We spent a long time together. I finally said I had to go home. I took her to her house and no one was there but I didn't even try to kiss her; when I went to leave she took hold of my arm and looked at me and said, "Don't you like me?" I said, "Of course I like you." She said, "Well, you don't act like it." I grabbed her arm and gave it a squeeze and then I turned around and walked away. I almost started crying. It was unbearable. It was like a pain and I had to get away from her. I walked home and from that minute . . . It would have been better to have gone on the way I was; I'd grown comfortable. That meeting was too much. Now I knew no matter what happened, no matter what, I knew I had to have her. I couldn't do anything but think about her and want her, to have her and protect her and look at her and smell her, just to brush my hand against her arm.

We started meeting and talking. We'd ditch school a lot. We'd walk around. I didn't try to do anything sexually with her for a long time, but we kept seeing each other, and then I kissed her, and then we started messing around. Sometimes, if my grandmother wasn't home, we'd go over there. I'd borrow my cousin's car, and we'd go park, and we'd pet.

I met her mother. Her mother had been married to a musician who'd treated her bad. I could see that that was going to be a problem. I had to sneak around to see her because her mother was afraid of me, but I had fallen in love and I think Patti had, too. One day her mother woke up with a pain in her stomach, and she died that evening. She had gangrene of the intestines, I think. She had had several abortions, and probably those caused that. Patti was sent to Arizona to some relatives before she could contact me. She wrote and told me what had happened. I was miserable. Finally, she came to visit an aunt in Glendale.

They were going to send her away again, and I couldn't stand that. We wanted to get married. Patti was sixteen and I was seventeen. My dad thought we should hold off and see how we felt in a year or so, but to us that seemed like a lifetime. I borrowed my cousin's car and we went to Tijuana to one of those places, and some guy married us. He called in his secretary and a guy from the street and they witnessed the ceremony: "Do you take this woman to be your lawful wedded wife?" In broken English, and we were married. I wanted it all to be legal. I didn't want that love ruined by our living together without being married because at that time I was extremely moralistic.

We came back with our little certificate and there was nothing the families could do but okay it. My father was furious because he wanted to have us married in the house with my grandmother there. I was his only son and he wanted to do it right. We had another ceremony to satisfy him, and then we rented an apartment down by Adams above Fiqueroa.

Before we went to Tijuana we'd work each other into such a state it was unbelievable. She kept asking me, telling me she wanted me to do it, and once I tried, but it was a horrible, horrible scene, and then she started bleeding. So after we got married, it was agony trying to have intercourse without hurting her, but finally I got through, and it was perfect from then on. As I look back I see that all we had was sex, that beauty, and we made love continuously. I remember once we made love eleven times in one day and I came all those times.

For a while, before we got the apartment, we stayed with my grandmother. We'd wait until she left the house and the minute she was gone we'd take our clothes off and start making love. We'd do it in the front room so we could look out the window and watch for her. When she was home we weren't able to contain ourselves, so we'd go out to the old garage in the back, which was filled with stuff; there was a place at the top where there were two mattresses on the beams we could climb up onto. Patti would wear a cotton housedress with nothing on underneath, and we'd go make love by the hour. Sometimes my grandmother would come calling us and we'd stop and hold on to each other and not breathe and be giggling up there. I'd finally found someone who loved me.

3 | The Avenue

1940–1944

WHEN I WAS at San Pedro High, because I was a musician and played for the dances, I began to get popular. All the chicks dug me and would vie for me, smile at me, and flirt with me. The guys came around, too, and listened to me play, and they wanted me to hang out with them. And one day this guy Chris came to me, him and a couple of other guys, and they wanted me to join the club they belonged to. It was an honor.

In San Pedro at this time there were a lot of different gangs. Chris had a gang called the Cobras. I thought I might be happier if I was with other people more and I also wanted to join because I figured it would impress my dad: the Cobras had a reputation. I joined and got a jacket with a cobra on the back.

We used to go to the Torrance Civic Auditorium to the dances, and Chris, who was the biggest guy in our group, would find the biggest guy on the floor, who was a member of some other gang, wait until the guy was dancing, and then go up to him and tap him on the shoulder to cut in on his date. The guy would say, "Hey, there's no cutting in here! Get lost!" Chris would just hit him on the shoulder again, grab him, turn him around, and Sunday him, you know, punch him. And when he'd hit a guy, he was so good that no matter how big they were they'd go down. The guy would go down, and everybody would get all excited, and Chris would tell him, "We're the Cobras. We'll meet you at so-and-so."

There was a street where some city or county lines met—Wilmington, San Pedro, Torrance, I'm not sure. The street was right in the middle of these lines, and there was some idea that this was the safest place to fight, which was ridiculous because the police would bust you anywhere—they didn't care about lines. But this was where we'd go. It was a country type place and at night it was deserted. There was an old lot with a stand where they sold vegetables in the daytime.

I was never afraid of a one-on-one situation boxing or fistfighting, but when you get into gangs then you have to worry if someone's got a knife or a gun or a piece of steel. We'd drive to this lot, the cars would stop, and out would jump Chris and all the guys and the guys from the other gang, and they'd meet and start fighting. I would have to get out and fight. We'd fight until one side or the other won, or, if we were losing, we'd jump in our cars and split. And afterwards, we'd go to this drive-in and eat and talk about the fight. They'd laugh and everything. That was, like, great fun. We'd strut around the school the next day. And we drank. We drank Burgermeister ale and Gilbey's gin to get the nerve to go into these things. That was the trip and it wasn't me.

Finally, during one of these fights, some guys brought out a chain, and a couple of knives came out, and a couple of guys got cut real bad, and I started thinking, "Wow, I don't want *this!*" I thought, "If this is being part of society . . ." That was society for me. Now, if that was what I had to do to belong, I didn't want any part of it. So that was when I started getting with Johnny Martizia and Jimmy Henson, musicians I'd met playing at dances. They were in their early twenties, and they had other friends whose thing was playing music, and it was a good thing. I got along better with them. I withdrew from the guys in school, and the gang ranked me: they thought I thought I was better than them, that I was stuck-up, that I had a big head, and every now and then I'd get challenged by one of these guys and have to have a fistfight, but it was better than being part of that gang. I quit the Cobras and that's when I really got into the music thing.

———————————

(Johnny Martizia)   I was about eighteen. I was playing with a little dance band, high school dances, and I kept hearing all these, you know, stinking saxophone players, out of tune, honking sounds, and I went to this rehearsal, and I heard somebody warming up, playing scales and so on, and my God! I said, "What is *that*?" It was such a gorgeous sound. It was like a real artist, and I looked, and it was this little kid! He looked about fourteen years old. It was Art. I couldn't believe it. I said, "Who the hell are you?"

Art and I got real friendly. He'd come over to my house. I played him some records and I played some jazz myself. Not well. He said, "How do you do that? How do you jam?" That was the word—jam. I explained about chord progressions and I said, "You make up your own melody." And boy, he got it right away. He's got great ears. He'd hear something once and he'd have it. He must have had a good teacher, too. Art knew all his scales, and that's very important.

I had started out playing cowboy songs, "Home on the Range," things like that. Then, somehow, I happened to hear some Django Reinhardt. That was really incredible. I still have some of the records—78s. I listened to them over and over and tried to copy all his licks. I started taking *down beat* magazine, listening to all the big bands, and going with the other guys to hear people like Coleman Hawkins and T-Bone Walker when they were in town. We'd get friendly with them and they'd tell us, "Hey, man, we're going to go down to this after-hours place and jam, do you want to come?" Of course we'd go. We'd stay all night.

Well, Art started going out with us, going to bars to play. We didn't even have a car; we'd walk sometimes for miles. Zoot Sims was one of the guys then. We used to call him Jackie, Jackie Sims.

Art was a very clean-looking, Italian-looking kid, normal height, good weight, very, very healthy, good-looking. He was a very exciting kid, kinda naughty, you know, a raise-hell kinda kid. One night we went to a club to jam and all of a sudden I turn around and here's Art having an argument with an old guy. Maybe he wasn't so old; he seemed old to us. The next thing I know, Art's rolling on the floor, fighting with this guy. Art was a very energetic kid. Always jumpin' around.

WHEN I was nine or ten I liked the big bands that I heard on the radio—Count Basie, Duke Ellington, Artie Shaw, Benny Goodman, Charlie Barnet. After I got my clarinet, I started buying their records. It became my goal to play Artie Shaw's part on "Concerto for Clarinet." Finally, after I'd been playing for a few years, Mr. Parry bought me the sheet music. I practiced all alone and with the record, and I was finally able to play it. It was a difficult piece.

Johnny Martizia was a guitar player; Jimmy Henson played trombone. I got together with them at their houses to play. Johnny would strum the guitar. He told me, "These are the chords to the blues, which all jazz emanates from. This is black music, from Africa, from the slave ships that came to America."

I liked what I heard, but I didn't know what chords were. Chords are the foundation for all music, the foundation jazz players improvise on. I said, "What shall I do?" He said, "Listen to the sounds I'm making on my guitar and play what you feel." He strummed the blues and I played things that felt nice and seemed to fit. We played and played, and slowly I began to play sounds that made sense and didn't clash with what he was doing. I asked him if he thought that I might have the right to play jazz. He said, "You're very fortunate. You have a gift." I wanted to become the greatest player in the world. I wanted to become a jazz musician.

I ran around with Johnny and his friends. We'd go into bars and ask if we could play. Sometimes they said yes. I was fourteen or fifteen. These guys took me down to Central Avenue, the black nightclub district, and asked if we could sit in. The people there were very encouraging.

I played clarinet in the school band in San Pedro but when I got to Fremont High I stopped playing in school and started working more jobs. I had been playing alto saxophone since I was twelve, and now I got a job playing alto with a trio at Victor McLaglen's. I began going by myself to Central Avenue. I met a lot of musicians there. I ran into a bass player, Joe Mondragon, who said he was going with Gus Arnheim in San Diego. He asked me if I wanted to go with the band. I was still going to school but I wasn't going regular. I went to San Diego and stayed for about three months.

Gus Arnheim was in a big ballroom down there. It was a

very commercial band and I didn't fit in because there were no jazz solos to play—you just read music. It was good practice, but it got tiresome, so I left, came back, went to Central Avenue again, and ran into Dexter Gordon. He said that Lee Young was forming a band to go into the Club Alabam; they needed an alto player. I auditioned and I got the job. I think I auditioned at the colored union. They had a white union and a colored union. I had already joined the union when I lived in San Pedro.

This was in the early '40s and things were so different from the way they are now. Central Avenue was like Harlem was a long time ago. As soon as evening came people would be out on the streets, and most of the people were black, but nobody was going around in black leather jackets with naturals hating people. It was a beautiful time. It was a festive time. The women dressed up in frills and feathers and long earrings and hats with things hanging off them, fancy dresses with slits in the skirts, and they wore black silk stockings that were rolled, and wedgie shoes. Most of the men wore big, wide-brimmed hats and zoot suits with wide collars, small cuffs, and large knees, and their coats were real long with padded shoulders. They wore flashy ties with diamond stickpins; they wore lots of jewelry; and you could smell powder and perfume everywhere. And as you walked down the street you heard music coming out of every-place. And everybody was happy. Everybody just loved everybody else, or if they didn't, I didn't know about it. Gerald Wiggins, the piano player, Slick Jones, the drummer, Dexter Gordon, and Charlie Mingus—we would just walk out in the street and pee off the curb. It was just cool. We'd light up a joint; we had Mota, which is moist and black, and we'd smoke pot right out in front of the club.

The dope thing hadn't evolved into what it is now, with all the police activity. I'd never heard of a narco, didn't know what the word meant. Nobody wanted to rat on anybody or plant their car with a joint or with some stuff. You didn't have to worry that the guy that asked you to go out and smoke a joint was a policeman or that the chick that wanted to take you over to her pad and ball you was trying to set you up for the cops. People just got high, and they had fun, and there were all kinds of places to go, and if you walked in with a horn everyone would shout, "Yeah! Great! Get it out of the case and blow some!" They didn't care if you played better than somebody else. Nobody was trying to cut anybody or take their job, so we'd get together and blow.

There was no black power. I was sixteen, seventeen years old, white, innocent, and I'd wander around all over the place, at all hours of the night, all night long, and never once was accosted. I was never threatened. I was never challenged to a fight. I was never called a honkie. And I never saw any violence at all except for an occasional fight over a woman or something like that. It was a whole different trip than it got be later on.

The club Alabam was the epitome of Central Avenue. It was right off Forty-second Street across from Ivy Anderson's Chicken Shack. There were a lot of other clubs, but the Club Alabam was really one of the old-time show-time places, a huge room with beautiful drapes and silks and sparklers and colored lights turning and flashing. The bandstand was plush and gorgeous with curtains that glistened. The waitresses were dressed in scanty costumes, and they were all smiling and wiggling and walking around, and everywhere you looked you saw teeth, people laughing, and everybody was decked out. It was a sea of opulence, big hats and white fluffy fur. And the cars out front were real long Cadillacs with little mudguards, little flappy little things, shiny things.

The band had two altos, two trumpets, a tenor, and a rhythm section. On the show was Avery Parrish. He was the one who wrote "After Hours" and made that famous, and when he played the whole place rocked with the music. There was Wynonie Harris, a real handsome guy, light skinned with glistening eyes and the processed hair, all shiny with every hair just perfectly in place. He had a good blues voice and just carried the audience away. The walls would start shaking; the people screaming and clapping. Every now and then they'd get up and start wiggling in the aisles next to their tables. Moke and Poke were on the bill, far-out comedians. When they came on they'd do this walking step, laughing, one right behind the other, moving in perfect synchronization. After their act they'd run into their dressing room, rip off their clothes, and throw on silk robes and come back and do this walk around the audience; every now and then, when they were walking, if the audience was really good, they'd have it so their joints would flop out of their robes, flopping in time, in perfect unison, and the chicks would go, "Ahhhhh!" And we'd just be shouting in the background, playing these real down-home blues. I'd go in there and play and get so caught up in the feeling that I never had a chance to think about anything bad that might be happening to me or to worry at all. It was such an open, such a free, such a beautifully right time.

There was a place on Vernon, right around the corner from the Club Alabam, called the Ritz Club. You went through a door into an empty storefront and walked through a curtain. You took bottles in, and they served mixes and food. The music started at two in the morning and went on all night. People would come and sit in: Jimmy Blanton, probably the greatest bass player that ever lived—he was so far ahead of any jazz musician on any instrument it was just ridiculous; Art Tatum came in; Louis Armstrong, Ben Webster, Coleman Hawkins, Roy Eldridge, Johnny Hodges, Lester Young. You can imagine what a thrill it was to be in the same room with these people. I used to go sit in after my job at the Club Alabam and play with them. Then the management decided to hire a regular band at the Ritz Club so they'd always have somebody there to play when people came to sit in, and I was hired. That's when I started smoking pot; I was already drinking every night and taking pills.

I was hanging around with Dexter Gordon. We smoked pot and took Dexedrine tablets, and they had inhalers in those days that had little yellow strips of paper in them that said "poison," so we'd put these strips in our mouths, behind our teeth. They really got you roaring as an upper: your scalp would tingle, and you'd get chills all over, and then it would center in your head and start ringing around. You'd feel as if your whole head was lifting off. I was getting pretty crazy, and right about that time, I think, Dexter started using smack, heroin.

Dexter Gordon was an idol around Central Avenue. He was tall. He wore a wide-brimmed hat that made him seem like he was about seven feet tall. He had a stoop to his walk and wore long zoot suits, and he carried his tenor in a sack under his arm. He had these heavy-lidded eyes; he always looked loaded, always had a little half smile on his face. And everybody loved him. All the black cats and chicks would say, "Heeeeey, Dex!"

you know, and pat him on the back, and bullshit with him. I used to stand around and marvel at the way they talked. Having really nothing to say, they were able to play these little verbal games back and forth. I envied it, but I was too self-conscious to do it. What I wouldn't give to just jump in and say those things. I could when I was joking to myself, raving to myself, in front of the mirror at home, but when it came time to do it with people I couldn't.

Lee Young was worried about me. I was so young. I think he felt he had an obligation to take care of me. Lee looked like the typical black musician of the '40s, the hep black man with the processed hair. He was light complected, very sharp, with diamond rings; he wore his clothes well; and he was a cat you'd figure could conduct himself in any situation. His brother was Lester Young, one of the greatest saxophone players that ever lived in this world. The most fantastic—equaled only fairly recently by John Coltrane. Better than Charlie Parker. In my humble opinion, better than Charlie Pa er, just marvelous, such beauty. And Lee, Lee played nice ums. He was capable but was in the shadow of his broth , and I think he felt that. He loved his brother and was very proud of him, but I don't see how he could help but feel sad that he couldn't have played with his brother and really set the world on fire.

Lee was very nice to me and thoughtful. To show you what kind of a person he was—I was playing my parts and nobody else would have worried about me. Why go out of their way to worry about a little white boy, you know? But Lee dug that I was hanging out with Dexter, and we were on that road, and he sat down with me. He said, "I've talked to Dexter, man, and he's got a way to go. There's cold awful dues he's got to pay and he's just going to have to pay 'em, I'm afraid. But you, man, why don't you—boy, I'd love to see you not have to pay those dues." I said, "No, I'm alright. I'm okay." He said, "Art, I really like you. I'd sure love to see you do right."

At that time Jimmy Lunceford's band lost Willie Smith, who had played lead alto with them for a long time. He went with Harry James. So Kurt Bradford, who had been with Benny Carter, went to Jimmy Lunceford, and Lee got me an audition with Benny. He tried to get me a job where he thought I'd be protected. I auditioned and I made the band.

(Lee Young) I started the band that Art was in after I left Lionel Hampton. Well, when I first quit Lionel's band, Lester left Basie, and we formed a band out here. Jimmy Rowles happened to be in Seattle, Washington, and he came down here to be in the band. Now, I don't want to make this a black and white thing, but at the time we're talking about it was an exception to have a white guy in a black band. Only we didn't say "black"; we said "colored band," "colored players." Music has always been the same to me. It never had any color to me.

Lester and I took our band to Café Society in '42—that's in New York City. Then our dad died. That broke up the band because I was very close to the family. I came back home to L.A. in the latter part of '42 or early '43.

I told you about the Jimmy Rowles thing because for some reason it seems like every band I had, I always had a white player. I don't remember where I heard Art, but I just believe it might have been at a jam session because that's all I did all the time. I kept my drums in the back of the car. They had all kinds of jam sessions on Central Avenue; it was against the union rules to play them, but I did it *all* the time. They must have fined me a hundred times. I'm certain that's how I met Art, and when I got the gig for the Club Alabam he was one of the first people I thought of because when you build a band you think of the first-chair man. And Art did play lead alto.

We had three saxes, one trumpet, one trombone, and piano, bass, and drums. We had to play two shows and we played for dancing. The arrangements we had were made by Gerald Wilson; Dudley Brooks and Nat Cole also used to write arrangements for us. I don't know if that was when Art was with the band or not. Nat always wrote in pencil. That'll let him know. Gerald Wiggins wrote for the band and played piano. We used to call him Wig. I've been all over the world since this—and talk about how times change—Art was just one of the band. We didn't know any different down on Central Avenue at that time. It wasn't about "whitey" this and "whitey" that. It was about good musicianship and people respecting one another for the talents that they had. I don't know of a single incident that occurred. We never thought in

the terms that they seem to now; maybe white people can't go
now on Central Avenue for some reason or other, and that
reason I don't know.

I remember when Buddy Rich first came here with Artie
Shaw and Vido Musso; they used to always be down on
Central. Harry James, he used to be on Central Avenue
jammin'. That's where everybody hung out. Everybody. They
had so many little clubs. Next door to the Alabam was a
Mexican restaurant, and she had a piano in the back, and
piano players used to go in there, and I'm speaking about *Art
Tatum*. Adjacent to that was the Downbeat. Within two blocks
they had about six clubs where musicians were working, and
so, like, we used to take long intermissions and go across the
street and listen. We'd go next door and they'd come over to
hear us play. It was like a west coast Fifty-second Street, but you
never really heard of Los Angeles that much, then, where music
was concerned. Everybody thought all the jazz and all the
better jazz musicians came from the east. The writers for
Metronome and *down beat* used to segregate it. They had what
they called "West Coast Jazz"; they thought it would be
different. I think that's because the east wanted to really be up
here and have the west down *there*, whatever that was. Music
is music. Either you can play or you cannot play. And I've
found that music is an international language. One of the best
bands I ever heard was a band in Buenos Aires, in Argentina.

But let me tell you this about Art. At that time, I think
everybody in the band was young, but, at seventeen, Art was
the youngest. And about musicians, you can always tell when a
guy is going to be great because the potential is there, and the
only thing that needs to happen is for him to get out and play.
It's like my brother, Prez. I know how much he could play at
seventeen, and I think that what happens is that they could
play *snakes* at that age, but they just have not mellowed into
the type of style they're going to play. I think that's all that
happens after that. When a musician is young, every idea they
have, they try to play at once. They're not necessarily any
better—Art probably wasn't any better at twenty-seven than he
was at seventeen; he probably didn't know the instrument any
better; but he knew what to do with it. He knew how not to

overplay. You learn to pace yourself. *But* if he was not able to play all those notes and hear all those things, then he would never have been able to create a style. He was destined: nobody at that time was taking a seventeen year old and putting him into a band. The nearest I remember is when Harry James had Corky Corcoran. He played tenor. At that time he was the child wonder; I think he was sixteen or seventeen. But he was never destined to reach the heights as a jazz player that Art reached because you knew then, in hearing Corky play, that he wasn't the instrumentalist, the technician, that Art was. Stan Getz was very young, too, but Stan, he copied a lot. Stan copied Prez. Now, I never did hear that in Art.

I lost track of Art for a long time, and then he did a lot of things on his own. When he went with Benny Carter, that's understandable. He went from nine pieces to fourteen, fifteen pieces; he went from three saxophones to five. That was an education in itself. And then to go on and join Stan Kenton, that's beautiful.

Art was talented, but let me tell you, I never would have hired him if I'd thought he didn't have the right personality. If it's going to be one of you and a lot of another race of people, you could have a problem. I didn't just take Art blindly because I thought he played so well. I knew he'd be able to get along with the guys. And I knew the type of guys I had in the band. They would only judge him by his playing. He was quiet, the way I remember him. As a matter of fact the whole damn band was quiet! Hahahaha! That was a *quiet* band, but it was a good band. It could play.

The Club Alabam had had many names. When I came out here as a kid, you know, I used to be a singer and dancer, and it was one of the first places I worked. It was called the Apex. That was in the thirties, when all the movie stars used to frequent the club, so it was really a big business. And the same man who owned the Apex wound up owning the Club Alabam. How can I describe it? You had to buy your tickets at a ticket window, and then you'd go in, and they had tables all around the dance floor, maybe three deep, and they had a balcony, and right on the railing they had tables all the way around. I think you could get nine hundred people in there. And there

was a long bar, maybe eighty, ninety feet, and all the hustlers
and pimps, they stayed at the bar to fire their shots, so it was
like something you see in the movies now, with the gangsters.
But these guys were harmless, guys that gambled, no guns or
that type of thing, and always shirt and tie and hats and coats.
The dance floor was about fifty feet; you could get a lot of
couples on the floor. And the show—they had eight or ten
chorus girls. Oh yeah! That's why I always took the job!
Hahahaha! We always had a shake dancer, chorus, comics, and
a headliner, and you couldn't get near the place on Saturdays
and Sundays especially. Most of the black people would be
there on weekends, and all during the week the clientele was
white.

That club was a nice place to work. But it all came to an
end with the change of times and with the people moving out. I
think it was the influx of transients; there was a lot of that.
During the war, I went on the staff at Columbia Studios, but
Central was really jumping then. It was almost like Broadway.
After the war, the clubs started closing. I don't know if it was
hard times or what it was. I never really thought about it, but I
observed it happening. As a matter of fact, it's been years since
I've been there because it was such a drastic change. If you've
grown up used to something and it deteriorates . . . The
Downbeat turned into a dump, a lot of winos hanging around.
And they started holding people up and mugging people. It was
just the times, I guess.

WHEN I went with Benny Carter I played all my jazz by ear. I
was good at reading, but I didn't know about chord structure,
harmony, composition. Also, I had never played much lead
alto, so with Benny I played second alto, he played lead, but in
my book I had two parts written in most of the arrangements
and sometimes, if there wasn't a large audience, Benny would
just get off the stand and let me play his parts. I'd get all his
solos. I learned that way how to play lead in a four-man saxophone section. And I learned a lot following Benny, listening to
his solos, what he played against the background. The guys in

the band were all great musicians—Gerald Wilson, Freddie Webster, a legendary trumpet player, and J.J. Johnson, a jazz superstar. We played all over L.A. We did well. I was making fifty dollars a week, which was big money in those days.

The band went to Salt Lake City. I took Patti with me, and we stayed with Freddie Webster and his wife, with a colored family, on the outskirts of town. Freddie was a nice-looking, kind of a strange-looking, little cat. I had a strong affection for him. He was a little man who could back up the little man complex; his playing was incredibly beautiful. And he always carried an automatic pistol. He felt that because he was black and because of his size, somebody was going to push him into a corner and he'd need an equalizer. When we finished the job at night, I'd go stand in the street and flag down a cab. Freddie would hide. Then I'd go to get in the cab and hold the door open, and he'd run and jump in. Because they wouldn't pick up a black guy. And I was always afraid the cab driver would say something and Freddie would shoot him. I was happy and comfortable with the guys in the band, but my dad hated blacks. He hated blacks and policemen and rats, informers; those were the things he raved about all the time, and he was angry that I hung out with "a bunch of niggers, a bunch of goddamned jigaboos." The band was going down south and Benny told me it would be too dangerous from the blacks and the whites both for me to go along. I couldn't understand why I had to leave the band and I didn't know what I was going to do, but Benny talked to his manager, Carlos Gastel, who also managed Stan Kenton's band. Stan had an exciting new band, very glamorous; they were from Balboa and all that. Jack Ordean, who played alto, had just left Kenton, so an audition was arranged and I was hired by Stan Kenton when I was still seventeen.

(**Benny Carter**) I was greatly impressed by Art's talent, his sound, his concept of playing lead, and his creative ideas. He was a handsome, clean-cut, and most mannerly boy with a very affable disposition. I wasn't aware at all of Art drinking heavily or using drugs. I liked him and have only positive memories of him at that time.

———————————

THANKS to Benny, when I got with Stan I was able to play lead. But while it had been possible to play solos by ear with Benny, with Stan things were different. He had a syncopated style, very original; things were built on an eighth note, three quarter notes, and another eighth note. It wasn't easy to hear when you played a solo, and it got increasingly difficult. Finally, when we played the first record date that we did, on Capitol Records, and I did a solo on "Harlem Folk Dance," it was just impossible. That's when I realized I *had* to learn something about chord structure and the theory of music, so I started asking the guys in the band, "What happens with this? What happens with that?" And I gradually learned to read the chords. Red Dorris helped me a lot. He played tenor and sang with the band. He sang on that first date "Do Nothin' Til You Hear From Me."

Patti came to the jobs. She never did anything to excess. Sometimes she'd have a drink, and later on she smoked a little pot, but all she cared about was making love to me and watching me play. There I was. I had been a child living in my fantasies. Now I was a married man making lots of money. One of the first things I did, when I was still with Benny Carter, I took Patti downtown and bought her a watch with diamonds and emeralds. I remember that watch cost me a hundred and seventy-five dollars, almost a month's salary. I'd buy her sexy panties and when we were riding on the bus I'd put my hand up under her dress when nobody was looking. We'd play games. Sometimes I'd make her pay her own way on the bus and we'd sit in separate seats like strangers. Then I'd start talking to her. We'd end up getting off the bus together and all the people would see it; it was so obvious. Guys would watch: "I didn't think she was *that* kind of a girl! He must have a great line." I'd look back and they'd all be staring. We were living down toward Los Angeles, downtown. We'd wander around and see an old hotel or one of those apartment houses and walk in the front door and down the hallway. We'd sneak into the hall bathroom, lock the door, and lie down on the floor and make love.

We'd go to the market together, and coming home I would slow up and walk behind her. We did this so many times and neither of us ever did anything to ruin it. I'd say, "Oh, pardon me, young lady, do you live around here?" She'd say, "Yes, I live down the street with my husband." And I'd say, "I thought so because I've seen you and you sure are beautiful." She'd say, "You shouldn't say that because I'm a married woman." I'd say, "I just can't help it. You're so gorgeous. I'd give anything in the world if I could make love to you." I'd walk home with her. She'd go up to the house and look in. She'd come back and say, "Well, my husband isn't home. I don't know where he's at. I guess you could come in. You could maybe kiss me or something." I'd get all excited. We'd go in. I'd put my arms around her. I'd kiss her. Then she would say, "Please stop. I told you I'd give you a kiss but that's all. I'm sorry, because you are a nice boy; you are handsome; and if I wasn't married . . . " I'd say, "Oh, please, please, please! Anything you want I'll give you. I'll do anything. Just let me look at you. Just let me look at your breasts." "Don't say that!" "Oh, please!" "Will you promise that's all you'll ask of me?" "I promise. I swear." So she'd pull up her sweater and take her brassiere off and stand there posing with her titties hanging out. And I'd ask if I could just touch them . . . .

I used to like to scare her, too. She'd go to the store and I'd hide in the closet. She'd come home and she'd shout, "Art? Where are you? Come on, Art, *please*. I know you're here." Then I'd start making noises. Growling. She'd say, "Come on out. Don't act silly. Please!" And she was always scared. I'd sneak out of the closet, and she'd turn around, and there I'd be with this horrible Frankenstein look I had. She'd say, "Oh stop it, honey, please." I'd yell, "Hhhrrruuuuuaaaahhh!" And she'd shriek, "Stop that!" I'd be coming toward her with my hands in front of me; I'd be jumping—little, fast, jump-steps. I'd be bouncing and I'd have this *horrible* look on my face. She'd scream, "Stop that!" And she'd start running. "Stop that, Art!" I'd be bouncing after her, "Pt-pt-pt-pt." She'd be hysterical. I'd chase her all around the room, into the kitchen and into the bathroom, and she'd scream, "Please! Please!" Finally, I'd kiss her, and everything would be alright.

I was doing well. People were getting to know me in the music business. I was starting to get a little following. And I was in love—after seventeen years of loneliness. I knew it couldn't last. Then, one day in the latter part of 1943, after six months of marriage, I got my greetings from Uncle Sam.

4 | The Army

1944–1946

THAT WAR was a real war. Every day the papers had casualty lists showing thousands of Americans killed. You'd go to movies and see newsreels of bodies. I was praying for some miracle. I was just one little person. Maybe they'd make a mistake and overlook me. And then I got the greetings.

I wish I could describe the feeling. It was as if I'd been given six months of happiness and now I was going to be killed. I did everything in my power to get out of it. I wanted to fail the physical so I kept taking the strips and bennies and drinking. I'd get in the shower on a cold night, put my clothes on, and, still soaking wet, walk around the block barefoot so I'd catch TB or something. I stopped eating. I stayed up for days at a time. I ran into a chiropractor. He checked my heart. I had a slight murmur, and he said I didn't have anything to worry about. He wrote a long letter to the draft board to take with me when I went to my physical. I didn't know that the word of a chiropractor is valueless, so I paid him and continued my escapades, and when I went to my physical I was so weak I could hardly get to the place. I went through the first part; they tell you to touch your toes fifteen or twenty times and they listen to your heart. I touched my toes once and was going down the second time and blacked out and nearly fell over. My heart was pounding, and I thought I had it made, but it didn't work out that way.

I was inducted into Fort MacArthur on February 11, 1944. My dad drove me down, and I went in. I was a loner. Even playing with the bands, I was a loner. The only times I could act out or talk were when I was drunk. Sober I was completely cut off. Now I was in the army. I had trouble going to the bathroom; I couldn't urinate in front of people. I couldn't do the other thing.

I stayed at Fort MacArthur having physical examinations and being miserable, and then they sent me to Fort Sill, Oklahoma. You took seventeen weeks' basic training to prepare you for overseas. We did everything imaginable at Fort Sill. We marched. We drilled. We scrubbed. It was a field artillery base so we fired all kinds of weapons. Whit, one of my stepfathers, had taught me how to shoot a .22, and I was an excellent shot. I got an expert's medal. After that we threw hand grenades, and then we went through obstacle courses, climbing ropes, and infiltration courses with barbed wire around them. You crawl up onto the course from a trench and you have to stay flat on the ground because .50-caliber machine guns are being fired over your head, four feet in the air. If you raised up, you'd get killed. They had holes with land mines, and the land mines would explode, so you'd feel as if you were in battle. Since we were in Oklahoma there were water moccasins and copperhead snakes. They used to crawl down on the course, and a couple of people were killed while I was there because they ran into a snake, flipped out, stood up, and got shot. You go through it twice in the daytime and once at night, and at night every fourth or fifth bullet in the machine gun clip is a tracer, which means it lights up. You could see these flashing bullets going over your head.

The only other person that wasn't from the south in my platoon of seventy-eight men was a guy named Dennis from Kansas. All the rest of them were from Texas and Oklahoma and Arkansas, and they really disliked northerners and me especially because I was from California—"Hollywood" they called it. They used to make fun of me so I got into a lot of fights.

Dennis was a real towhead with cowlicks and everything, a Dennis-the-Menace type kid; he was open for anything; he just wanted to have fun; and we liked each other. We used to go into town on weekends, Lawton, Oklahoma. They only had three-two beer, but you could get drunk on it, and every now and then you'd run into a bootlegger who'd have whiskey or gin smuggled in from Texas.

One night Dennis and I went to town and really got wiped out. We came back to the post at about two or three o'clock in the morning and went into the latrine, a big, separate building out in front with showers and rows of toilets and rows and rows of sinks. There was nobody in there but us, so we started acting crazy. We were so uptight and frustrated we started knocking things down. We broke things. Then we took the toilet paper out of the supply room and threw it all over and we lit it; it really started to blaze. We didn't know what to do then, so we ran out. We snuck out of the latrine and into our barracks.

Reveille rang in the morning. They'd blow a bugle. The sergeants screamed at you to get up. You threw your clothes on, ran out of the barracks, and lined up in the little parade ground. Each group of barracks had their own parade ground out in the middle. We ran out, me and Dennis, really hung over. We lined up and looked at the latrine. It was a mess. It hadn't burned to the ground but it was burned bad. They had roll call. Then the lieutenant came. The captain came. They started wigging out to see who had done it, and everybody in our platoon looked around at me and Dennis. They said they'd better find out who did it or the whole company would be put on quarantine; there'd be no passes. They dismissed us, and then when we started to go back into the barracks our platoon surrounded us. They said, "Where were you guys last night? We know you did it. You're the only guys that would do anything like that."

We all went to the latrine and we all had to clean. Everybody kept ranking us, accusing us. Finally I flipped out. I remember saying, "I didn't do it, but I wish I had! That's what I think of you bastards!" They tore our clothes off and threw us in the shower. They gave us a "GI bath" with strong brown soap with lye in it and scrubbed us with big brushes made out of wood sticks. We were hollering and fighting, and finally I told 'em, "Yeah, I did it, you motherfuckers!" Then somebody came and stopped it, one of the officers. And so they put us on KP for a couple of weeks. From then on it was open warfare, me and Dennis against the rest of the platoon.

When I first got to Fort Sill I used to cry at night and think, "How can it be? How can I be here?" I couldn't believe that this could be happening to me. I couldn't believe that I might die with these people I hated.

Before you finish basic training you're allowed a visit. The family chipped in, and Patti came to Lawton. I hadn't seen her for three months. It's hard for regular soldier's wives to get rooms in towns like that; if you're not an officer they think you're scum. But Patti had such a nice way about her, she talked a lady into renting her a room in a house in town, and finally the night came for me to go to her.

We had had an especially hard day. I'd had to go over an obstacle course, climbing and running and doing all sorts of outrageous things. I took a shower and cleaned up. I was all excited. I got a bottle of something and went to town; I went to the place and the lady of the house came to the door, a nice southern lady with the accent and everything. I introduced myself and then Patti appeared at the top of the stairs. She had a silky, clinging dress on with all kinds of colors in it; it set off her white skin. She was wearing those high-heeled pumps that made her legs look so pretty, and her hair was just hanging down. Her eyes were glowing and glistening and she was smiling. And when she smiled she had little dimples that showed. Her face looked like a child's.

I was so happy to see her. I couldn't stand to have anything to do with the girls I'd see in town. One time I was drinking some beer in a bar, and this little chick that looked nice came up to me and said hello, and we talked, and for a moment it was pleasant, and then she called me "Joe." I said, "What did you call me that for?" She said, "Well, that's what we call you soldier boys." I said, "I'm not a soldier boy!" I got so angry I wanted to strangle her. Joe! I'm not Joe! So seeing Patti I was seeing someone that was mine, somebody I meant something to, and it was wonderful.

We went into the room and had a couple of drinks. We talked and kissed and Patti told me how worried everybody was and how unbearable it was for her: she was so lonely. She cried. Then we got into bed and started making love. Up to this time, so that she wouldn't get pregnant, I had pulled out. I assumed that that was what I would do this time, and when I felt I couldn't keep from coming I told her, "I'm going to come!" But as soon as I said that she threw her legs up over my back and held me, and she threw her arms around me and grabbed me, and she had so much strength, and it had been so long since we'd made love, and I was so passionate, and I was fighting her to get out of her, and I couldn't do it, and so I came. And I remember thinking how marvelous it felt and what a shame we couldn't always do it that way. And I thought, maybe just this one time, maybe nothing will happen, maybe she won't get pregnant. But I *knew* that she would. I knew as soon as it happened that she was going to get pregnant. She held me and told me that they had decided she had to have a baby. My folks had told her to force me to come in her in case anything should happen to me overseas—so there'd be something left of me. And she said that that was what she wanted.

I felt awful because I didn't want to have children. I *knew* that I didn't want to have any children. I had even gone through one of those operations because I didn't want to have any children, ever; I didn't want to share Patti with a child. I knew I wouldn't make a good parent.

The doctor who performed the vasectomy had been a friend of Patti's mother's. He had tried to talk me out of it, but I told him, "Man, I want it done!" I got on the operating table, and I had no anaesthetic. They shaved me, put Mercurochrome all over me, and then he made an incision in my testicle. The pain was beyond description. He pulled out the cord with some prongs, and he took a needle filled with Novacain, and all the time I'm going through this the doctor's got someone he's showing how he does the operation. I can hear them talking. This person says, "Isn't the pain bad?" And the doctor says, "Well, it's just for a moment, and this is the best way, really, to nullify it. From then on, once you get the needle into the cord . . . " And so he stuck it in, and after a while it took effect, but while I was still pulsating from the pain he started interrogating me. I'm delerious, and he's asking little questions. Finally he said, "When's your birthday? How old will you be?" So he discovered that I wasn't eighteen, and he couldn't perform the operation. He sewed me back up without cutting the cord. I didn't know. I waited to have the test that would tell whether I was sterile or not, and at last he told Patti, and she told me.

I waited until I was eighteen and went back to the same doctor to have him perform the same operation. He cut the cord this time, but he didn't cut a piece out of it. He tucked it underneath a membrane, in case I changed my mind, so it could be repaired. The cord found itself back together. And later, when I gave a sample of my sperm to see if I was sterile, I wasn't.

Twice was all the courage I could muster. I couldn't go through that thing again. But you can see how I felt about having a child, and when I realized that Patti was going to get pregnant I was really angry. I was mad at my folks and at her. That was the only time I came in her, that one time, and she went back to Los Angeles, and she was pregnant.

When I finished basic training they shipped me to Camp Butner, North Carolina, and put me in the combat engineers. And while I was at Camp Butner I heard that Benny Carter's band was going to be in Durham, and they were having their concert on a Saturday night when I'd be free.

I went into Durham and found the auditorium. I bought a ticket. I noticed the ticket said "loge." I said, "What's the loge?" The guy tells me, "That's upstairs." I said, "I used to be with this band: they're old friends of mine and I'd like to be close to the stand, where I can say hello to them." The guy says, "Well, you can't do that. Whites aren't allowed downstairs." When Benny had told me I couldn't go with the band down south I didn't understand it. I had been all around Central Avenue for years as a kid. I couldn't understand what he was talking about, and my eyes were still closed at this time. I was shocked, and I tried to argue with the guy, but he said, "You either take a loge ticket or you don't go in."

I went in and took my seat. I looked downstairs. The whole bottom floor was black. The people upstairs were white. The band started playing, and I started drinking, and finally I just walked downstairs because I had to see them. I snuck through the dancefloor. I walked real fast and as I approached the stand I could feel the people staring at me, and then they started moving and all of a sudden they just closed me in. All of a sudden there was a circle of black people around me and they were saying, "What are you doing down here? What are you doing down here, white boy?" I said, "I used to play with this band. I want to say hello." They said, "You get outta here!" And they all started yelling. One guy screamed, "You killed my grandparents, you son-of-a-bitch, you white bastard! You beat my grandparents to death, you son-of-a-bitch!" I said, "I didn't kill anybody! I didn't do anything!" But they kept raving, so I got mad. I shouted, "I don't want to hear any of your fuckin' shit! I didn't do anything to you!" Someone said, "You better get outta here, boy, if you know what's good for you!" I said, "Fuck you all, man!" They grabbed me and one guy hit me in the back; another punched me, and I was screaming and swinging around; by this time I was close to the bandstand and the people taking the tickets saw what was happening and rushed out. I was raging, "I used to play with this band!" I think I hollered, "Benny!" And he jumped off the stand and ran down there. The ushers were saying, "You've got to get out of here! Someone's gonna kill you!" Benny comes up to me and says, "Oh, man!" I said, "What is this? What kind of shit is this? I just wanted to say hello!" He said, "This is what I was talking about before. I thought you knew about these things." I was crying by this time. They despised me. They wanted to kill me. Benny said, "There's nothing I can do, man. Come around after. We'll see you outside, around by the bus." The ushers escorted me out.

I was going to wait to see the guys, but if I had gotten together with one of those black guys from inside I would have killed him or gotten killed. I left the place and found me a jug and drank it and wandered around the town. I was mad. I was really confused. I was hurt. And finally I got on the bus and went back to the post.

I was drafted too late to get into a band. They needed people for combat, not for bands, but I had my horn sent to me anyway, at Camp Butner, so I could play. I was stationed right next to the 225th Army Ground Force Band, and when I realized that, I took out my horn and started practicing in my barracks, playing out the window so they could hear me. They ran over and just wigged out when I told them who I was. They had all heard of me because I'd been with Stan Kenton, and they started a campaign to get me into the band.

It was a difficult thing to do, but there was a warrant officer in charge of the band who played oboe and really dug me. He was a classical child prodigy from a wealthy family. I think he played with the Pittsburgh Symphony. He had blue eyes, blond-ish, curly hair, a pouting mouth and effeminate ways, delicate hands, long, slender fingers. He had a very refined manner of speaking and was brought up, I think, as a loner, like myself, only he was rich. He didn't really care for anyone else in the band, and he had found a friend in me; in fact, he was a little overly friendly and I always felt strange around him. He never made any sexual advances, but whenever I'd mention my wife or anything like that he'd get uncomfortable and change the subject. It's a thing I've run into lots of times, guys who liked me with almost a homosexual intensity but with no overt actions. This warrant officer had a lot of pull, and he kept working, and, finally, just before the outfit I was with went overseas, I got a transfer. That was right before the Battle of the Bulge, and most of the people in the outfit I was in were killed, but I got into the band.

When it was time for the baby to be born I got a furlough and went back to Los Angeles. Patti was living with my grandmother on Seventy-third Street. Her stomach was real big, and it was strange to feel the baby move. I was praying she'd have the baby before I had to go back, and just before I was supposed to leave she started getting labor pains close together. We took her to the hospital, and I sent a wire to the warrant officer requesting an extension. I got a wire back. He said if I came right away he'd guarantee we'd stay in the U.S., but if I didn't come back I'd be AWOL and I'd probably be transferred into another outfit and sent overseas. I had to leave Patti in the hospital.

When I got to the base there was a telegram waiting for me saying that the baby was born, a girl, six pounds, eight ounces. She was born January 5, 1945, the day after I left. I thought, "Well, anyway, I won't have to go overseas." But the reason the warrant officer had told me to hurry back was that the band was going overseas *immediately* and he wanted me to go with them. We were shipped to Camp Miles Standish in Massachusetts and loaded onto a boat in a convoy and sent to France.

Everyone was scared. The war was raging. The trip was okay until about the fourteenth day on the water, when it got stormy. It was a bad storm, and everybody was seasick. In the latrine, the vomit and the urine would roll from one end of this long tin urinal to the other, hit the end, and fly out onto the floor. It was hard trying to stand up with all the vomit and the piss. And then, one evening, just as the storm was abating, I felt a huge lurching of the ship and heard an explosion. There were two more explosions; it sounded like they were right under the ship; and then all the lights went out.

They started talking to us over the loudspeaker, telling us to be calm, not to panic, and to put on our life jackets. Finally they called our group to get up on deck. We filed up, and it was night. The motors were all shut off. The captain kept talking over the loudspeakers as softly as he could. He told us the convoy had been infiltrated by German submarines. We were about twenty-six ships and there were six navy destroyers with us. On the trip sometimes we'd see them running through the convoy.

I was fortunate enough, when I came up, to get fairly close to the rail. I was able to see down, and even though the motors were off, the ship was drifting, and where it was floating through the water there was phosphorous. That was the only light. You could see it to the left and to the right and in front; the light of the boat cutting through the water.

I had my life belt on. It was cold. It was February, and we were just approaching the tip of England, going through the Channel. This was the spot where the German submarines used to lie in wait to get the convoys. We were all scared to death. Every now and then the captain, I assumed it was the captain talking, would say that they were going to set off depth charges, don't be frightened. And that's what I'd heard at the beginning. We saw a huge explosion off the back side to the right, and a little while after that there was another. Two of our ships were hit and exploded. We thought at any moment a torpedo was going to hit us.

You can never find out what happens, but I heard later that three submarines were hit. They kept testing by radar until they found that all the subs had left and, after a long, long time, they turned the engines on and we started moving again, but we had to stay on deck just in case. Sometimes they'd turn off the engines and lay on the bottom and wait—the radar picked up the engine vibrations—and then start up again.

Up to this point we hadn't known for sure where we were going—England, France, or North Africa—but at last we entered Le Havre, and I'll never forget the sight of that harbor.

There were all kinds of ships, sunk, huge hunks of wreckage, and I guess the harbor was shallow because they were just lying there in the water. There were gun turrets blown to bits; you could see these huge howitzers, broken, all bent. The harbor itself was nonexistent: there were no more docks, so the Seabees had made landing places out of metal stripping.

The people started unloading and we watched from a porthole, but when our ship's turn came to go to the landing area everybody was unloaded except us. We didn't know what was happening. It was too good to think we wouldn't have to get off there and go to the Battle of the Bulge. We had been trained in stretcher bearing. If we did go we served as medics, helpless, no chance of defending ourselves. At the end of the third day there was no one on the ship but the crew and the band. Our warrant officer couldn't find out why we hadn't received orders to debark. We wanted to know if we could get off the ship and see the town, so he inquired and found that no American soldiers could go walking around Le Havre because the French would kill them. The Germans had taken the town at first, and there was a little damage, but they did just what they had to do, nothing more. Then the Americans came and took Le Havre back from the Germans and just mutilated the place. They were barbarians, animals, and the French despised them. We weren't allowed to get off the ship.

After five days we were frantic, but at last the warrant officer came back. He said, "I've got great news!" We'd been ordered to Bournemouth. We landed at Southampton, where they had trucks waiting for us that took us to a convalescent center in an old city in England, a huge camp filled with people who'd been wounded in battle. If they weren't dead but were wounded so badly they could never fight again, they were sent to the States, but if there was any chance at all of mending them up enough to put them back into battle, they were sent to England to one of these centers. Our function was to play for these people and give them a little entertainment, a little joy.

I stayed at the convalescent center for eight or nine months, playing and watching the V1 and V2 rockets fly overhead, bombing London, and then I became an MP.

At the end of 1945 a lot of people were released from the

war. They were sent home if they had enough points for longevity. Most of the guys in the band had been in the army for years so they qualified to go home, and rather than getting replacements they decided to do away with the band. I was put in the MPs and sent to London.

(Alan Dean) It was in the forties toward the end of the war, and I was singing with a small band in a hotel in Southampton. Southampton in those days was quite a place because it was more or less a clearinghouse for all the G.I.s who has fought in various areas of Europe during the war. They would come back to Southampton, and, according to priorities, would be put aboard troop ships and go back home, As I remember, Art and the guys that played with him in the military band had the unfortunate job of playing for them every morning as they took off to go back to the States. Of course the band remained behind.

I first met Art, I suppose, one night when he and a couple of other fellows came to us and said, "Hey, we like your band. Can we sit in?" We were, I must admit, a little reluctant at first, because it had been our experience that when a G.I. would say, "Can I sit in with you, I used to play with Tommy Dorsey," it usually turned out that he hadn't played with Tommy Dorsey at all. He could barely play his instrument. And it was bit embarrassing. But these guys seemed to be genuine, so we said, "Sure. By all means, sit in." Well, of course, when they started to play we knew that they were fine musicians, particularly Art, who just . . . absolutely . . . just stopped us in our tracks, he was so good. And, after that, they would come into the hotel almost every evening and sit in and play a set with us, and we became good friends.

The engagement, which was for several months at this hotel, came to an end, and we went back to London, and almost at the same time the military band that Art was playing with was disbanded because some of their members were being sent back on the priorities system. They broke it up and sent Art back with a few of the other guys to London, and, of all things, made Art an MP, which I don't think he was very happy about. He wasn't cut out for that kind of action.

London was really quite an exciting place to be in those days. There was a sort of free-for-all atmosphere. The war had taken away a lot of the stuffy social stigma that I remember England having before the war (I haven't lived in England for many, many years now). I know the war made people more together. They had nothing to lose so they had a good time. I know I did. Oh, there was rationing, and they had lots of bad air raids and that sort of thing, but generally life wasn't that bad.

My dad had a pub in London, which is only significant because good liquor was very hard to come by during the war, and my dad, having a pub, used to get a fairly good supply and would always keep a few back for me or himself or his friends. Whenever Art and the guys needed a drink, they'd just buzz me, and I could usually rustle something up. I was always amused when I'd get a phone call from Art sometime around midnight, and he'd say, "I can't take this MP thing. Have you got any gin?" I would say, "Yeah, I can get a bottle of gin." "Well, get in your car and meet me on the corner. . ," of Picadilly and something or other. I'd get in my car and park, and suddenly, out of the darkness, this small figure with a huge white hat would loom up, and it would be Art, and he'd take a quick look around and hop in the back of the car and dispose of about a half a bottle of gin, and he'd say, "Well, now I feel more like it." And back he'd go on the beat again. Studiously avoiding problems. He went the other way when he heard a fracas. He just wasn't interested, and I didn't blame him either.

The fellows came to my house on many occasions, and we used to sit 'til all hours of the morning playing records and getting boozed. On one occasion, one of the guys got hold of something that resembled grass, but I don't think it was. I didn't smoke anything, even ordinary cigarettes; I still don't, so I didn't participate. Fortunately. Because the other guys smoked whatever it was and were all violently ill and fell about the place. I don't think they tried it again.

Jazz was pretty hard to come by in London in those days, but there was this one place run by a man called Feldman who had three sons who were aspiring musicians—Robert, Victor, and

Monte. Victor, who was then about ten, played the drums, and of course, it's the same Victor Feldman who's one of the top guys in the studio scene in Hollywood now. He played amazingly well as a child, and then took up vibes and piano, and, as you know, he's quite a giant.

Feldman's was the place where jazz happened, and Art would go there and sit in and play and, of course, made a tremendous impression on the musicians around him because his technique, his fluency, his complete command of his instrument, was far ahead of any of the other musicians around. None of the English saxophone players . . . There were some good ones, but they just didn't have it all together like Art did. I think perhaps one of the reasons . . . I can't remember knowing anyone, ever, quite so dedicated to their music as Art was. Even when he was doing those awful MP things, walking around until five o'clock in the morning with a great white hat and a nightstick, he would grab a couple of hours sleep and a shower and go straight to a rehearsal room and practice his instrument for hours and hours on end with very little sleep. For him it was more important to maintain his ability and improve, and he did it studiously, without any hesitation. No matter what else was going on *that* had to happen. And I always admired that tremendous ability he had to dedicate himself to his work.

One time in Feldman's, a young fellow, oh, he wouldn't have been more than sixteen I suppose (I was about twenty at that time), a young kid, asked if he could sit in with us. We asked him, "What do you play?" He said clarinet, and we said, "Don't you play saxophone as well?" He said no, only clarinet. We said, "Well . . . alright." He played beautifully, and we asked him what his name was, and he said, "Johnny Dankworth." He said, "I'm actually studying to be a classical musician, but I love jazz, and I thought I'd like to try it." And I remember Art asked me who he was, and I said I didn't know. Art said, "Well, he has more promise than any musician I've heard in England to date." And I think he was very perceptive where that's concerned, because Dankworth, as you know, turned out to be one of the finest jazz musicians England has produced, and he's still very prominent along with his wife, Cleo Laine.

Art, of course, and the other guys subsequently went back
to the States, and I didn't hear from them again until 1951, by
which time I had become a name pop singer in England. I had
won all the popularity polls and I had made a few recordings;
some of them had sold very well. And, travelling around, I
worked with a few cats from the States, and they suggested I
try my hand in the States. I decided to do just that. Late in
1951 I emigrated. I brought all my records with me under my
arm and a lot of press clippings and whatever money I had and
off I went. A few days after I got to New York, I saw an ad
that the Stan Kenton Orchestra was going to be playing at
Carnegie Hall. I had every one of his records I could lay my
hands on, and the thought of seeing the Kenton band live was
just too much. I bought tickets in the first or second row and
sat there waiting for the band to come on. When they walked
on, who was sitting right in the middle of the sax section
playing lead alto but Art Pepper! I was thrilled to death. I ran
around backstage afterwards and we had a big backslapping
contest—"How are you? What the hell are you doing in the
States?" And that was actually the last time I ever saw Art.

I got an engagement as a singer in a nightclub in
Washington D.C. and was very well received, and was then
signed up by MGM Records. I had a few near hits, or near
misses, whichever way you want to look at it, and my career
went very well for me. I never got to star status, but I did very well
until the advent of rock-and-roll which brought me undone like
a lot of other people.

WE lived right by St. James Park in one of those old, four-storey
tenements, across the street from King Peter of Yugoslavia; he
was in exile or something at the time. At first I worked at the
Marlborough Street jail. We stayed there for twenty-four hours
and then we were off twenty-four. The prisoners were
American soldiers who were AWOL and deserters. If they had a
long time to do, we would transport them to Paris because they
didn't have space enough in London. We'd fly them to Paris
carrying sawed-off shotguns and .45s. I'd fill a small suitcase
with soap and nylon stockings and cigarettes and razor blades,

things you could get through the army that people in Paris couldn't get at all. We'd deliver the prisoners to the Paris detention barracks, and then we'd get a three-day pass. Somebody had given me the name of a woman in Pigalle, so I'd go to this lady and she'd buy whatever I had. She'd give me francs and I'd stay in Paris for three days and spend them.

They put us in some billets the army had taken over, miserable but cheap. I never went with any of the other guys. I'd stay by myself, wander around, riding the subway, drinking cognac, and every now and then I'd run into some pot. They had what they called Gunje, which was black, and I got some absinthe a few times, when it was the real stuff, and got wiped out.

Once in Pigalle I went into a club where there was a group playing jazz; they were from South Africa or Morocco. One guy played saxophone. I was drinking, so I went up and talked to them. I got across to them that I was a musician and that I would like to play. The guy let me use his horn, and they were amazed that I played so good. After I finished, this beautiful French girl smiled at me. She didn't speak English, but we sat together and I bought her a drink and then we left together. We walked until we came to a gate. She said, "You have money?" I said, "A little." She rang a buzzer and a light went on over our heads. A buzzer rang back, and the iron door opened, and we walked in.

It was a whorehouse. It was a place where the women take their tricks, but she didn't seem like that. I'd been to Tijuana when I was a kid and I'd been to San Bernardino when there were whorehouses there, and they were really a drag. This was different. I gave them a certain amount when I checked in, and that paid her; it paid for the room and it paid for the drinks. We had a couple of drinks and went upstairs to a room with one of those little French balconies. It was really like making love. It was almost like being with Patti. The girl was gorgeous. She had short, straight, black hair with a little wave at the bottom; beautiful skin; small, perfect breasts; and a beautifully rounded ass. She was really a woman. She seemed to have character and depth. She had little lines around her eyes, and she had such soul and such feeling. We made love all night long. She talked to me in French. She had a beautiful voice, and afterwards I thought about her a lot. I went back to Paris once more after that and looked all over for her, but I couldn't find her. I never saw her again.

The English girls had blotches on their legs, red blotches from a lack of protein. The English people never got eggs or anything like that. When I was in Bournemouth we'd have dances, and to get the girls to come, the girls from the surrounding territory, they'd get out all the old cheese and salami and "horse cock" bologna and make these godawful sandwiches using dry bread and stale mustard. They'd have old fruit all messed up and no good. They gave this stuff out, and no one was allowed in the dances except the girls. And the girls would come, and you could see them sneaking the food inside their clothes and then going over by the door, where their mother or grandmother or a little kid would be hiding out in the bushes. They'd sneak them a sandwich. That's how the girls got paid off. Some of them would ball you for a bar of soap, a pack of chewing gum, a piece of chocolate, a stale piece of cheese or salami; they'd cut the mold off.

It was very hard to get liquor. The English would line up by the pubs because at a certain hour each pub would have two or four fifths of gin which they'd put in the spigot and start selling, first come, first served, and that would be it for the evening. The soldiers used to get Old Kuchenheimer 100-proof rye whiskey at two dollars a quart; it cost us ten shillings (we got paid in English money). I'd buy it and I'd buy up the rations of a couple of guys that didn't drink so I always had my footlocker filled with alcohol.

I had been transferred to patrol duty in Picadilly, and when I had the day off I'd wander around the parks or Picadilly Circus, get drunk, observe things. This one time I went over to St. James Park, and there was a girl there, very pretty; her skin wasn't like most of them, pale, pasty, sickly looking; their teeth were all bad. This one looked pretty good. She was sitting on the grass. It was morning, around ten o'clock, and I had a sack with two quarts of whiskey in it. The girl smiled, and I noticed that she had a beautiful body, so I walked over and said hello. She said hello, and I said, "What are you doing?" She said, "Just relaxing. What are you doing?" I said, "Nothing. I got the day off." She said, "What have you got in the sack?" I said, "Oh, I have some goodies. Do you drink?" She said, "Yeeeesss!" I'd even brought a couple of little paper cups so I could drink outside. I went and got a cup of water from the drinking fountain and sat down beside her on the grass.

It was a pretty day. There's very few days in London that are warm and pleasant, so when you have one it's a joyous thing: everyone's outside and happy. I filled the other cup with Old Kuchenheimer and we started drinking and talking, and I told her I was a musician, and I think she had heard of me. When I was in London I played at the Adelphi Theatre. George Shearing was on the card. They had jazz concerts, and I was the young American, the Yank. I played at the London Palladium as a guest star with Ted Heath's band, so my name had been in the subways.

We talked and drank, and the time went by. She was pretty and I was very lonely. I balled only rarely, and then I'd suffer terrible feelings of guilt. And I'd look at myself every time I'd urinate. I'd be afraid there would be something dripping out the end of my thing, that I'd have a disease. But this girl appealed to me and I'd already made up my mind. We started lying close and goofing around with each other, and time kept passing. I asked her what she would like to do and she said, "Oh, don't worry about it; everything will be alright." At one point I said I could rent us a room but she said, "Don't worry, everything will be fine." It got later and later. At last I said, "There's no point in laying here in this park. Why don't we find some place that's a little more private?" And she said, "Alright, let's go."

She lived way on the outskirts of London, so we got on the subway and rode and rode and rode, and by the time we got there it was dark. Then we walked. And as we're walking, all of a sudden she says, "Well, it was nice meeting you. We'll have to get together again." I said, "What are you talking about?" Here I'd spent the whole day! We'd drunk almost the whole two quarts of Old Kuchenheimer! And I'd given her cigarettes! I said, "What do you mean? Yeah, naturally it's been nice, but where are we going?" So then she said, "Well, I've got to get home, and my parents are home. We can't go there." I said, "Why didn't you tell me? I told you I would have rented a room." She said, "But I just met you." Here she'd been rubbing up against me and spreading her legs! It was outrageous and I thought she was joking. I said, "Look, I went through all this thing with you and spent all this time, I'm not going to waste it. We're going to make love regardless!" She said, "No, we're *not*!" And she started to get snotty. I thought, "This fuckin' broad is not going to make a chump out of me! No!" I really hate prick teasers.

We were walking. I looked over to the right and saw a church there and a cemetery. We were way out in the country and hadn't passed anybody since we got off the subway. I said, "We're going to make it one way or another; either you're going to do it peaceable or . . . Suit yourself! She really got indignant and she started to pull away from me, but I held on to her and dragged her to this cemetery and threw her down on the ground. I said, "Come on! Are you kidding?" I thought she was playing a game with me. She said, "No, I can't! Please believe me! I would if I could, but I can't." I said, "Are you having your period?" She said, "No, I can't!" I said, "Well, you're going to!"

It wasn't even enjoyable. I spread her legs and got my thing out, and as soon as I got it in her she started fucking, and I came real quick, and it was nothing, and after I finished I said, "Oh, shit." She said, "You're going to be sorry." I said, "Fuck you." I hated her guts and I really despised myself. I would have liked to have killed her for causing me to go through such feelings as that. It would have been bad enough balling her if we'd been in nice surroundings and she'd wanted to ball. She walked off and I found my way back. I felt sick when I went into my billet. I showered and scrubbed myself as if I could wash the filth off me.

Right after that, word came that we were going home. I was so happy. They give you examinations before you go, and they found out I had the clap.

I tried to get out of going back but there was nothing I could do. And in those days you had to wait three months, period, before you could ball again or you might give it to the other person. So I had to come home to Patti and tell her that we couldn't make love. She cried, and, oh, I cried, and I told her that the girl didn't mean anything, and she knew that that was true. Patti marked the days off on the calendar. We went a month and three days, and it got so bad I had to do chin-ups on the doorsill of the bedroom because I hurt inside, because I wanted to make love so bad. Then finally the time came, and she forgave me. But that's retribution.

5 | Heroin

1946-1950

WHEN I CAME HOME Patti was staying with my dad and my stepmother, Thelma. And when I came to the door my daughter, Patricia, was there; she was walking and talking. She didn't respond to me: she was afraid of me. I resented her and I was jealous of her feelings for my dad. Naturally, she'd been with them so she didn't feel about me the way I wanted her to, and that started the whole thing off on the wrong foot.

I was bitter about the army and bitter about them making me have a kid I didn't want, bitter about being taken away when everything was going so good. I was drinking heavily and started using more pot and more pills, and I scuffled around and did a casual here and there or a couple of nights in some club, but nothing happened and I was getting more and more despondent when finally, by some miracle, Stan Kenton gave me a call.

Stan Kenton was incredible. He reminded me a lot of my dad, Germanic, with the blonde, straight hair. He was taller than my dad; I think Stan was about six, three, slender, clothes hung on him beautifully. He had long fingers, a long, hawklike nose, and a very penetrating gaze. He seemed to look through you. It was hard to look him in the eye, and most people would look away and become uncomfortable in his presence. And, just like my dad, he had a presence. When he spoke people listened. He was a beautiful speaker and he had the capacity to communicate with any audience and to adapt to any group of people. We would play in some little town in Kansas and he'd talk to the people and capture them completely. We'd be in Carnegie Hall and he'd capture that crowd with another approach. We'd be at the Kavakos in Washington, D.C., a jazz club filled with the black pimp type cats and the hustling broads and the dope fiends—and he'd capture them. He would observe, study the people, and win them.

One time we did "City of Glass" at the Civic Opera House in Chicago. It was written by Bob Graettinger, a revolutionary composition, an incredibly hard musical exercise; it was a miracle we got through it. Bob conducted it, a tall, thin guy, about six, four: he looked like a living skeleton conducting, like a dead man with sunken eyes, a musical zombie. He took us through it, and he finished, and he turned around to the people, and he nodded, and the people didn't do *nothin'*. The place was packed; we'd played the shit out of this thing and now there wasn't a sound. They didn't know what to do. We didn't know what to do. I'm looking at Stan and I'm thinking, "Well, what's going to happen now? What's he going to do *now*?" Stan looked at the audience. I saw his mind, you could see it turning, and all of a sudden he *leaped* out onto the middle of the stage, gestured at us to rise, swung his body around again to the audience, and bam! They started clapping, and they clapped and clapped and clapped, and then they stood up with an ovation that lasted for maybe five minutes. He did it all himself. Stan did it with this little maneuver.

Once when I was interviewed for *down beat* they asked me about Stan, and I told the interviewer, "If Stan had entered the field of religion he would have been greater than Billy Graham." And Stan didn't like it. But he didn't understand it. Maybe he thought I was putting him down; maybe he thought I was belittling religion and ranking him for being a phony, but that wasn't my intention. I was talking about his strength. He was the strongest man I ever met.

I traveled with the band: Shelly Manne was playing drums; Conte Candoli was playing trumpet; Bud Shank was in the sax section; June Christy was singing; Laurindo Almeida was playing guitar; and I was featured with the band. We played a lot of different places, and I was getting a name, a following. At first Patti came along with me, so it was fun, but one day in New York, while we were working at the Paramount Theater, Patti got a telegram from my father saying that Patricia was sick. I don't remember what she had. I didn't even pay attention to it, I was so angry. To me it was as if Patricia had gotten sick purposely to rank things for me. So Patti left, and that was it. For all intents and purposes that was the end of our marriage. Patti started feeling it was her duty to stay with Patricia.

It was impossible to take Patricia with us. We tried to take her once to Salt Lake City. We drove instead of traveling on the bus. I bought a car, but all the oil ran out of the car, and we got stranded, and then Patricia got sick. It was impossible. It was too impossible. The mileage we had to cover was too demanding. They both went home, and I sold the car, and that was the last time Patti was on the road with me.

I really became bitter then because I was so lonely and I couldn't stand not having a woman. There were chicks following the band that were very groovy, that really dug me; they'd send notes and hit on me and wait for me after the job, but I'd rarely have anything to do with them because I felt so guilty when I did.

In 1948 we were playing the Paramount Theater again in New York. Vic Damone was the single attraction. Sometimes we'd play seven shows a day, and there were a bunch of young girls who used to come around to all the performances. One day after a show, four of these girls came backstage and left a note. They wanted to meet me. I went to the stage door and said hello to them. I brought them into the dressing room and talked to them; they were sixteen, seventeen. They said they wanted to form an Art Pepper Fan Club. Would I mind? I thought they were joking at first, but they were serious, so I told them no, I wouldn't mind, that I'd be flattered. But I couldn't understand what a fan club would entail.

We had just started at the Paramount. I think we played for thirteen weeks, and it was jam-packed. I was living at a hotel on Forty-seventh and Broadway, and these girls kept coming around so I'd take them out. We'd go to the drugstore. I'd buy them sandwiches, and they took pictures of me. They were fairly nice looking, and they must have been from the Bronx because they all had that accent. Finally they told me that they really cared for me, that they had a crush on me, and they would like to, you know—they'd work it out among themselves and come and visit me one at a time. I said okay, but I was thinking, "They're pretty young." And I didn't know for sure if *that* was what they wanted. The next day, the one they had elected president of the club was at the Paramount after the first show. This was in the morning, and we had two, two and a half hours between shows. She said, "Shall we go to your place?"

The president was about seventeen. She looked Jewish, and she had a slender body but nicely shaped. She had pretty eyes. She was the most attractive of the four, with lovely skin, dark coloring. We left for the hotel. The guys in the band were watching, giving me those looks. The president was really enthused. She had a pretty dress on, and her eyes were all lit up. Her whole manner had changed. She'd suddenly become sexy and sure of herself and very womanly.

We got out of the theater and it was chilly so I helped her on with her coat. And that was the part I felt bad about. Because when I'm with a woman and I'm very polite and mannerly it becomes like a love situation. I felt guilty when I put her coat on. And then she clutched my arm and it was as if we were lovers. I was hoping we could have got where we were going without all these formalities, walking on her right on the sidewalk, helping her across the street.

It was too cold to walk to the hotel. Ordinarily, it was a nice walk, and I had hoped it would relax us, although she seemed completely relaxed. I was the one who was nervous. I hailed a cab and opened the door for her, and there was another little pang. We walked into the hotel and I really felt strange. I started feeling that the house detective was watching or the guy at the desk. Walking from the elevator to the room I thought, "What am I letting myself in for? Maybe this is some sort of weird plan to blackmail me or take pictures. Maybe somebody is going to break in and beat me up." I remembered all these stories I'd heard about people being in the big city and getting taken; there were a lot of young people mixed up in terrible crimes. We got to the room. I closed the door. Locked it. My heart was pounding and I was almost to the point of telling her, "Let's forget it." But I had gone too far to stop, and I had been away from Patti for a long time, and I was going to be away from her for five months more, and the girl seemed so clean and nice.

I had a bottle in my room, a bottle of vodka. I poured some in a glass and some orange juice. I asked her if she wanted a drink. She said, "Just a little one." I drank mine down and then took a great big, straight shot of the vodka. She's just standing there waiting for me. She's still got her coat on. I took her coat and hung it in the closet. She's still standing there, looking at me with this adoring look, and at last the feeling that was coming from her, this admiration, started getting to my ego, and I began to relax, but I didn't know exactly what to do yet. I didn't want to do anything that would spoil it—make a mistake or seem foolish. I sat down on the bed and started making small talk, "It's a shame this isn't a nicer place but being on the road we just have to take a little place like this because all we do is sleep in it." She just kept gazing at me. I rattled on and on, nonsense, talking and talking. All of a sudden she sat down next to me, put her hand on my arm, and she said, "You're the most beautiful man I've ever seen."

She had her hand on my arm and her head on my shoulder. I put my arm around her and she shuddered. I could feel her whole body vibrating. She had short sleeves on her little dress; it was a jersey dress, and you could feel her body through it. I rubbed her arm with my hand and she shuddered and pushed herself up against me. She put her hand on my leg, and I immediately got an erection. She smelled good. A lot of times I've been out with a woman that looked good, but when I got close her hair didn't smell nice or her breath, and it would turn me off because it would seem like she wasn't clean. This girl smelled good; her hair had just been washed; and she was so soft.

There was no mistaking at that point what was going to happen. I bent down and turned her chin up so I could kiss her, and she started to squirm and tremble. I probed gently in her mouth with my tongue, and I could tell she was really inexperienced, but little by little she relaxed her mouth till I could feel the tip of her tongue touching mine. We kissed for a long time. I started kissing her eyes and everything, and she just flipped out and lay back on the bed. I put my hand on her leg and started rubbing really easy. She had stockings on, but she had them rolled, which has always turned me on. I pulled her dress up. Her skin was beautiful. I bent down and kissed her leg just above her stocking, and I ran my tongue around her leg. She starting moving and grabbed my hair. I looked at the crotch of her panties. They were soaking wet. She had a great smell. I started kissing the outside of her panties. I don't know if she'd ever had anybody do that before because she really wigged out: she started murmuring things, "I love you." I stuck my tongue inside her panties where her lips were, and it was so moist. I rubbed my tongue up all around her, and then I pulled back her panties so I could get at her. I licked her really slowly, and she started quivering, and she grabbed hold of me, and she came immediately; almost as soon as I put my mouth on her she came. Then she said, "Wait a second!" She said, "My mother will see my dress." She got her dress off and her bra, and she was really beautiful. She had small breasts, but the nipples were hard. And she was very cute. I started to take my clothes off and got everything off but my shorts, and they were just standing out, and she said, "Come here." She sat on the edge of the bed and pulled me over to her and started caressing me through my shorts, and then she pulled them down real slow until my joint popped out, and she put her head against it and hugged me and put her arms around me and rubbed her face and her hair against me, and she started licking me. I could tell she didn't know how to suck on me; she just kissed it and licked it. I didn't want her to give me head because I was afraid I would come immediately, and she was so passionate I wanted to put it in her.

I put her on the bed and got over her and gradually put it in, and it felt wonderful. She was tight and moist. I finally got all the way in, which was hard to do at first because she was small, but she was completely turned on. I kissed her breasts, and she kept hollering, "I love you! You're the most beautiful man in the world! This is the greatest thing that ever happened to me! I'll never forget this moment as long as I live!" And I thought, "Wow! This is my fan club, and there's *four* of them!"

Usually when I'd ball the chicks that hung around the band,

the minute it was over I'd have to leave. I'd have get away from the girl because after my need for sex was satisfied I couldn't stand her. Her smell on my body was like a curse on me, and I'd have to wash myself and scrub because I felt so dirty. But this girl was so sweet that I felt some love and warmth for her, so later I *really* felt guilty, a million times more guilty. Because I felt like cuddling this girl, because I cared for this girl, I'd really betrayed Patti.

Sex was in my thoughts all the time, and because of my upbringing I felt it was evil. That made it even more attractive to me, and the alcohol and the pills I took made my sex drive even stronger. I was obsessed.

I used to room with different guys in the band, but if I had the money I'd room alone so I could fool around with the maids. The maid didn't exist for me as a person, so there was nothing Patti could be jealous of. Sometimes they would suck on me or something like that, but what I really wanted wasn't the consummation. I was away from Patti and, so that I wouldn't go out and goof, I wanted to have these experiences which would provide me with vivid mental pictures I could conjure up at will whenever I set about relieving myself by playing with myself.

If I was rooming alone I would wait for the maid to come; I'd peek out the door to see if she was there. I'd leave the door locked, but not from the inside, then she'd think I wasn't in the room. I would lie on the bed and expose myself. I'd fix the covers so the maid could see my joint. I'd pretend I was asleep and put my fingers over my eyes so I could peek out at her, and she'd come in and turn on the light and look and see me, and I used to wig out with their reactions. Some of them would go, "Oooohh!" and practically run out. Some would act nonchalant and just walk out. Others would stand and stare. Some would get nervous and uptight, but they'd be aroused. And then, after they'd leave, I'd throw a robe on and run out and say, "Do you want to get the room now?"

Down south the maids were great. They went along with whatever you wanted because they were afraid for their jobs and they were kind of naive. I'd say, "Well, come on. If you want to get the room, get it now." Or I'd make up an excuse, saying that I had to do this or that, or somebody was coming—

anything to get them in there. Then I'd sit down on a chair and fix it so my robe was open just enough so they could see me, and I would offer them a drink and talk to them. I'd peek at them while they cleaned the bathtub. Usually in New York the chicks were too hep. I didn't even bother with them. If you came on they'd say, "Yeah, sure, if you want something give me five dollars," and I'd never do *that*.

But one morning at the Forrest Hotel a maid knocked on the door, and she said, "It's late, and I'd like to get the room. It's the last on the floor. I'll be able to go home after . . ." She was beautiful. She was some latin type with light olive skin. She was about thirty years old and voluptuous. That word really describes this maid. She had on a black uniform with buttons down the front. It was made out of some light, silky stuff, and I noticed that the button at the bottom was open, and the button at the top was open. I said, "Go ahead."

She had green eyes. I'll never forget that, black hair and green eyes. I sat in a chair opposite the bathroom door. The door had a full-length mirror on it, and it was opened in such a way that I could see her in the mirror, but I was half in a daze. I really wasn't paying much attention because I had a heavy hangover. When I woke up I always had a hangover, and if I could get to a bar, I'd have a Bloody Mary. If not, I'd have a few shots in my room. So I was having a drink when I looked up and looked into this mirror, and I couldn't believe my eyes. She was cleaning the toilet bowl. She was standing, bent over but with her knees straight, which caused her dress to come up almost over her rear end, and she had black lace panties on. They usually wear white pants, something durable. She had these sexy panties on, and I could see the beginning of this little mound and some wispy black hairs sticking out the sides of these little panties. She had gorgeous legs. It was a beautiful sight, and I thought, "This is too good to be true!" When she came in, she'd closed the door behind her. Some of them leave the door open a little bit. When they leave it open you've got to sneak over and try to push it closed and catch their reaction if there is one. You hope there's no reaction.

I went and stood in the bathroom door, just looking at her. She's cleaning away. After she finishes the toilet she bends over to get the floor. She's wearing one of those half-brassieres, and with that button loose, I can see her breasts. I can see everything but the nipple. I can see down her dress to her navel. Needless to say I've got an erection. I move a little closer to her and she bends over the bathtub, and her uniform is all the way up over her ass. It was too much for me. I had my drink in my left hand; I put my right hand inside my robe and started playing with myself. If you can picture this ... I'm standing in the bathroom right behind this beautiful creature who's bent over so her ass is practically in my face, with those lace panties, with hair sticking out of the panties, and I'm jerking myself off, and I came that way, and as soon as I came I looked down, and she was looking at me through her legs. Her hand was on her cunt, and she was rubbing her cunt.

I went to the closet, got an old shirt and wiped myself off. I went back and sat in my chair. I poured another drink. She kept rubbing her cunt, and I guess she came because she stopped, pulled her dress down, and finished cleaning the bathroom. She came out. She made the bed. Never a word passed between us. Then, as she started to leave, she turned and said, "Is there anything else?" I said, "No, that was great." She gave me a smile, walked out and closed the door. I checked out the next day.

I felt as long as I didn't know a chick and nothing was said, then there was no love involved, and I wouldn't feel as guilty. I used to go to all-night movie houses and sit next to some chick and rub my leg against her leg, and I've had chicks jerk me off, and I've played with them, and then I'd just get up and walk out. A lot of times the girl would say, "Let's go to my place" or something like that. I'd say, "Just a minute. I have to go to the bathroom." And I'd sneak away and go to another theater to try to find another chick to sit next to. Because I didn't want to ball them.

I spent hours and hours fooling with the maids and fantasizing and playing with myself and going to all-night movies. I was going insane. I had a little drill I carried with me. I'd bore holes in the doors in the hotels and then peep into the next room at night and watch the people make love.

I was playing with Kenton's band in L.A. on West Broadway at a nightclub. We did an afternoon job and then we had a few hours off before our night job at the same club. Everybody was eating or fucking around, so I went for a walk. I was in my band uniform. I walked down the residential streets near the club and it was just dusk, right before the street lights go on. When I walked I always watched the windows. When lights went on I'd go over to see if anything was happening.

So I was walking and I saw a light go on in a bathroom window. There was a driveway next to the window. I'd hardly ever walk into a driveway, but I noticed there was a house in the back so I'd have an excuse for being there. I walked back by this window. It was open, and I heard water running so I knew it was a bathing scene. I didn't know if it was a man or a woman, and I tried to peek in, but the window was too high to stand and see. Down at the bottom level, near the ground, there was a kind of vent. It had little slats where I could put my foot so I stood on it and reached up to the sill.

I peered in. It was a woman. She was in a brassiere and panties, and she was evidently going to take a bath. The tub was right under the window; the toilet was to the left; the washbasin was to the right; and there was a little scale. She got off the scale and then she stood looking in the mirror over the washbasin. This chick was very pretty. She had blonde hair and white skin, and when she took off her bra and panties I saw she had blonde hair on her cunt and her nipples were hard. I thought, "What am I *doing*, man? What if somebody sees me or the slats break and I fall?" But I was all fired up. I held on to the sill and peeked in.

She's standing in front of the mirror. She takes her breasts and hefts them in her hands, and then she rubs them around in a circular motion, looking at herself in the mirror, and she starts to get a glazed expression, and she rubs and tweaks at her nipples with her fingers. She does this for a little while and then she runs to turn off the bathwater. She stands and looks at herself. She starts rubbing her cunt, rubbing down her legs and rubbing her cunt. She sits on the toilet and spreads her legs and takes the first two fingers of her left hand and rubs up and down on her cunt, and she closes her eyes and she's got her head back and with her other hand she's tweaking her nipple, and she starts quivering and shaking and then she holds her hand real hard on her cunt, and I guess she had come, and then she got up and looked at herself again and she kissed those two fingers, which really turned me on. I just couldn't help myself. I had unzipped my fly and reached in and grabbed my joint and started rubbing across the bottom of my joint, and I came right about the same time she did. And then I really panicked. She got up and got into the tub, and I jumped down to the ground. I was scared to death. I thought, "What if somebody's seen me? What if somebody looked out a window and called the police?" I got back to the club and sneaked into the bathroom. I had come all over my shorts and the top of my pants. I wiped myself off, and when I buttoned my coat it covered the area. I felt awful and I thought, "What's happening to me? What would Stan think and the guys in the band?" I thought, "I've got to stop this!" Heroin stopped it for me.

In 1950 I was in Chicago at the Croyden Hotel. That was the hotel all the musicians stayed at. I was rooming with Sammy Curtis. He was a tall guy with a roundish face, rosy cheeks, blonde, curly hair, and he had this lopsided grin; he played the little boy bit. He thought it was charming. He was very talented.

I think we played the Civic Opera House that night. I was featured. I got all the praise and applause, and it was great while it was happening, but after everybody left, there I was alone. I wandered around the town. I went to all the bars. I ended up back at the hotel and went into the bar there. I just had to continue getting loaded; it was a compulsion; I had demons chasing me. The only way I ever got loaded enough, so I could be cool, was when I passed out, fell out someplace, which is what I used to do almost every night. They kicked me out of the bar at about four o'clock in the morning, and I didn't know what to do. There was no place I could get a drink. It was getting daylight, and I couldn't peep in any windows. There was no one on the streets.

I went back up to the room. Sammy was there and Roy King, a tenor player, and Sheila Harris, who's a singer, and some piano player. They were all using heroin. Sammy had been using stuff for a long time, and I knew it, but I never would try it because I knew that the minute I did it would be all over for me. I asked them if they had anything other than stuff, and they didn't. I was so unhappy, and Patti was two thousand miles away, and there was nothing I could do. I had to have something.

Sheila came over to me. She was a good singer who worked with another band. She was about five foot, two, and a little on the chubby side—what they call pleasingly plump. She had nice breasts, large, but nice, and although I've never liked chubby women she was one of the few that turned me on. She had long eyelashes and large eyes, bluish-green. Her face was oval and full, and she had full lips, and her eyebrows were full. Most women in those days plucked their eyebrows, but she had let hers grow, and I liked that. She had long fingers and nice nails. And she was a nymphomaniac. When she looked at a man she was thinking of sucking his cock; that was her thought and she turned you on because you could feel that; everyone could. And you were turned on by the stories. She was a legend among musicians. Whether they had ever made it with her or not they'd all tell stories about balling her. She was purely sensual, but only in a sexual way, no other. No warmth, no love, no beauty. When you looked at her you just saw your cock in her mouth.

She came over to me and offered me some stuff, just to horn it, sniff it. She said, "Why don't you hang up that jive and get in a different groove? Why don't you come in the bathroom with me? I'll show you a new way to go." I was at my wit's end. The only thing I could have done other than what I did was to jump out of the window of the hotel. I think we were on the fourteenth floor. I started to go into the bathroom with her, and Sammy saw what was happening and flipped out. He caused a big scene. He said, "I won't be responsible for you starting to use stuff!" But Roy said, "Man, anything would be better than that jive booze scene he's into now. What could be worse? That's really a bringdown." We cooled Sammy out, and me and Sheila walked into the bathroom and locked the door.

When we got in there she started playing with my joint. She said, "Do you want me to say hello to him?" She was marvelous, and she really turned me on, but I said, "Wait a minute. Let's get into this other thing and then we'll get back to that." I was all excited about something new, the heroin. I had made up my mind.

She had a little glass vial filled with white powder, and she poured some out onto the porcelain top of the toilet, chopped it up with a razor blade, and separated it into little piles, little lines. She asked me if I had a dollar bill. She told me to get the newest one I had. I had one, very clean and very stiff. I took it out of my pocket and she said, "Roll it up." I started to roll it but she said, "No, not that way." She made a tube with a small opening at the bottom and a larger opening at the top. Then she went over to the heroin and she said, "Now watch what I do and do this." She put one finger on her left nostril and she stuck the larger end of the dollar bill into her right nostril. She put the tube at the beginning of one pile, made a little noise, and the pile disappeared. She said, "Now you do that." I closed my nostril. I even remember it was my left nostril. I sniffed it, and a long, thin pile of heroin disappeared. She told me to do the same with the other nostril. I did six little lines and then she said "Okay, wait a few minutes." While I'm waiting she's rubbing my joint and playing with me. I felt a tingly, burning sensation up in my sinuses, and I tasted a bitter taste in my throat, and all of a sudden, all of a sudden, all that feeling—wanting something but having no idea what it was, thinking it was sex and then when I had a chance to ball a chick not wanting to ball her because I was afraid of some disease and because of the guilt; that wandering and wandering like some derelict; that agony of drinking and drinking and nothing ever being resolved; and . . . no peace at all except when I was playing, and then the minute that I stopped playing there was nothing; that continual, insane search just to pass out somewhere and then to wake up in the morning and think, "Oh, my God," to wake up and think, "Oh God, here we go again," to drink a bottle of warm beer so I could vomit, so I could start all over again, so I could start that ridiculous, sickening, horrible, horrible life again—all of a sudden, all of a sudden, the demons and the devils and the wandering and wondering and all the frustrations just vanished and they didn't exist at all anymore because I'd finally found peace.

I felt this peace like a kind of warmth. I could feel it start in my stomach. From the whole inside of my body I felt the tranquility. It was so relaxing. It was so gorgeous. Sheila said, "Look at yourself in the mirror! Look in the mirror!" And that's what I'd always done: I'd stood and looked at myself in the mirror and I'd talk to myself and say how rotten I was—"Why do people hate you? Why are you alone? Why are you so miserable?" I thought, "Oh, no! I don't want to do that! I don't want to spoil this feeling that's coming up in me!" I was afraid that if I looked in the mirror I would see it, my whole past life, and this wonderful feeling would end, but she kept saying, "Look at yourself! Look how beautiful you are! Look at your eyes! Look at your pupils!" I looked in the mirror and I looked like an angel. I looked at my pupils and they were pinpoints; they were tiny, little dots. It was like looking into a whole universe of joy and happiness and contentment.

I thought of my grandmother always talking about God and inner happiness and peace of mind, being content within yourself not needing anybody else, not worrying about whether anybody loves you, if your father doesn't love you, if your mother took a coathanger and stuck it up her cunt to try to destroy you because she didn't want you, because you were an unclean, filthy, dirty, rotten, slimy being that no one wanted, that no one ever wanted, that no one has still ever wanted. I looked at myself and I said, "God, no, I am not that. I'm beautiful. I am the whole, complete thing. There's nothing more, nothing more that I care about. I don't care about anybody. I don't care about Patti. I don't need to worry about anything at all." I'd found God.

I loved myself, everything about myself. I loved my talent. I had lost the sour taste of the filthy alcohol that made me vomit and the feeling of the bennies and the strips that put chills up and down my spine. I looked at myself in the mirror and I looked at Sheila and I looked at the few remaining lines of heroin and I took the dollar bill and horned the rest of them down. I said, "This is it. This is the only answer for me. If this is what it takes, then this is what I'm going to do, whatever dues I have to pay . . ." And I knew that I would get busted and I knew that I would go to prison and that I wouldn't be weak; I wouldn't be an informer like all the phonies, the no-account, the nonreal, the zero people that roam around, the scum that slither out from under rocks, the people that destroyed music, that destroyed this country, that destroyed the world, the rotten, fucking, lousy people that for their own little ends—the black power people, the sickening, stinking motherfuckers that play on the fact that they're black, and all this fucking shit that happened later on—the rotten, no-account, filthy women that have no feeling for anything; they have no love for anyone;

they don't know what love is; they are shallow hulls of nothingness—the whole group of rotten people that have nothing to offer, that are nothing, never will be anything, were never intended to be anything.

All I can say is, at that moment I saw that I'd found peace of mind. Synthetically produced, but after what I'd been through and all the things I'd done, to trade that misery for total happiness—that was it, you know, that was it. I realized it. I realized that from that moment on I would be, if you want to use the word, a junkie. That's the word they used. That's the word they still use. That is what I became at that moment. That's what I practiced; and that's what I still am. And that's what I will die as—a junkie.

———————

(Hersh Hamel) We were playing at a place called Esther's in Hermosa Beach, and I was with Jack Montrose. Jack and I were friends. They used to have a session at this place almost every night, so we had gone down there to play, and Art came down, and we all enjoyed ourselves together. This must have been in the late forties. Art was serious about playing, liked to laugh; he was drinking, smoking pot. Art immediately hit it off with Jack and I, and we all decided to meet there again, and we did, on succeeding days. Art was very handsome at that time, lean and dark, black hair combed back, and very fastidious. Art was a very interesting player, swinging and very intense, sort of trying to do his own thing under the cloak of the strong sentiment and strong popularity of Charlie Parker. Art was trying to create a style of his own.

Art was married to Patti and they were living somewhere between Washington Boulevard and Adams in a nice, little place. Patti was a sort of naive girl who wasn't terribly interested in music, jazz. She was very pretty. She was blonde and very pretty. Very much a take-care-of-business type of girl. She did her thing. Around the house. Wasn't lazy. Sort of serious and not terribly talkative or friendly with any of the musicians. She had her own set of friends, whoever they were.

She was always nice to me, said hello, but Freddy Rivera—we got to know Freddy; he would always be around Art, you know, coming over to the house, and I got the impression that Patti didn't like Freddy, didn't like Freddy over there. Art wanted Freddy there. Art got a big kick out of Freddy. Found Freddy amusing. So, there was a little tension between Patti and Art about Freddy. As for me, when I came over and picked Art up or whatever it was, she was more friendly with me, but I felt I was still one of the musician friends of Art's.

Patti and Art seemed to be on different mind levels. They didn't seem to have the same likes and dislikes. There wasn't a great rapport between them, although, you know, Art seemed to love Patti. And Patti's ideas about the way a marriage should be didn't coincide with Art's. I don't think Art really thought about it that much. He was very involved with his music and his emotional ups and downs with his music. They took a great toll out of him, so he wasn't able, really, to grasp the reality of the marriage situation. That was my feeling.

We used to go out playing all the time. Go over to the east side, play at different places. Sometimes, out of seven nights in the week, we'd be playing five nights, and we had a different place for each night. Even if we weren't working we'd be, like, together, as a group of guys: myself, Jack Montrose, Art, Sammy Curtis, sometimes Chet Baker, sometimes Jack Sheldon, Bill Perkins, Gene Roland, Bob Braucus, Bob Neal. Sometimes Shorty Rogers even came along.

Some nights we'd play at a place called the Samoan in East L.A., right in the Barrio, off Whittier and Atlantic. We knew the owner there; he was very mellow, and he liked us to come in. He knew Freddy. Al Leon had a place for us to play in El Cerrito. And the Mexicans loved Art. I think they thought that Art was part Mexican; he has that Latin look. I don't think they realized he's more Italian than anything else. He was just a hero to them. They'd come in and take us outside and get us high.

At that point Art was just drinking and smoking pot, maybe a diet pill from time to time. And he could always drink me under the table. I remember one night we were at the opening of a record store in East L.A. It was about ten at night, the grand opening, and we played, like, a jam session. The owner asked us to. They closed up the store at about one and we played until four in the morning, and Art, while I was standing up playing my big bass fiddle, Art was pouring this gin down my throat and it was running down my neck. Well, I got so drunk! Art drank more than I did, and I got terribly sick. Art didn't really even show the effect. He was drunk but he wasn't drunk drunk, like I was. He took me home, and my clothes were all screwed up, and Patti washed my clothes and cleaned me up. I was a mess. It was a lot of fun. It really was. The point was, Art was able to consume a lot of stuff, no matter what it was, and show very little effect from it.

About that period, Art went back on the road with Kenton, and the way I heard it from Art was that he was initiated to heroin while he was on that tour. I remember he came back and he was involved with heroin. It seemed like he got involved pretty fast and pretty deep. When Art wasn't on the road with Kenton, he would do some things by himself, and I remember he was down at a place on Sixth and Western called the Surf Club. Hampton Hawes was down there with him, and I remember how loaded Art was on the gig, really zonked. I remember going down to see him and being disturbed about him being so stoned while he was working. His playing was fine, but it seemed like Art began to feel like he couldn't play good enough unless he was on heroin.

Art's really a gifted and talented player. He's given his great talent to jazz, his style. And he did retain himself through all the Charlie Parker years, some pretty rough times. I remember there was a club near Hollywood Boulevard where we used to go play sessions after hours. This must have been 1960, something like that. I was standing outside the club and Art was going in and Joe Maini was going in and somehow there were words between Joe and Art. Joe said something: "Hey, faggot!" About the way Art played. He didn't mean Art's demeanor as a person. And they got into a fistfight and were rolling around on the concrete hitting each other over the style of Art's playing. Art was defending his playing by engaging in fisticuffs with Joe.

You know, there are Charlie Parker influences in Art's

playing but Art was able to retain *himself*; whereas most of the alto players emulated Charlie Parker and therefore they didn't have as much of themselves to give as Art did. I think that's a great thing.

(Freddy Rivera) At that time, I was completely lost. I didn't know what the hell I was doing. I wasn't even close to having an idea of what I was doing. In reality I was doing nothing. Getting drunk. Running around the streets. Screaming. At times it was enormous fun, but much of the other time it was frightening, really, not knowing what the hell's going on. Art was frightened, too. He was frightened of life. At one time, we went into a shopping center and people were going in and out of the doors and he said, "They're making it. Those people are making it." One time we were in a car and we were talking and somebody said, "You know, a lawyer makes eighty thousand a year. You, Art, you're not making anything at all. You should be making as much as a successful lawyer or doctor." It was the truth, too. Art was making, what, twenty dollars a week? Of course, when he was with the bands he was making more money. But he *was* capable of making eighty thousand. He rationalized it, "It's a rotten world. People are cold and conniving. They won't give a person a chance. There's no justice."

I met Art when I was nineteen, around 1946. I was a drummer. I met him through Al Leon, the piano player; he brought him over to my house. We went out to this place in Bell; they had sessions over there. Zoot was there most of the time and Jim Giuffre, Stan Getz. The sessions were usually on Sundays. And we used to hang out, ride around, smoke dope, drink, talk.

Art and I were able to talk to one another. When two people like one another, sometimes they don't even know why. I guess there was some kind of empathy there as far as emotions, attitudes, feelings, sensitivity. And, of course, another factor was youth. When you're young, you can be very open. You make friends more easily.

Art's attitude toward music is difficult to describe

accurately. He's a marvelous musician, always has been. Very exact, with the right sound, whatever that means. The sound I like. Marvelous vibrato. But very exact. Does it right. And of course a lot of guys can do it right, but they can't swing. And there's depth in his music. Insight. When I think of Art, I think of Lester Young, and I think of Mozart, too. The quality—it appears to be easy, but it's never easy. If it were easy anyone could do it. I think there's a strong classical feeling there. I'm using the word to mean a feeling for form and for proportion and whatnot. He's just naturally a musician. He came out of the womb a musician, and I'm positive he always had a commitment to it. But you wouldn't find him, like some guys, practicing eight hours a day, constantly trying to get connections, get ahead, get the gig, achieve power, fame. He was afraid of any responsibility. He just wanted to fuck around.

Patti was a friendly person, an emotional, warm person, but she wanted Art to be more active and to seek success more vigorously, go after it, take care of business. And I imagine, as his wife, she wanted security, whether it was expressed immediately in more money or whether it was expressed in his attitude and in his ability to take care of himself, so she could at least feel that she was with a secure person who had a sense of direction, control of his life. Patti was very attractive. Physically, she was an exciting-looking woman, erotic in appearance, although she had something of the, you know, clean-cut, midwestern look about her and considerable charm. I think Art felt a need for her, an emotional need to draw upon her. I would think he had a strong feeling of physical attraction, emotions of abandon with her.

Art was very sensitive and I would say cunning in many ways. A real paradox. He had an inability at times to really take care of things and deal with his life in a forceful, direct way, to change things, but at the same time he showed a cunning in his relationship with people. The cunning was a result of great natural intelligence, but it was really a form of childishness. Instead of taking the form of advancing his career and getting work, which he had every right to have, it was diverted into the manipulation of flunkies: "Take me to the job." "Bring me home." "Yeah, come on over. Bring a jug." And people

did this, of course—out of admiration for his talent. And I
know what they got out of it. Feeling like nothing themselves,
not having any identity, they were able to incorporate
themselves into something else that was larger, that was great.
So they more or less had themselves swallowed. And Art—I
don't think that anyone could benefit from that. It's almost a
hundred ten percent self-destructive because everything is false
and there's no room left to grow and to do things for oneself, to
actively walk into the world: "*I* am going to drive myself to the
gig. I can do it." But Art was emotionally very young. The child
must be take care of. He must be given things. Infantile
gratification. For an infant it's perfectly appropriate; he's
weaned in three years.

One time we were at a place and I bought him a pizza and
then I wanted to take a bite. He wouldn't let me have any!
Hahahaha! What would you call that? That was selfishness.
And then, of course, he would have a student, a guy named Joe
Martin, and the student would drive him everywhere and do
things for him. The *Master!* We must serve the *master!* That type
of thing. Art used it to the hilt.

Art had considerable charm. Intelligence, a very natural
ability to understand things. He was a very handsome man. A
great natural talent. These are attractive qualities. His
humor tended to burlesque. It could be vicious. Mimicking
people. And often very accurately, very perceptively, with the
intelligence working. But mostly, it was burlesque. Sometimes
playing hillbilly music he'd shout, "*Tarnation!*" and "Shit fire
and save matches!" Hahahaha!

Art *is* sensitive even though at times the sensitivity is largely
an expression of selfishness. He's sensitive to such a degree
about *himself*. A person can be like this and be insensitive to
other people at times. Not always. Often he could be very warm
and very friendly, and you could talk to him. At times his
concern for other people would be expressed as sentimentality:
"I really *love* you, man." Even histrionics. Being stoned and
being emotional. But I question whether at any time the
concern with the self was ever put aside.

I saw a definite change in Art when he started using heroin.
It was rather dramatic. The change, I think, consisted essentially
in the intensification and exacerbation of traits that were

already there: indulgence in the self, a desire to escape the external world, reality, to sink into the self almost entirely. To be passive. As a musician . . . In the case of Art, the musician is a person who expresses himself and does send something out, but even this could be passive at times. It showed in feelings of intimidation in the presence of another strong musician, a reluctance to blow out if there was somebody around, another strong player, or in one of these very sticky social scenes in jazz, tribal games, "Who's number one?" Heroin intensified Art's tendencies to withdraw, not to fight, not to assert. And that was the easiest thing to do at the moment, although it made his life more difficult in the long run.

I was able to use heroin from time to time just for fun. I think we all have a predisposition in our systems for certain types of behavior and certain drugs. With some people, you know, *booze* is really their messiah, their mission, their destiny; they're just going to be *soaked*! I didn't have the need for heroin. I don't know why. I got off scot-free. At times I had the need to get stoned, whacked, and I thought of taking heroin for that purpose, but it was never the heroin itself. It was never *love*. Deep, natural, flowing *love*.

Art said to me once that all of his life all he'd really ever wanted was to get high. And the first time he stuck that needle in his arm he said, "I finally got high."

6 | On the Road with Stan Kenton's Band

1946–1952

AFTER I SNIFFED IT that morning in Chicago, I bought up a whole bunch of heroin, got a sackful of caps. We traveled back to Los Angeles. I guess it took us three months to get back, playing all the stops in between, and at this time we had a little vacation from Stan, about a month before we had to go out again. I told Patti I had sniffed a little bit, but it was okay, it was alright. She felt bad but she went along with it. Then I ran out. I got totally depressed and my stomach hurt. My nose hurt something awful, terrible headaches; my nose started bleeding. I was getting chills. I was vomiting. And the joints in my legs hurt.

I had to go to a session so I got hold of some codeine pills and some sleeping pills and some bennies, and I got a bottle of cough syrup and drank it, and I went out to this session because I still couldn't believe I was that sick.

Everything was real clear to me. Everything was so vivid. I felt that I was seeing life for the first time. Before, the world had been clouded; now, it was like being in the desert and looking at the sky and seeing the stars after living in the city all your life. That's the way everything looked, naked, violently naked and exposed. That's the way my body felt, my nerves, my mind. There was no buffer, and it was unbearable. I thought, "Oh my God, what am I going to do?"

I looked around the club and saw this guy there, Blinky, that I knew. He was a short, squat guy with a square face, blue eyes; he squinted all the time; when he walked he bounced; and he was always going "Tchk! Tchk!"—moving his head in jerky little motions like he was playing the drums. Sometimes when he walked he even looked like a drum set: you could see the sock cymbal bouncing up and down and the foot pedal going and the cymbals shaking and his eyes would be moving. But it wasn't his eyes; it was that his whole body kind of blinked. He'd been a friend of mine for years and I knew he goofed around occasionally with horse, heroin, so I started talking. I said, "Man, I really feel bad. I started sniffing stuff on the road and I ran out." I described to him a little bit of how I felt and he said, "Ohhhh, man!" I said, "How long is this going to last?" He said, "You'll feel like this for three days; it'll get worse. And then the mental part will come on after the physical leaves and you'll be suffering for over a week, unbearable agony." I said, "Do you know any place where I can get anything?" He said, "Yeah, but it's a long ways away. We have to go to Compton." We were in Glendale. At that time they didn't have the freeway system; it was a long drive but I said, "Let's go." We drove out to Sid's house.

As we drove I thought, "God almighty, this is it. This is what I was afraid of." And the thought of getting some more stuff so I wouldn't feel that way anymore seemed so good to me I got scared that something would happen before we got there, that we'd have a wreck. So I started driving super cautious, but the more cautious I was the harder it seemed to be to control the car. The sounds of the car hurt me. I could feel the pain it must be feeling in the grinding of the gears and the wheels turning and the sound of the motor and the brakes. But I drove, and we made it, and we went inside, and I was shaking all over, quivering, thinking how great it would be to get something so I wouldn't feel the way I felt.

Sid was a drummer also, not a very good drummer, but he had a good feeling for time. He was a guy I'd known a long time, too, a southern type cat with a little twang of an accent. We went in and Blinky told Sid I'd started goofing around and Sid said, "Ohhhh, boy! Join the club!" He said, "What do you want?" I said, "I don't know. I just want some so I won't be sick." He said, "Where do you fix at?" I said, "I don't fix. I just sniff it, you know, horn it." He said, "Oh, man, I haven't got enough for *that*!" I said, "What do you mean?" He said, "If you want to shoot some, great, but I'm not going to waste it. I don't have that much." I said, "Oh, man, you've got to, this is horrible. You've got to let me have something!" He said, "No, I won't do it. It's wasted by sniffing it. It takes twice as much, three times as much. If you'd shoot it you could take just a little bit and keep straight." I said, "I don't want to shoot it. I know if I shoot it I'm lost." And he said, "You're lost anyway man." I begged him and begged him. I couldn't possibly leave that place feeling as sick as I did. I couldn't drive. I couldn't do anything. I didn't care what happened afterwards, I just had to have a taste. Finally I said, "Okay, I'll shoot it." He said, "Great."

They both fixed, and I had to wait. At last he asked me what I wanted. I asked him how they sold it. He said they sold it in grams: a gram was ten number-five caps for twenty dollars. I said to give me a gram and he said, "Whatever you want." I said, "I thought you only had just a little bit." He said, "I only have a little bit but I got enough." It was just the idea that he wanted me to fix. I knew that. So I'd be in the same misery as he was. He said, "Where do you want to go?" I looked around my arms. I didn't want to go the mainline, the vein at the crook inside your arm, because that's where the police always looked, I'd heard, for marks. I asked him if he could hit me in the spot between the elbow and the wrist, the forearm.

Sid put a cap or a cap and a half of powder into the spoon. He had an eyedropper with a rubber bulb on it, but he had taken thread and wrapped it around the bulb so it would fit tight around the glass part. He had a dollar bill. Here came the dollar bill again, but this time instead of rolling it up as a funnel he tore a teeny strip off the end of it and wrapped it around the small end of the dropper so the spike would fit over it real tight. That was the "jeep." He put about ten drops of water on top of the powdered stuff in the spoon and took a match and put it under the spoon. I saw the powder start to fade; it cooked up. He took a little bit of cotton that he had and rolled it in a ball and dropped it in the spoon, and then he put the spoon on the table. He took the spike off the end of the dropper and squeezed the bulb, pressed the eyedropper against the cotton and let the bulb loose. When he had all the liquid in the dropper he put the spike back on the end of it and made sure it was all secure. Blinky tied me up. He took a tie he'd been wearing and wrapped it around my arm just below the elbow. He held it tight and told me to make a fist. I squeezed so the veins stood out. Sid placed the point of the needle against my vein. He tapped it until it went in and then a little drop of blood came up from the spike into the dropper and he told Blinky to leave the tie loose and me to quit making a fist and he squeezed the bulb and the stuff went into my vein. He pulled the spike out and told me to put my finger over the hole because blood had started to drip out. I waited for about a minute or a minute and a half and then I felt the warmth—a beautiful glow came over my body and the stark reality, the nakedness, this brilliance that was so unbearable was buffered, and everything became soft. The bile stopped coming up from my stomach. My muscles and my nerves became warm. I've never felt like that again. I've approached it. I've never felt any better than that ever in my life. I looked at Blinky and at Sid and I said, "Oh boy, there's nothing like it. This is it. This is the end. It's all over: I'm finished." But, I said, "Well, at least I'm going to enjoy the ride."

After I left the house I went to a drugstore that Blinky knew. At that time you could buy spikes easy, so I got four number-twenty-six, half-inch hypodermic needles, an eyedropper that had a good, strong bulb on it, and went home. I had about nine capsules of heroin left. I walked into the house and Patti met me at the door. I went into the kitchen. I put this stuff out on the table, and she looked at it, and she said, "Oh no!" I said, "Yeah, this is it. You'll have to accept it." I got a dollar bill and tore a little piece off the bottom to make the jeep. I got a glass out of the cupboard, a plastic one so it wouldn't hurt the end of the needle when I put it in to wash it out. I took a cap and put it in the spoon and put some water in it, and all this time I'm talking to Patti, trying to explain because I loved her and I wanted her to accept this. I got a tie out of the closet and asked her if she would tie me, and she wrapped it and held it and she was trying to be cool and be brave, and I stuck the thing in, and the blood popped up, and I told her, "Leave it go. Leave it go." I looked up, and I'll never forget the look on her face. She was transfixed by the sight of the blood, my own blood, drawn up, running into an eyedropper that I was going to shoot into my vein. It seemed so depraved to her. How could anybody do anything like that? How could anybody love her and need to do anything like that? She started crying. I took her hand away and took the tie off. I shot the stuff in, and when I finished I looked at her. She turned her head and cried hysterically. I put my arms around her and tried to tell her that everything was alright, that it was better than the drinking and the misery I'd gone through before, but I couldn't get through to her.

After I got the outfit and started fixing, that was my thing. I still drank and smoked pot, but I was a lot cooler. Things were going great for me. I was featured with the band and we played all over the country. We'd go from one state to another and the bus driver we had at the time was a beautiful cat who knew what all the liquor laws were—some states were dry—and he'd stop just before we crossed into a dry state and say, "This is the last time you can buy alcohol until such and such a date." We'd all run out of the bus. We'd figure out how much liquor we'd need. If we went to Canada and had to pass through an inspection station we'd take our dope, the guys that were using heroin, our outfits or pills, and give them to the bus driver to stash behind a panel. We'd go through the station and get shook down, and then he'd open the panel and give us our dope back. And wherever we'd pass through we'd buy different pot. In Colorado we'd get Light Green and in New Orleans it was Gunje or Mota. There were a lot of connoisseurs of pot who'd carry little film cans of it and pipes with screens to filter it, and when we had a rest stop we'd jump out of the bus and smoke.

Me and Andy Angelo roomed together for a long time and before that it was me and Sammy, and we each had our outfits. I had a little carrying case, like an electric razor case. I had an extra eyedropper and my needles, four or five of them. I had my little wires to clean the spike out in case it got clogged. I had a little bottle of alcohol and a sterling silver spoon that was just beautiful and a knife to scoop the stuff onto the spoon. I used to carry this case in the inside pocket of my suit, just like you'd carry your cigarettes or your wallet. I even carried a little plastic glass. I would set up my outfit next to the bed in the hotel with my stuff in a condom—we used to carry our heroin in one to keep it from getting wet. I'd wake up in the morning and reach over, get my little knife, put a few knifefuls in the spoon, cook it up and fix. It was beautiful.

It was wonderful being on the road with that band.

Everyone liked each other and we all hung out together. When the bus left Hollywood we'd buy bottles of liquor and start drinking; that was just standard procedure: it was a celebration. I always prided myself on being able to stay up longer than anybody else, drink more than anybody else, take more pills, shoot more stuff, or whatever. I remember once when we left L.A. we kept drinking and drinking and smoking pot and having a ball until the bus just ceased to be a bus. We wandered up and down the aisle talking and bullshitting. We kept going and going until, after about twenty hours, everybody started falling out. When it got to thirty-six hours only a few of us were still awake, and finally there was nobody left but me and June Christy. She could really drink. I don't remember how many quarts we put away. We drank continuously, I guess, for a good forty-six hours and we were going to keep it up until we got where we were going, but she fell out, too, so there I was all alone. That was awful and I panicked. I couldn't stand for anything to stop once it had begun; I wanted it to continue forever. I went up and started talking to the bus driver, and I stayed awake the whole time.

We hardly ever flew to a job, but a couple of times we had to when it was too far and we couldn't possibly make it in time. Once we flew to Iowa and rented a bus and the bus broke down when we were out on a little, two-lane highway. The weather was bad, like it is in the midwest, alternately raining and snowing, and ordinarily we would have been drug, but we were all in such a happy frame of mind we just played right over it. We were goofing around, and we had a habit, like, in the bus, we would blow sometimes. Andy and I would sit together and scatsing. We'd sing the first chorus of a song together, bebop, and then blow choruses, trade fours, and do backgrounds. Sometimes other people would join in and we'd really get into it and take out our horns, the ones you could reach easily in the bus. I'd get my clarinet and play some dixieland; maybe June would sing and we'd play behind her. So, as it happened, we'd all been drinking and were having one of these little sessions when the bus broke down.

Our regular driver was back with our regular bus trying to get it ready, and this driver we'd just hired didn't know what to make of us. He was fascinated. He made an announcement. He was going to radio ahead for help. We said okay and kept on playing, and all of a sudden we just found ourselves marching out the door of the bus. It was freezing cold but we had our coats on and our mufflers, and before we knew it there were twenty guys out there, with horns, marching down the highway. There were farms and stuff, you can imagine, cows and dogs and things. We're going down the highway playing marches.

June Christy was a pom-pom girl strutting down the road. She was a cute little thing with light hair and a little, upturned nose. She had a lot of warmth and she was sexy in that way, no standout shape, but she was nice and everybody liked her, and she had crinkly marks around her eyes from smiling a lot. Her husband was Bob Cooper, who played tenor with the band. He was very tall with blonde hair and the same crinkly thing around his eyes. People used to wonder why she had married him, being June Christy. People thought that she and Stan might get something going, and there were a lot of guys that dug her, but she married Bob, and I understood it. He was one of the warmest, most polite, pleasantest people. He was completely good if you can imagine such a thing, just a sweetheart, and he got embarrassed easily, and he blushed a lot. And he used to drink with June; he would look after her; they were a great pair. And they were marching down the road.

Ray Wetzel was marching, a fat funnyman, always laughing and smiling. He had a lot of jokes and little comic routines he used to do, and he was a wonderful trumpet player with a beautiful sound. Shelly Manne was out there in a big Russian overcoat with a fur collar and a big babushka or whatever you call it on his head. Shelly's like the picture "What Me Worry?", and he's always making jokes, and he doesn't drink, and he doesn't smoke pot: he's naturally high. He's playing the snare drum, playing wild beats and walking like he's crippled. Bart Varsalona joined in playing his bass trombone, another comedian.

Bart was a sex freak, and he had an enormous joint, one of the biggest I've ever seen. Occasionally on the road he'd invite some of the guys down to his room, where he'd have some real tall showgirl-hustler. He'd haul out his joint and slam it on the table top, and then he'd have the chick do a backbend or something and give her head while we smoked pot and drank and watched. A lot of the guys in the band considered themselves real cocksmen, but I'll have to admit that the kings—for pure downright sex and the number of freaks they knew in each town—were Bart and the bass player, Eddie Safranski. And Eddie was there, too, on the highway.

Al Porcino was up in front, a marvelous trumpet player, a nice-looking guy about six feet tall. In his room sometimes he'd take Ray Wetzel's pants and put them on, the pants from his uniform. He'd fill himself up with pillows and dance in front of the mirror. A couple of times he even went out on the stand like that. He always wanted to be a band leader. He had a book full or arrangements, and wherever he went, all his life, he'd get guys together and rehearse them like a big band. So he was out there with June, leading us, twirling his trumpet like a baton, marching backwards and shouting out commands, and we were doing all these movements, and we were all drunk and running into each other.

Bud Shank was marching, playing his flute, playing all those trills like they do, and Milt Bernhart—he had a big moustache at the time—he looked like Jerry Colonna. He was the lead trombone player and nobody could play louder than him. He had the most fantastic chops of anybody I ever heard. He was playing his slide trombone and walking, pointing it up in the air and going "Rrrr rruuuhh uhhh!" And we went into "When the Saints Go Marching In," and we were just shouting. And we really believed that we were marching in the Rose Parade or something. Cars and trucks were coming, and it was so far-out for this to be happening in that spot that they pulled off the road to watch, and they had cameras and kids and dogs, and they had the whole place bottled up, and the highway patrol finally came and made us get back in the bus. We were blocking the road. That was one of the great times. We had some great times.

STAN TURNS MINNEAPOLIS 'INNOVATIONS' INTO MUSIC APPRECIATION SESSION *by Leigh Kamman*

Minneapolis—Stan Kenton blew into Minneapolis in March with a

North Dakota blizzard, and the storm converted his first concert into a music appreciation session. With two concerts planned, at 7:30 and 9:30 p.m., and only several hundred spectators there for the first concert, Stan decided to combine the two at 9:30.

In appealing to the audience Kenton said, "Thank you very much for climbing through the storm. We appreciate very much you all being here.

"I wonder if we might ask a favor? So that everyone may enjoy or reject what our music offers, we would like very much to combine the two performances into one.

Meet the Band   "Meanwhile, we would like very much to have you meet the band . . . get acquainted with violins, cellos, violas, brass, reeds. If you want to know something about drums, see Shelly Manne. If you have questions about vocal music, see June Christy. In fact, we invite you to come on stage. If you can't get up here, we'll come down there."

Forty musicians and several hundred spectators swarmed on stage and through the audience. Shelly Manne demonstrated percussion. Maynard Ferguson spoke for the brass section. June Christy talked to aspiring young singers. And the local musicians checked their ideas against those of the big band musician. The local cats and fans did some genuine worshipping while the Kenton crew did some genuine responding with answers and autographs.

Session   In spite of storm and a serious air crash within the city limits, the crowd grew as 9:30 approached. At 9, Art Pepper, Bob Cooper, Buddy Childers, Don Bagley, Bud Shank, and Milton Bernhart played a jam session.

The crowd gathered in front of the stand while the Kenton men honked. By 9:30, some 1,200 persons had plodded through wind and snow to Central high auditorium. And at 9:45, the concert got underway with everyone happy and receptive for "Innovations." down beat, *April 21, 1950. Copyright 1950 by* down beat. *Reprinted by special permission.*

(Lee Young)   I always liked Stan Kenton. A beautiful person. As a matter of fact, I think he used to be rehearsal pianist at the Florentine Gardens on Hollywood Boulevard. The first time I met Stan, I met him with some disc jockey. Stan's one of the warmest people you would ever meet. He's just an *elegant* man. I'm talking about years ago; when you meet him now, the man's just the same. The man's the same. So you wonder, they must have thrown the pattern away. When you see what goes on today with people, you wonder how . . . Seems like all the wonderful, compassionate people were born a few years ago. Seems that way.

Bob Cooper and June Christy

(Coop) We were all very young when we got together with Stan, and he was like a father to us. He worried about people's problems and tried to resolve them when he could, so we had a high regard for him. And, of course, Stan had people across the country that worshiped him, idolized him, and that was part of the magnetism of the band, Stan's personal magnetism.

(Christy) I've often said that if Stan wanted to run for president, it would be a landslide because he had that powerful personality, that ability to win people over. No one's perfect, but he was great to his people, and we were his children, and we were all protected. I think you'll find very few people who'll say anything negative about him. I can't really think of anything.

(Coop) We always thought we should make more money.

(Christy) That's true.

(Coop) That's about the only thing.
I joined the band in 1945. The band Art joined—that was probably my favorite of Stan's bands. Art was there and Bud Shank, and I was getting to play more solos than before because the band was getting into a younger trend of music that we enjoyed. Shorty Rogers started writing some arrangements, Gene Roland, the more swinging things. I think all the jazz soloists in the band enjoyed it much more than Stan did. He still liked the flashy type of arrangement. And I never felt that Stan really knew when the band was swinging its best. We would wait for the moment when he got off the stand to go check the box office or something, and then we'd call all the music that *we* liked to play.

(Christy)   The audience reaction to that band was usually
great, but it depended upon where we played. If we played for
an audience who expected to listen to the band and not dance,
they were avid fans, and they wouldn't budge a muscle. They'd
just listen with their eyes wide open and their ears wide open,
but, as we often did, sometimes we'd be booked into a dance
palace, and people looked at us as if we were freaks because
there was nothing to dance to and the band was always loud.
So, if you weren't a Kenton fan, the band wasn't that popular.
For the most part we played for Kenton fans.

Traveling was no joy, but we were so young, and I, for one,
was so thrilled at being with the band because that had been
my ambition ever since I can remember. I started singing when
I was about thirteen in my hometown, and I *had* to be a girl singer
with a band. I would have settled for any band, but *Stan*, who
was at his very hottest at that moment! I was in seventh
heaven.

I had promised my mother I would finish high school before
going to the *big* town, Chicago. And I did. I was all packed the
night before graduation. Packed! I had two dresses and one
pair of shoes.

It was a fluke thing that I got the job with Stan in the first
place. I'd heard that Anita [O'Day] had left the band and I
figured that this would sure be an opportunity. I'd heard that
the band was coming to Chicago. I thought at the time (I was
totally wrong) the first place they'll go is the office that books
them. Stan hates those offices as much as I do. But in this case
I guess he needed a singer, and he needed one fast. The first hit
record the band really had was Anita's, "Her Tears Flowed Like
Wine." I don't think Stan ever cared for singers really, but at
that time he felt he needed one. I was sitting in the reception
room. I would have sat there all day long on the assumption he
would be there, and he finally came in. I gave him my little test
record. He played it and said, "I'll let you know in a couple of
days." I never suffered so much as I did during those two days
waiting to hear from him. He finally called and said, "Well,
we'll try you out for a few weeks and see what happens."
Years later—we used to do all those disc jockey shows because
they were important in those days—we were coming back from
one of those things and I said, "Stan, you never did tell me, am

I permanent?" I'd been with the band for about eight years! "Tampico" was my first record and it was, I think, one of the biggest hits the band ever had. I got paid scale for it. I'd been with the band for only a few months when we recorded it. I *hated* that song.

We used to joke about "The Bus Band in the Sky" because we never seemed to get off the bus. There were a lot of times we didn't have the time to check into a hotel and we'd have to do the gig and then get back to the bus and go to the next job. And particularly for a girl it was not too much fun because I think a woman has a little more to worry about, to look good, to get her hair done.

(Coop) But you were the envy of most of the girl singers around at that time. The band was very popular, and singing jazz . . . To quote the late Irene Kral, she said that when she was in high school she could hardly wait for the band with June to get to town so she could watch June and hear her sing: "That was the hippest shit in town."

(Christy) That was one of the nicest compliments I've ever received.

(Coop) Of course, the itineraries, they just went month after month, sometimes with no days, no nights off. And if we did get a night off, it might be traveling on the bus all night long. After a few years it got very tiring. Especially after we got married. Then it was even more of a chore because we were looking forward to settling down and having a home and so forth. It was tough, no doubt about it.

(Christy) And if we hadn't liked what we did so much, there was no way we could have done it.

(Coop) The particular bus I enjoyed the most was the first Innovations tour. We had two buses.

(Christy) That was when we had the strings and so on. Stan was really out to prove something.

(Coop) Our driver was Lee Bowman, and we had such a good time on his bus, at the end of the tour we bought him a watch for tolerating our drinking and stopping in the middle of the night to go into a bar and get more beer or whatever. It was called "The Balling Bus."

(Christy) And the other bus was called "The Intellectual Bus." And we, as a matter of fact, were quite sure that *we* were far more intellectual than they, or else why would we be on the right bus?

Whoever booked that particular tour was out of his mind, though, because he should have realized that you can't get that many people into a hotel all at once. We usually arrived all at the same time, and people got very mean and fiendish. We have a picture of some of the guys actually leaping over the registration desk in order to get there first so they could get to their rooms first. I learned a great lesson from that. I used to just sit in a corner because I figured I was a little too short to fight all of them. I did a tour a while after that with the Ted Heath band, and that tour was a rough one also, but when the bus stopped at the hotel the *gentlemen* of the band stood by and said, "Oh, Miss Christy, you must go first." That's when I first learned that it's awfully nice to be a lady and to be treated like a lady. I don't mean to imply that the guys in the Kenton band were not nice to me, because they certainly were, and by the same token I respected their privacy. If I felt that it was dirty joke time or something like that, I would go and stand by the bus driver and allow them to have whatever privacy you can have on a bus.

To tell you the truth, the band was kinda, like, clannish. That's the best word I can come up with, and I think Art was a little reluctant to join the clans for some reason or other. I think he was a bit withdrawn. Art was—I haven't seen him for so long, that's the reason I'm saying "was"—he was a very attractive young man, and I'm sure everyone else felt the same way. Art was a very good-looking guy, but some of his illness began to show up at certain times. And, as we all know, when you're ill, you don't look quite as good. It didn't show too much in his playing, but it did in his attitude. He became even more withdrawn.

I think Art is one of the greatest jazz musicians alive today.
I say that because I believe it. I haven't heard him play for a
long time. I haven't seen him. But with the Kenton band . . . My
experiences listening to him . . . I honestly feel that way about
him. Art didn't have a chance to be exposed with the band as
much as he might have been, which is a tendency of Stan's. He
likes the full, big-band sound, and he's reluctant, really, to let
anyone be the star, so to speak. The musicians appreciated Art's
abilities, but he wasn't featured with the band that much.
Maynard was, and of course Vido Musso. I've never been able
to figure *that* out. It's perhaps because I'm married to one of
the finest saxes that there is and I always felt that Coop should
be featured as much or more than Vido.

(Coop) I always felt that Art's major influence was Lester
Young; that came out more clearly when I heard him play tenor
a few times. Maybe not so much now as in his early days. And
to transfer that beautiful sound to the alto! He was really the
only one doing that at the time, and I think his sound was by
far the *best* alto sound at the time. Since then there have been
other marvelous alto players, but I think that perhaps Art was
a major influence in their sound. I always enjoyed his solos;
naturally, one of the highlights of the band was Art's solos.
And I still think that the solo piece Shorty Rogers wrote for Art
is one of Stan's best records. It's a lovely record. It'll probably
last for all time.

(Sammy Curtis) The Innovations band was great. It was
one of Stan's bold moves in music. It was a very aggressive
thing he did. He added a big string section and French horns,
and the band had a physical structure kind of like a symphony
orchestra. At that time no one was thinking in those terms. The
band was playing great music, and there was a very brotherly
feeling among the musicians. We felt we were participating in
something very important. There were a lot of string players who
weren't, you know, "us" jazz guys, and they loved it. They felt
it was important to them to be part of it, too.

Stan was a very devoted musician. The orchestra, it was so
big, a lot bigger than other bands; they had to build special

risers to set the band up on and carry all this equipment on the road. I could be wrong, but I've been told by a lot of people that would have to know that Stan was financing the thing out of his own pocket, which, the final line in that story is, he lost a lot of money. But that's the kind of guy he was. He believed in it so much, he put himself into it physically, spiritually, just to the hilt, and that's where he was coming from. He was beautiful.

Art was . . . His music was number one to him. That's all he talked about. We were very close. We'd go and hang out after work, go blow in clubs. Art had a lot of solos in the band; he was featured on a lot of things, and if he'd had a really good night playing, he felt great, but some nights he felt he could have done better, and he'd just get depressed. What he did in his music kind of dominated the way he looked at the whole world.

Art was and is a great player. I'm not going to say the greatest in the world because I don't feel any one guy is. But at the top of the gang is a select group of five or ten, just a few guys. When you get up that high on the ladder, you can't pick one as better than the other. That's where I place Art. He's one of those special guys. As to what made his playing so special, that's a hard question, and the only way I can answer it, to be honest with you, I think it's a gift of God. I think it's not something that Art did. God loved him and gave him this gift.

If you were Art's friend, he loved you. He would, I feel, have done anything I asked. Not that I asked anything special, but I felt that kind of brotherly thing. And he respected my work in music, and that was a part of it. You know, I may sound like I'm trying to make something special out of myself because I was not that nice a . . . I wasn't walking with the Lord then and I was a different kind of guy.

There were a lot of Monday night sessions around town in L.A., and guys'd just drive around in cars and go to clubs and sit in. Art would call me up and say, "Hey, you want to meet me, and we'll go sit in at this club, and then, if there's time, we'll go to another one?" It was just fun to hang out. Chet Baker would come and Jack Montrose, at that time; Jack Sheldon was one of the guys; Shorty Rogers, Hersh Hamel. We'd fill the whole car up and drive to a club.

Something that sticks in my mind—it shows a part of Art's

personality, how very sensitive he is. On Kenton's band, we were playing at a place in Dallas, Texas. It was a funny kind of setup. It was an outdoors nightclub, all tables, but in Texas there was some kind of law that you couldn't sell liquor over the bar, so everyone came with bottles and bottles of booze and instead of buying liquor they'd buy soft drinks for mixing. I don't know why, but the bus brought us there early by mistake, and all the people got there early also, and they just loved the musicians and it turned into a thing, like, "Hey, you don't have to work yet. Sit down and have a drink." Well, before the job started, I mean, including yours truly, just about the whole band was juiced out. Stan got there, and we started playing, and everything's fine, under control, but by the last set, I mean the whole band was just wasted, and Stan was counting the band off, and some of the guys would *interrupt* him counting off. It turned into one of those things. It was kinda humorous, but Stan was kinda stern and resentful of all this. He could have gotten angry at me or at anyone on the band, but for some reason he picked on Al Porcino and Art and told 'em to get off the bandstand. He kicked them off the stand. I was rooming with Art; that's how I remember. We had the next two or three days off, and Art didn't show up at the hotel for two days. I got worried about him. Al Porcino, the next day, he didn't remember anything that had gone on. But when Art finally showed up and I got talking to him, he said that when Stan did that, kicked him off the bandstand, it really hurt his feelings and he just kinda wanted to be by himself and had drifted around town there. But it's always stuck in my mind. He was just having fun, and then this incident occurred that hurt him very badly, and when he did show up the poor guy was totally depressed. It happened a few days ago! The other guy doesn't even remember it; it went in one ear and out the other. Art just hung on to it.

(Shelly Manne) I think it's important to find Art's position as a jazz alto player in the history of the saxophone. I think he has a very important part to play because of his distinctive way of playing. He's very individual. You can hear it. You know it. Art was a very lyrical player. Especially at a time when most of the alto players were in a Charlie Parker bag, Art had a distinct style of his own, very melodic.

Art was a big influence on a lot of people. He had quite an influence on Bud Shank because Bud was very young when he joined the Kenton band and, of course, Art was third alto, the jazz alto chair. In fact, when I settled down out here, finally left Stan and made the first album for Contemporary Records, *West Coast Jazz*, something like that, I was going to use Art; he was supposed to do the date but for some reason he couldn't make it, so I used Bud. And that was the first jazz record with a small group on a prominent jazz label that Bud had done; it helped establish his career—a tune called "Afrodesia" that Shorty Rogers wrote with Art in mind.

Art was always a quiet, introverted, sort of one-on-one person. He was never strongly outgoing, but he was always loose with the guys, fun to be around. He'd join in with the groups, with the guys, and he'd go anyplace to play. He wanted to play *constantly*. So even though we weren't close socially, we were close musically. I know that. And that kind of business that happens between musicians, musically, is a very strong tie.

We were all happy when Art joined the band because he was really a true, dyed-in-the-wool jazz player, and Stan needed that kind of thing in the band. We had plenty of strong ensemble players, and Art gave it another dimension as far as giving a jazz feeling to the band.

Stan Kenton was great. He was a father confessor to the guys. You could always go to Stan. And Stan's answer was the word of God, the final word, and you were confident that he'd steer you right. He took a personal interest in everybody in the band, and everybody that worked for him was devoted to him whether they agreed with him in his social life, his political thinking. I always felt Stan was to the right politically, and I was on the liberal end, and we always argued about things politically, but it never interfered with our friendship.

There are a lot of leaders if they get too close to the band they lose the respect of the musicians. Leaders will travel in a different car, stay in another hotel, and just see the band when they get on the bandstand. Stan usually had to go ahead and do interviews or set up; he had his own car on the road but he was with us most of the time. And you never felt aloofness from him. You could say anything you wanted to Stan. And it showed in the music. I think one of the main reasons Stan's band was such a great success, as was Duke Ellington's band—which was, of course, the greatest jazz band of all—was that, like Duke, Stan wrote for the individuals in the band instead of writing charts just with an anonymous band in mind and having the musicians play it. He knew our creative abilities; he knew what we could add to the band; and he knew we didn't want to just take it off the paper and play it. We gave something of ourselves to the music. In Art's case, Stan used Art, his individual talent, when he'd write charts with him in mind. The band had a very individually creative sound.

It's always hard doing one-nighters. You look back now, there are some good memories. For some it's good memories. Everybody has a different kind of constitution, a different ability to take a beating on the road. You travel three hundred miles a night every night on a bus, and in those days you'd have to make a 9:30 in the morning show, something like that, so it was difficult at best. You'd get into town and the rooms wouldn't be made up, so you spent four hours sleeping in the lobby waiting for checkout. It's hard, but I think there's a frame of mind that makes that all part of growing up and maturing and part of enjoying life.

Those are the experiences that later on, difficult as they were, you look back on with a lot of joy because, you know, you try new restaurants, see new places, meet new people, play for new people all the time, which is, in itself, an inspiration. But some guys, now—I'm not sure, I'm just taking a wild guess here—some guys weren't made up physically for that kind of life and I think Art maybe was one of those guys. I think Art had great difficulty coping with all the temptations of the road.

PROFILING THE PLAYERS

. . .

ART PEPPER, alto sax: He's 25, says his ambition is to be the best jazzman in America. Art joined Kenton prior to going into service in

1942. Has played with Vido Musso, Benny Carter, etc., and considers Al Cohn his favorite musician. Dislikes the road and the fact that "real great musicians can't make it unless they smile prettily and talk with gusto." down beat, *April 20, 1951. Copyright 1951 by* down beat. *Reprinted by special permission.*

· · ·

THERE'S a thing about empathy between musicians. The great bands were the ones in which the majority of the people were good people, morally good people; I call them real people—in jail they call them regulars. Bands that are made up of more good people than bad, those are the great bands. Those are the bands like Basie's was at one time and Kenton's and Woody Herman's and Duke Ellington's were at a couple of different times.

There's so many facets to playing music. In the beginning you learn the fundamentals of whatever instrument you might play: you learn the scales and how to get a tone. But once you become proficient mechanically, so you can be a jazz musician, then a lot of other things enter into it. Then it becomes a way of life, and how you relate musically is really involved.

The selfish or shallow person might be a great musician technically, but he'll be so involved with himself that his playing will lack warmth, intensity, beauty and won't be deeply felt by the listener. He'll arbitrarily play the first solo every time. If he's backing a singer he'll play anything he wants or he'll be practicing scales. A person that lets the other guy take the first solo, and when he plays behind a soloist plays only to enhance him, that's the guy that will care about his wife and children and will be courteous in his everyday contact with people.

Miles Davis is basically a good person and that's why his playing is so beautiful and pure. This is my own thinking and the older I get the more I believe I'm correct in my views. Miles is a master of the understatement and he's got an uncanny knack for finding the right note or the right phrase. He's tried to give an appearance of being something he's not. I've heard he's broken a television set when he didn't like something that was said on TV, that he's burnt connections, been really a bastard with women, and come on as a racist. The connections probably deserved to be burnt; they were assholes, animals, guys that would burn you: give you bad stuff and charge you too much, people that would turn you in to the cops if they got busted. Most of the women that hang around jazz musicians are phonies. And as for his prejudice, not wanting white people in his bands, that's what he feels he should be like. He's caught up in the way the country is, the way the people are, and he figures that's the easiest way to go. One time he did hire Bill Evans for his band, but people ranked him so badly and it was such a hassle that I think he became bitter and assumed this posture of racism and hatred. But I feel he's a good person or he couldn't play as well as he plays.

Billy Wilson plays like he is. When I knew him, when he was young, he was a real warm, sweet, loving person. And he plays just that way. But if you listen to his tone, it never was very strong; it's pretty and kind of cracking. It's weak. And when he was faced with prison—because he got busted for using drugs—he couldn't stand it. He couldn't go because he was afraid, and when they offered him an out by turning over on somebody he couldn't help but do it. He's a weak person. That's the way he plays. That's the way he sounds.

Stan Getz is a great technician, but he plays cold to me. I hear him as he is and he's rarely moved me. He never knocked me out like Lester Young, Zoot Sims, Coltrane.

John Coltrane was a great person, warm with no prejudice. He was a dedicated musician but he got caught up in the same thing I did. He was playing at the time when using heroin was fashionable, when the big blowers like Bird were using, and so, working in Dizzy Gillespie's band, playing lead alto, he became a junkie. But he was serious about his playing so he finally stopped using heroin and devoted all his time to practicing. He became a fanatic and he reached a point where he was technically great, but he was also a good person so he played warm and real. I've talked to him, talked to him for hours, and he told me, "Why don't you straighten up? You have so much to offer. Why don't you give the world what you can?" That's what he did. But success trapped him. He got so successful that everyone was expecting him to be always in the forefront. It's the same thing that's happening to Miles right now. Miles is panicked. He's stopped. He's got panicked trying to be different, trying to continually change and be modern and to do the avant-garde thing. Coltrane did that until there was no place else to go. What he finally had, what he really had and wanted and had developed, he could no longer play because that wasn't new anymore. He got on that treadmill and ran himself ragged trying to be new and to change. It destroyed him. It was too wearing, too draining. And he became frustrated and worried. Then he started hurting, getting pains, and he got scared. He got these pains in his back, and he got terrified. He was afraid of doctors, afraid of hospitals, afraid of audiences, afraid of bandstands. He lost his teeth. He was afraid that his sound wasn't strong enough, afraid that the new, young black kids wouldn't think he was the greatest thing that ever lived anymore. And the pains got worse and worse: they got so bad he couldn't stand the pain. So they carried him to a hospital but he was too far gone. He had cirrhosis, and he died that night. Fear killed him. His life killed him. That thing killed him.

So being a musician and being great is the same as living and being a real person, an honest person, a caring person. You have to be happy with what you have and what you give and not have to be totally different and wreak havoc, not have to have everything be completely new at all times. You just have to be a part of something and have the capacity to love and to play with love. Harry Sweets Edison has done that; Zoot Sims has done that, has finally done that. Dizzy Gillespie has done that to a very strong degree. Dizzy is a very open, contented, loving person; he lives and plays the same way; he does the best he can. A lot of the old players were like that—Jack Teagarden, Freddie Webster—people that just played and were good people.

Jealousy has hurt jazz. Instead of trying to help each other and enjoy each other, musicians have become petty and jealous. A guy will be afraid somebody's going to play better than him and steal his job. And the black power—a lot of the blacks want jazz to be their music and won't have anything to do with the whites. Jazz is an art form. How can art form belong to one race of people? I had a group for a while—Lawrence Marable was playing drums, Curtis Counce was playing bass—and one night I got off the stand, we were at Jazz City, and a couple of friends of mine who were there said, "Hey, man, did you realize what was happening? Those cats were ranking you while you were playing, laughing and really ranking you." I said, "You're *kidding*, man!" I started asking people and I started, every now and then, turning around real quick when I'd be playing. And there they were, sneering at me. Finally I just wigged out at Lawrence Marable. We went out in front of the club and I said, "Man, what's *happening* with you?" And he said, "Oh, fuck you! You know what I think of you, you white motherfucker?" And he spit in the dirt and stepped in it. He said, "You can't play. None of you white punks can play!" I said, "You lousy, stinking, black motherfucker! Why the fuck do you work for me if you feel like that?" And he said, "Oh, we're just taking advantage of you white punk motherfuckers." And that was it. That's what they think of me. If that's what they think of me, what am I going to think of them? I was really hurt, you know; I wanted to cry, you know; I just couldn't believe it—guys I'd given jobs to, and I find out they're talking behind my back and, not only that, laughing behind my back when I'm playing in a club!

There's people like Ray Brown that I worked with, Sonny Stitt, who I blew with, black cats that played marvelous and really were beautiful to me, so I couldn't believe it when these things started happening. But you're going to start wondering, you're going to be leery, naturally, and when you see people that you know . . . I'd go to the union and run into Benny Carter or Gerald Wilson and find myself shying away from them because I'd be wondering, "Do they think, 'Oh, there's that white asshole, that Art Pepper; that white punk can't play; *we* can only play; us black folks is the only people that can play!'?" That's how I started thinking and it destroyed everything. How can you have any harmony together or any beauty when *that's* going on? So that's what happened to jazz. That's why so many people just stopped. Buddy DeFranco, probably the greatest clarinet player who ever lived, people like that, they just got so sick of it; they just got sick to death of it; and they had to get out because it was so heartbreaking.

But all that happened later on. In 1951, musically at least, I had the world by the tail. That was the year I placed second, on alto saxophone, in the *down beat* jazz poll. Charlie Parker got fourteen votes more than me and came in first.

At the end of 1951 I quit Kenton's band. It was too hard being on the road, being away from Patti, and I grew tired of the band. I knew all the arrangements by memory and it was really boring. I didn't get a chance to stretch out and play the solos I wanted to play or the tunes. I kept thinking how nice it would be to play with just a rhythm section in a jazz club where I could be the whole thing and do all the creating myself. As far as the money went, the money never changed. I was one of the highest paid guys in the band, especially among the saxophone players; Stan didn't think that sax players were the same caliber as brass players or rhythm, and we had to play exceptionally loud and work real hard because we had ten brass blowing over our heads. Also the traveling got to be unbearable. At first I enjoyed it, but after a while, being nine months out of the year on the road, one-nighters every night ... Sometimes we'd finish a job, change clothes, get on the bus, travel all night long, get to the next town in the daytime, check in and try to get some sleep, and then go and play the job. Sometimes the trip was so long we'd leave at night after the job and be traveling up until the time to go to the next one. We'd have to change clothes on the bus and go right in and play.

Also I became more and more hooked and I went through some unbelievable scenes—running out of stuff on the road, not being able to score, having to play, sick, sitting on the stand spitting up bile into a big rag I kept under the music stand. I guess I looked sort of messed up. People started talking. Kenton became more and more suspicious. I imagined he knew I was doing more than drinking and smoking pot. So it seemed best that I leave the band and try to do something on my own, and I gave my notice. A lot of us quit at the same time. Shelly Manne quit. Shorty Rogers quit.

At first I was apprehensive. I had a lot of bills and I had a habit, so right away I did some recording with Shorty. One was *Shorty Rogers and His Giants*, and on one of the sides, "Over the Rainbow," I was featured all the way through and got great reviews. It became one of the most popular things I've done. Then I formed a group of my own. I got Joe Mondragon and on drums Larry Bunker, who also played vibes. We worked out some things which we could do without the drums while he played vibes, or if he did a ballad I'd sit in on the drums and play a slow beat with the brushes. I got Hampton Hawes, an exceptional pianist. It was just a quartet, but it was very versatile.

Because I had my own group, I wanted to do my own material, tunes that would express my personality, not just standards. I had fooled around writing little things out when I was with Kenton. Now I tried writing seriously and found I had a talent for it. I wrote a ballad for my daughter, Patricia, probably the prettiest thing I've written to this day, and I wrote a real flag-waver, a double-fast bebop tune, very difficult, and I named it "Straight Life."

We worked at the Surf Club and got a great review in *down beat*. In that same issue, announcing my starting a group of my own, I was written up in another article with another new leader who was going to throw his hat in the jazz band ring and see if he could make it, and that person was Dave Brubeck. We all know now, anyone that follows jazz, that Brubeck became, and still is, one of the outstanding leaders of a jazz group, but at that time, if you read the articles, I was the one they felt was more talented and the one that would make it bigger and make more money and be more popular. I was more of a jazz player. I swung more.

Everything was perfect. I bought a tract house on my GI bill. I had finally gotten to know my daughter and was just mad about her, really loved her. We had a little white poodle named Suzy, and I had a car. I had everything. I was making good money and I didn't use any of that money on my habit—I was dealing a little bit of stuff to musicians, friends of mine, to support my habit. And I felt that I wasn't doing anything wrong because I wasn't taking food out of my child's and my wife's mouths by using. But I was really strung out.

I realized I had to get away from the stuff. In the latter part of '51 there began to be newspaper stories about dope. It was beginning to hit the limelight. I realized that things weren't going to be the same, things were going to tighten up. And that meant either I had to kick or I had to go to jail. That would really ruin my career. I was thinking how nice it would be to just stop, be cool, and not pay any of the real heavy dues that you usually have to pay. So that's what my thinking was when my dad came out to the house I'd bought in Panorama City and asked me if I'd like to come and have a drink.

My mother had gone to my dad, who was living in Long Beach, and she told him I was using. I had asked her not to say anything to him because he hated junkies; he'd always told me don't ever do *that*. But he found out and came to me and said, "Let's go out and have a drink." He used to come with Thelma, but this time he came alone and he said he wanted to talk to me.

We went and had a drink, and then he looked at me, and he put his hand on my arm. We were in a bar in Van Nuys, a bar I later worked in with a western band. He said, "When did you start on that stuff?" He put his arm around me and got tears in his eyes. And the way he put it to me I knew that he knew. I think at first I tried a feeble "What do you mean?" But he grabbed my arm. I had a short-sleeved shirt on. I had marks all over my arm. He said, "You might as well be dead." He said, "How did it happen?" So we talked and I tried to explain to him. I had tried to minimize the feelings I had, but it was so good to be able to tell somebody about it, to let him know how awful I felt and how really scared I was. He said, "What are we going to do?" I said, "Oh God, I don't know. I want to stop." He said, "Tell me the truth, if you don't want to stop nothing is going to do you any good." We talked and talked. Before he'd even come to me he'd inquired and found a sanitarium in Orange County, and they said they'd take me in. He made sure the police wouldn't hear about it; I wouldn't be reported. He said, "Will you go to this place?" I was afraid because I was afraid to kick, and I was afraid I might goof, and I didn't want to disappoint my dad. I felt miserable when I saw how miserable he felt. He said, "Anything I can do, no matter what it costs, don't worry about it. Don't worry about anything—I'll take care of you." That's when he started crying, and we hugged each other, and we were in this bar, and it was really strange, but I felt wonderful because after all these years I felt that I'd reached my dad and we were close. And so he asked me if I'd go to the sanitarium, and I saw that he wanted me to real bad, and so I said yes, alright, that I would go.

(Sammy Curtis) As to drugs, it's like the thing going on

now. It's a peer thing. A lot of guys are doing it, gettin' stoned.
It *did* feel good. People enjoy feeling good. You don't know
what it's going to lead to. You don't think of that. I'm a
follower of Jesus now, and I look at everything spiritually, so I
think that anyone drinking, getting stoned, you name it, is
looking for the Lord. They're looking for something greater but
they don't know how to go about it, to find it, and
unfortunately, in the search they fool around getting stoned,
and it feels better. But it's a temporary and destructive thing.
I've been there, and getting closer to the Lord feels much better.
It's cheaper and it's constructive not destructive.

DOPE MENACE KEEPS GROWING

Dope is menacing the dance band industry. It has become a major
threat and unless herculean effort is made by everyone concerned to
halt its spread, it may well wreck the business. We are not talking
about marijuana, benzedrine, or nembutal, although these are the
first steps leading to the evil.

We are referring to real narcotics, heroin principally, and too
many well-known musicians and vocalists are "hooked," as they say
in the vernacular. This is serious business and it constitutes a triple
threat to the future of dance music.

It is demolishing the professional as well as the personal careers of
the addicts themselves, many of whom cannot be spared from the
ranks of working musicians because of their talent.

It is giving a bad name to ALL musicians and jeopardizing their
living. We know instances in which bookings have been refused to
clean units and bands because of undeserved reputation.

Most important of all, the example set by musicians who are addicts and who also are well known, is a wrong influence on
younger musicians and on youngsters who may become musicians.

down beat usually has not given prominent display to news stories
about musicians who run afoul of the law because of their habit. We
did not wish to be accused of sensationalism. We knew, of course,
that Miles Davis, the trumpet star, and drummer Art Blakey were
picked up recently in Los Angeles on a heroin charge. We did not
print it.

Now we are becoming convinced that we are doing a disservice to
the industry by not giving wider publicity to such facts. We are begin-

ning to believe that we should name names and state facts, even in the instances of musicians who die from the habit, without attempting to thinly disguise the cause of death as has been done in two or three cases recently.

The grapevine is flooded with rumors and rumors of rumors. A name girl vocalist and her musician husband both are said to be hooked. One of the five top tenor sax stars has flipped, it is reported. Another femme singer, who has been in trouble before, walked out after playing three nights of a two week club engagement because her chauffeur was picked up with heroin capsules in his possession and the law began to stalk her again.

We can't print names on the basis of rumors alone, even those which seem to be substantiated. There must be an arrest or other official record. When there is, and it is only a matter of time in nearly all cases, *down beat* intends to print it as a small effort to help stamp out this traffic.

One name band leader has seen the light. He is eliminating, one by one, his sidemen who are known to be using the stuff. There have been half a dozen replacements in his band recently. Other leaders should follow his example. It's a tough decision to make, turning out an otherwise capable instrumentalist who may well have stellar talent. But it's better than having the entire structure collapse.

It's a pity, too, that such musicians should practically be deprived of making a living by the only means they know. Too many of them, however, are not making a living even when they are working. The dope pusher takes most of it. It's better that they should be forced to work out their own destiny alone, rather than be permitted to remain and infect others, like a rotten apple in a barrel. down beat, *November 17, 1950. Copyright 1950 by* down beat. *Reprinted by special permission.*

Perspectives

CRITIC DEMANDS JUNKING OF WEAKLING JAZZMEN *by Ralph J. Gleason*

The most important question in the music business today is not who's going to make the next hit record, but rather is something nobody talks about, particularly for publication.

Apparently operating on the ancient myth that you can conceal illness by not recognizing its existence, nobody, from bandboy and sideman up to bandleader and booker, will speak openly and frankly on the cancer that is infecting the business. I don't have to state it any plainer than that for you to know exactly what I'm talking about.

Jazz Is Big Business   Jazz is big business today. It's an important and money-making part of every major record company's activities and a major part of most minor firms' work. The jazz clubs flourish all over the country. In the opinion of a veteran publicist in San Francisco, a man connected with show business, the entertainment world and publicity for years, the jazz clubs are a strong part of the backbone of the entertainment field today and in the near future will be the biggest thing in the business.

Today's youngsters are the potential night club patrons of ten years from now, and what today's kids want is jazz. They are giving up the Joe E. Lewises for the John Lewises and the Sophie Tuckers for the Sarah Vaughans. Every year the older entertainment world loses another generation of customers. And the new order gains one.

Time To Clean House   With this in mind, please consider the possibility that it is time for the musicians, the jazz fans, and the musicians' union if necessary, to clean house. But good. It's up to bandleaders and bookers, sidemen and managers to see to it that the cancer is contained, that the infection is stopped and a thriving business, that is also an art and a way of life, is not penalized by the twisted attitudes and hysterical flight from reality of a very few. And they are, relatively, a few. Even though they may be a talented, articulate, and amazingly active few.

How can you respect a man who does not respect himself? There is no reality on Cloud 9, and there is no clearer perception of life. If the music business, itself, doesn't do something about it, we will all be losers in the long run. Frankly, I can think of no re-orientation too severe for certain of our so-called stars for their behavior in recent years. An addict is a shame and a disgrace to the very word "musician."

"Special Privilege" Gone   Time was when camaraderie between the races and the colors and the factions in music was the rule. The residue of history when musicians were strolling players, a group apart, and as artists and special human beings enjoyed special privileges. It's getting so the word is one of opprobrium rather than praise.

Sure the papers exaggerate; sure the hysterical columnists shoot off a lot of nonsense. But you know what's happening, don't you? Is it good? No one can cure it but you. It's time the hipsters got their hip cards punched, but in the right place. down beat, *December 2, 1953. Copyright 1953 by* down beat. *Reprinted by special permission.*

(Shelly Manne)   Drug use was prevalent among musicians then. That was why I originally left New York. People hitting on me for money to score. Leave something on the bandstand, turn around, and it's gone. Friendship goes right out the window. People turn into animals. But there are different extenuating circumstances in everybody's life: the need to be accepted by a group of peers who maybe are using drugs or alcohol at the time, the need to be accepted as one of the guys, the need to be considered hipper by doing that, by being a far-out cat, or the discontent with one's own playing. Maybe he feels that a stimulant or a depressant might somehow enable him to get his head together so he can cut the crowd out and get totally into his playing. Who knows. There's a hundred reasons why. It might be something in your personal life which a friend wouldn't necessarily know about, in your background, in your bringing up, in your environment. It's too hard for me to speculate on why a guy would use heavy drugs or heavy alcohol. I know that to do it just for fun — smoke some pot, take a few drinks with the guys, just partying it up — or because there's a lot of tension on the road, just as a release, was cool. We used to have a lot of fun. We'd get stoned or something and just enjoy ourselves. But when you start getting into heavy drugs, you're getting into another area, and it's a terrible vicious circle because it's a losing battle all around. You're not only leading a life on the road that is debilitating to your body, to use heavy drugs as a relief from the stress of being on the road creates another disability to your body. And finally your body breaks down, and finally you break down, and finally you have no control or will power, and the whole thing just goes down the toilet.

I was fortunate because drugs scared the hell out of me. When I was young, in New York, playing on Fifty-second Street, when I was eighteen I looked fifteen, and all the musicians I was playing with—Ben Webster, Coleman Hawkins, Trummy Young, Dizzy—all those musicians, kinda were very protective. Even when I hung out in a saloon, the White Rose, on Fifty-second Street, with all those guys and somebody'd offer me a drink (I didn't like alcohol), they would put them down, "No, give him a Coke." I'm very grateful to them for that, being protected like that. And, of course, what helped me, too, was being accepted by those guys. It gave me strength and confidence. I felt self-assured about what I wanted to do, where I was going.

7 | Busted

1952–1953

THE POINT was whether I really wanted to do it or not. A month at the sanitarium cost two thousand dollars, and there was no sense in spending all that money if I was just going to come out and start using again. But I felt I wanted to stop. I was *hoping* I felt that way.

My dad phoned the sanitarium and they told him I should go and stay with him so they would know exactly how much I was shooting a day. He put his house in mortgage and took his money out of the bank. He bought dope for me. I'd make a phone call to East L.A. and line it up, and he and my stepmother would drive me to score. We did this for three days. Then they made the appointment for me to go into the sanitarium.

Before I left, my dad got a hammer and we all went into the kitchen. Patti was there. He handed me the hammer and told me to do it right. It was like a ceremony. I broke the outfit into a million pieces and took the pieces into the backyard and threw them as far as I could. I felt that I'd be able to make it with my dad behind me.

When I got to the sanitarium I was already sick. They got me into bed and took the standard tests, and then the doctor came in with the nurse and talked to me for a while. Heroin isn't like drugstore dope: you never know what you're getting. He tried to estimate how much I'd been taking a day but he couldn't do that, so he said, "I'll send the nurse back with a shot of morphine and after you get the effects of it, call for her and let her know how you feel, if it takes away the sickness, because I don't want you to be uncomfortable." The nurse came back with a syringe and injected the morphine under my skin instead of into the vein. (Later on I tried to get her to let me fix myself in the vein, but she wouldn't do it.)

The morphine helped me quite a bit but I still felt bad. So I called the nurse and told her to get the doctor; I was still sick. She came back with another shot of morphine. They set the dosage at a certain point and keep it there for four days, and then they gradually decrease it. You get a shot every four hours. After the second shot I felt just fine but I told the doctor that I was still sick and got another shot, and after that I said, "I still don't feel comfortable." He said, "Well, I don't understand it, but alright, we'll give you one more shot." By this time I was just wasted. I was sailing. So I finally told them that I felt okay. I could make it. Hahahaha! I could stand the pain.

The next day they put me in a whirlpool bath and a guy gave me a massage, the most beautiful massage I've ever had—he was an artist. Here I was in this gorgeous room, comparable to any hotel I'd ever stayed in; I had my own private patio with flowers and lawn and birds chirping; and every four hours this pretty nurse would come in and give me an enormous shot of morphine. And I was just *blind*: I tripped out and sang to myself and made funny noises and looked at myself in the mirror. I stood in the bathroom for hours looking at myself and giggling, saying, "Boy, what a handsome devil you are!" I had a beautiful body. I'd get in the shower and bathe and get out and take the hand mirror and put it on the floor and look at my body from the floor. I'd look at my rear end and the bottom of my balls and the bottom of my joint, and I would play with myself until I got a hard-on and then gaze into this mirror and say, "What a gorgeous thing you are!"

I mentioned that as a child I used to play a lot alone. I loved sports and I made up a baseball game that I played with dice, and I never played it with anybody. I'd choose the names of the best players and roll the dice to make up fantasy teams, six or eight teams in the league. I would make up names like the New York Bombers, the Philadelphia Penguins. I had a typewriter that my mother's husband, Whit, had bought me, and I'd type up a sheet for each team listing all the players including pinch

hitters and relief pitchers. I'd set up a page with the team standings and I kept batting averages, home runs, runs batted in, the
whole thing. I had meetings for the managers, and I would talk.
Sometimes I'd have trades. If a team was really losing I'd have
them buy somebody that had a good batting average. And
when I played the game, I was the radio broadcaster; I was the
manager; I was the ball player; I was everything. I'd roll the
dice. Each roll of the dice meant something. I'd say, "Ted
Williams is up. Warren Spahn is pitching. It's the first pitch.
Strike one!" I'd keep the standings and the percentages, and
then I'd have my own all-star game with the leading batters. I
even rolled the dice to get attendance.

I hardly ever cheated. Naturally I'd form favorites, and
there would be certain players that I'd like better than others,
or somebody would get close to a record legitimately and then it
would be very hard not to cheat a little. A pitcher might have a
shutout, two outs in the ninth inning, and somebody would hit
a single, Then I might get angry and re-roll, but the few times I
did that I felt bad about it. It spoiled the record, and I swore
that I wouldn't do it anymore.

And so, when I was twenty-seven years old, I still had a
baseball league going, if you can imagine that. It was something
Patti could never understand. I'd be loaded and be up all night
in the kitchen playing games. And when I went into the
sanitarium, I took my notebook with my schedule, my dice,
erasers, pencils, ruler and the whole thing, and I'm playing my
league in my room. The nurse came in a couple of times and I
explained it to her and she couldn't believe it.

There were some women and a couple of men who had
rooms in this place. It was like a hotel. After a few days I
started getting out and talking to the people. I met one lady who
was about forty-five. She had diamond rings on and just reeked
of money. Her pupils were pinpoints. She said, "Oh, hello! Are
you the new boy in number seven?" She said, 'I'm Mrs. So-and-
so." We started talking. She said, "What's your trouble?' I said,
"I'm a dope fiend." She said, "Tsk, tsk, tsk! Oh, what a shame!"
I said, "What's your trouble?" She said, "Well, I have this condition—my veins don't function correctly—and I have to have
morphine. It opens up the veins into my brain. And I have trouble sleeping: they give me morphine to help me sleep. And I

need the massage—I have muscle problems, you know—I have pains in my back, in my legs, in my lower legs." She showed me her legs.

I met the other patients and they all looked wealthy and they were all stoned. I found out that these people just checked into the sanitarium from time to time, stayed there, and stayed loaded. They get their morphine and their massages, and who can tell what else they get. You know, the guy massaging them—probably whatever they want they get. I thought, "Wow, these people really have it made. No police involved. No jail." I thought, "How beautiful!" I mentioned it to my doctor and he said, "Yeah, but unfortunately you're not in that position, are you, financially?"

I kicked after about two weeks, and I was in pretty good shape with the whirlpool and the rubdowns and the vitamins and the food, but I had a terrible mental craving and I'd have nightmares about dope, just continuously. I was worried. I thought, "Well, here I am checked into this place, and it's costing all this money, and right away I'm trying to get the dosage up." I knew that wasn't right.

It came time to leave, and I went home to Patti, and after we made love she said that she'd decided that maybe it would be better if we didn't stay together right away—just to see how I did—because she was afraid I'd start using again. My feelings were hurt but there was nothing I could do. I stayed with my dad and Thelma for a while and then I went up to my mother's house. And immediately, as soon as I got there, I got ahold of this guy Henry and scored.

Right after that, I went to a jam session with some guys at a place called the Blue Room in Santa Monica. I was playing and drinking and I got sick to my stomach and had to vomit, so I went to the bathroom. Everybody at the place was guys that I knew, so I left my horn sitting on the stage. When I came out it was gone. I said, "Did anybody see my horn?" Nobody said anything. I said, "Man, *somebody* must have seen it!" They all just froze. I looked everywhere. The case was gone; the horn was gone. One of them just stole it off the stand. I thought, "These are the kinds of people I'm dealing with. These are my friends." Here I'd just gotten out of the sanitarium; I'd lost my saxophone; I had no money; my wife didn't want me in the house I'd bought; I was completely alone; and I was getting hooked again.

I started working with a borrowed horn at different little gigs with a trio or a quartet or as a soloist with somebody else's rhythm section. I had run into this girl Penny. She was short and had a gorgeous shape, black hair. She was Jewish. Extremely pretty. She kept calling me and wanting me to score for her. She had a little car and she'd drive out and meet me and give me the money, and I'd go to East L.A., and then we'd go someplace and fix.

I remember the first time. We went back to my mother's house to fix, and my mother was asleep. There was a garage in the back that wasn't being used so I had Penny park her car in there, and then we went into the house, snuck into the bathroom, and locked the door. I fixed about three or four caps and put half a cap or a cap in the spoon and fixed her. I started to go to the sink to clean the outfit, and all of a sudden she looked up at me, put her arms around me, pulled me down to her, and she kissed me. That was her thing, kissing and having that intimacy at the same time the stuff was hitting her. She was so sweet and so nice, I couldn't believe she was actually using heroin. All of a sudden I hear a noise, a voice: "Junior, is that you in there?" I whispered, "Cool it. It's my mother." I said, "Yeah, it's me. I'm just going to the bathroom." "I thought I heard voices." "No, I'm here all alone. I'm just going to the bathroom." "You don't have any of that stuff, do you?" "No, ma, go back to bed. Everything's alright." "I thought I heard a girl's voice." "Don't be *silly*, ma, go back to bed. There's nobody here but me." I waited, and meanwhile this girl is kissing me, trying to hold on to me. She put my hand on her breast and was rubbing up against me. She was grabbing my joint. I told her, "Cool it! Cool it! We've got to get out of here! Just be quiet!" I opened the door and looked out in the front room. There was no light. Straight ahead was the front door. I told her, "Come on!" We ran out and into the garage, and I pulled the door closed.

Usually heroin kills your sex drive, but for Penny it was like Spanish fly. We got into the back of her car and she was all over me; as I say, she had a beautiful body, and she was so excited she got me excited. I got most of her clothes off. In fact, I got all of her clothes off, and there she was naked in the car, and I started making love to her. She was clean; she smelled good; and she begged me to take my pants off, so I did; she started licking me and sucking me and she said, "*Please* put it in!" I didn't know how old she was. She looked very young to me. She said, "Don't worry. I'll be alright. I've got a diaphragm." So we had intercourse, and it was really nice, and when we finished she started telling me "I love you." and everything. "I wish we could live together." She was really far-out. I told her, "Well, give me a call, like, whenever you want." She left and I went back to the house.

There were lights on in the front room and the bedroom and the bathroom. At first I thought it might be the police, but I looked in the window and saw that it was just my mother. She was in the bathroom with the door open. She was down on her hands and knees. She had forbidden me to fix in the house, and I hoped I'd cleaned up everything. I walked in and said, "What's wrong?" She says, "I was *right*! There was a girl!" Penny had left a little scarf and her purse in the bathroom. My mother holds out her hand. Here are these capsules, three empty capsules. She flipped out and told me, "If you ever do that again I don't want you coming back here!" We had a terrible argument. I said, "What do you want me to do? Get busted? I'm not hurting anyone coming here. I'm not putting any heat on you." She said, "I just don't like it! It's not right!" I told her alright, I won't do it again.

I got a job at a club in Inglewood with a Hawaiian name. It was a well-known place in those days for jazz sessions, and I told Penny about it, so she came to the club. Right before this I'd run into a guy that was a merchant marine. He'd been to Saudi Arabia or some place where he'd gotten some incredible heroin. Sometimes with stuff, when you put the water in it in the spoon and you put the match under it, it'll dissolve but dirty particles and residue will be left. His stuff would cook up perfectly. It was a light shade of green; I'd never seen anything like it; and it was just dynamite. I had some of this with me, and it came intermission time, and it was an afternoon session, and I wanted to fix. Penny said she was sick and would I please give her a taste.

I couldn't figure out any place to do it, so we went for a drive. I didn't have very long. Then I saw a gas station that looked fairly deserted. There was only one guy working there. It was early evening. I parked the car around by the restroom, and I figured that this guy would be pretty busy. He was waiting on somebody out at the island, and he couldn't see the bathroom. It was a pay toilet. I opened the door of the men's and I said, "Come on."

I used my belt to tie up, and I fixed first. As I say, the stuff was marvelous; it was all I could do to keep from falling out. I cooked up just a little more, and I'd just started to fix Penny when I happened to look up and see, on the frosted glass of the door, a black sleeve with a white insignia. It was the arm of a policeman's uniform, and he was working on the lock. They were trying to break in without making noise. As soon as I saw that, I shot the stuff in, and "Mmmmm, oooooh, that's goooood." I whispered, "Shut up! The cops are out there!" She said, "Ohhhh!" I said, "Shut up!" I looked at her. Her eyes were going back in her head and I thought, "Oh, God, this is too strong for her!" She's got a little trickle of blood running down her arm.

I put my belt back on. I grabbed her and pulled her over to the sink and washed the blood off. I threw the stuff and the out-fit into the toilet. I put the spoon in my mouth to suck off the burnt part. I'm doing all this—it's incredible how fast I'm doing it. I stick the spoon in the bottom of the trash and that's when I hear, "Open up! Police!" I flush the toilet, praying everything'll go down. I'm telling Penny, "Straighten up! Put water on your face!" I yell, "I'm coming right out." I open the door and see two cops and this gas station attendant, and just as we walk out a detective's car pulls up. One of the cops grabs me and says, "Alright, what were you doing in there?"

I thought they knew we were getting loaded. I heard the attendant say, "Yeah, well, I peeked in, and she was bent down, and I'm sure she was, they were, you know." I got the impression that they thought she was giving me head and I thought, "Thank God!" And then I realized that that was why they hadn't broken the door down. They wanted to catch us in the act.

I immediately told them a story. I told them that I was playing in a club over here and we'd had a couple of drinks and we were out looking for a place to get a sandwhich when she'd gotten sick at her stomach, so we stopped at the gas station. She was sick and wanted me to be with her, so I took her into the men's toilet. I didn't think there was anything wrong with that. And the harness bulls, I think we had them licked, but then the detectives came over.

The detectives shined their lights in our eyes. They pushed me up against the wall and shook me down. They went into the bathroom and started going through it and came up with this spoon, and they said, "Aha!" You know. They made me take my coat off and roll up my sleeves, and they saw the marks, and they said, "Were you fixing in there?" I said, "No, I wasn't fixing in there." They said, "Well, you're going to jail." I told them, "I'm working at this place. My horn's out on the stand. What's going to happen? Give me a break, man! What are you doing?" They took us to the Inglewood substation.

They separated us and interrogated us, and finally a guy came in and said, "Well, it's all over. The chick copped out." He said, "I don't know if you know it or not, but she's a minor. You're going to prison for fifteen to life." I said, "I thought she was nineteen or twenty!" He said, "Well, she's seventeen." Fortunately, I stuck to my story and she stuck to hers. They'd told her I copped out, too, but she didn't go for it.

They kept us all night. They threatened me. The next morning they took us to the old county jail downtown. They allowed me one phone call, and I called the club and asked them to put the horn away. I never saw Penny again. They cut her loose the next day. But they told me they were going to prosecute me for furnishing to a minor.

They couldn't make anything stick, see: I'd only been out of the sanitarium a few weeks and I'd fixed only a few times at varied places. It would have been very hard to get me on a marks beef. They didn't have anything to hold me on but I didn't realize that, so when they told me they'd give me a break and send me to the psychopathic ward of the General Hospital and then to a hearing before a judge who'd send me to Norwalk or Camarillo for ninety days, I figured anything would be better than fifteen to life and I said alright.

They drove me to the hospital, handed me a paper, and told

me to sign. They told me it was for my property. The attendant took me upstairs, put me on a table, and wheeled me into a room. I looked around. Here's an old wino next to me. He's naked. He's strapped to a table, and he's screaming. And he's peeing. Pee's shooting up in the air. There's another guy, and he's playing with himself and growling. I stayed there for two weeks. They put me in a room with eight other people, all nuts, and they filled me with downers, all kinds of downers, millions of downers. I could hardly walk. I slept nearly all the time. That's the way they keep you cool.

They wouldn't allow me to shave, so I looked awful, and one day I woke up in this corner they kept me in and there was Patti sitting on the edge of the bed. She looked at me and said, "Why did you do this?" I said, "Well, I thought everything was finished: you didn't want me to come home." She said, "I was going to have you come home right after you got out of the sanitarium, but we decided it would be better to let you have a little time on your own so you'd really appreciate coming home. And then . . . " I said, "Well, it's a bum beef." She said, "It's not that! I found out from your mother that you brought some little whore, some little tramp off the streets, into the house, and you were shooting dope and making love in the bathroom! You took this girl out to the garage at night and made love to her!" She started crying. "How could you do anything like that?"

I realized that I'd fallen into a trap. All I would have had to do was just be cool for a little while. I started crying, I tried to hold on to her, and I said, "Please give me another chance." She said, "It's impossible. You're hopeless." She said, "It's useless. Look at you." She said, "Your dad will be at the hearing. He'll help you." She shook her head and got up and walked out the door.

When the day came, they marched me down to the hearing in pajamas and a robe. We went to a courtroom that's right there in the building, and here's my dad and Thelma and Patti. All the other cases were for people who had done outrageous things—threatening their families with butcher knives, peeing out in the front yard. They brought up my name and the judge started talking. He said, "We're going to send you to Norwalk and try to save your life. You've tried it with a private sanitarium and you found that that didn't work, so we're going to send you to an institution." Then my father started shouting: "He's not going to go to any state institution! I've heard all about them! They're corrupt, lousy places! And you're not going to get money out of the misery of people like this! You're not going to get it out of my son! If he needs to go back to a sanitarium, I'll pay for it, but he's not going to go to a California mental institution!" The judge really got angry, but my dad kept raving about graft and corruption and the system, and the judge finally just wanted him to shut up so he yelled, "Alright! But mark my words: this boy'll be—I won't even give him a year—he'll be in a state penitentiary instead of a hospital! You mark my words! I'll stake my reputation on it! Alright! Get him out of here!"

I went to my dad and hugged and thanked him. I kissed Patti. Then I got my stuff, changed clothes, and walked downstairs, and when I got to the gate the guy said, "Here, sign this thing." I signed it, and as I signed it I read it, and I saw on the paper where it said "committed by" and it was *me*! I had committed *myself*! The police had just put a shuck on me and the funny part was I had spent two weeks in this place and if it hadn't been for my dad I would have been sent to Norwalk for six or nine months or maybe a year because I had committed myself voluntarily and didn't know it.

In 1953 I was separated from Patti. I stayed in Long Beach with my dad for a while and then I ran into a girl, Susan Douglas. She had been married to Kendell Douglas, the bass player, but before that she was married to another guy who was very wealthy and he was in some kind of asylum back east. He was giving her money and she was living up on the Strip in an apartment hotel. I saw her a couple of times while I was staying with my dad, and she told me she would like to have me live with her. She'd like to take care of me. I realized that I couldn't live in Long Beach because it was too far away from the jobs, so I moved into L.A. and got a little room in Hollywood.

Susan kept wanting me to visit her and stay with her, but she wanted to make love and I didn't want to make love to her. There was something about her; she didn't move me in that way. And she was a beautiful girl, too. Her hair was a chestnut color, and she was very seductive, a real feminine girl, and she was young and unworldly and easily led; I could have led her anywhere. But I couldn't have intercourse with her because she didn't move me, and she was so nice I couldn't act like anything was happening that wasn't happening. She was the kind of girl you wouldn't want to hurt. I wouldn't.

During the time I was going to see her, Susan would let me use her car whenever I wanted. She had a custom-made Cadillac that her husband had given her. A special paint job. The whole thing. When I stopped it at a stop sign people would walk over and say, "Wow!" A couple of times driving downtown, where there was a cop directing traffic, he'd walk over and say, "Boy, where did you get this car? What a beautiful car!" It was a greenish color, but unlike any green I've ever seen. It was a lightish green that had gold flecks in it. A greenish gold that you could see forever into. It was like looking into a lake. It had a white top, a convertible. The seats were covered with actual cowhide and the rugs were white shag. It had every device known. The aerial had a button; the trunk had a button; the hood had a button; and not only the windows but the wind-wings had a button. There was a light that went on if the doors weren't locked, and it had a button you locked all the doors with. It had a radio with four speakers, two in front and two in the back. It had an ashtray for the driver and an ashtray for the passenger . . .

I was scuffling. I wasn't working too much, but I'd done a lot of recording and I was well known, so the Martin Company had given me a horn for advertising. I woke up one morning, sick, and I took this horn down and asked Susan if I could borrow the car. I took the Cadillac and drove down to Main Street and pawned my alto. I went from there to East L.A. and got a gram of heroin. I was very sick and wanted to fix where I'd got the stuff, but the guy lived with his wife and mother and there was no place we could go, so I had to drive all the way back to the Strip. I had this gram rolled up in cellophane, ten number-five caps in a row, wrapped in cellophane. I didn't want to hold them in my mouth, but after I got off the freeway and I'd gotten almost to the Strip I decided I'd better put them somewhere, so I put them in my sock, the ten caps, down in my right sock, thinking that that would be cool, which it always had been before.

I stopped the car out on the street near Susan's. I got out and looked around. Everything looked alright so I walked through the parking lot. I always went through the back because I wasn't registered in the apartment. I had stashed my outfit outside in a hedge by the side of the building. Before I went in I reached down in this bush to get the outfit, and as I reached down I felt something cold on my head, I heard a click, and I heard this voice, "Federal narcotics agent. One move and you're dead." I heard a holler or a whistle and a door opened, and I looked out of the corner of my eye and there was another one, and they both had guns pointed right at my head. The first guy said, "Lean against the building." They frisked me for a weapon, found the outfit, and then they said, "Come on."

They walked me to the back stairway, walked me in, marched me right to the door of Susan's apartment, and they said, "Knock on the door. Don't say anything or you're dead." There was nothing I could do. I knocked, and the door opened, and there she was. They ran into the apartment. They told Susan and a friend of mine, Joe Martin, who was there, "Don't move!" Susan is an innocent little girl; Joe had never been in trouble or done anything wrong except fix a couple of times with me. They were bewildered. Susan said, "What's happening? What's going on?" And one of the guys said, "Well, we got your boyfriend. One of our snitches told us he was a big dealer." She said, "A big dealer of what?" He said, "Don't play coy with us, sister. We know what's happening." He took the outfit and threw it down on the coffee table. He said, "Where's it at?" I told her, "Susan, don't say anything to these fuckin' guys." I said, "She doesn't have anything to do with what you're talking about. Leave her alone." They said, "Oh, yeah, yeah, that's a likely story." They looked at Joe and said to me, "Tell Tonto here not to get any wild ideas or we'll break his fuckin' jaw!" Joe was Italian but he looked Mexican, I guess. They told us, "Sit down!"

The feds started searching the apartment. I said, "You can't go through this place! I don't live here!" I turned to Susan: "They can't go through your place! Ask them if they've got a search warrant!" She said, "They can go through my place. I have nothing to hide!" I said, "I don't *live* here!" One detective turned around and said, "We know what's happening, man. We were told the whole story. You were picked up here for your last job." And so right away I had a pretty good idea who informed on me. I think it was Sammy Curtis, but I was never able to find out for sure.

I kept talking to them. They kept searching the pad. Susan had been modeling; she had posed for a lot of shots—not nudes but semi. One of the guys said, "Ohhhh, look at this! Is this what you show your tricks?" I said, "What the fuck are you guys talking about?" He said, "Well, isn't she your whore?" I said, "You motherfuckers!" He said, "Watch out, boy, we'll break your head open."

They went through everything and then they said, "Alright, little girl, close your eyes. You've probably seen everything, and if you want to watch you can, but we're going to strip these two assholes." Joe took his clothes off. He was clean. Then they told him. "Alright, bend over and spread 'em." Joe said, "What?" The guy said, "You know what I mean, asshole. I'll beat your fuckin' brains out if you don't do it! Spread your ass open, punk!"

I stripped. I got everything off but my shoes and socks. In those days you could take your pants off over your shoes. I thought once this was over maybe they'd stop, but as I started to bend over one guy said, "Hey, get your shoes off!" And my heart sunk. I had loafers on. I took my left shoe and sock and pulled them off in one motion. I did the same with my right. Then I stood up and spread my cheeks and waited. They weren't even looking at me. They were looking at my shoes. One guy grabbed the left one, hit it, pounded it, threw it aside. The other took the right one, pounded it, threw it aside. Finally they got up. "Bend over." They looked. "You're clean, motherfucker." I grabbed my clothes and started to put them on, but as an afterthought one fed went over and took my sock, my left one, and shook it. He stretched it out and threw it down and I thought he was going to give me a pass, but he went on to the other one, shook it, stretched it, and the ten caps fell out in the cellophane.

The cops were so happy, man. They looked at Susan and they said, "See what we were talking about, little girl?" "Yeah, well, there it is! There it is! Now what have you got to say?" They told me that the guy who'd turned me in had said I was a big dealer. I said, "What kind of a big dealer?" I pulled out the pawn ticket. I said, "I went and pawned my saxophone, man. Here's the ticket. Today's date." I had pawned the alto for twenty-five dollars. I had bought a gram of stuff for twenty dollars. I had bought a couple of packs of cigarettes. I had put some gas in the car. And I'd bought a burrito. What kind of a dealer could I be?

I said, "I spent the night with this chick. She doesn't even know that I use. This guy is a friend of hers. He doesn't know *nothing*. I spent the night here, got sick, grabbed the car keys off the table, went out, hocked my horn, and bought the gram. I never even got a chance to fix. Here's the gram." They realized they'd gotten some bum information but they said, "Alright. Great! Great! We'll add car theft to that."

I had told Susan that if anything ever did happen to say she didn't know about my taking the car, to say I stole the car and file a stolen report on it. That way they couldn't take it away from her. I wouldn't have gotten any more time; the charges would have run concurrently. And it was such a beautiful car, this Cadillac. So after they found the stuff, I immediately said that I had taken the car, but then the chick jumps in. She says, "He didn't steal anything from me! He can have anything he wants! Anything he wants he can have! He can have anything of mine! I love him! I *told* him he could use the car *anytime* for *anything* at *anytime*! He didn't steal the car, and I *gave* him the keys. No matter what he wants it for he can have my car!" The cop said, "Ohhhh! So you told him he could take your car? You *knew* he took your car? You gave him *permission* to take your car?" She said, "Yes!" So that was it. She had voluntarily given me her car; I had used it for transporting narcotics; and they ended up getting the car.

They went to Joe and looked at his arms and found four or five marks. They said, "Alright, we're going to book you for marks." The feds didn't have a law for marks, but they were going to take him down and turn him over to the state. They looked at Susan and found two marks. "Oh, you don't know anything about it, huh?" They really got rank. I said, "What's *wrong* with you guys? You've got me. Give the girl back her car and take me down." So the guy said, "Well, I'll tell you what we'll do. If you cop out that the stuff was yours and sign a statement, we'll cut 'em loose." I said alright.

We all went downtown to the federal building. I signed the paper. I said that I'd gone down to the Central Market, the produce market, and I saw a Mexican there in a leather jacket, and I thought I'd seen him someplace before. I went up to him and asked him, "Hey, you got any carga?" He said, "How much you want?" I said, "Un gramo," And he said, Hora le!" I bought it from him, but I didn't know his name. It was totally ridiculous, and they didn't go for it, but there was nothing they could do. Then one of the guys says, "Well, we're going to take the car." I said, "What do you mean, man? I signed the paper!" He said, "You didn't give up no names." He said, "If you want to take a ride with us and show us where you got the stuff, then maybe we can talk about the car."

They told me if I came up with a dealer they'd turn me loose. I guess they figured a musician is weak. It was a musician that set me up; I guess the feds figured, "Well, here's another musician." I must be weak, too. And maybe I would know somebody that was dealing. I had a lot of connections in East L.A. I could have turned over. They said, "Here, we'll give you the gram, the car, cut all of you loose, and all you have to do is take a ride and point out somebody." I have to admit that the thought of being free and being able to shoot the gram was very tempting, but I couldn't do it. When I first started using, this friend, Henry Garcia—we used to cop together—told me, "Do you know what you're doing? If you do this you may get busted and you may have to go to jail. If you're not willing to go, just don't do it." I'd said, "No, I realize and I'll be able to go when the time comes." And I thought, "Well, here's the test." So that was it. I knew I couldn't inform on anyone because I would never have been able to relax. There's one thing you have if you don't inform: you don't feel bad about yourself. No matter how bad things get, you have that. It's something that a lot of people don't understand, but anybody who's been in that position realizes what it is and knows what I'm talking about. So they kept after me, and I told them no.

I told Susan, "File a theft report. Say I stole your car and get it back. They can't hold it and I'm not going to turn over on anybody to save it." The feds walked us across the street to the L.A. County Jail, where they house you even if you're a federal prisoner. Just before we went upstairs one fed said, "Well, this is your last chance. You don't have to go up there. Take a ride, make a buy, and that's it. We'll cut you loose and you can go to your pad and get loaded." I was deathly sick. I told them no. I said, "Are you going to keep your promise about cutting Joe and Susan loose?" The fed motioned to this other fed and he told them, "Okay, you're free. Say goodbye." Joe shook my hand. Susan said, "Oh, Arthur, I love you!" She said, "Is there anything I can do?" I said, "No, take care of yourself." She asked the detective, "Can I kiss him goodbye?" She grabbed me and kissed me and held on to me. She was just, like, a little girl, you know, that had cared for me. I had never cared for her but she was so sweet and I felt so sad. I watched them walk off.

The feds pushed the elevator button and we got in. They pushed the jail floor; I think it was nine. The elevator opens and they walk me to the gate and they say, "One for booking, federal narcotics." One of the feds says, "You got any money for cigarettes?" I said no. He reached into his pocket and gave me a five-dollar bill. I almost fell over. Then the guy put out his hand and said, "Come on, man, this is our job. This is what we have to do. I hate a fuckin' informer and I just want to shake your hand, not being a rat." I shook his hand, and the other guy patted me on the shoulder and he said, "Good luck."

8 | The Los Angeles County Jail

1953

WHEN YOU'RE BOOKED into the Los Angeles County Jail they put you in a cage with a wire gate, and you have to wait while they type up a whole bunch of stuff. You lie there and sit there, and then, when enough people are ready, the guards call out the names and you walk to another section, where they take your fingerprints. They do each finger and your whole hand, and they take your picture. Then you wait again, and there's no place to sit. You lie on the cement floor, and people get sick—they're vomiting. I was sick before I got busted; I was sick before I went and hocked my horn; so I was deathly ill by the time I was waiting. And it took thirty-six hours to be booked in.

The agony of kicking is beyond words. It's nothing like the movies, *The Man with the Golden Arm*, or things you read: how they scream and bat their heads against the wall, and they'd give up their mother, and they want to cut their throats. That's ridiculous. It's awful but it's quiet. You just lie there and suffer. You have chills and your bones hurt; your veins hurt; and you ache. When water touches you it feels as if it's burning you, and there's a horrible taste in your mouth, and every smell is awful and becomes magnified a thousandfold. You can smell people, people with BO, their feet, and filth and dirt. But you don't scream and all that: "Kill my mother, my father, just get me a fix and I'll do anything you want!" That's outrageous.

The depression you feel is indescribable, and you don't

sleep. Depending on how hooked you are, you might go three weeks or a month without ever sleeping except for momentary spells when you just pass out. You'll be shaking and wiggling your legs to try to stop the pain in the joints, and all of a sudden you'll black out and you'll have a dream that you're somewhere trying to score. You'll get the shit and the outfit, and you'll stick it in your vein, and then the outfit will clog, or the stuff will shoot out the rubber part of the dropper, or somebody'll get in the way—somebody stops you and you never get it into your arm. I used to dream that my grandmother was holding me and I was hitting her in the face, smashing her in the mouth—blood came out of her face—and I could never get the dope in. You'd have terrible dreams: you'd flash to a woman, your old lady; she'd become a dog and she'd have a peepee like a dog instead of a cunt like a woman; and all of a sudden you'd come and immediately you'd wake up, and you'd be sticky and dirty and wet.

The first time I went to the county jail, I went seventeen days and nights without sleeping at all, I was so sick. I kept vomiting and couldn't eat. Seventeen days and nights, and all they gave you was aspirin. You could get three of them at night when they had sick call come around. And at night they had salts and soda. You could get either one. Salts to make you go to the bathroom or soda to settle your stomach.

In the county jail for a while they had a kick tank. They'd lock you up in a solid cell all alone. I knew a young Chicano cat who got put in the kick tank, and he started vomiting. He vomited and vomited, and he called for the guards but they ignored him. He kept vomiting and he ruptured a blood vessel in his stomach and bled to death, choked in his own blood. That's the treatment that the dope fiend got.

I was once in jail with a Chinaman. He had been shooting "black" (opium) for years and years. Chinese didn't get busted for a long time because the Chinese as a whole are much stronger than the whites and the blacks. But then some of the young Chinese got out and started shooting regular heroin, hanging out with the other dope fiends, and they got Americanized. And so, when they got busted they ratted on their elders. This Chinaman was an older guy; he looked like a skeleton; and he was really strung out. He was shaking so much he could hardly walk. They assigned him to a cell but he said, "I can't bear the cell. Just put me on the freeway." The freeway is the walkway that goes by the cells. They put him out there, and for two weeks he did nothing but sit in one position. He didn't eat one bit of food. Every now and then he'd drink a little something, take some broth out of the stew. For two weeks he sat with his feet on the floor and his arms around his knees in a corner on the freeway not saying a word to anybody, sweat pouring off his face. When he got a little better I talked to him and he said that he was trying to put himself into a trance, to leave his body, to get over the misery. I've seen guys put their pants legs into their socks and tie strings around them so no wind could get to their bodies. Then they would walk up and down the freeway for days, walk all night long, and they wouldn't sleep for weeks except for these horrible moments.

So kicking is the most insidious thing. It's a million times worse than they portray it. It's not an outward, noisy anguish. It's an inner suffering that only you, and, if there's any such thing as God, like, maybe you and He know it.

The amount of time it took to be booked in was incredible. That first time the place was jammed with people, people that stank and derelicts. I looked around and thought, "What am I doing here? What did I ever do to get put in a place like this?" And I had no conversation during the whole thirty-six hours that I was being booked in.

As I said, when you're sick the sensation of water touching your skin is like a physical pain. So the first thing they make you do, they force you into a shower, a funky shower; the floor is filthy, and the soap they use is yellow soap that you wash clothes with, floors with. Then, after you've showered and you're shivering and your pores are wide open, before you get a towel, you walk out and they've got trustees there with the guards. The trustees have big cans with long handles on them, like fly spray cans, and they make you raise your arms and they squirt this bug juice underneath your arms, and it's so strong it goes right into your pores and burns. They make you pick up your balls and they squirt it all around your joint. They make you bend over and spread your cheeks, and they squirt it in your ass, and it runs down and burns like fire. They squirt it on your hair, and it's horrible-smelling stuff. I made the mistake of thinking that trustees would be cool so I said, "Could you go easy?" As soon as I said that they shot more on me. Then they give you a towel to dry yourself. You put on these clothes that they give you that don't fit, and then you go to the linen room and get a mattress, a "donut" they call it. You get an old, funky blanket and a filthy pillow that smells of urine and vomit and come. You get a mattress cover that you use as a sheet and an old, beat towel.

I was so sick by that time I didn't know what was happening. You go to the hospital and they have you stand there and drop your pants, grab your joint, and squeeze it to see if you've got a venereal disease; if you don't that's it. They take you to whatever cell you're going to. I was white and I was a heroin addict, so I went to the white hype tank. That was 12-B-1. As you walk up to the front of the tank the guys come and look at you and they give you the coldest looks imaginable. And then you go inside. They finally open the gate, and you walk inside.

If you have money, anything over six dollars, they put it with your property, with your rings or your watch, but you can keep six dollars on you, cash, to buy candy and cigarettes. They give you an envelope: it's like an ID and it shows your charge, your name, and how much cash you kept. If you're a narcotics addict they stamp an N on your envelope so they'll always know you're an addict. Then, if you go for visiting and you get underwear or socks or anything, they'll soak them first in water because people sometimes cook up heroin and pour it in an agreed on spot in the shorts or whatever, and when the guy gets them in he can cut that part out and put it in the spoon. If you're an addict everything is soaking wet when you get it.

In the block there's about eighteen cells, and the number one cell is the trustees' cell. These aren't trustees like the ones that were squirting us, trustrees dressed in brown who live upstairs and do the work in the jail. These were just the trustees that run the tank. They interrogate you. Where are you from? Who do you hang out with? Who busted you? What officer? Have you got anybody running for you on the streets? Your old lady? Is she going to send you any bread, any dope? They want to know if there's a chance of you doing them any good. If they think you've got something going for you they'll try to put you in a better cell. Fortunately, I knew a couple of people there and I was pretty well known because of my music, so I was spared a lot of indignities. But the other people who come in, if they're not known or they're grasshoppers, busted for pot, the tank trustees might march them into a cell at the back of the tank and take all their six dollars. If the guy won't come up with it they might sneak up in the night and cut his pockets with a razor blade and take it. And they'll sell him his own food.

Once a week they'd have a horrible stew. Instead of potatoes, it had parsnips and turnips in it, just awful. But there would be a little bit of stew meat. So when the pot of stew came, the trustees and the people in the number two and three cells, the strongest or most popular people, would put up a rope at the end of the number three cell and say, "Deadline," so nobody from the back could walk up there. Then they'd take the pot into the number one cell, take out all the meat and put it on a tray, and they'd keep the bread, too. They'd eat all they wanted and send the remains to the back cells, and then they'd sell sandwiches, late at night, to the other guys for fifty cents apiece. Any little treat that came in special, like peanut butter, the trustees would hide and sell. There were vendors that came around selling cigarettes and books and candy, and when the candy man came the guys in the front would butt in the line and crowd back in and buy up all the candy. Later they'd sell it to the grasshoppers and the weaker, less known fiends for fifteen, twenty, maybe twenty-five cents a bar, when the candy was five cents a bar.

Sometimes, before he brings a new guy in, the guard will say, "Well, nothing better happen to this guy." That's the same as saying, "He's a rat." So when the rat comes in first they take his money and later on they get him. They make him sit on the floor in one of the back cells and put his legs up on the bottom bunk, and someone gets on the top bunk and jumps down on his knees and busts them backwards. They then kick him in the head. Blood comes out of his ears and eyes and nose and mouth, and he has to say, "Squeal, squeal. I'm a rat."

Two guys came in one time and they said, "There's these two rats that are going to come here soon. They turned over on us and got us busted, and if we leave before they get here, really take care of them." Everybody said okay, and these guys were shipped out to max at the farm, Biscaluse Center. A couple of days later here come two more guys and they had the same names as the first two said had turned over on them, so before they could say anything the guys in the tank just beat them to death. Well, one guy died later in the county hospital. Right after that, another guy came in and said, "Did So-and-so and So-and-so come through here?" They said, "Yeah, we really took care of the two rats." But the new guy said, "They weren't the rats!" And it was the ones that had come through *first* that were the informers! They immediately sent word out to max and they got them out there, killed one of them and beat the other nearly to death. But the poor guys that weren't rats . . . And there were many cases like that. If somebody didn't like you, they'd just make up a false jacket. There were always people who were hanging bum jackets, people who were weak or were jealous or had got burned by somebody or thought some guy had balled their old lady. So you were always afraid because you didn't know who was going to say what. Knowing yourself, that you were alright, had no meaning as far as those people went. Sometimes they'd just beat people up because there was nothing else to do.

I thought the army was bad. Now here I was in jail. The army was a warm place in comparison. I was lonesome; I wanted love; I was losing Patti; I wanted to cry. But there was no privacy at all in jail. There's eyes always watching. Even at night when you're trying to sleep there's people not sleeping; they're sick; they're watching. There's always lights on because of security. I wanted to pour my heart out to somebody; probably a lot of the people felt the same way, but you had to be strong and act like nothing bothered you. I had to be tough. I had to ridicule anything that indicated weakness. I had to be real cynical and act like the only thing that was important was getting loaded. I was double tough and real cool, and I was miserable.

My father helped get me out on bail, and I went back to plead. I thought they would leave me out until sentencing, but I pleaded nolo contendere so they jerked me off bail and put me back in the county jail. I was sentenced to two years. At that time I could have gotten probation by the feds or I could have gotten a year. They gave me two years and sent me to Forth Worth.

9 | The U.S. Public Health Service Hospital at Fort Worth

1953 – 1954

THERE WERE THREE PEOPLE from the L.A. County Jail and a couple of people from San Diego, five of us altogether, that went on the chain. The U.S. marshals took us. We went down to the Union Station and they put us on the train. We had a pullman; it was the law; they had to give you a pullman if you were going to be traveling more than twenty-four hours. They paired us off. I drew a dope fiend from San Diego named Kantola; his name came before mine alphabetically. We were put together in one bunk. They had leg irons on us and we had to sleep that way, in a top bunk, and Kantola was sick.

When we went to eat they took the leg irons off and put us in handcuffs. We walked into the dining car and sat down; one of us had to eat with our left hand and the other with our right. People were staring at us so I played the role, like I was a big gangster. I had a double-breasted suit on with a white shirt, and I took my tie off, and I was very handsome. I gave people cold looks, the porters, and if chicks would stare at us I'd give them evil looks. You could act any way you wanted because nobody could bother you—you had the guards there. So you'd glare at people and they'd look away because they'd be scared.

We got off the train at Fort Worth, and they lined us up and put chains around our stomachs and handcuffs on our wrists.

They drove us out to the U.S. Public Health Service Hospital, a little ways out of town on a big hill. We went into a building and down in an elevator, and that was the last time I would be outside for nine months. It was nine months before I got an out-doors pass. You walked to the different buildings through underground tunnels. There were three hundred addicts and eight hundred mental patients who were connected with the coast guard, their families—people who had lost their minds or were in the process of losing them.

We got there on a Sunday. There was no activity and nobody around. We went through the different stages of getting booked in and of course it was nothing like the county jail. I thought, "Maybe this will be good for me." I had messed up everything, and as far as my playing, nothing was happening right anyway, so I started thinking, "Maybe I'll be able to straighten out, and when I get out everything will be like it was before. Again. And I'll be back with Patti. And I'll enjoy play-ing." Two years seemed like an awful long time, but I'd spent three and a half years in the army. And there was always a chance of making parole after a part of my time was up.

The buildings were tall and there were about seven of them. One big building had all the administration offices in it and the doctors' offices, where the psychiatrists did their work. There was a building for the women and three for the extreme mental patients. Part of one building was a school, and part of another had a regular hospital in it. These buildings were spread out over a large area and were joined by the tunnels. We went to 201, the place they took the newcomers to see what kind of shape we were in. Me and Kantola told them we were sick. They really didn't believe me. I didn't appear to be sick. But I wanted to get some dope and if you were sick they took you off with liquid methadone, liquid Dolophine they called it, and they had chloral hydrate to make you sleep at night. If you were *really* in bad shape they'd give you morphine a few times, but all I got was one little taste of methadone and one little taste of chloral hydrate, and then they wouldn't give me anything more because I had come there from the county jail and they knew I was alright.

There were a lot of people in there who'd been getting stuff for ages. These were people who came in off the streets to kick.

They'd sign themselves in and stay sixty or ninety days and then they'd leave. We called them "winders." We talked a couple of these guys into giving us a taste of their medicine. They had to drink it in front of somebody, but they'd put it in their mouths and act like they'd swallowed it and then come back and spit into a cup, and we'd drink it. It was kind of nasty, but when you want dope it really doesn't seem to be very nasty.

We stayed a while getting physical examinations, and then they assigned us to the place where we were going to do our time. It was like a dormitory. It had a big dayroom and another room with rows of bunkbeds separated by little, five-foot boards, making cubicles, two guys to a cubicle.

In the morning a bell would ring and we'd get up, go to the bathroom, wash and dress, and walk down to breakfast. The mess hall was in another building, quite a ways from where I was staying, so I'd walk through the tunnels with the nut patients. They'd be shuffling along with their hands in their pockets and their heads hanging down, and every now and then I'd see one of them standing in a corner, peeing against the wall. I'd walk into the mess hall, and we, the fiends, would eat on one side, and they, the nuts, would eat on the other. The food was very good.

I was lucky in Fort Worth. When I got there, there were very few musicians and eventually they appointed me head of the music department. It really wasn't a department, but they had to have somebody to order things, so every now and then I'd make up an order for reeds and drumsticks and things like that. Then I started doing a little teaching and it was good because instead of cleaning the tunnels or working in the kitchen I got to work in the music room. I'd go to the band room in the morning, sweep the floor, clean the place, and make sure everything was locked up, and then I'd get out my horn. I'd close the door in this little room and just sit there and practice. I did that every day, and it was the first time I'd ever practiced, and I really got down with music. Then I formed a little group. I got a drummer and a bass player, who weren't very good, and a piano—the piano player was very good, a guy named Abdullah Kennebrew, who was black and short, and we argued all the time. The piano had wheels on it so we could roll it. We had a little cart to carry the drums and bass and we'd go around and play for different wards. We'd play in the closed wards for the mental patients. We'd walk in and set up in a corner and just start playing, no announcement or anything. We were a regular jazz group, and we played bebop, and the patients had no idea what we were doing.

Each patient had his own little thing. There was one guy who just walked around making the sign of the cross. He'd bow down on one knee as if he was praying and mumble. They had a bench that extended all around the dayroom, and one guy would sit there and count money all the time; every now and then he'd put his fingers to his mouth and wet them as if he was counting bills. Then there were catatonics, who would just stand in one position and never move, and there were people who'd sit or lie on the floor and play with their toes. Now and then, there would be one that would look at you, but as soon as you looked back, he'd turn away and giggle and hide behind a table or something.

We played, and while we played I noticed that almost all of them showed some signs of hearing the music, moving their feet or some part of their bodies in a semblance of the rhythm we were playing in. Some of them would even smile—a silly smile. And that showed us that what we were doing was getting through to them. I talked to the aides and the nurses and asked them if they thought we were doing any good, if there was any point to it, and they said that they thought there was because on the days we played, they found that the patients were a lot more manageable; there were less violent flare-ups. It was as if we anaesthetized them with our music.

One day a week, sometimes twice a week, we'd play in the women's section. These were the wives and daughters of people in the coast guard. A lot of the women, I was told, had syphilis, cases that had progressed to the stage where, when they were finally aware of the fact that they had it, it was beyond cure. The nurses and doctors said that in the end the patients got to the point where they would have to be locked in a cell, to die there a horrible death, writhing and beating themselves against the padded cell, ripping at their bodies.

We'd play for these women and it was sad in actuality, when you look back at it, but at the time it seemed very funny.

There was one woman, about twenty-eight, and I noticed that if you looked at her, she'd get excited; she'd really get frantic. So I'd be playing and she'd be standing, her left hand grabbing at her stomach, bunching up her robe, and I'd stare at her, and the longer I looked . . . She'd start shaking all over; she'd stamp her feet; she'd start screaming and calling me names: "You son-of-a-bitch!" And then I'd stop, but I couldn't help doing it again and again. There was another girl. She had long, black hair, and I guess at one time she was sort of pretty, but she was really wasted. This girl would lie on a couch while we played. Once while I was playing I happened to look over at her, and I noticed she was staring at me. I looked away. I played. I looked back again, and I saw her glance around to see where the nurse was. When she saw that the nurse wasn't looking, she took her robe and opened it up, and she had nothing on underneath. There she was, just lying there with the robe pulled back and her legs spread. She was looking at me and I was looking at her and then all of a sudden she closed the robe. She'd keep opening it and closing it, and a couple of times the nurse saw her and made her stop.

I started taking nutmeg. They had tunnel crews that cleaned at 2, 3, 4 A.M., when all the action stopped. They'd wash down the tunnels with big hoses and scrub them because the mental patients would urinate against the walls and sometimes shit on the sides. These guys brought papers of nutmeg and mace smuggled in by the guards, and I took it because it was very difficult to get anything else.

They sold it in penny matchboxes; one box cost four packs of cigarettes. You'd put it in a glass with hot water and stir it up. It wouldn't dissolve: it would kind of float around. It was very hard to drink. I gradually increased the amount I took and finally got up to four matchboxes a day. The guy would wake me at about four in the morning and give me the nutmeg. I'd get up, go to the bathroom, put it in my glass, get it down without gagging, and then go back to sleep. I'd wake up again at about 6:30 or seven, when they rang the bell, and by the time I was ready to go to breakfast the nutmeg was hitting me and I'd really be sailing. It makes you feel like exceptionally good pot; you giggle; you laugh; everything is insanely comical. I'd walk down the tunnel with another guy (we'd take it together), and we'd pass the mental patients walking with their eyes on the ground, dragging their feet. We'd pass the one that was praying and the other one counting the money, and we'd start laughing. Sometimes five or six of us would take it at once. We'd go to the mess hall and rush to the table. They'd have coffee on the table in a big pot, and it was really delicious. We'd put our trays down and sit, and by the time we'd finished one cup of coffee we'd be completely out of it, goofing around, acting crazy. That's at about seven o'clock in the morning. And I did this every day for about six months at one period. It's a wonder I didn't kill myself.

The nutmeg made you think about sex. The bad thing about Fort Worth—it was both good and bad—there were a lot of women there. Every sixty days a different group of student nurses came in. They'd be going to different hospitals for their training. They'd be seventeen, eighteen years old, walking around in short uniforms, walking through the tunnels. There were also the women that worked in the administration building, office women who dressed real sexy—you could see them wandering around; then there were the nurses and the Grey Ladies and the Red Cross. So all kinds of intrigue went on. People would be hiding, staring at women. I guess a third of the addicts were Puerto Ricans. The Puerto Ricans used to stick little mirrors on their shoes: a guy would go to the library and stand by some chick; he'd have the pockets cut out of his pants, you know, and he'd put his foot underneath the girl's dress and play with himself.

There was a choir and a lady who came out to give choir practice who was very pretty. She had brownish-blonde hair that came down to her shoulders, and she wore lipstick and rouge and had her eyebrows plucked and everything. She was a southern belle. She had pretty skin coloring, sort of like a peach. She'd wear a sweater that was cut low or a white silk blouse with one of the buttons loose and a low-cut bra, and she'd always manage to get in a position where you could see her breasts. If she got anywhere near you she'd rub her ass against your leg or something, but real innocent, and she kind of flapped her eyelids at you. She had blue eyes and she'd give you this look.

She led the choir, and I sang with them a few times, and I

noticed that she was flirting with me a little bit. Then one day
she said, "Oh, would you stick around after? I want to talk to
you for a minute." Everybody left. She was sitting at a table
with a book of songs. She said, "Would you look at these
songs?" Instead of sitting down next to her I just stood and
looked over her shoulder. She had a blouse on that was cut
fairly low. I moved up against her, and I started to get a hard-
on. I'm standing right against her shoulder, pressing myself
against her shoulder, looking over her shoulder at the music,
and she's all red in the face and kind of trembling. Finally, she
had to leave. She asked me if I would help her, getting something together, some arrangements for the choir.

A few days later a guard came and said that I was wanted at
the school. They told me I had a meeting with the choir teacher.
I went. She was in one of these rooms with a piano, alone. The
guard said, "I locked the door because I didn't want people
bothering her." He opened the door, and I pushed the lock
when I went in. She said, "Hello. I hope I didn't disturb you
from anything you were doing, but we agreed to get together
about these arrangements and I want to get something worked
out so we can have something for our choir rehearsals and start
them as soon as possible and get the ball rolling and have
something to work on right away." I said, "Oh, no, no, that's
fine. That's fine." She had a real cute southern accent. She
looked like one of those Tennessee Williams girls with the low-
cut dress and the breasts just straining at the top of it. The
guard said, "You just holler if you need anything. No one'll
bother you, so if you need anything, just holler." Looking at
her, you know. He closed the door, and I'd locked it, and after
he left I looked at her and she looked at me and her eyes got
kind of crossed. She's married and has children, a nice, upper-
class lady.

This room was on the first floor, but from outside you'd
have to pull yourself up to look in; no one just walking by could
see. The piano was facing the wall. If we were sitting at the
piano our backs would be to the windows. I didn't want that.
So I took a table and put it in front of the piano so we could sit
at the table, and if any activity was going on under this table
nobody would be able to see it from the window or any place
else. I had some music paper I'd brought with me, and we sat
down. I said, "Okay, now, what did you have in mind?"

I noticed that every time I looked at her she'd get this cross-eyed look, and I was starting to shake a little myself. Before I went to the school, when I realized what it was, I excused myself, went into the restroom, and took my shorts off, so all I had on was white, khaki-like pants and a white shirt that hung out (that's what we wore, white). I had undone my buttons, but with the shirt out you couldn't see that. She said, "Well, I brought a list of songs. You can look them over and let me know what you'd like to do first." She was sitting on my left; the piano was behind us. She had a short-sleeved dress on. By looking I could see between the buttons. I could see part of her breasts, and I knew from our last encounter that she knew where I was at. She said, "Will anybody bother us here?" "No, no one'll bother us. They'll probably listen." I said, "Let me see the list." She handed me the paper and our arms touched, and you could almost feel the electricity shooting through. I looked at the songs. I said, "Oh, that's a nice tune!" She bent over, exaggeratedly, so she could see which tune I meant. She's got perfume on, and she's got her head right next to mine. Then she said, "Can anybody see in?" I said, "No." I'm whispering. "Nobody can see in." Then I said, out loud, "Oh yes, that's a *nice* tune. I *like* that tune. What key would you like to do it in?" She said, "Well, A flat is a good key." I said, "A flat? That sounds good." And I put my hand underneath the table and touched her knee. I said, "What other tunes do you like?" She said, "This one's nice." I'm slipping my hand up under her dress. She had her stockings rolled about three inches above her knees, and I reached the bare flesh, and it excited me something awful. She started to quiver, and I looked at her, and her eyes . . . She just looked insane, insane with passion.

I said, "Well, let me try this tune." I turned around to the piano and started playing chords just so anybody listening would know that everything was cool. I played and I said, "Well, I think that key sounds good. Sing the first notes." I had her sing a couple notes. She's singing away, and I'm playing the piano, and I'm shaking all over. I said, "Sing some of the melody with the words; I'll write the words down." By this time I had a huge hard-on, so I reached in and grabbed my joint and flipped it out of my pants. I had my shirt over the top of it so she couldn't see. I said, "Tell me the words, and I'll write them down. Move over a little bit." She moved and I took her hand

and put it on my leg. I held it there and I said, "Okay, now, tell me the words." She started singing, "Sometimes I wonder why I spend the lonely niiiiight . . . " I keep pulling her hand up my leg. She's singing, "The melodyyyyy haunts my uhhhhhhh!" I said, "Cool it! Cool it!" I had taken her hand and put it on my bare thing, and I was all wet from being so passionate. She whispered, "Oh, no, no somebody'll see!" I whispered back, "No, no they won't! No they won't!" I said out loud, "Okay, let's hear the words again." She started again, and I finally got her to hold on to me. She's half singing the words, and her voice is cracking, and she's rubbing me, and I put my right hand up under her dress, and every now and then I reach my left hand over and play a chord so if anybody's listening they'll hear the sound of some kind of music. I finally touch her panties; they're soaking wet, she's so passionate; she's playing with me, and all of a sudden I grab her hand because I'm going to come. I whisper to her, "You wouldn't kiss it, would you?" "Oh, no! I can't do that! What if somebody comes in?" I would have given anything in the world if I could have pulled her pants off and got her to sit in my lap, but there was no way, and I was looking down her dress, trying to grab her breasts. I didn't know what to do, and she's singing, "The stars were briiiight . . . " She's quivering and her voice is shaking, and I whispered, "Jerk on me!" And I came in her hand.

I took a sheet of music paper and tried to wipe the come off. I asked her, "Do you have any Kleenex?" She reached in her purse and gave me some Kleenex. She whispered, "Do you really like me?" I said, "Oh, you're just too much. You're the most beautifully sexy woman I've ever met." I put myself away and buttoned my pants, and she wanted to kiss me. I didn't want to. I figured I might get lipstick on me. I whispered, "No, we better not." I kissed her on the cheek and said out loud, "I'll start the arrangement in A flat on 'Stardust' and have it ready for you in time for the rehearsal." We walked out. I had a couple of sessions with her like that, and I wrote two arrangements for the choir. "Stardust" and "I Can't Give You Anything But Love."

In Fort Worth I never noticed any homosexual activity. I'm sure it went on to some degree but there couldn't have been very much. I think that because there were so many women, everybody had his own little thing going. They all had somebody they'd get cleaned up for, try to do well for. They'd fantasize about a certain woman and write notes back and forth, especially with the student nurses. So it was healthy, but it was extremely hard as far as doing time. In fact I told my psychiatrist, "Sometimes I feel like I'm just going to grab one of these girls and take her in the band room and rip her clothes off and rape her."

The doctor I had was named Graetitzer, Dr. Arthur Graetitzer. Doctors could go into the coast guard as an alternative to the army and practice their specialties there, so that's what this guy did. Dr. Graetitzer had had a big practice in Saint Louis with a wealthy clientele, and he joined the coast guard and was sent to Fort Worth to do his two years. I was one of his first cases. I saw him three times a week, Monday, Wednesday, and Friday, for an hour privately and then Tuesday and Thursday we'd have a five-man group with Dr. Osborn, the head of the hospital.

I realized that as soon as I could convince these doctors I had a chance for rehabilitation they would recommend me for parole, and once I got their recommendation it was automatic: they were in charge. So at the beginning, every word I said, all my actions, were directed at creating a certain level of sickness so I could recover from it. And I kept going on the premise that I was directing things, that I was molding the thoughts of both doctors.

I started reading everything I could get my hands on about mental illness. I got tight with the chick that was running the library. I got access to books that the inmates weren't supposed to read. I got a great book on abnormal psychology filled with case histories, and I adopted certain symptoms so I could recover from them. And I thought I'd really fooled these guys, and maybe I had to a certain extent, but one day I was in my bed reading this book and I looked up and before I could make a move to stash it, Dr. Graetitzer just walked right into my little cubicle. He said, "Yeah, I've been through your area a couple of times and I noticed the things you were reading. I don't think it's . . . Why are you reading these things?" I told him, "I was just interested, being as we're dealing in psychiatry. It's just very interesting." He said, "I don't think that at your, in your position, in your condition that it's wise to be reading things like this. I think it would tend to hinder the work we're trying to do. You can read what you like, but I don't think it's to your advantage to do so." I said okay, and then, finally, I got so interested in what was happening I decided I wasn't hurting anyone but myself. So instead of playing this game I figured I'd better use the time to my advantage and learn something that might help me. I started leveling with the doctors, trying to find out if there was anything *to* psychiatry, if there was any way that you could change anything by knowing about yourself. I got very serious, and everything I did during the day, I would talk about at these sessions. I talked about Ping-Pong.

I was playing a lot of Ping-Pong. It got to the point where I played a little every day, and if I had the time I'd play four or five or six hours straight. And the same things that had always been wrong with me before, happened there, playing Ping-Pong. I got very good, but I wanted to be the best and then that whole thing of being afraid, of worrying, of lack of confidence hung me up. It was the same thing I'd gone through in school and in music. I found that certain people have a lot of confidence. I don't know if it's something they really have or if it's a front, but it would really come out playing a game like Ping-Pong. If I'd play a black guy and he'd start talking and ranking me, telling me how he was going to beat me, that would really unnerve me. When the blacks would signify, talk all that shit that they talk—"Yeah, baby, you ain't got no chance against *me*, suckah! I'm the *king*! That's my *road* game, jack!"—all that shit, I hated them for it. And I realized that it was a weakness on my part to allow that not only to make me afraid but to make me crumble. I would fall apart. And I would lose to a guy that I actually had more skill than. When I was able to relax and disregard that stuff—if I was loaded—then I could play over it and not let it get to me. And I'd destroy the person; I'd wipe them out; I'd win without question. So I realized a lot of things that were wrong with me in playing that game, and it was very interesting.

I think it was ten months that I was being analyzed. I began to understand my parents. I learned why they couldn't get along. I understood why my mother didn't want a child; it was a hopeless situation. I realized that. And I learned all this, *but it didn't change my feelings.* I felt that I wasn't wanted and that I wasn't loved, and I sort of liked that feeling. It was an excuse for me not to do anything. An excuse for anything I might do that was wrong. I could say it wasn't my fault: nobody cared about me so they couldn't blame me for being antisocial or being a little strange. If I hadn't been so talented, it would have been easier. I would have been an outright failure and a bum or a real criminal. But it just so happened I was picked by something, maybe I was reincarnated, but I have a genius that was given to me. I have a genius, however it's given, and I knew in myself that I was wrong in the things I was doing, and that made it even worse. That made me feel guilty. I wasn't doing what I knew I should do. But the pattern was set. The mold was cast. It was just easy, it was fun, and I liked it. I liked getting up in the night and sneaking away from Patti, who was clean and pretty, and going to an old, beat bar down on Main Street, putting my money in the juke box, and asking for "Cottage for Sale" by Billy Eckstine or "Ol' Man River" by Frank Sinatra. Sad songs. I'd sit in the bar and drink and fantasize being some way-out gangster, some murderer-lover. Dangerous. And I thought of myself as the most handsome person on the street. I thought I was so handsome that anybody who saw me said, "Wow! Look at that guy!" I believed that any woman that saw me thought, "Oh, Jesus, what I wouldn't give to have *him!*" That's why it was so far-out for me to be going into bars and down alleys, following chicks, sitting next to ugly chicks in filthy movie places, playing with their cunts. It was a Jekyll and Hyde thing. It was exciting because I felt as if I was really a prince. I always thought of myself that way and still do. I still do. I stopped voicing that opinion because people think you're kind of crazy, but I really believe it. I believe I'm above anybody I meet. Anybody. Everybody. I think that I'm more intelligent—innate intelligence; I feel that I'm more emotional, more sensitive, the greatest lover, the greatest musician; I feel that if I had been a ball player I'd have been in the Hall of Fame. There's no question in my mind: if I ever became crazy I would probably be Jesus. But, unfortunately, I've never been crazy. I've just been totally sane.

I used to go to these psychiatric sessions high on nutmeg. My eyes were all red. He must have known. He was just very cool. He wanted to go through with it; he didn't care what I was. And, as I say, I learned all these things about myself, and I know that I could have completely turned my life around had I wanted to. But I didn't want to. I enjoyed the excitement. And, as I knew I would, I made parole just as soon as it could be made with the highest recommendations from everybody.

During this time I was in Fort Worth, Patti had some lawyers from Reno send me a paper so they could represent me because she wanted to get a divorce. But she wrote that she was just divorcing me so that when I came out we could start courting, and if we still loved each other we would remarry. I believed this. I had to believe it.

When I got out, I went to my father's house in Long Beach. It was wonderful seeing Thelma. We talked, and I had a few drinks with my dad. And I remember shaving and bathing and getting all dressed up. At first everything was beautiful, but then, when I started getting cleaned up, I felt these strange vibes from my father and from Thelma a real sadness. I asked my dad if I could use his car. He said, "Yeah, if you take care of it. I don't want you shootin' none of that dope and drivin' it." He said, "Where're you goin'?" I said, "Oh, I want to go uptown." Thelma said, "Where are you going, Junior?" And I said, "Well, I wanted to go see Patti." My dad walked out in the backyard. I looked around. I was all dressed up, and I looked marvelous. I'd put perfume on. I looked at Thelma and said, "Well, naturally, I . . . " She said, "Well, Junior, don't you think it's best that—why don't you start a new life? Why don't you start a new life and try to find happiness? Maybe it just wasn't right." I said, "I'd like to, but I love her. I've got to see her. I'm going to try to win her back." And Thelma said, "Oh, Junior!" I said, "What do you mean? What do you mean 'Oh, Junior!'? What's wrong?" She started getting tears in her eyes and I thought, "Oh, God!" I said, "What's wrong? What's wrong?" And she said, "Oh, you poor baby." She put her arms around me and I thought, "Oh, God, what's happening?" She put her arms around me and she said, she said, "Patti is married."

And I . . . I just . . . I can't . . . If I could have died from heartbreak and shock I would have died right then. I thought I would come out and visit her and take her out and make love to her and win her back. And we would be married again. Ours was a love that was a lifetime, a mating in heaven. I just couldn't imagine . . . Thelma said, "Junior she got married right after the divorce. That's why she got divorced in Nevada." She said, "Patti wants security. She married Remo Belli." I said, "Remo Belli!" He was a drummer, one of my "friends" from back east. He came to town traveling with a band, Tex Benecke I think it was, some stupid band, or Glenn Miller, or somebody. I had invited him out to the house. And as soon as I got busted he "just happened to stop by" Patti's house. She lived in Panorama City, which is *way* out in the valley. He lived in Hollywood. He couldn't "happen to stop by" there. No way in the world. He'd have to travel thirty miles. And he had invented a drumhead, and it developed into a factory; he's probably close to a millionaire by now. I guess he gave her the money to get the divorce.

Thelma cried. We cried together. I got in my dad's car. I was going to go out to Patti's house and kill her. Then I thought, "Oh, fuck her." I drove the car to East L.A. I found some people I knew, Rachel and Mondo. I went to see Henry. We got together and bought a gram of stuff, and so I fixed. And I thought, "Here I am. I'm finally with people that are cool, that are real, that are happy to see me." It was like a party. I thought, "These are my people. Fuck Patti. Fuck all those kinds of people like that." And that was my homecoming from Fort Worth to my dear, sweet, one and only, lifetime, true love. Women!

———

(Thelma)   The first thing I noticed about Patti was how beautiful she was. She was such a beauty. A perfect shape. And the second thing I noticed was how *determined* she was. She was always determined to do what she wanted to do.

I don't think Junior should *ever* have been married. You see, he didn't want a child. He wasn't used to children, and he didn't care nothin' for little kids. Now, they lived with Grandma when he come back, and, you know, a little girl,

fifteen, eighteen months old, they ain't got no table manners.
She'd be eating peas, for instance, and drop some on the
tablecloth, and he'd get so angry and he'd smack her hands
until they was as red as blood, caused all kinds of dif-fugue-
ality. So we just took Patricia, and we had her until she was six
years old.

Patti and Junior went on the road with Stan Kenton's band.
It was a whole year once that Patricia didn't see either one of
'em. And kids, you know, can be so cruel to other children, and
the other kids in the neighborhood would tell her, "You don't
have any momma and poppa. You only have a grandma and
grandpa." And, ohhhh, she'd cry and cry and cry. But I always
made sure that she knew about 'em. I had a picture of each of
them and at night when I'd put her to bed I'd say, "Now, you
say goodnight to your momma and goodnight to your daddy."
So she didn't forget them.

Patti finally stopped going on the road with Junior. Kenton,
he flew, but they sent the gang in an old bus, no heat, and no
cooling system in the summertime. And they must have been
going over some awfully rough roads because Patti got a crack in
her tailbone. She was sick for quite a while over that. Her
doctor told her, "Now, don't you ever ride on that bus ever
again."

That was when Patti went to work for Arlene's of
Hollywood. Patricia stayed with us. Patti came down every
weekend to see her, never missed a time, but she had to live in
L.A. because that was where her job was and she had to work
because she was determined that she was going to get enough
money together to make a down payment on a house. She was
just obsessed with a home of her own.

I remember Patti crying to me, saying she wished Junior was
a truck driver or anything but . . . She wished that he had a job,
a steady income, came home nights. I think they would have
been ideally happy if he could've done that, but of course he
couldn't. You can't put a musician in a position like that. One
time when they was livin' in L.A. on Hope Street, when Junior
got out of the army, he did have a job in a meat-packing place.
That was before he went with Kenton, and Patti's always said
that that was the happiest time of their lives. He went to work
in the morning and came home at night.

Poor Patricia was sick all the time, all the years that we had
her. One time I was sure she was going to die. They had her

in the contagious ward of the Children's Hospital: she had
diphtheria. But when Patti took her, when they moved out to
the valley, she stopped getting sick. The doctor told Patti it was
the climate in Long Beach that didn't agree with her. Now, we
didn't know that.

But that was a heartbreaking thing. When Junior and Patti
got their house and moved to the valley and Daddy and I went
to see them—of course, to us, Patricia was our little girl, our
child. When you take care of a kid for that long, they become
just like your own. Poor little thing. She'd get her little suitcase,
she'd put some things in there, and she'd say, "I'm ready to go
home!" Well, of course, we couldn't take her. And when our
car'd start off, well, she'd follow the car, you know, running
out in the middle of the street with her suitcase, just
a-screamin' and a-bawling her eyes out. Hollerin' at the top of
her lungs. Ohhhh. It got so bad, we stopped going. We knew if
we stayed away she would realize that that's where she
belonged. It was a couple of years before we could even take
her home. It was too hard for her and too hard for us.

Millie [Art's mother] was the one who suspected that Junior
was using drugs because she's the one that told us about it. So
the first thing Daddy did, he went to somebody he knew, a
lawyer or somebody, to ask how he could help Junior, and the
lawyer was the one that suggested we put him in that
sanitarium over in Garden Grove. So that's where we put him.
For a month. But it didn't do no good.

Daddy was just devastated when he found out Junior was
using drugs. He couldn't hardly stand that. He would have done
anything in the world to get him away from that. He couldn't
understand how Junior could get hooked on it like he did
because, Daddy said, "I was exposed to drugs all the time I was
sailin'. It was nothin' at all to get drugs." He went all over the
world in his shipping days, and it was as easily accessible as a
cup of coffee, and he never was tempted to use it, and he never
was able to understand why Junior took it up.

I never did know how Patti met Remo. I just know that all
of a sudden, there he was. She was in the valley then, and she
came and left Patricia with us. She told me she was going over
to get a divorce. She knew that if she waited until Junior came
back, she'd go back to him, and she'd had so much grief over
him. And it wasn't because she didn't love him. I don't think
she'll ever stop loving him. She still loves him. He's like a

disease with her. But she knew she couldn't live that way anymore, and she knew that if she didn't make it final, she'd take him back, and they'd start all over again. And they weren't good for each other. He couldn't live her way of life, and she couldn't live his.

John and Millie Noble

(John) Art and Patti were in school when I went into the service, and they got married before I got back. I can't talk about Patti too well. We never got along real good. Now it's different, but when she was a young girl she was always nosy to the point of being downright *personal*. She'd be around me for a little bit; it'd be okay for a few minutes; and then I'd try to get away from her because she'd start asking me about my girl friends and what we did and what time I got in and all this stuff, you know, that was absolutely none of her business. And, Christmastime or something, here's my presents all under the tree, and she couldn't wait to just tear 'em all up and see who sent me what. She'd go in my drawers and look at my love letters from my girl friends. She'd say, "I can't help myself." I used to get pretty vocally violent with her. I couldn't stand her for very long at a time.

I don't know how to describe her. Sometimes she was a witch to me. If she wanted to be, if she applied herself, she had a pleasing personality, but most of the time she didn't apply herself. She was good-looking, and I guess she could have been called a good figure. She did model in San Francisco, I think it was. But it was hard for me to get close to her. She knew she was a nice-looking person. She had real nice eyes if she wanted to look at you and talk to you nice, but if she wanted to probe you, then I didn't like the way she looked. And she tried to probe everyone. But I lost track of them after Art started getting into trouble.

(Millie) We saw him down at Thelma and Moses' a couple of times. Remember, once he saw our little kid dancin', and he got such a big kick out of it, and he tried to talk Johnny into letting Jimmy take music lessons, and Johnny said, "No way in hell is my kid going to take music!"

(John) I followed Art's career, different places, and I associated a lot with those people. I wasn't in with them, but I was right alongside of them. I listened to them; I saw what they did. I just didn't want to encourage Jim to get into that type of entertainment field. There are some fine people, but you need a real straight, hard back and a good head.

You know what? In my opinion Art just didn't know how to say no. If someone'd come up to Art, even some of the times we'd go out together, "Well, John, I'll have to see you later. I'm going off with So-and-so." And I wouldn't argue with him. I'd say, "Okay, Art. See you later." He couldn't say no. Whether it was a man or a woman or what. If they got to talkin' with him and wanted him to do something, they'd keep persisting on him for a little bit, and he'd just break down. Away he'd go. He couldn't say no.

Before he started all that, shortly after he got home from the war, he was playing in San Diego—I can't remember the ballroom—and Patti wanted me to take her down there. So here I was with Patti, and by the time we reached San Diego we was at one another. We went in and I wouldn't dance with her. I danced with other girls around there. And Art was supposed to come back with us, but he went backstage after we talked, and pretty soon he came out and said, "John, do you mind taking Patti back home?" And I says, "No, I won't." He says, "I know you two don't get along too well. I've got some friends that want me to go out to a jam session, and I don't know if Patti'd like it." I said, "That's between you and Patti." And I went back myself.

(Millie) Do you think it would have made any difference if he'd married a different type of woman than Patti?

(John) No.

(Millie) Well, was it Grandma and Moses? They didn't handle him right?

(John) No. He didn't have a chance to be handled right.

PART 2

1954–1966

10 | The Los Angeles County Jail: Integration

1954 – 1955

I STAYED in Long Beach for a little while and then moved to a hotel in Hollywood, and I ran into a girl named Didi. I ran into her in a jazz club. She was a chubby, Jewish girl, a hairdresser, and she really dug me. I was getting strung out, and she told me if I'd like I could stay at her place. She had a nice apartment about a quarter of a block off Hollywood Boulevard. I figured it would be good to live with her for a while. I'd have the use of her car, and she made good money. Her mother was married to a guy who was part or whole owner of a huge business. I stayed with her, and it enabled me to spend all the money I made recording and playing in clubs on drugs.

After a while it got to be a drag staying with Didi. She was getting demanding; she wanted me to ball her. I balled her a few times at first, but she didn't appeal to me sexually and finally I couldn't do it at all anymore. I just could not do it. Period. She ignored it as long as she could, and finally she asked me what was wrong. I told her she just didn't move me and that I couldn't help it. That put the handwriting on the wall. I couldn't ball her, so I knew I was going to have to move. I got a room on Hudson above Hollywood Boulevard, Didi drove me over, and I moved in.

The very next day I went to a hotel in Hollywood to see some people, to cop from them. They'd just come in from Detroit. There were three of them. There was a broad, a funky broad, real skinny and ugly, a friend of Tony's, and Tony

DiCorpo, who plays tenor saxophone, and he was a dog, just a dog, no morals. I've run into a lot of musicians like that, people that don't care about anybody but themselves. They use people, but more than that, they don't have any warmth; they don't have any honor; they're not kind. Even when I've taken advantage of someone, like with Didi, I was always good to her and honest and I tried to do right. And I was clean. This Tony was dirty, physically dirty, and coarse and shallow and weak. I've always hated people like that, but I went over there. It was just one of those days when nobody that was around that I knew had anything. And I used to cop for these three. They had called me and asked what was happening. They said *they* could score, but the shit wasn't quite as good. I figured, "Well, I'll go over and get a taste." I went to their apartment and gave them the money, and they went, Tony and the other guy. They left the broad behind with me, and I was in their pad so I figured it would be cool.

They were gone for quite a while. I waited and waited and waited. I said, "What's happening with these guys?" The broad said, "Don't worry about it. Everything's cool." This chick was the kind of person not even a mother could love. She was skinny, no looks, no personality, and nobody in his right mind would give her a nickel to let her give him head. I don't know how these people are made or where they come from or where they go. I've met a lot of them and she was about the worst I've ever seen.

While Tony was gone, I happened to look around the house and I noticed some cottons lying around. Then I noticed an outfit. Then I found another outfit and about three or four dirty spoons all burnt black and with blood, caked blood in them. I said, "Jesus, what *is* this?" In case the police should come, you know, I was dead. I had marks and I'd been out of jail only four months. I asked this chick, "Is there anything else around?" "No." "Well, let's get rid of this stuff!" She said, "Ohhhh, it's awright." I said, "No, let's get *rid* of it!" "Ohhhh. Okay." I said, "Take it in the hall or do something with it. Put it somewhere but get it out of the room." Just then there was a knock at the door. She went to the door. She took off the chain. I said, "Don't open the door! Find out who it is!" But before she could get the chain back on, the door was pushed open, and here was the narcs. And here were Tony and his friend. They'd gotten rousted and gotten busted and been brought back to the pad. The narcs find the outfits; there were three altogether. They look around and they find some dollies, some Dolophines. Then the police come.

They took us all to jail, to Lincoln Heights. Tony has twenty dollars of my money. As we're going through this scene I'm trying to get him to hand me the bread. He's acting like he doesn't know what I'm talking about. I couldn't come out and ask him. I didn't want to let them know I had given him money to score with. I wanted him to slip it to me. But he knew what I wanted, and he kept it—played dumb and kept the money.

They booked us on suspicion, marks and outfits and possession with the Dolophine. I'd just gotten out of the federal joint; I had CR, conditional release. Tony and the other guy said, "Well, man, why don't you take ... Why don't you say everything was yours? You're on parole. They're going to send you to jail anyway. Why don't you say everything was yours and we didn't know anything about it?" I said, "Are you *kidding*?" I said, "You've never been in jail. Why don't you say everything was *yours*?" They said, "Oh, we can't do *that*!" And I said, "Oh, man, well, fuck you."

They called their names. They rolled 'em up, and they left, Tony and his friends. I don't know how they cut them loose or why; there's no telling what they must have done to get cut loose. They held me. I had nothing to hide in the little court I was staying at so I gave the key to the police, who went back to my room and searched it. And Didi, when she moved me, had taken some pills of her own and given them to me, put them in my things, and I didn't know it. They were Empirin with codeine. A doctor friend of hers gave them to her on prescription because she had headaches and because she just liked the codeine. They found the pills and dropped the "marks" and filed a possession against me of codeine. And when I heard what it was I couldn't tell them whose they were. All I would have had to do was say they belonged to Didi. They would have got her and she would have explained. But I couldn't do it because that would have been ratting on her.

They moved me to the county jail, and I had no money on the books. Tony had kept the money. Finally Didi came to visit me and I told her, "Man, they've booked me on possession with those pills. Why didn't you tell me you took those pills over to my pad?" She said, "Well, I figured you could use them." I said, "*Yeah*, I could use them. It was *nice* of you to give them to me, but I didn't know that they were there. Now all you've got to do is tell them you got 'em on a scrip, right?" It was all legal. But she said that nobody from her family had ever messed with dope and she was afraid to say the pills were hers because her mother would have gotten upset and her stepfather, the businessman, wouldn't have liked it. I said, "But I'll go to *prison!*" She said, "Well, I just can't help it. I can't do it. I'm afraid I'll get in trouble." And she walked away.

She wouldn't have gotten any time. It would have been a little inconvenient and kind of a drag for her mother to know that her daughter was taking codeine tablets when she had a headache. But I guess that's what I get for using her. You know, I really believe in retribution. I stayed with her, drove her car, took advantage of money from her; she cut my hair. I used her, and I was paid back. She left some money downstairs for me but she wouldn't say that the pills were hers, and for possession of three or four Empirin codeine tablets the judge found me guilty, and I was sentenced to six months in the L.A. County Jail.

(Hersh Hamel) After Art had been in jail a couple of times, Patti flew the coop. We were close during all those years. He had another old lady for a while—Didi, the hairdresser. I knew all his old ladies. Didi was not really a good-looking woman. She was sort of chubby. She loved Art. Art was still a beautiful man, features and body. Didi just took care of him, didn't let him do anything himself, which wasn't very good for him. All Art liked to do was lay back and get stoned and watch TV and go play when he wanted to play. That period was a little strange. I think that was in between some jail . . . And he took a bust for her. He wouldn't cop out on Didi. That's the way that went.

I HAD a federal parole hold, but they don't tell you until you get out whether you're going to be reinstated on parole or whether you're going to have to do more time for your violation. I knew I was going to be in the county jail for about six months.

They put me in 11-B-1. That was the white hype tank at that time. They'd changed it from 12-B-1 because the women had been right above on the thirteenth floor, and guys would talk to the chicks through the air vents. Guys would holler up and say, "There's a little broad up there named Louise; she just came in; this is her old man, Richie. Call her to the phone." And some chick would go call her to that particular cell, and they'd run their cases. "I ran this story to them—did you cop out?" Aside from that guys would just flirt with chicks, "Yeah, baby, I'm So-and-so. I'm getting out on bail soon. What's happening with you?" "I'm waiting to get out on bail, too." "Well, where do you hang out at? Why don't we get together?"

They'd line things up. Maybe the chick's a hustler, or they can pull some robberies together, or maybe it's just the contact, talking to a chick, because you get very horny when you get clean. There were water pipes going from floor to floor, and they dug out the hole around the pipes, so there was a spot where a chick could send down a note on a string. The chick would take a piece of paper, rub it around her cunt, pull out some pubic hairs, fold them up in this paper, and send it down. Then the guy would get it and smell it and talk to the chick on the phone, you know, "I got your paper; you sure smell good. Boy, I sure wish I could be lickin' on you now." And he would jerk off at night with the paper, and the guys would pass it around.

In order to stop all that, the bulls moved the hypes from the twelfth floor to the eleventh floor and onto the twelfth floor they moved the regular convicts who were nothing, just regular people in for traffic violations. They might have some armed robbers in there but no dopefiends, and the dopefiends were the ones that were the hustlers, the people that were playing at being gangsters and real hep and all that. When I went back to the county jail I noticed that on my legal status they'd stamped 11-B-1, and I said to the first officer I could find, "Man, what's happening? I'm a dopefiend. I want to go to the hype tank." He said, "That is the hype tank. We moved you assholes so you wouldn't be fuckin' around with the broads upstairs." I said, "Well, that's okay then." I just wanted to be sure I was with the dopefiends so that if any action came down I'd be with people that were cool. People that were like me.

I went through the thing of saying hello to everybody, bullshitting with everybody, and I got word that people were hollering about integration. That was in '54, '55. The guys had said, "Never, man! Never! We're never going to have any spooks or greasers in our cells." The Mexicans had their own tank and the blacks had their own tank. But you never called them black then. You respectfully called them colored or suedes. If you called them black they'd fight you. And we called the Mexicans Chicanos.

I was in the tank for several months, and then I was sent out to the farm, Wayside Honor Ranch. But after I'd been there for a week they found out I had a federal hold on me and sent me back to the county jail, and when I got back I noticed that everybody was uptight. I asked someone what was happening and he told me they were trying to integrate the tanks and these guys weren't going to allow it. He said, "It's really been a scene; they're putting down ultimatums, the police, and they've taken a couple of guys out and put them in solitary confinement, in the hole."

It's afternoon and everybody's kind of lazy, laying around, and there's three or four guys walking up and down the freeway. I'm lying in my cell when all of a sudden the gates start racking and "Clear the gates!" Bam! They close them. Usually they shake them a while for a warning because if you get caught going in or out the gates will break your leg. This time they closed them all of a sudden, and here are these four guys locked outside on the freeway, and here comes the goon squad. They ran in and grabbed these four. I think they got Tubby Whitman, who was just a monster, one of those guys that looked like he could punch a hole through solid iron, and they got Jew Bill Irving and Jim van Eyck, and they might have got Blackie Levinson. All tough guys, bad-acting cats. They threw them against the bars and started beating them up. It was like a free-for-all. They dragged them out of the cell block and opened the gates again. All of a sudden these guys were gone. I said, "What's happening, man?" I hit on a guy that had been there a while, and he told me, "They're trying to break the power of the white hype tank so they can integrate it." The bulls had to get the tough guys out; they took them and put them in Siberia. They'd been ordered to integrate, and that's what they were going to do, and the guys were saying, "It's a battle to the death!'' And I'm thinking, "Oh, God!" They're refusing the food! Doing time is hard enough without all of that. We couldn't get visits, and all we ate was emergency rations. There was no telling what might happen; the guys were getting crazier and crazier every day. I'm thinking, "Oh, man, all I want to do is get out of here." All I wanted was something nice to eat and peace and quiet.

Finally, one day the guards came in and I heard, "Pepper, roll 'em up." I was so happy to hear them say that. I rolled my shit up; I was so glad it was unbelievable. The guys in the tank went to the front. They said, "What do you want him for?" They wanted to make sure the bulls weren't just fucking with me. The guards said, "He's doing time here. He's got to go the cages upstairs." I tried to act like, "Wow, what a drag. I won't be able to fight this thing with you." I said, "Well, man, good luck and everything. Keep up the battle." They took me out of the cell and marched me upstairs, and one bull said, "Did you really mean that? You hate to leave there?" I said, "Are you kidding?"

It was already integrated upstairs. And instead of cell blocks, we had cages like animals are kept in but with no doors. They didn't bring your food to you; you went to a mess hall and they gave you *nice* food. You're on the roof, on the very top of the jail. You can go outside. They've got a couple Ping-Pong tables and different things, and you can look out over the roof and see the city. It's almost like being free after being locked up in the tank. And you work different jobs.

Just before I got out I happened to be waiting for the elevator—I was a trustee so I had a lot of freedom. The elevator stopped and out walked Jim van Eyck, Blackie Levinson, and another guy, friends of mine from the tank, and they'd been in the hole, the black hole for all this time. They looked like death. The guards had finally broken the segregation. They'd locked the ringleaders in the hole, and then they'd gone in with firehoses and turned them on everybody else.

After that they used little name cards. At the front of each tank there was a board for these cards showing all the cells and one white, one blue, and one orange card for each cell. White was white, blue was black, and orange was Mexican. That's how the officers checked to make sure the cells were integrated.

I don't know where all the pressure came from. I'm sure it didn't come from the black or Mexican prisoners. They *wanted* to be segregated. They just wanted the same rights. I don't know who pushed this thing, the city council, the mayor, or the governor, but it was a political thing.

I didn't have occasion to see this system in operation until several years later when I got busted again for possession. Then I went in and saw the cards. I saw a white card, a blue card, and an orange card and I looked and saw three black guys in the cell. The tank trustees had got ahold of these cards and just wrote a guy's name on whatever color card looked good on the board. That's how they integrated the L.A. County Jail.

They had music in the cages. You'd wake up in the morning to music and then at night you'd hear it. In the tanks there was no radio, no nothing. I went five or six months without hearing a note of music before I went up to the cages. So, if you can imagine, being a musician, or just being any person . . . For most people, music is an important part of their lives, and to be deprived of it completely is terrible. So what I'd do to keep myself from going crazy, I would play my cup. We were all issued one. They give you a tin coffee cup with a little handle on it. I would hold it up to my mouth, leave a little opening at the side, and put my hands over it like you do when you play a harmonica or a Jew's harp. And I found that I could hum into the cup and get a sound sort of like a trumpet. I could do a lot with it. And in the jail, with all the cement and steel, that small sound could really be heard, especially from the corner of the cell. So I'd play to myself, and the guys would hear me. I'd look up and see that there were guys standing all around outside my cell, just digging. And I found that they got a lot of pleasure out of it, especially at night. We had one guy named Grundig, who had played drums at one time. He'd take the top from a trash can and beat on it with a spoon, and I'd play my cup, and the guys would clap, and we would have, like, a regular session. You'd have to be in that position to realize how much joy you could receive from something as crude as that.

I was in 11-B-1 then; it was before the tanks were integrated. And it so happened that one day I looked across the tank into 11-A-1, the black hype tank, and saw a guy I thought I recognized. This guy hollered over, "Hey, Art Pepper!" He said, "My name's Stymie." I said, "You look familiar to me, man." He said, "Oh, well, yeah." And that was Stymie from *The Little Rascals* in the movies, and he looked just like he had when he was a kid. We started talking. He said, "I heard you were over there." He'd been out to court. He told me he'd been in jail for a couple of years fighting his case. I said, "Boy, what a drag, man, no music." He said, "It's terrible. What I do . . . I can't stand it. We get together and we sing." I said, "Oh, man, I'd sure love to hear that." He said, "Well, you'll hear it." I think this was on a Tuesday. Nothing happened. I'm waiting and waiting, but I don't want to push him because I know that music is a personal thing and you can't force it, especially under those conditions.

Then Sunday came. They talk about God and religion and make fun of it, but when you're in prison and then Sunday comes, you get a certain feeling. Instead of all the anger and brutality that runs through all the other days, on Sunday everyone becomes quiet, and you feel a presence, like, there is a God. On Sunday it becomes evident that something different is happening. Everybody becomes introspective; everybody is in their own little worlds; you can feel everybody delving into things. So it was Sunday, and all of a sudden I heard a voice. I walked out of my cell and looked down the walkway. I heard a voice and it's singing "Gloomy Sunday," of all songs, man. It was a voice like usually only the black men have, almost a feminine voice, high, and very, very pretty, very sensual and warm and very much in tune, with a sweet sound and a nice vibrato, and it's Stymie's voice. I looked at the guys in my tank. They were all quiet. They were all listening—Jew Bill, who used to go around with a guy from Tennessee; they broke in on a black dealer that was keeping a white woman and pistol-whipped him, made him piss on the white chick's head calling her "white tramp," "nigger lover"; they beat the dealer half to death and stole his dope. I saw these two brothers, armed robbers, who took so much coke that one time in a hotel they flipped out and started shooting through the hotel doors. I looked over at the black tank and saw other guys who'd done terrible crimes. And everyone was just sitting or standing or leaning on the bars of the tank, looking out the windows, looking out on the parking lot, out at the freeway going toward Hollywood, out at the free people. I saw them standing against the bars and I thought, "They're going to the penitentiary. They may never get out again. They've left the woman that they love out in the streets. And here they are listening to this song, sung by a black man, listening to this sadness and this beauty." And I thought, "Where's the justice? Why do these things happen? Why do we do these terrible things? What causes us to do these things?" Some black guys started humming along with Stymie, and it was so pretty and so sad that all the ugliness was forgotten and all the hatred, and for that short while we were, like, brothers. And that's why I talk about Sunday and God and the beauty of music. Everything was wiped away, and we were just human beings sharing a common sadness.

(Freddy Rivera)   As Art started going to jail, there was a further intensification of the traits that were already there. More dependence. More disregard for reality. A heightened refusal to take any direct action. Or to be more careful. I also know that he liked prison. He liked the brotherhood. I do think that he liked being told what to do, being taken care of, having someone else organize his life. And, lacking self-esteem, he could go into an environment where he could *identify*, believing unconsciously that he was a black sheep, ostracized from the "respectable" world. Feeling that way all of his life, he could readily identify with all these other outcasts. Furthermore, going into prison, he is a famous musician. Rightfully so. He really is somebody. And I say that he is somebody out of prison; that's a fact. But in prison, you see, he's with people who, often in their own hearts and in the minds of the outside world, are total rubbish. So when he comes into this environment, now we have a demigod. He told me even one of the guards spoke to him admiringly, very surreptitiously, sotto voce. Even the guard, huh? So this was an environment where he could get a great deal of support and admiration, feel more comfortable, and have a constant, ongoing family—whatever they do, rapping cups on the bars, screaming across . . . Always a family. It's almost like being in Italy. Hahahaha! And you're not alone. So when he makes the statement that criminals are better . . . Of course they're better. They love him. He was really somebody. I'm not dealing with the question directly because there *can* be, in prison, fine people, great people. If you don't believe me, ask Lenin. We also know that in prison we have people that are hardly to be called human. Just as we have them on the street, out here, too. And in the government, and in Beverly Hills.

———————

I THINK I did nine months altogether in the county jail; I did three months, dead time, waiting for my trial. Finally my release date came, and I walked up the spiral staircase to an iron gate, and these two guys came over to me, two guys in suits, older guys; they had big hats on and they looked just like marshals. One of them said, "I'm Marshal So-and-so. I'm sorry to tell you that your conditional release has been violated and we're taking you back to prison." I said, "Where?" They said, "We're taking you to Terminal Island."

They handcuffed me and walked me out of the jail and over to a car. When we got to the car I saw the street and all the people. I said, "Oh, God, man, I've been in this jail here for nine months and now I've got to go to Terminal Island." We got in the car and drove. We went past the docks at Terminal Island. I'd been there a lot with my dad as a kid when he was working on the boats as a winch driver. And while we were driving I thought, "When's it going to end?" I felt as if all of a sudden I would wake up and it would be a dream or somebody would say, "Oh, well, that's okay. This was just a little test we were putting you through, and it's all over now. You can go home." We'd turn around and the marshals would say, "We're just friends of your dad's; we were joking around. Your dad wanted to see if we could scare you a little so you wouldn't use any more drugs." It was like a play, a farce: it couldn't be real. And then we pulled up to the penitentiary.

Terminal Island had been a naval prison at one time. It comes right out of the water on big stones, and it's all green on the sides of it. The gate opens, and they step inside. Another gate opens, and the marshals say, "One." You know, "We got one from the county." They march me in, and they say goodbye, and here I am in Terminal Island Federal Penitentiary to start doing three hundred and fourteen days just because this fucking broad Didi wouldn't cop out.

11 | Diane

1955 — 1958

I WALKED into the prison, an old, old prison with a big yard in the middle. I went through the booking routine and they put me in a cell. Outside the cell you could hear the water bouncing against the rocks. I went over to the window and I looked out. I looked out and I saw San Pedro.

I saw Beacon Street, where my dad met my mother. I saw Fort MacArthur, where I'd been inducted into the army. I looked up to Daniel's Field, Navy Field, where as a kid I used to watch the football games. I could see the streets I'd lived on then: Twenty-fourth Street and Alma, Thirtieth and Gaffey. And here I am in prison looking at all this. What happened? How could I be here? For no reason. Up until that time I'd never committed any kind of crime at all. Ever. Nothing. Now here I was with people who were forgers and bank robbers.

I was so despondent and so drug with having to be there, I told them I wouldn't work. They looked at my jacket and saw that I had a high IQ, and they wanted me to work in the school or do something constructive, but I said no. They gave me a job with a little pan and a little broom and I swept the yard. In the morning, after everybody went to work, I would go out and sweep for a couple of hours, and then after supper I'd sweep for maybe an hour, and it was really funny. I wouldn't do anything else. Here I was, probably one of the most handsome people in the place—I could probably have been a movie star or a great engineer at Cal Tech—and here I was with a little broom sweeping up spit and cigarette butts and seagull shit! Hahahaha!

We had a saying: "To loosen your wig." When you got up-tight and really nervous, then you'd "unscrew your cap," and that was the only way I could stand doing the time. I'd get silly and nutty and make weird noises. I'd walk like a spastic. Every-body would be lined up to go to work, and I'd walk right by them shaking and kind of slobbering. And that's when I started getting a reputation as a nut, and I saw that even the toughest convicts started looking at me with a kind of fear.

I met a guy, Myaki, and we became pretty friendly. He was a slender Chinaman. He had a bony face; you could see the bones all over his body. And he was a real warm guy, one of those guys who'd do anything for me. He worked in the hospital, and he was a very good criminal. He could open locks and was an expert at breaking into safes, so he used to steal things out of the medical locker. He'd get alcohol and make up different concoctions. He'd get sleepers and lay them on me for nothing. And he's the one that told me, "You're getting that rep of being a loner and kind of flippy, and that's a good front to have because you gotta have a front in jail so nobody'll mess with you. People'll leave you alone. They won't try to steal your commissary or fuck you in the ass or use you or rob you or kill you. They won't bother you because a nut—there's no telling what a nut might do." So I'd make my noises and stare into space, and when I was eating I'd let the food fall out of my mouth onto my clothes. And I noticed people, like, "Wow! *Dig* that cat! Boy, that Pepper, man, that musician! Isn't that that musician? Boy, that cat is way out! Dig him, dig him. *Dig!* Boy, he's really *strange*. Is he jivin' or is he for real?" And Myaki would run me stories about guys coming to him saying, "Hey, man, you're a friend of that guy, that Pepper, man. What *is* that? Is he kidding around or . . . ?" And Myaki would say, "Ohhhh, I don't know, man, We're friends, but he's kinda . . . He's told me some strange things. I get kinda leery. I get kinda scared sometimes. I think he's got a lotta violence in him, man. He's a weird cat, a weird cat."

One day they called my name and said, "You have a visitor." I ran to my cell and got cleaned up as well as I could. I walked into the visiting room and there was Patti and Thelma and my daughter, Patricia. She was ten years old, and she saw the whole thing—me being brought in by guards, a terrible person who had to be locked away, who must be evil because he couldn't be let out with the other people. And I felt that Patti did that purposely so she would have something to back up her degrading remarks about me. I felt so awful when I saw them that I cried. It was one of the worst moments of my life. I looked at Thelma and thought, "Couldn't you *stop* them?" And she looked at me and started crying, as if she knew what I was feeling.

The time in Terminal Island was very strange; it was a strange prison; there wasn't too much happening there so it was "hard time." Unlike Fort Worth. And the worst thing was . . . Every now and then I'd be in the yard or in my cell and I'd hear the fog horn. In San Pedro, at Point Fermin, there's a fog horn that goes "Booooohhh-oooooooohhh." I used to hear it as a child. I used to lie at night and listen to it. Now I heard the same fog horn in prison, and I relived all my childhood over and over, and it was a terrible, terrible three hundred and fourteen days. And when the time came to get out, I thought, "Oh, man, I don't ever want to go back to prison again." I got out and got a room in Hollywood, a little room on Yucca, right off Hollywood Boulevard.

The first night I was out, you know, I wanted a woman. I went to Jazz City, which was on Hollywood Boulevard right off Western. There was a girl there, a waitress, and I knew she had eyes to ball me. I went to the club, and she wasn't there, and I didn't have any money to be hanging around. I talked to a girl I knew who'd worked there for years. She probably would have made love to me just to give me relief, but I didn't care for her sexually. Then while I was sitting I noticed another waitress, one I'd never seen before. She was an Oriental-looking chick. She kept glancing at me as she walked by. And when they went to their stations, to the bar to get their drinks, I noticed that she and the other girl were talking together and I saw them motion toward me. Finally, the girl I knew said, "There's one of the waitresses that would like to meet you." She brought her over and said, "Diane, meet Art Pepper. This is Diane."

I said hello, and she said hello, and a little later she walked over and said, "Would you like a drink?" I said, "I don't have much bread." She said, "I know that." She said, "What would you like?" I asked for a screwdriver and she brought me one, and from then on she kept dropping off drinks for nothing. She asked me, "Would you like to go and have some coffee after? If you can stick around until I get off . . ." She took care of her checks, and then as we left I said, "How are we going to go? I don't have any wheels." She said, "I have a car."

We went around on Western to the lot. I said, "Which one?" There were five or six beat cars and one yellow Cadillac convertible, really pretty. She walked me up to that car and said, "This is it. Would you like to drive?" To make me feel like a man, you know, *that* style. I said, "This is yours? Wow, what do you do on the side?" She said, "I'm married, and I work, and I do whatever I want with my money." She gave me the keys.

This chick was fairly nice looking. As I said before, she looked Oriental but instead of the slender, oval face she had a square, squat, Filipino face, and her body was like her face, squat and kind of dumpy. She had black hair, but it was prematurely grey, and she didn't seem to know how to fix her hair right. She had something wrong with her upper lip. It was a little deformed, which at times was ugly, and at other times, it was a thing of beauty. Probably her best point was her eyes, a little slanted and black. And her skin was nice.

She said, "Where would you like to go?" I said I didn't care, so she took me to an all-night restaurant where the show people went, and we ended up just talking and talking. Finally I said, "Don't you have to go?" She said, "Yeah, I guess so." She drove me to my hotel and I said, "Why don't we stop someplace or park someplace?" No women were allowed at my hotel. She said, "Well, why don't we wait?" I said, "What do you mean?" She said, "I'd rather wait until . . . we have a nicer setting." I said, "Well, you're married, so we can't go there." She dropped me off and she said, "I'll see you tomorrow." I said, "You know, all I need, all I wanted to do—I just have eyes, you know. I've been locked up a long time and I just want, I just want some female companionship. I don't want you . . . It's a drag that you're married because, you know, I don't feel right about things like that." She told me that she didn't dig her husband

and didn't ball him. He had begged her to stay with him; that was the only reason she was still there. She let me off and I went to my room. And then I walked out on Hollywood Boulevard. I walked along trying to pick up a chick, trying to thin of some chick I knew from before. I went to an all-night mov. Nothing happened. I just wanted to get laid.

I was supposed to have called Diane at the club the next night, but I decided I didn't want to get involved with her. I forget what I did that night, the same thing I guess. I wandered around looking for a chick, but I couldn't find anybody I knew so I went back to my hotel. It was late. I started up the stairs to my room, and there she was.

It was Diane. She was sitting on the stairs waiting for me. There she was and she said, "I thought you were going to call me." I said, "I don't want to get involved, you know. You're married." She said, "I told you how that is. I've really thought about you. I've seen you before, and I like you. Last night I didn't want you to think I was just some chick you could ball right away. I've thought about you every second since then. I couldn't sleep thinking about you. I want to make love to you. I don't care what else happens. I just want to make love to you. Let's go, please. Please." And so, you know, I hadn't balled in all that time. I said okay, she handed me the keys, and we drove down Sunset to a beat motel. We bought a jug on the way and had a couple of drinks, and then we made love. She was nice. She made love well and I enjoyed it because it was a release for me, but she didn't move me that much and I didn't want to get involved in anything. I just wanted to be left alone. I just wanted to have chicks I could ball when I wanted to ball. And I could tell she was really hung up on me. She drove me back to my room and I said, "Great." You know. I really tried to be nice. And I felt guilty because I didn't care for her and had made love to her. And she was married and had two kids, I found out.

From then on she was continually waiting for me. She called me. She left notes. She wanted to give me money. She wanted me to use her Cadillac. She wanted to drive me places. And it was just no good. You see, I've never wanted to take advantage of anybody: I didn't want to have them under false pretenses, have them believing something that wasn't true. I've always thought of myself as an honest person, and I really didn't care for Diane.

I thought about Patti all the time. Patti would call me. She even came to visit me once. She came at about 8:30, when I was still in bed. I heard a knock on the door and, "It's me, Patti." I didn't have a robe so I threw my pants on. I didn't have any shirt on, no shoes. I opened the door and there she is. She walks in and she's wearing one of those flaring skirts with the pattern all bright. She's wearing a blouse that's cut down off the shoulders, and you can see the vee of her breasts. She had on pretty pink sandals, and her hair was fixed beautifully, and she smelled wonderful. Here's the woman I would have given anything to have had, I thought. She divorced me to marry someone else. We talked; it was awful; then she left. But she kept calling me, and she was hanging up everything for me as far as anybody else. I couldn't imagine how, under any circumstances, she could have married someone else. Why weren't *we* married? I loved her so much. I wanted her so much.

Right at this time I made an album. I think it was *The Return of Art Pepper.* I was recording a lot and playing beautifully. Diane kept coming around and coming around, and she finally talked me into going to her house one day. I met her husband. He told me that nothing was happening with them, that it was all over. He loved her, but she didn't care for him. They had a beautiful house in Burbank with a great big swimming pool.

One day Diane came to my hotel and said, "I'm getting a room. Would you please let me get a room with you?" I was scuffling. I'd started to use. I got weak. I said okay. The thought of having a car . . . I just got weak. I'd told her all along that nothing was happening, that I was still in love with Patti, that it would take me a long time to get over it. She said, "I just want to be with you. I love you and I want to take care of you. I don't care how you feel about me. I'm happy being with you."

We moved to a house. I think it was on Fargo, on an incredibly steep hill. And it was nice at times, but the minute I moved in with Diane, Patti found out about it. Among musicians everything is known. She called: "I don't know why you want to *live* with that woman! She had two kids and a husband and left them. She's a tramp!"

PEPPER BACK; DATES PILE UP

Hollywood—After a 20–month absence from the jazz scene, altoist Art Pepper is once more active here. He has joined forces with composer-arranger-tenorist Jack Montrose and will record, work with, and go on the road with a new Montrose quintet.

In the offing are record dates for three labels on which Pepper will be featured—a Pepper-Chet Baker album for Pacific Jazz; an LP for Liberty on which the alto man will play with Montrose and Red Norvo; a further album for Atlantic to be recorded this month.

Montrose told *down beat* he intends to use Pepper on his soon-to-be-recorded jazz ballet, which will be released later in the year on Pacific Jazz, after which the two hornmen plan to travel east with a rhythm section.

Pepper's first gig after his long absence was a date at Paul Nero's The Cottage in Malibu June 29. down beat, *July 25, 1956. Copyright 1956 by* down beat. *Reprinted by special permission.*

ART PEPPER . . . TELLS TRAGIC ROLE NARCOTICS PLAYED IN BLIGHTING HIS CAREER AND LIFE *by John Tynan*

"At the end of 1954 I was using 40 caps of heroin a day . . . "

This is not a random quotation from some detective thriller, nor is it to be found in the text or script of *The Man with the Golden Arm*. These tragic words were spoken by altoist Art Pepper in an exclusive interview conducted July 20, 1956, in the Hollywood offices of *down beat* a few weeks after Pepper was released from the federal penitentiary on Terminal Island, Calif. He had just finished serving a term there for his second conviction on narcotics charges within three years.

There is ugliness in the story that follows, as there necessarily is in any frank discussion of narcotics addiction. But there's courage here, too, and a high mindedness of purpose on Art Pepper's part. For expressly to help others, this is his story, in his own words, of how he became addicted; what dope did to him; what he lives and hopes for today in his fight to kick the habit forever. Overriding all else is an obtrusive dissonance, a general tragedy that is not exclusively Pepper's but haunts the lives of all who seek to conquer reality through the jab of a dope charged needle.

The entire interview was taped by local jazz disc jockey, Don Clark, who also participated in the questioning. The truth, unfolded softly, often slowly by Art, now becomes public domain with his permission.

John Tynan: Art, who introduced you to the use of narcotics?
Art Pepper: Well, it was just friends.
JT: Musicians?
AP: Yes.
JT: Here or on the road?
AP: On the road. I think possibly if I had been here . . . Well, maybe it would probably have happened anyway. I think I *had* to go through it first.
Don Clark: Are there pushers in the music business that you know of?
AP: No. Outside the business—outside, definitely. There are none in the music business.
JT: No matter how badly a musician may get hooked, you've never seen any who would push dope?
AP: No. Absolutely not. As a matter of fact, you'll find that any musicians who're users still won't do it, even if they see turning another person on will help them personally, because they have enough respect for the other person's life. They won't do it unless the other person himself asks them. But I've never seen any musician go out and collect a recruit or something.
JT: Art, did you mess around with marijuana before you used heroin?
AP: Oh, I went through the whole routine. I started drinking at a very early age, maybe when I was about 15, getting drunk and so on. Then pills. I started smoking pot (marijuana) but found that I wasn't able to manipulate. It was too difficult, too much of a strain. I didn't have control of myself. I'd go on the stand in a night club and feel I wasn't able to do what I wanted with my horn.
JT: How old were you then?
AP: In my late teens or early 20s. Then I saw that it couldn't go on, that I couldn't continue that way. I had to abstain completely from the use of any type of stimulant or else go onto something that would be more desirable.
JT: Can you recall the circumstances of the first time you used heroin?
AP: Oh, yes. It's just as if it happened yesterday.
JT: Would you describe it?
AP: I'd been on the road for quite some time, away from my wife. Being as unstable emotionally and as immature as I was at that time, I couldn't stand the thought of being away from her. I needed a woman. I had like a mother complex, and I was always searching for some-

thing that wasn't there. So this particular night we played a concert and I went up to the bar in the hotel afterwards. The bar closed at 4 o'clock in the morning. I went up to the room and these people were there. I was just in one of those, uh, moods.

And I felt a strong desire then and there to leave the band and go home. I guess I was pretty down. I saw that there was this thing going on up there in the room and I realized, that as weak as I was, I should never try it once because I knew what it would lead to. But just in one of those moments it was offered and I accepted. When I made it, it seemed at the time to be an answer to all the problems.

DC: Did you think about making heroin before that night?

AP: Oh, yes, yes. I had it offered to me for several years prior to that. But I knew, I knew inside of myself that if I ever once gave in to it, that it would be fatal, so I just kept from it. If I had been stronger, a little more stable, I maybe would have been able to withstand the temptation altogether, which I wish I'd done.

JT: After that night in the room when you first took heroin, when was the next time?

AP: Well, I started horning it at first. I didn't shoot it. In other words, I sniffed it through my nose. At first it was all right. I could make it just whenever I would run into it. If somebody would have some, I'd make it and I was all right. Maybe next day I'd feel a little funny, but I was still juicing and everything and felt fine. But then, just little by little, it got more and more—and I got to the point where my nose would bleed constantly and my stomach was getting upset from swallowing the mucous. . . I realized I just couldn't make it to horn it anymore, so I fixed and that was it.

The minute that I fixed—from that moment on it was just an every-minute thing. My whole life was just stopped. Everything that I'd ever wanted, everything that I'd loved was destroyed. . . You become selfish, you care for no one but yourself. You're scared of everyone, of everything. You don't trust anyone. You can't possibly enjoy any type of an emotional or intellectual scene at all because your mind is so completely taken up by the fear and pressure that you're under.

Being hooked on junk becomes a way of life. You exist for it and it alone. Nothing else matters because it gives you a purpose in living. And that purpose is to get more junk. You haven't got a true, honest thought in your head. And as far as creating anything, it's impossible. There's no creation at all.

JT: Besides heroin, what else did you shoot?

AP: Everything. Even pills. But shooting pills has a very bad effect on you.

JT: Art, when was the last time you worked steadily?

AP: That was in November, 1954, at Jazz City. I was guest instrumentalist with the Barney Kessel quartet. I'd come on and do just about 15 minutes.

DC: When did you get arrested the first time?

AP: 1953, in Hollywood.

DC: How long were you in that time?

AP: I did 15 months. A little time in the county jail, then I went to Fort Worth. That's a public health service hospital.

DC: Was it a gradual withdrawal?

AP: No, just a cold turkey. You got arrested and just thrown into the county jail to sleep on the floor and sweat it out.

DC: Was there any treatment there? Did anybody talk to you about treatment or about anything that could help you?

AP: At Fort Worth, yes. But outside of Fort Worth there's no treatment.

DC: What did you do when you got out?

AP: Well, I got out in May of '54 and felt I had things pretty well under control. But during this time my wife sent me a divorce and had remarried just before I got out. I think I used that as an excuse to go on heroin again. I still hadn't gone through enough agony . . .

JT: When were you arrested the second time?

AP: Dec. 7, 1954. I spent nine months in the county jail, then about 10 months in the federal pen on Terminal Island for parole violation. Of course, this makes me a two-time loser. If I goof again and get busted, I can get 30 to 40 years in prison under terms of a new federal law. . . At the end of 1954 I was using 40 caps of heroin a day. I was really in terrible shape. Weighed 128 pounds and I wasn't able to do anything. I couldn't play at all. My blowing was—was just cold. There was no soul, no nothing in it. It was just something I was doing because I needed the money.

JT: If you were using 40 caps in a 24-hour day, how often did you have to take heroin?

AP: Well, I would fix maybe five or six caps every time. Actually, I could've been using maybe a hundred caps a day in another month if I had access to that much, because the demand just builds and builds. Using that much junk you're just the same as you are right now. You know, it's like getting on one of those little assembly line things that are moving. You get on it and you can't get off.

DC: Do you think that working in clubs was part of the cause for your falling into this?

AP: Yes. Yes, definitely. But with me there were other things, too. I got married at a very young age, when I was 17 years old, and in a way I was successful too quickly. Things were too easy and I think it was a little overwhelming to me. I started playing professionally and almost right away I went with a big name band and things were going fine. Then, in 1943, I was drafted into the army and I just couldn't understand why I should have to go. I wasn't old enough at 18 to accept the fact that I had to go. So it was a very hard thing for me to do. I started drinking quite a lot in the army. I guess I felt sorry for myself. I was very immature.

After 2½ years in the service, when I came out, I wanted to be free in a way. You see, my wife had since had a child and the responsibilities were, I think, a little bit too much for me at that time. I resented my wife and child because I felt they were holding me back in my career. My wife could no longer travel on the road with me. Then I started going on the road again—and the road itself is such a difficult thing. One-nighters with a big band, you know. Little by little I ran into these . . . "opportunities"—and through my own immaturity I, like, sought an escape.

The escape proved to be heroin. So, I'd make the heroin and it would satisfy all my frustrations from being away from my wife whom I really loved. (Long pause.) It seemed to be an answer at the time.

DC: Did you ask yourself at that time what the eventual outcome might be?

AP: Well, I just didn't want to admit it to myself. I just wouldn't look at it. . . I thought of what so many people had told me and I'd seen examples of guys who had been completely ruined by it. I guess I thought I could be the one who could do it and still be all right. But I knew really deep down in my own heart that I couldn't possibly end up any other way than the others.

JT: You mentioned recently that for all the years you made good money you now have absolutely nothing to show for it, not even clothes. . .

AP: Nothing. I have an old blue suit that was given to me when I got out of the joint, the time before this, and a couple of pairs of slacks that were bought for me by a girl friend—and that's it.   .

DC: How long do you think it will take you before you know for certain that you've licked the problem?

AP: Oh, I figure possibly a year or two.

DC: Do you have any nagging thoughts about what it would be like to go back?

AP: No. I went through it so completely that there's no more wonderment or mystery about it. I know exactly what it is and what it leads to. There's no enjoyment in it at all. It's without enjoyment for me.

JT: How is your health now?

AP: Well, I'm very fortunate. My health is good, real good.

DC: You ready to start over again, right from scratch?

AP: I'm not worried about that. I figure that I love music, I have a definite feeling for it. I know that that's what I'm going to do, what I have to do. And if I don't make it, to become a really great success, uh, I'll be happy as long as I'm able to make it for myself and stay straight—because I'd rather stay straight and play music for my own amusement. I would be happy even doing that.

JT: What are you planning musically for the immediate future?

AP: To play as much as I can. I'll be making quite a few record dates for different labels here and I'd like to get a little group of my own. Meanwhile, I've been working with Jack Montrose. I really like his writing and he's a wonderful person to work with.

JT: What would you say to young musicians starting out today who might be entertaining ideas of taking junk for kicks, then staying away from it?

AP: If a young guy starts using junk, he'll never ever learn how to play a horn. I'm sure of that. It's impossible. There's no way he can do it because in a little while his whole life will be revolving around junk. He'll have no time to develop. He can go out every night and blow and it won't do him any good in the long run. Pretty soon his mind will begin to stagnate like all those who've used junk . . .

If many young musicians hadn't used junk, they would have really been wailing. The junk is just destroying the whole talent. It's just killing it. Nowadays I think of all the young cats that start using junk, and it completely destroys them so you never hear what they might have had to offer. Maybe some might have been the greatest musicians ever, yet no one will ever hear them, nothing will ever happen from them because they'll just destroy themselves.

And it can only lead to eventual suicide—if a person has the nerve — or life in the penitentiary, or getting shot during a holdup or something. It'll eventually come to that.

JT: Do you think there is any way to head off an individual who may be on the way to drug addiction, or must he solve his problem by himself?

(In answer to this particular query, Art Pepper felt that the extreme importance of the question required additional consideration by him so that he might give a clearer, more adequate reply. He submitted the following answer in writing:)

"I think it's up to the individual. It's like telling children not to do something—they'll do it every time until they finally decide that they themselves don't want to do it anymore. An addict is a sick person and should be treated as such. I think the work in the U.S.P.H.S.

hospitals at Ft. Worth and Lexington is doing a great deal of good for those who sincerely want to stop and straighten themselves out. My doctor at Ft. Worth gave me some invaluable assistance which is now beginning to take effect.

"The percentage of addicts who have stopped is around 1 or 2 percent, which is far from a happy situation, but I think I have an explanation for this. The small percentage is a good excuse for not stopping—a person may say, 'Well, I guess I shouldn't feel so bad about not stopping because nobody else can either.' It's a warped justification for being weak.

"Actually, it's really not too difficult to stop if you've finally made up your mind to do it—of course, you've got to want to more than anything else in the world. I lost a wife, whom I loved very deeply, a wonderful child, a home, etc., but it still wasn't enough to make me stop.

"It can't be for any one person or anything that you stop—it's got to be for *yourself*. It's only for yourself that you can quit, believe me—and with God's help I think I'm now well on the road to recovery and a full and reasonably happy and moderate life." *down beat, September 19, 1956. Copyright 1956 by down beat. Reprinted by special permission.*

DIANE was still working as a waitress in jazz clubs, and I was recording and playing with Jack Montrose at the Angel Room in the Crenshaw area. So I was doing well, but I was goofing, and I was really getting strung out.

The Chicanos dug me. I used to play at the Diggers and at the Coral Room, clubs in East L.A. They liked my music, and they liked me because I was a regular, one of the few musicians that went to jail and did time without informing on anybody. They envied me my talent and the opportunities I had, and they couldn't understand why I would want to put myself in *their* position. They said if they had what I did they would never, ever do what they were doing, dealing and robbing. They only did these things because they never had a chance to do anything else.

One night a heavyset Chicano came into the Angel Room. He was a real gangster type. He introduced himself; his name was Mario Cuevas; and he was a big dealer. He liked me. He liked the way I played. So I hit on him if he had anything; he said yeah and he laid something on me. A condom. It must have had about a quarter of an ounce of stuff in it, which is a lot. He gave it to me.

The next time Mario came by he said, "Why don't you straighten up? If you like, I'll get you some Dolophine." Which is pills (Methadone) you kick with. I said, "Wow, I'd sure love to." I knew all the time I wasn't going to do it. Mario got me the Dolophines, and I cut down with them, used them when I was sick, but I didn't kick. He came around again and he said, "What happened?" I said, "Oh, man, you know." And he said, "Well, you just want to continue this rat race." He laid some more stuff on me, and I started buying from him. He said, "I'd rather give it to you myself than have you go out in the street, taking a chance of getting rousted or picked up, busted. And at least with me you're getting decent stuff." I went from a quarter a day to half a piece a day, and this was stuff that wasn't cut for the street. This was stuff that was strong. This was stuff that would be taken by a guy who was pushing on the street and cut by that guy two or three times. You can imagine the habit I built up.

Diane didn't know what to do. She'd never been around a junkie before. She'd never taken a pill, smoked pot. She'd worked in jazz clubs, and that life was exciting to her, but she didn't know what it was like when you finally go *home* with those people. She saw what was happening but she couldn't stop it. I blew the gig at the Angel Room, and little by little I started blowing all the gigs and stopped going out asking for gigs. People would call and I wouldn't go to the phone. I'd make an occasional record date, something like that, but all I wanted to do was stay in the pad, lock the windows and doors, and just fix all day and night.

And all during this time the phone was ringing every day, and it was Patti saying, "You'd better leave that chick. I'm warning you." And I'm in agony because I want Patti. And I want to get rid of Diane, but now I'm feeling sorry for her and I don't know what to do. Her car's all messed up. I wouldn't allow her to spend money on her car or on anything else. Gradually, everything started falling apart, and every penny I had, I'd give to Mario.

Mario reminded me of a modern-day Zapata. He had a lot of

Indian qualities. He was a big guy with a full, round, moon face, straight, coal-black hair, dark eyes, the whites real white, and everything about him denoted strength. The Mexicans I've met that had a lot of Indian in them were very strong people, very proud, very down-home, down to earth, and very honest. And if they like you, they really like you, and if they don't, that's it. There's no phoniness. Mario, whatever he told you, that's what it was. He was an honest, beautiful person and a great friend. He would never, ever have anybody else do his time for him or suffer for something that he got pleasure out of. I later wrote and recorded a song for Mario, a tribute to him. He was one of the greatest people I've ever met in my life.

Mario lived over by Riverside Drive. He'd come every other day, and I'd wait for him. He'd come in. I'd ask him if he wanted some coffee. He'd be dressed in a suit—real sharp—and real healthy because he'd stopped using. See, he used for a long time, but the last jolt he did was in McNeil Island, ten or fifteen years, and he didn't want any more of it. Now he was just dealing to make money. He didn't deal to individuals. He had people he'd make drops for that dealt, that had people dealing for *them*. He'd never put himself under the gun, you know, with handling stuff or put himself in a position to get caught. So he really took a chance on me, carrying stuff into my house when I could have gotten him busted and would never have had to go to jail again because he was so big. He'd come, and we would talk, and I'd be looking at him, and he knew the whole trip, what was going on in my mind. It was like a game. Sometimes he'd get all the way out the door before I'd say, "Uh?" He'd say, "Oh!" you know, and then he'd walk back in, reach in his shirt pocket, and take out the condom. It was half an ounce. He'd hold it in his hand, and my heart would be pounding because I wanted to leap on it. He'd throw it on the floor and say, "You better get that quick!" I'd jump for it, and he'd start ranking me, "You better get it quick! You better get in the bathroom and get that stuff in you! Boy, oh boy, you're too much!" He'd stand there. I'd just be wigging out because I wanted to run into the bathroom, and he knew that. He'd shake his head, "Go on, go on. Go in the bathroom!" But I'd wait and it would seem like ages before he finally split, and then I'd rush into the bathroom feeling really rank. Three different times he gave me Dolophine, but I never did kick.

At first, when Mario gave me half ounces, they'd last for two or three days. Then I started using more and one day I ran out; I couldn't call and ask him to come because he'd just been there. I couldn't tell him I was already out. I was going to have to go out and hustle, go out in the street and score.

Diane and I had just had a terrible argument because all I did was sit in the house and nod out. Whenever I came to, I'd just cook up again. Sometimes the spike would be lying on the floor or still stuck in my arm, so when I woke up I'd have to clean it out, get it unplugged. I'd start cutting the light fixtures. I'd be cutting the cords and the plugs to get wires to stick into the spike to clean it. I would have ripped up anything in the house to unplug that needle. And there was blood running down my arms and burn marks all over the place from my cigarettes when I'd nod out—on the rugs, the couch, the chair, everything. Diane couldn't stand it, and we'd had this argument when I told her I had to go out and went into the bathroom to get cleaned up. Then I heard a noise. I ran out and saw the car pulling away. Diane had taken all my pants, every penny, my horns, and the car and she'd split, and there I was trapped on this huge hill.

She didn't come home for two days, went to friends' houses, her mother's, her father's, and she called me over and over but she wouldn't come home, and I was really sick. On the second day Mario dropped by and laid some stuff on me. When Diane came back I flipped out and threatened to kill her if she pulled that again.

Diane woke me one morning and said, "You have a record date today." I hadn't been playing. I hadn't been doing anything. I said, "Are you *kidding*? Who with? And where? And what?" She told me that she and Les Koenig from Contemporary Records had got together. The only way they could do it, they figured, was to set it up and not tell me about it so I'd be forced into it. They knew that no matter how strung out I was I would take care of business if people were depending on me. Even at my worst I was always that way. She told me that Miles Davis was in town, and they had gotten his rhythm section and set it all up with them. They were going to record with me that day: Philly Joe Jones on drums, Paul Chambers on bass, and Red Garland on piano.

I wouldn't speak to Diane at all. I told her, "Get out of my sight." I got my horn out of the closet, got the case and put it on the bed and looked at it, and it looked like some stranger. It looked like something from another life. I took the horn out of the case. When you take the saxophone apart there's the body piece, the neck, and the mouthpiece, and those three pieces are supposed to be wiped and wrapped up separately when they're put in the case. Evidently, the last time I'd played I'd been loaded and I'd left the mouthpiece on the neck. I had to clean the horn because it was all dirty. I had to oil it and make sure it was operating correctly. On the end of the neck is a cork, and the mouthpiece slips over that. I had to put a little cork grease on it. I grabbed the mouthpiece and pulled. It was stuck at first and then all of a sudden it came off in my hand. The mouthpiece had been on the neck for so long that the cork had stuck inside it, and on the end of the neck was just bare metal. It takes a good repair man four or five hours to put a new cork on. It has to set. It has to dry. It has to be sanded down. I didn't have time for that. I was going to have to play on a messed up horn.

And I was going to have to play with Miles Davis's rhythm section. They played every single night, all night. I hadn't touched my horn in six months. And being a musician is like being a professional basketball player. If you've been on the bench for six months you can't all of a sudden just go into the game and play, you know. It's almost impossible. And I realized that that's what I had to do, the impossible. No one else could have done it. At all. Unless it was someone as steeped in the genius role as I was. As I am. Was and am. And will be. And will always be. And have always been. Born, bred, and raised, nothing but a total genius! Ha! Ahahaha!

There was no way to fix the neck so I put the mouthpiece back on it with the cork and fitted it where it was. If I wasn't in tune, or if it started slipping or pulling loose or leaking, I was dead. I wrapped some tape around it. I took the reed off. It was stuck on the mouthpiece, all rotted and green. I got a new reed, found one I liked, and I blew into the horn for a little while. Then Diane came to the doorway. She was afraid to come in the room. She said, "It's time for us to go." I called her a few choice words: "You stinkin' motherfucker, you! I'd like to kill you, you lousy bitch! You'll get yours!" Then I went into the bathroom and fixed a huge amount.

I had no idea what I was going to play. Talk about being unprepared! The first albums I'd made, I'd always had something I'd written, a couple of tunes. We drove to Melrose Place, where the recording studio was, and there was Les at the door. He gave me a sheepish grin and said, "Well, how're you doing?" I said, "Uh." He said, "It'll be alright. Everything'll be alright."

Les Koenig was someone I'd met in the early fifties. He'd been a movie producer at Paramount, a good producer with a lot of credits (He co-produced "Detective Story," "The Heiress," "Roman Holiday"). But right after the war they started a big campaign to rid the movie industry of communists; I think it was the McCarthy thing. I guess after Goebbels and Hitler they saw what a strong force propaganda was, and they were trying to clean up, rightly or wrongly, the people that started it. Probably they were thinking right, but like anything else that starts out like that it becomes a monster after a while and a lot of people suffer. So the people in the industry were asked to sign a paper saying that they didn't believe this or believe that or had never been a communist or had never attended a meeting or *would* never attend one and all this nonsense. And the people were called before a committee and asked to name communists in the movie industry. Most of them signed the paper and named names. They just said, "Well, fuck it—this is my livelihood." But there were a few that were such real people, such honest people, honest to themselves, that they would not cooperate. And Les Koenig was one of these. He wasn't a communist actually, but he refused to go along with it because he felt that the committee infringed upon his rights. And so he was ostracized and kicked out of an industry where he'd become a producer.

After he left the movies he had to find something to do. Les was a person that liked good things. He liked art; he liked good writing; he loved music. And so he started Contemporary Records. Les was the first to record the legendary Ornette Coleman when no other company would touch him. He recorded many young, far-out people and gave them their first opportunities to be heard. And he recorded Sonny Rollins, Shelly Manne, André Previn, Hampton Hawes, Barney Kessel, and many more. I had made albums for different companies, but I'd never gotten the right shake on my royalties, things like that. (In fact, all the records I made prior to my association with Les are still being sold in this country or in Europe, in Japan, and I don't get a penny in royalties from them to this day.) I just figured that was how the record business was. Then I was approached by Les. He offered me a contract, and his whole operation was very different. I saw that here was an honest man, and I felt very safe with him, and so I signed, and I've never had any regrets. We developed a beautiful friendship over the years. When I was really troubled, I could talk to him. He helped me a lot.

So here he is at the door, and I walk in, and I'm afraid to meet these guys because they've been playing with Miles and they're at the pinnacle of success in the jazz world. They're masters. Practicing masters. But here I am and here they are, and I have to act like everything's cool—"Hi" and "What's doin'?" "Hi, Red, what's goin' on?"

When the amenities are over and Les gets everything set up, the balance on the horn and all the microphones, then it's time to start making the album. Red Garland is looking at me, and my mind is a total blank. That's always been one of my faults—memory. I have a poor memory, and I can't think of anything to play. Red says, "Well, I know a nice tune. Do you know this?" He starts playing a tune I've heard before. I say, "What's the name of it?" He says, "You'd Be So Nice to Come Home To." "What key?" "D minor."

It came out beautiful. My sound was great. The rhythm was great. And I remember in the reviews, by people like Leonard Feather, Martin Williams, they said, "The way Art plays the melody is wonderful. He's so creative. He makes it sound even better than the actual tune." Well, what I'm doing, I don't know the melody so I'm playing as close to it as I can get, and that's the creativity part. It does sound good because I play it with a jazz feeling, and it's like a jazz solo, but I'm really trying to play what I recollect of the song.

Les suggested we try a ballad for the next side, so Paul Chambers said, "You know what would be a nice tune for alto and the way you play? 'Imagination.' Do you know that?" I said, "Yeah, I've heard that. Bah dah dah dahhhh dah . . . "

Red said, "That's A flat." I said, "Well, I was just goofing around." We ran through the melody and the bridge and then I said, "What should we do at the ending?" Red said, "Just do a little tag kind of thing. Just make it a free kind of thing." I played the melody and then I blew; Red played; Paul played; I came in and just followed along, a little series of chords; and then they stopped and I played a little ad lib kind of thing and we went into the ending. It was just *fantastic*. "Imagination" on *Art Pepper Meets the Rhythm Section*. It sounded as if we'd been rehearsing for months.

That's the way the whole thing went. We played a lot of things I'd liked but never done. And I really moved them, you know. And that's something. They'd been playing with *Miles*! And me being white! They were all real friendly and said it was beautiful, and they dug the way I played. Diane looked at me, like, "Would I forgive her?" and "Wasn't I happy?" And I was so relieved it was over I told her, "Everything's cool." So that was the session, and when it came out the people really liked it.

ART PEPPER

ART PEPPER MEETS THE RHYTHM SECTION—Contemporary C 3532: *You'd Be So Nice to Come Home To; Red Pepper Blues; Imagination; Waltz Me Blues; Straight Life; Jazz Me Blues; Tin Tin Deo; Star Eyes; Birks' Works.*

Personnel: Pepper, alto; Red Garland, piano; Paul Chambers, bass; Philly Joe Jones, drums.

Rating: ★ ★ ★ ★ ★

At time of writing, this album is exactly one year in release. Why it has not been reviewed until now is quite unfathomable, for it certainly was one of the best jazz albums of last year and probably Pepper's most mature recording to date. The session was held Jan. 19, 1957, when Lester Koenig availed himself of the Miles Davis rhythm section, then in Hollywood with the trumpeter to play a local night club.

The altoist and rhythm section are indeed well met in this balanced set of eight tunes ranging from a purely played *Imagination* to some intriguing three-quarter jazz in *Waltz Me*. The solos of all concerned are of consistent interest, with Pepper at times reaching heights he's seldom attained even under most congenial conditions in a club. In *Red Pepper*, a down-homey blues, Art's Lester Young-like phrasing in his opening chorus clearly shows where the roots lie.

As soloist and comper, Garland is authoritative and original. He can be alternately strong and delicate, sparely laconic, and ripplingly virtuosic. The bass-drums team here is peerless, with Chambers getting off some well-conceived pizzicato and arco solos. Jones' brush chorus in *Waltz Me* bears endless replaying for its taste and humor.

This memorable meeting deserves a favored place in anybody's collection. (J.A.T.) down beat, *June 12, 1958. Copyright 1958 by down beat. Reprinted by special permission.*

(John Koenig) My father always told me Art was the best alto player in town. He responded to Art early. And he told him early on, "Look, if you respect anything about my judgment, you better stop taking dope. It's gonna mess you up." Art said, "Yeah." And that was that.

They recorded a few albums in the early fifties. He thought Art wasn't getting a chance to play with people that were up to him, which was why he wanted to make those records like *Meets The Rhythm Section* and *Gettin' Together*. But, unfortunately, Art started getting into trouble, and that effectively took him off the scene. He would come back for a brief stay and try to get something together. Les was genuinely disturbed but he couldn't prevail upon Art to stop.

I'd say the first thing Les liked about Art was that he didn't play like anybody else. He wasn't anybody's man but his own. Art was the best player around then. (I'm not saying that he isn't now.) There were a couple other good alto players in the country at the time: there was Cannonball, and there was Jackie McLean, Phil Woods. It's hard to think of anybody else that you could identify as a powerful individual force. And Art was here. Les responded to Art basically because Art was something special.

Les was always interested in—whatever the human endeavor, he was interested in something unusual. Even to the extent that he would prefer an unusual idea that wasn't carried off as well to one that was normal and carried off letter-perfect.

That's probably what made his identity as a collector and a record producer. He was kind of contrary, you know. He was the first person to record Ornette Coleman. And Les was the most meticulous person I ever saw. He was meticulous, and, if known for nothing else, at least in this business he's probably remembered for being about the most honest person in the record industry.

I was a little kid when Art started coming around. I heard stories that he was a dashing kind of guy, in a way a stereotype of a hard-living jazz musician of the time, with all the dope and all the women and all the playing. But I think Art was a more legitimate jazz player than any of the other ones out here. He went along with the life-style. I don't mean the dope, but Central Avenue and that whole thing; whereas I listen to the other records of white players in town at the time—they're good records but Art came from a tradition. He was the genuine article.

Art was very unsure of himself after he got out, after his big ordeal. He'd come around, and my father would ask him how he was doing, how he was playing, and my father would try to encourage him. Every time Art would leave, you'd get the feeling, what a waste. My father was genuinely upset. They developed a personal rapport which was a kind of private thing.

PEPPER'S PROGRESS By John Tynan

"For the first time in my 32 years I've got a piano at home."

Art Pepper smiled happily, snuffed out a cigarette and continued, "I got it in August. You've no idea how much it means to me—not only where my music is concerned, but psychologically. It's like a symbol of a new life."

Symbol of a new life . . . a phrase in which the key word stands out in brilliant contrast to the living death of heroin addiction which entombed the altoist for some of the most vital years of his young manhood and musical creativity.

It has been truly opined that, to an artist, the "public" is a most fickle mistress. Consider the following statistics:

In 1951, when Art Pepper was alto star of the Stan Kenton band, final tabulation for first and second places in the alto sax division of *down beat's* Readers Poll read as follows: Charlie Parker, 957 votes; Art Pepper, 945.

In 1955, when Pepper was imprisoned in the federal penitentiary for violation of parole stemming from his first arrest two years previously, he had plummeted in public favor to 18th place in this magazine's annual poll with votes totaling 31.

But in 1956, just a few months after his return to music, with no out-of-town appearances for new albums on the market to his credit, he had soared to 9th place. In the just-finished 1957 poll, he moved all the way to second.

What of Pepper today, his problems and aspirations? What has kept him away from heroin—and inevitable further imprisonment—for one-and-a-half years? As may be surmised, he is reluctant to discuss so painful a subject. He did, however, make the following observations with characteristic candor and the reiterated hope that others might profit from his own experience.

"So far as problems are concerned," he said thoughtfully, "the biggest one I've had since I got out was being back in the same environment. By that I mean night clubs, mainly. And having to contend with the creeps who approached me with the idea of selling some junk. At first, this was a constant problem and temptation. It wasn't until word got around that I'd put down that scene that the pushers began to ease up."

He raked his dark, unruly hair with nervous fingers and lit another cigarette. "My own personal problems, of course, also had to be met—the complexes I was left with after goofing for years; the inability to have confidence in myself and in my playing.

"In June of last year, for example, when I first got out, I felt it would take a long time to get back my chops. In fact, there were many times after that when I was convinced that I was through in music. I was nervous, unsure of myself, afraid I wouldn't know the new tunes, or that I no longer was hip to what was happening in jazz. Most of all, I guess, I was deathly scared that people wouldn't like the way I played."

His brow was deeply furrowed. "There were some people, too, who made it tough for me to make a living in music. But here I've got to draw the line. There's just so much I feel free to say . . . "

Responsible medical opinion holds that an individual, once hooked on heroin, is forever unfree from the sometimes intolerable "yen" for just one jolt of the drug that once dominated his every waking moment. How does Pepper combat this tearing desire to "fix just once," that twists every addict after he has kicked?

"The yen is still there, of course," admitted Pepper grimly. "I dream about it. It's a very real thing. There are pressures within myself arising from the knowledge that once you've used, it's the simplest escape there is. You *never* forget that. You forget all the bad parts of being addicted; remember just the good. And the worst is, you rationalize about it until you've almost forgotten what it will lead to.

"But, like a person with a bad stomach, you learn to live with it and do what you can to take care of yourself. When the yen for a fix becomes bad, I've gotten into the habit of performing a sort of ritual that helps to keep me straight.

"It's just a thought process . . . I think about the progressive steps that'll result from my goofing. First of all, I consider, the narcotics detail gets the word and before long I get picked up. This has got to happen; there's no escape. Then I get sent up for maybe 30, 40 years. My record takes care of that. I think about never again seeing my wife, my friends . . . never again being able to play, which is the thing I want to do more than anything else. Well, by the time I'm through with this line of thought, I'm shaking with fear, so scared that the feeling is gone."

At 32, Art Pepper feels he is just approaching maturity. He now believes that you can't avoid the everyday responsibilities of living and that meeting them is actually easier than avoiding them. In this, he acknowledges his wife, Diane, as *the* constant stabilizer. ("You have to be loved; you have to *know* that someone loves you. When you do, everything is easier.")

Those early fears and feelings of musical inadequacy when he returned to professional life, seem now dreamlike and wispy to the altoist. Not only has he "got his chops back," but he is increasingly regarded by critical authority as one of the most important contributors to contemporary jazz. The ever-present depth and passion in his solo playing, stemming possibly from the suffering in his life, gives to his musical conception a strength and basic emotional quality possessed by few of his contemporaries.

Since last summer, Pepper has recorded for several west coast labels. When he badly needed funds, shortly after his release form the penitentiary, a tempting bonus offered by the owners of Intro Records (an Aladdin subsidiary) induced him to exclusively sign with that company. All but two of the albums he made for Intro have now been released. But that company has abruptly swerved from a jazz policy (its basic catalog is almost wholly rhythm and blues) and Pepper's contract is on the block to the highest bidder. At this critical point in his career, Pepper is without a home label.

Since his return to jazz, considers Art, he hasn't noted any progressive changes. "Matter of fact," he declares, "so far as I can see, the music has stagnated. Nothing new is happening now, there's no progress evident like when I was a kid. Another thing I've noticed is that there's no spirit of camaraderie among jazz musicians anymore. They all seem to follow the attitude of the nation: competition. 'Keeping up with the Joneses' is keeping down the jazzman.

"When I was coming up," Art reflected nostalgically, "there were 13 or 14 big swing bands. There was a need for blowers. Today, who are the blowers going to blow for, themselves?

"But then there are hardly any really good young musicians. Just Bird and Miles imitations—all the way. And to make it worse, today it seems like nobody is helping anybody else, saying, 'blow, man, blow.' So it's really not the young cats' fault."

For a jazz musician who unequivocally states, "I dig blowing by myself; I feel I play better," Art Pepper's biggest ambition is somewhat surprising! He'd like to have a big band of his own—12 or 13 pieces.

"I want a band that could shout, along the lines of Kenton's or Woody's, with way out arrangements. But," with a sigh, "money is imperative. And then, if Barnet can't make it all year round, how can I? No, I've got no hopes at all of ever having a band like that."

Reflecting on the future, Art murmured with a wistfulness somehow lent substance by perceivable resolve, "In my 50s I'd like to write a symphony." Then, strongly, "I make no distinction between jazz and classical music, so I don't see what's so strange in my wanting to write an important long work, do you?"

Reverting to the more immediate future, however, "I'd really like to come up with something original. It would have to be a swinging thing. To find a sound ... something of my own, though, not like a chamber group. *Jazz*, in the purest sense of the word. Maybe a combination of alto, tenor, trombone, and rhythm; or alto, tenor, and rhythm. Anyway, whatever it'll be, I'd like my own group to have the popular success of, say, Chico Hamilton's."

The Art Pepper of December, 1957, is remote in spirit and ambition from the pitiable addict of three years ago. For helping him on the road to recovery, he expresses deep-felt gratitude to Richard Bock, president of World Pacific Records, ". . . and all people who've helped me. When I got out of jail," he said, "I had no wife, no girl—zero. But Dick Bock contacted me then and gave, just *gave* me money to put me back on my feet. How can I ever forget that? He's helped me many times since when I didn't know what I was going to do.

"But my wife is the one who's made me happier than I've ever been in my life. Now I really look forward to my older years. I used to be scared of growing old—but not now. Diane has done more for me in one year than all others did in my life's entirety.

"Whatever I may do in music from now on and whatever credit I may get for it belongs to her. She didn't give me back just my self-respect and career. Diane gave me back my life." down beat, *January 9, 1958. Copyright 1958 by down beat. Reprinted by special permission.*

ART PEPPER
"Living without love is like not living at all"

For over a decade, Art Pepper has been recognized as belonging in the top echelon of modern jazz alto saxophonists.

This sensitive, serious minded musician, at 33, is perhaps at the height of his creativity.

Pepper was born in the Los Angeles suburb of Gardena; is thus an original "west coaster." His earliest jazz influence, he says, was tenor man Zoot Sims.

While playing with the Stan Kenton orchestra, with which he first attracted national attention, Pepper was featured in a solo work, *Art Pepper*, composed and arranged by Shorty Rogers. Under the pseudonym "Art Salt," he was featured in Rogers' Capitol album, *Modern Sounds*, one of the first examples of what came to be labeled "West Coast Style."

In recent years Pepper has been working around the Los Angeles area, San Francisco, and other western states with his own quartet. Next month he hopes to make a trans-atlantic hop to Milan, Italy, where he expects to record an album for World-Pacific Records followed by a tour of the continent.

For the following *Cross Section*, Pepper offered his views on the following topics:

THE RHYTHM SECTION (PHILLY JOE JONES, PAUL CHAMBERS, RED GARLAND): "I was fortunate enough to make an album with these three. All I can say is that if I could play with them every night for a year, I feel I could *really* get with my horn. They're the greatest!"

ZOOT SIMS: "He's the most natural, swinging musician I've ever heard. I think I could achieve complete satisfaction playing with him in a small group. Add Miles for the third horn and going to work each night would be the ultimate."

GIL EVANS: "His writing for Miles on *Miles Ahead* to me was the most perfect thing I've ever heard done for a soloist with band. Gil's understanding of Miles was perfect. I'd love to have the opportunity of doing an album with Gil with the same writing approach."

CRITICS: "Although I've been very fortunate in receiving fair critical comment as a whole. I really can't say that I'd want to be a critic myself. Even with 23 years musical background, I just wouldn't feel qualified to judge another's performance."

FOOTBALL: "The greatest of all games. And the Los Angeles Rams are number one by me."

RHYTHM SECTION: "It's very difficult to find a section that plays for the soloist. Piano players seem to think it old-fashioned to play the basic chords, leaving the soloist free to improvise with altered notes, etc."

ELIZABETH TAYLOR: "She is such a gas. Wow!"

COMPOSERS: "Aside from Gil Evans, I most appreciate Al Cohn, Gerry Mulligan. Bill Holman, and Quincy Jones. So far as classical composers are concerned, there are many—but Stravinsky, Milhaud, and Ravel are my favorites. Ravel's *Daphnis et Chloé* (parts 1 and 3) is the most complete and perfect composition I've ever heard."

LITTLE ROCK: "I feel that the situation there is one of the worst tragedies of our time. We can never hope for goodwill from the outside world as long as this state of affairs persists. It is in complete defiance of the Constitution."

STAN KENTON: "I've never encountered a stronger personality. If Stan had chosen the field of evangelism I'm sure he'd have been as effective as Billy Graham."

MARRIED LIFE: "My first experience failed because of my immaturity. But my second venture has proved a lifesaver. Diane, my wife, is just the greatest. Living without love is like not living at all."

CARL PERKINS: "His loss hit me very deeply. We had worked together many times. Carl's talent was very great and as a person I thought of him as a rare friend. The last recordings I made under my own name were done with Carl. Unfortunately, they are owned by Aladdin (Intro) Records and have been released in stereo on Omegatape only. Carl's playing on these two albums was his greatest recorded work."

BOB WATERFIELD: "He was so poised. I've yet to see a football quarterback who did everything so perfectly. I'll never forget seeing Bob kick a 48-yard field goal with ten seconds left to play—to beat the Bears."

MASS COMMUNICATION MEDIA: "It's amazing the way they mold the minds of the people in any way they please. Coming home from England after World War II, when Russia was being praised as our ally, an officer seated by me on the boat said that within 10 years the Red Star would be the symbol of villainy instead of the Rising Sun and the Swastika. How true!"

MILES DAVIS: "His development has been phenomenal. I've listened to *Miles Ahead* by the hour and his warmth, choice of notes, and beautiful simplicity has touched my very soul." down beat, *October 16, 1958. Copyright 1958 by* down beat. *Reprinted by special permission.*

----

12 | Suicides

1958-1960

I NEEDED MONEY so I started working at the Tiffany Club with my own group, still shooting half a piece a day. One night Diane's sister, Marie, came to the job with a boyfriend to hear me play. She said, "Where's Diane?" She said, "I'll give her a call." I had just finished the first set; Marie went to the phone; and then I heard her scream my name: "She's killed herself! She's killing herself!" I grabbed the phone. Diane said, "Goooodbyyye, Aaaart." She said it was no use, she couldn't stand it anymore, and she wanted me to know she always loved me. Goodbye. She had taken some sleeping pills. Marie kept her on the phone, kept her talking, and I ran to the bar, where there was a private phone. I called the police and the Georgia Street Receiving Hospital and gave them the address.

The police and the firemen got to the house at the same time. Diane had moved all the furniture up to the doors: they had to break the windows. By this time she was out. They put her in an ambulance, rushed her to the hospital, and pumped her stomach. They didn't know if she was going to live or not. The police had a note for me that she'd written saying goodbye. Now, if Marie hadn't come to the club I wouldn't have gotten home until three o'clock in the morning, and Diane would have been dead.

She came out of it two days later, and when she'd been in the hospital about four days I brought her home. She was like a drunk. I had to do everything for her—take her to the bathroom, pull down her panties—and she loved that, the fact that I was doing these things for her.

I tried to straighten up a bit. I hit on Mario once more for some pills; and I almost stopped, but then I goofed again. And right about this time, during the night, I heard a noise and found the loan company breaking into the gargage. We were behind on the payments, so they took the car, and that fucked everything up. Here were were trapped on this hill (it was practically impossible to walk up) with no car. Then Mario got rousted; one of his dealers got busted and turned over on him; so he was hiding and that ended him. I was going out on the streets trying to score. Finally I did manage to clean up a little. We got an old car from Diane's father; I kept on working; and we moved to Glendale, into a little apartment house.

It was a nice place. There was a pool, and we'd swim. There were a couple of young girls there and they'd flirt with me, and I would probably flirt a little bit with them, and Diane was just, she was getting into that frame of mind. She felt I didn't really dig her. She was acting strange. She accused me of all kinds of things. I was goofing now and then as far as getting loaded, but I was working and I wasn't out of line that much. But she had these things going on in her mind, and I don't know what they were. I don't know if she felt guilty about leaving her kids or what it was.

One night I went to work and as I was coming home after the job for some reason I had a strange feeling; I kept picking up weird vibes out of nothing. I got to the apartment house, went upstairs, and opened the door. The chain was hooked. I said, "Diane, let me in. Open the chain." There was no answer, and the light was on in the front room. I couldn't figure out what was happening, but I knew it was something bad. I kept knocking and calling, but there was no response. Fortunately there was a louvered window close to the door and it was cracked open, so I was able to take the screen off, push it open, reach my hand in, and get the bolt loose.

I hollered her name. There was no sound. I went to the door of the bathroom. She had taken the knob off and locked it from inside. When I saw that I got scared to death. I was afraid to go in, but I had to. I put my shoulder to the door and hit it. Nothing happened. I hit it again, and it gave a little. The third time the door broke in, and I looked to my right, and it was a sight I'll never forget.

Diane had on a dress I was really crazy about. It was white, crocheted. Tiny crocheting. Handmade. It was a lacy, white dress you could wear to a wedding. She had put this dress on, and she was sitting on the toilet with her head hanging down on her chest, her arms laid out on her thighs and her hands hanging palms up. And I saw the red.

I couldn't stand to see it all at once. I turned and looked at the sink. There were three or four razor blades in it with blood on them. There was blood all over the sink and the floor. I looked again. There was blood all over this white dress. I looked, and she had cut both her wrists. I didn't know if she was still alive, but I saw, when I was finally able to look at her, that she was breathing, heavy, kind of sobbing, and I said, "Oh, my God! What happened? Why did you *do* that? What did you *do* that for? What's wrong with you? Jesus Christ." I grabbed each of her wrists over the cuts and held them as hard as I could to stop the blood and pulled her up off the toilet. I held her like that and just screamed at her, "What's wrong with you? What's wrong with you? Why did you do it? Oh, God!" I was getting sick because the sight of blood just makes me . . . I'm terrified of blood.

I dragged her into the front room. I didn't know what to do. I was trying to revive her. I got her on the couch over by the phone. I put one of her wrists in my armpit to hold it and dialed a number. I got an ambulance, got a doctor to come, got ahold of her sister, all this time hanging on to her, and it seemed like forever. Finally there was a doctor there; there was police; and somebody came and took her away from me. She came to as they were carrying her out. She looked at me and said, "I'm sorry," and started crying.

When Diane came home I asked her why? She told me that she felt she couldn't reach me. That living with me was like being alone, and she loved me so much she couldn't stand it. She couldn't stand it and she wanted to die. I was really trapped then. I felt so sorry for her. It was a horrible situation. Patti kept calling. I just felt so guilty. We'd gotten an old car from Diane's dad; I think it was a '47 Pontiac. We drove to Las Vegas in this car and got married.

When we got back, I received word from the court that a hearing would be forthcoming. Remo and Patti were going to adopt Patricia. Then I got a phone call from Patti asking me if I'd got the papers. I said, "Yeah, but that won't do any good. I'm going to contest it." Patti said, "Well, I'm sorry, but we're going to win by default—by your not being there." She said, "I don't think I'd go if I were you. If you do, I just want to tell you what's going to happen." She had hired a private detective to follow me, and she proceeded to tell me all the places I'd scored at, all the things I'd done, the people who would get busted if I went to that hearing, and what would happen to me if those people got busted. It would be told to them *how* they got busted—because of me.

There was nothing I could do. I knew Patti must have told Patricia that I was a fiend. A sex fiend. A monster. She had set this whole thing up when I was in Terminal Island by taking Patricia to see me. The hearing was held. I couldn't go. Remo adopted Patricia.

Afterwards I got very frantic thinking about it. I remember one night it hit me more than usual. I'd been drinking. I told Diane, "I'm gonna go out to the valley and see them." I was going to kill them. Diane got scared. She wouldn't let me go alone. We got in the car, and she drove me out to Panorama City, all the time trying to talk me out of it, but I just kept raving, getting more and more worked up. I told her where to turn, and we stopped in the front of the house. I'd brought a hammer along. I got out of the car and I said, "You wait here." He not only took my wife but now he'd taken my daughter, and they were poisoning her mind against me! They'd tell her I hadn't contested the adoption because I didn't care about her!

I was really crazy. I'd been drinking in the car, and I'd taken a bunch of speed. I walked up to the door and I was saying, "You motherfuckers! God, how I hate you!" I pounded on the door with my hammer. There was a light on in the house, but there was no answer. I pounded again. Then I heard Suzy. That was my little dog! Remo had everything! My wife, my house, my dog! He had all these things, and he wasn't content with that! Now he was going to take my daughter, even in name! I hammered again. Suzy and I had really loved each other. She would always leap on me and jump up and down, and I think she knew who it was and she was leaping at the door. I could hear her as I pounded. No one was there. Suzy kept on yowling and whining. I started crying. I said, "Little Suzy." I felt so miserable and so lost and so alone. I walked out on the front lawn and took the hammer and threw it at the house. I got back into the car, and I cried and cried and cried, and Diane drove us back to Glendale.

After we got married I got a job playing at the Blackhawk in San Francisco with my own group. I guess this was in 1957. The Blackhawk was a big jazz club at the time. We drove to San Francisco in this old Pontiac, which was another whole scene—it was a fantastic trip. And we stayed in a hotel which was right down the street from the club.

I think Diane thought if we got married I might straighten up. It was just a prayer she had. But I was still using, and we kept arguing about that. I told her I just couldn't stop and as long as I'm taking care of business and doing my job please don't bug me. Maybe if I'd been madly in love with her, *maybe* I would have been able to do something, but I doubt that. When I was with Patti I was using, so certainly I wasn't going to stop for Diane. We were having these arguments, and Diane was getting outrageous, and I went to play this session at the Blackhawk.

I'm in there playing and there's this guy Brew Moore, who plays tenor saxophone, plays very well; his old lady, Diane got to know her, and so here comes Diane into the club with this chick. We had had an especially bad fight before I went to work. I saw her come in and I hoped she'd be cool, but I noticed she was drinking pretty heavy and all of a sudden—I'm at the mike just before the intermission, introducing the guys in the band—and she starts shouting, "Hey, big man! Yeah, there's the *big* man, big Art Pepper, the great jazz musician, big man, big shot!" I say to the people, "Pardon the interruption. I'm sure that that table will maybe do us a favor and leave before the next set and go to a bar that's more befitting their character—down in the Bowery, where all the rest of the drunks are." She really flipped out then: "Son-of-a-bitch! Bastard!" I said, "It's intermission. We'll be back in fifteen minutes."

I walked over to the table and grabbed her. I told her, "Come on, let's get out of here! This is my *job*! Save this shit for the room, you fuckin' asshole!'' I got her out the door. This club was right on the corner. It was a Sunday afternoon and it was a nice day, so people were looking out their windows and we really attracted attention. Diane just kept coming on and coming on. I wanted to get away from her. I told Brew Moore's wife, "Why don't you take her someplace? Take her to your house. I've got a job to do." I said, "We'll argue later all you want. Please give me a break now." But she wouldn't stop. She kept cussing me out and suddenly she grabbed my right hand: she got my two fingers and bent them back and said, "I'll stop you from playing, you bastard! You son-of-a-bitch!" She bent me down to the ground. Later I had to go to an emergency hospital, where they put a splint on my fingers. I flipped out and grabbed this thing she had around her neck and pulled her; the necklace broke and stuff started rolling down the street. I slapped her and told this chick to get her out of there before I killed her. She's calling me every name— "Bastard! Dopefiend! Motherfucker!" I walked away while she screamed after me, and when I came back she wasn't around.

When I finished the gig I went back to the hotel. The key wasn't in the box so I went up and knocked on the door. I could hear water running. She wouldn't answer. I went downstairs and told the desk clerk that my old lady must have taken the key and could I get another key. He found one and let me have it. I went upstairs, and she must have heard me coming because when I opened the door there she was, sitting on the window-sill, bending back. This was, I guess, the seventh or eighth floor, and the room faced one of those wells. She had a razor blade at her throat and her hair was all stringy; she was almost foaming at the mouth and she said, "You come near me, I'll cut my throat and jump out the window, you motherfucker!"

I heard the water running and ran into the bathroom. There was a big bathtub with a shower, and the shower was on. The hot water was going full blast. In this bathtub was everything I owned. I had some nice clothes. I had a beautiful black cashmere overcoat, and here was the coat and all my after-shave, perfume. She'd thrown the bottles in the bathtub and broken them. I had just bought a Buffet clarinet that cost about four hundred dollars. She had taken it out of the case and dumped it in the bathtub! My clarinet that I just loved! I ran out. I shouted, "Oh, you bastard, what's *wrong* with you?" She yelled back, "Don't come near me! I'll kill myself!" I said, "Oh, go ahead and kill yourself, you son-of-a-bitch!" I said, "Why are you doing this to me? Why don't you just leave me alone?"

I was afraid she was going to jump out the window. I would have gotten busted. I had marks; I had stuff there; I had an outfit; and she was screaming all this shit: "Junkie! Lady's boy!" Finally, I walked out the door. I said, "Do whatever you want." I walked down the stairs. I didn't know what to do. I went back upstairs, and she was gone. I went to the window and looked out. I looked for blood. I didn't see anything so I went downstairs again and asked the guy at the desk if he'd seen my old lady. He gave me a weird look. He said, "Yeah, she went out of here just a little while ago. Is there anything I can do?" I said, "No, it's just one of those hassles." He said, "Yeah, I know, I've been through it two or three times myself. Boy, they sure are a drag at times." I said, "They sure are a fuckin' drag."

I walked all over, looked all over. I went for hours looking for her and waiting and waiting. I went back to the place and what seemed like days later she finally walks in.

She'd changed completely. She'd gone to the emergency hospital and told them she wanted to kill herself, and she wanted them to put her in the nut house. They sent her to a psychiatrist, and he listened to her story. Thank God, you know. Finally he said, "Do you love him?" She said yes. He said, "Well, you can do one of three things: You can leave him; you can stay with him the way things are now; or you can join him. Or you can kill yourself, but you'll just hurt him, and you won't solve anything that way." She said, "Well, I can't leave him, and I can't stand living with him the way it is, because I feel that he loves *that* more than me." He said, "Well that leaves one choice open. You can join him." So she'd decided that that was what she was going to do, and nothing could change her mind.

I begged her. I tried to reason with her. I told her it was the end of her life. Unfortunately, she knew the people I was scoring from, the houses I went to, and she said, "I'll go and score from them myself." I knew they'd give it to her because they love to turn a chick on; maybe they can get some head or something. They're real assholes, especially in Frisco, the people that deal. I was trapped. She said, "You can watch me now, but you have to go to work." There was nothing I could do except fix her. She was going to anyway, and I would rather do it myself because there was no telling what might happen to her. I was afraid she'd get an overjolt. I had to do it. I gave her a taste, and she loved it. I thought, "Here we go." She really loved it. And it was too bad. But it ended all the suicides, and our life became much more peaceful.

Diane's sister, Marie, was going with a guy named Bill who had been with the Four Jokers, a singing group. Bill's mother had a lot of money, so she set him up running a hotel in Palm Springs. It was more like a motel, but fairly large; there was a bar. Bill had a comedian playing there, Yuki Sharon, a Jewish comedian who played piano and told jokes; Bill tended bar and sang and played a little snare drum with the brushes. Marie and Bill gave us a call and asked us to come up there, and Bill offered me a job working with Yuki. He said he would give us a place to stay and he would pay me a salary, so I said yeah.

Yuki Sharon looked like a caricature of a Jewish comedian. He was like a fat Sid Gould, and Sid Gould was the most Jewish-looking Jewish comedian I've ever seen. And he was the dirtiest Jewish comedian I've ever seen. He used to work for Blinky Palermo in Philadelphia in the underworld after-hours club. Yuki Sharon looked like him, with the big circles under the eyes, and Yuki was a great wit. He told good jokes and loved good jazz, the old jazz, and he played sort of like Fats Waller, simple but pleasant. It was easy work. We'd blow together and then he'd stop and tell a joke in the middle of the tune; I just followed him; and then, on a couple of songs, I was featured—he'd play behind me. It was enjoyable, and Bill gave me a good salary. Since we ate there and got our room for nothing, whatever I made was clear. We saved most of it because we had stopped using.

We stopped because it got impossible for me to support two habits. Now I was getting Percodan from a doctor, and we were getting Dexamyl Spansules, and we were drinking Cosanyl cough syrup—Cosanyl had dihydrocodeinone in it, which was very strong. So between the Percodan and the Dexamyl and the Cosanyl and pot and juicing very heavy I was doing good because I wasn't using heroin.

The first day we went to Palm Springs, the police were waiting for us when we came back to our car. They put us up against the car and searched it, the whole thing, because a '47 Pontiac sedan was an East L.A. or a Temple Street gang car. It wasn't like anything they had in Palm Springs. I explained the situation, the fact that I had a record. I had to tell them the truth because I didn't want to take a chance of anything back-firing on me. They told me to go to the police station and get a work permit and they said, "Once the cops get to know your car everything will be okay, but if you could get a better car you'd save yourself a lot of grief." In Palm Springs they try to keep up a certain air of respectability.

It was embarrassing, and we felt bad, so Bill said, "Let's go down and look around for a car. I'll give you an advance. We'll work something out." This was in '58, and we found a '57 Lincoln that was just beautiful. It was a convertible. It had a fantastic maroon paint job and a white top. Inside there were fur rugs, actual fur, and every single thing had a push button. It had been made for the shah of Iran. He'd ordered eight cars, all special, but two he hadn't taken, and this was one that had been used by somebody in Palm Springs and then traded in. It was in perfect shape. I told Bill, "God, I'd love to have that." I was afraid he wouldn't go for it but he said, "Well, you don't have anything else to spend your money on. Okay. If we can get it through, great." He signed for me. We got the credit, and the payments were ninety-nine dollars and fifty cents a month. At that time that was really high. I stayed on that job for quite a while, and Diane and I were getting along pretty good because there's nothing like success.

And then—I forget what happened—I think Bill's mother got angry at him. At any rate, she cut him off; he blew the hotel; and it ended the job. We had to go back to Los Angeles.

When we got back to L.A. we moved out to Studio City into a motel, and I looked in the newspaper for a job because I wanted to keep the car; I was really in love with it. I became an accordian salesman. I'd go to people's houses and give the kids musical aptitude tests. I'd play a note and then another note and ask them which one sounded higher. I'd ask them little rhythmical questions. I'd put this pretty little accordian on the kids, the keys all mother-of-pearl; they'd fall in love with it.

My territory was East Los Angeles, downtown L.A., Glendale, and Pasadena, a pretty large area. I'd get three leads a night, and if I sold the kid, if I could get the parents to give me ten dollars, then the kid got a certain number of lessons and he'd use one of those accordians for a while. I'd keep the ten dollars. After he finished this series of lessons the high-pressure salesman went out. *He'd* say he's taking the little accordian away, but if the kid wants to *continue*, he can march in the Rose Parade and all that. And the salesman would show him a great big accordian that cost a fortune. The kids would cry, and the parents, who were just scuffling and starving to death . . . It was really sad. But in another way it was good because some of the kids really did have musical talent.

I did that for a while and did fairly well. I remember my first time out I sold all three leads and got thirty dollars. But it was hard work, and it became harder and harder to mantain the payments on the car, and a Lincoln, it costs a lot of money to get them repaired. You have to keep them up. Fortunately, instead of starting to use again we continued with the Cosanyl. I was getting fat, and people saw me and thought I was clean. Finally, this guy Steve White—who is kind of a legend around L.A., extremely talented and likable but totally crazy—I ran into him; he was playing with a rock group from North Carolina and he asked me if I wanted a gig—replacing him on tenor with that group. So I started working at this club in the valley called the Palomino.

Then Les Koenig asked me to do another album. I was really down with the tenor so I made *Art Pepper plus Eleven* playing alto, tenor, and clarinet. Marty Paich wrote all the arrangements. They were modern jazz classics, and I used large bands, well-known people, good musicians. When I did that, things started to open up for me. Diane and I moved from the motel to a nice little house in Studio City. I got a job at the Lighthouse working steady. Marty Paich started using me on a lot of Mel Tormé's things and with other singers.

THE RETURN OF ART PEPPER by Jack Tynan

Hollywood—For Art Pepper the long, lean years are over.

Fast reestablishing himself as one of the most important altoists in modern jazz, busy with Howard Rumsey's Lighthouse All-Stars five nights a week and Sunday afternoons, the 35-year-old musician today has put his troubled times well behind him and is now seeking greater expressiveness as an artist.

So busy is Pepper, in fact, that it is hard to believe that only a year ago, he was selling accordions—along with lessons on the instrument—to make a living. He had no work to speak of, and had become a stranger in the recording studios where his name had been linked with the foremost experimenters a scant five years previous. To those musicians with whom he occasionally came in contact, he seemed a ghost of his old self. He appeared to have lost all interest in jazz and the playing of it.

"It's true I was pretty disinterested in music at that time," Pepper admits today. "But I began to put down the *music* rather than the circumstances."

In Art's case, the "circumstances" stretch a long way back. They cover his youth in Gardena, Calif.; his early days of sitting in with jazz greats when Los Angeles' Central Avenue and Main Street were swinging with all-night sessions; his first big break with the Benny Carter band when, as a 17-year-old, he sat alongside the late trumpeter Freddie Webster and trombonist J. J. Johnson; the great days with the Stan Kenton orchestra, and the oblivion that followed.

All these "circumstances" added up for the sax player to a total sum of disillusionment with music and a jazz world that did not seem exactly ready to welcome back Art Pepper with open arms. There was a brief period of recording in 1955–56, and an alliance with tenorist Jack Montrose that came to little but scattered night club engagements. The albums that emerged in that period were uniformly good, mostly quartet discs that showcased Pepper's flexible and dynamic style. The last of the quartet sessions, recorded for the Aladdin label, was never released on LP, though it is available on Omegatape. It is of special interest due to the presence on the date of the late pianist Carl Perkins. It was Perkins' final recording.

Withal, the deadly "circumstances" found their mark. Pepper became more depressed at the lack of recording calls, and at the repeated attempts to launch his own group in a town of clubowners ready to buy music for clowns. And so he withdrew from music, retreating into a personal shell that was made a little less lonely by his wife, Diane.

Today Pepper can say, without undue display of emotion, "Diane's understanding saved me; I owe so much to her." And it is true that in Pepper's darkest hours, when making a living in music seemed nothing more than a bad joke, Diane stiffened his will to endure and, finally, to return to jazz more eloquent than ever. *down beat, April 14, 1960. Copyright 1960 by down beat. Reprinted by special permission.*

THINGS were getting good. I bought a dog for Christmas for Diane. Actually, I bought it for myself. It cost three hundred dollars, a little champagne poodle, and we named her Bijou. I got more and more work. I got a call from André Previn at MGM to do the soundtrack on *The Subterraneans*, and I got to play a lot of solos. Then I got a call from Mickey Whalen, the music director at MGM, and I did *Bells Are Ringing*. I was drinking the Cosanyl, which is very fattening, and I was steadily putting on weight. I went from a hundred and fifty up to a hundred and ninety-five. People would see me and say, "Boy, you really look great!" And, "It's great to see you clean!" Between the two of us Diane and I were drinking three pints of this stuff a day and I was juicing heavy, but all our bills were paid; there was money in the bank; and I still had the Lincoln.

I had gone through a crisis and survived. Now I had a tenor, an alto, a clarinet, and a bunch of suits. I had just about everything I wanted, but I wasn't happy with Diane, you know, because I never had loved her. I married her because—I don't even know why now—I felt I owed it to her and I thought maybe, maybe I could just *learn* to love her, but it never happened. Right at this time Les wanted to do another album so he got another Miles Davis rhythm section: Wynton Kelly on piano, Jimmy Cobb on drums, and Paul Chambers, the only holdover, on bass. I was really prepared for this album, *Gettin' Together*, and it was excellent. I played great, and I wrote some of the arrangements. I wrote a tune that I recorded for Diane.

Well, I wrote a tune and named it "Diane." It was a dream of somebody I would have liked to have had, and I called it "Diane" because I figured it would make her happy, and it did. The tune was way too beautiful for her, but what was a name?

I had the world by the tail. There was no end to what could have happened for me at that time. One night I had a record date—I forget who it was with, a singer—and after the session I was riding home on the freeway from Hollywood to Studio City, which is a very short distance; I was riding in my Lincoln, and I had the radio on, and I remember Ray Charles was singing "The Outskirts of Town," and all of a sudden I got very sad, I just got very sad, and I thought, "This isn't it. Something is wrong." I took my turnoff on Whitsett and turned left under the freeway and, without even thinking, I just made another left turn back onto the freeway; now I was headed toward Hollywood to the Hollywood freeway, which goes to the Santa Ana freeway, which goes to East Los Angeles, which is where all my old connections were, all my friends from my heroin days.

I turned the radio up and drove. I took the cutoff on Brooklyn Avenue, and there I was. I drove to this broad's pad that I used to know, Rachel. She and her brother, Boy, still lived at the same place, and they were so happy to see me. It was really a homecoming. They said, "Wow, look at the car!" Hora le, Art!" They were talking Chicano to me, and I was talking Chicano back, and I asked them if they had any stuff. They said, "Yeah, what do you want?" I said, "Can you still get a quarter for fifty dollars?" I had a whole pocketfull of money. I reached in my wallet and gave them fifty dollars. Boy said, "I'll go. I'll be right back!" He came back with a condom with a quarter of an ounce of heroin. I said, "You got a 'fit, pistolo?" He got it out, and I said, "Let me go first, then you can go." I took a fix and I said, "Wow, this is it!" I was happy again. I stayed there bullshitting for a long time, and then I took the shit. I said, "You got an extra spike?"

I went home, and as I drove up the dog started barking. I parked the car and walked in, and Diane said, "Where've you been? I've been worried." I took the condom and threw it on the table. I threw the outfit out and I said, "Go ahead." And that was it. The beginning of the end. Six months later I was busted, on my way to San Quentin, and Diane was in the Orange County Hospital on her way to death.

ART PEPPER

Art Pepper Plus Eleven—Contemporary M 3568: *Move; Groovin' High; Opus De Funk; 'Round Midnight; Four Brothers; Shawnuff; Bernie's Tune; Walkin' Shoes; Anthropology; Airegin; Walkin'; Donna Lee.*

Personnel: Pepper, alto, tenor saxophones, clarinet; Pete Candoli or Al Porcino, Jack Sheldon, trumpets; Dick Nash, trombone; Bob Enevoldsen, tenor saxophone, valve trombone; Vince DeRosa, French horn; Herb Geller or Bud Shank or Charlie Kennedy, alto saxophone; Bill Perkins or Richie Kamuca, tenor saxophone; Med Flory, baritone saxophone; Russ Freeman, piano; Joe Mondragon, bass; Mel Lewis, drums.

Rating: ★ ★ ★ ★ ★

This is a highly satisfactory album for which Marty Paich, who conducts and did the arranging, deserves a full measure of credit.

The tunes read like a jazz hit parade of the '40s and '50s, and Paich has treated them with the reverence and seriousness they deserve while still retaining wit and a freshness of view. Pepper, in the context of this group, turns out one of his best performances on record. As an altoist, he immediately assumes his place again in the front rank with the added virtue of successfully escaping the tyranny of Charlie Parker's spirit and still keeping that full-blown swing. He is surprisingly sensitive and moving on clarinet (*Anthropology* of all things!), and if he ever gets seriously down to work on that instrument as his major, there's room to believe he might be the one to bring it up to the point of development of the other solo horns.

On tenor he is a solidly swinging, toughminded soloist, but it is on alto, still, that he shines. The whole album is in excellent taste, the solos by Freeman here and there are a gas, too, and Lewis provides a fine, swinging foundation. (R.J.G.) down beat, *February 16, 1960. Copyright 1960 by down beat. Reprinted by special permission.*

(Marty Paich) In the fifties, when I first came across Art, shortly after World War II, when we had a quartet in town, it seemed like there wasn't that much anxiety as there is today. That is, people played, and they enjoyed themselves. Today there's such an emotional stress on performers; this total commitment to try to be number one has really destroyed a lot of artists, and record companies and agents and managers have sort of manipulated the artist, trying so hard to make him number one. It has become very difficult. With so much money in the music business today, so many people are pressing, and it has a definite effect on the artist.

When I first met Art he was the greatest saxophone player that I had heard. Far above anybody else. I couldn't believe how beautifully he played. And at that time there was the battle going on: a lot of writers were writing about East Coast Jazz and West Coast Jazz. Art to me was the sound of West Coast jazz, that melodic style he played, rather than the hard-driving, New York style that a lot of players were playing. I just fell in love with him the first time I heard him. And then eventually we worked together.

I didn't work with Art for a long time, until he went over to Contemporary and he wanted me to do some writing for him. I was with Shorty Rogers at the time, and Art used to come and sit in an awful lot, and I was starting to write a lot of arrangements in the early fifties. Art liked certain things I did, and that's when he asked me to the *Art Pepper plus Eleven*. We collaborated on that album. Incidentally, that album got five stars in *down beat*. It was an incredible album, and I got a lot of letters from people talking about that album, and they still are talking about that album.

I felt, and I feel to this day, that Art is the number-one saxophone player around for my particular taste. I liked him so much; well, we were doing a lot of commercial sessions. I started to get very busy arranging, and I had a lot of albums to do. At that time, I was working with a lot of singers so I'd bring Art just in by himself. On Jesse Belvin's album; I think he played on Lena Horne's album; he played on several albums that I did at RCA Victor when I brought him in just to hear him play. Then we became good friends. Of course, my direction at that time was going more and more into arranging, and Art still had his quartet, so we really didn't see each other too much except when he was in town. I'd try to get together with him and call him and have him come down and play.

Art was, he looked like a movie star to me. He was in good shape, pitch-black hair; he looked marvelous, you know, he looked like Tyrone Power; he was so handsome, and he had a lot of poise, very quiet, a lot of class. When he came on, people quieted down, and when he played he played with such authority. There was standing room only for Art when we played a lot of clubs or when I went into a lot of clubs to hear him. And people just loved to be associated with him. Everybody loved to be in his company. When Art was in the room there was a certain magic that was happening. If he was there, that's where the action was. When the word got around that we were going to do *Art Pepper plus Eleven*, I had innumerable calls from practically everybody in town, top players, wanting to be on the session because they had the feeling that . . . It was just electrifying all the time Art was around. I can't say enough about him. And when he called me to do the *Plus Eleven* I was just elated that we were going to work together. We spent a lot of time together, and I really gave my all as far as writing is concerned. I felt I had to prove myself to Art. I wanted to try and come close to his stature, you know what I mean, and that's where we were at that particular time. There have been saxophone players that have come and gone, but Art's in a class by himself. There isn't even anybody close.

Art is just a simple human being. Simple, artistically, and very easy to understand, for me. He just wanted to play. His personality was just beautiful all the time. I didn't associate with him too much, I'm talking about socially, but when we worked together I found I never had any problem with Art Pepper, never one small disagreement. He said to me, "Just do what you think." And he did what he did, and I made suggestions, and Art would say, "Fine." Very soft-spoken, very laid back, never any problem. Whereby today, if Art and I were young kids working, there might be disagreements because of the way things are, the stress. A lot of players today are so concerned with the success factor. In our situation, we were striving for the artistic thing rather than trying to think of agents and managers and a lot of money, which is involved today. In those days, we didn't even *think* about the money aspect. We just wanted to play and to write. Today guys half play, and then the other half of it is money right away. And the minute money enters into it, it's a totally different ball game. Art and I just hit it off, and it has always been that way, and everybody I knew felt exactly the same way. And not too long ago, when we used him on Melanie's album, he just came in; fifteen years had gone by and he was exactly the same way.

I was never involved with drugs myself. Certain players striving for total excellence, trying to go as far as they could artistically—a lot of them felt they needed it, most of the players that I knew. Well, like I say, I didn't get involved in too many of their lives socially, you know. I could only stand by the side and hope it wouldn't happen because in the end it has a devastating effect. I never was around Art when I thought he was out of control. He always had that same composure and played beautifully, and I couldn't tell whether he had been on drugs or if he was straight. There were one or two times that Art showed up late on my sessions, but I understood what the situation was and it didn't bother me at all. I just loved him so much that I sort of bypassed it and worked around it because I knew when he got there, everything was going to be fine. And this came later. Not in the earlier times. It was later that the problems started to happen. But, you know, people in this town at that time: if you showed up late, it got to be a scene, and the word would get around, and things like that, but, listen, that is *nothing* compared to today. Today players show up two or three hours late with nothing said, so, you know, signs of the times.

One thing musically that I definitely have to stress, and that is the fact that in addition to Art playing such beautiful notes . . . There were many players that did play a lot of nice notes, but they floated. They sort of moved around the swinging part of it. They were so engrossed in the technical aspect of what they were doing to get the notes, the swinging suffered. But Art had them both together. He had the notes, and he was swinging all the time. That's very important. I hope you mention that. Art *always* swung, and that's the thing that put him above everybody else. And he played all the instruments, and he played them all exactly the same. He put them in his mouth, and it was Art Pepper. I don't care if it was baritone, tenor, clarinet. He's the greatest. He always will be.

(Steve Kravitz)   I think it was in the early part of 1960 that I met him. I was Art's student until probably a month or two before he got busted.

It was really weird. I had some class in high school and for one of the assignments you had to interview someone in the profession you wanted to go into. So all these people in the class were making appointments with accounting firms. I went to the Lighthouse because Art was playing there with Conte Candoli, and I asked Art if I could talk to him, and he said okay. I listened to the band, and then they took a break, and Art said wait a minute, and Conte sat down and started talking to me. I was so naive at the time. He was layin' all this stuff on me, like, "My family doesn't know I'm out here playin'. They think I'm back in New York sellin' dope." I said, *"Really?"* I was sixteen years old. As soon as he said that and I reacted to it honestly, I realized that he was puttin' me on. Art was still in the kitchen, and Conte wanted to know what I was doin', and I told him that I was here to interview Art for this project, and Conte said, "Why the hell don't you study with him?" I said, "Well, uh." It never occurred to me that somebody like that would teach. I didn't know anything about musicians. To me, Art, guys like that, were *stars* like Marlon Brando. It never occurred to me that I'd get as far as I'd actually gotten. I had his albums. I listened to them all the time.

Art came out of the kitchen, and Conte left, so I asked him the questions. They gave you a list. Then I asked him about studying with him. My heart was goin' like this. And he said, "Oh, yeah." I remember he had an incredible Lincoln car. I remember it being pink; maybe it was maroon. It had to be the biggest car ever made. I asked him, "How do you make it from the valley to the Lighthouse?" And he said, "Well, I spend most of my paycheck on gas."

He gave me his address and told me to call him and we would set up something. I was so stupid. I didn't even know about answering services. I called him and got the service, and

in my mind . . . They just said, "Art Pepper." I thought I'd got
the maid. I figured if a cat was that famous, he had a lot of
bread. And this was a period when he was really goin'. He'd
made the *Art Pepper plus Eleven* album. He was really tight
with Marty Paich, and he was doin' all that stuff.

We set up a time, and I went out there. He lived on Ventura
Court. It's an alley. One little street north of Ventura Boulevard
at Whitsett. It was three doors up, small living room, one
bedroom, shower. It was right behind a bar that's now called
the Queen's Arms. The first time I went out there I couldn't
find Ventura Court to save my life. I drove around for half an
hour. You know, Whitsett goes right up the hill, so I drove up
the hill because I was still on this trip about the maid and the
big house. It had to be in the *hills*. I finally stopped and called
and it turned out I was right across the street. When I got
there it was kind of a surprise.

I guess he had me play. I don't remember how we got
started, but I do remember he writes out all his lessons. They're
beautiful. He'd write out an exercise and a duet and a jazz
étude, and for my assignment I had to write an exercise and a
duet. It wasn't just playing. We played through some stuff, and
he had me do some sight-reading to see how I did. He hated the
mouthpiece I had. He was always handing me his. I had a
metal mouthpiece, and his was rubber. I hated the way I
sounded on his mouthpiece. Little did I know. When you switch
from metal to rubber you get a darker sound at first, and that's
what I was hearing. He didn't push it though. The lessons were
around an hour and a half. I pulled out my wallet to pay him
at the end of the first lesson and realized I'd left all my money
at home. I almost went through the floor. He got really nervous.
He was still playing at the Lighthouse, so I said, "I'll bring it
out there tonight." He said, "I've really got to have the money."
I was so embarrassed I could have crawled under anything. I
went that night with a friend of mine to the Lighthouse, and I
remember when I walked in Art waved to me, which was a big
thrill. I just handed him the bread, right there in front of . . . I
was so excited. I had no idea what was going on. To me he was
just Art Pepper, my idol. I had no idea what was going on at
all.

Diane was always there at the lessons, and she was always

nice. And they had a little, white poodle, nice and friendly. I went there once for a lesson and Art picked up his clarinet because he didn't have his tenor. He said it had gotten stolen, and I felt real bad. Now I realize he'd probably hocked it. He picked up the clarinet and he played this incredible, beautiful bebop lick, and I, oh, wow! So many people love Art's clarinet sound. They hate everybody else, Benny Goodman, Artie Shaw, Jimmy Giuffre, Buddy DeFranco, and they love Art Pepper on clarinet. He played this lick that really knocked me out. I think this was the second lesson.

I had been told to write an exercise out. He'd said, "It's an exercise so make it difficult, something that will make you *work*." I wrote this incredible, unmusical, impossible exercise. You know, leaps from the top of the horn to the bottom, silly rhythms. I'd done a little writing in high school and I really went out of my way. He tried it and he couldn't play it. Nobody could have played it. And he said, "Well, you'll never have to play anything *this* hard." He wrote out some more études and another duet, and we worked them out.

One time he came to my house for a lesson because I lived near his father and he was going to be out that way. And that was really a trip. Art Pepper's comin' over! I'd been working on a little blues tune and I wasn't sure about some of the notation, so he wrote it out, helped me with that, and put a title on it, something to do with me, and that made it really exciting. Then we had some coffee, standing outside and talking, and I remember he was saying he was playing one of Bud Shank's altos because his alto had been stolen, too, or he'd sold it. This was when he was playing an old Martin. All his admirers were playing old Martins.

I don't remember the intervals between the lessons. I think it was every week, and I think I only had four or five lessons. I had met an older guy who was studying with Art also. This guy was in his twenties, a good tenor player, a serious, dedicated musician. He was the one who said, "You know, I think Art is on heroin. There's a lot of funny stuff going on. I'm going to stop studying with him soon because I don't want to get involved with that." And I thought, "Hmmmm." I think I only had one lesson after that. I got real nervous about this dope thing. I drank, but the dope thing was totally foreign to me and it really bothered me. I think what happened was I just didn't call Art back again because I couldn't decide what to do. And then he got busted. That was the end of it. He didn't recognize me when we first met again playing in the Magruders' rehearsal band. Maybe it's the beard.

Art didn't play like anybody else. He wasn't a technician. He chose the notes. His lines were beautiful. He had a whole different approach to alto. The sound he got, the phrasing. I always got the feeling the notes were, like, bouncing out of the horn, and it was the way he was accenting and phrasing them. I dug his tenor playing, too. It was a very fat, dark, different sound. The album that I really loved was *Art Pepper plus Eleven*. He played alto, tenor, clarinet. I have that on tape in my car. Still. That's about eighteen years and it's still . . . I used to wear that album out. The charts were great; the band was great; and the clarinet solo on "Anthropology!"—the way he built that solo still knocks me out. The first chorus was all down in the low register, kinda laid back; the next chorus was kinda in the middle; the last chorus he played up on the high part of the instrument. It started somewhere and it went somewhere, like, I'm gonna get in the car and go from my house to yours, and I know I'm gonna get there, and Art was playing that solo, and he knew where he was going, and he got there. That's the way all his solos hit me.

I wasn't into changes then. Probably if I'd kept on studying with him, we'd have got there. So, I wasn't hearing the changes in an intellectual way. I was hearing it on a purely musical level: the sound, the notes, the whole thing—the excitement, the beauty, the music!

I don't know if this was true or not. I was at somebody's house, somebody that knew Art and knew what he was doing, and he explained—the few of us that were there were on the ground, dying laughing—about what Art had to go through to get up in the morning. It was, like, a pint of vodka that he'd have at the bed and drink that. Then some scotch. Then he would get up and head for the beer. He would drink more booze in the first hour of his day to get the strength to go out the door and score than most people drink in a month. But I never saw him drunk or strung out. His manner then was the same as it is now.

I've noticed with Art . . . He probably saw Perk and Coop and all the guys who used to make albums with him—they're all doin' studio work now. Suddenly Art's saying, "Wow, man, I've got to play piccolo and flute!" Runnin' around buyin' all these horns. "I'm fifty years old. What am I gonna do?" He says, "Hey, Steve, how do you do this? Who can I call up to play flute duets?" I guess he's come out of that now. But it's easy in this town to be influenced that way. Like, I never set out to become a doubler. I never figured I'd take up flute, piccolo, buy a bass clarinet, get into the bassoon. It just turned out that way. My whole musical scene has been "I want to work on those changes but I'd better practice the flute." I ended up being a doubler, never really getting into jazz playing like I wanted to. And in this town, if you're doing studio work, you're a success. If you're not, you're not a success. Of course, also, that's where the money is. But, when I was twelve years old I didn't take up clarinet because I was thinkin' about how much money I was gonna make. I was thinkin', "Wow, man, I made a note! Wow, man, listen!" But it's true. You can't play jazz and make a living.

The fifties, that was really a stormin' time for recording jazz. And that was great music. Today you have to be really strung out just to sit down and listen to a lot of this stuff. It's like background music. I'll be in the car and turn on the jazz station and they'll be playing some fusion thing, and ten minutes later I'll realize that they're still playing the same thing and I haven't even been hearing it. That stuff Art does, did, does, that's just guys playin' themselves, makin' music. He went through a period where he was playing all that ugly crap. You know, I figure that was just a time when he was trying to explore another direction, see what that was all about. I didn't run into anybody who liked Art during that period. But I'm sure the reason he's playing like he is now is because he allowed himself to go through that period. A lot of guys would say, "Wow, I can't play like that. Nobody's gonna hire me." But that's why there's a book. That's why he's doin' what he's doin'. Because he's always been true to whatever's been going on inside of him.

13 | Stealing

1960

I'VE OFTEN THOUGHT that maybe I was in the wrong thing being a musician. The people I met, the musicians I met playing in clubs or at recording sessions, seemed very unreal to me, insincere, two-faced. I never knew where I stood with them, and I never felt at home with them, and the only way I could relax with them was to be loaded. I'm that way to this day. They're gossips, real politicians. They come on, "Oh, hi!" but behind your back they'll rank you and if they get busted they'll rat on you. And I found when I'd come out of jail they were always looking at my eyes and looking at my arms to see if there were any marks while they were smiling at me and saying, "Oh, how good it is to have you back!"

When I'd started using drugs I ran into a different kind of person. In jail I found people who had honor. They were real. They said what they thought. If someone bad-rapped you to a friend of yours he'd say, "Hey, man, don't talk about him like that! The cat's my friend!" The dopefiends were warm to me and open with me, I felt. And so, on the way home, as I say, I made the turn; I went to East L.A. and scored and saw the people and I had some idea that here were people I could communicate with.

I started using, and for a while I was able to do it. I had so much money. Diane had a fur coat. For a while I was able to buy dope and continue living the way I had been. And the heroin was actually better for me than the Cosanyl. I felt healthier. But that wasn't what I wanted. I had to get really far-out and have everything change, and in order to do that I started using just a ridiculous amount of heroin. And so I put myself in a position where I was no longer able to function, really, where it became obvious to everyone what was happening.

I started coming in a little late, nodding out at the sessions. Little by little people started saying, "Uh-oh, there he goes." Some people tried to talk to me, "Is everything alright?" You know, the few who really cared about me. But I wouldn't accept any help. I didn't want any help. They thought this was something that was happening to me, that I had no control over. But *I* was doing it. Purposely. Purposely doing it for some end that I'm not really sure what it was except that I knew I wasn't happy in this false paradise I had carved out for myself in Studio City.

I guess in order to really make things difficult, I burglarized a doctors' office—I didn't *have* to—in close proximity to where we were living, to put pressure on myself. I couldn't find any money but I got a whole bunch of dope, millions of pills. Diane was really getting messed up. She had decided to go wherever I went and however I went, and I felt bad because what I was doing to myself I didn't want to do to her. I thought, "Well, maybe I'll use these pills to get us cleaned up." And then maybe I could figure out some way to keep her from going down the tubes with me.

We tried to clean up. We went through an unbelievable scene in the little house we lived in, for four days, taking hundreds of pills. I remember I fell down over a table at one point and broke a lamp and cut myself. Diane would fall. It was a nightmare of falling on the floor looking for pills. Diane had dropped the bottles and they broke. Diane was trying to get out of the house. Right near us was a wash, by Ventura Boulevard, with a big drain like a storm drain, and she wanted to go to this wash and fling herself over the bridge. It would have killed her, and she would have done it, but she couldn't get out the door. She couldn't find the door. She never found the door. I swear to God, she could not find the door.

On about the fifth day I came to enough to see that the poor dog was just terrified and starving. I knew I had to take care of the dog. I had a pain in my arm. I looked down at my clothes and they were covered with blood. I wondered if I had killed her, Diane, in my delirium, to be rid of her. I panicked and ran into the other room, but there she was, alive, lying on the floor amidst the broken bottles. She had cuts all over her from trying to find pills on the floor. I fed the dog, and I realized I had to have some heroin. I was so sick I couldn't believe it, and I had no money, no nothing. I left the house and got into the car.

The car, I'd let it go—no oil change, and I was using cheap gas. And that day, as I was driving to East L.A., I ran into the back of another car at a stop sign. No one was hurt but it ruined my car; both front tires were cut. When I finally finished with the cop, I left it where it was and started walking.

I was in Lincoln Heights when I had the wreck, at Five Points, a little area where five streets come together. I walked to East L.A. and found Rachel and Boy. I told them I was deathly ill and I had to have a taste, but I didn't have any money. They saw what awful shape I was in so they turned me on. I said, "I've got to get something for Diane." That's one of the few times people have come through when I really needed dope. Boy said, "I'll drive you home." He couldn't believe his eyes when we got into the house. The dog was so frightened she peed all over the floor when we went in, and I felt so guilty for the poor dog. Diane was crawling on the floor. Boy helped me put her in a chair. I fixed her, and it brought her back to life. She looked around and told me that she had been trying for days to find the door to get out to throw herself off the bridge.

I saw that I couldn't stop like that. I didn't want to stop. I had completely messed up my jobs now—missed a couple and ruined everything. I was already just about written off by everyone.

About four months after I made that trip on the freeway and just after this attempt to clean up, I went down to East L.A. to score and I ran into a couple of friends of mine, Frank and Ruben, and they wanted to rob a nightclub in Studio City. Both of them were old-timers, been using a long time, and they were pretty sharp.

Frank and I had been friends for a while. I'd scored from him, and he'd helped me out occasionally. Frank made me think of a Mexican Mickey Cohen. He always wore suits, and he had a nice car, the big Thunderbird, which was a classy car at that time. He had a cold look about him; he was an intense person. He wore glasses and was very intelligent, spoke good English, knew his way around. He was really respected in East L.A. in the drug culture.

Ruben was a real relaxed, down-home type cat. Chubby. I don't think he even owned a suit. He wasn't intelligent as far as schooling went, but he was very smart in the ways of the streets and he was smart in the ways of crime. Ruben was very open and warm and friendly, and we really got tight. He was always laughing and a lot of fun to be around.

Ruben's father did landscaping. He had a gardening truck, so Ruben and I used to get together and go around, just for kicks, in this truck and do a couple of gardening jobs to get money to cop with. And while we were doing that we would be boosting things, stealing. I'd never done anything like that until after I came out of jail, but then, little by little, each time I went to jail and came out it got a little easier accepting that role.

Frank and Ruben saw that I was really strung out again so they asked me if I would be interested in making a little bread. Frank said, "There's a nightclub out in the valley I've been casing. We'd like to burglarize it. You're in if you'd like to do it." I said alright. I was broke by this time. I'd gone through just about everything and was already owing rent. I said, "Where's this place at?" Frank said, "That's one of the problems. It's right next to your house." The club he was referring to was one of these great big places on Ventura Boulevard, next door to where I was living. I realized that if I did this job I'd probably have to move, but I said okay. I wanted to see if I had the nerve to do something like that. When I was in jail I'd heard guys talk, and I wanted to see if I could do a righteous burglary like that, with weapons, so I said alright.

About a week before the job, Diane and I left the house. We didn't tell the landlady. We went and stayed with Frank in East L.A. We took everything out of the house, but we moved our stuff just a little at a time so the neighbors wouldn't know we were leaving and notify the landlady. We had to have access to the house to burglarize the nightclub.

They decided to do it on a Saturday night, actually Sunday morning. We drove out there in the Thunderbird. Frank had a black leather jacket on and a pair of black slacks. And he was wearing a hat, a stingy-brim hat. He was a dapper cat. There were two guns, and I wasn't allowed to have one. They were afraid with my inexperience I might get nervous and fire when there was no need to, which was a drag for me. I felt I should have one just in case. I was voted out of having a gun.

We parked in back and entered the house through the back door. We didn't turn on any lights. We used candles. When it got to be about 2:30 Frank went down the street to a pay phone and called the club. Somebody answered. He asked about reservations and came back. At 3:15 he called again, and there was no answer. He waited and called again. No answer. He let it ring and ring. Then he walked by the club and looked at it from all sides. There were no lights, no cars in the lot. He came back to the house and said, "Everything is ready. There's no one there."

The plan was to cut a hole in the wall. The hole would come out in the kitchen area. They would go from there into the club itself, search that, take whatever was stashed, and then go upstairs into the manager's office, where the safe was, with the money. Ruben was one of the best safe men in East L.A. Guys would pull burglaries; they would have the hole already drilled and cut; and then they'd go get Ruben to open the safe.

Frank said to me, "You're going to be the lookout. That means I want you to look out the front windows and the side windows and keep circulating, keep your ears open. If you hear anything take this flashlight and signal us." I saw them getting the tools out and I said, "Why do you have to go through the wall?" They said, "You can't go through the doors because there's alarms on the doors. You have to go through the roof or a hole in the wall."

They went out and started the hole. I could see them from the bedroom window. Their manner was very businesslike. They didn't waste any time. It was almost like surgeons working, you know: "Chisel. Wire cutters." The side of the building was stucco, but every so often as they went through the wall they'd find a big piece of wire mesh (I think there were about three of them, to make the wall strong), and each time they came to the mesh they had to cut—they had to make a hole large enough for a body to get through. It was hard work, and every now and then I'd hear an "owwwww!" when they'd cut themselves or when they'd be straining to bend the wire back.

I'm listening, pointing, and it's very spooky at this time of the morning. Very cold and damp. I'm walking around this abandoned house that's just a mess, with the broken pill bottles on the floor and a few old pieces of furniture. I'd wanted to fix before we did the job, but they had rationed the dope out. We'd fixed at around nine o'clock so we'd be clearheaded. After a certain length of time, about three or four hours after you fix, you become very aware, keenly aware, and as you start to get sick you really become conscious and supersensitive to everything—feelings, sounds.

They kept working, working, it seemed like forever, and then I heard, "I think that's it." "Yeah, I think so." They both came into the house and Frank said, "Alright. We're going in. You've got to really be careful now, man. If anything happens you've gotta run to the hole and holler inside." Both of them put handkerchiefs around their faces, and they took their guns out.

Frank went first and then Ruben, really not knowing if there was someone waiting inside. I kept running from the back of the house to the front, into the yard, listening, watching, and every now and then I'd hear a car or a siren. Finally, they came to the hole and called for me. They had a bundle, bottles of whiskey, and they had a bagful of change, money from the machines—cigarette machines and things like that. We put it in the car. I said, "Is everything alright?" Ruben said, "I don't know, man." Frank said, "There's an office upstairs, just like I thought, where the money is, but the door to the office is locked and it's wired. There's an alarm system into the office and, I don't know, there could be someone hiding in there, sleeping in there." We were standing in the bedroom of the house; they were debating what to do; and I was thinking that we'd gone through all this hassle and we weren't going to get anything. Ruben said, "Well, I think I can take care of the alarm. Run it back into itself. Rewire it." I said to Frank, "Why don't you give me a gun. Let me go into the office." I really wanted to do something that would be exciting and dangerous, and I really needed the money. Frank said, "I'll do it. That's okay." Ruben went in. After a while he came back to the hole and said, "Everything's cool. I got the thing turned around." Frank went in and he said, "Keep your fingers crossed."

They had hoped to have everything done while it was still

dark; now it wouldn't be long before daylight, and I'm getting panicked. We should have already been out of there, long gone out of there. We don't know if a silent alarm has been tripped, if the police are sneaking up to get us coming out with the stuff. Here I am without a gun. I can see myself getting hung with the whole thing and them getting away. I'm standing out by the hole, and all of a sudden here's Ruben, and he's got a big smile on his face. He says, "Help me out of here, man." He was too tired to push out of the hole. I pulled him and I said, "What happened?" And here comes Frank. He says, "Here, take this." He hands out a box, a little box, and I say, "What's this?" He says, "That's it." He comes out and I say, "That's it?" He says, "That's it."

And the money wasn't in a safe. It was in a strongbox. He handed me this box, and boy, my heart was pounding, and I said, "Is this it?" He said, "Yeah, man, we really lucked out. There was no one there, and everything's cool. Let's get outta here!" We covered the hole with brush to keep it from being visible. We got into the car, and Frank said to me, "Why don't you drive, man?" Both of them were tired and cut up from breaking into the hole. It was daylight now.

I got on the freeway, the same freeway I'd taken my little excursion on when I'd decided to go back to my dopefiend life. There's no cops, no black and whites, no motorcycles. And so, after we'd traveled a certain distance I realized that we had made it. I looked over at Frank and said, "Man, let me have a drink." He handed me one of the bottles with the pouring spouts on them. I took four big shots. I was already starting to get sick. I was really strung out but I was just so happy. We're driving along, and Frank opens the box and says, "Wow!" I look over and I see that there's just stacks of money. I felt so happy. I had never felt any elation like that before. It was a feeling of power, a feeling of accomplishment. I really felt like a man. I don't think I've ever been so satisfied with anything I've done. I looked at the other people on the streets and I thought, "They ain't nothin' compared to me! I'm a giant! King Pepper! King Arthur! Mr. Jazz! Mr. Everything!"

We went to Ruben's house. He had a place in back of his parents', a little shed. Sometimes he'd go back there with guys to fix, and his parents knew he did that with his friends. It was cool to do that. We went in to count the money. Naturally I wouldn't get as big a share as they did. They were the brains behind the thing. They had the guns. They had the plan. They had cut me in. I had done a good job, but naturally I wouldn't get as much as they did. We counted up the money. They were going to throw the checks away but I said, "No, let me have them." They said, "You know you've got to be awfully careful. You've got to hold them for a while, and when you finally do pass them you've got to be careful where you pass them. And if anything happens, that's you. Period." I said, "I know that. You don't have to worry about me." They said, "Well, you've been in prison. You know what it's all about." And I did. It made me happy that they trusted me, and I had no worry about my ability to stand up under a bust and to take whatever I had to take. I said, "Let me have the checks."

Frank gave them to me, and then he handed me a little money sack. I didn't question or count or anything. Whatever I got was what I deserved. We left Ruben at the pad, and Frank and I got in his car and went to his house, where I was staying. The Mexicans that are married have a life separate from their wives'. The wife stays home and takes care of the kids and the house, and the man goes out. That's the way it's always been. The wife doesn't ask any questions. Frank drove me to the pad and said, "Tell Lupe I'll see her later on. I'm going to get some Menudo." He was going to see his mistress too. He let me off. I said, "Man, thank you!" I was so elated. I was talking a mile a minute, and he was kind of chuckling. I wanted to kiss him I was so happy.

I walked to the house and looked around to make sure everything was okay. I've got this money sack, and I hold it behind my back. I knock on the door real quiet. We were sleeping in the front room. Diane comes to the door, sees it's me, and opens it. She says, "What happened?" We were really late. Frank's old lady comes and she says, "Is everything alright?" I say, "Yeah." And I took this bag, and I opened it, and I turned it like *that*, and money flew all over the room.

We got all the money together and counted it. We had over thirteen hundred dollars in cash. That was my share. There was three or four thousand in checks, but it remained to be seen whether I could cash any of them. As it worked out, we cashed a lot of them. When you have checks like that you give them to certain people: you take a percentage and they take the risk. They go through them and take the ones they think they can cash, on consignment, and they pay you as they cash each one. When they finish, they lay the rest back on you. We made almost a thousand dollars on that, so I ended up with about twenty-three hundred dollars for one night's work, and I felt like a real success. I felt that my dad would be proud of me. I wished he could have seen me and gone through the whole night with me, being aware of what was happening, what I did.

I was really sick. I had forgotten all about it; now it hit me. I said to Lupe, "Man, here!" I laid some bread on her and I said, "Give me a quarter." She said, "No, here," and she gave me ten back. She gave me a quarter for forty dollars, and it was good stuff. I put it in the spoon. I told Diane, "I'm going to go first." She said, "Go ahead." And for about a week we were in heaven.

The money from the burglary went fast. When you're doing nothing but using, money really goes. Diane went. I'll talk about that later. Finally, all I had left was Bijou, the poodle, and I was going out boosting every day to get money for dope.

I usually went with a guy named Rudy who had an old Plymouth. We'd drive out together and steal tools. We'd go to building sites in East L.A. When the workers ate their lunches they'd all sit facing the same way, facing the street or the sun, and they'd leave all their tools hooked up, the drills and sanders. One of us would sneak up over the big piles of dirt where they were digging foundations and unhook the tools, get as many as we could carry, and get out. You'd have to crawl, and it was scary because if these guys ever caught us . . . They were rough guys, construction workers, and you were taking their tools that they worked to pay for. As soon as you got out, the other guy would drive up and you'd jump in the car and get away.

I was just moving around, staying at motels and different people's pads, and I didn't like to leave the dog behind so I was taking Bijou with me when I went out boosting. And one time we were driving, me and Rudy and Bijou, near Olympic and Indiana, and we spotted an auto paint place so we stopped. Rudy would go one way, and I'd go another; we'd grab what we could get and meet at the car. We both got out. I left Bijou and walked around the corner to the place where they were painting cars. I looked inside and saw a big hydraulic jack; you pump it and the whole car goes up. I snuck into this place and grabbed the thing, and once I grabbed it and started to move it, it was too late to leave it, and what I didn't realize at first was that it had steel wheels, and when I started pulling it, it made this awful noise going over the sidewalk. It made a terrible noise, and I pushed it down the street just as fast as I could.

I get to the corner. I look for Rudy. He's down the other way. I wave. I want him to come immediately, but it's too late, and I can't leave this thing. I roll it to the car. We'd parked on a residential street right off the main thoroughfare, and I saw some people sitting on a porch a few houses down. They were watching me, but I was getting sick, and anyway it was too late to do anything but what I had to do. I open the door, and I'm trying to get this thing into the back seat of this old Plymouth sedan—it was a real beat car, kind of a rusty red color—and I'm just killing myself. I've got grease on me, and the handle hits the roof and rips out what upholstery's left. And there's nothing I can do with Bijou. She's jumping up and down. She wants to play.

I don't know how I got it in the car. It must have weighed a couple tons. I get it in, and I look around, and there's Bijou down by this house with the people on the porch. She's running around the lawn, barking. I holler, "Come on, Bijou!" And I go after her, but she thinks I'm playing so she's running like poodles can. Her ears are flying back, and she's got this smile on her face. She's running like the wind, barking and leaping up in the air. Her tongue is hanging out, and her tail is wagging, and she pounces down on her front paws, stops, looks at me; I get almost up to her and then she runs real fast and, oh God, I said, "Come on, Bijou! Hurry! Please! *Please!*" Some other people come out of their houses to watch. I see Rudy up at the corner. He doesn't have anything, and he's running, and I think, "Uh-oh, something's wrong!" Here he comes, man, and he says, "Let's go! Let's go!" I say, "We gotta get Bijou, man!" So now we're both going after her. Finally I catch her; I get her in the car; and we pull out with all the neighbors looking and her still barking. I thought sure someone would take the license number or something, but what saved us was the fact that this was East L.A. and everybody minds their own business.

I sold Bijou to Ruben. One day I was really sick, waiting for Rudy to come over, and Ruben said, "Why don't you let me take Bijou, man?" His old lady liked her. I looked at the dog, and I knew I couldn't keep her, so I said, "I'll let you take her, but as soon as I get settled I want to buy her back." He said, "Okay, man, but you're not going to get settled. You're just going to jail." I sold Bijou for twenty dollars.

Later on, after I got busted and got out on bail, I went over to Ruben's to see her. I looked out in the yard and couldn't believe my eyes. I said, "Is that *you*, Bijou?" Always before she'd hold her tail straight up. She'd wag it. She'd prance. I saw this dog slinking around with her tail between her legs. She was fat, and she had grease on her. Her head looked like a lion's head. Ruben had trimmed the hair off her body but he'd left it on her head because he was afraid he might hurt her eyes or her ears. She looked at me and started to wag her tail, and then she said, "Ohhhh, God. I look *awful.*"

I talked to Ruben and I said, "What happened to her?" He said, "Oh, she's fine except for her haircut." I said, "Well, how'd she get so fat? She used to be so groovy." He said, "Oh, she likes tortillas and beans, man. We've been feeding her tortillas and beans." I went through a big scene with them, but they finally agreed to sell her back to me. I took her to a grooming parlor. All the other dogs were there, strutting around, and there were beautiful cats sitting in people's laps. I walked in with this fat dog in a rope collar. She didn't even want to go in the door. I had to carry her, and she hid her head so nobody would see her. The nurse took her on the leash, and the dog looked at me and then slunk out of the room hiding her eyes. And all the animals were looking at her, like, "Who is *that*? What is *she* doing here?"

It took a couple hours or a couple days, I don't remember, and I came back. They called my name. The door opens, and here comes Bijou, just prancing out. I had bought her a collar and given it to them, a little diamond collar with blue, beautiful against her champagne color. They'd cleaned her and clipped her. She walked out with her tail up. She strutted out. She looked marvelous. She looked down her nose at all the other dogs and at the people, and then when I petted her she went and peed on the floor as if to say, "There. Take that!"

I kept her until it was time to go back to jail. Then I gave her to Diane's sister, Marie. She had a nice, big home in West L.A.

Boosting is hard. Every day you go through the hassle of stealing some little thing, taking a chance of getting busted, trying to sell it to a fence, going out to score, and by the time you do all that and fix, usually you've shot up all the dope that you got and it's time to go out and steal something else. It was a continuous job. It was a drag.

I'd go to bed at night and maybe I'd have a little bit of dope left. I knew if I had a getup, if I could fix in the morning, I'd be able to get started. But what would happen, I'd go to sleep and dream about dope. Dream about police chasing me. Dream about jail. And I would wake up at three, four o'clock in the morning, soaked with sweat and panicked. These dreams had just taken all the dope out of me, I felt. And so I would invariably shoot my getup, go back to sleep, and then wake up at eight and not have anything and be sick. And then that thing would start of running around trying to figure out how to get money and where to score.

So many things could go wrong. There's been times when I'd be going to one connection, and everything was running along smooth, and then one day I'd make the phone call and some strange voice would answer or his old lady, "Yeah? He's not here anymore." Or, "He doesn't live here." I would have to find another connection. I'd have to go all over. Then I'd run into somebody, and I'd ask the guy does he have anything, and he'd say, "No, man, I just sold my last gram, but I know where I can score for you, man." So you don't want to, but the only thing you can do is go with him. And here you are with some guy in a car in all kinds of weird neighborhoods. You're in places where it's real hot as far as the heat goes, and you don't feel safe. And you're trying to figure out some way to score without putting the money out in front because you might get burned, but the guy says, "Man, I gotta have the bread. I *can't* take you to the man. I gotta have the bread to buy the stuff. If you don't trust me, forget it, man." He'd get indignant. So you had to be cool, and you might give him twenty or fifty dollars, and that's *it*. That's your money, and you're sick already, and you think, "What if he doesn't come back?"

I've had guys let me off on a corner, and the police are going by, and I've got to find a place where they won't see me vomiting, but there's nowhere to go. I'm waiting and watching every car. The guy says, "I'll be back in ten minutes." And you look at the time, and it seems like an hour, and it's only been eight, nine minutes. Pretty soon it's twenty minutes. Then it's an hour, two hours, three hours, and you panic but you can't leave the spot because if you leave the guy's got a perfect excuse to burn you. You have to stay. And you're thinking of all the things . . . You could get rousted. You could get picked up for marks; in those days if you had marks on your arms they could throw you in jail. And then you'd have to go to jail sick. You're thinking of how wonderful it feels when you put the needle in. It takes all the cold away and the chills and the agony from your mind.

Finally the guy comes back. He drives up and he looks at you and shakes his head, kind of frantic, and right away you know there's some kind of game going. The guy'll drive by and pretend that the heat are behind him, and then he'll sneak back to the street and whistle at you, and you'll go over, and it'll be, "Oh, man! I almost got busted, man! Hijo!" He'll be raving on and on and you'll know, "Oh God, I'm burned." The guy'll say, "I gave him the bread, man, and he went into the house to get the stuff, and all of a sudden the narcos came, and they broke in the door, and I was hiding in the back alley. All this time! I was afraid to run. Wow, man, I'm sorry. Hijo, I'm sick, too. You got some more money, man? Maybe I know another guy." And oh, Jesus, God. You have to go out and get more money and you're sick. Sick. And even when you get the money, you don't know whether you can cop.

Other times the guy comes back with the stuff, but you're out on the street so you can't get at it to taste it. Even if you do, it might have a lot of quinine in it, which makes it bitter so it tastes like stuff. So you get to the outfit. You go into some toilet in a gas station or in a laundromat. You put the stuff in the spoon and pour the water in it, and then you see the stuff floating! It's floating on top. It's floating on the water. It's baking soda. You try to cook it up anyway, even though you know you've been burned, and it turns into a paste. It just bubbles into a paste.

Other times you cook up, and it's the real stuff, and you've gone through all these things to score, and I've been in a shitter, and all of a sudden the needle will clog, and I can't fix, and there's nothing I can do. I've got to get out of there and find some way to get a spike. It wasn't legal to sell them anymore. They got harder and harder to get. Or the rubber on the eyedropper might break or the jeep might leak, and you go to shoot the stuff, and most of it shoots out the end of the dropper instead of through the needle.

So I'm doing this little penny-ante boosting, making enough to get a gram or two grams at a time, and then I'm out again, and I'm thinking, "What am I doing? What am I doing with my life?" My friends were telling me, "Hey, man, what are you doing out here stealing things? Why don't you straighten up? Go to work. Make an album." I'd get letters, "Want to record? Play here?" I was too fucked up to do it. I got more and more angry at myself, hated myself for what I was doing. I'd let so many people down by not taking care of business. The talent I was given, I was wasting it, throwing it away.

And I was bitter. Bitter that I had had to go to jail. Friends of mine, musicians I'd played with, roomed with, they'd been using for years and never went to jail. I know they got busted, so they must have just ratted on somebody to get out of it, you know. And here I am, because I'm trying to be a decent human being and not be a rat, I'm in jail all the time. Why? I'm not hurting anyone just getting loaded. I got bitter at people.

I was angry and bitter. I would be out hustling, trying to score, I'd be sick, and I'd see people going to work in the morning, all in their nice cars, dressed nice, clean shaven, and clearheaded. I'd see them going to work, and I'd still be standing on the corner waiting for some guy, freezing someplace, in the evening as they were coming home. Here come the same cars back, and they're all smiling and happy. Just the guys in the neighborhood in East L.A. And they go into the market, and they get a check on Friday, man, and they cash that check, and they buy their juice, and they're happy. They're not sick.

I hated them. I was envious of them. I would say, "Look at those chumps! Fuckin' assholes! Lames! Fuckin' rabble! Sheep! Animals! Following the leader! I'm not like that! I'm different! Fuck them! Fuck society!" I'd rave like I used to hear my dad rave about the rabble, the scissor-bills, the kikes, the spicks, the niggers, the tramps and floozies, on and on. Each time I got sick there was more and more fear and hate, knowing I was trapped and I couldn't stop, knowing I was going back to jail. I was full of animosity and so jealous and all I wanted was a lot of money, man, so I could lay up and really drown myself in heroin, saturate myself with it, so I wouldn't feel or see, so I wouldn't want to cry or die. All I wanted was lots of money so I could make myself totally oblivious to everything.

When I was in jail I heard a lot of stories. Guys gather in little groups. You walk down the freeway and look in a cell and there'll be four or five guys talking about shooting this stuff and that stuff. Or someone will come up to you and say, "Hey, Art, take me on a trip." And so you tell about something you did, something that happened to you, the whole thing, you paint a picture. On the street nobody will listen to anyone else for more than a minute, a couple minutes at most, but in jail people will listen, if a guy can talk, for two or three hours straight without ever saying a word. Some are better than others at it and they'll paint some beautiful things, sometimes about women but mostly about different junk they've had, how good it was, and about big scores they've made. They'd pull a robbery and instead of buying a gram or a quarter they'd buy a piece or two or three or four pieces and sell a little bit and lay up and just fix and not have to go out on the street. So now, what I wanted was to find somebody to help me pull an armed robbery. I wanted to go in with a gun, get the money, score, get away from the scene, and cool it.

I went to person after person looking for someone to do it with. Every now and then I'd run into somebody who in the joint had talked about what a big man he was and how many armed robberies he'd pulled—which I'd believed. I'd see him and now it was, "Oh, man, I just got married and my old lady . . ." Or, "I just had a kid." Or, "Man, the heat is so hot. It's too hot around here. I'm afraid that the man has got the pad staked out." What it boiled down to was that the guys were just chicken. They were just bullshitting in the joint, and they were really nothing but street hypes running around stealing the easiest things they could find.

I kept looking, and I kept asking Ruben. I told him, "Man, let's do something, or are you just a bullshitter, too?" He finally said, "Okay, but we're not going to do it like a couple of idiots, like these guys that run into these little markets and get shot for twenty or thirty dollars. Let's take our time and look around and find someplace where we can get something worthwhile."

There was a bar in East L.A. All the gangsters and the big dope peddlers hung out there. Ruben said that we could really get a haul. It was a hands-off place. An in place. You just don't rob a place like that because if those gangsters found out who it was, they would kill us.

We cased it. Ruben found out where the bread was. We staked it out for three weeks. We were going to do it in the morning when the cleaning guy, the mayate, the spook, cleaned it. We figured they might have twenty, thirty grand, which was a lot of bread, a *lot* of dope. But it wasn't only the bread or the dope. It was the idea of having the balls and the heart to do it. Everybody would be out to kill us. Me. Art Pepper. And I wanted to have a gun because I wanted to be able to kill somebody so I could be the cat that was the violent one—from prison, from the movies, you know. I wanted to shoot two or three people because I thought it would prove my strength.

The time comes, and we meet, and Ruben gives me the strips of wire to tie up the spook, thick wire like baling wire. I fold it up and put it in my pocket. He gives me a crowbar and I say, "Where's my gun?" And he says, "I'm not going to give you a gun, man. You're too crazy." You see, they all thought I was insane. It kind of knocked me out. These were violent, killer-gangster type cats. Guys that had stabbed people in prison and killed them, and they thought *I* was too violent. Me. A musician. Real lovable, a loner, a real melancholy type person. They were afraid to give me a gun, and that flattered me.

We went to a gas station across the street from this bar and fixed one last time, in case we were killed, so we'd be straight. I had the wire in my back pocket and the crowbar and Ruben had the gun. We parked the car the way we planned it, and we watched, and all of a sudden two mayates come out and start cleaning the windows in front. There's *two* spooks instead of one. It's the first time there's been two. I said, "I *told* you you should have let me have a gun! What's going to happen now? If I go in the back or in the front or wherever you go, I'm going to be without a gun!" He said, "It's too late now. Do you want to forget it?" I said, "I just want the money, man. Let me have the gun, man. Let me do it by myself. Let me just go in and kill them." I'd lost interest in seeing if I had the balls or not. I knew I had the heart. I could have killed anyone, twenty people if I had to, just to get the money to get the dope.

Ruben said, "I'll go in the back. I'll subdue them. You stand by the front, by the door. You wait, count to a hundred, and then walk in." I said, "*I* walk in! What if they got a gun? They'll just kill me!" He said, "You want to do it or not?" I said, "Alright. Fuck it. Go ahead then."

This was Monday morning. They were going to take the money to the bank at ten o'clock. It was starting to get daylight. The people were waiting at the bus stop to go to work. Here I was. I was just going to walk in dead through the front door. Ruben went to the back. I waited and waited. I counted. Then I went in. Ruben had one guy down, lying on the floor; the other one had his hands in the air, and Ruben had the gun on him, a violent, old-looking gun. The guy was just praying, "Don't kill me! Don't kill me! Please don't kill me!" I walked in and he saw me and just flipped out. He was shaking all over and Ruben said, "Tie him up." I started walking toward him. I reached in my back pocket to get the wire, and he thought I was reaching for a gun and he went completely crazy. He broke and ran. He started running toward me, toward the door. He was a great big mayate. I grabbed at him and tried to hold him, but he pulled away. I yelled at Ruben "Kill him! Shoot him!" And Ruben had the gun on him, but he didn't fire, and the guy just ran right through me and out the door screaming, "Help! Help! They're going to kill me! Help!" I ran to the door to try to stop him, and then I ran back. I said, "What are we going to do now? Why didn't you shoot him? Boy, what a fucking asshole you are! Talk about having balls—you haven't got any heart at all! Where's the money?" And I ran around behind the counter and started ripping out cabinets and tearing things apart to try to find the money. Ruben ran out the back door. The other guy was still lying on the ground. I couldn't find the money. I ran out, thinking that any minute a bullet was going to hit me. I could hear noise and people screaming, and I ran around the corner, and Ruben had started the car. He was making a U-turn. I ran to the car, grabbed the door, jumped in, and we drove away, and I kept yelling, "You lousy motherfucker! Boy, what a yellow cocksucker you are!"

Ruben stopped at Rachel's house, where I was staying. He said, "I'm going to let you off." I said, "What do you mean? We haven't got any money! Let's go rob some place! Let me have the gun!" He said, "No, man, I'll see you later." I said, "What a yellow motherfucker you are." All these people that were supposed to have so much nerve! I felt that I had way more balls than they did, and I didn't think I had any heart at all. I thought, "Who am I supposed to look up to? Who am I supposed to follow? Who am I supposed to like? And what am I supposed to pattern myself after?"

It's morning. I'm sick. No money. No dope. And at any minute I might be picked up by the police or killed by the Chicanos if they find out who tried to rob this place, and it's all for nothing. I went to Rudy's. I said, "Oh, man, let's do something." I didn't tell him who I went with, but I told him what had happened, and I said, "Here I am sick, man, and I don't know what to do."

We went out. We went to a gas station. He turned the guy, and I took a battery charger. We went to a fence. I think we got sixty dollars for this beautiful battery charger. We bought a quarter of stuff, and I was so drug and unhappy, we just shot it and shot it.

14 | The Los Angeles County Jail: The Hole

1960 - 1961

DIANE had left me. The thought of Diane made me ill. She didn't have any heart at all, no spirit. She was always sniveling, whining, crying. She was using, but she never earned any money. I didn't want her to be a whore! I would never want a chick that would be a whore. We were living with some people, and she just laid up and waited while I went out and burglarized some place or boosted and came back with the dope. Finally she couldn't stand it anymore—I don't know *what* she couldn't stand. She wasn't *doing* nothing, and this guy Boy, that we'd been staying with, moved to Orange, and he'd always had eyes for her, and I guess he must have told her to come on up there and he'd take care of her. So she split.

I had had two occasions at this period when two different Mexican hustling broads hit on me and told me that they wanted to take care of me. All I would have had to do is, if somebody messed with them, go pistol-whip the guy; you know, just be behind them so they'd have a man. The girl would go out and hustle and get the money, and I would go out and get the dope and fix her and keep everything straight. They liked me because I was a famous musician, and I was kinda handsome, and they'd heard I had a lot of heart. They said, "Man, what are you doing with that stupid broad? She's just laying up on her fucking ass not doing nothing, and you're such a groovy cat. Why don't you come with me?" This happened twice, and these were chicks that made a bill (a hundred) a day at least. I didn't put them down, but I couldn't get involved with them. I knew I'd get hung up on the chick. They were both beautiful girls. I knew I'd start having a feeling for the girl, and if she was balling different guys it would eat me up. I've always been moral. I couldn't change it. Old-fashioned. And I felt sorry for Diane. If I left her she'd just die. She was such a weakling. So I came back to this place one day, and there was a note from Diane that she'd left, and I thought, "Thank God, she's gone. She's made the move. Maybe now I can get myself together and be cool, support my habit."

When I robbed the doctor's office in Studio City, I had got one huge bottle filled with phenobarbital. I didn't know this, but Diane had taken the bottle with her when she left. I heard from Rachel, Boy's sister, that when Diane went to Orange, all of a sudden she realized . . . well, I don't know what she realized,but I imagine she saw how disgusting, how weak she was, and so she took I don't know how many of these pills, and Boy found her, and he didn't know what to do. He and some friends carried her out to his car. They figured they'd dump her on me. They were driving along, and the rollers stopped them, and Boy told them Diane had taken an overdose of sleeping medicine, and they were trying to take her some place where she could be helped.

The cops took her to the Orange County Hospital. All she had left at that time was what she had with her, a blouse, a skirt, a little blue sweater, a pair of flats, and a purse. Everything else was gone, the furs, the dog. She nearly died. It's too bad she didn't die. It's too bad she didn't die the first time she tried to commit suicide instead of the way she finally did die. She would have been better off.

Diane never contributed anything ever. She was totally inept at everything. She couldn't even keep house. The first time I went to Diane's pad when she was still married to her husband, it was just like a pigpen. It was a beautiful house with a pool and everything, but it was unbelievably dirty—junk and clothes. There *was* one thing Diane could do; she used to work crossword puzzles. Every day she'd go buy the *New York Times.* Later on I learned that that was the epitome of crossword puzzles. She'd go to magazine stands and buy ten or twelve of the most difficult puzzle books and sit and work them all. She was very good at that, but she did nothing at all to help me in any way, shape, or form. All the time I was supporting my own habit I was able to do it. When I had to support hers, too, it just got too much for me. It got to be too much.

Later on, when I was no longer with her, Diane stayed in Manhattan Beach with some friends of mine, Ann Christos and her old man, John James. She lived with them and was stealing money out of John's pockets, going through the house stealing their dope. Finally they told her, "No good. Either you're going to have to do something or get out. You're just too heavy. It's all we can do to carry our own weight. Do something or hook it up." See, when she was with me she was never forced into anything. They told her, "The only thing you got is your ass; go peddle it. Want some dope? Go sell your ass." So she finally got up off her lazy ass and went out to turn a trick. She went into Manhattan Beach. There's millions of clubs down there. It's the easiest place in the world to turn a trick if you want to. She wanders around, looks around, has a few drinks at a few different bars, and finally she hits on a guy and he's a . . . He's a vice officer! Hahahaha! And she got busted for offering! The story of Diane—The Great Zeeeero.

(Hersh Hamel) I know Diane very well, or did. Diane was a waitress at Jazz City, 1956, '57. It was a big club during the fifties. They struck up a relationship. Diane had a couple of children, so I understand. She claimed she gave her children up for Art. It seemed more like she wanted to give her children up. Art was the excuse.

Diane started out very pretty. She's Filipino and had those island features although she wasn't real small. But she smoked incessantly, cigarettes, which later on deformed her lip. She had to have a lot of teeth taken out, and she had a little groove in her lip from the cigarettes. She had a very pretty body when I first saw her. Of course, later on . . . She didn't use anything when Art met her, and she was determined to straighten him out. Of course she became a huge junkie, worse than Art. She lost her looks.

Diane wasn't terribly bright, terribly intelligent. She was a waitress. She was very lazy. She used to just like to lay in bed. They used to, like, get stoned on horse and lay in bed a lot. I remember she got this thing from the Akron—one of those pillows with arms on them so you can eat breakfast in bed, sit up and read. And she was just *thrilled* over that. Just thrilled. She was trying to help Art, but she gave up somewhere along the line. She didn't know how to help him. She was really a good person; she just lost herself to dope like a lot of people do. It's very easy.

I DIDN'T know Diane had taken these pills. I'm running around East L.A. pulling burglaries and boosting and trying to get ahold of a gun, and they're going to give Diane ninety days or something like that. So what she does, in order to get out early, in order to make them like her and help her, she says, "Well, I'm Art Pepper's old lady." All the narcs had heard of me and they said, "Oh? Where is he?" She said, "He's in East L.A. robbing and stealing, just strung out like a dog."

The police can't arbitrarily stop someone and search them without a reason. If they do, their case isn't any good. But when Diane told them about me, that was the "show cause," and they went to their files and gave pictures out to the heat in East L.A., my pictures. And when I got busted, the show cause was Diane's statement. She had informed on me.

At this time I was so hung up I had no one to go with me anymore. I was just walking the streets, burglarizing houses, going into stores, no car or nothing, just carrying stuff down the street—televisions, clothes, power tools—carrying them to the connection, hiding in alleys and parks. But then I did an album for Les Koenig, *Smack Up,* and I got some bread, and the next day I went to Stone Street in East L.A. I went to Frank and Lupe Ortiz's house to cop, and I bought a half a piece of stuff; the house was under surveillance; and the police had my picture in their car.

I got two condoms of stuff. I had had a student of mine drive me; he was parked three blocks down, on Wabash, a busy street. I turned the corner onto Wabash; there's a Bank of

America and a lot of people going and coming. I'm walking by
the bank, and the car is just a few feet away, and two guys are
walking toward me, I'm trying to pass them, and all of a sudden
somebody grabs me from behind, around the neck, and starts
strangling me, and one of the guys drops a badge and says,
"Sergeant Sanchez, L.A. Narcotics."

There were four of them: MacCarville, Salazar, and this guy
who had me around the neck, Solagi, and Sanchez, who's a
total illiterate madman. I'm trying to get my hand to my mouth.
There was no way I could have swallowed the stuff because the
guy had me so I could hardly breathe, but Sanchez saw me and
grabbed my arm. I fought as much as I could and screamed,
"Help! Help! Robbery!" hoping some citizens would jump in
and give me just enough time to get it into my mouth and
swallow it, but I was dead. They had me. They were too strong.
Sanchez opened my hand, and there were the two quarters.

They got me in the car and drove about three blocks. I'm
handcuffed with my hands behind my back, and this ape
Solagi, he's sitting on my right; Sanchez is driving; and MacCarville is sitting next to Sanchez. All of a sudden we stop; I fall
forward; and Solagi smashes me in the stomach with his elbow.
Sanchez whips out his gun and hits me in the head with it. He
clicks it and says, "I'm going to kill you, you motherfucker! You
stinking bastard! Open the door!" Then he yells, "Open the
door! Throw him out! Run, you bastard! If you don't, I'm going
to kill you right here!" I said, "Ohhhh, man, what are you doing?" He'd cut my head with the gun. I said, "Just take me to jail
and book me, man!" He said, "We know where you got the
stuff. You got it from Frank and Lupe Ortiz, and you're going to
tell us that or we'll kill you!" I said, "I didn't get it from anyone.
I had it. I had it before I went to the pad."

They drove me to the Hollenbeck Station. They parked in
the lot and Solagi said, "Get out!" I went to get out, and he
kicked me in the legs so I fell. I would have busted my teeth out
because I fell on cement, but I turned and hit my head. They
grabbed me and dragged me in.

They had two holding tanks in the Hollenbeck Station. They
took everyone out of one of them and threw me in it. Then
Sanchez pulls my belt out and hits me in the stomach and the
back, and he knocks me down again. They said, "You're going

to cop out on these people or we're going to kill you." I had about a hundred and eighty dollars on me. They took my money. They knocked me out and left.

When I came to, I crawled to the bars and hollered at the two bulls on the cells, "*Please* undo the handcuffs!" They're not supposed to put you in a cell with cuffs on. They wouldn't even answer me. I said, "You motherfuckers!" The guys in the other cell said, "Hey, putos gavachos, you motherfuckers! Why don't you help this guy?" They screamed at the bulls, but they wouldn't do anything.

This was in the afternoon. At about eleven o'clock that night two detectives came to the door. They said, "What *is* this?" The bulls on the cells said, "Well," and they started whispering. These were guys from downtown, from robbery detail. One of them took out his handcuff keys and undid me. I was cut. Blood was running down my wrists. My hands were swollen. There was no feeling in them. They said, "You won't try to get away, will you?" I said, "No, I can't do nothin'." They said, "We don't want to handcuff you." They put me in a car and drove me down to the Glass House, which is the jail downtown. They booked me in. They no sooner book me in than I'm dragged out of the cell, and here I am in an office with Sanchez. He put me through all kinds of shit again. He said, "You'll talk eventually."

They took me to the old county jail, and this booking in took eighteen to twenty hours. I get into the hype tank, and in the morning I'm vomiting bile, and all of a sudden here come all the dope fiends to the cell door and one of them throws a newspaper at me: "JAZZ MUSICIAN BUSTED ... Art Pepper, renowned jazz saxophone player, was arrested by So-and-so at such-and-such place .... *Pepper said he bought the heroin from Frank and Lupe Ortiz.*" Then I realized what Sanchez meant when he said, "You'll talk. We'll get you." They just put it in the paper that I had ratted on Frank and Lupe.

So now I'm laying there. I'm so sick I can't move. I've been in jail a lot of times. I've seen people killed. I've seen them beat to death, with thick blood running out of their ears and eyes, every bone broken. That was what was waiting for me. I looked at these guys. I said, "Man, there's nothing I can say. Sanchez told me he was going to get me. I didn't say a word. Didn't say nothing, and this is what he did. If you're going to kill me, kill me. I did not rat on them. I've never talked, ever." I laid there, and I thought I was dead. They went outside and had a conference. Then they came back. They said, "We're going to wait and find out from Frank for sure."

When Frank got busted they put him in the tank that I was in. Maybe they thought he would be so unthinking he'd believe the newspaper story and have me beat up real bad, and then, before I died, they thought I would cop out on him. But he came by the cell, and he said, "You didn't say anything, did you, Art?" I said, "No, you know that." I told him what had happened. He put the word out. "Don't let anything happen to Art Pepper." He was an intelligent guy, and we had a good friendship.

I testified for Frank at his trial. I said that when I went to his house I had the dope on me, that I had just stopped by his house to help him move, which I *had* done, and it helped Frank, and he straightened everything, and that saved my life. But to this day there are people who read that story in the papers who believe that Art Pepper is a rat. And there is nothing that ever happened to me that was more horrible.

When I went to testify for Frank, I went under cover; the narcs didn't know what was happening. Before they did know I was already in the courtroom in the custody of a deputy sheriff. When I came out, as I walked with the deputy, I told him, "I'm afraid. I'm afraid these detectives are going to kidnap me and kill me." He said, "Don't be silly. Nobody would try anything like that." We walked down the hall and around a corner. There's Solagi, Sanchez, and MacCarville. They're sort of lounging in the hallway. I tell the sheriff, "There they are!" They give me a cold look. They walk up to the deputy and flash their badges. They tell him, "We'd like to take Pepper, here. We've got permission from the jail." They made up some story. Solagi says, "It's okay. It's all clear." Now, they were going to take me out and they might have killed me, but what happened next was incredible. It was like a movie. This deputy sheriff unbuttons his holster, puts his hand on his gun, and says, "I'm sorry. He's in my custody. I brought him here; I'm taking him back. You can come along with us, and when he gets back into the jail you can present your papers and take him from there."

They tried everything. They joked with him, and they grabbed me, and I said, "No! No!" and held on to the deputy sheriff, "Don't let them take me!" And they laughed. Sanchez glared at me. But this guy realized that what I had told him was true, and he would not let them take me.

The deputy took me to the jail. He told the desk sergeant, "If anybody comes for this guy make sure it's legal and everything's in order." They took me back into the jail, and then Frank came. So I was vindicated with everybody in the tank. The way it ended up they finally got Frank for some ridiculous thing. They framed him, but it had nothing to do with me.

END OF THE ROAD *by John Tynan*

For detective sergeants Ed Sanchez and Ray MacCarville of the Los Angeles police department's narcotics division, it was a routine stake-out.

Inside the house that they were watching, at 1113 Stone St., Lupe and Frank Ortiz went about their business of the moment as they prepared for a visitor. The Ortiz' business was alleged to be the sale of heroin; the expected visitor was Art Pepper.

To the waiting detectives, Pepper's appearance and entry into the house was a trigger for action. For an hour they waited expectantly. Then Pepper reappeared.

"We followed him for about two or three blocks," MacCarville said later. "Then we picked him up. He had a half-ounce of heroin on him and admitted being a user."

At police headquarters on Oct. 25, Pepper was booked for possession of the drug (estimated value: $240). Bail was set at $12,000. A three-time loser, he faces a sentence of from five years to life imprisonment.

Contrary to erroneous reports in the metropolitan newspapers, the bail was not posted. Pepper was left to the agonies of withdrawal in tank 11D-2 of the county jail. ("He's hooked real bad," said an officer the day after his arrest. "He was real sick today.")

To the police, Pepper was merely bait. On Oct. 26, narcotics officers closed in on the Ortiz operation, and the house on Stone St. was crossed from their list.

The police had Pepper dead to rights. Some three months prior to his arrest for possession, the altoist had been picked up for needle marks by a county sheriff's radio car, had pleaded guilty to addiction in court, and was sentenced to serve 90 days in the county jail. Before the full term of that sentence had expired, Pepper was released. A good-behavior release of this nature is not unusual.

But it was patently clear that the "monkey" had claimed a victim, and Art Pepper's troubled career had apparently come to the end of the road. Affecting adversely an application for parole is his record as a parole violator for which he served his last prison term in the federal penitentiary on Terminal Island, Calif., in 1955–56. He was released in June of that year.

Pepper's first narcotics conviction (for heroin) was in 1953. He served some time in Los Angeles county jail at that time, then was transferred to the U. S. Public Health hospital at Fort Worth, Texas, from which he was discharged in May, 1954.

The ravages of heroin on human life have perhaps never been demonstrated more clearly than in the story of 35-year-old Art Pepper. As it does with us all, his life touched and affected the lives of others. His first wife, who divorced him during his term in Fort Worth hospital in 1954, is now happily married to a San Fernando Valley, Calif., businessman. Pepper's daughter, now a teenager, lives with her mother and stepfather. Thus, while heroin shattered Pepper's first marriage, only he was permanently scarred.

In 1956, out of prison and still on parole, Pepper was given a second chance for happiness. He met his present wife, Diane. During the ensuing four years, he repeatedly stressed his debt to her for "keeping him straight."

At the end of 1957 Pepper could say with conviction, "My wife is the one who's made me happier than I've ever been in my life" (down beat, Jan. 9, 1958). "Now I really look forward to my older years. I used to be scared of growing old—but not now. Diane has done more for me in one year than all others did in my life's entirety."

"Whatever I may do in music from now on," he continued, "and whatever credit I may get for it belongs to her. She didn't give me back just my self-respect and career. Diane gave me back my life."

And a bare seven months ago, Pepper declared just as categorically (down beat, April 14), "Diane's understanding saved me; I owe so much to her. My marriage now is permanent and so very different from before. No words can describe what it means to me."

On Sept. 22, one month and three days before the altoist was left in a county jail tank to kick his habit "cold turkey," Diane Pepper was admitted to Orange County, Calif., general hospital in a coma induced by an overdose of phenobarbital taken to combat the withdrawal symptoms of heroin.

According to the report of two medical examiners at the hospital, numerous needle marks were found on her body. In the opinion of the examiners she "had been a heroin addict for a number of years."

Acting on an affidavit filed against her for narcotic drug addiction by Detective Sergeant Robert Manning of the Orange police department, Superior Court Judge Crookshank ordered her committed voluntarily to the California state hospital at Norwalk, Calif.

To detective Manning, it was an old and ugly story. He told of finding her slumped in the back seat of a car he had pulled over because, he said, he spotted two known narcotics violators in the automobile.

Rushed to the county hospital for emergency treatment, she later told Manning she had swallowed 30 phenobarbital tablets to ward off the pain of withdrawal. At ¼-grain each, Manning estimated, the dose totaled 7½ grains of the drug, "enough to kill anyone else." Why hadn't the overdose proved fatal?

Said the detective. "There was still enough reaction from heroin in her system to keep her alive."

Diane admitted to Manning, the officer said, that she had been "turned on about two years ago by her husband." She added that she had "wanted to kick, but Art wouldn't go along with her."

Manning said she told him she was "shooting about four grams a day and that Art was shooting seven."

"That's around two spoons," observed the detective. "Quite a bit of junk."

The life of fantasy in which the heroin addict exists is productive of strange, often inexplicable thought processes. In the case of Art Pepper, deep feelings of anxiety and self-pity seemed to dominate his thinking. He was given to dark moods of depression, and the persistent delusion of persecution, like the drug his system subsisted on, was never far away. And the constant stream of optimistic thinking, running like a broken thread through his life as an addict, was merely self-delusion and a stark symptom of inner despair.

Yet, for all the fantasy and inner-life induced by heroin, Art Pepper at times exposed himself to brief and brutal flashes of reality, of true consciousness about what dependence on the drug meant to him as a human being and to those he yearned to love.

He knew what continued addiction meant. He knew it spelled death.

In the summer of 1956, when he tape-recorded a long and frank interview for this magazine on his mental illness, he said, "Of course, this (his 1954 conviction) makes me a two-time loser. If I goof again and get busted, I can get 30 to 40 years in prison under terms of a new federal law ..."

During the same interview, he noted "I've been working with Jack Montrose. I really like his writing and he's a wonderful person to work with." Montrose at a later date was arrested for heroin addiction and possession.

Again, reflecting on what a future narcotics arrest would mean, Pepper told this writer a year and half later (*down beat*, Jan. 9, 1958), "I think of the progressive steps that'll result from my goofing. First of all, I consider, the narcotics detail gets the word and before long I get picked up. This has got to happen; there's no escape. Then I get sent up for maybe 30, 40 years. My record takes care of that. I think about never again seeing my wife, my friends . . . never again being able to play, which is the thing I want to do more than anything else. Well, by the time I'm through with this line of thought, I'm shaking with fear, so scared that the feeling (for a fix) is gone."

Somewhere along the line this fear was conquered—by heroin.

And to the last, to the time of his final arrest on Oct. 25, Pepper's emotional defense mechanism against the outrages of the mess that had become his life went to bat for him. He told arresting officers MacCarville and Sanchez, they said, that he felt he was still a young man, and he figured when he got out of prison, he'd still have his life before him.

Earlier this year, Pepper had begun to reassert himself on record dates as the superlative musician he is. He had begun to make his own albums once more, and it was unanimously agreed by all who heard them that the altoist was expressing himself as he never had before. His horn was heard on a variety of albums recorded for several labels and on the sound track of the motion picture, *The Subterrraneans.* Things were at last beginning to look up for Art Pepper.

His friend and constant collaborator, Marty Paich, was responsible for much of the unveiling of the "new" Art Pepper. Paich constantly called him for record dates, and last spring told this writer, "I feel the situation between Art and myself is similar to that between Miles Davis and Gil Evans. We understand each other." Paich described the altoist as a musician "of the utmost jazz caliber. There's no one else I would write for because the minute he hears the background, he makes an immediate adjustment to the arrangement." Paich summarized his feelings by declaring, "Art Pepper is probably one of the most dedicated musicians I know. He just lives for that horn."

What Paich did not know at the time he made the statement was that there was a compulsion driving his friend more overpowering than music, than the loss of heaven and the fear of hell, than eating or sleeping, than love or hate, than life or death—the craving and the physiological and psychological need of heroin.

When told of Pepper's arrest, a stunned Marty Paich could only comment haltingly, "During the last few months, I used him on record dates a few times, and he acted awfully weird. I tried to talk to him about it, but it didn't seem to do any good."

Ironically, Paich had been trying to reach Pepper the week of his arrest. He wanted to use the altoist on another record date. But there is no phone in tank 11D-2.

For this gentle, introverted, mentally tortured artist and for all the Art Peppers, society has sanctioned a law—"Thou shalt not find *this* way out." Because he sought whatever release heroin brings, and found in it his personal panacea, this musician became a criminal in the eyes of the law. And the law is absolute.

To the officers who arrested him, to the judge who may send him to prison for the rest of his life, to Federal Narcotics Commissioner Harry Anslinger, who has expressed contempt for all addicts, the life of Art Pepper may be summed up by the cynicism, "file closed on one junkie." To those who appreciated and were fulfilled by his music, it must be, "File closed on one artist." down beat, *December 8, 1960.* Copyright 1960 by down beat. *Reprinted by special permission.*

(Ann Christos) I first met Art at the Lighthouse. Actually, back in Minnesota my husband, a musician, used to listen to his records and he'd say, "Now, listen here! This is Art Pepper!" And then when I came to California, I went down to see him, and I was fascinated by him. I started following him around; he thought I was insane. I heard that he was sleeping in East L.A. in a car, and I remember I woke up at about 3 A.M.: the passage of the moon by the window, the light, had awakened me. I got up and went down to East L.A. and drove up and down the streets looking for him. I saw him the next night and I said, "I looked for you." He said, "I was sleeping in a car on such-and-such street." He was playing at the Lighthouse. I don't know what he was doing. He was on the streets. I don't know what drove me, but I felt I just had to help him. I talked to a black trumpet player, Joe Gordon, and he said, "Don't get involved with him. He'll just drag you down." I said, "It's not sexual or anything. I don't know what it is. I just feel that he needs help."

Two weeks after I looked for him in the car, I heard that he was in jail. I was at work, and it came over the radio, and I went down to Esther, a waitress at the Lighthouse. I said, "Art's in jail. Let's bail him out." It was about five hundred dollars and he didn't particularly want to come out. He really thought we were insane. We got him an attorney, too, but Art said, "Don't waste your money." What year was that? 1960?

He went to Esther's house, and he wanted to fix real bad, and she wouldn't . . . She had eyes for Art sexually. Art knew it and he wouldn't give her any satisfaction, but I think he did that time and then he tried to manipulate her from there. She wouldn't give in so he took a hammer after her. She called me up, "He's insane! He's insane!" Hahahaha! So she brought him to my house. He sat down at the piano, out on my porch, and that's when I recognized his scowling "smile." I looked at him, and I realized that he wasn't smiling, he was scowling. Then he started working on me, silently, and finally I took him to East L.A.; he stayed there for a couple of days.

I wasn't using at the time. I was just drinking. I came out here, and I think I used the first six months, and then I cleaned up, got out of it, you know. And Art says, "That won't last long." It's such fun tripping with Art. Art's like fast motion; he walks fast. We'd find ourselves tripping to the connection, just talking, and the excitement of going! And Art's animation! If there's something waiting for him, no matter how sick you are, there's a happiness that sets in; we'd start joking and laughing because we knew that soon things were going to be alright. And we'd get there, and sometimes there's a wait, there's a hassle, sometimes it's immediate. You never know. I guess all this is part of the game.

Art was very handsome. Very, very handsome. I thought he had a strong face, but others say there's weakness in it. I hear strength in his blowing and I guess I see it in his face.

While Art was out on bail, he recorded for Les. Les gave him a fifteen-dollar advance. Art's folks had told Les, "Don't give Art any money." But he talked Les out of fifteen dollars, saying that at least we could buy a soda and go to a movie. I had an old, '47 Dodge, and I had a fifth of vodka in the car. Les gave me the fifteen dollars, and I was taking Art home to Thelma and Pops's. Art drank the whole fifth straight down and then he said, "Give me my fifteen dollars." I said, "No, I need that for gas." And while we were still in Hollywood, the generator or something crapped out and the car stopped. Art got out of the car and said, "Give me my money! It's my money! I worked for it!" And I knew he was right. He makes you feel guilty. I said, "But we've gotta get the car fixed." He had to get home. We didn't have cab fare or anything.

That was the night he beat me up. He turned into an ape, huffing and puffing and stomping. He'd disappear behind a house and hide behind a bush—like an animal. And then he came out and grabbed my purse, turned it inside out, threw it across the street. This must have lasted an hour. And he pounded me on the chest and then he hit me in the face or something, and my glasses fell to the ground, and we both looked at 'em, and he picked them up and handed them back to me. Hahahaha! I was scared stiff, but that indicated that he was . . . he was a Milquetoast. He wouldn't hurt anybody. I still didn't give him the money, and he kept threatening, and he said, "You're so ugly! You're so ugly, and you got a bad body! And . . ." I can't remember, just venom, degrading things, degrading to me. And I kept saying, "I know. I know that." And he'd stop. As soon as I said I knew it and it didn't affect me, then he'd try something else to demoralize me. I was aware of all my deficiencies so there wasn't anything he could do to me. And then he started to laugh when he realized he couldn't get me in that area. There was a party going on and I remember going and sitting on the porch at that party and, like, daring him. He came over and he sat down, too, and he said, "Please give me my money." And I said okay. I gave him the money, and I called up Pops, and he came and got me. Art was gone for three days that time.

While Art was still out on bail, Diane got out of Norwalk. Art asked if he could bring her out to my house in Manhattan Beach. I said sure. I was curious. He brought her, and she was very paranoid at first because she didn't know what I was to Art, but I had nothing to hide. In fact, I told Art he didn't have to pay back anything because it was given. I asked nothing in return. Diane could recognize a female threat and I wasn't. I've had a lot of male friends that way. Art and I became friends because he knew I wasn't asking anything of him, sexually or emotionally. I just wanted to know him. I accused Art one time.

I said, "You're so stingy. I bet you don't even have a peepee!"
And he pulled down his pants, and he showed me, and he said,
"And it really gets *big*, too!" He ought to remember that one.
We just cracked up.

Art had Diane in anklets and tennis shoes and cotton
dresses. Frumpy. I asked her why she dressed like that and she
said, "Because Art likes it." Then he went back to jail, and
Diane was living with her sister, Marie, and she called me up
and she said, "Why don't you come to Hollywood and pick me
up. I feel like doing something." I didn't recognize her on the
street corner. She had her hair done and she looked sharp and
pretty. She was Polynesian or something. She had a small nose;
wide, very, very dark eyes. Her mouth—the bottom lip had a
nice contour but the top lip was in two points instead of round.
And she was always sort of smiling when she spoke. Diane was
very articulate, very fastidious, took good care of Art, kept him
nice. But when he went to jail, boy, she came out! She looked
like she was on the street, whoring, only high-class. A high-class
call girl.

Diane could be mean to Art. Going to score in East L.A. one
time, I was driving, with Art in the front seat and Diane in the
back, and Art was whining or something. Diane said, "Art, stop
it!" He wouldn't, so she took her purse and just beat him over
the head with it. Art had my radio, and he took this radio, laid
his head on it, and buried himself in the sound.

During the times Art stayed with me, he never listened to
music. I played his records and he was forced to hear 'em, but
when I was at work he'd just watch TV. He wasn't interested in
what anybody else was doing. He didn't have to hear it. He had
his own thing, his own feelings, his own thoughts. Music was
nothing Art ever had to struggle with. It was always there, it
seems. He never practiced that I know of. He could pick up a
horn . . . One time he blew a horn—the upper register was
out—and he just blew around it. His mind eliminates any kind
of hassle, say, pads falling off. He just ignores it. And Art has
no tolerance for imperfection in other musicians. Frank
Strazzeri had started out as a classical pianist and had just
recently been blowing jazz, and they were at the Lighthouse,
and Frank wasn't blowing to Art's satisfaction, and I guess Art
put on that scowl. People look at him and think he's smiling. I
guess it's for the audience so they don't really know what he's

thinking. But the musicians know. When they got off the bandstand, Frank came up and started apologizing to Art and Art wouldn't even listen to him. He just turned him off. Like, if a musician doesn't blow good, he doesn't want them apologizing anyway. But when things are movin' right, behind him, and then he blows! Actually, he sets the beat, he's so solid himself. (He used to test Diane to see if she really was hearing. And he told me once that he found out that she didn't know what was happening, that she was a phony. And then he'd pull it on Christine. He did it to me a few times, but I was listening and I knew what was happening. Art and Christine were living downstairs, and he got a gig at the Blue-something-or-other. It was a trio, and he came off the stand, and he said, "Good drummer." I looked at him. Christine said, "Yeah, he really swings." And I said, "He rushed!" Art smiled at me. Christine got furious because I was right. He *was* rushing. But that's Art's testing.)

I guess the only thing that I know of that has *really* been important to Art in his life is dope. I think dope slows him down. See, I'm hyperkinetic, and so's Art, I think. Sometimes I travel at a fast pace inside myself; the exterior doesn't reveal it. I think Art is that way, too. One time after we'd scored we were sitting there, and I was moving my hand, and he says, "You know, you're keeping time." I was keeping a beat, as fast as I could go, and didn't even know I was doing it. He says, "I'm that way, too." He needs something to calm him down. And, another thing: when you're on drugs, I've heard this stated many times, you don't give a shit what the public thinks out there. You just shut 'em out and do what you want to do. You can't feel criticism, looks.

Art's life-style is complaining and bitching. That's part of his personality. People that know him, they just hear it and forget it. Some people want to do something to correct some of these things that are ailing him and they extend whatever services—like, if he doesn't feel good; or, "If I only had a drink or a fix." Some people go out of their way, like I did. And I never got anything back for what I did. I can't explain it. I was lonely, and Art was company, and when he's happy he's a pleasure. When Art's happy, he's funny. When he's happy, he's like a little kid with new toys.

Listen, when Art gives a little bit of his mind, his thoughts, or even spits out some of his hate—I don't know how to say this—when he shows you a part of himself, no matter what part it is, that's an extension of his friendship because Art doesn't say much to anybody. But if he even gives you some of his humor, his laugh, it's such a gas.

Oh, Art's always polite to his fans. With his square fans, always. But with the dopefiends, the really down-and-out junkies, to them he's a star; they make him a star. And he's even more gracious to them because he knows that. They need his fame, and he gives them some of it when he talks to them, and he knows that, too. There are some people who love him, but they're very destructive. I feel like I was one of them at one time. They'll give him dope for nothing, even when he's trying to stay cool. And he has tried. But he can't say no to them. He doesn't want to offend them and he's not strong enough to resist. People'll come up and just give it to him for nothing. To buy his friendship. But that doesn't buy Art's friendship. That's what they never find out.

Art used to think I was insane. He'd say, "There's that crazy girl." Because I'd always go see him. He was worth traveling to see, forty miles, whatever. To me Art is beautiful. I'm not in love with him. I love him.

I WOUND up in the first cell wth my old boosting partner, Rudy. He got busted about the same time I did. We were made tank trustees.

One day I was wandering around, walking up and down the freeway going "Woe is me" and thinking about how groovy it would be to get loaded, when I happened to look out to the front of the tank. When a newcomer comes in, he carries his little donut, his filthy mattress, and blanket and cup, and he puts the donut down and waits for the guard to come and open the tank. I heard a donut hit the deck, and I looked up and saw this guy, and I said, "Oh, no! It can't be! Wow, that's David Arbedian." I wanted to run up to the front, but I tried to be cool. I had a feeling as soon as I saw him; I thought, "Maybe he's packing something."

There's two ways of carrying dope into jail. Either you

swallow it and vomit it up, or else you've got it stuck up your ass and far enough to where in a shakedown they can't see it. David's parents owned a business, he had a lot of money, and he'd always had a lot of dope. I just figured if he had a chance he would bring something in. I looked, and I had a feeling.

Now, it has to be a real friend of yours for you to get in on anything, and David was a good friend of mine. We'd been in Fort Worth together. We'd hung out together. I'd eaten at his pad, at his parents'; I'd wrecked his father's car. I had to be cool because of all the people watching: there's all these hustlers, and everybody's got their eyes open to see if anything's going on, and they can really pick up on it because that's their life, seeking dope.

I walked up to the front, and it *was* David. He was always a handsome guy. He always had some groovy chick with a Corvette and all that. He was strong looking with white teeth and a handsome face and a solid jaw, but babyish, with a boyish grin and black, curly hair. He was the kind of guy women want to take care of, and he always played on that. He'd just gone through that shower thing. His hair was all messed up, and he looked kinda crazy, kinda disheveled and lost. Then he saw me—he saw a friend in the jungle and he got a warm look on his face and he nodded to me. I said, "What happened?" He said, "Ohhhh, man, I got busted for possession, dead bang." That means there's no way out. He had no case.

The guys were standing around. They're looking at me, and they're looking at David, and one says, "Heeeey, jack. What's goin' on, baby?" A black guy. He's strutting along and then he kind of sidles up. The black guys have really got an image going; the real fiends, they're so suave. They'll talk to people they don't even know. The Mexicans are different. They're closed off and won't say anything even when they're dying for some stuff. This guy comes up and says, "Heeeey, jack," and he looks around to see where the heat is. He gets up by the bars and he says real low, "I *know* you didn't come dry, baby. And I *know* you're gonna look after old dad." The guy doesn't even know who David is! A lot of white guys are that way, too, and they talk like the black guys with the same inflections. Some white guys talk like Mexicans. Everybody's got his own little game. David says, "No, ain't nothin' happenin'." "Ohhhh,

that's too bad, man. You wouldn't lie to me, would you baby?"
"No. Nothin' happenin'."

I'm standing there hoping it isn't true. The guy saunters
back. David's still outside the tank waiting for the guard to let
him in. I look at him, and he looks at me, and he kind of nods
his head. He smiles. I give him a quizzical, like, "What?
Really?" It was just a meeting of the eyes, no words said, but in
those expressions I knew something was happening.

The guard let him in and called for the trustee. I was there. I
took his name. The two trustees take care of the whole tank.
We have all the names listed and line everybody up for count in
the evening.

The number one cell is the biggest cell in the tank. There's
two bunks against the wall and there's a toilet and washbasin
and a metal partition that comes out. The tank was crowded so
I told David, "Just put your stuff here in number one, man."
That was a dangerous thing to do because people would
wonder. But I made it clear right away that the guy was a friend
of mine and because it was so crowded I was going to let him
catch the floor in number one.

When we got to the point where we could talk I whispered
to David, "You holding?" He said, "Yeah." I said, "How?" He
said, "I got a keester stash." He was already getting sick, and I
was wigging out from waiting, but he had to wait till nighttime
to get the stuff because people were walking by and looking
and trying to feel it out.

Time passed, and the night came. They call salts and soda,
and then the bulls come in a team and run up to all the cell
blocks and rack the gates, and all the gates in all the cells are
roaring and rattling and clanging. They're all shaking, and you
have to get in one. They leave one cell open for the people
sleeping out on the freeway so there's a toilet for them to use.
The bulls holler, "Number five cell open!" It was fortunate that
the place was completely filled at this time. Bad in one
way—because there were so many eyes—but if it hadn't been
filled, it would have been harder to get David into our cell. I'd
told Rudy what was going on.

We're locked in the cell; the lights are out; David gets his
stash; he makes it. He's wiped out. I say, "I'm going next. How
good is it?" He says, "Well, here, I'll put it in the spoon." I say,

"Put a little bit more. If I'm going to go out, I want to go out happy." David bends over and lights a match so I can see the vein. I mainline it rather than trying to hit a small vein in my hand, even though it's a dead bust. If they'd said, "You're going to die after," I would have said, "Okay, just let me do this first." I fixed, and it was so great. Rudy says, "Come on! Come on! Hora le, Art! My turn!" I feel so good. I'm grabbing David; I just want to kiss him. I'm telling him, "Oh, God, David, I love you! Thank you, thank you, thank you! Kill me, Sheriff Pitchess! Blow up the whole county jail! Who cares!" I was so happy. I once said that there's nothing like the first time, but there were a lot of good times, and that was one of them.

The next day people were looking at us. David's supposed to be kicking, but he's not. I told him, "Act sick." Our eyes were pinpointed. Rudy and I were running the tank, and we were both wasted, and the guys picked up on it. Guys came to me, "Hey, man, I thought we were tight." Guys I knew real well. I said, "Man, there ain't nothing happening." These were cats I would have loved to have turned on, but I couldn't do it. I said, "I ain't got nothin'. You know that." People got angry.

The next night comes. We go through the same thing. David gets loaded; I get loaded; and then it's time for Rudy. He's all ready and all of a sudden I hear a noise—running! I say, "Here they come! Ay viene! La jura!" (Here comes the fuzz!) Rudy doesn't know what to do. All he had to do was palm the thing and act like he was asleep, but instead he's trying to get it in his arm. I'm in the top bunk and I look down: Rudy's got the outfit in his right hand, he's got his left arm over his knee, trying to find a vein, and here's a *flashlight* right on this whole action! They scream, "Don't move! Don't move!" They're trying to get to the water to turn it off, but they can't get in. (The rollers have to get the key to get in; it's a security thing.) I'm telling Rudy, "Get rid of it!" David takes the spoon and cleans it. I tie the stuff up in the condom and throw it to him. He puts it in his mouth and swallows it. They're yelling, "Don't move or it's all over for you!" I tell Rudy, "They don't have a gun! They don't have guns here! Hurry, before they shut the water off! Get rid of it!" He gets up. *Finally.* "Don't move! Don't move!" My heart is pounding. "Get rid of it!" The bulls are running for the water, and once they reach it we're dead, outfitwise, you know. He goes to the toilet and says, "I gotta take a piss." They're holler-ing. Boy, are they mad. He drops the thing into the toilet and hits the button. No sooner does it go down, I swear to God, you hear the flush and then "Whoooch—clunk." They'd shut the water off. If he'd waited another second we'd have been stuck with it.

So. David has swallowed the stuff; we'd got the spoon clean; we'd flushed the outfit; and now we hear the keys clanging. The front gates are clashing, and they're telling the people, "Get in one!" They get all the people that were on the freeway into cells; they get everyone locked up; and they run into our cell and grab us: "Get outta there!" They throw us out on the freeway against the bars. They shook us down and went through the whole place, just tore the cell apart. Didn't find nothin'.

While we were standing out on the freeway I said to David and Rudy, "Lookit man, lookit. This is what we're going to tell them. We found an oooold outfit that was made out of a toothbrush and a lightbulb." I'd never tried it but I'd heard about it and the police believe it. They've found things like that. I said, "We got ahold of some aspirin, and we were goof-ing around. We crushed it up. We were trying to shoot it." We had to cover for the marks. "That's our story, and just stick to it. We gotta have a story, and that's it." I was very proud of myself that I'd made it up like that.

They took us before the doctor. We closed our eyes and made our fingers meet in front of us. Touched our noses. He looked at our eyes, looked at our arms. The doctor said, "These men are loaded." We denied it. They interrogated us and we all told the same story. They said, "Who do you think you're kid-ding? How do you think we came there? We were *told*. We were told that you had stuff and that you've been getting loaded for the last three or four days." I said "Oh, that's great."

They took us to the hole. I'd never been there but I'd heard about it. They opened the door and took Rudy away. They made me and David go through a gate, and they took all our clothes off and gave us each a pair of longjohns. I couldn't but-ton mine. They came to my knees and barely fit over my shoulders. David's were just as bad. They took David to his cell.

They opened the door, a solid steel door, smashed it open, and I looked in and saw a pitchblack cell. They told him, "Whenever you hear us coming just crouch in that corner, and if you're anyplace else we'll kick your teeth out when we come in." They threw him in and threw an old, dirty blanket after him. No shoes. Nothing. They opened mine. They told me, "Whenever you hear this door open you be crouched in that far corner or we'll kick your teeth out!" They slammed the door and the reverberation was so loud it went through my head and through it and through it. I had half a blanket and that was it, that and the cold cement floor and a toilet. And there was a grating in the wall. You could hear water dripping. You could talk through the grating. I heard Rudy hollering for us. I thought, "Well, if I can hear him, and David can hear him, then the police must be listening." I said, "Rudy, cool it, man. We told them the truth. There's no use making up any false stories. They're listening to us now."

Time passed. The next day came. I could tell by the sound of the racking of the gates, and then I heard keys rattling and doors banging, and I crouched in the corner. A guard came to the door and slammed it open as hard as he could. I put my hands over my ears. The guard had a trustee with him who shoved in a little paper plate and a paper cup with a top on it. The cup had water in it, and the plate had some food slopped over it. He slammed the door shut again. I tried to eat a little of the food. They'd warned us, "Don't put the food down the toilet. If you stop up the toilet you'll be sorry."

The next day came. I heard the noise, and here they are. The door slams open. I'm crouched in the corner. The trustee reaches in, and he's got a board. He's pounding around the plate with it. I look and see hundreds of cockroaches running off the plate. He pulls it out, throws it into a pail, and puts in another water cup and another plate of food. I see the cockroaches running away and then, in the light from the open door, I see them turn around and head back to the new plate. The door slams shut again.

If I was scared before, when I saw that I was terrified. There's nothing more scary than cockroaches when you can't see them. I felt that they were crawling in my nose and in my asshole and in my ears and eyes and mouth. I didn't touch the food at all. I opened the cup a little bit and drank the water. During this time I heard David. He's talking to me through the grating. He's kicking. He's saying, "I'm really sick. I feel awful, man. I don't know what to do, Art." He said, "I saw the cockroaches and I'm scared." I said, "Don't put your food in the toilet, man." He said, "I already did and it's stopped up and water's pouring out in my cell." I heard his cell open. Evidently, water had run out through the door and they'd seen it. I heard them raving at him. They made him wipe the floor with his blanket. They hit him. They smashed him against the wall. They slammed the door and left him in the wet longjohns. I was curled up in my little blanket trying to keep any part of my body from touching the floor. I imagined that big spiders and bugs were coming out of the grating. David was crying.

The guards came twice a day with food and water. They asked us, "Well, are you guys ready to change your story?" We told them there was nothing to change. It seemed they were just going to keep us there. There was no way we could get out; we couldn't get a lawyer. There was no help we could get. David was deathly ill. He told me, "If there was any way I could kill myself, I'd do it. I just don't know how to do it." I said, "Oh, man, just hold on. Hold on."

We were there for five days; it seemed like eternity. Finally they took us back to our cell block. They figured if they put us back in the same tank the guys would beat us up. We weren't trustees anymore. We were shot back in the second section and treated very bad. David told the guys in the tank, "Come on! If you're going to do anything to us, do it and get it over with, and we'll get some of you as we're going out!" But they let it go. I told my friends, "It wasn't my stuff. There was nothing I could do. If it had been my stuff I would have given you a taste." So it blew over.

At my arraignment my bail had been set at one hundred thousand dollars. The DA's office gave a speech. They said I was involved in a huge network of dope dealers and I was dealing to Hollywood and the near valley. I was reputed to be a big gangster in a narcotics ring. The people I was scoring from were big people, but I was just buying from them. I wasn't dealing at all at the time. The judge finally said, "Well, what was found on the suspect?" They said, "Oh, that's inconsequential. That has no bearing on the case." The judge said, "How much was it?" And the guy said, "Two quarter ounces, a half ounce total." They recommended that bail be set at a hundred thousand because they didn't want me to get out and inform the rest of the "gang." They said they had things in the works; everything was set up; they had people under surveillance. The judge went along with them, and they put me back in jail.

When I went to my preliminary hearing the judge said to the DA, "Well, where's this gang and all the things you were going to tie in?" He realized that it was all bullshit but he wouldn't lower the bail to fifteen hundred dollars, which is what the public defender asked for. He put it to five thousand, and I still couldn't get out.

I got ahold of Les Koenig. I think I had my dad go see him. Les was interested in having me make an album, and for that I usually got about five hundred dollars in front. Ann Christos and this chick from the Lighthouse put up a couple of hundred as a deposit, and Les called the bondsman and assured him of the rest, and I got out on bail. I went down to the studio with a horn I borrowed from a student, a Martin with a good sound. That was *Intensity* with Dolo Coker and Jimmy Bond, and that was the last album Les had that I did, so he kept it. This was in 1960, and he didn't release it until 1963.

My dad wanted me to have a lawyer. I said no. I told him, "I don't have a chance in the world." He said, "I still want you to have a good lawyer." He had already paid out all the money he'd saved, so the only way he could get a lawyer was to put another mortgage on his home in Long Beach, and he did that.

The lawyer came and talked to me. He told my folks that he'd talked to the police, and if I'd get on the stand and sign a paper against Frank Ortiz they'd cut me loose. They'd drop the charges. My dad had gone through all this—I had told him it was useless—and then the lawyer presented us with this solution! My stepmother and my mother just wanted me to be safe. They didn't know anything so I didn't care, didn't even want to know, what they thought. Diane said, "Oh, man, those guys wouldn't do anything for you! They don't care about you! Turn over on them! Later for them!" She'd gotten out of this nuthouse, Norwalk, where she'd been. My dad didn't say a word. He was waiting to see what I'd do. I looked at this lawyer and I said, "Man, are you kidding? We're paying you all this fuckin' money for advice like *that?* I could have done that in the beginning if I'd wanted to! I'm not a rat!" I cussed him out and ranked him, and my dad was sitting there, and I glanced at him, and he was just beaming. He was so proud of me. The lawyer said, "Well, if that's the way you want to be, there's nothing I can do. Maybe I can get you on the N number program." (They had just started a special program for people who were convicted of using drugs or of possession. Rather than give them an A number, an adult prison number, and send them to a regular state prison, they'd give them an N number, a narcotics number, and send them to a special narcotics prison.)

David Arbedian and I had the same background, the same kind of record. We were in Fort Worth together. He'd gotten busted recently on possession, just like me, and he got out on bail, like I did. He got busted *again* on possession while he was out; I didn't. And David didn't have a work record. He worked for his dad occasionally. I had a good work record, for years, with my music, so I figured that if anybody would be acceptable to the N number program it would be me. I had no crimes on my record. David had been picked up for burglaries, suspicions of robberies, but he got on the program. He didn't turn over on anybody; he was just accepted as an N number. I wasn't because they said I was a hardened criminal. I was beyond rehabilitation. There was no hope for me, and the program was only for young people that could be saved. So I wound up doing four and a half years. David did eight months. That's justice.

I got sentenced to two to twenty years in a state prison, and I waited for the chain. You go back to the tank and you wait two, three, four weeks. Then they call out your name and take you to Chino, which is a guidance center in Chino, California. At Chino, they run you through all kinds of physical and mental tests. At that time they were checking your skull, the width of it, and the width of your eye slits and where they were placed and the width of the strands of your hair because they believed that criminals' noses went off to one side and they thought they could tell something by the formation of your facial features.

At the guidance center, they determine where to send you. They can leave you in Chino proper, where you get nice visits with picnic lunches. They can send you to a camp. They can send you to Soledad, which was a vocational type place. They can send you to CMC, California Men's Colony. They can send you to Vacaville, a medical type prison. Or else they can send you to San Quentin or Folsom. Folsom is for the real old guys that are hopeless, completely hopeless. Quentin is for the ones that are too violent to go to any other prison, people that have been busted several times for things like robbery with violence and murder. And where do you think they sent me? To San Quentin.

Your name comes out on a list. They post lists for all the different prisons. I saw my name under San Quentin, and I couldn't believe it. Everybody had told me, "Oh, man, they'll just take you across the street to Chino. You'll have visits with your family. You wear your own clothes on the weekend, nice shoes." And they sent me to San Quentin. Not only was I not eligible for the N number program, I was also not eligible for Chino or Soledad or Vacaville or camp! Probably if I'd been older, they would have sent me to Folsom, which is the graveyard. So that was the treatment I received, and as I look back and try to figure out why this happened, I remember Sergeant Sanchez and I remember his words: "Before we're through with you, if you're *able* to think or reflect, you'll just continually regret the fact that you wouldn't cop out on these people and cooperate with us."

15 | San Quentin

1961

FOUR WEEKS after seeing my name appear on the list I was on the "Grey Goose." That's that horrible, horrible grey bus you see going by with prisoners in it. They put you in white flying suits with elastic around the ankles. They put handcuffs on you and run leg irons all the way through the bus, and you've got two guards with rifles, and there you go. And all these guys were, like, "Heeeey, baby, heeeey, jack, uuuuuhh, is Louie still up there? That suckah. Boy, when he see *me* drive up there again he'll say, 'Boy, there's that suckah *again*, man!' " The only people besides me that seemed dazed or surprised were a couple of murderers, killed their wives or something. They called my name, put these clothes on me, I got on the bus, and we headed north.

We stopped at Soledad and they put us in a wing for people that stay overnight. There's a school there and a lot of shops—welding, machine, electric shops. They classify people as to age and priors and some of the younger people go to Soledad because they feel there's still a chance for them to be trained, so when they get out they can be successful in something. The people in Soledad aren't branded as hardened criminals but they are; they're just on the way up.

They have tunnels through the cell blocks. We walked through one of them to the mess hall. There were a bunch of guys hanging out in the tunnel, and it all reminded me of being a jazz soloist in Stan Kenton's band because you've got these flying suits on and you're going to San Quentin and that makes you more of a criminal than the people that are there. It gives you status. The guys look up to you because that's their world.

They kept us segregated in the mess hall. We had guards guarding us, but guys would make signs to us or nod, things like that, so we strutted. It's your last little moment of glory before you get to San Quentin because there's no glory there. So you strut and look mean. We ate and we spent the night. Guys would come to the cell, sneak into the block: "Hey, So-and-so says to say hello. Need some cigarettes? Anything you want?" All of a sudden you find yourself in a world where everybody takes care of you. The convicts take care of you because they like you. The people that have it feel good sharing it with someone—if you're right. That's the only criteria. If you're right, not a rat. If you're a regular; if you're righteous people; if you haven't hurt anyone; if you haven't been rank to people; if you haven't balled some guy's old lady when he went away. The word filters through.

A couple of cats snuck up to my cell. It happened that they'd got some smack in, but they couldn't get at it. They were hoping we'd be there in the morning. A cat was going to bring an outfit and a taste to make the bus ride nice. He was just going to lay this stuff on me. If he got busted, he'd get another ten or fifteen years. I'd never met the guy, never seen him before. He was a friend of a guy I'd known on the street and he'd been told that I was jam-up people. I was really impressed. I thought, "What wonderful people, man!" And they were all Mexicans. They were all Mexicans. They were beautiful, man.

I guess the blacks were good to their people, but I started forming a dislike for them in jail because I thought, "Here I am, a guy that played jazz, had black friends. Why wouldn't they talk to me, help me out? Because I'm white? I'm not a Mexican. The Mexicans help me." They liked me, and anybody that likes you, man, you like them. People that don't like you, pretty soon you don't like them.

As it turned out, they woke us up before it was even light, and we left too soon to get loaded. And as we left I saw this guy. He made a motion. He spread his hands: "It's too early. There's

We rode to the town of Richmond and then across the Richmond–San Rafael bridge. As you start across the bridge you see San Quentin on your left with water all around it. Soledad looks like a big trade school or a college. San Quentin looks like a prison. It was a greyish cement color, beaten by the winds and the sea and the fog. Doom emanated from it. I've always been a fan of Sherlock Holmes; it had that feel, like it should be on the moors. I got nervous, so I looked around at the guys. I figured these cats had really been around. They were cool. I figured I'd draw strength from their reactions. I looked, and everyone was the same. They were all quiet, and they had the weirdest looks in their eyes, guys that had been there. I saw fear in their eyes. I'd heard a lot of stories I'd tried to dismiss from my mind, but I saw these guys and they weren't joking and kidding as they had when we left the county jail and when we approached Soledad. All that had changed, and everything was stripped to just the realization of where we were going, where we would soon be.

We turned off the highway and into the litle town where the prison employees lived. We pulled up to the prison, and a couple of guys on the bus called out, "Hey!" to the trustee at the gate, but he just shook his head. We went through the gate. We went through another gate. We got out of the bus. There were a few trustees who were working outside the prison, gardeners, things like that, and a few of the guys from the bus knew them and called out, "Hey! Hello!" But it was real quiet and dead.

It was late afternoon. We gave our names; they checked us off. We went through a little interrogation, and finally they took us through the last gate into the prison itself. I looked to my right and saw a chapel, and on my left I saw the prison within the prison. San Quentin is like a city. People who can't make it in the city get put in jail. The guys were talking, "That's the adjustment center. If you really fuck up that's where you go."

We walked straight ahead, past the clothing room, an ancient place that looked like it was from the 1800s. Instead of stopping us there, they said, "We'd better give them dinner. It's getting late." We walked into the upper yard, "the big yard" it's called; it's world famous. I'd heard about it when I was a kid, seen movies of it, and I said, "My God, here I am in this yard." As we walked into the yard, a guy said, "Look to the right." I saw a little, red light bulb. "That goes on when someone's getting gassed."

A few of us had to go to the bathroom. They walked us into a huge bathroom right off the upper yard. It was next to the north dining section. I went in there to take a piss; I happened to look up and I saw a walkway and a guard on it holding a .30–06 rifle. He's got his finger on the trigger, and the rifle is pointed at us. And I noticed that everywhere I looked, indoors and out, there was a walkway a storey above us. The guards get their ammunition and guns from the tower and then they walk around the entire prison on these walkways—mess hall, cell blocks, everything. And there's no way you can get to them, but anywhere you're at, they can be there in a moment a storey above you with a gun. I had to marvel at whoever planned the prison. It was perfect.

We walked out into this huge yard and saw all the people in line waiting to eat. We're in these white jumpsuits. Everybody else was in blue. When I was there, there were six thousand people in a prison that was made to hold fifteen hundred. Can you imagine looking into this mass of people? And everybody's watching us. The most evil-looking people I'd ever seen. Some guys are looking us over to see who they can get for a punk—who they're going to drive on with a shank to tell them they're going to fuck them in the ass, or if some guy's a rat, they're going to kill him, or who they're going to rob.

The mess hall was filled. There might have been two thousand people sitting there when we walked in. Everybody eats facing the same direction. We walked to the front of the mess hall and all the way through the serving line, and all those eyes were on us. I saw people with part of their chins blown away or an eye gone. Hideous people, little white sissies, spooks' punks, with all kinds of jackets on to protect them if they got shanked. It was a sea of faces and not one smile. Just looks. Evil, cold, penetrating looks. I thought, "Is this what I'm going to do for two to twenty years?"

We walked to the mess line, and the guys serving food gave us the same cold looks. It was like a comedy. It reminded me of when I was a kid looking in the mirror practicing mean looks after a Frankenstein or Dracula movie. I would see a face. A guy would nod. And I'd see that the guy looked familiar, but there was no smile, and I felt that the whole world was against me. We got the food; I couldn't eat; I was too scared. Then they got us up and marched us to the South Block.

The South Block is the biggest, longest, five-tiered cell block in the world. We waited. We heard names being called out. Now, I may not always have acted it, but I'm fairly intelligent. I can spell. And even though during those periods of time when I was dealing with criminals I tried to make myself sound like one of the guys by saying "ain't" and purposely making my English bad, I *did* speak well at one time. So when I heard these guards read off the lists of names, they sounded like complete morons to me. They'd mispronounce things and say things over and over to make sure they hadn't fucked up. If it were coming from my side it would have been alright. I would have thought they were hep, that that's the way to be, that they made up for it in other things. But coming from the guards it really seemed funny.

They got us in our cells. As you face the cell, on the left are metal beds; small, steel-ribbed metal bunks, one on top of the other. You can pull them up against the wall, and they hook with a chain. On the right is a space just big enough for one person to stand and walk to the back of the cell. There was a toilet directly behind the bottom bunk. When you sat on the toilet your knees touched the bunk. The guy's laying there with his head right at your knees when you're trying to take a shit. When you piss your ass is at his head. The toilets had no seat over the top. They were white porcelain. They were square. They were set up on a block of cement, so when you sat on the toilet your feet didn't touch the ground and you had to hold your knees up with your hands to try to shit. Right next to the toilet was an old washbasin, discolored and rusty, and there was no hot water. If you know San Francisco, it gets cold there. You'd wake up in the morning, and the water would be so cold it hurt. The plumbing system is so ancient that at certain times of the year when the tide drops the toilets wouldn't flush for days at a time. In order to flush the toilet they gave you a five-gallon tomato can, and you had to use it to pour water in the toilet. But the can didn't fit into the washbasin enough to fill it, so you might be an hour pouring until finally something happened, and a turd might go down. It always stank. All those toilets, cell after cell after cell. You'd get a wooden board to cover the toilet so it wouldn't smell so bad. There were two of us. Neither of us had ever been to this place before, and we just looked at each other, and we looked at this fucking thing.

It was evening. We still had our flying suits on. I'd let this guy have the bottom bunk. He was scared, really sad. He was a Mexican kid, thin; he had all the tattoos. When I first saw him I thought he'd been in prison before, and I guess he had—Youth Authority or something—because in the crook of his right arm he had a black panther with red blood on its claws. Sometimes the eyes are red, too. That was the usual thing the young gunsels would have done in places like Tracy and Preston. He reminded me of those kids that hang out on the corner in East L.A., real cocky and confident because they've got all their friends. Now here he was without his gang. All of a sudden he's alone with me in a cell in San Quentin. I wanted to say something to him, but I didn't know what to say. I felt as bad as he did.

I got up on my bunk and just sat there. Then I happened to look out of the cell and I saw these hands coming up over the floor of the walkway in front of the cell! I see these arms, and I think, "How can anybody come up over the bottom?" As I watch, a guy climbs up. He looks all over. He's holding a can about three inches wide and a foot long, and it has a little handle on it. I see that it's something that would fit through the bars. Another hand appears over the side, and a second guy climbs up. They both look loaded to me but not loaded from stuff. They're giggling and all that. The first guy was a white guy with curly, sandy hair, freckle-faced, a nice-looking guy in a rugged sort of way. Blue eyes. He had the look of someone who'd just stolen a dime out of the church box. He had a little shit-eating grin on his face. The other guy had black, curly hair. He was one of those white, white Mexicans with milky skin, not a mark on him, not a blemish, doubly handsome. He looked like one of those old Spaniards. They were both wearing the prison blues. The first guy was clean but rumpled and relaxed looking. This other cat was all starched, his shirt collar; everything fit perfect. His pants were a different color than the ordinary blues. Later on I found out that these were blues made from the old material, which everybody wanted. They had been bleached out so they were very light and real pretty.

I noticed that both these guys had the same animated look about them, and their eyes were sort of red. Right away I thought, "Juice!" They each had a can. They whisper, "Art Pepper?" And I say, "That's me." The first guy says, "I'm Don Proffit, man." He says, "I've been a fan of yours for years. I'm an actor. I heard you were coming. This is my friend, Huero." Huero says, "I've known a lot of cats that have known you. They say you're good people. We figured since you just drove up it must be a little scary, so we brought you something to take the edge off." Huero puts his can through the bars and Don puts the other one through. It's pisco, a drink they make out of all kinds of things, fruit and yeast. It's home brew. It looked like a dull orange juice, kind of pissy looking, and it tasted like rotten beer. I looked at the other cat in the cell. They asked him, "Who are you?" Huero said, "I hope you realize that in a place like this if someone does you a favor you never say anything about it or get them in trouble. You're with our friend and we don't want to leave you out, so remember, if anything happens, you get too drunk or you get busted, you ride the beef." The guy was so sad. I said, "He'll be alright."

We started drinking this stuff and talking. Don told me about his acting. Huero loved my music. All four of us got really loaded; we had a ball. We finished the two cans, so Huero climbed back over the walkway, and a few minutes later I saw his arm coming up again and this can, and here he comes after it. They went through this whole scene and never got busted. It was like the thing that happened in Soledad. I was afraid San Quentin would be different, that there was some other breed of people here. But I saw that it's just people, and there's groovy people everywhere. I drank so much I got sick. They left and they said, "We'll see you tomorrow." I vomited, and I got up in my bunk, and I thought, "Well, maybe it's not so bad after all." And I got that warm feeling of having friends, male friends, good people; I was liked and it made me feel good. I passed out.

All of a sudden I heard this clanging of gates. It was a horrible sound, and I woke up and looked down and saw this toilet with vomit all over it. My cell mate was still asleep. I couldn't understand how he could still be sleeping with all the noise that was going on. I threw some ice water on my face, and they racked the gates and called us out, and we went to the mess hall.

The coffee tasted good. After we ate they took us to the clothing room and we got our blues, a blue shirt and pants made out of a kind of denim, and brown shoes—"Santa Rosas"—old man type shoes with the line across the toe. I was very happy to be out of the jumpsuit; I felt less conspicuous. But I found out later it wasn't the clothes that made me conspicuous. I learned that even with six thousand people I couldn't just blend in with the crowd. Everyone knew we had just drove up. One of the guards told us some of the details. He told us what we should and should not do. He told us you get one to life for attempted escape. He pointed out the walkways and told us the guards were all expert shots. He said just do right and everything'll be okay.

It so happened we got there on Friday, so my first day was a Saturday and we were more or less free until Monday. When I arrived I'd seen several people I'd known before, and when I walked out of the clothing room here was a real good friend, Little Ernie Flores. He was one of those prematurely grey people, his hair had turned almost completely. His bone structure was Indian, but he was very small and dapper. He saw me and he said, "Heeeey, Art!" I looked at my clothes. They were old, wrinkled blue denim. He was wearing the same thing but it was that slightly different color, and he was all pressed, real sharp. Instead of the Santa Rosas he had loafers; they were shined. He looked great. The last time I'd seen him on the streets he'd had a lung operation and he was really messed up. Now he was healthy and clean, and it made me feel good to see him like that. He said, "Come on, I'll show you around." He noticed me looking at his clothes and at my own and he said, "Oh, don't worry about that, man. I'll fix you up. Come on."

Little Ernie was working in the employees' dry cleaning plant. He was the lead man there. We had some small talk and walked around, and he said, "It's not as bad as it seems. I know how you feel because I felt the same when I first drove up, drug and panicked, but you've got friends here, and everything'll be alright."

We walked around the big yard, and he showed me the canteen line. You can buy a book with duckets in it, coupons for however much money you draw, which you use to pay for things from the canteen. You get a new book each month, and no one can steal it from you because only you can cash your own duckets. You can buy these books if someone sends you money, or you can have someone that's in the jail put money on your books, or you can get a job and get paid. Eventually I got a job paying six dollars a month, but the prison deducted a dollar and eighty cents from that for the "inmate welfare fund," which they said was for movies and canteen, leaving me with four dollars and twenty cents a month, still a lot of money.

Little Ernie showed me the big yard. The cell blocks formed the walls of the yard and right in the middle was a tower with a shed on it and a walkway so the guards could walk out to it with rifles. I looked around this big area and everywhere I looked I saw groups of people and I could see that they were, like, cliques. A group of Mexicans, a group of blacks, a group of whites. Each group talking, and all kinds of action going on. In the middle of the yard, to the left of the shed, was a bunch of picnic tables. I saw guys standing around them real intent. I walked over with Ernie and he said, "This is the domino tables." They played dominoes because cards weren't allowed. They made their own dominoes out of plastic and wood and glass, and they were beautiful. They played for cigarettes—that was money in prison. And I learned that many people were killed because of debts incurred at the domino tables. In San Quentin you could work or not work. If you chose not to work, you'd just wander around the yard. Those were the guys that played dominoes. Those were the guys that if any dope came in they had some action. They were living just like on the streets, hustling and scuffling.

Ernie said, "Let me show you the lower yard." The lower yard has a football field, a baseball diamond, and handball and basketball courts. We started down the stairs and as we went down I saw a guy coming up, and he looked really strange; he looked like a ghost. He had his hands on his

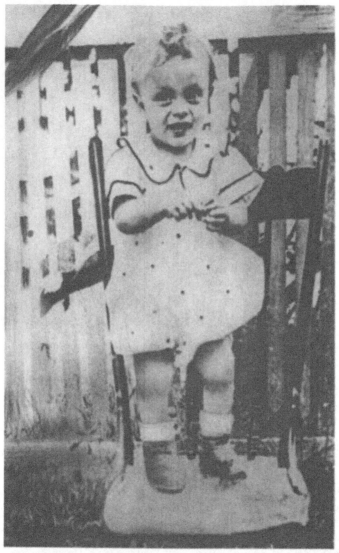

Me at about age one. "There was another time when they were separated for nine months and Junior lived with Grandpa Joe and Grandma in Watts. Grandma took care of him then, and that's when he made the most progress physically." Photo courtesy of Thelma Pepper.

The only photograph of my mother, my father, and me together.

My father who, more than any other person, molded my personality and way of thinking. Photo courtesy of Thelma Pepper.

My grandmother and my father. Photo courtesy of Thelma Pepper.

(Left) Thelma, later my stepmother, in 1932; one of the nicest, most sincere and honest persons I've ever known. Photo courtesy of Thelma Pepper. (Right) Me (on the left) with Thelma's children—Bud, John, and the little one, Edna. Photo courtesy of Thelma Pepper.

My mother and I in downtown Los Angeles. I was about 13.

Me in the uniform of the Cleveland Boys Band, San Pedro, California, under the direction of James E. Son. This was my first exposure to a musical group.

Benny Carter and his band at Billy Berg's Swing Club, Hollywood, about 1944. From left to right: Sonny White (piano), Benny, Jimmy Cannady (behind Benny), Harold Clark, Tommy Moultrie (bass), Bob Graettinger, Joe Epps, Willard Brown, Candy Ross. Second row: Percy Brice, Charles Johnson, Bumps Meyers, Al Gray, Calvin Strickland, John Morris. Photo courtesy of Benny Carter.

Me as a soldier boy in 1944.

Playing football at Fort Sill, Oklahoma. I'm on the left, carrying the ball.

A rehearsal with the Army Ground Forces Band at Camp Butner, North Carolina.

Me, Patti, my mother, and my "cousin" John in Tijuana, just after World War II.

My first wife and first love, Patti.

Right after the war, before rejoining Kenton, I toured with The Lou Olds Group for a short time and had this picture taken in Arkansas. The inscription says, "Love! to my beer drinking buddy—your goofy son. Pepper" My mother and I drank and smoked pot together.

Stan Kenton, a powerful man, who was the only person I knew to approach the stature of my father. I'm on the left with my sax. New York's Commodore Hotel around 1948.

On the road in Iowa with Kenton's band. The bus broke down and it was freezing cold. We made a good thing of it, though, and had an impromptu march down the highway. Ray Wexell is the leader and behind him, left to right, are Bob Fitzpatrick, Bart Varsalona, and Harry Betts. Photo courtesy of Buddy Childers.

Bob Cooper and June Christy in their Kenton days.

The Stan Kenton band on Catalina island, 1951. Left to right, first row: Stan, Jay Johnston, Bob Cooper, me (suffering with a terrible sunburn), Bud Shank, Bart Caldarall, Bob Gioga. Second row: Shelly Manne, Dick Kenney, Harry Betts, Bob Fitzpatrick, George Roberts, Milt Bernhart. Last row: Ralph Blaze (on guitar), Don Bagley, John Coppola, Buddy Childers, John Howell, Shorty Rogers, Maynard Ferguson. Photo courtesy of Ray Avery.

Pepper Spices Offering At Surf

Hollywood—Art Pepper, alto man who took first place in the beat's 1951 poll, launched his new quartet at L.A.'s Surf Club recently. Unit is hailed by modernists (down beat, February 22) as the most musically refreshing new group on the coast since Dave Brubeck's. With this issue's Scanning subject are Hampton Hawes, piano; Joe Mondragon, bass; and Larry Bunker, drums and vibes. down beat, March 7, 1952. Copyright 1952 by down beat. Used by special permission.

Modern Jazz Is Lighthouse Beacon

Hollywood—Onetime Kenton bass man Howard Rumsey started Sunday afternoon sessions at the Lighthouse Cafe, Hermosa Beach, two years ago. Now it's a fulltime operation and a notable west coast spot for the friends of progressive jazz. Sitting in when this photo was taken were, left to right, Teddy Edwards, Art Pepper, Doug Mettome, Shorty Rogers, bassist Rumsey, and Shelly Manne...down beat, August 24, 1951. Copyright 1951 by down beat. Used by special permission.

In 1956 Diane and I lived on one of the steepest hills in Los Angeles, on Fargo Street. I woke up one morning to a phone call from Bill Claxton, the photographer, saying that he had to take my picture today for the cover of The Return of Art Pepper. I had run out of heroin and was very sick, and I was unable to score before Bill got there. We climbed to the corner, and he snapped this picture of me in agony. Photo by William Claxton. Used by permission.

ART PEPPER
Exclusive CONTEMPORARY RECORDS recording artist.

My grandmother, Diane, my father, and Thelma, about 1958. Diane and I were both fat because we'd been drinking Cosanyl. Photo courtesy of Thelma Pepper.

Diane and Bijou, about 1965. I left them both with Marie. Photo courtesy of Marie Randall.

The Buddy Rich band of 1968. My spleen had ruptured and was removed, and I rejoined the band (too soon, it turned out) at the Riverboat in New York. Woody Herman is on the extreme left, Jack Jones is holding the microphone, Don Menza is sitting on the far left in the sax section. I'm right next to him. Photo courtesy of Don and Rose Menza.

(Facing page.) Bassist Jim Krutcher took this picture of me, 1967 or '68. Photo courtesy of Jim Krutcher.

Activities board in the main lobby at Synanon, 1971. Photo by Laurie Pepper.

Jamming in Synanon. Phil Woods came to visit. From left to right, Phil, me playing tenor, and Frank Rehak.

(Left) My fourth and greatest love, Laurie, on the beach at Synanon, 1970.
(Right) Laurie and I in one of those photo booths, 1975.

Conducting a clinic. I'm instructing the saxophone section of a college band.
Photo by Laurie Pepper.

A publicity picture, 1976. Photo by Laurie Pepper.

Laurie. Photo by Mirandi Babitz. Used by permission.

Les Koenig presiding over a 1977 record date for Art Pepper: No Limit. From left to right: Les, Carl Burnett, George Cables (seated; I call him "Mr. Beautiful." He's my favorite pianist.), and Tony Dumas. Photo by Laurie Pepper.

The first Japanese tour, 1977. Cal Tjader and I after our concert in Tokyo, holding flowers given us by pretty followers of jazz. My reception there was overwhelming and frightening. I feel a strong obligation to return to Japan again and again and to justify, in my playing and recording, the devotion of the Japanese fans. Photo by Laurie Pepper.

A live radio broadcast from Tokyo in 1977. Photo by Laurie Pepper.

On the cover of the Newport Jazz Festival issue of the Japanese magazine, Swing Journal, July, 1977. The photo was taken at the beginning of my U.S. east coast tour. Photo by Nobuo Hiyashi. Used by permission.

In the kitchen of the Village Vanguard at the end of the east coast tour,
August, 1977. Photo by Mitchell Seidel. Used by permission.

At a photo session for **Swing Journal** in Tokyo, 1978. One of the photographers took this picture of Laurie and me.

Japan again in March, 1978. We traveled and performed eighteen days out of nineteen. My band, from left to right: Milcho Leviev, Bob Magnusson, and Carl Burnett, all fine musicians. We played large, medium, and small halls and tiny nightclubs. This is a rehearsal in a huge hall in Hiroshima. Photo by Ted Kimura. Used by permission.

One of the most pleasant record dates I've ever done—Art Pepper: Among Friends, September, 1978. From left to right: me; drummer, Frank Butler; bassist, Bob Magnusson; and pianist, Russ Freeman. Photo by Laurie Pepper.

I like this portrait Laurie took of me at the Among Friends date, September 2, 1978, the day after my birthday. Photo by Laurie Pepper.

This picture was taken recently at Dontes, a Los Angeles jazz club. I've played there many, many times, and each time it's a battle; I'm out to conquer the audience. I feel my whole musical life is on the line with each performance. In this picture it looks like I'm winning. Photo by Laurie Pepper.

At Dontes, ready to try to win again. I think my expression in this picture suggests how hard it is to play jazz. Photo by Laurie Pepper.

With Ralph Kaffel, President of Fantasy Records. "He was everything Art admired in a man . . . a gentleman." At Fantasy Studios, at the Straight Life session, September 1979. Photo by Laurie Pepper

Art and producer Ed Michel at the Winter Moon session. Art said this ballads-with-strings album was the best record he ever made. Fantasy Studios, September, 1980. Photo by Laurie Pepper

TOP: Art and Laurie, backstage at Yubin Chokin Hall, Tokyo, July, 1979, during the Landscape tour. Photo by K. Abe, used by permission

MIDDLE: Art and Laurie on the book tour, San Francisco, the Jack Tar Hotel, November, 1979. Photo by Phil Bray, used by permission

BOTTOM: Art and Laurie at Fantasy Studios, Berkeley 1981. Photo by Phil Bray, used by permission

"Art, onstage, during those years, was a riot. . . . He didn't tell jokes, he told stories."
At Donte's, circa 1980. Photo by Laurie Pepper

The Art Pepper Quartet wearing their band jackets: Carl Burnett, drums; George
Cables, piano; Art; David Williams, bass. The background, including other people
in the backstage area of a nightclub, has been airbrushed out, but this was taken in
Australia in August, 1981. Photo by Laurie Pepper

With George in Japan, on tour, November, 1981. Photo by K. Abe, used by permission

"I remember a day." Off Seattle, circa 1980. Photo by Laurie Pepper

stomach, and I saw that there was blood running out all over his hands. As we got close to him he let go of his stomach to grab the rail because he was starting to fall, and he was just covered with blood. I said to Ernie, "Oh, man!" And I started to go to the guy's aid, but Ernie grabbed me and said, "Come on, come on, *come on!* Hurry!" He was frantic. We got down the stairs, and as we reached the bottom I looked back, and here was the guard on the walkway above the stairs with his rifle pointed at the guy. Ernie said, "Now, if we had stayed there to try to help him we would have been right in the middle of this shit. There's no telling what might have happened. I know it's cold. We haven't been brought up that way. But you have to mind your own business and keep walkin'." I said, "What happened?" He said, "Oh, those things happen here all the time. Somebody shanked the guy. They get a piece of metal from the machine shop and sharpen it into a dagger, and they put tape over the handle part."

We got to the lower yard, and I was feeling kind of sick, and Ernie said, "Now, dig these cats here." There were a bunch of courts where the Mexicans were playing handball, and there were two full-sized basketball courts. I saw these guys playing basketball that looked like Mexicans, but they weren't. And then I realized that they were righteous Indians, American Indians. Ernie said, "Dig these guys and get a good look at them, and if you ever find yourself in any close proximity to them get away as soon as you can. Never let them see you staring at them. Never bump into them. Watch yourself because they're dangerous. They hate everyone but themselves."

You stay in D section for a while and then you're moved to another section. I was kept in the South Block and moved up to the fifth tier.

Twice a week they'd have a shower run. They call out, "Showers!" You take your blues off; they rack the gates and run you downstairs to the showers in sections. There's about ten shower heads in these open showers, and there's this huge number of men in line waiting to get in. So as you go into the shower you throw your underwear into a bin and then you try to figure out some way to get under a shower head. There might have been five or six or ten people to a shower head, so you got clean the best way you could and then you got in line by the white room. When your turn finally came they'd give you a towel, and you'd give them your size. They'd give you the closest thing they had to your size. If you wore size thirty-two shorts they might give you a thirty-four or a thirty-six all torn and miserable. Then you'd dry yourself and put this stuff on. Cold cement floors. The windows all broken. The wind whistling through the windows. And the groups of people, the noises they made, the whole vulgar scene . . .

Maybe there'd be a sissy, a black sissy. There was this one guy, they called him "Chocolate Bar." He had a joint that was maybe twenty inches long. It looked like a snake. And he would squeeze his legs together so his hair would form, like, a cunt in the front and then in back there'd be this long thing like a tail dangling, his joint. And he would be wiggling and swishing and singing, and all these guys would be saying, "Saaaay, baby! Saaaay, beautiful! Saaaay, honey! Boy, I'd sure like to have some of *that!* You're sure beautiful, gal!" All this sickening shit, guys looking at you, animals. There are guys that lift weights, that got all kinds of muscles, and they're flashing and posing and trying to prove something I didn't know what or to who. I thought, "What kind of creatures are these? What are they trying to do?" What they were doing, they'd see some guy that was young and tender looking and they were trying to impress him. They were trying to get him hot. Can you imagine a bunch of men trying to make another man hot? And make this little kid want *them* rather than some big spook or some double-ugly southerner? Then you'd see other guys, just terrified, guys with pimples all over their backs, people with big scars and horrible deformities. And you're there, and there you are, and then some asshole just purposely rubs up against you.

And you had to run and be like an animal just to get a shower. You had to act like the animals in order to make it. They only left the water on a little while so you had to fight, and once you got soap on you, you had to push and to touch a male body . . . It's the most sickening thing in the world. But you had to push them out of the way to get into the shower because you had these guys that thought they were real tough and they'd stand right in the middle. You were taking your life in your hands. They had fights all the time. And the guards were standing up on the walkway with rifles trained on the showers.

The dregs of humanity, boy, that's what they are. The only thing I can liken it to is when I was in the army in England and France, the American soldiers. They were ordinary people that you'd see on the streets at home; they had mothers and fathers; and they were just human beings that go to church and are polite—actual humans that can get on a bus and pay the fare, transact business. And I saw them overseas screaming at women pushing baby carriages, "Hey, baby! Hey, you fine-assed, high-cunted bitch! Hey, baby! How'd you like to suck on my big cock, you beautiful motherfucker you?" That's how they talked, and that's what they did, and it was the same in San Quentin. I thought, "Am I one of these?" I thought, "Here I am again." Only it was worse because I was locked up. I wanted to kill them all. I thought if I just had a knife or a gun or some poison gas.

I realized I couldn't stand the way I felt during those first few showers. I realized if I stayed like that I wouldn't make it. I'd kill somebody or get killed and never get out. I'd never, ever be able to play again. I'd never be able to get up in the morning and go for a walk. Never see happiness and beauty. I'd never have any loved ones again, any love at all, anything decent. I'd never be able to feel the warmth of a woman's body. I'd never know the companionship of a woman's love, just to be in a house with her and be able to hold her and look at her and to feel that I had the comfort and care of another human being. The pleasure of lying together, watching TV, touching one another, waking up in the middle of the night and feeling her body, her hair, having something of beauty there. I thought, "I'll never make it." I would have to kill someone or they'd have to kill me because I hated them so much. Every person. And I hated, above all, everybody who had a hand in putting me there, all the circumstances, all the ... There was no way to define them. I was helpless and just carried away in hatred. Can you imagine these showers? Twice a week? And that's all you could bathe no matter what happened. You couldn't ever be clean at any other time because it was freezing cold water in your little cell with the filthy toilet and the tiny sink. And to be locked up from four in the evening until the next morning with somebody that you had no rapport with, that you despised. You could never be alone. Not for one second. You couldn't shit alone; you couldn't piss alone; you couldn't jerk off alone. I looked around and saw these guys laughing and others almost in trances who looked like they were just wiped out. Oh, a few of them were loaded but very few. I wondered how they could stand it.

That's when I started talking to Little Ernie and Woody Woodward, a huge guy, solid muscle, with fists like ham hocks, but a warm person who played tenor saxophone and painted pictures and loved me because I was a musician. He had committed so many armed robberies before he went to Quentin that they had him in the newspaper, the all-time winner of armed robberies with violence: he'd done about two hundred of them up and down the coast. I talked to Jerry Maher, a Richard Widmark type, slender, with steel-cold, blue eyes; I'd seen him in situations with guys that were ten times bigger than him and meaner, you would think, and he was always at ease, had no fear at all. I talked with these people and others. I knew so many—Frank Ortiz was there and Ruben—and I asked them, "Man, how do you stand it? What do I do? I don't want to die here. How do I survive?" And I think it was Jerry Maher who told me, "You have to loosen your cap." He was kind of joking. He said, "I got a cap wrench, man, if you want it." He meant you've got to get a little crazy and a little dingy when you get too uptight. He told me, "Act like you're crazy. It'll keep these idiots away from you. Make noises. Talk to yourself. Mumble. Sing to yourself and groan. Act weird."

That's what I'd done in Terminal Island, but it was nothing to the extent that I did it in San Quentin. I went completely out of it. When I went to the shower, I would stumble like the people in Forth Worth. I'd kick my feet and go, "Grrr-rghhuuughhh!" I'd look at people and go, "Uhhhooooohhhh!" I'd get in the shower and throw the soap up in the air, and I'd put the water in my mouth and scream, "Aaaeeeeeeeee!" They'd look at me and then they'd move away so I could shower. I would bad-rap people. It's a miracle I wasn't killed. I acted like a real maniac and the most violent person imaginable. I'd go to the mess hall with John Wallach—we were in Fort Worth together; we'd go to eat and instead of sticking the food in my mouth I'd stick it in my cheek or bury my head in the plate. We'd put our arms around the plates and eat like animals, slurping and slobbering. I took every kind of pill, every single thing I could get my hands on no matter what it was. There were some pills, they called them "black-and-whites," Dilantin and Phenobarbital; they were for epileptics. Most people were afraid to take them because they really messed you up, but they gave you a nice high so I took them all the time. I'd wake up early in my cell and get my can, and I'd take some wax paper or toilet paper and make a bomb—roll it up into a ball and light it to heat the water—and make some coffee, and I'd take the pills with my coffee and be wiped out when I staggered out of my cell. You lose your equilibrium. You can't walk. So I got a reputation for being really insane. People were afraid of me. And I found that the things I thought I wouldn't be able to live with I was able to play over. I'd mumble to myself and slobber, and that's how I survived. There's nothing like being locked up.

When I went to the guidance center at Chino in '60, we went by alphabetical order, and the name right before mine was Penn, William Penn. Penn was a nice guy, kinda sweet, slender. He had pretty skin. You know how a girl looks when she's young and she goes to the beach a lot, a blonde, when her hair is kind of brownish-blonde on her arms and the sun hits it? Well, Penn had hairs on his arms like that, and he had real pretty hair, little curls, and he had beautiful blue eyes. He looked like a little sparrow, and he loved me because he loved jazz, and he'd follow me around. We were on the chain together to go to Quentin. They called, "Penn, Pepper." So we were handcuffed together. We got on the Grey Goose and we sat together; it just happened to work out that way. They took us off the bus at Soledad and they called the names for the cells, and it's "Penn, Pepper" in the same cell, which was nice because he's clean, very neat, and he adores me. I had someone to flatter me, and he's telling me the records he's got and when he saw me at so-and-so, how much he loved it, how much his old lady loved it. The next morning we got back on the bus and it was the same thing: we sat together. So people see us come; we're handcuffed together; we eat together; we go through the physicals and the different things you go through when you go in and we're always together because of our names. And, evidently, a few people decided this cat was my kid, my punk, my girl friend.

You get very aware in prison. You're careful to observe things. It's a jungle; there might be a snake there or a centipede. You never walk around half conscious. When you go into a toilet you look at every person. If you're in line you look at everybody behind you. It becomes a habit. Eyes are always moving. So I noticed this one guy, kind of cold-eyed, who was watching me. He was about five, nine, and there was nothing violent looking about his build, nothing physical, but he had a scary way about him and I never saw him talk to a living soul.

I noticed him watching me. I'd be standing someplace in the upper yard, and I'd look over, and he'd be behind an iron girder looking at me. I'd look at him and he'd lower his eyes and turn around. I'd look away and back, quick, and he'd be staring at me again. He'd lower his head. I'd find myself in the canteen line, and there he'd be standing at a distance, but I'd feel his presence. And I really started getting worried.

I hit on a guy I knew. I said, "Man, don't look now. I don't want this cat to know I'm pinning him. But this cat standing over by So-and-so . . . " And I said real low, "Do you know that cat?" And my friend said, "I sure do, man! That guy is murder three. Everybody's terrified of him. Nobody messes with him, and he doesn't have anything to do with anybody. He's a real death-shank type cat. He does everything single-O." I hit on another guy. Same response. I hit on another guy and he said, "Man, don't have any dealings with him and don't ever do anything he doesn't like or you're dead." I thought, "What is this cat looking at me for?" I hit on another guy and I copped out. I asked him, "Well, why do you think the cat's watching me?" The guy said, "Well, there's only one reason I can think of. He's a lifer. He's gonna be here for life. He's looking at you. That means he has eyes for you." He wasn't a fruiter. See, the guys that are doing life, rather than just playing with themselves, with books, they learn to make it with a man and think of the man as a woman. They're not fruiters in that sense of the word. Maybe if I was there for life I'd do the same thing. I doubt it though.

Finally, one day a guy that was a friend of Penn's, Bob,

came up to me and said, "Wait a minute. Don't look now but—now look! See that guy standing over there by the third girder?" I looked and said, "Oh, man, are you kidding? That cat's been looking at me for weeks now. I'm terrified." Bob said, "Well, he approached me the other day, and he wants to make a meet with you." Bob said, "I don't know what he wants, man, but you gotta see him. You gotta make a meet with him and find out." I said, "Okay. Tell him I'll see him downstairs in the lower yard."

I go down to the handball court. The guy walks up to me. He says, "Art Pepper?" I say, "Yeah." He says, "Man, I hear you're a great musician." And right away I think, "Uh-oh, that's what the cat wants. He's intrigued with me." I say, "Yeah, why?" He says, "I been watching you." I say, "I know that, man. I could tell you were watching me. What's your story?" I was trying to act tough. I was scared to death. He says, "Well, I been watching you, man, and, uh, you, you got a lotta friends. A lot of friends. A lot of friends. I've been asking about you. Quietly. I noticed that a lot of people like you. You talk to Chicanos. You talk to suedes. You talk to everybody. Everybody seems to like you. You have a lot of friends. I'm not like that. I'm here for murder. You've probably heard that. I'm here for murder—a couple of times. And I've killed a couple people in jail since I been here. I don't think I'm ever going to get out. I don't like people. People don't like me." Then he says, "I'm lonesome." And I think, "Oh God, here it is. The cat's lonesome." I say, "Yeah, well, I'm lonesome, too. God! I'll say I'm lonesome, man! I'd give anything in the world if I wasn't here and I had my old lady or some chick that really dug me." He looked at me and he gave me the funniest look. He says, "Chick? That's a thing from another world." And I think, "That's it! That's what the guy wants! He wants me! What am I going to say to him? What am I going to do?"

I'm looking in his eyes, and they're a dead, pale blue. There's nothing there. I say, "Yeah, man, yeah. We're all lonely, man. I feel for you. At least I'm going to get out one of these days." He says, "Well, I just want you to understand my position, man. I'm lonely, and I can't stand it anymore, and I've got to have someone." I say, "Yeah?" He says, "I've got to have someone." I think, "What am I going to do?" He says, "I've got to have someone. You know that little cat that you got?" I didn't understand what he'd said. It didn't sink in, I was so scared. I thought he was going to hit on me. I said, "What do you mean?" He says, "You know. *You* know. Penn. Your little friend." I say, "Penn? Oh, you mean, oh, you mean *Penn*." He says, "Yeah, yeah. Penn, your little friend." I say, "Well, what about him, man?" He says, "Well, man, you're popular, like I told you. Here I am all alone." And then he says, "I've got things to offer. A *lot* to offer. I'm clean. . . ."

He started telling me his good points. He says, "I've killed a few people, but that was just circumstances. They got in my way and there was no way out. I had to do it. And," he says, "maybe I'm a little crazy." And I thought, "A little!" It was a cold day. Northern California. Wind's blowing. It must have been thirty degrees, and I was sweating. He says, "You could have anybody you want. I've seen Mandy, like, looking at you. She'd give you anything you wanted, man. I've been looking and looking. That little guy, Penn, just turns me on. I really love him." And *then* the whole thing was clear to me! I said, "Well. Great, man, great!"

I was so relieved. I said, "Oh, *wonderful!*" I almost broke into some insane laughter. I was so scared I almost peed in my pants. I thought he was going to stab me right there because there's some strange people, man, and all the stories I'd heard about this guy! I said, "Well, that's great, man, why don't you talk to him?" And he says, "*I* can't talk to him. That's your, that's your old lady, man." I say, "No! No he's not!" He says, "Alright, now, lookit . . . " You know, he wouldn't believe me. I tried to explain, but he thought I was trying to get out of making a deal. He says, "Alright, I'll tell you what. You decide what you want for him. I'm appeal.ng to you now. I'm appealing to your good nature. You can have anything you want. With me, I'm hung here. I saw him. I like him. I want him. I need him. I *have* to have him. I know maybe you care for him, too, but you could find somebody else. Please. Could you do me a favor? Please. You tell me how many cigarettes you want for him, and whatever I can give you outside of that. If any dope comes in—you're a dopefiend, right?—I'll kill somebody and get some dope for you. You make a price, moneywise," meaning cigarettes, "and I'll get it and pay it to you." I say, "It isn't that way!" He says, "Think it over, decide what you want, and I'll talk to you again." I said, "But . . . " And he was gone.

I'd read books about prison life and seen movies, but I'd never, ever heard of selling somebody for cigarettes. If I hadn't been involved I would have laughed and laughed. It would have been a great story to tell. But I *was* involved, and it wasn't funny. I went to Bob and ran down the conversation. I said, "What am I going to do?" He said, "*Sell* him!" I said, "He isn't *mine!*" He said, "Any death play, any shank play involved, we're in it fifty-fifty, if you want to do it that way, and we'll split the bread." I said, "I can't do that. I cannot *do* that." He said, "The guy believes that you and Penn are making it. Nothing's going to change his mind. What else you gonna do?" I said, "I don't know *what* to do?" He said, "Sell him! Sell him! If you don't sell him I will. I'll go to him and tell him *I* got control over the cat, and he'll listen to me, and then you'll be out the bread." I saw that the guy was serious. This guy was a friend of Penn's, not of mine. He was a friend of Penn's from the streets, this guy.

I went to Penn and told him the story. He said, "Oh, God! Oh, Art! God! What am I going to *do?* Don't sell me! What am I going to *do?*" I said, "Are you a sissy?" He said, "No!" I said, "Why does this guy think you're a sissy?" He said, "I don't *know!*" And then I looked at Penn for the first time in that way. He had full, pretty lips like a woman, blue eyes, blonde hair; he was really beautiful. I looked at his arms and I saw the hairs. He said, "Oh, help me, man, please! Don't sell me!" I said, "How could I sell you? You don't *belong* to me!" He said, "You're my friend. Help me!" I said, "Well, you better talk to this guy who *says* he's a friend of yours." And I told him what Bob had said.

We both went to Bob. We told him, "Man, you can't do that." Bob said to Penn, "Lookit, lookit, I'll tell you what we'll do. We'll sell you to the guy; we'll get the bread; and *then* . . . we'll *kill* the guy!" Penn looked at me, and I looked at him, and we both looked at this other cat. I told Penn, "Come here, man. Come here." We left Bob. I took Penn to the lifer. I told him, "Man, this guy's name is Penn. My name is Pepper." I ran down the whole trip. "He's married. We're like, next to each other in our names. We were chained together. We were celled together.

We became friends. He likes jazz. I play jazz. We became friends. He's not a fruiter. I don't make it with fruiters." I talked and I talked and I talked so well, and we were so open and honest with the cat that he finally realized what was happening. Then we told him about this other cat, Bob, and he got mad. We found out later that Bob was the guy that had developed this thing. He said to me, "I'm sorry. I was told that that was what was going on. Bob is going to hear about this."

Three days later Bob was transferred to Vacaville. He had asked for a transfer. The guy had drove on him with a shank. From then on the guy became a good friend of Penn's and a good friend of mine. He started coming around, listening to jazz. This was a guy that had never had anything going for him. We started eating with him sometimes. And so, he acquired a couple of friends, like, out of the whole thing.

16 | San Quentin: Learning the Ropes

1961–1964

WHEN I BEGAN to learn the ins and outs, and I started loosening my cap, life became a little more bearable. Finally I got a job. You fill out a card. They ask you to put down your skills and qualifications, so I said I knew how to type. I'd learned in junior high school and thank God because it really came in handy at this time in my life. They saw my IQ, and I had neat handwriting, and that impressed them. They needed someone to work in the paymaster's office.

In San Quentin they had maximum, close, medium A, medium B, and minimum custody. There were people that were locked up all the time, and there were others that were allowed out in the yard but who had to report to the little police shack there every hour. For this job I wanted in the paymaster's office I had to be a medium B or minimum, and I was a medium A when I arrived there, but they saw I had the ability to do the job so I had an interview with the head of the office, and they put me up for reclassification. This got me out of the jobs I had been doing—cleaning jobs, dirty jobs that were really a drag—and hanging out in the yard, and that's where you get into trouble.

When I got the job I had to get up at the 4:30 unlock; the only people in the South Block that were unlocked at that time were the kitchen people. I didn't live in their section. This time the bureacracy worked to my advantage. They moved me to the

289

North Block, a semihonor block, though I wasn't eligible yet: I didn't have enough time clean with no beefs.

In the South Block you were locked up from 4 P.M. on, period, but in the North Block, after supper, at different times, they'd have unlocks and you could go down and take a shower. This meant a totally different life from the one I'd been leading. I'd spend less time in my cell, and I'd be able to go to movies in the evenings instead of only on the weekends—when I'd be able to borrow a horn and play.

I'd wake up at 4:30, wash my face with freezing cold water, throw my clothes on, and then they would rack the gate. I'd go to the mess hall and eat at the early line. Then I'd go through the gate, and it would be dark, pitch-black out, and I'd walk all alone through this prison. There'd be no one there but the guards; at different points you could see them flapping their hands together, huddled around these little towers, where they'd have a stove, and you could see the steam coming out of their mouths. I'd walk to the between-gates. I'd go through a little passageway and there would be Fourposts, the police shack, to my right; to my left was the clothing room and the gym. Further on there were the chapels: a Catholic chapel and a Protestant chapel right next to each other. They were very pretty; they had built them new. At that time they didn't recognize the Muslim religion, but any other faith could take a room and have their little services. I think they had AA meetings in the chapels, too. In Fort Worth and in Terminal Island I had gone to AA meetings and I'd even sung in the church choirs, but in San Quentin you were locked up so much you only had time for a few activities. I worked ten hours a day during the week, so my weekends were spent playing music, reading, and trying to get loaded.

I'd walk to the gate. The guy would open it and say hello. I'd go into a place and sit, and then they'd open another gate for me. They'd pull my card. It was really elaborate. Then I'd be outside the inner prison. In front of me was the gun tower. And then there was another gate and a machine that checked to see if you had any metal on you. There was another gate, the firehouse, the officer's club, some of the guard's homes, a library for the guards, and then the final gate. Beyond that there's a parklike area for the guards' families and the warden's home, a big place. To my left was a large building where the free people worked.

The paymaster's office was just a cement building set on the outside of the South Block. It was right next to the walkway going into the gas chamber. I'd walk to the door all alone. I was the first one there. It would be foggy, and the fog horns would be going. I'd open the place and put the lights on and go to my desk. The paymaster's office had a dual purpose: we kept the hours for all the people that worked in the prison and all the state employees and we doubled as a cleaner and laundry service for the guards and the free personnel. I'd start work at 5:30, and people coming to work would bring their clothes in. I had a little book. I'd go to the counter and write up a ticket, whatever it was, two pants, one jacket, and charge them so many ducats. They bought books and used ducats so the convicts wouldn't deal in money.

The guy I worked for, I'll call him Mr. Williams. He was a black guy, dark. He was very neat, a studious-looking guy. He loved jazz, and if we were alone he'd ask me about when I was with Benny Carter's band or when I was with Stan Kenton's band and how it was being a traveling jazz musician. And he asked me how I could use drugs to the extent that I gave up my music, how I could allow that to happen to me. He was very nice, but he was a free person. He could go out and ball a chick that night. He had money. He had a car. And he'd tell me that he went to North Beach and saw some jazz player or other. I almost got the feeling he was lording it over me at times; I'd get angry at times and find myself hating him. But then I'd realize that whatever I had done, *I* had done it and it would do me no good to have those feelings. I only hurt myself.

Mr. Williams was a good person. A lot of times the six of us, the convicts that worked in the paymaster's office, we'd do little things that were illegal. We'd steal a steak from the ODR, the officers' dining room, or we'd take the food out of the trash cans from the gas chamber or get a cheeseburger or a chocolate malt illicitly from the snack bar. We'd hide this stuff in the toilet in the back of the office. We'd eat in there or cook the steak in there, and sometimes Mr. Williams would catch us; he wouldn't come all the way in but I'd know he smelled the food. And he'd give us a pass. We knew that he knew, but he never busted us for any of these things—and these were beefs that go against you as far as getting in an honor block, or they can take away your movie privileges. If you get too many they can cancel your board appearance.

Sometimes I'd be playing music in the yard on a weekend, and I'd look over, and there would be Mr. Williams, standing unobtrusively against the wall listening. I'd catch his eye, and he'd nod at me, and then the next day at work he'd say, "Yeah, I heard you yesterday. You were smokin', man." Every now and then he'd give me a message from somebody. "Sonny Stitt says to say hello." Mr. Williams had mentioned that I worked for him in San Quentin, and Sonny had said, "Give him my best and tell him to get out here and start blowin'!" He'd boost my spirits like that, so I knew he was for me, but he was cool enough to know that you can't be a righteous convict and make it in San Quentin if you have any association with a guard, which is what he was. It wouldn't be good for your reputation. He realized that, and I think that's why he was so aloof. I think he would have liked to have really been friends.

There was a guy that came into the paymaster's office all the time, Sergeant Metzger or Metzler, a big, square-headed guy. He had a Will Rogers air and he was real kindly looking, but I had strange feelings about him. I got weird vibes. One day after he left I mentioned it to this cat that worked in the office. "Who is that guy, man? I just can't figure him out, that Sergeant Metzger." He said, "Oh, man, you've never heard of him?" He went over to the pay book, where there was a printout with all the guards' names, and he said, "Look at this." By Metzger's name there were all these extra figures—"$175.00; $175.00." I looked under the code and it said, "death house duty." That was the gas chamber. He told me, "He's the guy that has worked every execution for the last twenty years, him and another guard that they pick at random."

They had two slots leading into the gas chamber and they had two guards, Sergeant Metzger and another guy. Each guard had a pellet of cyanide like a large jelly bean. On a nod from the deathwatch lieutenant, when the victim was all strapped in with the hood on and ready, at that nod they both dropped their pellets. The pellets go down little ramps and fall into pots which are out of the guards' eyesight. One contains water and one contains acid. In the pot that has the water nothing happens, but in the other pot the acid eats away the coating on the pellet and the gas is released and kills the person. The guards don't know which of them is responsible, but this guy had been doing it for twenty years or so. There's no telling how many people he'd killed. He got one hundred and seventy-five dollars for each one. He had requested the job, and he had seniority, so they just allowed him to do it all the time. Some of the guards wouldn't do it, which is a great thing to be said about guards. I wanted to ask him about it, but I would have been completely out of line.

When Baldonado, Moya, and Ma Duncan were to be executed they took her from the women's prison at Corona and brought her to San Quentin to be killed. I saw them when they drove up. The next morning, when Metzger came in, I said, "Uh, yesterday I saw Ma Duncan drive in." He said, "Oh, did you see 'em? Yeah." I said, "Wow, it's sure far-out, huh? She looked like a little ol' mother." He looked at me. When he saw I was trying to draw him out, he gave me a straaaaange look. It wasn't a scary look. It was a haunting look. He wasn't threatening me. It was a cold, detached, penetrating look, and I tried to read it, and we looked at each other for a long time. I was writing up his ticket, and he was waiting for me to finish, and I found myself shaking. I would have given anything in the world if I could have met him on the streets as a free man and gone into a bar with him and talked to him and tried to pick his mind and find out what he felt, what he thought, if it bothered him that he'd killed all those people, if he had a reason for wanting to do it, if he felt a moral duty to rid the world of evil, if he was so desirous of money that he didn't care how he got it, if it was sadistic. I just wanted to know. It fascinated me.

It takes a while to learn the ropes of being in prison. It's like anything else—being in the army or being at a new job on the outside. If you work at a factory you have to learn what you can and can't get away with and who are the people to know. It took a little while to learn what was happening, how to do my time, and how to get little benefits and to use situations to my advantage.

I found out after being there for a while and working in the paymaster's office that that gave me a lot of advantages I wouldn't have ordinarily. A lot of people just stay out in the big yard and play dominoes. They loan money and are collectors, and they do all kinds of things that are very dangerous, and they don't have any juice, any status as far as the guards go. But I had a responsible job that set me above most of the people in the prison. I dealt with people's pay. I dealt with their clothes. I dealt with things that were valuable to the people that worked there.

After you shower, you line up to get your whites. The guys that work in the white room handle the towels and socks and shorts and T-shirts. If you have a friend in the white room, if you've got a contract, you do something for him, he does something for you. I knew a guy, Spider Barrucho, an evil-looking cat with blonde hair and a Zapata moustache. A great cat. We'd been friends on the streets. I'd come up to the white room and say, "Hey, Spider!" He'd say, "Hey, Art! What's goin' on?" And if he wasn't handing out the particular item I wanted he'd nod to the guy that was. They had the new stuff stashed. Now, you could get twenty dollars a month, which was your allowable draw, plus getting money on someone else's name. You'd get somebody on the outside to put money on another guy's books. He would draw the twenty in ducats and give you fifteen in cigarettes and other commissary and keep five. That's the standard rate. So, some guys, if they had a lot, they'd pay so many packs of cigarettes a week to the guy in the white room and get brand-new shorts, socks, T-shirts. The guy in the white room had a hell of a job. He made a lot of bread—until he got busted. He'd work so long, and then the heat would bust him. The guards knew everything that was going on because of informers, and they were very sharp. But if you had juice, that's what I'm saying, they'd say, "Well, that's Art Pepper. He works out of the paymaster's office. Let's give him a pass." And they wouldn't come down on me for my starched clothes or my new underwear even though those things are against the law. That's how you get the goodies.

And that's how you don't get rousted a lot of times for things. Sometimes we'd be out on the yard and the guards would walk up to a group standing against one of the blocks and grab everybody and shake them down for contraband. They'd find shanks, narcotics, outfits, gasoline for bombs. They would find stolen items and dirty books that were smuggled in by the guards. (The convicts pay the guards and then rent out the books, two to five packs a night.) They would find glue that people sniff, in hand lotion bottles, white glue from the shoe factory. You might have contraband shoes on. Your shoes have your number on them. My number was 64807. I might be wearing shoes that didn't carry that number. You've paid four cartons of cigarettes for those shoes, or you've stolen them from someone, or someone in the shoe factory might have made them. Sometimes a guard will bring shoes in to a certain convict. He'll wear shoes that will fit this convict and take them off and put on the convict's old ones. And if you were wearing starched clothes—say it's a weekend, you're expecting a visitor, you can't get back to your cell, you're locked out, and you've got these clothes on that you paid two or four packs of cigarettes to get. You've been saving them for this day to look sharp. The guards will roust you and strip your clothes off right there in the yard and march you to Fourposts and interrogate you. They'll try to get you to cop out on who you got the stuff from. And they'll take your starched clothes and throw them in a big tub of water. They have a pile there of the oldest, beatest clothes in outlandish sizes, with tears in them, and they'll just throw you a pair of pants and a shirt, and that will be what you wear until you can get into your cell again.

Now, I've had them walk up for a shakedown, and they'd see me standing there, and they would draw the line at the guy standing next to me: "Alright, let's clear the way. Clear the way. Let's just move out. Clear the way." And they'd get everybody in the area right next to me, and they wouldn't shake me down because I had juice.

We got the guards' clothes and the clothes of the women that worked outside, and we'd send them to the employees' dry cleaning plant. A panel truck would come. The same kind of truck that took the bodies away from the gas chamber. When the truck came in the morning at ten I'd take off the dirty clothes I'd worn to work and put on some others I'd stashed in my desk. I'd put my blues under a guard's overcoat. Ernie, who was in charge of the plant, would have straightened the guy that was driving the truck or else I would lay a couple packs of cigarettes on him, and when I was loading the truck I'd motion to the guy that this was for Ernie from me, but the guard would be watching so I'd have to do it real cool. I'd just shake the coat or flick it back so the driver could see there's blues underneath. He would take them to Ernie, who'd wash them, starch them, press them, and send them back in the afternoon. Then the driver would touch a certain overcoat and nod to me, and I'd know my clothes were under that. I'd take the coat inside. Guards were coming in to get their stuff; they'd be waiting; and if somebody came in and saw his coat and wanted it and my blues were underneath I'd be in trouble. I'd get somebody to turn the guard, and I'd grab the thing real fast, go into our little shitter, take my blues out, and sneak back in with the guard's coat. It was really a scene, and it was exciting. It was very exciting. And after work when I went through the gates the guards could see that my clothes were freshly pressed. They'd look and give me a little smile.

I'd do a favor for a guy who worked at the ODR, take his clothes and shoot 'em through, and he would give me a couple of steaks. I'd put them in our toilet, and I'd eat one. I'd take the other and stash it down in my shorts and sneak it in to Ernie. And then, again, going through the gate, the shakedown was very light.

If any of the guards did shake us down or do anything bad to any of the six of us that worked in the paymaster's office, when their clothes came in, to let them know they couldn't get away with that, we'd take a razor blade and cut the linings in their coats. If they brought shoes we'd cut the insides out. We'd do it in such a way that when the coat went to the cleaners they could clean it; it would hold together. And we had an understanding with them there that if they noticed any tears or cuts they'd ignore them. The guard would pick up his coat, and then the next day when he'd put his arm into it the whole lining would shoot out the sleeve. In his pants the seat would rip when he sat down. The linings would come out of his shoes. And he would know what had happened, but there was nothing he could do. Too many people had access to his stuff. He'd know, but he couldn't do a thing, and when he came back he'd give us one of those looks and we'd say, "Oh, hello, Officer So-and-so, nice day." And he wouldn't shake us down again.

We kept the books on the guards' hours. They got overtime for going on a deathwatch or whatever. We recorded it in code. If all those things weren't recorded accurately by number, when the books went to Sacramento the computer there would throw them out and the guy wouldn't get paid his overtime. It would take forever. He'd fill out a form, and we would lose the form. He'd know that we had goofed purposely, but he couldn't prove it. So when he was going to shake us down or shake down our cells, the guard would think, "Oh, no, I don't want to go through *that* again." And he'd turn his back and give us a pass.

As you entered the paymaster's office, in the front, to your left, was the counter. Across from that, on the right, was a big bin, and everything that was lost in the laundry would be put in this bin. Now, you know how women are—they love secondhand shops and sales and bargains, so they'd come in sometimes to look in the bin when I was alone in the morning or late in the afternoon. And there were some real pretty ones who worked in the offices, and no one ever saw them, no other convicts. They'd come in when I was alone, and they'd do little things. Like, when I was writing the ticket up they'd show me something on their clothes and they'd reach so their hand would touch my arm, and that little, teeny contact . . . Or one of them would come in and I'd say, "We have some new stuff in the bin there. Why don't you look through it?" She'd say, "Well, I don't think I lost anything." I'd say, "Oh, that's okay. Look through it. We're just going to throw it away, and if there's anything you'd like to have, take it." She'd walk over to the bin, and I'd immediately walk out from behind the counter and join her. I'd purposely arranged this thing so she had to bend way down to get into it, and I'd stand where I could see part of her breasts or her brassiere. And from being locked up like that, just seeing that, I'd almost come right then. I'd move a little closer to her and say, "Oh, how about this? This looks like something you might use." I'd reach down and across her and raise up so my hand touched her breasts. I'd tell her to take her time looking, and I'd bend down as if I was straightening out the shoes that were in a row on the floor. I'd try to see up under her dress.

I felt that they knew what they were doing because a couple

of these little chicks would bring in silk pajama type outfits to be cleaned which had stuff in them, as if they had come in the pants. We'd all smell them and save them for the other guys so they could smell them, and if they were really far-out I'd take them back to my cell with me and put them over my head and play with myself at night. You became so obsessed with sex that the smell of something like that just drove you insane.

When you first came in, in order to keep yourself from being run over by any group or any person you would have to pass that first test. Somebody'd test you, try you, bump into you, call you down to meet with them in the lower yard with a shank just to see what you would do. If you chickened out then everyone would just take your commissary and run all over you from then on. You go to the store and buy your cigarettes and whatever else you need. Some people bought all their stuff for one month at a time. So you'd walk out of the line with a big sack or two sacks full of stuff, and a couple of guys would walk up to you, and one guy would tap you on the shoulder and engage you in conversation, and the other would hit you on the back of the head, and then they'd take your bags and run. Sometimes the guard up on the walkway would see this. Sometimes he didn't. Sometimes he'd fire his gun into the yard.

There was a black guy that killed a girl at the University of California in the library. He was a fat, slobby guy, and everybody hated him, including the blacks, because he killed this pretty girl for no reason. Every time he went to the commissary, whoever happened to see him in line would just beat him up and take his stuff. And the guards saw it, and they wouldn't do anything because they hated him as much as everybody else did. He never got any commissary. People would spit on him. That's the way guys were treated that killed women or anybody that molested a child. Gangs were excepted. There were a lot of Mexicans who used to go around, and that was their kick, to go out and rape a chick, that was part of their gang experience. That showed they were men and they got away with it because they were in a group and had a gang to fight for them. But any loner that killed a woman . . . Murderers were treated awful because they weren't a part of any group.

No matter if you were white, Mexican, black, Indian, there was something everyone had in common—if you were sharp and hep and talked the language of whatever society you might be in, then you were accepted as a regular, okay, we all live the same kind of life. They don't want to admit it, but it's an unwritten law. And if you have that, you have something going for you out front. But if you're a murderer that just killed somebody, a passion killing, because somebody took your old lady out, well, you haven't been robbing or stealing or living that life so you're really an outsider. They wreak havoc on that kind of person.

When I first got to San Quentin I could feel people watching me. They look for weakness. They observe you for a day or so and watch who talks to you. And if somebody comes in that's young and pretty and doesn't have a lot of friends, then all the little splinter groups and the black group as a whole, they may want him for a sissy. They'll have talks among themselves about who's going to get him, and then they'll drive on him with a shank and tell him they're going to fuck him, and if the guy doesn't attempt to fight back it's all over for him. They'll just take him and fuck him and he belongs to a group. They'll turn him into a punk. If he fights it's different. He's accepted as one of them because he's got nerve. I didn't have to prove myself because I knew so many people. I was sort of a celebrity, although that was both good and bad. It was good in this one respect: I had many people come to me and say, "If anyone messes with you let me know." Guys that were real bad, tough people that were feared. On the other hand, some guys would say, "Oh, that punk motherfucker. He ain't nothin'. That lousy motherfucker, he's probably a rat, that stinkin' cocksucker. He's a convict just like we are, that cocksuckin' motherfucker. Who does he think he is?"

Nearly everyone in San Quentin seemed to be in some gang or other. Being a musician, I had friends that were black; I had a lot of friends that were Mexican; and I had friends that were white. I had more friends that were Mexican, so the whites really got on me. "What are you doing with those cholos? Those beans? Aren't you a white man?" Or when I'd play music with the black guys in the yard, they'd say, "What are you, a nigger now? Have you turned nigger?" It was scary, and I'd been told by different guys that they were going to kill me because they didn't like the way I was carrying myself. And the black musicians, because they were afraid of pressure from the Muslims, when they were in a group they'd act like they didn't know me, but when we were alone we were the best of friends. I wanted to belong to every group but I couldn't, so the only way I could make it was just to be loaded all the time and act crazy and go from group to group. But then, when I started getting way out, some of these Mexicans I knew came and jacked me up and told me, "Man, what are you *doing?*" They ranked me because I was acting weird and taking black-and-whites. They'd say, "Ain't you got no class? If you act like that, when something good happens, when some stuff comes in, you're not going to get any. We won't be able to give you any because you're too crazy. The guys'll say, 'No, he's too nuts.' "

There were other people that shunned gangs, but instead of doing it the way I did, they gambled. Cards were illegal, so they played dominoes. They played all the time, and they played for cigarettes. From the minute they finished breakfast—sometimes they'd start before breakfast and not eat—until lockup that night, they were at the tables. Even in the rain. The tables were under the shed in the big yard. Some guys made a lot of money, and some guys lost a lot of money, and that caused some terrible things to happen.

There was this young white guy, a young gunsel, a real gangster type supposedly; we'll call him Charlie. He was gambling all the time playing dominoes, and he finally went through everything he had. But he had a mother that loved him, so she sent money to everyone he could imagine. She'd visit him, he'd give her a name, she'd send money to that name, and the guy would take five and give Charlie the rest in cigarettes. Sometimes his need for money became so immediate he couldn't wait for that, so he'd send her a letter saying he had to see her, and she would come, and he'd tell her he's got to have money right away. She'd put the money in her mouth and pass it to him when they kissed goodbye. But he finally drained her dry. He couldn't get any more money from her, so some of the guys he was in debt to told him, "Alright, we've got a proposition for you." The proposition was this: they would send a friend of theirs to make contact with Charlie's mother; they formulated a plan using the guy who cleaned up the visitors' waiting room; Charlie had to talk his mother into this; he told her, "If you don't do it I'll be killed." So now, not only does he have his mother smuggling money to him, he's got her smuggling heroin. She's just a poor mother that loves her son.

This is a classic example of what happens through the domino tables. She was given instructions. She would visit him and drop the heroin into the big ashtray in the visitors' waiting room. She made the drop. The convict got it. Charlie was paid off in his debt. They even gave the mother a few dollars, but now she was trapped and she had to keep doing it. Finally somebody talked in the yard, and the guards and the police set something up and pulled a bust. They busted the mother and the guy picking up the stuff and the people delivering it. Now the mother is in jail. They're going to send her to prison because this is a serious charge, and the only way she can get out is for Charlie to talk. So he feels a little remorse. They promise him immunity. They'll put him in protective custody. He goes to court in San Rafael and testifies. He cops out. Then, the time comes for him to go back to prison and he thinks they're going to put him in another prison and protect him. They just put him on the Grey Goose and take him back to San Quentin. Evidently he had incurred the wrath of somebody on the staff of the prison who wanted him done away with. They put him in between-gates and he's screaming, "I can't go in there! I can't go in there!" They say, "Get in there, you son-of-a-bitch!" And they threw him through the second gate, and now he's in San Quentin. There he is, he's just there, he's in the yard. There's nothing he can do. He panics and runs to Fourposts. They tell him to get out of Fourposts. He runs into the gym. He had been back, I guess, about two hours. He went into the gym back by the weights. He was only there a little while when word came out that Charlie was dead.

Some people who run up a big debt aren't lucky enough to have a mother like that, so if they can't pay they get killed right out in front. And that's where the loaners come in. They loan cigarettes or cash money. You can't hide too many cigarettes but you can hide cash. There are people that have five or six hundred dollars stashed in their cells, and they lend it out.

The little drugs, that's cigarettes; heroin you get with cash unless you have access to an outfit. You can get a taste for carrying an outfit from one block to another. But if somebody wants to buy some stuff he'll go to a money loaner. If the loaner gives him twenty dollars he has to give back thirty. The big moneylender has a guard running for him. The guard takes the money out and mails it to the guy's family or to whoever he's getting the dope from, or he drops it someplace. There's a million different ways you can get money in and out. But people who don't have anybody on the outside are in trouble if they get in debt to the loan sharks and can't pay because then they have to face the collector.

The loan shark can't do anything violent because he has too much money stashed away. He can't afford to be suspected so he has a collector, a guy that's real tough and hasn't any fear. The loan shark tells him, "So-and-so owes me so much." If the collector collects it, he gets a certain percentage. So he goes to the borrower, puts a shank on him, and tells him he's dead unless he gets the cash or the cigarettes within a certain amount of time. If he doesn't get the money, the collector has to stab him. He has to kill him if it's a big enough debt—to preserve his reputation. In order to make people fear him, the collector has to do a certain number of stabbings.

And then there's ordinary borrowing. Say somebody borrows three packs of cigarettes from you, which is nothing, and he doesn't pay you back. Well, you have to go to the guy and make him pay because if you don't, word gets around that you didn't collect and then everybody burns you. Everybody runs all over you unless you show that you're strong. People have been killed for one or two packs of cigarettes because the person that did the lending had to collect for the sake of his reputation. During all the time I was in San Quentin I rarely borrowed or loaned cigarettes and then only with people I knew real well. I never played even one game of dominoes.

As I said, nearly everyone was in some kind of group. The whites and the Mexicans were all broken up into little splinter groups. A Mexican might have a cousin that lives a couple of blocks away; maybe one guy lives in Monte Via and the cousin lives in White Fence. These guys will be in separate groups that fight each other, plus all the other Mexican groups, plus all the white groups, plus all the blacks. The whites were the same: you had the white armed robber clique, you had the white dopefiend–armed robber clique.

There's one white group that does stick together. It's the Nazi party. It's a very small group. They spend their time plotting what black guy is the most obnoxious, the ugliest, or the most popular, or the one that they might fear the most, and then they start a small but severe campaign. You couldn't reach a person's bed through the bars with your arms, so they might get a stick with a wire on the end of it and put it underneath their coats, and they'd use that device to put notes on the guy's bunk. They'd do this for a long time. They'd drop off a piece of paper with a little drawing showing a black guy laying on the floor with a knife sticking out of him, and they'd draw red blood on it and put Nazi marks all over the paper. They'd say, "We are watching. You will *die* at such-and-such a time." They'd make up little poems. They'd keep this up until the guy was really panicked, and then they'd stab him and throw him off the fifth tier. And then they'd start on another one. This is the kind of place you were living in.

You had to hand it to the blacks and the Indians. The Indians stuck together completely. All they did was play basketball. Every minute. They wouldn't hold any jobs. They wouldn't go along with any program. No matter what kind of weather it was, if they weren't playing basketball they were huddled together in some corner of the basketball court.

The blacks had total solidarity. That's where they get their power. It's the same way they get their power on the streets now and the reason they're so strong. They talk about "my people" and all this nonsense, which to me is utter nonsense because they don't feel it; they don't believe it, most of them, but at least they *do* it; and it makes a weak position a strong position and a smallness in numbers turns to their advantage. In the daytime they go down into the yard and gather and do calisthenics, training for the war to overthrow the white race. They line up and do these outrageous things, chant and make strange African noises: "Kill them all! Kill the whites! Cut them to ribbons! Destroy their women!" And everybody stands around and hates them, wants to kill them. They're generating fear.

They're going through these strenuous wartime calisthenics openly in the yard. They do it in the morning and in the afternoon. For a while they'd gather by the laundry. There was a big laundry with corrugated tin walls. They'd stand against this and face the rising sun and the preacher would run them through these little routines; to me, and I was watching, I felt that it was all geared to make the rest of us fear them. And it worked. The guards would be on their walkways and they'd get orders from the captain to shake the Muslims up a little, so they'd shoot over their heads with their rifles and hit the laundry walls. Now and then they'd hit one of them in the shoulder or the leg, and that would break them up for a while. They'd have to change their position.

Most people had to go through a shakedown. But if the blacks were shook down they'd holler, "Prejudice!" And they wouldn't have to submit. They didn't have to scrub floors or do anything they didn't feel was dignified, and there's hardly anything that's dignified if you're a prisoner. Anything that had to do with cleaning, anything that had to do with laundry, anything that had to do with sweeping, mopping. So the whites and the Mexicans did all the cleaning and scrubbing.

The younger blacks coming up have a lot of nerve. They're getting to the point where they're so intent upon being strong that, just like they do in sports and like they do in music, they spend every second trying to be strong and fearless. It has become an obsession now with them. They will give their lives to show that they're not cowards as they were always thought to be in the past.

There's lots of black people in prison that don't want any violence. They don't want to have anything to do with all these hate groups. They don't want it but they have to be a part of it at least outwardly; they have to make those noises because if they don't they'll be set upon by their group. The musicians would have to act the part even though they didn't feel it. I'm talking about some of the black musicians. And because they were a little smarter than the run of the mill black in the joint, they in some cases developed into leaders.

There was this one guy I'd know in Detroit; he was a drummer. I'd been to his house, we'd copped together, we'd been friends. After about a year in San Quentin I ran into him. He was a warm guy, but he'd had occasion to have a couple of fights and he had a scar on his face that made him look mean. And he was smart. He'd studied the Muslim religion and learned all the little sayings, and he became a preacher. I asked him, "Where have you been?" While we talked he kept looking around because he didn't want the blacks to see him talking to me. They're not supposed to have any communication with whites unless they have to, to gain some other end. And they can't shake hands. They can't touch them. He said he'd been in the adjustment center. And he said he had something going. He said, "I know it's hard in here. We're friends, and I'm in a position where I can help you. When you see me, don't talk to me unless I nod that it's okay." I didn't know what was happening at the time, but later he told me he was a preacher and the blacks were continually giving him things, goodies, although the guards would continually harass him.

So I saw this guy one day and he motioned to me; he was alone. He said, "I'll meet you here later." He named a time. I was there, and he appeared with a big sack behind his back. He looked around and set the sack down. He talked off, away from me, and he said, "Well, I've really got it made right now if I can stay out of the adjustment center." He said, "Whenever any stuff comes in, I get it, and I'll lay it on you. But we got to be really careful because if the blacks ever saw me messing with you it would be all over for me. I'm going to leave now. Pick up this bag." In the bag there's cigarettes and coffee and a new razor and razor blades and perfume and aftershave that cost a lot of money, that the blacks gave him. He just laid this stuff on me, and this happened several times.

In the county jail there wasn't any TV, and in San Quentin in the South Block and the East Block there was nothing like that, but in the North Block they had a TV and we used to watch movies and all the sporting events. When we watched the boxing if there were two black boxers, it wasn't so bad, but if there was a Mexican and a black or, God forbid, a white and a black, it was just unbelievable the hatred that came out.

The Mexicans are quiet people. They're clannish, they're secretive, and they don't believe in infringing on other people's rights or annoying them. You can sit in a room full of Mexicans watching a thing like that and nothing will be said. So everything would have been fine but the blacks would get together in a group to aggravate everybody else.

See, the whites and the Mexicans, they sit wherever there's a seat, but the black guys all sit together. So, if you're sitting on a bench with a couple of blacks and there's no room for another person, well, some black guy will just come up and, "Heeey, baby! Saaay, home boy!" There's not enough room for him to sit but this guy sitting next to you says to the new guy, "Heeey, baby! Come on up here, blood!" And they'll just sit right on you. Either you can stay there and have them pushing you off the bench, being so loud and obnoxious that you can't enjoy anything, or you can fight with them and try to kill them, or else you can move. And that's what the white guy does or the Mexican. He moves. All you want to do is enjoy what you came to see, the TV. These blacks don't come to see TV: they come to get together. Any black guy will tell you that if he's honest. They come to annoy everybody else. Everyone in prison is consumed with resentment and hatred, and I guess the most convenient target for your anger is some other race of people. Maybe that's what these blacks were doing, assaulting us with noise, disrupting everything. You have to move. And then they look around, like, "Hey, boy, what's wrong?" There's nothing you can do, and they know that.

The fight starts on TV, and they start yelling: "Hey, brothah! Look at that brothah up theah! *Git* that white boy!" Whatever the white guy is, he's no good. The black guy is the greatest. Baseball, the same thing. They don't care about teams. All they care about is the black brothers and "blood" and all this, man. They've got their reasons, but why do they have to take their hate out on *us*, whites and Mexicans who have been discriminated against, raised just as badly or worse than they were? *We're* suffering just as much. *We've* been sentenced to prison. *We're* away from our loved ones.

As I said, the nonblacks are quieter about their anger, but after a while they can't stand it so they start in, too, raving, "Get that jigaboo! Kill that black punk!" And the Mexicans and whites join together because Mexicans in prison hate the blacks regardless of what they try to do with black power and brown power. They scream and rage in Spanish, and so much hatred gets going that the tension becomes unbearable and you can't enjoy any sporting event—football, basketball. The movies are even worse, with the blacks talking loud, making obscene remarks about the white women on the screen. It might be a beautiful love story but, "Boy, I'd sure like to have some of *that!* I bet she'd like to suck on this big, black cock of mine! After she had some of my big joy stick she wouldn't want any white man ever!"

Of course there are black guys that haven't succumbed to this thing. The blacks that were friends of mine, they'd look over at me when this happened and shake their heads: "What can you do?" A lot of times you'd see them just walk away and lock up in their cells because they couldn't stand to see this. But when the black guy gets up to leave, the others will say, "Saaay, where you goin', jack?" So a lot of them, in order to survive in prison, have to placate these maniacs, hang out with them, laugh, and, "Yeah, baby!"

You've worked to get into an honor block so you can do the time a little better, and now you get to watch TV, and there's something you want to see, but you cannot watch it. They will not let you watch it. So you lock up in your cell and you're thinking, "I wish I could kill all those people! I wish I could drop a bomb in the midst of them!" Your guts are churning; it aches. No wonder you get ulcers. And you can hear them in your cell, no matter where it is, fourth tier, fifth tier, you can't shut them out.

When I think of prison now the worst part *used to be* not having sex, being locked away from the good things, just not being free. But *now*, when I think about it, the thing that hits me first and is the most horrible part of it is to be locked up in an area where you have to listen to that hatred and that hollering—"Git that white boy!" "Kill that nigger!"—over and over and over, and you can't get away from it. I couldn't go to jail again. I just couldn't. I think I would have to kill myself rather than go through that again.

———————

(Ann Christos) Art saved my honor. When Art was in San Quentin, some black dude came by the beach house, and he ended up in San Quentin. All of a sudden I get a letter from him asking me to write to him, and I was very naive. Art used to tell me, "You're like an open window." I said, "Sure, what's a letter?" Then Art wrote to me saying that this guy was going around saying that I was his "white ho." But Art said, "I straightened him out." And I never got another letter. Art knew me and he knew that this guy was just flashin'. Nobody had ever went to any lengths to protect my honor before, and it meant a lot to me.

———————————

17 | The Check Protector
1964 – 1965

WHEN I GOT OUT of San Quentin Shelly Manne helped me. They sent me to Tehachapi, and he wrote to me there and said if there was anything he could do he'd do it; he'd like to have me play in his club. Once you make parole you have to have a job to go to in order to get out. They gave me permission to write to Shelly and I told him I was coming up for another parole hearing, and he wrote a letter saying he would hire me.

I got out and finally got together the money to get back into the musicians' union. I've rejoined that union so many times. I would have been a life member long ago if I hadn't gone to prison. I worked for Shelly, and then I got an offer to go to the Jazz Workshop in San Francisco.

I was on the Nalline program. When you come out of prison you go three times a week to get a Nalline test. It works like this. You go in; once you're in the door's locked and you can't get out; you sign in and sit there in subdued light for about twenty minutes and then they call your name. There's a doctor there, and he's got this green light, and you look in the light, and he looks at the pupils of your eyes in profile and measures them. Then they give you a shot of Nalline. They skin it in your arm, and you go out and sit down for another twenty minutes before they call you back, and the doctor does the same routine again with the green light. If your pupil hasn't gotten smaller than it was the first time, you get an "equivocal," which is enough to hold you for. If your pupil gets larger, you're dirty, you've been using heroin; they immediately put you in a cage and then they take you down to the county jail. You go three times a week, and when you go you meet all the people you've been in prison with. Everybody that's there is junkies. When you get the shot of Nalline, if you're clean, you get loaded: you get a little buzz as if you've shot some stuff, and when you walk outside the little buzz goes, and then you get a headache, and you get depressed, and you start thinking of that little taste that you just had, and you want to get loaded.

You start using again, and through the grapevine you find out that if you take steam baths just before you go, and drink wine, and take bennies, you can pass the Nalline test. So that's what I used to do then, when I was chippying, and later when I was using. I had a friend, Hersh Hamel, who played bass, and he had a membership card for the Beverly Hills Health Club. He'd take me as his guest, and I'd go into the steam bath and stay there until I was almost dead, my skin hanging off my body, the sweat pouring out of me. Then I'd go get a couple of fifths of port wine or muscatel and drink it down and take five or six Dexamyl Spansules, or if I had some crystal (speed) I'd shoot it, or if I had some bottles—bombidos they call them in New York, here they call it methadrine—I would shoot that. I'd pass the test, but it destroys your body.*

At any rate, I went to San Francisco and took my tests up there at the San Francisco police department, and I played at the Jazz Workshop, one of the greatest clubs going. It was almost an all-black club, run by black people, and I went in there with an all-white band. They had all-black bands all the time. But people were making these little remarks about whites and honkies. People would come in and say, "What do we got here? Where's the brothers and sisters at?" And they'd tell the guy that was running the place, "Say, blood, what is this up theah? What is these guys tryin' to do? That's ouahhh music. *Black* music." And we had to put up with all that shit. And they say white people can't play jazz, but I disproved *that,* you know, because I played jazz, and all my white people played jazz. I had Bill Goodwin on drums, a great young drummer; I had Frank Strazzeri, an Italian, on piano; and I had a Jew, Hersh Himmelstein—he'd changed his name to Hamel—on bass. (I'd call out his introduction, "Hoishie Himmelshtiiiiine!" I used to wig out announcing him.)

* The California Department of Corrections discontinued the Nalline program.

(Hersh Hamel) Art was at Quentin or someplace, and I had
bumped into Diane. She told me Art was going to be out in
about a month and asked if I could help, come by, drive him
around, get some clothes for him. They didn't have a car, and
she knew that I really dug Art and I'd help.

Art got out, and I took him around to get some shoes, some
clothes. I took him to his Nalline tests downtown, and if it
looked like he wasn't going to pass the test, he was messing
around a little, I'd take him over to the Beverly Hills Health
Club, get him in the sweat bath, stay in there for a couple
hours to try to sweat it out of him.

At that time, we decided to form a group. I was running
around with a drummer, Bill Goodwin, who's a great drummer,
and we got Frank Strazzeri, myself, and Art, and we went up to
my brother's house, who I was living with in Laurel Canyon,
and we rehearsed and got some music together. Art had written
some tunes in Quentin which were very interesting, "D
Section," "The Trip," "Groupin'," nice tunes, and I wrote a
couple tunes, so we had a little library of original things. When
Art first came out, he wasn't using much at all; we played a gig
at Shelly's Manne Hole and Art had a tremendous lot of fire.

Art was very influenced by Coltrane at that time because he
was in jail with some pretty radical players. Art heard those
guys in Quentin, and at first he didn't like it so much, he said,
but after hearing them practice day after day, he started to pick
up on what they were doing and to like it more and more. And
then, when he came out, he was pretty well exploding, I can
tell you, musically. So much so that when we went into Shelly's
in 1964, Shelly Manne and some of the other guys criticized
him terribly, "Oh, no, that's not the old Art." You know,
"Doesn't sound like Art Pepper." And Art is so sensitive. When
people start criticizing, he immediately starts bending. So he
started coming off what he was doing. He started using shit
again because he was getting some criticism. Diane said she
liked the "pretty" Art Pepper better. She didn't like the
harshness he was playing with. And I think some of the harshness came from the fact that Art had spent a lot of time in jail.
There was a lot of hostility, a lot of pent-up emotion, and when

he played he was barkin', boy! It was raw emotion, and it was great. Incredible. Whether he might think so now or not. If we could have recorded at that time! Les recorded us on a few tunes, but he didn't like it.

We went up to San Francisco at that time. I got some jobs for us and we worked at Don Mupo's club in Oakland for two nights. We started Friday night; on Saturday night the last tune we played was "The Trip," and the people were standing on top of the tables. I kid you not. The place was packed solid. You couldn't get into the club or out, hardly. People were standing on the tables, cheering, while we were playing. I've never seen anything like it; in jazz this very rarely happens.

Art wasn't using much then. Drinking some. But a couple of months later we came back to Frisco, to the Jazz Workshop, and he was using. Funny thing, on a night when he wasn't using, he'd come in and complain about Frank Strazzeri and be real uptight with all of us and be really nervous about all the tunes. One night we played our ass off, the rhythm section just *burned*, and he was uptight all night. The next night, he came in all stoned out of his mind, and I didn't think we sounded anywhere near as good, and he was just smiling, knocked out with everything. So it wasn't really the way the band sounded, it was the way Art felt. But at that time, the level we were play-ing on was very, very good.

———————

(Shelly Manne) When Art came out of prison, a lot of music had been happening. I always loved the way Art played. His lyricism was the main thing I really loved, a very emotional way of playing. And very coherent, well-constructed solos. Well, sometimes a musician feels challenged, feels that he's going to be left behind, that what he's saying isn't the in thing at the moment. The problem is, too many people, critics, magazines, newspapers, they make music a competition like a sporting event. It's not a sporting event. You don't go to a museum and say, "Well, I give four votes for Rembrandt and five for Van Gogh." You can't do that. Each person, if they can really play and they are artists, which I consider them to be because jazz is definitely an art form, if they have that inner ability, that creative drive to say something very personal . . . There are no "greatests," you know what I mean?

If I tried as a drummer to play like Tony Williams or Elvin Jones, I'd fall on my ass. It doesn't make me not love them any less as artists because *I* can't do it. And in my own experience, I found myself going through a period, when I owned a nightclub, of having these guys work in my club, and the next thing you know, I'd be trying to play like them because I'd be so strongly influenced, so delighted, by what they're doing. And I saw how the crowds reacted to it. I thought, "Oh, they consider me old hat." But I'm older and a little wiser: the festival I was just on, there were a lot of drummers there and I didn't go up there fearing that they're watching me or that I'm not going to play my best. I just go, play, and have fun because music is fun.

Everybody should try to improve; their playing should constantly change by absorbing playing from other great players. You should never stop growing. But the one thing you have when you're playing the way you feel, you have an individual way of playing. And I felt when I first heard Art, when he came out of prison and did his first club date, I didn't like what I heard. Not because he wasn't doing it well. But I didn't feel that it was an honest expression of the person I was listening to, after listening to him for all those years. It's okay to borrow from somebody like John Coltrane, but Art lost a lot of that lyrical quality that I love about him. When Art overblows his horn, the individual sound he has just disappears. I love Art on tenor, too. He has an individual sound, which is one of the things all the great players have, whether it be Charlie Parker, Lester Young, Art. He was destroying that, and I was sorry to see it, and now, more recently, I heard him reverting to himself. And that other stuff is absorbed into his playing and is expressed by his own identity, which makes it still an individual thing. But there was a period when I thought he was losing his way as far as Art Pepper is concerned. That happens to a lot of players, but they find that the best thing to do is just go *play the way you feel* because nobody can do it the way *you* feel, and if it's good, it's good. And not to be influenced by what's happening at the moment. Everybody has great favorites of the moment.

———————

WHEN I went into San Quentin I didn't know what was going to happen with Diane. She'd gotten out of Norwalk after her suicide attempt, and I told her if she wanted to go ahead and get a divorce she could do that. There was no telling how long I'd have to stay in San Quentin. I'd rather have her get a divorce. But she said, "Oh, no, no! I love you! I want to be able to take care of you! I want to do everything I can for you! Please, please don't deny me the chance!" So I said alright—against my better judgment.

Diane came to visit me after I'd been in San Quentin for several months. She got a ride up with someone. She'd been straightening up, and she looked like she was fairly clean, and I thought, "Well, maybe she'll be cool." She went back and wrote all the time, nice letters, and finally she got another ride up and came to visit me again. She told me she couldn't stand to go back to L.A. She'd decided she was going to get her stuff and come and stay in San Francisco and wait for me to get out. I didn't feel that she was together enough, and I didn't want her uprooting herself. In Los Angeles she had her mother, who was a lesbian, but nevertheless she was her mother and would help her. She had her sister and her father, who was a good man, and her father's wife. But I couldn't talk her out of it. She went back to L.A. to my dad and, I didn't know about this, but she told my dad I had said it would be okay for him to give her all my things. She wanted to move to Frisco and she wanted to have everything of mine there so when I came out I would have a place and all my stuff. She got all the things I'd sent my dad—shoes, a lot of nice clothes, and scrapbooks and pictures and stuff. I had all my school things, report cards, pictures of my army career, mementos of my time with Kenton, clippings, awards I'd won, and a bunch of music. My dad didn't want to do it, but Diane conned him out of my stuff.

She moved to San Francisco, rented a little place, and she got a job in some nightclub, some bar. She put my clothes in the closet and the music and scrapbooks all around the little apartment so it would look like I was living there. And she told me she was imagining that I was just out playing someplace and I'd be back. She lived in a little dreamworld, and I thought, "Oh, well, I guess it's alright if she can make it." She seemed to be doing fine.

It was approaching Christmas. That's the only time you're allowed to receive anything in San Quentin. They give you a list of things you're allowed to have. You're not allowed cigarettes but you can have candy and nuts and cigars. There were a bunch of different things listed, and they had to be packaged and sent from the factory or from the store so no one could inject dope into them. You only have one sheet, one list, and you have to pick one person to send it to; if that person doesn't come through with your present you're out of luck.

Diane came to see me and she asked about Christmas, and I made the mistake of telling her about the list. I told her I was going to send it to my dad. It would give him something to do. I didn't tell her I was doing it that way because I trusted him and not her. She said, "Oh, you've got to let *me* do it! I'm your wife! I love you!" I told her if anything happened and she couldn't send it, it would really hang me up. You have to have been in prison yourself to realize what getting these little extra things means. It's blown all out of proportion by the circumstances.

Diane said, "Please, please, please! I would never hang you up. Of course I'll send the stuff. I'll get everything on the list. The most expensive things that there are!" She took the paper. I signed it over. This was three months before Christmas. She said goodbye. After that visit I never once heard. Never got a letter. Never got a visit. Nothing. Christmas came. I never got a package. I never heard a word, except every now and then somebody would come in and I'd pick up these vibes. People would look at me. Little things would be dropped. Finally some friends came to me and told me that some black guy that had just come in had told them about Diane, Art Pepper's wife, in Frisco. She was strung out on this stuff that was famous there in those days—Percodan and yellow jackets and meth (methadrine) mixed—and she was really a derelict. She was making it with these black guys, and they were laughing at me and talking about me behind my back. That's why I'd wanted her to divorce me in the first place—because I didn't want to go through anything like that. People are really cruel in prison. And I heard nothing from her.

Me and Jerry Maher worked in the paymaster's office together, and we used to get loaded together on weekends, and he had the same situation with his old lady. He'd given her his sheet for Christmas and hadn't heard from her since, but he'd get word that she was balling this guy and that guy, friends of his, and that his kid was left someplace, squalling and dirty. I'm half German and half Italian. He's full German and violent. We would spend hours and hours together: "Here's another Diane story." We would get together and talk about what we were going to do to our wives when we got out. We devised tortures. Our favorite plan was to rent a house with a cellar. I'd get Diane and he'd get his old lady and we'd put them in this cellar and chain them up. Then we'd get a real powerful stereo set and put speakers all over the walls; we'd have sounds of trains and airplanes and war sounds and people screaming; we'd turn the speakers on at all different times of the day and night; and they would never know what time it was. They would never see daylight. We would come in with black hoods over us and beat them with whips. We'd make them give each other head, and then, just before they'd come, we'd beat their cunts with whips. We'd pour ice water on them. We would go on for hours, and there was nothing we didn't envision: water tortures, lighted sticks under their toenails.

I was in San Quentin for three years. Then I was sent to Tehachapi, and that's when I went to the parole board and got a release date. I don't know how she found out about it, but after I got my date, they called my name one day and said, "You have a visitor." It had been two years since I'd seen Diane. When I saw her, my immediate reaction was I wanted to kill her. I wanted to beat her to death. But I wanted to contain myself until I could get at her, so by an unbelievable strengthening of my will and the greatest acting job I've ever done I acted cool.

She looked at me and burst out crying. She said, "Oh, I'm sorry!" She said she had flipped out, and she was sorry, and how can I ever forgive her. She loved me and missed me, but she was so fucked up from the methadrine and the Percodan she was ashamed for me to see her in that state. She couldn't stand to see anybody so she'd hid in the room; she'd nearly gone insane. And somebody had stolen all my stuff out of this room. Everything was gone. And she's sorry, and she loves me. She had finally got back to Los Angeles. She said she was straightening up and she wanted to save money and take care of me. What could she do for me? Would I ever forgive her? I said, "Oh, don't worry about it. I understand. I understand what dope does." Don't worry about the scrapbooks and things I had saved since I was a little kid. That's alright. I was shaking inside. When I touched her it made me cringe. I got ill thinking about all these guys she'd balled. But I was able to play over my feelings, and I told her that if she wanted to visit me it was okay. I told her I had a release date.

Diane came to visit me every week. She brought food and all that. And every now and then she'd look at me strangely and say, "Are you sure you forgive me?" And I'd say yeah. All I wanted to do was get out and have her under my power. Finally the day came. Diane came to pick me up. She'd rented a place on Sunset Boulevard in Hollywood. I got her into the pad. She took a shower and put on some sexy negligee. I started kissing her. I got her all excited sexually. I got her all worked up until she's wigging out with passion. I got her just to the point where we're going to ball and then I looked at her and spit in her face: "You slimy, stinking, bastard bitch!" I grabbed her by the throat. I told her, "No, I'm not going to kill you. I'm going to make you suffer like you've never suffered in your life before!" I let her go and backhanded her as hard as I could in the mouth, and I threw her against the wall. I smashed her head against the wall and I told her, "Don't touch me, you slimy, filthy bastard!" She begged me, and she crawled along the floor. She had blood running out of her mouth, and I almost had a feeling of pity for her, but I thought of what she'd done to me and I said, "Don't touch me, you dirty bastard!"

I stayed with her. And whenever she got to the point where she was ready to go kill herself I'd ball her and pretend that everything was alright. Then, when she thought everything was cool, I would turn on her again. I found this beautiful little Hollywood girl up the street and balled her, and I let Diane know about it. I put her through hell, and I felt she deserved every bit of it. But what happened is I got hooked and I couldn't continue it. And then we were both hooked, and that ended my revenge.

Three months after I got out of San Quentin I hung up my Nalline tests. I couldn't make it, so I went into hiding. My parole officer came around. He told Diane, "Tell him to give himself up, and I'll make sure everything'll be alright. I'll get him a dryout, so he won't have to go back to the joint." I agreed to give myself up, and he took me to jail. They gave me six months in Chino. It was better than going back to San Quentin. Chino Institute for Men. They had a narcotics program there. They keep you in barracks instead of cells, and there were three barracks filled with dopefiends. They had women dopefiends, too; I'd see them drive up, the beatest looking bags in the world.

We were all getting counseling. There'd be a social worker or a parole officer, and he'd have a "group." The whole idea was to get people to rat on each other, to try to expose people so they would "learn" and do better. I had never seen anything like it. People *informing* on each other! We'd meet and "I saw you doing this! I saw you . . . " I realized that the only way to make it was to say as little as possible and try to con the people as much as possible to get out. It was a wasted experience. The only thing I can recall of note is that in playing handball I fell over a metal faucet and cut my leg and then from favoring my leg and continuing to play handball I got an inguinal hernia and had to have an operation there. Talk about inhuman. They give you a little something to put you out, but after that, because you're a dopefiend and a prisoner, they won't give you anything to help you through the pain. I got through it and got okay and got out of Chino, and I went back to Diane. My parole officer didn't want me to go back to her. He kept telling me it was a mistake.

A friend of mine, Arnold, was in Chino with me. His old lady would visit him, so she started bringing Diane. Diane moved to an apartment in Glendale, near Arnold's wife. Arnold got out a little before me, and what happened was he was involved in a burglary, and Diane got involved, too. He'd gotten hold of a check protector and a bunch of blank checks.

I got out, and I went to this place Diane had, and I was surprised to see that it was such a nice apartment. I started looking around and I saw all kinds of *things*. Every drawer was filled. There was every kind of light bulb and every type of writing paper, every kind of soap and perfume, and every kind of cleanser. It was like a warehouse for a grocery store. And everything was brand-new. The cupboards were filled with food and cheese and nine different kinds of crackers and canned goods, canned meats. The place was jammed full of stuff and I said, "What's happening here?" Diane had clothes, clothes still in the packages, sweaters and shirts and socks, and I said, "My God, what's happening?" Diane said, "Well, I've got a little thing going. I didn't want to tell you because I was afraid you'd be drug, but I was, like, scuffling and Arnold asked me to help him, so I said okay." I said, "What *is* it?" And then she told me about the check protector. She went behind the couch and pulled out this machine that writes checks for a company, protects them, and makes them legal. This and the checks had been stolen in the burglary. Diane had gotten a phony driver's license and a phony birth certificate. She'd write the checks out and Arnold would drive her to the stores. There were some markets that didn't have the call-in system at that time—I think it was the Market Basket chain. They'd search around for a Market Basket; she'd go in and buy thirty, forty dollars' worth of groceries and hand them a payroll check for a hundred and fifty, a hundred and seventy-five. Arnold would wait for her. She'd wheel the stuff out. She got a certain percentage of the cash, and they split the groceries. And so, here I am into this thing with all this shit in the pad.

I'm home a couple of days, and here's a knock at the door. It's my parole officer. He comes in and we talk. He's sitting on the couch with his arm along the top, and in back of this couch is the check protector and the book of checks. He's talking, he looks around, and he mentions how nice the place is, and I have to tell him, "Well, my old lady's been working and I'm going to start playing." Finally he leaves.

There's a guy I know of from Pasadena; he has a bad reputation—he's got a reputation of being not quite trustworthy. I think he's a rat. One day this guy comes to my door. He says his name. I say, "What are *you* doing *here*? What do you want?" He says, "Oh, uh, Arnold wanted me to pick up something for him." I say, "Arnold who?" He says, "Well, Arnold, you know. He wants me to pick up a couple checks." I said, "I don't know what you're talking about, man! There ain't no kind of checks here! There ain't nothing happening here! Get out! I don't want to see you around here again, and whoever this Arnold is, tell him not to send anyone else! We're moving right away, and if anyone comes out, if the police come out, it's all over for you!" He says, "Ohhhh, man!" I say, "Get the fuck out!"

He left, and I figured the police would be coming at any moment. Diane wasn't home. I grabbed the check protector and the checks and ran outside in the night. I didn't want to throw the machine away because I didn't want to get involved with Arnold in that kind of thing, but I wanted it out of the house. I called Arnold. I told him, "Man, I want you to get this shit out of here immediately!" He said, "Man, I can't keep it *here!*" I said, "I don't care! Get it out of here!" Diane comes home and she brings some stuff; so we fix and then I tell her that the shit's out and that's it. I said, "You've never been in jail. You don't know what it's like. I don't want to go back to San Quentin." I don't know what she said. I fell out.

The next morning there's another knock on the door and here's my parole officer again—here he is and he's got two detectives with him. He says, "I want to talk to you. Is your wife home?" I say, "Wait a minute." And they waited for a minute, which I couldn't believe. I ran into the bedroom: there was an outfit and stuff in there. Another "possession." I woke Diane up. "The heat are here!" I said, "Take this. Get rid of it. Flush it. I'll keep them in the front room." I went out and said, "She's getting up." I closed the door into the hall. I said. "Well, what is it?" They said, "We've been informed that you know something about a burglary. We have to check you out." One of the detectives said, "Have you got anything in the house?" I said, "Anything what?" He said, "Anything anything. Anything at all." I said, "No." He said, "Do you mind if we search the place?"

They started their search and they found all these groceries.

They'd look in a drawer and look at each other and raise their eyebrows and nod. My parole officer told my old lady, "We've got a complaint. We have to take him in." They took me outside, put handcuffs on me, and put chains around my stomach to hold the handcuffs. They told me to get into the front seat of the car. They drove me down to the station in Pasadena and put me in a cell. I couldn't find out what was going on, and I waited there for three days until finally they called my name. I walk out, and here's my parole officer. "We want to know if you'll give permission for a polygraph test. You've been accused of certain things. Our informant has given us definite information. If you're innocent you don't have anything to worry about. If you're guilty you won't want to take the test, and we'll just violate you." They had checked me for marks. I had marks. They could violate my parole. My only chance was to take the polygraph test.

I walked into a room, and here's the machine all set up. The guy introduced himself. He said, "You're taking this of your own free will? You haven't been coerced?" I said, "I guess you can call it that. If I don't take it, I'm admitting guilt. It's a nice game you got going." The machine looked like something out of science fiction with lights and dials and bubbles. I'm scared to death because I know exactly what they want to know. Even though I wasn't involved with the check protector and hadn't participated in the robbery, I was aware of what was going on and I was a recipient of its benefits.

The detective said, "I'm going to explain something." He hooks the machine on to me so when I answer a question they can tell by my heartbeat and perspiration the emotions the questions are evoking. If I tell a lie the dials register it. He said, "Just to show you that we don't want to trick you I'm going to read the whole thing to you before you start the test." This is the most diabolic part of all. I didn't realize it at the time. He said, "I'm going to start out by asking you your name." And he told me all the things that would be asked of me in the order they were going to be asked. When he finished he said, "Just to make sure there's no question about it, I'm going to run through it again." One of the questions was "Do you have knowledge of the burglary that took place at so-and-so?" And after that, "What was your mother's maiden name?" And then, "Do you own a dog?" Then, "Did you ever see a check protector?" And, "Do you know a person by the name of Arnold Samsa?" He would go back and forth like that, and because he went through it twice I knew the exact order of the questions he was going to ask. So when he asked me, "What did you have for lunch?" I knew the next question would be "Have you ever seen anyone forging the checks in question or forging a signature on the checks in question?" I could feel my whole body moving and vibrating, the blood pumping through my veins, the sweat forming on my forehead and underneath my arms; my voice sounded strange to me. There was no way I could control all that. Then we went through it *again*. By this time I knew every question. Three questions before, I knew when he was going to ask the real question, and I could feel myself getting excited. My mouth got dry. All these things were measured, and they were a dead giveaway I knew something.

When I finished, the detective didn't say anything. The parole officer didn't say anything. They sent me back to my cell and left me there for three more days with no word. At last they called me out, and my parole officer said, "The test shows exactly what I figured. You know something about the checks. It's up to you." He said, "Do you want to talk about it?" I said, "There's nothing to talk about. I have nothing to say." They sent me back to my cell. I stayed for three more days. Then they came and interrogated me. I said, "I'd love to help you out, but I don't know anything at all. If you're going to send me to jail, send me to jail. I can't help you."

They released me. I called Diane to come and get me. I've got a big beard. I haven't shaved in nine days. We go to the house, the same apartment, and I don't know if the police are outside or what, and Diane goes to a drawer and pulls out a condom of stuff and an outfit! Here she is, as if she's got a legal pass to do all this shit! But I'm dirty and miserable and here's some heroin, the only thing that's friendly and warm and good. So I fixed. Then I went into the living room and, just as a formality, I kind of glanced around the pad. I happened to look behind the couch and here it was *again!* I couldn't believe it. I could not believe it. The check protector and this big book of checks. I just couldn't believe it, man.

I told Diane and I told Arnold—I got this Arnold over

there—I said, "Take this fuckin' thing out of here!" I told Diane, "If that's what you want you can go with the machine and the checks and just get the fuck out!" She said, "Well, this is *my* place!" I said, "Alright, fuck you! *I'll* get out!" And then she said, "Ohhhh! Noooooo! Art!" And she started whining. Finally Arnold took it away.

We stayed in Glendale. We had all these groceries. We had nothing, really, just all this nonsense, and finally it went. I was on the Nalline program again, killing myself trying to beat the tests, and we didn't have a car. I was riding the bus to East L.A. to score. Finally I hung up everything—the Nalline program, my parole—and so we had to move. I had to hide again. We moved in with a relative of Diane's, an aunt; Diane's mother was staying there, too. I remember walking the streets, picking up cigarette butts. I'd work occasionally, and every penny I made we spent on dope and cough syrup.

Finally a guy offered me a job at a jazz club out in Orange County. I was afraid to take it, but the money was very good and I felt that even though I'd hung up my parole they wouldn't look for me that close. I told the guy I'd work the job if he didn't advertise in the paper. I told him he could put my name on the club. I got a kid I was giving lessons to to drive us out there. Diane hadn't heard me play in a long time and she wanted to come along. As we approached the club I got a feeling, a premonition, that something bad was going to happen. I told the kid, "I'm afraid to have Diane in the club. We know some people out here in Orange County. Please drop her at their house, where she'll be safe. Then you can come back." I told Diane, "Just before the job ends give me a call at the club and I'll tell you if everything's okay. Our friends can bring you over." I had the kid drop me a block and a half from the club. I walked. I had my alto case in my hand, and I saw they had my name out front, which I'd said they could do. I didn't know this: the owner had also put an ad in the Orange County papers.

I went into this club still very nervous. I had quite a few drinks, and then I got up on the stand with the rhythm section and started to play. I had been playing for almost an hour and it was time to take an intermission, when a waitress came up to me. She motioned to me while the piano player was taking a solo. I bent down, and she said, "There's fuzz in this place. I think they're after you." I said, "Is there any way out of here?" She said, "No, the back is padlocked. There's only the front door." I said, "Well, bring me a drink, a big one."

She brought the drink, and I remember playing. I played beautifully, and the people loved it. I really reached them. I played "Everything Happens to Me." I stayed on the stand, and the guys were looking at me. They didn't say anything, but we'd been up there for about an hour and a half. I realized there was no way out. Even if I stayed on the stand the whole night the cops would grab me, but I figured I'd play as long as I could and give the people their money's worth—so I'd have something to remember and they'd have something to remember me by. At last I announced the intermission. I introduced the guys in the band and told the people, "It's beautiful playing for you. You're a marvelous audience." Then I said, "It's just a shame that all of you aren't like most of you are." I started talking in circles. I was rapping to the people, and I think they saw some of the sadness I felt. I put my horn down, and turned to the guys, and I said, "Yeah, it was a great set. Thank you." And the minute I left the stand a guy walked up to me and said, "Please follow me. I'm a police officer."

I knew I had no chance. I walked outside, and the guy said, "Alright. Up against the wall." I said, "Ohhhh, man, why don't we get away from this club?" He yelled, "Against the wall!" So here's the front of the club, my name in big letters, and me against the sign getting shook down. "I have a warrant for your arrest. We have an APB out for you. Parole violation." They handcuffed me. All the people were out there watching and I felt that they were really with me. Some of them said, "Is there anything we can do?" It was a touching thing, but these cops couldn't have cared less. "Alright! Come on!" They threw me in the car. I was glad Diane hadn't come along. She'd had an outfit in her purse. They asked me, "Where's your old lady? How'd you get here?" I told them I'd hitchhiked. They said, "Yeah, sure." This kid I'd come with was practically crying. He came up to the police car and I said, "If you ever run into my old lady, tell her goodbye for me."

18 | San Quentin: Tattoos

1965 - 1966

THEY TOOK ME to the Orange County Jail, and finally word came back from the parole department: "You've been violated. You'll be taking the chain back to San Quentin as soon as the bus is ready." And I said, "Oh, that's great. That's just great."

It was at this point I thought, "Well, man, I am a criminal." See, now, when I was a kid I read books about murders, mystery stories, detective stories. I saw all the movies about the "Big House." I loved things like that and I would have been happy to be a criminal until I saw the people who really were criminals: most of them were dumb and stupid and stank. But there were a few that were sharp and hep, and every now and then I'd see some real armed robber and I'd think, "Well, what do I like about this guy?" I thought, "I've got to make myself the kind of convict I like, a hep convict. I want to be proud of myself." I'd look at him and see that he had tattoos—a skull and "Hate" and "Death to All."

A Mexican guy I knew in the Orange County Jail was good at tattooing, so I asked him to give me one. He said, "Man, are you kidding? You've been in the joint twice and you're going to get a tattoo now?" He said, "Look at me." He had tattoos all over. "I'd give anything in the world if I hadn't started putting these things on." I said, "No, no, don't talk me out of it."

He had a bunch of pictures that he'd drawn, and I could choose one. I saw a pretty one of flowers with a place to put a name, and I said, "Let me have that one." He said, "I'll put your old lady's name there. What's your old lady's name?" I said, "Diane, but, wow, I don't want *her* name there." He said, "Oh,

325

it doesn't matter. Once you start you'll have a million of them."
He had to get a needle and some ink smuggled in, and we had to
hide and point for the bulls, and it hurt bad, but he finally got it
on, and it looked beautiful. Georgeous, Every time I took my
shirt off I'd stand and gaze at myself in the mirror, and it really
knocked me out. I didn't want to wear a shirt anymore. I started
walking around in an undershirt.

One day I noticed that the tattoo had started to fade, and I
asked the guy what was happening. He said, "Oh, man, that's
the trouble. Sometimes they give you India ink and it's not
pure. I think I got burned, man. They gave me watered ink." It
kept fading and fading, and I said, "What am I going to do?"
The guy said, "All I can do is put it on again." I said, "Jesus,
man, it hurts so bad." He says, "Well, you wanted a tattoo." So
I said okay, and he put the whole thing on again, and it took
ages, but it looked beautiful. And then it started fading *again*.
He said, "Well, the guy burned me again, the son-of-a-bitch,
man! He burned me again, and after all I've done for that
asshole, man! Well, all we can do is put it on again, or it'll fade
out completely." I had gone through such pain, I couldn't stop
now. He put the whole thing on again, and it looked beautiful
again, and to this day you can't see it. Right now you can't even
see it. For a while, though, it looked great.

They took me back to San Quentin and that was my thing,
to get tattoos. I'd see guys I'd known before and they'd say,
"Oh, man, what's *that*?" I'd say, "I'm going to be covered with
'em. I'm not going to have an empty spot on my body. I'm gonna
be a real gangster." I kept looking around for guys that did tattooing. One guy did one of Pan. Pan played his little horn and
all the women followed him. He'd take them into a cave and
ball them, and then the women would disappear. They'd never
find them again. I had Pan put on my left forearm, and
then—I've always liked Peanuts—a guy put Snoopy and Linus
inside my left forearm. I got the smiling and the sad masks on
my right forearm. On my right bicep I got a Chinese skull, with
a long moustache and a Van Dyke beard, smoking an opium
pipe. Above my left breast I got a naked lady, a rear view of her
squatting, but that one faded. And then on my back I got a
chick doing the limbo, going under the bar, with little black
panties on. That one came out nice. Just before I got released, I

was going to get a vampire. A guy had done a drawing of Dracula, and it was going to be on my right arm over my vein. The mouth would be open over the vein, and then when I fixed I could say, "Hey, wait a minute! I gotta feed mah *man*! He's hungry, jack!" You know. "Come on, baby, I gotta go first. Mah man's hungry. He needs some *blood*!" But I got out before I could get it, and I always wanted that one.

One day I was sitting out in the yard. I was taking black-and-whites, which were easy to get, and I'd finally succumbed to the lowest and most dangerous thing to do in prison, which is sniffing glue. It causes you to hallucinate, it's bad for you physically, it's bad for your mind, and it's degrading. I got with a guy named Sleepy, and I was sniffing glue with him. You could buy a bottle of white shoe glue for four packs of cigarettes, which is cheap. You take a towel and cut it up into strips and pour the glue onto a strip and roll it up in your hand; then you cup your hand, put your fist to your mouth and suck in hard two or three times, and your ears start ringing.

So me and Sleepy were sitting out on the yard sniffing glue, hunched over, with our knees up, when a guy came up to me and said, "Can I talk to you for a minute?" I said yeah, and he said, "There's a friend of mine wants to talk to you, has eyes for you. She, er, he likes you. He's been watching you." I didn't know what to say. I told the guy, "Well, I'm not, I don't play any of that homosexual thing." He said, "Well, why don't you talk to him? He could do you a lot of good and he could also be a bad enemy." I knew from hearing people talk that there were some dangerous homosexuals in prison, and I knew the names of these guys, so I said, "Well, who is it?" The guy—I could tell he was a little swishy himself—said, "Mandy." And I thought, "Oh, my God, Mandy!" I'd heard stories about this guy. He was a white guy, nice looking with cold, blue eyes. He was well known in prison, dangerous. It was rumored that he'd killed two or three people and stabbed several others; he was considered insane. My first reaction was to tell the guy no, there's nothing happening, but when I heard the name I thought I'd better be careful. I told the guy, "Yeah, well, I'll talk to him." He said, "He's waiting for you down in the lower yard."

Sleepy had heard the whole thing. He said, "Man, I'd give anything in the world if that cat sounded me! Oh, man, he's a clean guy. He's, like, a nice-looking guy." This Sleepy had done more time than me for longer periods, and he'd only fallen into sniffing glue recently, but he'd been pretty sharp as a hustler in the joint. He knew all the people and all the angles. He said, "Man, I would give *anything!*" I said, "Yeah, but I'm not a homosexual. I don't dig them." He said, "What's the difference? Just close your eyes. All he wants to do is suck on your joint, man. All you gotta do is close your eyes and think of some beautiful girl, man, and just for that little thing, this guy will really take care of you. You won't have to sniff glue. Whatever's around he'll get it for you. He'll get you food, good clothes, cigarettes, coffee, all the best. And nobody'll mess with you because she'll let everybody know that you're her man. They'll have to answer to her, and they're really afraid of her. I'd give my right arm if she'd hit on me. You've got the chance of a lifetime!" I said, "I can't make it, man." And Sleepy said, "Well, be careful then. Don't offend her."

I get downstairs. I'm nervous. I don't know what I'm going to do. I walk down the same stairway I'd walked down my first day in Quentin with Little Ernie when we saw the guy with blood pouring out of his stomach. I'm tripping out about all the things I've been through in San Quentin. I look up, there's a guard on the walkway looking down at me. If I make a wrong move he'll kill me. I'm going to meet a fruiter that digs me, and I don't want to incur the wrath of this fruiter or I may get killed by him. I get down to the lower yard, and here are all the Black Muslims on the football field going through their exercises to get strong so they can kill all the whites. And here's Mandy.

I go over to him. The other guy, the messenger, stands off a little ways like a bodyguard. Mandy says, "Hi, Art." I say, "Hello, Mandy." His eyes are cold as death. He's dressed perfectly. He's got nice shoes, almost impossible to get, and they're shined. He's spotlessly clean. He smiles. He really looks deranged. He says, "Let's walk over here." We sit down on the lawn and he says, "Look at these black motherfuckers." He says, "One of these days, I'd like to form a group and wipe 'em out. Kill 'em all. Aren't they ridiculous! Look at that monkey-looking motherfucker!" He's raging and his eyes are beaming with lust for the violence he's going to perpetrate on the black people. "But," he says, "That can wait till later. That's something for the future I'm working on." Here's these white maniacs hating the blacks, and the blacks practicing and training to kill all the whites, and the Mexicans are standing there silent. I'm thinking, "What's going to happen one of these days when all this stuff comes to a head? What's going to happen to this country?" Mandy says, "Maybe they haven't been walking over here. I don't want to sit anyplace that they've been near, those stinkin', yella-teeth motherfuckers, big, black niggers!" We're sitting on the grass, and I look up, and from the lower yard you can see Mount Tamalpais. It's close, and there are beautiful homes on it. Little wispy clouds are floating across the sky, and the sky is blue. I'm looking at the mountain, and then my eyes drop back into prison, and I see the walls and the guards with their rifles and all these people full of hate. And then I look at this madman sitting here, going to tell me that he loves me.

Mandy says, "I've been watching you. Even when you were here last time. At that time I had an old man and I was in love with him, but I kept looking at you, and you really move me." He had never been out. I'd been out and come back. I think he'd killed a couple of people in an armed robbery. He said, Now, things are different." His old man had gone home. "I like the way you carry yourself and I don't like to see you sniffing glue. You deserve better than that. You've got too much class to be doing that. I like you. You're clean and neat and you're talented. Whenever you play out in the yard I sit in the distance and listen and watch you. You're wonderful. I really care for you. If you could feel the same way you'd never have to worry about a thing. Clothes—look at the way I'm dressed." It was the epitome of dress in the joint. He says, "Dope—when anything comes in I'll go to 'em and jack 'em up and get part of it or else. Every night in your cell, until I can arrange to move you into my cell, every night you'll be delivered steak sandwiches. Anything you want. Canteen. From now on, if you have eyes, you won't have to draw any money anymore. Just take whatever money you got and keep it. Save it for when you get out. You won't have to worry about a thing—cigarettes, coffee, chucholucos. Anything you want you've got. And if anybody ever messes with you, or if there's somebody you don't like, tell me and I'll take care of them. That's it, man. I just want someone to be close to and someone to love."

Most of the guys in the joint go for whatever situation they're in. That's how they conduct themselves. I'd asked a lot of guys how they could make that scene and they said, "Well, it's just something you do while you're here, and then when you get out it's different." But I couldn't do it. I just could not do it. I've seen three or four guys get some cigarettes together and pay them to a fruiter; they meet someplace and he gives them each head and they don't see anything wrong with it. But I couldn't do it. It would have been much easier if I could. I looked at Mandy and I said, "Man, I'm sorry. If I made that scene you'd be the one I'd want more than anyone else, but I've just never made that scene, and I can't do it. I can't do it." He said, "Well, let's be friends and we'll see what happens."

I got away from him and I got nervous. I talked to some friends of mine. I talked to Frank Ortiz. He said, "Man, watch out for that cat because if you accept anything from him you'll put yourself in a position—he might think you led him on." And right away Mandy started offering me things, so I told him no, that I couldn't take them because it wasn't right. He got drug, and he got hurt, but then he said, "I appreciate your honesty. We could have had a ball. But I can't rank you for being honest, and I admire you for not trying to take advantage of me and get something for nothing." And from then on we were friends.

I finally quit the glue sniffing, but I kept taking black-and-whites. I'd take sixteen or eighteen of them every morning in my cell with my coffee. With black-and-whites you lose your equilibrium. You fall down and run into things. There were three or four of us who'd been taking them, hanging out together. One day I was sitting with these guys on the yard, sitting on one of the domino tables, and I dropped my cigarette. I went to pick it up. I bent down and fell off the table. I cut my head and got all bloody. When blood is drawn it's a serious thing. The guards think you've killed somebody or somebody's shanked you, so my friends stood around me while one of them got a wet rag and cleaned my forehead. I'm goofing around, and right away I fall off the table again and hit my head in the same place. Now, they get a guy to sneak in the hospital and get some bandages to stop the bleeding. That night we're all lined up to go into our cells. I get into line, and we round a little bend. I go to take a step and I step too high. I fall back, hitting my head on the cement. The guards rush out and grab me and take me to the hospital. They interrogate me. Finally they put me back in my cell. The next morning walking out of my cell on the fourth tier, I walked straight out and smashed into a bar. If I hadn't hit the bar I would have fallen over and killed myself. The guards took me to Fourposts. They interrogated me again. They had had a lot of reports about me. They took my blues and put some old, beat clothes on me and walked me to the adjustment center.

The adjustment center is for people that stab people and things like that. They said, "This is where you have to go." A guard came in and said that the psychiatrist thought I was trying to kill myself with the black-and-whites. He said, "What are you doing this for? Look at you!" I said, "There's nothing wrong with me. I just want to get out." He said, "Well, you're never going to get out this way."

In the adjustment center you only leave your cell for about five minutes each Saturday when they walk you down, one at a time, to take a shower, with guards watching you through a glass. They bring you your food in your cell, push it through a slot. You sit there for the whole time in a cell, and that's it. I was there for about two months. You never see anyone because there's nothing across from you, just a wall, but everybody knows what's happening and who's there. On my second day a guy down the way asked me, "How're you doing?" I said, "Terrible." He said, "Well, I'm So-and-so. I'm a friend of So-and-so's. I'm going to send you down something." He hands something to the next cell, reaching outside the bars. He says, "Pass that to number seven." The guy passes it down to me, and I open it up, and here's about twenty-five black-and-whites! I took them and got wasted. For two days I had a ball.

It had a lot of romance, being in the adjustment center. People look up to you for being there and being cool, not whining. There were guys in there waiting to go to trial for murder or for shanking people, and I was digging this whole scene. I'd hear the others talk, and I started thinking how great it would be to kill someone and really be accepted as a way-out guy. As a rough cat. All the guys that were really in would know about it. "Man, that cat, Art Pepper, he wasted a cat, cut him to ribbons. Stabbed him and stabbed him, blood pouring all out of the guy. Don't fuck with him, man." I started dreaming about it and thinking about it and seriously planning it. I was all ready to do it and could have done it. I had the nerve, I had the shank, and I was in the process of choosing my victim when I got my date to get out.

————————

(Jerry Maher)   I'd seen Art play before I ever met him. I first met Art, I think, in Quentin through John Wallach. John Wallach and I were working on the waterfront together, and him and Art were close for years. I was working at the paymaster's office in Quentin, and Art decided he wanted to work, so I got him a clerk's job in the paymaster's office. It was me and him and Joe Coletti and a guy named Larry Steckler. We worked there for a couple of years. There were some trips in that paymaster's office, really some trips.

Art was a pretty good-lookin' dude then. When you first meet Art, he's pretty quiet and introverted, but after you get to know him well, and he's around people he feels comfortable with, he falls his loony hand, you know. He's pretty comical. And we used to have a lot of laughs together. But right off the top, right after you meet Art, talk to him a little bit, you snap that he's extremely sensitive. And I also snapped that he was highly uncomfortable in that setting. You know, I've been raised in YA's (Youth Authorities) and joints, so I was as comfortable as you can get when you're surrounded by a bunch of lunatics, but Art doubted his own ability to cope with it and was a little ill at ease behind that. His music and gettin' high was his refuge. I used to get on his case all the time behind his talent, fuckin' off that talent in the pen. I told him I wish I had that much talent doin' anything, you know, and we used to argue about that all the time. That and niggers. Art was tellin' me Ray Charles was a genius, and I told him there wasn't any nigger alive that was one step above a blithering idiot.

I was a little bit in awe of the guy: he was older than me and he had so much talent. And I used to just sit and trip on it, you know, how come some people are born with so much talent and others none. I also see something in Art, which he's quick to admit to, which is almost a suicidal, a real strong self-destructive, drive. Like those black-and-whites. We used to get on him about those black-and-whites because he'd get like a zombie, just slobbering. He was sittin' at the domino table one day, on the yard, and just fell forward and gave himself a black eye. The corner of the domino table hit him in the eye. One day he got up to go to the head on the yard and made a big, staggering U-turn and wound up pissin' on this little stage that was set up against the East Block wall, a little raised stage about two feet up in the air and about six by six. There was a stool on it where the yard cop could sit and be elevated about two or three feet above everybody, you know. Art took off from the domino tables goin' in the opposite direction, to the head, and wound up makin' a big, staggerin' U-turn around the yard and standin' there pissin' on this. He thought he was at a urinal when they arrested him.

I used to tell him, "Man, you're just a walkin' bust. Get yourself together." And Johnny Wallach, he's another dude with a heavy suicide... And John and Art kind of reinforced each other's sickness. Both beautiful dudes, man, but they'd get on those black-and-whites together staggerin' around, and they didn't know who they were for days at a time. John finally fell out in the North Block with convulsions one day. Took him out of the North Block on a gurney. Art wound up, I think, in the hospital too. Either in the hospital or the hole.

I was in Quentin doin' a forgery beef. I'd started at Soledad, and I got popped in Soledad makin' it with a secretary. I was workin' in the procurement office. I was twenty-one at the time, and I hooked up with this little twenty-one-year-old secretary. She hit on her husband for a divorce, told him why. He snitched on us. Got her fired and me transferred. I did about two years on that, got out, got a violation and came back, and got out and got another violation and came back.

Next time I saw Art on the streets—I got out the day Marilyn Monroe committed suicide, August of '62. I was livin' in West Hollywood with my second old lady, Yolanda the

Snake, and I ran into Art one day on Santa Monica Boulevard. He was just comin' out of the unemployment office. He was livin' in a little apartment behind a barber shop off La Brea and Sunset with Diane. I was dealin' at the time, and he hit on me to score, so I wound up sellin' him some stuff.

I took him out to this little old hooker's pad in North Hollywood. I had a couple of workin' girls, and one of them, I had just sold her my last quarter when Art called to cop. So I went out, and Yolanda and I picked him and Diane up and took 'em out there. I fixed Art in the bathroom and he immediately OD'd on me. He fell down on the floor. And that's when I started hating Diane. I was cookin' her fix when Art fell out, and I stopped, naturally, and turned around to help him, and she said, "Oh, he's alright. He'll be alright. Go ahead and cook my fix." I said, "You cold-blooded, stinkin' son-of-a-bitch! Your old man is layin' on the floor turnin' blue and all you can think about is gettin' *fixed*?" Anyway, I turned around and fixed her, and *she* fell out on me. And I found out, they copped later, that they'd been drinkin' Cosanyl all day. That got me hot, hot, hot because I, you know, I had to work on them for about an hour, hour and a half, somethin' like that, and I threw 'em in the back of the car, soakin' wet, both of 'em, and drove from North Hollywood back to their pad at about eighty miles an hour at night with the cold air blowin' on 'em, and Art kept groanin', "Man, roll up the window! I'm freezin' to death!" I told him, "Fuck you. I hope you do freeze to death, you ignorant bastard!"

As for Diane, well, at one time Diane was a beautiful girl. I've seen pictures of her. When I met her, she was a dog. She looked like she was a hundred years old and had lived every one of 'em on her face. All her teeth were gone: completely false uppers and lowers. Haggard, tired, worn. She'd put herself in the gutter and wallered in it long enough to where she couldn't ever get back. It sounds kind of cold, but her dying wasn't any loss to anybody in the known universe. In my opinion she wasn't nothin'. She was a tramp. And that wasn't Art's fault.

Art's very dependent, and in my opinion Art's relationship with women is one basically of dependence. Because of that, I could never accept the idea of Art being responsible for anything Diane did. I'd have to look at it to the contrary. I think that any man-woman relationship Art's gonna be involved in, the woman is going to have more influence with Art than Art's gonna have with her.

Art doesn't have an evil bone in his body, and he's—I don't mean this in a demeaning manner because on Art it's totally acceptable, you have to know him—but Art is a pathological physical coward. I guess it's the way he was raised and he's been in music all of his life, moving with that element of people. He's never been called upon to get violent or be violent. I remember an instance in the joint. I can't remember if it was Big Woody Woodward or Tubby Whitman. It was one of the notorious hogs that had some words with Art. They got into a hassle, and the guy told Art, "Man, I'll tear your head off and shit in your neck!" Somethin' to that effect. He had no intention whatsoever of doin' it; he wouldn't have laid a hand on him. But Art took it seriously, and he came to me and a half a dozen other people, and he was just in a panic: "Oh, God, what am I gonna *do*? That animal's just gonna *ruin* me, man! That guy's gonna break my spine, gonna tear my arms off!" I can't remember who it was, but I went and talked to him: "Man, what is this shit with you and Art?" The guy said "*What*?" I ran it down, and the guy cracked up. He said, "Man, you know me better'n that, Jer. I wouldn't put my hands on that guy." I said, "I didn't think so but Art goddamnsure believes it." Art was panic-stricken; "Oh my God, it's all over. I know it's all over. Fuck it, this is it!"

────────────

I WAS released in June of '66 with another guy that got out on the same day, a friend of mine, Richard Fortier. They gave us each a package and a suit—a cheap, single-breasted, black suit, but at least it fit well. I paid the guy some cigarettes to have it fixed. I put a white shirt on and a tie. We went through the gate and they gave us our ticket home and a little money. Richard had been there a long time. This was his second time, too, so we both knew all the guards. They said, "Well, good luck, man, hope we don't see you back here again."

We walked out into the little town of San Quentin and got a

ride to San Rafael, and when we got there we stopped at a bar immediately and we both got brandy. Everybody could tell we had just gotten out of the joint. The bartender said, "It must be a great day." We had a few drinks and got a nice buzz and rode into San Francisco. I didn't have to be back in L.A. till Monday to report to the parole department, so we decided to goof around in San Francisco for a while.

We got off the bus on North Broadway, right in North Beach. They'd given me a package with some extra stuff in it—a couple of khaki shirts, khaki trousers, work boots, sport shirt, "dress" slacks, and assorted underwear and socks. I just took it and threw it in the trash can. It was a beautiful day, sunny and warm, and we were wandering around, and we heard music. We walked toward the sound of the music and saw a little, narrow street blocked off for traffic. There were some people in this street and they were dancing. They were having a festival. We walked in and looked around.

There were a lot of pretty girls. I saw one wearing a long peasant dress with long hair and beads and bracelets and rings. I noticed that they wore rings on their first fingers, which I'd never seen before. This girl really looked good, so we walked closer to the group, but as we got nearer I saw that the bottom of her dress was all torn where she'd stepped on it. It looked like she'd dragged it through the gutter. It was wet and soiled. Her clothes were wrinkled, and you could see dirt in her hair. She had strange things painted on her face. She looked like a death's head, white makeup, and her eyes were all blackened. No lipstick. Her hands and fingers and her fingernails were filthy. You could almost smell her.

When you're in prison you acquire a passion for cleanliness. You "talachi" your cell all the time, scrub it out until it's spotless. You can eat off the floors of the cells. Me and Ernie Flores when we celled together used to walk on our floor in our stocking feet to keep it clean. And Richard and I had these pictures in our minds of women, how pretty they were and how clean and how sweet smelling, a whole fantasy about what we wanted them to be. So we went to the worst place we could go: North Beach in 1966.

I looked around and saw the guys in Levis, matted dirt on their clothes, boots run over at the heels, ugly, dirty, long hair sticking out, and beards, scraggly and ugly. We noticed that there were a lot of black men. No black women. Just the men dressed in outrageous costumes with weird hats from the *Three Musketeers.* I guess they figured that even though these chicks were filthy they were still white, and they were dancing with them, hanging all over them and strutting around, and I could see on their faces this look of "Yeah, I got this white 'ho." I thought of all the things that went on in the joint. Richard said, "Look at that fuckin' nigger. Look at that trampy white bitch with that black animal!" I noticed some people looking at us strangely, and I realized that they probably thought we were police. I said to Richard, "Man, we ought to play a little game that we are police. Jack 'em up, take 'em in the alley, and beat 'em half to death."

We went into a bar and had a couple of drinks and we saw the same thing in there: girls dressed in ridiculous costumes acting like they were really into something when they were into nothing except dope and filth, hanging over these black guys who were strutting around. It was disgusting to us. We sat in the bar and kept drinking, and I got pretty juiced. Finally I happened to look over and saw for the first time a halfway decent-looking girl. She must have been about sixteen. She was at the bar, and this real pimp type black guy was slobbering all over her. I walked up to the bar and said to her, "What kind of a fuckin' tramp are you?" The guy started to say something. I said, "Oh, shut your mouth, you black punk!" I turned to the chick and said, "You filthy tramp bitch. What are you doing in here with this black motherfucker? Where's your class at?" She wigged out: "Oh you white motherfucker! You honkie sons-of-bitches!"

I realized the hate that I had, and it scared me. I was a madman. I wanted to kill people. Richard felt the same. And we were so violent these guys were actually afraid of us. Richard said, "Come on, man." We left North Beach and went downtown to the Tenderloin. That wasn't as bad. At least there were some people there that dressed like human beings. I didn't want to have anything to do with the young people. They were so corny.

We ate and got a cab, and Richard took me to the airport. He told me, "Man, you gotta be careful. You're out in this world now. You could have killed somebody in there and be right back in that prison." And I was close to it. I started fantasizing forming a white vigilante committee. People who'd stick up for the white race and not lay down and take all this hate that's coming from the blacks. Who'd be men. Who'd be proud of our heritage. The blacks were proud of *their* heritage. I envied them that. The whites were like little babies. They couldn't do anything. I was ashamed of being white. The blacks stuck together and did what they preached. I saw what they were talking about in the joint. They preach separatism and the formation of their own state, but then they turn around and preach the destruction of the white race by balling all the white women so the children will be black. And I saw that that was happening in North Beach, and the white chicks were all for it.

These chicks were rebelling against their parents. Their parents are weaklings who care only about money and anything to stay out of trouble. Who never stand up for any ideals. Who have no morals. Who don't make their children respect them. Who set such bad examples that the young white girls from Brentwood and Beverly Hills think that it's hep and right to go out with black people to show that they aren't like their parents. Their basic premise is commendable, but it's taken advantage of by these black guys that are full of hate. These guys have been oppressed for years. Now they're just using these white chicks for their own ends. They ball them not because they love them or want them but to satisfy their hatred against the white people, against the girls' parents.

I saw that I had to some way get rid of my hatred or it was going to kill me. For the blacks, it's beautiful to hate because everywhere they turn they've got people to support it and to join with them. And they can talk about it. It's a badge of honor, a badge of courage they can wear on their sleeves, and I admire them for it. But there was no one to join in with me. No one. The people that had the nerve and would be freethinkers were on this other kick of trying to undo the injustices they felt their parents had done. I was alone.

Before I left San Quentin, I became friends with a guy there, Joe, who had a sister living in Hollywood. She was a singer. Joe had written her thinking she could help me out and I could help her professionally. He gave me her number and wrote and told her I was coming out. I came in on the plane and got a bus to the parole department in West L.A. I got a parole officer and some money to get a place to live. I walked from the parole department down to Olympic and La Cienega. I was still debating whether to call Christine or not. I wanted everything to be completely new and open. Diane was in CRC. I thought, "Maybe I'll call. She can help me find a place." And I wanted to get laid, too. It had been a long time. I called her, and she said she'd pick me up. She told me she had a little yellow Anglia with a red stripe on it. I waited, and she drove up, and I looked down into this little car. Her skirt was almost to her pants line. I noticed that she was tall; she had red hair; and she looked pretty sexy to me—especially after doing all that time. She said, "Hi." And I said, "Hi." And she said, "Well, get in." She said she'd been hoping I'd call. She said, "What do you want to do?" I told her I had to get a place, and she said, "Why don't we go to my place? You probably want to relax."

We're driving and I'm glancing at her and she doesn't make any attempt to pull her dress down. She has long legs. They seem pretty nice. I looked at her face. She had a little black thing above her upper lip. It looked like a mole at first, but it was a tattoo. She had a hard, cold look about her, a bluesy, floozy kind of look, and when she talked and I looked in her eyes I could see that she'd been through a lot and was kind of bitter. But then I also felt compassion for her. She was like a whipped dog that still had a lot of guts left.

She lived in Hollywood in a teeny wooden house in back of another house on Gordon Street. We went in and she said, "Would you like a drink?" I said, "Well, I'd like to have some brandy." She said, "I've just got wine. I'll go to the store. You take your coat off, take your tie off. I'll be right back." She went out and while she was gone I looked around the pad. I saw that she had a hi-fi set and a piano and a lot of records and a lot of music. When she came back I drank the brandy, and she asked me if I wanted to smoke some pot. She got some out and rolled it, and I noticed that she rolled it better than any guy I'd ever seen. Everything she did ... A couple of times the phone rang, and the way she talked on the phone was real undercover, underworld. I found out she was dealing pot to support herself, and it was kind of exciting to me. I was going back into that same life, but she was so unlike Diane, who couldn't do anything at all. This one seemed strong, as if she could really take care of business.

We goofed around, talked about everything, and finally she said, "It probably was pretty hard there being without sex." And so we made love, without really any feeling. I noticed that she smelled clean, and her cunt was pretty, and she made love good. Then she said, "Where do you think you should stay?" I had to find a place to live for the parole department. She took me to a hotel and I got a room and she said, "Well, what are you going to do now? Why don't you come over to my place. You won't have to eat out. It'll be cheaper." We ate, and she said, "It's no use you going home. You're welcome to stay here if you want." So I spent the night, and instead of doing anything else I ended up staying with her. She was so strong. She eventually just always seemed to keep me around. That's the way it started. I stayed there. And pretty soon I was just there.

PART 3

1966–1978

19 | Christine

1966 – 1968

WHILE I WAS in Quentin the last time I got a letter from a counselor at the women's prison at Corona. She said that Diane was there at CRC, a lightweight prison for little kids and lame little girls that I was never able to go to: I was too evil and bad, a wild monster convict. Diane wanted to write to me, so her counselor wrote first to make sure I wanted to correspond. I wrote back and said yeah, sure, because I was already formulating a plan.

I had never been able to do all I wanted to do to Diane. I'd put her through a lot, but we'd gotten hooked again and that had stopped it. I wrote to her, and she answered. She had written Les Koenig at Contemporary Records. She'd used my name and begged him for my albums. He sent her about seven of them, and she had the albums all up in her room. That was her claim to fame at CRC. She was the Great Art Pepper's Old Lady. All the chicks would say, "Wow, is that your old man?" We corresponded, and she tried to clean up for all the things she'd done when I was in Quentin before and she was in Frisco. I wrote back, "Don't worry about a thing. I can hardly wait until we get back together again. Everything will be different." I had her completely strung out, and she thought everything was cool, but I'd never forgotten what she'd done. I'd heard millions more stories about her being used by black pimps, and balling chicks, and blowing everything I owned.

As it happened, I got out first and went to Hollywood and called Christine, and we started making it together. But I kept writing to Diane, telling her I was out and everything was great and I was going to send her money and I was going to come and visit her. Here I was for the first time with her in prison and me out, and she's dying for a visit. I'd tell her, "Don't worry. I'll be up as soon as I can. I'll send you money. I love you." And she's falling all over herself telling the girls, "He's coming to see me! He's going to send me money!" She's getting all prettied up. I wrote and told her, "I'll be up on the weekend. Get all ready for me." Which she had done to me. I had waited week after weekend all dressed up. I wouldn't even sit down because I didn't want to wrinkle my pants. I'd paid to have my clothes pressed to be as clean and handsome as I could, and I'd stand out in the yard waiting for my name to be called, and week after week passed without a word, and I never saw her, never got a penny from her, nothing but stories from people saying she was balling this cat and that chick.

I didn't visit her. I wrote her and said, "Wow, I'm sorry, but something came up and I couldn't make it. I'll be up next weekend without fail. Be all ready. I'll be there at such-and-such a time." Again, I didn't go. I wrote her. I said the same thing and then I didn't write again. Not a word. And that was the end of it. I never saw Diane again. She got out and went back, and when she got out again she was dying, and she tried to reach me, but by the time I heard about it, it was too late. She was dead.

———

(Ann Christos)   I think Art's fame attracted Diane. It was important to her. She liked important people, being with important people. I think Diane would have made it to a higher level if she hadn't got involved with Art and drugs. I think Diane started using because she couldn't control Art. She told me she decided to join him, maybe that would work. But they tormented one another. She attempted suicide. He did. One time Art said he was going to slash his wrists, and she went and got him a razor. Just games. And for Art, I think it was habit that kept him with Diane. Art's balled lots of women, but he's a moralist, a purist, and when he gets involved with a woman he usually sticks until something breaks it apart. They had established this niche, and they were alone. I know because I've been in those niches.

When Diane came out of CRC the second time, she got tight with her kids; her boys came to live with her. Then she found out she had cancer. Diane got all the morphine she wanted for her pain, and her son started to rob her of her pills. He was a doper. So she went to live with her mother. (Her mother was a dyke, dressed in manly clothes and things like that.) That's when she requested to see Art. He was in Synanon and they didn't give him the message: they didn't want to upset his tranquility. She wasted down to under eighty pounds. I was at CRC at the time.

Actually, Diane was the only woman I could ever talk to and discuss things and banter with without, you know, how you say something and people get offended—they take things personally. You could just talk to her and be honest and be critical, and she was the only woman that I'd ever encountered that had this open type mind.

———————————

(Marie Randall)   We were both born here in L.A. Our parents were divorced, and we were much closer than sisters usually are. It was she and I against the world. Diane never felt loved as a child. Being the older sister, she said that when she was a little child, she would try and hug and kiss my mom and dad, and they really didn't go for it, and she said, "And when you were little, they'd try and hug you or something, and you'd just turn your back and walk away." She didn't admit it to me until not long before she died: "They'd be nice to you, and you'd just walk away from them." That's probably why they were nice to me—because I wanted no part of them. So this, I think, was the beginning of all her problems. I've had all these years to think about it.

I was five and Diane was seven when our parents were divorced. In our conspiracy against the world, if we were living with one parent and we didn't like what was happening there, if they didn't let us do something, we'd say, "Okay, we'll go live with our mother." Which we would do, until things cooled down, and then we'd pull the same jazz on whoever we were with: "I'll go live with my father." It was easier living with our dad. He was the stronger of the two. Our mother drank.

Neither of us had to study in school. We both got very good grades. And Diane was extraordinarily bright. Gee, on her Stanford-Binet test I think her score was a hundred thirty-five.

Diane was very wild as a teenager, very wild. Well, it was really shocking at the time, but she'd have one boyfriend at a time. She didn't go out with everybody every night. She smoked early. So did I. Things other girls didn't do at those times. She met Ted, who was her first husband, and she had a baby when she was seventeen. I guess she thought she found the love she was looking for. But he was also seventeen, and she grew, and he didn't. So even if Art hadn't come along, that would have ended. He was into motorcycles and things like that, and his parents had enough money to take care of him, and when they wouldn't, Diane would—working in an ice cream parlor, something like that, trying to keep the family together.

Diane met Art the day he got out of San Quentin in a shiny blue suit and white socks and brown shoes and ten dollars or something. She was in her early twenties. She was gonna save him. Hahahaha! She had actually led a reasonably sheltered life, and she was gonna save Art from old demon dope. Even though she'd been working in a jazz club and all that stuff was around her all the time, she didn't even know how to drink. One time I took her to Reno and she's trying to be very sophisticated. She ordered a screwdriver in a zombie glass and needed a water chaser for it. And she spent the whole night on one drink, chasing it with water.

Diane was working in a jazz club. She needed the money, and she liked the hours. Neither one of us ever liked to get up in the morning. Ever. And she could be with the kids in the daytime. I had done it first, and she saw that I made a lot of money and my hours were very short, four or five hours a night, and it was easy work that any dummy could do.

I've always thought Art looked like Marcello Mastroianni He was a very good-looking man in those days, and Diane was always attracted by good looks. She didn't care how nice someone was, they had to be handsome. Well, she was gonna straighten Art's hand. I said, "What about the kids?" She said, "That's no life for them being around . . ." But she didn't mean that, because she was a very selfish person and she just wanted to be alone with Art. She didn't give a damn about the kids. Even before Art, when she was their mother, she would buy them fifty-dollar suits, which was a lot of money for a five-year-old kid in those days, or very expensive presents, with the money she made, but she didn't give them the love that she didn't get. Bought 'em things constantly.

I think Art connected the night he got out of San Quentin. She fought it at first, but it would have happened whether Art had come along or not. You see the signs. She used to sit down and eat a whole banana cream pie sometimes or bake three dozen cookies and eat every one of them. Now, that's compulsion. And it's only a symptom. As drugs are only a symptom. And if it hadn't been drugs it would have been alcohol or some other excess because she always had a problem.

When I saw this happening, it really disturbed me. That's when Art and I would have terrible scenes. They would be broke constantly because they were shooting everything up their arms and they would come and bum on me, stay with me. If I knew Art had something, I'd threaten to call the police, and he'd have to go flush it down the toilet and want to kill me. I know he would have killed me if he thought he could have gotten away with it. And I thought it was all his fault. I blamed him for everything. But I had great feelings of ambivalence because I really liked him when things . . . when bad things weren't happening. You know, we'd go to a drive-in movie, the three of us, and they'd stop off at a pharmacy first to buy a quart of Cosanyl, and we'd sit at the movie and have a ball. They'd pass it over to me: "No, thanks." Brown bagging it. They must have liked me to offer to share it. Hahahaha!

They had a great deal of affection for one another, using baby talk. He tried to please Diane. I was married to a man in Palm Springs, and they came down there, and Art went into hock for her. He bought her a beautiful diamond and sapphire ring for Christmas one time on the Friendly Credit Plan. He bought her a Lincoln convertible. My husband didn't have any money, but his mother was a millionaire, and Art wanted Diane to look as well as I was looking. And that's certainly affection and love and not just status.

Art bought her a poodle at about that time. Zsa Zsa. That was a very neurotic dog. She used to eat everything—furniture, clothes. She came with us on a crazy trip the three of us took to San Francisco, when we got all the flat tires. Diane and I could laugh at anything. We thought all these flat tires and crazy Zsa Zsa were funny, but Art saw absolutely no humor in the situation. Every time we got a flat tire, Diane and I would get the giggles and say, "How many more can you get when you only have four tires?" Things like that to us were funny, and that's how I miss her so much. 'Cause we could laugh ...

Right before we found out she was going to die, Diane bought the most beautiful bed you've ever seen, a mattress and box spring with a twenty-year guarantee. We got to giggling after she found out she was dying: "All my life I've wanted this bed. I buy it with a twenty-year guarantee, and I'm gonna use it a month or two!" One day, after they opened her up and found out how hopeless it was, she's in the hospital, we're sitting there smoking, and the doctor comes in and says, "What are you doing, smoking?" She says, "What's it gonna do to me now?"

She regretted all those wasted years with Art. They could have been productive years. When they were married, all the jobs Art got, he got because of Diane. She really pushed his career, and it was a constant frustration to her. She did everything to help him, his talent. Of course, she could shine in the glow of it, but, other than her own selfishness, she truly wanted him to be a great star because she thought he deserved it.

Art got Diane another poodle after Zsa Zsa. Bijou. Art loved Bijou so much. They paid three hundred dollars for her, I understand, and do you know, he hocked her to a connection! And Bijou never forgave him. After he got her out of hock, the very first time she saw him, she turned her back on him. He didn't even exist. She was never friendly to him again. She was the most sensitive person that there was. You know, they lied and stole from me, broke into my house, but hocking her was just beyond the realm of believability. They gave her to me, and Bijou became my whole life.

Diane's suicides—that was another very funny thing. They

lived off Glendale Boulevard on Fargo, the steepest hill in Los Angeles. And I had a friend, Frank Sinatra, Jr., who was Frank Sinatra's cousin, and he was going to take us to the Mocambo for Sinatra's opening show. So, Diane, knowing she had a deadlock cinch that I was going to be there to pick her up, took fifty or sixty phenobarbital. I arrive, all gussied up for this show, and there she is. She took 'em an hour or so before I got there, knowing I was going to be there to save her. Well, called the ambulance, all of that. The hill was so steep the ambulance couldn't get up it! Hahahaha! The only way they could get up to save this dying girl—they had to *back* up Fargo hill!

She wasn't really trying to kill herself. These attempts were a cry for help. She never really tried to kill herself without a guarantee. I'm a very dependable person, and she would do it when she knew I would get her. And what she wanted was more attention. What does anyone want from a suicide attempt?

Every now and then, Diane would see what she was doing to her life, and that really wasn't the way she wanted to spend the rest of her days. She tried to straighten her hand, but her need for love was stronger than her need for survival. Art meant more to her than her whole, entire life. She loved him to the day she died.

When Diane got out of jail and Art was living with Christine, she was terribly upset. She wouldn't even tell me how horrible things were. But it was obvious. You just had to look at her. As for Christine, Christine was not a likable person under any circumstances. The only thing that comes to mind is—unpleasant. I don't really even remember too well what she looked like. I know we encountered her a couple of times, and she was just unpleasant, just a bitch. And Art's such a weak person that if Diane wasn't available someone had to be.

Diane came to live with me, as usual. I got her a little job, but she decided that wasn't what she wanted to do, so she screwed me again. We'd had such a good relationship until Art came into her life, and then she used me, he used me. Oh, God, it was terrible what they did. Well, being away from Art all that time, she was compelled to go back to drugs. The next thing I heard, I got a bill from an ambulance company in Long

Beach dunning me. She'd gotten busted and tried to run, and a cop had hit her on the head or something, so they'd had to call an ambulance for her. And she went to jail.

I'm sure she was staying with Ann Christos at those times. She got busted in Long Beach. And then where did she go from there? I know I spent my life bailing her out. It all runs together, it happened so much. But CRC was a marvelous place. It was like a country club. I couldn't believe how well they were living there. They used to have mixed group, so I had to take her eyelashes to her just because they were going to be around guys. I took her makeup. It was cute. It was very good for her, too. When she got out, she was really trying to straighten out.

Diane and I only had each other to tell things to. And even today something will happen—like this. Or I'll see a television show or read something in the paper and think I should tell Diane. I've got no one like that left, and I'll never have anyone like that. She was a marvelously witty, bright, intelligent person, and it just killed me to see her life go that way. But the second time she got out of CRC, she'd really, truly learned a lot and she was going to straighten her hand. That's why we got back in touch with her children. She was going to be a decent, responsible human being. And then she started coughing up blood.

Well, we were sitting on the bed here one day, watching television, talking, and she was coughing, and there were little blood spots in the Kleenex. That's not really extraordinary if you've got a bad cold or something. I said, "Here, let me give you some throat lozenges." Hahahaha! She was with a guy named Tony Kennedy at that time. He was a CRCer, too, a really good guy though, an Oakie guy, very down to earth, who just worshiped her. Tony and Diane were living in Torrance or Gardena, and the blood spots appeared, and they got progressively worse. She went to Harbor General and they X-rayed her, gave her a TB test, and said, "Well, you better come in. We've got to explore the problem." Tony was still with her. They opened her up and found cancer attached to her heart, lungs, and aorta. Knew right then and there that it was hopeless.

There used to be a house next door, and I arranged for Jeff, Diane's son, to have the house. I wanted him to have some family. He was a very disturbed young man, had chippied around with drugs. Diane leaves Tony, plops in with Jeff: "I'm your long lost mother. Now that I'm about to die, you can take care of me." Well, her younger son, Mike, was sixteen when she came back into his life. He was just a normal teenager, skinny little kid. Her coming back so distressed him that he blew up like a ballon. He became the Crisco Kid, and he had never had a weight problem in his life.

Well, she moves in with Jeff, undergoing cobalt, chemotherapy. She was still in pretty good shape, but she was the most demanding bitch. Poor Jeff—my husband, Jack, had given him a job—had to get up at 4 A.M. to go to work. At midnight Diane would decide she wanted some ice cream or something, so, "Jeff, get up and get me some ice cream." She became more demanding, more bitchy.

Jeff had married a girl that we hated, because he knew we hated her. It disgraced him even more. This girl he married was the anatomical wonder of all time. She was a fat junkie! Have you ever seen a *fat* junkie? When it got to the point where it was difficult for Diane to drive to the hospital to get her morphine, this girl would say, "Okay, I'll drive you, but you gotta split it with me." Diane could get as much as she wanted, so what did it matter?

When Diane was staying with Jeff here, she called Synanon. Even though she loved Art desperately, she did just want to say goodbye. She wanted to go down there and say goodbye to him. She was terribly distressed when those sons-of-bitches wouldn't let her talk to him.

Diane was the only person in the history of the Nalline program that was on five hundred grains of morphine a week and passing her test! Hahahaha! We used to joke about that, too. She had to keep going down for her Nalline test because of the red tape. They *knew* she was on morphine.

I wasn't nice to Diane. And I know why now. I tried to avoid her because it was just breaking my heart watching her die. Can you imagine loving someone so much that you don't want to see them? Being so selfish?

Well, Jeff finally . . . I couldn't let this go on. Mike was out on his own, working, had his own apartment. Diane goes to him, says, "I want to move in." And he comes to me, "Should I take care of her?" I said no because I could already see what she had done to him coming back into his life. He felt terrible about not letting her move in.

My mother and she got an apartment together. It was my mother's biggest thrill to be able to take care of Diane. My mother had lived her own life, and I never had loved her because she wasn't a good mother. She wasn't the kind of mother I wanted. She was a lesbian and a drunk, and I was always ashamed of her. So was Diane, but Diane wanted love so much, she found her more acceptable than I did. My mother waited on her hand and foot until her dying day. Diane was down to sixty pounds when she died. She looked like something out of Hitler's ovens. Just bones. She had just turned forty when she died.

After Diane, my mother had nothing left to live for. She died. Then our father died. And then—Bijou had had cancer a couple of times, breast cancer, and we had taken her down to Dr. Salk in Palm Springs, who's the best vet in the United States (he's the brother of Jonas Salk)—when Bijou died, it just shattered me. It was horrible to lose Diane and my mother and father, but Bijou, who had spent almost every night of her life with her face next to mine! I wanted to die.

Weirdest thing of all. About a week, two weeks before Diane died, my mother called and said, "Please come over and get us and get her out of the house. Things are really bad." I didn't want to. I didn't want to see her, but I felt guilty enough to do it. I drove down to their place in the valley, brought them over here, and Jack went down to Ah Fong's and got a great big mess of Chinese food and a big bag of fortune cookies, and I put 'em in a bowl. At random. Just dumped them in a bowl. We all took our cookie out and opened it. There must have been fifteen or twenty fortune cookies. The one Diane picked had no fortune in it. That has never happened to me in my life, and I've been eating in Chinese restaurants since I was a baby. We started giggling and Diane said, "Well, of course I have no fortune. I have no life."

———————

I HAD a hotel room a few blocks from Christine in Hollywood, and I kept that. I had a good parole officer for a change. In fact, they changed the whole idea of the parole department. Instead of going out of their way to send their charges back to prison, parole officers were going out of their way to keep them out. Of course, at this time I didn't trust him much, but the guy was good. His name was Mr. Dom. I found out that he had played clarinet as a kid and had heard of me. He liked the way I played so he was for me right away.

Mr. Dom would send me a card telling me when to test, which was once a week every week: I was on the Nalline program. Again. Five years on Nalline and five years on parole. I'd be put in prison for violating my parole, and each time I got out parole was set at five years. Some guys never get off parole because they continue to violate and go back. That's where they have you. Mr. Dom would send a message that he was going to come and see me on such-and-such a day, so on that day I would get up early, go to the hotel room I was renting, mess the bed up and try to make it look as if it was lived in. He'd come. We'd talk. He'd ask me how I was doing.

Christine had been a singer working little gigs, little jam session gigs. It was good with her at first because she was so interested in music. I had a tendency to get away from music by doing other things. I'd read the sports pages and listen to news broadcasts incessantly. Christine was always pushing music; she'd keep music on the radio instead. But when I listened to music, it brought back sad memories. I'd start thinking about the past. Listening to the news was like listening to the old-time serials—things were happening to other people, bad things. It took you out of yourself and instead of brooding over your own plight you were listening to and living in other people's problems. And it kept you company. Music put me in a melancholy mood. I'd want to get loaded.

I had a job at Shelly's Manne Hole when I got out, but I didn't have a horn. A horn cost five hundred dollars. I got a tenor on credit. Christine signed for me, but I paid for it. I could only afford one horn, and with the rock thing going the way it was I figured with a tenor I'd have a better chance of finding work. I played at Shelly's with a great group, and we did a lot of originals of mine. I'd been playing like John Coltrane more and more over the past few years. He'd impressed me so much. I had never been influenced like that before by anyone. I knew

I was playing great, but people kept asking me, "How come you're not playing alto?" They were thinking of the way I played before and couldn't accept what I was doing on tenor. It wasn't what they'd come to hear. That depressed me. Some guys came around to the club and they had some stuff, and before I knew it I was fixing again.

Christine had goofed around with stuff a few times but never got involved with it. She started fixing, too. I was only able to fix for three days, and then I'd have to clean up for four days so I could pass my Nalline test. Cleaning up meant going back to the Beverly Hills Health Club. I'd have marks all over my arms, I'd be kicking, and I'd go into the steam room and sit there while the sweat poured out of me. I'd feel like I was dying I was so weak. I'd look around and here were all these guys, all these Jews. They were wealthy, they had big Lincolns and Cadillacs, and I could hear them talking about companies merging, about producing and directing movies. After I left the steam room I'd sit with towels around me, sweating, the skin hanging on my bones. Where I had marks I'd rub with my hand, and the marks would peel off. I was sitting like this one day when I looked up and somebody said, "Hey, Art! How're you doing? It *is* Art, isn't it?" It was Pete Rugolo, who had written for Stan Kenton and was now a big man, writing for TV shows and movies. He said, "What are you doing now?" I said, "Oh, practicing and . . ." I wanted to get away from him and crawl into a hole.

Christine had a piano so I'd sit at the piano and mess around. She was always at me to practice and to go out and jam. She'd force me out at night and we'd go to different places and ask if we could sit in. I'd play, and she'd sing, and it was great except that we got so loaded. We'd drink and drink and drink. We'd hustle people for drinks and take any kind of pill, smoke pot, or shoot stuff depending on what period it was during the week. When it came time to eat, Christine would go to her mother's house in Torrance and borrow some money and get some food.

Christine introduced me to Red Mountain wine. You could get a gallon for a dollar and fifty-seven cents. We'd put the wine in these little plastic bottles orange juice comes in and take them in the car, and as we drove we'd drink. I don't know what the two of us were running from, but we were continuously on the move and we'd drink two or three gallons of this wine a day. We'd wander around looking for places to jam. We'd play games. I started getting Christine into the things I used to do with Patti. We'd go to a park and I'd walk ahead of her and then turn around and say, "Hello." And we'd find a secluded part of the park and make love. We'd drive down the street at night, she'd pull her pants off, and I'd unbutton my fly, and we'd play with each other riding along drinking our wine.

There was a place in Venice where we'd go sometimes. The piano player there had a little sign: "The World's Worst Piano Player." And he was. He was terrible. Christine had a brother who played banjo and guitar; he'd come along with us; we'd sit in and be completely blind. Christine would sing. One night we ran into some people there who lived in Venice and invited us over to their place. The girl was one of these artsy-craftsy chicks that makes things. She made earrings for people she liked—earrings that suited the person. She took a needle and jammed it through each of my ears. She made a special set of earrings for me and put them in. We went home, and the next morning I woke up with my ears hurting and found I had these earrings on. Christine said, "I don't think you should wear two of them." She took out the one in the left ear. After that, every time we went out and ran into artsy people they'd make me another earring, and I wound up with five or six of them. Christine had a little diamond, and I used to wear that one all the time. I grew a beard. I had my beard and my earring, and I let my hair grow. Christine had boots and a little tambourine. We started wandering around the Sunset Strip, going into different places, playing rock.

In my conversations with him, my parole officer always told me, "If anything ever happens, trust me. I want to help you stay out. If you goof, don't be afraid to tell me. If you start using, don't hide." I ran into a friend of mine from the joint who had a lot of stuff, and it was good stuff. He was living in Hollywood near us, so we'd do him little favors, drive him around. He didn't have a car and he'd lay some stuff on us. Naturally I got strung out, and I wasn't able make the Nalline tests anymore. I had to hang it up. We moved to Manhattan Beach, and I was hiding out from the parole department again.

My friend Ann Christos had a place right by the beach. Below her was a vacant apartment, and we moved in. One night while we were living out there, we went to a party at the house of a friend who lived in Venice; they were having a little session; the place was full of weird people—they really seemed loaded to me. The guy asked us if we wanted a drink. He brought in a couple of little tumblers: they had ice in them and the drink was clear with a light purplish color to it. I said, "What's this?" He said, "Vodka with a little something special." We drank our drinks and stood around and then all of a sudden I had feelings that were so strange that I went to the guy and asked, "What *was* that?" I was really getting loaded. And he said, "That was acid."

I felt good, extremely good. I had no worries. I felt I could do anything. He had a long, L-shaped front room, and the phonograph was on loud, playing rock, the Mothers of Invention. I walked out into the middle of the room and started dancing. Always before I'd been too self-conscious to dance, but the acid killed that. I was shaking and wiggling, and I really felt elated. I felt I could do anything with my body. I felt I could fly if I wanted to. I walked back to the couch where Christine was sitting and I said, "My God, I've spent twenty years taking everything in the world to try to feel like this. This is it!" I went back on the floor and started dancing again, and the guy whose pad it was came over. I said, "Boy, I hope I'm cool. I feel like I might just float through the ceiling." He said, "Horn some of this." He handed me an inhaler. I took a couple of big snorts and I'm holding on to it and he grabs it out of my hand; all of a sudden my whole body starts vibrating and I feel a ringing, roaring in my head. I feel as if I'm going to explode, I grab hold of the wall, and I keep going up and up. I said to myself, "God, if I ever come down from this . . . " I started praying, "*Please* let me come down." Finally I came out of it. The guy opened the inhaler. He'd busted a popper of amyl nitrate in it.

I don't know how we got out or got back home. The guy gave us four of these amyl nitrate things and he said, "When you're balling it's really great. Just before you come, sniff that." We got into the pad and ripped our clothes off. We grabbed each other and fell on the floor and started making love like animals. And then we opened one of the amyl nitrates and sniffed it before we came. About two hours later I started getting weird tastes in my mouth. I looked at myself in the mirror and my eyes were illuminated—they were all different colors. I looked awful. I was scared. I felt a pressure in my heart; I was afraid it was going to burst. Something was working inside of me and my body couldn't contain it. Christine was panicked. I said, "I can't stand this. We've got to come down some way." I ran upstairs to Ann and told her, "I've got to have some stuff. We took some acid and we're going crazy. Please!" We didn't have any money, but I begged her, so she made a phone call to a guy, and we fixed, and that brought us down. I said, "Oh God, never again!" That was my first experience with acid.

Christine went to see a guy she knew in Culver City and got some acid to sell. It was liquid with a purple hue to it. You'd put a drop of it on a piece of paper and sell that. To take it, you'd put the paper under your tongue; the acid would go into those little vessels there. You couldn't see what you were getting but it wiped you out. The first time we'd taken it, at the party, we were drunk and had been taking Dexamyl Spansules and had smoked pot. The second time we decided we'd take it sober.

We got up in the morning and took the acid. Then we got in the car. They were having a jam session at a club in Gardena; a waitress I knew invited us to come. I figured we'd better have a drink. We bought a bottle of Red Mountain.

At first the acid didn't affect us at all. While we were driving we had to be cool and concentrate, and we saw people dressed up to go to church—that whole thing of Sunday morning. Then we stopped the car in the parking lot, got out, and walked into this place where you couldn't tell if it was dark or daylight, where there were all these people who looked as if they'd been going for days, all the chicks laughing and everybody high on pot and junk and juice and acid. There was a jazz band playing, and it was as if we'd entered Dante's inferno. The acid took over.

We didn't have much money left but the waitress said,

"Don't worry about it. I'll take care of you." She brought us free drinks. We started talking to the people at our table, a guy and two sexy girls in low-cut dresses. At the time I didn't have a horn; I think I'd hocked my tenor so I was playing an old, silver soprano sax I'd borrowed from Christine's brother. The girls saw the case and said, "What's that?" I told them I was a musician and they started giggling and flirting with me. I looked at Christine and at that moment something snapped in my mind. I looked at these empty-headed women. I looked around me at all these crazed, laughing people hiding in the darkness on a Sunday afternoon, trying to deny the existence of any reality, and I realized that I was a part of it. I was doing the same thing I had done as a kid, searching for something and never stopping, never being satisfied with anything, always thinking something wild was happening in the next block or the next house. What I was doing with Christine was just the same. We couldn't possibly stop and relax and enjoy each other or enjoy life because we were so busy trying to find the wild things that we thought we were missing out on. After paying all the dues that I'd paid—prison and everything—here I was past forty, with my pierced ear and my beard, and I was still running. I thought of all the people that I knew, that I started out with. They're all living out in the valley with nice homes; and they have two or three kids, they're grandparents, they have nice clothes and cars and money in the bank, they're into businesses; and they long, long ago stopped this kind of life. I looked at Christine and saw that strained look on her face: she looked like one of those pachuca tomboy broads with the tattooed beauty mark. This crazy girl, this child, that wanted to be a jazz singer, playing a tambourine and borrowing money from her mother. It was outrageous. I'm here. I'm hiding from a parole officer, taking acid, and still trying to prove myself as a musician. I thought, "My God, this is insanity! Now, *what is wrong! Why am I doing this!*" I felt that maybe I was on the threshold of learning something. I thought I might be about to solve my problems so I could be happy and enjoy life and not have to be hounded all the time, loaded every second. Maybe I could finally realize that it all started with me, it was all within me, and all I had to do was stop.

I didn't even want to play at that point. I had more important things to do. But I was there, and I had the horn, and people . . . It was an obligation. So then it became the same old thing. The battle started. I had to play because I couldn't be a coward. I had to show the other people up and prove that I was better than them. I got out that old, silver soprano, that relic, and I had to play it as if it were a five- or six-hundred-dollar horn in perfect condition. And I had to cut all these young guys who'd been practicing and working and were really out to play and especially to cut anyone like me.

I played great, and afterwards I was basking in this little adulation I had to have, always felt I had to have. And for a while I was happy. And Christine was happy because she was getting the overflow: she must be pretty important to have me because I'm so far-out. That's the way they think. It came time to leave, and we walked out.

First there's the contact with your old lady. She's telling you how great you were, and you still feel good. But then, like someone on a rollercoaster, I was hit by a depression far greater than the high I'd just experienced. We approached this Anglia, this beat little English car that was just as phony as the whole life I'd led. It had a red racing stripe on it, but the car could barely do forty with its little, dinky wheels. I got in, and Christine said, "You want me to drive?" The sun's shining, and I look around and see the people on the street. A black and white comes by with the rollers; they're looking at us. And then everything came back at me. Reality came back. I started feeling my body and worrying about it and I got this taste in my throat that I always got when I took acid. I could taste my brains in my throat.

Christine started driving. "Oh, Art, fill my bottle." I looked down at the half empty gallon of Red Mountain sitting in a rumpled paper bag and smelled the stench of stale wine we'd spilled before, so many times, on the floor of the car. She said, "How 'bout if we go over to So-and-so's?" Her eyes were just crazy, and she wanted to go again. She wanted to go to this guy's house in Venice. She wanted me to play the piano for her so she could sing. So I would tell her, "Yeah, you sound great." So somebody would tell her that. She had to have that. All I wanted was to be left alone. I didn't want to have to generate all this thing so Christine could get her "fix" for singing, but I had to go with her to Venice and I felt really bad.

We bought another gallon of wine and started pouring it down with uppers. We got to the guy's house and I asked him, "Do you know of anybody that's got any smack? Do you know of *anything*?" He said, "Well, I know a guy that's got some bottles." He meant methadrine. I said, "Alright, man. We don't have any money." He said, "I'll spring for a couple bottles." I said, "We don't have a 'fit either." He said, "I'll see if I can borrow one." He left, and while we're waiting in the pad I started looking around.

There were two apartments above a market. His wife lived in one, and in this one he had an electric piano and books and pipes and paintings. And he had a daughter there that must have been around fifteen, sixteen, and I think he was balling the daughter as well as his old lady. The girl had on a little silk kind of thing that just fell away at her breasts. You could see her nipples. She had on a real short skirt and little, teeny panties. You could see the hairs coming out the side of the panties. She was just sitting around. When I'd get up to go to the kitchen or the bathroom she'd figure out how to be in the way, and she'd rub her tits up against me and all that. I'd watched the way they looked at each other, and I'm sure he was balling his daughter.

We were waiting for this guy to come back. Christine's sitting at the piano, pecking away at the piano. She says, "You were great." Then she says, "Sometimes I get the feeling you don't want to let me get my fix, you know. What's wrong?" I said, "Nothing's wrong. If you wanted to make it, you could make it. I just wanted to go home." I felt that all she wanted was to use me to gain her objectives. She wanted attention and I was the bait.

Finally the guy came back with an old, dirty outfit and two bottles. We fixed the methadrine. On top of the acid it really put us in a state. I felt as if my scalp was coming off. I played the piano, the few little things I knew; Christine sang; we drank and drank and drank; and pretty soon I was so far-out nothing mattered anymore. We stayed until about four in the morning, and finally we got in the car. Christine said, "I'll drive." She starts driving, and then she reaches over and unzips my fly and pulls my joint out, and she's playing with it. She takes my hand and puts it on her. We get to the pad and go inside and lock the door. And we made love, you know. And then we just laid there, glaring at the ceiling, each of us thinking our thoughts. I didn't know what I was doing or what I was trying to prove, and I was too tired to figure it out right now, and I couldn't sleep.

Mr. Dom kept trying to reach me, and by this time he knew about Christine. He called her and told her to tell me to come to the office or call him. Otherwise they'd put out an APB on me, and I'd be violated when I was caught and sent back to prison. I called him on the phone. He said, "Man, I want to help you." I said, "That's hard for me to believe." He said, "I really do." He said, "How much are you using?" I told him and he said, "Alright, clean up for three days and come in and take a urinalysis, and everything will be straight. I swear it."

I thought about it a lot. I was afraid that when I went into the office he'd lock me up right away and send me back to the joint. I hadn't tested for about three months. I decided I'd give it a chance. I couldn't really clean up that quickly, so we went over to some friends of Christine's who weren't using. I asked the guy to urinate in a little bottle, and I took that down with me and put his urine in the bottle they gave me as if it was mine. It came back about two days later, clean, and I was reinstated. I saw that Mr. Dom was really for me, and that made me feel good. I had to start taking the tests regularly again, and I had to clean up, which I did do, and I went back to chippying and sweating it out at the Beverly Hills Health Club.

After I'd been on parole for about two years the state passed a new law saying that when a person had done two of their five years on parole the parole officer could make recommendations about him to the board. At that time I couldn't get work in California, but I had offers of jobs in other places. In Canada. I told Mr. Dom, and he appeared before the board and spoke for me. The board agreed that being on parole didn't do me any good if I couldn't work and released me. That finally ended my parole and the Nalline tests.

At this point I started really thinking about what we were doing and it didn't make sense. I think if I hadn't had Christine during that period I might have straightened myself out.

The acid started these feelings. One time when I was loaded it came to me—the reason why I used heroin and the *solution*. I really found the answer! And unlike my psychoanalysis, where I found out why but found no cure, this time I had a foolproof solution. It was simple. I talked it over with Christine and explained it to her, and she understood it, and when we came down I remembered that I had found this thing, but I'd forgotten what it was. I asked Christine; she'd forgotten, too.

One of the last times we took acid we went to a place called Sperling's in Santa Monica. A steak house. There was a piano player there, and I jammed with him, and then Christine came up for the next set to sing. Afterwards, we're getting ready to leave, and Christine's looking at me, telling me how marvelous I sounded, and I know she's waiting for me to tell her how she sounded, but I had listened to her while she was singing, really listened for the first time, and it came to me then that she wasn't good at all. Acid makes you incapable of lying. You see things as they are. Christine made the mistake of asking me. She wanted to be praised, too. She asked me and I told her, "Yeah, well, it was alright."

She got very upset, naturally, because she thought she was a singer. Up until that time I'd never said anything. I'd tried to pretend that she was cool and hadn't been in practice or something. This time I said, "You just don't sing in tune. You don't have a nice sound: it isn't vibrant enough; it isn't full enough. I don't really like your phrasing." Everything was bad, and I told her, and she flipped out and called me all kinds of names. She said, "Well, I can't do anything around you! You've just smothered me, musically and artistically! Whatever I do you don't like! You don't think anything a woman does is any good! You think all women are inferior to you! You've just ruined me! All you want is—you want all the praise!" I said, "If I do something well, naturally I enjoy being praised, but only when I do something right. I don't want anybody to praise me when I don't deserve it. I don't rank you because you're a girl or anything. You asked me about your singing. It's alright. You just don't move me that much. You're not really a singer." She said, "Oh, you motherfucker!" I said, "Why do you have to call me that? That's all you know is 'motherfucker.' Don't ask me things! You should know how you sing!" She said, "Well, everybody else says I sing good! All the jazz musicians I've sung with say that I really sing just like a horn and that I'm great!" I said, "Yeah, well, that's because they're putting you on. Maybe they want to ball you or want a ride someplace or want to borrow some money from you. It's bullshit. You don't really sing good."

Christine was very artsy. She painted abstract paintings. She'd go around and search through garbage cans and get old wires and make things out of them. Her father was a construction worker for a long, long time. He was an alcoholic. He died a while before I met her. She had two brothers; one was a dope fiend, a real heavy junkie and an armed robber; her other brother had been to prison for using marijuana but was never a criminal like Joe was.

She was raised in Torrance, a place where there were a lot of gangs. She'd grown up in a hard and violent atmosphere and always had a chip on her shoulder. She was one of the tougher girls around, and she wanted to be a boy, I think, because her dad probably liked the boys. Later she got married to a guy who played piano, just a fun-loving kind of guy, not very intense, so she started taking charge. She started dealing pot and doing the things the man usually does, and he relaxed and let her. That was her pattern and I fell into it, too.

Christine had a lot of violence in her and hatred, and it was hard enough before to restrain myself, but when I got around Christine, who was so much like that, I found myself giving way to it, too. When I was driving the car and somebody would honk at me or do something I didn't like in traffic, I'd stop the car, get out, and holler, "Motherfucker!" and threaten their lives. It's a miracle I didn't get killed. And when I did that, Christine thought I was great because I was so rugged and tough, and she'd rank her ex–old man for being a sissy and a punk. She called everybody sissies and punks.

After this thing happened about her singing, life with Christine really got bad. When we went out together and she'd sing, she'd keep staring at me to get my reaction, with a challenging look; "What's wrong with *that*? I suppose you don't like that either, you bastard!" It got so I didn't even want to meet her eyes. Sometimes I'd want to fix and I'd run into somebody and make a taste and then she'd come home and flip out at me. Or there would be some girl, say, a girl friend of a friend of hers or his wife, and the girl would come on to me and Christine became very jealous. When we were driving around, and I'd look at the girls walking down the street, she'd glare at me and say, "What're you looking at, you son-of-a-bitch?" She started hitting me in the car.

We were really juicing at this time. We were drinking from the minute we woke up in the morning until we fell out at night. This one night all of a sudden I woke up and there were Christine's eyes in front of mine. I was lying on my back, and I felt a stinging in the side of my neck, and the first thing I heard was "You lousy, stinking motherfucker! I'll kill you, you bastard, you cocksucking motherfucker!" I said, "What's wrong? What are you *doing*? What are you, crazy?" And she shouted, "Don't say that to me, you bastard! I'm not crazy, you motherfucker! I'll kill you, you bastard!" She was straddling my stomach, she had her left hand around my throat, and she was very strong for a girl. In her right hand she had a knife she always carried with her, a pushbutton knife with a six-inch blade: it was stuck into the side of my neck. Her eyes were just crazy. I don't know how long she'd been sitting there looking at me like that. She yelled, "You son-of-a-bitch! I know you! You've been out balling chicks! You've been out fixing! You don't want me! You're trying to get away from me, you son-of-a-bitch! I'll kill you first, you bastard! You can't use me and throw me aside! I'll kill you!" I said, "I haven't been doing anything! I haven't been out with any chicks!" She kept glaring at me and cussing me out, and I was afraid of her, she was so insane.

She tightened her hold on my neck and stuck the knife into my throat. I could feel it piercing my skin. With that I smashed my arms out, hit her in the face, grabbed her by the throat, and threw her off me. She came lunging at me, and I grabbed her arm and got the knife out of her hand. I held her and I said, "Boy, what's wrong with you? Are you insane? This is too fuckin' much!" She said, "I'll kill you, you son-of-a-bitch, if you keep messing with me like that! You're not going to go out with any other chicks after all I've done for you, you bastard!" I said, "I'm *not* going out with any other chicks! I don't *want* any other chicks! Would you act like a human being?" Then she got emotional. She started crying: "You don't love me! You don't care for me! You don't like the way I sing! All you want to do is take my money! I've done everything for you! You wouldn't have a horn if it wasn't for me." I kept telling her, "I *do* love you. Everything's cool. Your singing's alright, man. I appreciate everything."

This went on and on. Sometimes she'd be painting. I'd go for a walk and be gone for a while and come back and she'd wig out and punch me in the stomach or the ribs. The thing with the knife—she did that two or three times. I was afraid to do anything to her because I was afraid to get started on a woman. I was afraid I'd kill her or any of them if I ever got started on them.

After I got everything straightened out with the parole department, we moved back to Hollywood. Finally I got a call one day. It was a trombone player—I forget his name. He asked me what I was doing and I told him I was just blowing around town. He asked how would I like to take a gig with a big band. I said, "Whose band?" "Buddy Rich." He said, "We need a lead alto." I told him, "I haven't been playing alto. I don't even own an alto." But he said, "We can get you one. I think Don Menza, who plays tenor in the band, has an alto. Maybe he'll let you use his till you can get one of your own." I said, "I don't know if I can play after all this time. I haven't played it in a long time." He said, "Yeah, you can play it. I know you can make it. It'll give you a chance to get back into the music business and start making some money. Get your reputation back. Get back where you belong." I said, "I don't know. I've lost my confidence." He said, "Think it over for the rest of the day, and I'll find out from Don if you can use his alto. I'll call you back this evening." I hung up the phone. Buddy's band was a hard band to play with, very demanding. I didn't know if I could do it.

Christine was all happy at first. But then she took my not wanting to go with the band . . . She said, "If you're worried about me, you don't have to worry about me. Just go ahead and go if you're ashamed of me." I said, "What are you talking about? I'm not ashamed of you!" She said, "You just used me until you got a chance to do something." I said, "No, I didn't. If I go with the band, you'll go with me. We'll have a ball."

It seems I've always been with women who have been a drag. I've almost always been in a position where I really didn't care for them. I wasn't the one who did the choosing. Diane chased me all over the place. Christine's brother gave me her phone number and then she said why don't you stay here and that was it. I didn't see a girl and go out and get her because I liked her. The only time that had happened was with Patti. I was thinking in my mind, "What will I do this time to get away from her? Will I go to prison? Will I die? Will she kill me?" I said, "Of course I'll take you with me. We'll have a ball." And I felt sorry for her. She'd never had anything nice, any of the good life. Maybe it would help her, soften her up. I told her, "We'll have a lot of fun. You'll travel with me, and being with Buddy's band we'll be respected. And instead of drinking wine we'll drink good brandy. We can buy nice clothes." She said, "That would be wonderful! Are you sure you want me?" I said, "Yes, I want you."

———————

(Hersh Hamel) Christine was sorta masculine, a little bit. A little rough. Rough talking, rough looking. A little bit too much tryin' to be one of the musicians, tryin' to play that role. Christine was involved in a lot of heavy traumatic scenes even before she met Art. I was a little spooked out by her. There never was any closeness between Christine and me, and it was hard to get through to Art with Christine there. She was like an invisible wall. She was such a strange chick. I wish I could put it into words. She was very protective of Art—whether it was protective or whether it was overbearing—and Art needed somebody. It was a strange relationship, not like any other relationships I'd seen him have. She's a very sick girl, very sick, mentally. She was not in reality. She made her own reality, and Art made his own reality.

(Ann Christos) I introduced Art to acid. He and Christine were living in a little apartment underneath mine in Manhattan Beach. He loved acid. He loved the grotesqueness, because that's what he saw. Acid's always been frightening to me, but Art enjoyed it, and Christine did, too, although she got very jealous. She got jealous of me and started to rank me verbally one time. And Art shut her up.

Christine was tall and willowy, and she had pretty green eyes, light skin, red hair, a nose with a sharp tilt on the end. She'd smile, but it wouldn't be happy. Her eyes were kind of dead. We never really ever had a rapport. She always considered me a threat for some reason. Diane never did.

I don't know what kind of person Christine was. I don't know her. I'll tell you what. We all got high on acid one time and Art said, "Let's go into Venice. There's a blind piano player in a club over there." We went to the club and Christine wanted to sing. And Christine can't sing. Art told her, which made her want to sing all the more. She was, what would you call it, challenging Art. Musically. Her ear wasn't bad, but it wasn't right. One of those things. She got up and sang, and it was terrible, and we were leaving, and I got awfully paranoid. Art was introducing me as "Mamby," their maid. I said, "Art, I don't think I can walk out of here! I'm too frightened!" Art took my hand and led me out of this mass of worms and people, that club, you know. He took over and led me out. And Christine got *nasty*, just nasty, that he did this for me, showed me a kindness. All I can remember is that she's nasty. That's all I can say about her.

(Jerry Maher) I saw Art again in '67. I was living in Orange County with my ex-old lady, Lynn, and one afternoon, out of the clear blue sky, got a call, and it was Art. He was callin' from the Manne Hole. I don't even know where he got my number. He said, "Why don't you come on out?" So I took Lynn and this Chinese broad, Virginia, and went out there that night. Art had Tommy Flanagan on piano, Will Bradley, Junior, on drums. After the last set we all went up to Art's pad. He was livin' with Christine at the time, not too far from the Manne Hole. He was drinkin' brandy; I was drinkin' VO. I had a little stuff. I was chippyin' at the time. He asked me if I had any, and I told him no, I wasn't usin', because I knew he'd want some.

It was a weird little pad. It was sorta like a maze you had

to go through to get into this one little room. Art went in there to change his clothes and he said, "Jerry, come here a minute, man." I walked in there, and he told me, "Check this!" He opened his shirt, and there were three big, huge gouge marks down his side. You could tell by the thickness and width of the scab on 'em that they were deep gouges, and I said, "Jesus Christ, brother, what happened to you?" He said, "It's that *bitch*, man! That bitch, she's violent!" I looked at him and asked him, "Can you whip her?" And he says, "Just barely, man." Hahahaha! "And I think she throws those!"

Christine was just a big, typical Hollywood, superhip, nothin' bitch. Stereotype. "Hey, baby, what's goin' on?" I never liked her brother either. I saw him the same way. I heard later he turned into a stool pigeon or somethin'.

———————————

20 | On the Road with Buddy Rich's Band

1968–1969

I WAS FRIGHTENED. And I was tired, really tired. I didn't want to do anything at all. I realized that all the time I'd been using dope I hadn't had to face anything because once you give yourself up to that life there's no decisions to be made: you just have to score, and you have the drive to score because you're sick, and if you get arrested you go to prison and there's nothing you can do about it. All I wanted now was to relax and stay home. I didn't want to perform. I didn't want to put myself in a position where I might fail. I was tired, and I wanted to spend the rest of my life just sitting someplace. I used to think that if I could only have someone take care of me, it would be wonderful just to stay in some house. As long as I had the rent paid and a few dollars for some food, a TV or a radio so I could listen to the ball games—that's all I would want forever. Then I got this call to go with Buddy Rich. I was given an offer, and there was no way, in all honesty, I could refuse it. Maybe if I'd been alone I could have said I had some kind of disease, that I went to the hospital for a checkup and they found out I had cancer or that I had TB and couldn't blow. I could have come up with something. But I was with Christine, and I felt obligated to make the money, you know. She had worked—delivering automobile parts, driving a little pickup truck, borrowing money so we could eat and pay the rent. I felt I had to repay her.

Buddy Rich's band was a very modern band. The arrangements were hard to read and loud, and they played a jazz-rock thing. Buddy Rich, I'd heard, was really a taskmaster and temperamental, and if you goofed at all he would hear it and rank you, ridicule you in front of everybody, which is something I've never been able to take. And I had a reputation—being a junkie, being in prison. Those were things Buddy didn't like. I was putting myself in a lion's den.

The phone rang and Christine said, "It's for you." I'd been afraid for many years to answer the phone; a lot of times I'd just let it ring. It was Don Menza. I'd heard of him. He's a great young tenor player with a fantastic technique. He's one of the new breed of musicians, a musician in every aspect. He writes arrangements, reads well, can jam, can do anything. He even makes mouthpieces and repairs horns. He says, "I hear you don't have an alto. That's unbelievable, man. That's like Bird not having an alto. I sure wish you'd come on the band. I've got an alto; it's in good shape; I've looked it over; I blew it just a little while ago. You're welcome to use it until you can get one. I'm leaving for Vegas in a few minutes. I have to be there a day early. I'll take it with me. When you get to rehearsal it'll be there."

We were going to play Caesar's Palace in Vegas. They got me a ticket that was paid for by the band and another for Christine that came out of an advance. They gave me another advance so I could rent a room in a motel. We got on the plane and there we were—one day riding around in our little car drinking gallons of Red Mountain and the next on a plane on our way to Las Vegas. We went to the motel and checked in, and there's a swimming pool, and the room's air-conditioned, and Christine's all excited. We've got two hours before the rehearsal. Christine says, "Isn't this wonderful! I knew you'd make it! Now these motherfuckers'll really hear somebody play!" I said, "I'm not so sure." She said, "Fuck 'em. You'll blow their minds. You're the greatest player in the world!" I said, "Did you see a liquor store on the way here?" She said, "Oh, man' you can't have a drink now, can you?" I said, "Well, I've gotta have a drink." She said, "I noticed one about a block away."

We walked to this liquor store. It was burning hot outside. You could see the heat rising off the street. I bought a fifth of brandy, we walked back to the room, I poured out a couple of big drinks, and Christine said, "Here's to success."

The rehearsal was at Caesar's Palace, a beautiful place with a huge fountain. I walked in with another guy from the band. I looked around. I didn't even know Don Menza. The guy who was with me pointed him out. I walked over to him—a red-haired genius with no weaknesses, completely out of my league. He said, "Hi. There it is in the bag over there." I had my mouthpiece in my pocket, a Meyer mouthpiece. I'd saved it, for-tunately, because with your own mouthpiece you have half the battle won. I took the horn out, put the reed on the mouthpiece, the mouthpiece on the horn, fastened the neck strap, and I was saying to myself, "Oh God, please play right." I tried it, and it played very, very good, and my fingers felt good on it. I looked up, and Buddy Rich had come in. He had somebody else who was going to play for him; he was just going to watch the rehearsal. Buddy's a little guy about fifty years old, one of the greatest drummers that ever lived, a monster on the drums, and a real arrogant little guy. Everybody's scared of him. I sat down. Don Menza was rehearsing the band. He called out a number. I looked at the music and it looked like Japanese. I told myself, "Am I *kidding?* I've spent five years with Stan Kenton. I've played the studios. I've been with all kinds of groups and done all kinds of things. Why can't I calm down?" The tune was beat off, and we started.

I guess it was just starting to play, getting into that familiar setting with the sound happening all around me. I began to lose my fear. I read through the thing without any mistakes, and I sounded good. Don gave me a little nod and a little smile. The guy playing third alto, Carlisle Owens, the only black cat in the band, he smiled at me, and the baritone player really liked me, I could tell.

Christine was sitting in the back, and she was really thrilled. She'd never been in such proximity to all this greatness. We played another tune and another, and I was afraid to look at Buddy, but I finally glanced at him out of the corner of my eye. He was staring at me, and I couldn't tell what he was thinking. Finally the end came, and Buddy walked up. He said, "How are you doing, Art? Did you meet all the guys? This is Art Pepper. We've got Art Pepper and we've got Al Porcino." That was his first day on the band, too (we'd been friends for years—he's one of the greatest lead trumpet players in the world). Buddy said, "Welcome to the band. Good luck." Underneath my arms was all wet, I'd been so nervous. We finished the rehearsal, and the trombone player told us what time we'd start that night. We had to get there early to have a rehearsal with Tony Bennett, who we were backing. I tried on some uniforms, found one that fit okay, and so I was a member of the band and I had won again. I felt good because instead of running I had faced it and made it. And something else happened that day that helped restore my confidence. I was playing alto again instead of tenor. I was playing like myself again.

When I was a kid I played clarinet, and my first influence was Artie Shaw. I heard him play on records and on the radio, and I thought he played beautifully, with a wonderful sound and a great technique. Then I saw a picture of him. He was going with or married to a movie star. She was beautiful. He seemed very glamorous to me and I thought, "Wow!" and I saw an opening for *me* at nine, ten years old. I thought, "Wow, there it is!" And I never doubted for a second that I could be as great as Artie Shaw.

I kept buying records. I remember I got "Annie Laurie" by Jimmy Lunceford's band; it was so swinging. In that band at the time was Joe Thomas, the tenor player. He had a full sound; he kind of moaned through his horn; he growled; he moved me. Playing alto was Willie Smith, and I liked the way he led the section. That saxophone section was the best I've every heard, even up to now. Later on I had occasion to hear the band in person at the Trianon ballroom: they were more devastating than they were on record. And I was standing in front of the band, listening to them, when all of a sudden this beautiful black chick came up. Dorothy Dandridge. She had furs on, and she stood there listening to the band and looking at Joe Thomas, and after they finished their set everybody fell all over her, and she went to Joe Thomas and started rapping with him. It was so glamorous. I loved not only the music, I loved the whole idea.

I liked a lot of people. I loved Johnny Hodges in Duke Ellington's band, the way he played ballads, and in that band was Ben Webster, who had a rich, full tone like Joe Thomas's but more subtle. Joe Thomas was a shouter; Ben Webster was more soulful. Then I heard Louis Jordan on alto: he knocked me out. I liked Benny Goodman. I liked Charlie Barnet, and then all the dixieland people—Wingy Manone and, oh, that guy that played cornet, "Livery Stable Blues," what was his name? I liked Roy Eldridge and, naturally, when I got with Benny Carter, I liked him, but I never attempted to play like any of these people. Never. I'd see little books—*Solos by So-and-so*, taken off the records—and every now and then I'd buy one and try it, but it just wasn't me, and it had no meaning to me at all, playing what was written. All these people influenced me, subconsciously, but I didn't feel like any of them and I didn't play like any of them. I'd go to sessions and hear other people playing and think, "Oh, that guy sounds like Willie Smith; that guy sounds like Johnny Hodges." And I used to think, "Well, maybe I don't play good. Maybe I'm on the wrong track." Just before I was drafted I heard Lester Young—he was with Basie's band—and, boy, I said, "That's the one!" But he played tenor and I played alto. I dug the things he did, but I didn't want to ape him. I ran into Zoot Sims; he knew all of Prez's solos and could sound just like him, and he'd hold the horn up at a forty-five-degree angle, just like Prez did. I thought, "Why don't *I* sound like anybody else? What's wrong with me?" Finally, I got with Stan Kenton's band, and then people started telling me, "Man, you sure sound great!" I'd ask, "What do you mean?" I'd want to know why. They'd say, "Man, I can tell it's *you.*" And I thought, "Well, that's what it is. I wasn't wrong after all."

I got drafted. I went overseas and played there, and everybody liked me. I came home three years later and just assumed everything was the same as it was when I left. I'm not home more than a few days when this friend comes over and he says, "Man, have you heard Bird or Diz?" I said, "Bird or Diz who?" "Have you heard bebop?" "*Be-bop?*" I hadn't heard a word, I swear to God. I was feeling good. I'd been playing in England, built up a style of my own.

He put on a record, Sonny Stitt and Dizzy Gillespie. On one side was "Salt Peanuts" and on the other was "Oop Bop

Sh'Bam . . ." Ahahaha! ". . . A Klug Ya Mop!" They played these charts—"Salt Peanuts" was so fast . . . Jimmy Lunceford used to have a tune called "White Heat" that was real, real fast, beyond comprehension at the time. These guys played faster than that, and they really *played*. Not only were they fast, technically, but it all had meaning, and they swung! They were playing notes in the chords that I'd never heard before. It was more intricate, more bluesy, more swinging, more everything. They had gone from one decade to another, one culture to another. Straight up! I heard it and I thought, "Oh, Jesus Christ! What am I going to do?" I heard this Sonny Stitt just roaring, flying over the keys, swinging, shouting. It moved me so much—and it scared me to death.

The guy said, "Well, what do you think of that?" I said, "Yeah, well." I had to protect myself so I said, "Yeah, but, boy, it's so . . . They never relax. When are they going to settle back and groove? Where's the warmth and the feeling? Their tones . . ." I tried everything. Anything to justify my own position. He played a thing by Dizzy and Charlie Parker, and I heard Charlie Parker, and I really didn't like his tone. It sounded coarse to me. I finally had something to hang on to. I said, "I don't dig his tone." My friend said, "Well, what about Dizzy?" I had to admit, "Yeah, he's got a nice tone. It's a little thin though."

He left. I got ill. What was I going to do now? I decided the only thing I could do was just practice and play and play and develop my own thing. The tenor was always the more popular instrument. It used to be there was never a solo written in a stock band arrangement for alto. It was all tenor solos—that was the "jazz saxophone." Charlie Parker made the alto popular, and I thought, "Well, that's good. That's good." I noticed that all the tenor players had switched to alto, and they all sounded just like Charlie Parker.

Books came out. Bird's solo on this, Bird's solo on that. They'd copy these things off the records and practice by the hour Bird's solos and his licks. Everybody sounded like him with the same ugly sound. Guys I'd heard before who had had beautiful tones now, all of a sudden, had ugly tones like Bird. Out of tune. Squalling. Squawking. I didn't want to play that way at all, but I realized that I had to upgrade my playing and I had to really learn chords and scales. So I didn't copy anyone. I didn't practice much, but I went out and blew and blew and blew. Then I rejoined Kenton, and I sounded only like me.

Bird had a great ear for changes, a great blues sense, great technical ability. He was able to play real fast, and his lines were beautiful. Everything was thought out and made sense. I never used to like his tone, but that's personal. A tone is like a person's voice. Now when I listen to him I love the whole thing, tone and all. He was a genius. But when I heard Coltrane!

In the late fifties I heard John Coltrane with Miles Davis. I heard the *Kind of Blue* album. On that album he played everything you can imagine. He played more notes than Bird, more involved than Bird, and I *loved* his tone. Everything he played held together and meant something to me, and he really moved me. He's the only guy I ever heard in my life that I said, "I'd give my right arm to play like that."

It happened slowly, but by 1964, when I got out of San Quentin and started playing again, more and more I found myself sounding like Coltrane. Never copied any of his licks consciously, but from my ear and my feeling and my sense of music . . . I went into Shelly's Manne Hole with a group, and a lot of people liked what I did and really thought I was playing modern, and a lot of others asked what had happened to the old Art Pepper.

When I got out of the joint the last time, in '66, I had no horns. I could only afford one horn, and I got a tenor because, I told myself, to make a living I had to play rock. But what I really wanted to do was play like Coltrane.

In '68 I got the job playing lead alto with Buddy Rich. And that day in Las Vegas, after the rehearsal, I was blowing Don Menza's alto in the motel room. I was jamming in front of the mirror, blowing the blues, really shouting, and all of a sudden I realized, "Wow, this is me! This is *me*!" Christine was there in the room reading a book, and at the same time she looked up and said, "Art, that's fantastic! *Alto*, that's you!" Then I realized that I had almost lost myself. Something had protected me for all those years, but Trane was so strong he'd almost destroyed me.

That experience—it lasted about four years that I was influenced so much by John Coltrane—was a freeing experience.

It enabled me to be more adventurous, to extend myself notewise and emotionally. It enabled me to break through inhibitions that for a long time had kept me from growing and developing. But since the day I picked up the alto again I've realized that if you don't play *yourself* you're nothing. And since that day I've been playing what I felt, what *I* felt, regardless of what those around me were playing or how they thought I should sound.

The first night at Caesar's Palace I sounded good, and everybody congratulated me. Afterwards, Christine and I went with some of the guys and had a bite to eat and some drinks, and then we went to somebody's room and smoked pot and put on our bathing suits and went swimming in the pool. It was fun, and it was great to be accepted into that world. I thought of all the things I'd given up in using drugs. I started feeling good about being a musician and about life.

Every night I got stronger and played better and more together with the band. Me and Al Porcino made the band swing in a different kind of way. I was playing good solos. There was talk about going to Europe pretty soon. We made an album. Then, all of a sudden I started noticing some little pains in my stomach. And when I put my uniform on ... One night I asked Christine, "Do I look heavier to you?" It seemed like every day I'd feel these pains. I felt bloated. I went to the drugstore and bought all kinds of stuff for gas and laxatives, but they didn't help. I got worried.

We finished the job in Vegas and went from there to San Francisco, to Basin Street West. Christine and I got a room right above the club. The pain got worse and worse, but I kept playing, until one night the pain was so bad I couldn't bend over to get my music out. I didn't want to go to a doctor because I was afraid—afraid of what it might be. I was hoping it would go away by itself. I walked out of the club that night, and Christine helped me up the stairs. I sat on the bed. I couldn't lay down. I started to fall over, and I thought I was going to die. Christine got me back into a sitting position and ran down the stairs and hit on Buddy Rich. He'd heard that my stomach was hurting, but he didn't know it was that bad.

Buddy found out from the owner of the club where the

nearest hospital was. He helped carry me from the room and drove me to St. Luke's. They weren't going to let me into the hospital because I didn't have insurance, but Buddy flipped out and forced them to take me. He signed for me.

They didn't know what was wrong so they couldn't give me anything for the pain. They put me in the intensive care unit. They put tubes in my nose and in my veins, and they stuck a tube from one vein into my heart so they could measure the way my heart was pumping. They had two things fastened on my chest that went to a machine that recorded my heartbeat. I remember looking at the screen and seeing it. It made a pattern and a noise, but the pattern would change and drop and the beeping would slow. I think I went into a coma for a little while, and when I came out of it I saw that the pattern of my heartbeat was very irregular and everyone had gathered around me. There had been two or three other patients in this room, and they had died. Now all the attention was focused on me. Then I saw the doctor. He was leaning on me, he had a big syringe in his hand, and I felt it prick my stomach. It filled immediately, completely with blood. He looked at it and at me and shook his head. He said, "Where's Mrs. Pepper?" They'd said she was my wife to make it easier. Christine wasn't there. He sent a couple of people to look for her, and he said, "We haven't got time to wait. We have to operate." I said, "I can't stand to have an operation. I can't stand to be cut." He said, "You've got to sign this paper. You can't live without the operation." I signed my name.

From then on, it was all hustle. They gave me a shot, and I was rolled through a hallway. I was in an elevator and in a room that was very bright. I still had all the tubes; the bottles were still hanging; people were holding them, wheeling them by me. I remember saying to the doctor, "Please put me out!" I remembered the operation in Chino. I can't stand pain and I can't stand to see blood. If I see a wreck on the highway I get sick. I got into this bright room, and they put something over my nose, and, mercifully, from that point I was out.

During this time, I later found out, besides going through the operation I was having DTs because I'd been drinking so much. I dreamed I was in a farmhouse with a gang, and we were selling dope and robbing and hiding from the police. We had piles of heroin. They didn't want us to shoot any, but I was begging for some of it. I was in such pain. Then the police came and started shooting at us, but I kept trying to get the heroin, and finally I got some. But every time I found a way to hide from the rest of the people the needle would clog or the dropper would break, and I could never get it into me. I wasn't hooked at that time, but I was still dreaming about dope.

I opened my eyes and saw the ceiling. I heard somebody say, "He's coming out of it. Call the doctor." I saw Christine standing by the bed. She grabbed me and said, "Thank God." The doctor came in. I was aware of a tight feeling around my stomach and a throbbing pain. He said, "How are you feeling?" I said, "I don't know." He said, "Do you know where you are?" I said, "Yeah, in a hospital." He said, "Where?" I had to think for a while. I said, "San Francisco." He said, "Don't be scared. You've had a bad time. We didn't give you a chance in the world to survive, but the way things look now I don't think there's any danger. First there's something I have to tell you, and I'm going to tell you immediately so you can start getting used to the idea. You can never drink again. We had to cut you open for exploratory surgery, and I noticed that your liver didn't look right, so we did a biopsy. It showed a cirrhosis condition. Your days of drinking are over." Then the doctor asked me if I had been in an automobile accident or a bad fight. I said no, and he said, "Well, when I put the hypodermic in your stomach, you were bleeding to death internally. All we could do was open you up, try to find out where it was coming from, and stop it. I made the incision, and blood just flew out of you, and when we got you cleaned up I saw that your spleen was ruptured. These things usually happen in automobile accidents." They had removed my spleen. I looked at the doctor and I saw that he was the leader of the gang in the dream I'd had.

I started getting pains in my upper back. I had contracted pneumonia right after the operation, and one of my lungs was filled with fluid. The doctor came in. "This is going to hurt, but it has to be done." He gave me a local anaesthetic and took a long needle and stuck it through my back and all the way into my lung. I sat on the edge of my bed bent over. He had Christine there and two nurses holding me. The pain was unbearable. He got the needle into my lung and drew the fluid out. When he was done he gave me a big shot of morphine. I said, "I don't think I could ever stand to go through that again." I looked at this monstrous jug: it was almost six inches full of a lightish pink liquid that had been in my lung.

During this period they gave me Demerol and morphine. When they started pulling me off these drugs, I dreamed and I saw things. I was being chased by police—these were dreams I'd had before—I'd be with my grandmother driving on the freeway trying to fix. She'd be trying to stop me and I'd be hitting her with my fist. I'd be running, hiding, and then I'd actually see things crawling around. Little insects.

Christine was very good. She'd stayed up with me for two days while they were trying to find out what was wrong, and when they'd decided to operate and couldn't find her, she was asleep on a little bench in a chapel they had. I kept searching my mind, trying to remember when I'd gotten a violent blow to my stomach, because the doctor said that that was the only thing that could have caused my spleen to rupture. And I remembered those times, just before I went with Buddy, when we were at our wildest, when she'd hit me so hard. I remembered that at those time I was in such pain from those punches I could hardly breathe. The first time I mentioned it to her, Christine really flipped out. I guess she thought I was blaming her. I was just trying to figure out what caused it, that's all. I don't know if she felt bad because she thought she had done it. I don't know what she thought.

While I was in the hospital—for about three months—I had visits from all kinds of people and cards and letters. It was amazing to find out how many people cared about me. There was a nurse there, a black girl; her old man dug me. When she told him I was in the hospital he got a TV for me. You have to rent them. He paid for the TV, and I never even met him.

A priest came and asked me if I wanted to talk. I said no. He came when Christine was there, and he inquired and found out she was there all the time. He asked about our financial situation. The priest made an arrangement. He paid for Christine's food, and they fed her and me at the same time in my room. That was a beautiful thing.

I didn't know how we were going to pay for the hospital. The bill was twelve or thirteen thousand dollars. Some people got together in Oakland and had a benefit for me. They rented a club in Jack London Square, and a bunch of musicians played for free. Roland Kirk played, and I had never even met Roland Kirk. It still surprises me that he would do that. They got about thirteen hundred dollars to help me pay my hospital bill. It was the nicest thing that ever happened to me. It was something amazing. I never could get over it.

For a long time after the operation, I was afraid to look down. The nurse would change the bandages, the doctor would check the incision, but I never would look at it. Finally the doctor gave me this long pitch saying, "You've got to accept yourself as you are and be thankful you're alive." He forced me to look. I got sick at my stomach. I had two incisions, one from the middle of my breastbone down to just above the pubic hair and another to the left. My bellybutton was gone. It was the ugliest thing I'd ever seen. When I was young, with Patti, she had to have a cyst removed from her ovary, and I paid a lot of money to a specialist to make a tiny incision where the pubic hair was and then go up to remove the cyst so there wouldn't be a scar. That's how I felt about those things. Now here I was with horrible scars all over my stomach, just ruined. I thought, "How in the world will I ever ball anybody? Have anybody see me?" It got to the point where I'd never take my shirt off. I hated to take a bath or a shower because I couldn't stand to see myself. And I still feel the same way. I still feel the same way.

Well, we went back to Hollywood, and I was in bad shape but I was healing. Then I got out of bed one morning, and I noticed a pain in the middle of my stomach and saw a little puffiness there. It kept getting bigger. Christine talked me into calling the doctor who performed the operation at St. Luke's in San Francisco. He said it might be a hernia.

I went to the Veterans Hospital in Brentwood, where they would treat me for free. They checked it out and said that's what it was. I was in pain. I'd gotten a bunch of pills from the hospital, and I took them all the time. I drank wine and shot stuff. A guy I knew came around with some Numorphan, pills I'd never tried before. I cooked them up and shot them. It was like shooting heroin and coke, and it took the pain away. Then I got a call from Buddy Rich. They were on their way to New York and wanted me to join the band as soon as I could. At the VA they said I could play even with the hernia. My dad loaned me a corset he wore for his back. I felt strong enough, and I knew that if I didn't get back with the band or do something I was going to get hooked and die. Buddy sent me my ticket. They were opening at the Riverboat. Fortunately, I wasn't strung out yet, so I cleaned up and got on the plane with Christine and joined the band. I'd been playing lead alto before, but now it was too much of a strain. They put me on third alto. I wore the corset; Christine would lace it up. I kept working as hard as I could. I was juicing and taking uppers. We played the River-boat for quite a while and then started back to L.A. on the road, playing Boston and Philadelphia. We played Chicago. The pain got worse and worse. By the time we got to Texas I couldn't make it anymore, and Don Menza and the guys in the sax section told me to just finger the notes. The last night was New Year's Eve, and the pain was so bad I had to stop playing.

I had a ventral hernia, and my stomach was all puffed out. We got back to L.A., and I ran into this guy again, and he still had Numorphan, so I started shooting it. It killed the pain so I could play. With that and some Percodan tablets I made it through the job we had then.

I went to the VA again and somebody else had a look at me. This doctor said I needed an operation. I told Christine, "I'm so scared I can't stand it. I wish I could die." I wanted us to make a pact—we would kill ourselves. The doctor said he had to make a big incision and then pull the flesh and wrap it around my insides to keep them from pushing out. He said it would be very painful and it might not be successful. I checked into the hospital. I was so messed up from the things I'd been doing it took them a month and a half with food and vitamins to build me up so they could operate.

I had the operation. I got pneumonia again. Finally I went home. I laid in bed and Christine gave me medicine. I couldn't lay on either of my sides or on my stomach. Fortunately we had a little TV at the foot of the bed. The guy came around with the Numorphan, and I bought some heroin, too. I got strung out like a dog. Then one day I noticed the little pain again. I looked at my stomach and saw a swelling. There was a little area right in the middle that was puffing out exactly the way it had the last time. I had the TV by the bed, and I left it on all day and all night.

Christine couldn't stand it anymore. She wanted me to go to her mother's house and stay. Her mother was sick, too. She had had an operation at the same time, and Christine wanted to take care of both of us at her mother's. I was using. I couldn't do it. She had to leave. She said, "You're just going to kill yourself! That's all you want to do! I can't watch it anymore!" She cried and called me every name under the sun. She left. I laid in bed and watched television.

In the icebox was a little lunch meat, a little jar of mayonnaise, and half a loaf of bread. I'd take my medicine. This guy would come with the Numorphan. The guy I was copping stuff from, he'd bring a taste over and lay it on me; I got him to go pawn my horn. Christine came back three days later. She burst out crying when she saw me: "Oh God, Art, you look like you're dead. Look at yourself!" She brought a mirror. I looked horrible. She said, "You've got to do something. Either do something or I'll call the police and have them take you away. What about Greg Dykes?"

I had first met Greg in the federal joint. When I saw him again, later, he said that if I ever got really hung up I could give him a call and go to Synanon. I told Christine, "I don't want to go there. People think that everybody that's there is a rat." She said, "Fuck what people think. You know what you are. I can't leave you like this. I'm going to call Synanon or I'm going to call the police." I said, "Alright, call Greg and see what he has to say, but I'm not promising anything." She called him, and she was crying over the phone. Greg asked to talk to me. He said, "Art, what's wrong?" I told him I was just ruined physically: "All I want to do is get loaded and die, but I don't have the nerve to kill myself." He said, "Ohhhh, man. Get down here! Come down and we'll take care of you! Please, man It's your only salvation. I really love you, man. I want to save you. Please come down." I said okay and I hung up. I looked at Christine and said, "Oh God, man, it's the end of my life."

(Don Menza) The Buddy Rich band of 1968 was a magnificent band, probably as good as any band I ever played on,
including the '61 Maynard band. It was dynamite, I thought.
Buddy had a lot of fresh writers, and there suddenly became an
awareness on his part where it wasn't all, well, I shouldn't say
that. I was gonna say it had all been show—and he can put on
a hell of a show—but he can also *play*.

We were out on a short tour, we got back to L.A., and an
alto player decided he was going to leave, so we started talking
about who was going to replace him. I was sorta the straw boss
on the band, and Art didn't even enter my mind. I didn't really
know him, and he had been off the scene for a while. Jim Trimble called me and said, "What would you think about Art Pepper coming on the band?" I said, "Great! I didn't even know he
was, like, here. Where is he?" Art called me, and he didn't
have an alto, and he was, like, panicked because he didn't
have any bread. I told him, "Look, I have an alto." I was really
excited because I remembered seeing him in the Stan Kenton
days and buying his records. For me, it was really a thrill to
know he was coming on the band.

I've listened to a lot of players. I can see their origins. I can
see where they come from. I can hear the Bird in Art, I can
hear the Prez in Art, and in the sound I can hear two or three
different people, but out of that comes Art Pepper. And when
you hear him play, you *know* it's Art Pepper. Whether he's
playing alto or tenor, I can hear a certain thing that still has the
Art Pepper stamp on it.

When Art came on the band, he didn't look well. Frankly, I
was shocked. I watched him desperately trying to hang on, trying to get better. We had already recorded the *Mercy, Mercy*
album in United Studios down here, and I remember talking to
Buddy and saying, "Hey, man, the band is so hot now. What
are you doing? You should record the band live *now*. You
should do the album over again. What you're doing now puts
the album away." And sure enough, two days later he comes to
me and says, "Tell the cats we're gonna record the whole
album over again, live at Caesar's Palace." I'm just glad I didn't
have to foot the bill, even if it was my idea, but that was a hot
band. Between Al Porcino and Art Pepper . . . Art sounded

beautiful on the band. He just roared right through it. Then we went up to San Francisco, and I could see very plainly that Art was really hurting. Really hurting. And his spleen ruptured. That's what happened, and he almost died.

Christine, she always talked about helping, but I don't think she did. I tried not to get too close to her. I could see trouble there. I remember her stealing horns on him; all of a sudden he'd be without a horn. I remember coming to town one time and he was all blurry eyed, didn't know where to turn. She had taken his mouthpiece. She had a tenor of his that he couldn't get back. I stayed as far away from her as I could. I don't think it put up a shield between Art and I 'cause on the bandstand or on the bus, whenever we had to come into a close contact, it was always a great deal of admiration for each other, and he was very encouraging to me, too. For me, it was a great spiritual thing that happened. But she really, she had that aura about her, where I just said, 'Uh-oh.''

Christine was a redhead. At one time she must have been a very statuesque woman, a very beautiful woman. It wasn't there when I saw her. It had all started to deteriorate.

Well, Art would come in, and some nights he'd feel better than other nights, and then finally it was just wipeout city. That's when he went to the hospital. Buddy, as I remember, was really good to Art. There's a great deal of compassion in Buddy Rich, which a lot of people don't believe, but Art can attest to it.

Somebody filled in for him in San Francisco, and we came back to L.A., and it was obvious he wasn't coming back right away, so I managed to get Joe Romano on the band. Then we went on a tour of England. Joe is an extremely physical player, and he's got great eyes. Art does, too, by the way. He really . . . Art sat down and looked at that music, you know, and he said his eyes weren't too good, he hadn't been sight reading, and he was gonna need glasses, and this and that. He just read straight through the book like he had memorized it. Anyway, Joe was there. Buddy didn't know who he was and, naturally, Buddy knew who Art Pepper was, so it was kind of a challenge to have to follow that. After a month or two, Buddy loved him, loved the way Joe played.

We got back. We get to New York, and Buddy gets a call

from Art. Art's ready to come back on the road. Buddy tells me, "Tell Joe he's got his notice." You've gotta do it to somebody. And I said, "Look, man, you tell Joe. First of all, I feel very excited that Art will be coming back. *However,* you better check out his physical condition. Can he play? they just sewed his stomach up. And letting Joe go—I would consider it very carefully." So he said, "Well, we'll have Charlie Owens play lead alto." I said, "You better think about that, too. I have to sit in the section. Maybe playing third for Art would be better. So he could hang on to somebody. That's a hard job playing lead alto. There's a lot of huffin' and puffin' goin' on. Here's a cat just comes outta the hospital. Make up your mind, let me know what you want to do, and you tell the cats." So Buddy let Charlie Owens go. Art came to New York and sure enough, boy, he was in baaaad shape. His stomach was bulging. He could hardly blow. He could hardly *talk.* I think he came out too soon. And if I'm not mistaken, Christine was still with him.

Things weren't getting any better. They got worse instead of better. Two months later I left the band. We were here before Christmas, and I gave a two-week notice, which they totally ignored, and they fired me. Typical road thing, so they wouldn't have to pay me vacation pay. I don't remember how it went down with Art, whether he left before I did or not.

Art's a sweet person. I never heard him talk bad about anybody. And it hurt everybody to see how he was hurting. Sometimes I'd be with him, and we'd be having such a beautiful time, but he'd be drinking. I used to try to get him to cool it, but . . . And then, of course, there were the people who came around the band, who knew who he was, who knew what he wanted, and you couldn't keep him away from them. In New York . . . It was scary.

I remember vividly Art coming on the band, and I remember the rollercoaster ride he had to take physically and emotionally. That wasn't easy for any of us to watch him go through that because you could see he needed help, and there was no way we could help him. He needed physical help and mental guidance, and Christine wasn't doing either part. She was more concerned with where, how, and how often *she* could groove.

————————

THERE wasn't anything left in the house but a few clothes. We threw them in the back of the car and drove to Synanon, which was way out in Santa Monica on the beach. I made Christine buy me a fifth of brandy. I could hardly walk. We got there. She went in. Finally, here she comes with three guys from Synanon. One of them looked at me and just shook his head. They helped me up the stairs into the place and told me to sit on this bench. It was a big, old building. It looked like an old-time hotel. I sat down, and everybody was staring at me, and it was altogether different from what I thought it would be. Instead of being dopefiends and people like me, the people there were all young or old square people. I wanted to get out of there. I started to stand up, and they said, "Where are you going?" I said I wanted to get my things. They said, "You stay there. We'll get them." I said, "Oh, no, I want to get them myself." I started to walk out the door, and they just grabbed me and dragged me back to the bench.

You have to have an interview before you can be taken in, to see whether you really want to get in, if you're really hung up, to see if you've got any money. They helped me up the stairs—the place was full of stairs—and we finally got to this room, and I nearly fainted I was so beat. Greg Dykes was in the room. I was so juiced I was seeing double, triple. They asked me if I had any money. I said, "No, I don't have a penny. If I did, I wouldn't be here." Instead of being nice I got belligerent. Somebody said, "Well, we have some rules here, you know. No physical violence. We don't allow any stealing. I started yelling, "What do you mean, stealing? I'm not going to steal from you fuckin' assholes! I don't steal from people who do favors for me! I'm not a fuckin' tramp rat, like you stinkin' motherfuckers are!" They said, "Cool it, man! What's wrong with you?" I said, "Oh, you're a bunch of fuckin' rats, all of you! That's why everybody hates you! That's why the people in prison just despise all of you! Because you're all weaklings and rats! I'm not going to steal from any of you rats! I don't want anything you have!" I raved and raved. Christine was trying to cool me down, and Greg was trying to calm me because he wanted to get me in. He's acting like my attorney or something.

I stood up and threatened them, and I almost fell down. They said, "Well, you're not in good enough shape to come in here. You're going to have to get an okay from a doctor." I said,

"What do you mean an okay from a doctor? You said to come out here to the fuckin' place! I drove all the way from Hollywood, and now you're not going to take me, you motherfuckers!" They said, "You have to get an okay from a doctor." They knew about the operations. They told me to go to the Veterans Hospital and find the guy who operated on me and have him sign a paper saying I wouldn't die if they took me in. They told me to go, and I was *so* happy. I shouted, "Alright, I'll go, you motherfuckers, but if I go and come back and you won't let me in, I'll burn this fuckin' place down! Or if the police come, and I go to jail, I'll know who's responsible and I'll send somebody with a bomb and blow this place off the face of the earth, you yellow-bellied, weak, punk, New York bastards!" Somebody said, "Get him out of here! Don't come back! We don't want you here, motherfucker!" I said, "I'll come back if I want to, you cocksucker! You don't tell me nothin'! I got more goin' for me in my little finger than you have in your whole fuckin' body! Every one of you put together! I'm a fuckin' genius! I'm a king compared to you assholes! I've *lived* all my life! *I* wasn't afraid to go to prison! I'm the strongest person you've ever seen in your lives, you lousy, milquetoasted, sop motherfuckers!" Greg was saying, "Oh God, Art, please!" And he says, "He doesn't know what he's saying! He's delerious!" Christine says, "He's delerious! He doesn't know what he's saying!" And I say, "*Oh yes I do*, you motherfuckers! If you don't take me back—if I want to come back—I'll blow this place off the face of the earth and all you little pipsqueaks with it!"

There were people lined up all over watching us go out the door. They were lined up in the lobby and on the stairs. We got in the car and I said, "I gotta have a drink." Christine had a few dollars so she bought some brandy. It was only a little way from Synanon to the VA Hospital. I said, "Let's go tomorrow. Please!" She said, "No, you're going tonight." We went to the hospital, and by some miracle the doctor that was on duty was the doctor that assisted in the operation I'd had. Christine told him what was happening. She told him I was using heroin and Numorphan and drinking a gallon, at least, of wine a day and taking uppers and sleeping pills. He said, "it's a wonder you're still alive! What's *wrong* with you?" I said, "I don't know."

They put me in the hospital. The next morning, at about five o'clock, I heard a bell ring and I found I was strapped down. I looked around and I saw people, but they weren't like the people from before in the hospital. These people were nuts! I was in the nuthouse! An aide came by. I said, "What's going on? What am I doing here?" He just gave me one of those looks and walked on. I yelled, "There's nothing wrong with me, man! I'm just sick! I'm supposed to be in the medical part! I'm not crazy! All these people are crazy! I'm not crazy! What are they doing?"

Finally they took the straps off. They made us get up and wash our teeth. They stood there and watched, helped some of them wash their faces. Then we lined up in the medication line. People were doing all kinds of weird little things—giggling, moaning, doing little dance steps, talking gibberish, bowing, and howling like dogs. I get up to the medication window and I say, "There must be some mistake. They put me in the wrong place. My name's Arthur Pepper. I don't belong here." But the guy says, "Oh yes, Mr. Pepper. Here's your name. Right here. Here's your chart. Here's your medication. Here it is. Right here." I say, "Well, it's a mistake. I'm not crazy. I'm cool. There's nothing wrong with me. I'm just a little rundown, that's all. *Physically* rundown. I shouldn't be here." He said, "Well, you'll have to talk to your doctor about that." He gave me my medication, and pretty soon I wasn't feeling any pain.

I was there for about three weeks. You get up early in the morning. It's still dark out. A bell rings, and you go to the bathroom, and when you finish with the bathroom they put you in the hallway and lock the iron gate. You get your medication, and then they put you in the dayroom. You go from there to eat your meal and then back again to the dayroom. March to your meal. Back to the dayroom. March to your meal. Back to the dayroom. Then they line you up for medication, open the gate, and shuffle you off to bed.

I spent two or three days just looking at people as if I was at a movie. I thought, "Boy, these cats are sure far-out." They weren't as far-out as the people I saw at Fort Worth, but they were pretty crazy. The third day I was sitting in the dayroom when one of the aides came over to me and said, "Would you like to play some dominoes? Some of the fellows are trying to get a domino game together." I looked at him. I thought he was joking. He was a black cat, and I thought he was just goofing on me. I said, "Yeahhhh! Hahaha!" He said, "No, man, there's some guys here—they want to get up a domino game—and I thought maybe you'd like to play." I said, "What guys?" I saw he was serious. I looked over and here were three guys. They were standing there with their heads drooped over, kind of slobbering on themselves. I looked at this aide, and I looked into his eyes and tried to search him out. I said, "You want me to play with them?" He said, "Well, I thought, maybe, if you guys would like to get together. It's good therapy for you, but if you don't feel up to it . . ." And I realized that he really thought that I . . . *he thought I was like them!*

I had been there three days, and I thought it was only because I had to get a paper signed. I had to get this paper signed because I had to go into Synanon because I had no place else to go. But, I mean, as far as really belonging there . . . Before this incident I thought that I could talk to the doctors and the nurses and the aides because they knew I didn't belong there, but now I realized that they were only doing their jobs and, really, the staff and everybody thought I was some kind of a nut. I couldn't imagine how they could think that way. I told the guy, "No, I don't want to play dominoes."

I went into the bathroom. They have mirrors above the washbasins. I stood and looked at myself in the mirror. I opened my mouth. I closed my eyes and opened my eyes. I smiled. I said, "You're not crazy, are you?" I answered myself, "No, I'm not crazy. Are you?" And then I thought it was very amusing. It just seemed very amusing to me that I had finally found someone I could communicate with. I got a pleasant feeling. I said, "Well, what's the matter with these people? We're alright." And the face in the mirror said, "Yeah, we're alright. What's wrong?" I said, "Nothing's wrong now. Everything's cool." And I laughed and turned to the side and gave my best profile, and I raised my left eyebrow. I learned how to do that when I was a kid, to look sexy. I forget who it was—Victor Mature or somebody did it, and all the women liked it. You raise just the eyebrow.

After three weeks the doctor told me I was alright. They would let me out. The morning came, and they gave me a little sack with some cigarettes in it, a candy bar, a package of gum, a toothbrush, and some tranquilizers. I walked outside and sat on the lawn waiting for Christine to come pick me up, and here she comes in this ridiculous little Anglia. It was hard for me to get up and down because I was in such pain. I walked over to the car, and as soon as I saw her face I knew something was wrong. I looked from her face to the back seat, and there were my clothes. She said, "Where do you want to go? Art, I just can't take it anymore. Here's your stuff. Where do you want to go?" She got tears in her eyes. I said, "Oh, man, cut the tears, that's so ridiculous." I got in the car. I wouldn't have got in, but I couldn't walk. I couldn't do anything. I thought for a minute and I said, "Let's go to Les Koenig's."

We went to Contemporary Records. I said, "You don't have to go in with me." She said, "I want to make sure you're okay." I said, "Fuck you." There was nothing I could do. I could fight her or kill her or something, but I couldn't keep her from walking in with me. I asked the secretary, "May I see Les?" She gave me a funny look. She said, "Just a minute." But Les heard us talking and he said, "Art! Come on in!"

I walked into his office. Les looked at me, and I could tell from his face that I really looked bad. He said, "What's happening?" I said, "They let me out of the hospital. Christine and I are breaking up." I knew he didn't like Christine anyway. He said, "What are you going to do? Where are you going to go?" I said, "I need some money. Can you let me have some money?" He said, "Well, I want to do the right thing. I want to help you. I don't want to do anything that's going to hurt you." He meant that he didn't want to give me money to buy dope with. He said, "There's a motel up the street. I'll give them a call and find out if we can get you a room. I'll come and see you every day and pay your rent, give you money to eat with." He called the place, but there were no vacancies. I said, "I guess I can go out to the valley to my mother's and spend the night." He said, "Why don't you go over to your dad's? Why don't you go out there and recuperate and then come back?" Les knew I could do nothing the way I was. I said alright. I said, "Could I have a few dollars? Just money to get out there?" He couldn't refuse me so he gave me ten or fifteen dollars. I thanked him and told him I'd go to my mother's and get my dad to come pick me up.

We got back in the car. I told Christine, "If I was strong enough to take a bus and there was a bus that would go there I would take a bus to my mother's." She started driving. I told her, "Stop here." I went into a liquor store and bought a fifth of brandy.

My mother's house was in a beautiful little area. We pulled into the driveway with flowers and birds singing and all that. My mother wasn't home. The doors were locked. I went back to the car and said, "She's not there." All this time I'm drinking my bottle. Christine's crying. She says, "I wonder when she's coming back." I said, "Oh, man, fuck you! Leave!" She looked at me. I said, "Get the fuck out of here!" She said, "Okay, if that's what you want." She screeched out of the driveway and then she stopped and looked back. She shouted, "Fuck you, motherfucker!" She gave me the finger, and she roared away. You could hear the motor fade in the distance. Then the silence came back. And I felt like I did when I was a kid, when my mother would be out, drunk, with the door locked, and I'd be sitting on the porch waiting for her. I sat on the front porch of my mother's house. I was forty-four years old, and I was finished with life.

21 | Synanon

1969

CHRISTINE had taken all the clothes and junk out of the car and thrown them on the porch. There they lay, all my worldly goods. That was it. That was me, sitting there with my bottle of brandy. It was funny, actually; I started laughing. That was me, the sum total of my life at this age.

I sat and waited, nipping off my bottle. I was really loaded by this time. I was mumbling and making noises. Then I hear a car in the driveway, and here she is, my mother. She looked all pleasant until she glanced over at the porch and saw me sitting there. What a sight I must have been. She made out my belongings in a heap and me hunched over like a grinning idiot with a bottle of brandy in my hand. She shook her head: "Oh, God, what has he done now? What's in store for me now?" I just sat there. I couldn't even get up. She parked the car and walked over and said, "Junior, what happened? What are you doing?" I said, "Well, I just came to visit." And I laughed. She said, "Oh, the landlady!" The landlady lived right in front. She said, "Oh, the landlady, the neighbors! Why don't you put that bottle away? You're not supposed to drink, are you?" I said, "Oh, later with the landlady!"

My mother had changed a lot over the years. She had found God. She had accepted Christ as her personal savior, and she'd stopped drinking and smoking. Since then she'd become badly crippled with arthritis. She said, "What happened? Where's Christine?" I said, "Christine's gone. She's gone. She's finished. She's gone. She left me here." My mother said, "Oh, Junior, you can't stay here! You know that. We've tried that before. It won't work." I said, "Don't get upset! Don't start flipping out, ma! I know it isn't going to work. I'm not asking to stay with you. I'm not going to stay with you. I know you don't want me to stay with you. You'd rather have me lay in the gutter and die than have me stay with you!" She said, "You don't have to talk like that." I said, "Well, it's true, isn't it?" She said, "Oh, Junior, *please!"*

I'd gone over there before—when I'd been hooked. I'd stay overnight now and then, and I'd burn things. When you're high on stuff you nod out and drop your cigarettes. She had a piano, and I'd put cigarettes down on the side of the piano and burn holes in the wood. And in her rugs. And in her couch. In things she couldn't replace. I said, "The only favor I want to ask you is if I could call my dad on your phone. Don't worry, I'm going to call collect. I'm not going to ask you for the price of a phone call." She said okay. She opened the door and she said, "You look terrible." I said, "I know I look terrible. I feel terrible." She said, "Bring that stuff in so the landlady won't see it." I said, "Fuck the landlady." She said, "Junior, watch your language, please." I said, "Oh, fuck the landlady and everybody else!" I took the junk I had and dragged it into the front room along with my bottle. I called my dad and he said, "Of course! You know you're always welcome here." My dad was sick. He had emphysema, and his eyes weren't good. He said, "Can I come up tomorrow and get you, so I can beat the traffic?" My dad and Thelma lived way out in Yucaipa. "If there's no other way, I'll make it out tonight." I said, "That's okay. You make sure and come tomorrow." I thanked him. I think I cried. He said, "Don't worry about anything. We'll take care of you."

I hung up, and my mother said, "Ohhhh, couldn't he come tonight? Oh, I wish he could have come tonight." She said that three or four times. I said, "Boy, you're too fuckin' much. You're my mother and you don't even want me to stay here and I can't even walk!" She said, "You're just hopeless. We can't get along. Especially when you're in *that* condition. I thought you were going to Synanon. What happened there?" I got into an argument with her and started cussing her out. She kept on and on. I got madder and madder until I couldn't stand the thought of spending the night at her house. I couldn't imagine it. It became an obsessison to get out of there right then. I got on the phone and called Synanon, and they put me through to Greg Dykes. I told him what had happened. He kept talking me into it. Anything to get away from my mother. I said, "Is there any way that you could come get me?" He said, "No, it's against the rules. You have to get here yourself." I hit on my mother and—anything to get me out of there—she got hold of Merle, her husband. He was working at a gas station. She asked him if he would drive me to Synanon. I told her to please call my dad. I realized it wasn't her fault. She was just afraid. She'd had such bad experiences with me.

I never thought that I would ever really go there. Merle agreed to drive me. He borrowed an old truck from the station, I grabbed my junk, and away we went. It was evening. I had a little bit of the juice left and on the way to Santa Monica I finished it and took the rest of the tranquilizers they'd given me at the VA. Merle didn't know where the place was. We stopped at a gas station and somebody told him, "Just go down Pico till you get to the ocean. Just go all the way as far as you can go." Finally I saw the big sign that said Synanon but one of the letters was gone—SYN NON—and I remember thinking of sin. It was a foreboding, old building made of brick. It looked like a gigantic YMCA or one of the old billets the army used to take over. We parked across the street. I'm looking at the place and I'm talking to Merle: "Jesus, I don't know, man. I don't think I can make this."

Merle was younger than me by about eight or nine years. He was tall, an oafish guy, but a nice guy. We'd always gotten along. He was kind of dumb, and one eye was messed up. He's one of those guys that bumps into walls and doors and things. But you couldn't blame Merle for anything. He'd had a terrible life. He used to sleep in people's garages. That's how my mother met him. He came and asked if he could mow the lawn and sleep in her lawn swing. She started feeding him and giving him little odd jobs. She felt sorry for him. Finally they got married.

Merle said, "You gotta do something, Junior. It's useless with Moham. You can't stay there. You gotta do something. Maybe this'll be good for you." After being locked up for all those years, to put myself in a position like that voluntarily! Merle helped me. He opened the doors—big, glass, swinging doors—helped me inside up the little flight of stairs. There were people standing around and all kinds of activity going on. I heard people going upstairs and I think I heard music.

Merle went to the desk. Evidently the guy on the desk remembered me from before and the doctor at the VA had sent his OK. I saw them looking at me and whispering. Everybody was staring at me as if I was some wild animal that had wandered in. Merle talked, and I looked at the people. It was all I could do to stand without falling down. A couple of guys that looked like house detectives came over and said, "Sit down right here. It's okay. Just sit down. Everything'll be alright." I sat on the little bench, and I looked to my right. You could see an area going into an enormous room where there were lots of people walking back and forth. I noticed a blackboard with times and meetings posted on it. Somebody asked me if I'd like a cup of coffee. I said no. A guy came up to me: "Where's your stuff?" I said, "Oh, I got a suitcase in the car. I'll go get it." I got up off the bench and started to walk down the stairs and almost fell. I grabbed hold of the bannister, and the guy said, "No, no, no, we'll get it for you." I had the same feeling I'd had before. I just wanted to get out of there. I thought that once they got their hooks into me there was no telling what they might do. I was frightened. They didn't look like dope-fiends to me. They weren't like me. They all talked like New Yorkers. They wouldn't let me get down the stairs.

Merle brought my suitcase. He said, "Well, I'm going." I said, "Wait! Wait!" They said, "No, no, you go." I said, "Wait outside for me!" People were looking at me. I didn't see anybody I knew. I didn't feel any feeling I liked. They walked me up the stairs and took me into the office, and there's Greg Dykes. They started asking me the same old questions. Did I have any money? Do I really want to do something for myself? I told them, "I don't have any place to go, man. I'm fucked up. I don't have any place to go." They told me just to go along with them and not worry about anything. They took me downstairs, and I had a chance to talk to Greg. He said, "Everything's alright. We're going to put you on the couch down here. It's just a procedure that everybody goes through, in case you get sick. We'll take care of you and you'll have somebody watching you around the clock. Don't get panicked and walk out. Just stay. We'll do everything we can to make you comfortable, outside of giving you medication. I'm sure glad, I can't tell you how happy I am, that you came here."

We walked into a gigantic room. I expected to see a globe with flashing lights like the old ballrooms had that I used to play in. There was an area that looked like a bar in the back, and I saw tables and people eating. On the right there were eight or ten big, high windows. It was a huge place. And there were couches and chairs and people sitting around, young people, old people. I asked Greg, "Who are all these people?" He said, "These are just the people that are here. These are Synanon people." They had great big couches, a whole bunch of them in lines. I saw somebody else lying on a couch. He looked terrible. Greg said, "That's somebody like you that's kicking. They look after him and get him things." I remember Greg saying, "This is the only time you're really treated good, so anything you want, ask for it. Anytime they offer you something and you want it, say yes." Somebody put sheets over an old couch and a blanket. They got a wastebasket and put a plastic liner in it in case I vomited. I sat down. There was a guy that was going to sit with me; he introduced himself. Greg said, "I gotta go. I'll see you in the morning. Relax and get some sleep. Don't be scared. Everything's fine. We're all friends here."

I stayed on the couch a couple of days, I guess, and there were just too many people bothering me, coming around. That's what they do there. In Synanon people won't leave you alone. They wake up in the morning and spend the whole day putting their noses in other people's business: "What's wrong?" "How do you feel?" That's Synanon—bothering and bugging everyone. That's supposed to make you well and make you all one big, happy family. I'd be lying on the couch feeling horrible when all of a sudden some stupid-looking broad or a couple of them would come over and say, "Hello! I'm Margie, and this is Wilma, and what's your name, and how are you, and we're fine. We're from so-and-so. Where are you from?" Oh God! I told the guy who was sitting with me, "I can't stand this. I've gotta get someplace where these people won't be bugging me."

I found out I had a "tribe leader." Everybody was in tribes, like the Indians used to be, and I had a leader. I said, "Well, where's my leader at? Let me find him." He's a real important personage. They don't know if he can be bothered now or not. Finally he came. He was a black guy, and, it turned out, he was a guy like me, a guy that had been around, an older guy and a nice guy, and he liked jazz, and thank God for that. His name was Bob Holmes. I told him, "Man, I can't stand all these wide-eyed, stupid little broads and idiotic assholes coming around. I thought this was a place where they had *dopefiends*. There's no dopefiends here. It's just a bunch of little kids. You've gotta get me away from here before I wig out and have to leave." He said, "Well, we'll see what we can do."

Bob talked to some people and came back and said, "You're still not well enough to go to one of our dorms because then you'd be required to carry on like everybody else does—with a job and the games. It would be too hard. But since you are in such bad shape I'm going to get you into the infirmary." The infirmary was in a building in a place they called the Clump, an apartment complex. I took a ride on the Synanon bus and checked in. Bob even left word that I was to have no visitors, so no one could bother me except the people that were in the infirmary. Fortunately, a couple of them were sick.

The next morning I looked around and saw that the infirmary was filled with Puerto Ricans. I was in prison in Fort Worth with Puerto Ricans. They acted the same in prison as they did here. They were clannish, and they never spoke English even when they could. I don't know if you've ever heard Puerto Rican, but it's fast and high-pitched, and they would talk and talk and *loud*. Here, just like in prison, they were as obnoxious as the blacks, getting together in groups and chattering when you were trying to rest or relax. The white guys talked softly. And if they walked into a cell where someone was sleeping, they would say, "Hey, your cellie's asleep. Let's go out there and talk." They'd leave quietly and go someplace where they wouldn't disturb anyone. But not the Puerto Ricans. They'd get right next to where you're trying to sleep and talk, talk, talk this machine gun language, all of them at once.

So I'm in this little infirmary in Synanon, and I hear these voices talking Puerto Rican just like lightning, and I think, "Oh, my God, am I going to have to go through *this* again?" Synanon was filled with Puerto Ricans, blacks, and people from New

York—who of all the white people have the least regard or respect for anyone. There were maybe one or two Mexicans in the whole place. There were maybe five or six people that I called real dopefiends that were from the coast. Righteous people. Regulars.

They moved me to a bedroom where my new roommate was a young guy, the son of a doctor. He was a nice kid. Later on I heard he'd started a revolt and tried to get the kids to overthrow the government of Synanon. I asked him, "What are you doing here? I know you're not a dopefiend." This kid, Peter Kuhn, was about sixteen. He was very tall with black hair, wore glasses. He was very intelligent. The more I talked to him, the more I liked him. I realized that there were a lot of things I didn't know about Synanon, and I figured that maybe for my own sanity I should try to squelch my hatreds for a while and find out what was happening. Maybe there was something going on that I didn't know about, so I started asking him, "Well, what *are* these people here? That isn't a dopefiend there. Who is that? What are all these children doing here?" And he gave me a little rundown.

Synanon had gone to Puerto Rico and recruited dope fiends. They got so much money from the government and a tax-free stamp for recruiting people. They went to Puerto Rico and New York and got these guys, who were now so far from home they couldn't leave. Synanon couldn't get people from California to come and stay. I found out that the young kids were put in Synanon by their parents or by the courts. Some had dabbled in pot and some had actually messed around a bit with dope. And then people brought little children in with them—little, teeny children and babies. Sometimes women gave birth to children there. And sometimes people left and left their children behind for Synanon to take care of. So there were the babies, there were the young people, the Puerto Ricans, the New Yorkers, the blacks, a lot of blacks, and then, of all things, there were the squares. "Life-stylers." Game players who had moved into Synanon.

There were squares that came down and played the "Synanon game," which is like group therapy. It was a club for them. They met and played a game one night a week. When I first got into Synanon they had their own games, just the squares, and then the residents, the dopefiends, one or two of them would play in each game with the squares, which seemed like an interesting thing to have happen. There were all kinds of people in the "game club"—businessmen, real players, those phony guys that say they're writers. Everybody had some kind of line, but in the games they'd be ripped apart. In the games you study people and try to find their weaknesses. You point out the bad things. The squares were people that were lonely, searching for companionship. Some of the women were just beautiful, some of them had a lot of money, and I used to wonder why they came to a place like this. At first I thought they came to hang out with dopefiends, to have some excitement in their lives, but after I was around them and observed them, I saw that even though that was part of it, the main thing was it was a place to go. They'd play their game, and after the game they'd congregate in one area of the club where there was a bar with big windows overlooking the ocean. It had tables and was like a real bar except there was no liquor served. They served coffee, ice cream, things like that. The squares sat there and talked. You could talk to any girl you wanted. Any girl could talk to any guy. If they *didn't* talk they'd be ranked later on in the games. It was an open sesame to meet people. They went out together. They were in games together and could find out about each other.

So the people in the game club were lonely people, and I found out that even the ones that had money and were good-looking and had way-out cars were just as hung up as everybody else. They didn't know how to communicate, they felt inferior, they were self-conscious, they didn't feel adequate. Synanon was great: it enabled them to release their hostilities in the games. They could make fun of people and say things they could never say outside. After a while they felt free. They found out about themselves, they found out that other people were the same, and it gave them self-confidence—they realized they weren't alone. It was ideal for *them*. They could come and go home, go home to their nice places.

There were squares who after a certain length of time decided they liked the Synanon way of community living, so they moved in. They moved into apartments across the street from the club and worked outside at different jobs and gave most of their money to Synanon. They spent all their free time in Synanon playing games and hanging out, and they could live there with their friends, away from the violence of the outside world, because there was never any violence in Synanon. That was a no-no. The main rules were no dope or alcohol and no physical violence, so Synanon was very safe in a world that's awfully frantic and crazy.

For a while it was all I could do to make it through the days and nights. Then I started feeling a little better. One day some people came into the infirmary with some tapes and a tape recorder, and I thought they were going to play music, but instead they put on a tape of some girl copping out about a guy, an Italian, who had balled a lot of chicks. She said she had been getting loaded with him. Here is this girl saying she'd gone with this guy and given him head in a Synanon vehicle. She's telling all these people, and it's on a tape! I asked somebody, "Is this chick still *alive*?" They said, "Yeah, what do you mean is she still alive?" I said, "Well, she just ratted on this guy. She's a fuckin' *snitch*, man!" They looked at me. They said, "Oh God, you're . . . Phew! Well, it figures." I said, "What do you mean it figures? What the fuck are you talking about?" They said, "Oh, well, just stick around for a while and you'll find out what's happening." I got angry. I said, "You're a bunch of rats!" Not only were they a bunch of Puerto Ricans, blacks, inconsiderate New Yorkers, and funky, bratty, snot-nosed, little kids, but they were a bunch of rats besides! So all the things I'd heard about Synanon and knew about it before were true!

Before I went there, even in the condition I was in, I had asked Greg Dykes if the place was filled with rats. He said, "No, man, there might be a few, but that's it." I said, "I don't want to ruin my reputation after doing so much time to keep it. I don't want to live with a bunch of rats." Then I got there. I heard these tapes. Here's this chick. After she finishes, other people start copping out on this guy and that guy and this chick and that one. He was using dope. She was giving that one head. I thought, "I should have known better."

After they finished with those tapes they played another, of Chuck Dederich, the founder, Mr. God, with his bullfrog voice.

It was a long, long tape, and he just kept repeating himself as if he was talking to some idiot five year old, croaking away about the camera's eye, saying that when you're loaded it's like having a camera that doesn't take all the frames of the movie. He's saying that you just get a part of it. He likened it to seeing *Gone with the Wind* with a bad projector that doesn't show all the frames. But then, he said, when you've been in Synanon awhile, the projector gets better and better, and after you're there for some length of time your projector, which is you, is perfect, and you see the whole movie, and you know everything that's happening, and you understand life and yourself and your problems and the world and your fellow man. He's running on and on with this garbage. An old wino. Well, I guess he drank whiskey, gin, and stuff, but here's a guy that had a big, old line of bullshit, some phony salesman out of the midwest who happened to land down on the beach and in order to live had to run some kind of a game up under somebody. He was a great bullshitter, so he found a little, beat pad, and he found some winos, and he got some dopefiends to come in, and he gave them some soup, and pretty soon he got some money from somebody. By the time I got there they had this huge, old luxury hotel and other places all over—Frisco, Oakland, San Diego—half a dozen places he'd built up from this scam. I'm listening to this tape and thinking, "How could he ever do it?" *How?* I couldn't believe it could possibly have been done from what I'd seen so far.

I saw a guy I'd known in jail and asked him what was going on. He told me, "You have to wait and see. Wait until you play some games. I couldn't explain it to you in a million years. The best thing to do is keep an open mind. You've *got* to stay here. You *know* you can't leave. Try to be cool and then when you get in a game you can rage and call everybody every name under the sun and get rid of your frustrations. That'll enable you to stand it until the next game. Believe me, it'll really be interesting. It's a hell of an experience, man." I thought, "Well, what the hell." I couldn't go. I could barely walk. The food wasn't bad, and from what I'd seen—the people were dressed alright—nobody seemed to want for anything.

They started taking me out by the swimming pool. The Clump was like one of those Hollywood apartment complexes.

There was a little coffee shop where you could get coffee and peanut butter and bread for nothing. I sat out by the pool during the day. I'd see people and chat with them. I was a celebrity. Chicks talked with me and flirted with me. I thought, "This ain't bad." Then, finally, "Well, I think you'll be okay," the doctor said.

I got my clothes, and a guy took me to an apartment in the Clump right near the pool. It was a large, two-bedroom apartment with two baths, and the front room was filled with bunk beds. The guy went to one that was empty. He said, "This is you." It was a top bunk. I said, "Man, I don't know how I'm going to make it up there." He went to the office and came back and said, "When So-and-so comes we'll move him up. He's young. You can sleep on the bottom." In a little while the kid came in, he put his stuff on the top bunk, took my stuff, and fixed my bunk for me.

It had a feeling like jail, only there were no cells. The Clump had a lot of units and little walkways. I learned that a couple of blocks down, on Kansas Street, they had another complex and more people lived there; that's where they had a school for the little kids. A few people lived at the club and in the apartments across the street from it, but they were squares or people who'd been in Synanon for a long, long time.

In one of the bedrooms of the apartment were two guys who'd been in Synanon for two or three years, "old-timers" they called them. The other bedroom had one bed. I looked in there. It was really classy. It had a big double bed with a nice spread on it. There were pictures on the walls and statues and knickknacks and a TV and a record player with two speakers. I glanced in the closet. The guy had a lot of shoes and clothes. He was really living it up. He was our dorm head. I didn't see him for three or four days, didn't even know who he was. Finally he came one night and introduced himself. He was a tall, black, pimp type cat. When I saw him I realized I'd seen him down at the club working at the Connect, the desk where the cars were given out and all the details of running the club were taken care of. He looked to me like he was loaded. I didn't know if he was or not. He was going with a white, square game player.

I started finding out what was happening and what was expected of me. There were eight people in the front room and three in the other bedrooms. That's eleven people in an apartment where ordinarily maybe only a man and wife and child would be living. Eight of us used one bathroom. You can imagine the confusion. The dorm head was supposed to coordinate everything, but he had a guy called the ramrod who did all the work. There was a set of rules and a set of dorm assignments which changed periodically. I think my first assignment was cleaning the bathroom. It had to be spotless, all the time spotless, with eight people using it. That meant you were cleaning it constantly, that is, if you did it right, which I did. Some guys did the carpet; one did the trash; and someone did the kitchen. We didn't use the kitchen very often—we ate in the main dining room at the club—but sometimes somebody would cook something. After you were there awhile you got "walking around money." It's called WAM. After three months you got a dollar a month; after six months, two dollars; and so on to five dollars; then, after five years, fifty dollars a month. So you could go to the store and buy something, a little popcorn, coffee, or maybe you could hustle something from the big kitchen at the club.

You weren't supposed to hustle anything, but, as in all places, there was hustling going on. Fortunately, right across from me in the bottom bunk was an older guy, Del, and he worked in the kitchen. Most of the live-ins were dopefiends, *supposed* dopefiends, but there were some heavy alcoholics, too, and that's what Del was. He must have been about fifty-five. He'd been a cook on the street, but he was one of those hustlers and he knew a million funny stories. We were in a game once, half women and half guys, and some chick was ranking Del because he was so old, and he said, "Well, dearie, I may not be able to cut the mustard, but I sure can lick the jar!" He cracked everybody up; he had a million of those old-time jokes.

Del was cooking in Synanon. He'd come home, and I'd be there, really unhappy, wanting to get loaded, especially during the first months, and he would start telling me great stories out of his past life. I don't know if he was making them up or what, but he'd get me laughing. He didn't trust the other guys because they were so young. He'd look around and then if everything was cool he'd whisper, "Want something to eat?" I'd say, "Yeah! Yeah!" In order to get our meals we had to take the Synanon bus down to the club, and it was a long trip. Del would hand me a big steak sandwich with tomatoes and pickles, the steak cooked perfect, about an inch and a half thick, tender.

People who worked in the kitchen weren't allowed to take anything out. That was a real bust. And, anyway, steak was something we just didn't have. We ate well, but only the people who'd been around a long time got steak. Jack Hurst, who was the director at the time, and the people who lived in the club, the big shots, would go in the back of the kitchen, get meat, carry it home to their families, and cook it. Bill Dederich, Big Chuck's brother, had an apartment in the Clump and he'd have barbecues on his terrace. You could smell the meat cooking. For a while the big shots even had their own section of the dining room, where they'd eat food like that, and you could see them, you know. It was sickening. But Del got that stuff, stashed it on his body, and brought it home to me.

The residents were divided into tribes of about sixty people who played the Synanon game together, and each tribe had a certain section of the Clump, maybe three apartments for the men and two for the women. If people had to be disciplined, the tribe leader did it. For drinking or stealing or using dope or physical violence, the punishment was a bald head or, for the women, a stocking cap, and if you had a good job or a nice pad you lost it and had to sleep in the basement and work scrubbing pots, and you'd suffer horribly in the games. (If you split, left Synanon, you were labeled a "splittee," and if you wanted to come back and were allowed to come back, the punishments were the same, only they lasted longer.)

In each tribe there were so many "elders," people who'd been around for a number of years, and we went to them when we needed anything—to try to get a pair of socks that fit or decent underwear. There was a Store where you got clothes for free, but the good things were in another store for the big shots; we got the old things they didn't want. If you couldn't find a pair of shoes that fit you, you could go to the elders and beg them and maybe they'd give you a voucher. Then you could go to a real store and buy shoes. If you wanted to write someone or make an emergency call—someone was dying—you'd have to go to the elders and seek permission. After you were there for three months, you could go for a walk but you had to get permission and you had to sign out; usually you had to take someone with you. Sometimes they'd change that: the whole place would go on "containment" and you couldn't go out at all. But that was the idea of the tribes. And if you did anything wrong or you didn't do your dorm assignment, that's what the games would be about.

You'd be in a game with ten or fifteen people and if somebody, like, pissed on the toilet seat in their dorm or something like that, you'd tell it. You'd accuse him of it in front of the girls. When your covers are pulled in front of women it's really a drag, so there'd be some wild shouting matches. They made up a lot of things, too, just to get you mad, to get you raving. Somebody'd accuse you of farting at night so loud they couldn't sleep, or some chick would accuse some broad of throwing a bloody Kotex in the corner of the bathroom, leaving it laying there. The idea was that ranking you and exposing your bad habits would make you eventually change. And it worked, you know, it worked.

When I got healthier, I got a job. I wanted a job. I was bored just sitting around. Because I'd worked in the paymaster's office in San Quentin, they assigned me to the bookkeeping department, which was in a building a little ways down from the Clump, a gigantic, old warehouse where they kept all the stuff they hustled for Synanon, all the donations, furniture, food. They had offices upstairs, and one was the bookkeeping office. Most of the people in the offices were women, and my boss was an old battle-ax named Faye. She was one of those old reprobates, one of those stout, husky broads that look as if they'd just knock you down if you argued with them, and there was another chick that really looked like an old dyke. And always before, in my experience, women I was able to charm, *always* in my life. But I ran up against some women here that were uncharmable. I don't know how they'd ever been dope-fiends, but they assured me that they had and talked continuously about what terrible lives they'd led.

I've never had any special schooling, but as a kid I was good at arithmetic and was always very neat, had an orderly mind, so I automatically fell into my job in the bookkeeping department and at first it wasn't so bad. I had a desk of my own. I liked that. I got into a routine, just as I had in San Quentin. I got hold of some pictures and put them under the glass on the desk. I got a good stapler and a whole bunch of pins. I've always been a hoarder, so whenever I could find anything or steal anything I'd take it. They had a little supply room. I'd walk by it and sneak in and grab cards, different colored cards, and notebooks and pins. I had my desk filled with brand-new stuff. They were always talking about saving and using things over; I just threw things away. If a pen just for an instant didn't make a perfect line, I'd throw it in the trash. When I opened a new box of staples I'd throw all the loose staples away, or if the box got wrinkled I'd toss the whole thing out. I didn't care about saving or conserving or the program they were trying to conduct. I wasn't trying to help anything along. I felt that they were hustlers and that they were conning people out of money.

Everyone around me was brainwashed into this Synanon system of brotherly love and helping each other. And everybody had a built-in guilt. If you did something wrong, you'd cop out on yourself. If you saw any of your fellow communers doing anything wrong, you'd immediately rat on them. That was being a good Synanon person and living the Synanon life-style. A group of rats. I've never been a bad person or a criminal type, but the naivete of these people was ridiculous. If Chuck Dederich or Jack Hurst were to tell them to jump out of the sixth-story window of the club they'd all jump because they'd think that that's the "Synanon Thing," the "Synanon Position," to jump out the sixth-floor window. These people talked about how they were dopefiends and hustlers and robbers and whores, and *then* they'd go along with this kind of program? There's no way in the world it could be so. But all these people were brainwashed. Innumerable people were brainwashed like this.

We had office games in addition to the three games a week we had in our tribes. In the office games they'd rank people for using too many pens or for having a bad attitude, for wasting coffee. Nonsensical things. I found that I could drive them crazy by speaking my mind. You're not supposed to bad-rap "on the floor," outside the games, say bad things about Synanon policies or Synanon people. I would just call it like I saw it. If somebody was an asshole he was an asshole, and I would tell him he was an asshole in a game or out of a game. If there was a rule and it was a ridiculous rule, I'd tell them it was ridiculous and I'd ignore the rule. In games they called me "sour." I'd talk about dope and getting loaded, and they'd say that that was "bad" and I was "evil." I called them names: "You fat, old, double-ugly bitch! I don't believe you ever used any dope in your life! Somebody as ugly as you never got anything given to them, and I know nobody would fuck you and give you money, and you're too dumb to steal." They said you shouldn't be prejudiced. You weren't supposed to have those feelings. Most white men fear the black man with the white woman. They're afraid he is really as superior sexually as he says he is. If I found out that some white broad was married to a black guy I'd rave at her in games and call her tramp, slut, whore. Most people tried to act like they weren't prejudiced, which is ridiculous. Everybody is filled with prejudice, and every now and then in a game if you could bring it out, they would admit, "Well, I used to be." They were hypocrites. But when it came down to the serious things, I played my cards right. I had jailed so much I knew how far you could go, and I found out you could do anything except drink, use dope, or use physical violence and get away with it.

The thing of it is, the people that ran Synanon had to keep everyone offguard and keep everything different. If they fell into a routine, if life became boring and fell into a pattern, they'd lose the people. So they would change. All the time. Just make changes for changes' sake. They'd paint the place where you were working or move the desks. The same thing in your living quarters. Every single room in Synanon, whether it was in the club, the Clump, Kansas Street, the school, each room had been maybe fifty different things in the last three years. You'd be here, so they'd move everybody over there. They move these people here, move you there, move this here, paint that. Make a rule: you can't have this. Then you can have it. They'd have "glut raids," which I'll get into later, getting rid of the opulence.

Or somebody would attain a high position after years of carrying out his faithful duty to the Synanon doctrines and the word of the great lord and master, Chuck Dederich; he would be rewarded; and then all of a sudden the gestapo would come and take away everything he had and make him wash dishes and scrub toilets and make his wife live in a dormitory with the other broads and newcomers. They did all this to keep everybody messed up. That was the basis of Synanon because dopefiends and nuts can't stand routine and when they get bored they have to do something crazy, so Synanon made the insanity. Themselves. The people that ran it caused the insanity.

Shortly after I arrived, the insanity took the form of changing the hours. Ordinarily people get up in the morning and set certain daytime hours aside for this or that. Synanon decided to do away with this. They instituted something they called the "twenty-four-hour day." There was a group of bigwigs, the "regents," or whatever they called them—a group of people who were in favor at that particular time with Big Chuck, you know, Big D., the god, the Old Wino. This group would have games together and call each other names and then they'd figure out, "Well, how can we fuck things up and disrupt everybody now?" They decided on the twenty-four-hour day. One day I was told, "Instead of working from eight o'clock in the morning until 4:30 in the afternoon, you're going to go to work at 11:30 at night and work until nine o'clock in the morning." Can you imagine that?

I'd go to work at 11 P.M. and at 3 A.M. a jitney would come pick us up and drive us down to the club to eat. We'd ride down the street; we wouldn't see a soul, no life, no cars; it was like death outside; and we didn't say a word to each other. We'd go to this ridiculous, old-time club that used to be a millionaire's hangout, now fallen into disrepair, a junk heap full of ignorant ex–dopefiends or whatever you want to call them, nuts, running around trying to be painters and carpenters and carpet layers. You can imagine what the place looked like.

We'd get out of our jitney at 3:20 and walk into this club that looked like some old movie set for Rudolf Valentino or Theda Bara. And here were these tired-eyed musicians. They were playing music, and the crazy people were standing around; chicks with no bras on were dancing. We'd walk into this mad revelry without drinks, without dope, and go into the kitchen and eat. We'd eat the same thing we had at supper: if we had breakfast at supper we'd have breakfast for breakfast; if we had liver for supper we'd have liver for breakfast; if we had meatballs and spaghetti for supper we'd have meatballs and spaghetti with dripping water running off the plate for breakfast. When we finished eating, the musicians would play a "hoopla," which was the standard dance of Synanon. Some nut invented this togetherness rock-and-roll dance: instead of dancing separately they all danced together, following the same steps. We'd walk out of the mess hall into this false gaiety. We'd sit around surrounded by posters proclaiming the twenty-four-hour day. We'd go to the bathroom. Then we'd get in our jitney and go back to this lonely warehouse, and nothing could be as desolate and miserable as the streets were during this drive, with the occasional sireeeen of an ambulance or a police car or an occasional old drunk staggering by and laying down in the gutter.

We'd drive up to the warehouse. We'd get out. We'd find the keys. They always had to look for the keys, they were so disoriented. Then we'd go back into the office and work until nine in the morning over figures and money matters. I'd sit and nod out over this thing I was doing, and one of the old hags would holler, "Hey! Wake up! Art! Wake up!" And I'd say, "Oh, you old bitch, shut up!" Faye would call me into her office and I'd tell her they could take Synanon and stick it up their ass.

That lasted a few months. It finally ended. Everything changed. Every now and then I'd run into somebody who had a little sense and they'd say, "Just cool it. Everything changes. It'll change tomorrow or the next day or next week." I knew I couldn't leave, so I'd go into my games and rave about how much I hated Chuck Dederich and his twenty-four-hour day. I was getting a reputation as the most "negative" person in Synanon. They'd say, "Why don't you just get the fuck out! We don't want you here! You're just ruining our thing!" And I'd say, "Well, I'm going to stay and ruin it for you dumb bastards as much as I can, and when I'm ready to leave I'll leave and not until, and *hope* you don't like it!"

While we were on the twenty-four-hour day, summer came, and the only thing I enjoyed at that time was going to the beach and riding the waves, trying to get healthy. If I went to bed when I got off work at about 10 A.M. it ruined the whole day, so instead I'd go down to the beach, stay until two, then grab a bite to eat, come back, and go to sleep. On one of those days I got off work at nine, walked back to the Clump, and I was standing there waiting for the Synanon bus to take me to the beach when I saw this car pull up at the corner. There were a few people waiting there for the bus. I saw this car turn the corner, and I looked, and just as I looked the person in the car looked at me, and I said, "Christine!" Evidently she'd been driving around trying to find me.

I should say that when you go into Synanon, for the first ninety days you're not allowed any communication with the outside, no letters, no nothing. I'd been there a couple of months, and I hadn't had any word from Christine. The other people were watching. I couldn't run out to her. I motioned to her hoping she'd understand. I wanted her to go down the street and wait for me. Evidently she got the picture. The bus came and everybody got on, but they were still watching me because they'd dug this little byplay. I started to get on the bus. I said, "Oh, I forgot something," to myself, like. As soon as the bus left I snuck down the street where she was parked. I jumped in the car and laid down in the seat and told her to drive.

She looked terrible. I said, "What's happening?" She said, "Oh, man, it's been awful." She started crying. I said, "What's wrong?" I thought she wanted me to leave with her. I said, "If you want me to, I'll leave." I wasn't ready yet, but I would have gone. She said, "No, let's forget it. You can't leave. You'd just die out here. What would you do?" I said, "There's nothing I can do. I'm too weak now to do anything." At the time I didn't know this, but later on I found out she was already living with some other guy. She still cared for me and she wanted to see me.

We had a terrible conversation. It was useless to pursue it and so I said, "I'll probably get in trouble for this ride and *have* to leave." She said, "No, I'll get you back." I laid down on the seat again, she pulled into the back of the Clump, and I jumped out of the car and hid. She pulled out of the driveway and looked back at me. She had tears in her eyes. She said, "Good-bye. I'll always love you."

A few people had seen me, but there were some groovy people there, older chicks who liked me, who'd been around. We were real friends. I went down to the club, and a few of these chicks took me downstairs. They asked what had happened, and I told them because I knew I could trust them. I cried. I wasn't crying for her. I was just crying for my life.

I went back into the club and I felt better about everything. I realized that that part of my life was past and, you know, when I was looking at Christine in the car I noticed that she had these panty hose on and they were kind of droopy. She didn't look sexy at all to me. But at that time I realized that I was thinking about sex again. I had had no sexual desire for a long time, since I'd gotten sick. I'd been getting ready to leave Synanon and go get loaded. I'd been thinking, "What's the use of trying for something I don't even want?" But when I started getting these old feelings, life seemed worth living and I didn't want to go out and ruin it by getting loaded and destroying my health.

Little by little it happened. I found myself looking to see who was going to be in my games, and if there was a groovy chick I'd watch to see where she sat so I could look at her during the game. Everybody was passionate because they weren't getting loaded anymore. Everybody was going through the same thing. I'd sit across from a chick; she would pretend that she was crossing her legs; and you know, they do little things so you can see up their dresses or they bend over. I started using these games. I'd talk to the chick and say, "Boy, I'd sure like to suck on your cunt!" Everybody would flip out and call me a dirty, nasty, rotten person, but I knew the girl I was saying it to liked it. Not the other ones. But you could say anything you wanted, and it was exciting, and the games changed for me from being nothing but hate sessions into a sexual trip.

I went to my tribe leader and said, "Man, I'm really getting a reawakening. I've really got eyes to get laid." He said, "How long you been here?" I think it was two, two and a half months. He said, "Well, being as you're an older guy, just start looking around and if you find a chick you have eyes for who has eyes for you, tell me and we'll talk about it. It's gotta be within certain guidelines. You're a newcomer so you can't go with an old-timer chick, and certain chicks are, like, bad news. We want a chick that's going to be good for you. Look around. See someone you like and let me know, and I'll tell you if it's cool." From that minute I started looking for someone to make love to, and I thought I might even get lucky because a lot of people had found love there.

22 | Synanon: Laurie

1969

THERE WAS a girl working in bookkeeping; she was Faye's secretary. She'd been married to a guy in Synanon Industries who I would later work for. Her name was Trudy. She was very neat and very smart, a great secretary. I used to make excuses to go in and see her just to talk to her. She had a little, upturned nose, and she was slender and delicate. She wore glasses. She had light hair, a light complexion, and a beautiful body. Every now and then I'd walk home with her from work and we'd eat together, things like that. I could tell she liked me.

I talked to her one day when we were having lunch together: "Boy, the one thing that's really a drag here, once you clean up you have a real strong sexual drive and it's such a hassle. You can't see somebody you like and make love. You gotta go through that whole thing." I looked at her and I said, "You really turn me on. I'd sure like to make love to you." She blushed and said, "You would, huh? Well, I feel a strong attraction to you. I'd like to if we could." I told her, "I've talked to Bob and I have permission if the person is acceptable."

I went to Bob. He was in his little office. Each tribe had an office of their own in the club. There were a few people sitting around. I said, "I'd like to talk to you privately." They all walked out of the room, and I closed the door. I said, "Do you remember the conversation we had the other day?" He said, "Yeah. You mean you found somebody *already*? It's only been two days since we had that talk!" I said, "Well, I've been looking all this time, and there's a chick—she's nice, she's not too young, and I'm sure she's not scatterbrained or crazy or anything." He said, "Well, I'm all for you having an old lady and going to the guestroom. It might help keep you here. It sure helped me when I was a newcomer. Who is it?" I told him and his face dropped. I was sure he'd bend over backward to get anything going for me, but I found out later it wasn't up to him. He'd get beat up by other people in the games if he didn't follow the guidelines. He said, "Oh, Art, I know Trudy well. She's a very attractive woman, and you two would probably make a nice couple, but I'm sorry. It can't be. The first thing, right off the bat, is that she's been here too long, five years. But the *main* thing is she's just been divorced and it was a traumatic experience for her. She needs somebody to help her get over him; that's something you don't need. It's too emotional, too involved. The third thing is she's a square. She's never been a fiend, and it just wouldn't be good. There've been people in the past who've wanted to get into similar relationships, and if you got to do it in two months, which is a very short time, it would create a lot of animosity and envy. It just can't be. It'll take you a while before you realize that the things that are done are done in your own interest. Trudy could drive you right out of this place. She'd probably like to leave since her marriage has broken up. Imagine you leaving with her! You'd die. Just keep lookin' around. There's all kinds of chicks."

So that was that. I started looking throughout the club and on the bus and everywhere, and I started asking girls how long they'd been in Synanon and how old they were. I got a reputation of being a real flirt, but I wanted to find someone and I wanted everyone to know I was available.

There was another girl, Rhonda, who'd been married to a guy that was there. We had always talked; she would give me things; and she'd told me, more or less, that we should get together. Rhonda was sexy looking. She had more outward sex appeal than Trudy, but Trudy had more class. Rhonda was kind of a dog in a way, but it was fun being around her. She had large busts and a fair body; her face was kinda strange. She was a tall girl, and her legs were a little too thin for the rest of her. She had straight, brown hair, and she was also very intelligent. She was a real climber. That was one thing I didn't like about her. She used people to further herself. We were sitting on the couch one day, and she was flirting with me like she always did, and I told her what Bob had said, that I could start looking around. I said, "Would you like to get together?" She said, "Oh, man, I wish you could have asked me a little while before! As you know, I'm ambitious and you can't offer me anything now other than the envy of the other girls who have eyes for you. I've got a thing going with So-and-so." This was a guy that was a big shot. He later became a director in one of the Synanon houses. They were going together, and he could really further her ambitions because he was well thought of by Chuck. He was being groomed for an important position and could really help her. She said she cared for him, too. I said, "You missed your chance." She kissed me and everything. She rubbed herself against me, but my feelings were hurt.

There was another girl I liked, a redhead I was working with in bookkeeping. She was a newcomer like me. One Sunday I saw her in the club and went over and started talking to her, and while we were talking a blond came over who had been around for a couple of years and she asked the redhead, "How would you like to go for a walk?" It was a beautiful day. She turned to me and said, "Would you like to come with us? Sonja is coming and there'll be four of us." We all signed out and went down to the boardwalk. I walked with the redhead, bullshitting and all that. We'd always flirted. We walked by the beach and it was hot. Somebody said, "Let's stop and get a Coke or something." We sat down at a table. I was sitting across from the blonde, and she really started coming on to me. She was another secretary. She was thin with a beautiful complexion, and her hair was cut short in little curls, an old-fashioned hairdo like a bob. I noticed that she had hardly any breasts, but she had a nice ass and she was tall and there was something about her eyes—they had a sexy quality. She had blue eyes. You could tell she was a natural blonde.

We left this restaurant, and now I was walking with her instead of the redhead. We got back to the club and the blonde said, "Why don't we go down to the beach?" The redhead and the other girl both had things they had to do, so this girl turned to me and said, "How about you, Art? Would you like to go?" I had my bathing suit down in the men's locker room so I said, "Okay, I'll put on my suit." She said, "I've got mine underneath my clothes."

Synanon had a private beach, and there weren't many people out at the time. We met. She had a bikini on. She had a beautiful stomach, beautiful legs, and nice feet, and she had blonde hairs on her legs. She already had a little tan. We laid down on the sand and started talking. I told her how hard it was to stay in Synanon when you didn't have any contact with a female. She said, "I know what you mean." I said, "Who do you go with?" She said, "No one. I really understand what you mean. It's murder." I looked at her and thought, "Well, what the hell. She's clean." And I liked the parts of her body I could see, and she had sexy eyes. I said, "I believe that anybody can be compatible if they want to be. How would you like to get together with me?" She said, "Do you really mean it?" I said, "Yeah." She said, "I'd *love* to!" The next day I went to Bob Holmes and he said, "She's fine if you have eyes, but make sure. If it's the wrong chick you'll pay a lot of dues to get out of it."

The next time I saw her in the club I asked her if she wanted some coffee. I had observed her a few times walking around and—when I really got into it—if I could have balled her that Sunday it would have been nice, but to have to go through all the "courtship" and then the "relationship" and the games with her . . . We just didn't mesh. I realized I'd made a mistake and something had to be done. I found out who her tribe leader was, a woman, and went to this woman and told her the story: "What do you think I should do?" She said, "I'm glad you found out now. That girl is very together. Just tell her outright you don't really care for her that much." That afternoon I had coffee with her again, and before I started speaking I could tell she knew what was happening. A very perceptive girl. I started mumbling something and she said, "You don't really have eyes anymore. It's good you told me now. I'm disappointed, but I'll get over it." She walked away from the table, and I saw she had tears in her eyes, and I thought, "Oh, man, what a scene this is! This is ridiculous!"

Things kept going wrong. A woman who'd been in Synanon nine years hit on me, but Bob wouldn't give his permission. She went to Chuck, but he wouldn't give his permission either, and I was really relieved because I didn't like her that much. A friend of mine who was a lesbian offered to get in a relationship with me, and I thought about it seriously, but I just couldn't do it. I went out with some nonresident women to a concert, and one of them drove me home and gave me head in the car, and that was great, but I still didn't have an old lady. I was raving in games that I couldn't get this one and I couldn't get that one because of this or that and they beat me up in the games saying, "Why don't you relax?"

Finally, I was in the club one day, walking up the stairs, and I looked ahead of me and there was this girl. She was real thin, with black hair cut short, and she had a nice tan. She had gorgeous legs and the most beautiful ass I ever remember seeing. She was wearing a short skirt, and I could almost see her panties but not quite. I followed her up the stairs, and when I got to the top, where she was turning, I walked by her and said hello. She gave me a funny look. She said, "Hello." She looked kinda scared, you know, and I walked on.

I saw her a couple more times, and each time I said, "Hello. How are you?" But I couldn't make contact with her. Then one day I got on the bus and noticed this same girl sitting right behind the bus driver facing the center of the bus, so I sat down across from her. She had on a little, short, purple dress. She really looked classy and very withdrawn. She had pretty eyes, very, very pretty eyes. She had thin lips, but they were sexy. Her whole thing was sexy. I looked down at her hands. Her hands were delicate, artistic. She was wearing little sandals, and she had the cutest little feet, like little doll feet, with cute little toes. I looked at her legs and saw that they were open a bit; I could see up underneath her dress; I could see these purple little panties. And that was so sexy and so exciting . . . . By then I didn't even bother to look away or to be cool. I devoured her with my eyes. The bus stopped, she got off, and she was gone. Instantly she was gone, before I could think of anything to say. I followed her and saw the place she went into. I asked somebody who the girl was in the purple dress and they said, "That's Laurie Miller." I said to myself, "That's it. That's for me. I'm going to have her. There's no question about it. I'm going to start a campaign tomorrow, and I'm going to get her or else."

The next day was Saturday. On Saturday night people would come in from the outside and visit. There was a speaker, and the band would play a hoopla, and the visitors — the prospective square game players — were taken on a tour. All the residents were supposed to go to the Saturday night party. The dorm heads forced everyone to go; it was mandatory.

Some people really did do the "Synanon Thing." They'd go to the club on Saturday night, and if they saw any newcomer that was kinda lonely or looked sad they'd talk to them and run them a bunch of "data," tell them how great it was to be in Synanon and try to find out why they were unhappy and make them feel accepted and wanted and part of the group so they'd stay. And report them if they felt they were going to leave. Be a rat. And they'd show the visitors around and explain the "Synanon Philosophy."

I dressed up as best I could and got on the bus to go down to the club. As I'm riding I'm looking out the windows and I'm seeing people, the real people, the people who have been able to manage their lives, the free people. They were on the streets with chicks and cars, going into liquor stores, laughing, and having a ball. I remember reaching down and putting my hand on my stomach, where after the operation I still had the hernia, and I felt the bulge there and the pain I always feel, and I thought of the cirrhosis that was in my body, and this rare Italian blood disease the Synanon doctors had just informed me I had. I said, "Well, I've made my bed, now I gotta lie in it." I thought of getting off the bus and walking back toward town, going into a bar or a liquor store and bumming enough for a bottle of wine, making a phone call. Then I thought of Laurie; I thought of her and those little purple panties.

I got off the bus and I looked at every face. I went into the club. I looked and looked. I didn't want to ask anybody if they'd seen her because I didn't want to tip my hand. I was afraid if somebody found out I had eyes for her they'd try to shoot me out—somebody that had been there longer. I was afraid if they saw I dug her they'd think, "Wow, if *he* digs her and he's been around as much as he has, she must be a way-out broad." I figured I'd better keep it to myself. Also I didn't want to have anybody running up to her saying anything. I wanted to make the move myself. I looked all over; the place was packed. Then, there she was sitting in the "bar" with a group of people. I went over and watched her, waiting for someone to leave so I could sit next to her. Nobody did. Finally she got up and walked away. I went to her and stood in front of her. I said, "What's your name?" She told me. She looked ill at ease: "Who are you?" I said, "I'm Art." "Art who?" "Art Pepper." I saw there was a sudden recognition. I had figured she was playing a game, a coy little game. I thought she really knew who I was. She said, "Art Pepper. I knew some people that knew you at Westlake School of Music." She named a bunch of people, Les McCann, Charlie Haden. I said, "I used to blow with Les McCann, and Charlie Haden—I gave him his first jazz job with my quartet." She said, "Oh, really?" I was trying to think of something to say. Usually when I talked to a girl the conversation would take a certain direction right away, but in this one nothing happened and I couldn't figure out how to break through. She looked around and said, "Oh, pardon me, I've got to circulate." I said, "What do you mean?" She said, "That's what the Saturday night party is for. There's some new girls in my tribe. I want to find out how they're doing." And she was gone.

What a drag. I started thinking maybe it was my stomach that had turned her off. I was really wiped out, and I didn't feel I was handsome anymore. But I felt that I had to have her. I couldn't give up. If I didn't make it, it wouldn't be because I didn't try.

The next day I went to the beach hoping she'd be there. I put on a bathing suit. I was worried about my stomach, but I wanted to show off my tattoos so I didn't want to wear a shirt. I got a towel and folded it over my arm like a waiter. I looked ridiculous. I had a long beach towel, so I put that around my neck and it hung right in front of my stomach. I held it with my left hand. It looked very natural. I could even leave my hands go. I figured if I laid down I'd lay on my back or on my stomach so the bulge wouldn't be noticeable.

The Synanon beach is right behind the club, and it has a fence around it with two little openings down by the water. I walked out the gate and toward the water and saw her. In a purple bathing suit. As soon as I saw purple—there was that beautiful little body. She looked like a little girl. In fact I almost felt guilty wanting her. I felt I was some lecherous old man wanting to ball a sweet little child.

She was lying on her back reading a book, one arm out to

the side, holding the book in her other hand, blocking the sun. I walked by her as if I was going to the water. As I walked I stared at her, and I could see the little, curly, black hairs coming out of the sides of the little purple mound at her crotch. Beautiful legs and little, teeny toes. I walked toward the water and stood there for a minute. I was hoping she hadn't seen me, and I got scared. "What's going to happen when she sees my stomach?" I was going to go back and put a shirt on. I decided against it. I was hoping my tattoos, especially the skull, might impress her, and I've always been pretty muscular. I pretended I was looking at the water, and then I kind of yawned and walked back and stood right over her, waiting for her to say something or look at me. She just kept reading her book. I'm standing there and standing there. I said, "Hello." She said, "Hello."

By this time I had asked some people about her. I asked a friend, Paul Rainbolt, and he told me she'd been going with this Jewish cat. I'd looked at him: he wore glasses; he looked like an intellectual type cat. So I decided she was an intellectual and kind of a snob and thought she was too good for most guys.

I sat down. I talked to her, forced myself on her, forced the conversation. Finally she put down the book. I said, "It sure is lonesome here, isn't it?" She said, "Is it?" I said, "What's anybody do here anyway?" She said, "Well, it all depends on what you want to do. Probably the things you want to do you can't do here." She was "running me data." I kept pursuing the lonesome thing. Finally she came out and said, "Are you hitting on me?" I said, "Yeah." I could see that when I said that at least I drew a kind of response from her. She was flattered. But the more I talked to her the more it seemed to me she didn't really want to get into another relationship. And I could tell she was very wired up in what she was doing in Synanon. She started talking about the school. She worked with the kids. When someone is involved with children they're really involved. The whole situation suddenly seemed very frustrating, and I thought for a minute that maybe I should just forget it and look for somebody else, but I kept looking at her lying there in that bathing suit. She had small breasts, but they were nicely shaped. At one point she turned and for a second I caught sight of a nipple, and it was hard, and that immediately turned me on. I thought, "I've got to have her."

I asked her what she had done on the outside, and she told me she'd been a photographer doing album covers and publicity pictures. I said, "Jazz groups?" "No, rock groups." And so from the little bit she told me and from what I'd seen of her I realized she'd been into that phony Hollywood trip. Maybe she thought I was the same kind of people. I leveled with her: I told her I'd really come to the end of the line, that if I left Synanon I would die. I told her about the things that were wrong with me physically. I wanted to prepare her for my scar. I told her that the only way I could make it was to have someone to care for, that all my life I'd been looking for a woman to love me. I don't know if she really trusted or believed me, but I think she started to think I was alright.

I enjoyed talking to her. I got a warm feeling from it, and I told her so. I told her how I felt about Synanon. I said I felt I was being held prisoner. I couldn't even go for a walk. She said, "Why don't you ask one of the guys in your tribe to go for a walk with you?" I said, "I don't like the guys in my tribe. I don't like guys." She said, "Well, I don't think you'd have any trouble getting some of these young girls to walk with you." She was about twenty-five. There was a bunch of eighteen- and nineteen-year-old girls who would giggle and flirt with me. A lot of the older guys had young chicks like these who admired them and were impressed by their reputations as big dope-fiends. I said, "I don't want any young girls." I told her that she could take me for a walk if she would. I told her again, "I *am* hitting on you." She said, "Well, I don't think you can just go with someone without getting to know them. You've got to be friends first." I said, "Well, let's be friends!" She looked at me and smiled for the first time, smiling with me instead of at me. At first, when I'd thought of having a girl, it had been purely for sex. Now I realized it was much more than that, and the prospect really became exhilarating. I said, "When can we go for a walk?" She said, "I'm busy today." I said, "How about tomorrow?" She said, "Okay, I'll take you for a walk tomorrow." I said, "What time?" She started reciting all the things she had to do. Oh, my God! I said, "When do you ever have time for yourself?" She said, "Well, you have to stay involved. That's the trouble with you. You just sit around thinking about what you'd be doing if you were on the street and mope and feel sorry for yourself. You can't make it that way. You've got to be involved and do things for other people. The kids are such a gas. It's a lot of responsibility taking care of them, and then there's the newcomers in my tribe—I'm a dorm head—and . . . ." Oh, Jesus!

That night as I went home I saw Synanon in a new light. The people on the bus nodded and said hello. The bus driver said hello. I got off the bus and walked into the Clump, and people I passed on the walkway said hello. I went into the coffee shop. Usually, if I couldn't find a place to sit alone, I'd get my cup and walk and stand as if I was looking for somebody outside, you know. Everyone else just sat anywhere. I always resented that. If someone sat down next to me I'd say, "What's the matter, you got nose trouble?" This time I got my coffee and was standing there and some people said, "Want to sit down?" I started to say no and then I thought, "Well, what the hell." I sat down and everyone was friendly, and I found myself talking with them. And I began to realize how much my thinking had been shaped by my prison experiences and how my hatred and anger had been consuming me. I went back to my pad, and instead of hating the people in the front room for being in the front room, I realized that they were there, just like me, trying to get some help.

We met in the club, in the living room. I said, "Oh, great! I was afraid you wouldn't be here." She said, "You'll have to get permission to go out." I looked around and found an elder of my tribe. I signed out and wrote down the name of the guy who'd given me permission and under "who with" I wrote Laurie's name. We got out of the club. I said, "Which way should we go?" There were really only three places we could walk to. We could walk toward Venice, past the Pacific Ocean Park pier, which had been closed down and then had caught fire several times. It was a strange fairyland that was all black and destroyed. There were twisted tracks where the rollercoaster had been, stands and old tin cans, and a diving bell, where people used to go down and look at sea monsters. There were fences all around, but you could walk along the water and look up and see parts of it. Beyond that there was a walkway that went along the sand past the city of Venice. There were old storefronts on it; a fruit stand; centers for elderly Jewish people, where they would go dance; and then there were the beat shops, where the kids, the hippies, sold jewelry and candles. Besides them there were the winos and the dope culture, which encompassed a lot of people, young and old. You had all these people wandering around, sitting on benches, and there was always some excitement. Every now and then you'd run into a group playing bongos and conga drums or somebody playing a flute, and a couple of these freaky, half-naked girls would dance. We could go to Venice, or we could walk into Santa Monica, to the shopping mall, or else we could walk north up the walkway and go to the Santa Monica pier.

We walked toward the Santa Monica pier. It was a beautiful day. Laurie was wearing a short, green dress, suede, like velvet, and she looked very cute. We walked to the pier and down to the end. On the way back we stopped at the merry-go-round. They have an old, old one there, still working. This old-time organ music was playing.

I felt wonderful. It seemed everything was working out fine. Laurie was very friendly and sweet and she really turned me on. We sat down on a bench and watched the merry-go-round. We made small talk, and I reached over and put my hand on her knee. She seemed to stiffen a bit, but she didn't say anything. I left my hand on her knee, and it really turned me on. I started moving my hand up her thigh under her dress. She let out a roar and jumped up. She said, "I think we'd better go back." We started walking back. I kept trying to put my arm around her, put my hand down her dress. She wouldn't let me. I said, "Look what you do to me." And I looked down to my front, and her eyes followed mine. I was wearing bathing trunks, and my pants were standing all out. I had a hard-on. She said, "Oh!" She really got embarrassed. I said, "Boy, I sure feel comfortable with you. I really feel relaxed." She looked at me and said "You feel *relaxed*? I don't feel relaxed. I feel like I'm with some wild animal."

We walked back to the club. I got angry then. I couldn't understand how she could say that. I thought it would be flattering to show someone they turned you on. It hurt my feelings. She said, "I'll see you later." I said, "Thanks for the walk. Thanks for being my jailer and taking me out of this rotten place."

I figured I had goofed the whole thing. That night I walked

over to the coffee shop and found this friend of mine there, Paul Rainbolt. He was a tall, skinny guy, a nice guy; I'd known him in jail. He was a real dopefiend and a criminal, so I respected his opinion. He'd been in Synanon for about four years. He said, "Oh, Art, I was looking for you. I want to talk to you." We walked out by the pool. He said, "I don't know how to say this. This girl was talking to me today. She knew I was a friend of yours. Laurie." Paul said, "She wanted me to explain things to you. She doesn't . . . She's a nice girl. They come in here, and they don't want to be treated . . . They want you to act like a gentleman and not come on coarse. You've got to cool it. You've got to go through the formalities. That's the routine here. To make it different from the streets. She wanted me to talk to you. You can't move so fast." I said, "It doesn't matter. I blew that anyway." He said, "Do you like her?" I said, "Yeah." He said, "Well, I don't think you blew it. Just act like a gentleman." I said, "Well, I thought that was a gentleman. It always was a gentleman where I come from."

After I talked to Paul I got some insight as to what was happening in Synanon. A lot of the girls that were into the dope thing—they weren't treated as ladies. Some cat just took 'em out, and if he wanted to ball he'd say, "Let's make it." And so the idea was to change that and to treat them as nice girls and also for the man to do something he'd maybe never done. To make it as much like the American way as possible, courting and getting used to living in society. I saw Laurie and apologized and asked her if she would forgive me. I said, "I still really have eyes for you and I'd like to get to know you. Is that okay?" She said, "We'll get to know each other and see what happens."

I would meet her after games and at different times when she was free, and we'd go into the club and have coffee and peanut butter sandwiches. I got to the point where all I thought about was her. During this period of time you weren't allowed to touch. There's no contact. Finally I asked my tribe leader, "What's supposed to happen now? What am I supposed to do? I want to keep everything on the up-and-up so it'll work out right." He said, "Well, I don't have anything against her. She's a lot more together, Synanon-wise, than you are. Now you get in a courtship. I give you my permission." I said, "Great! That's it then!" He said, "No, that isn't it. You have to go to her tribe leader and tell her you'd like to be in a courtship with Laurie."

Her tribe leader was Betty "Greek." Betty had been around a long time and was married to a guy named Jimmy the Greek, Jimmy Georgelos, who'd been around longer than anyone just about, ten years at least, and was really a legend around Synanon. He was a wild character. He was around sixty. Betty was a very together chick in her mid-thirties, very attractive. I said to Bob, "Wow, it's really going to be embarrassing going to her and asking her something like that." He said, "No, man, she's a great chick. It's just something you have to do, a formality. You'll grow behind it."

We were now on the "cubic day." We worked ten hours a day every day for fourteen straight days, no time off, and we really worked—two coffee breaks and a meal—but at the end of that time you had fourteen days off. The cubic day had a lot of good qualities because when you worked you really got into it. You excluded all else and were so tired by the time you finished your day's work and played a game you just fell out on your bed. If you didn't have a game you had to do your laundry, your dorm assignment. I found that I worked well on this system, and when I was off it was really great. "Motion" was your working period. I was in my "vacuum." It was still summertime so I could just go lay on the beach.

I was out on the beach with Laurie the next day, and I saw Betty. I realized that the longer I put it off, the harder it would be to talk to her. I got up and walked over. Betty was getting a suntan; she had her straps down; she had kinda large breasts. She was lying there and I was thinking, "My God, this is the most ridiculous thing I've ever done in my life!" I walked up to her and said, "Betty Georgelos?" She said, "Yes?" I found out later that Bob Holmes had already told her I was going to talk to her. She knew everything, the whole story, but rather than helping me any, she didn't say nothin'. I had to say every word. And she got very businesslike. She pulled her straps up. She got very dignified.

I said, "I'm Art Pepper." She said, "Yes, I know." I said, "Well, I want to ask you something." She said, "Yes?" I said, "Well, uh, well, uh, one of the girls in your tribe, a girl that caught my eye, and I really like her ... Laurie?" She said,

"Yes?" I said, "Well, I really like her, and she's in your tribe, and so, you know, I thought, well, you know." She said, "What?" I said, "Well, I would like to make it with her." She looked at me real shocked. She said, "What do you mean make it with her? I'm not a madam! This isn't a whorehouse! Where do you think you are?" I said, "No, I didn't mean it that . . . I mean, I like her and I want to go with her." She said, "Well, that's a little different. Does she know about this? How does she feel about it?" I found out later that Laurie had already talked to her. I said, "She's agreeable, too." She thought for a while and then she said, "Well, you know Laurie's a very nice girl. I want her treated like a lady." I said, "I really care for her. I'd like to go to the guestroom with her." She said, "There you go again! You can't go to the guestroom. First you get in a court-ship. That'll allow you a little more freedom. You can hold hands. You can kiss goodnight—just a plain kiss. And if that works out alright, then we'll see about the guestroom." I said, "Is that it?" She said, "That's it. You're now officially in a courtship with Laurie." I said, "Thank you." I went back to where Laurie was lying. I said, "Everything is straight. Isn't that nice?" I said, "Can I hold your hand now?"

There was this idiot Puerto Rican, had never been anything but a street hype, and he worked in Synanon security. They had, like, police cars that said Synanon on the sides, with walkie-talkie radios, and they rode around in these cars trying to find someone drinking a can of beer. And a lot of people you find that get put in positions of power, they can't handle them—President Nixon, that's the prime example. Well, this guy was another strata but just as bad. I forget his name; we'll call him Pendejo, just to have a name.

Laurie and I would meet in the evenings after our games. We'd go to the dining room. They had stuff out all the time, left-overs and garbagy food, like, "Feed 'em so much they can't do anything else." And most people ate like pigs. We'd eat and bullshit and then take the bus back to the Clump. There was a little area where there were some workshops that were closed at night. There was a board we could sit on. We'd sit there and kiss.

One night we were out there fooling around and we saw a light. I knew it was one of these security assholes, so I said,

"We'd better get out of here." We walked to Laurie's place and stood there at the door saying goodnight. I put my arms around her and kissed her, and all of a sudden there was a light shining on us, a spotlight, and somebody hollers, "Hey! What you doing there? What you doing? Stand still! Don't you move!" And this Pendejo comes running out. I yelled, "What in the fuck is wrong with you? Turn off that fucking light, you asshole!" He shouts back, "Don't you talk to me like that! I take you down to the club and shave you head! I have you head shave!" Laurie says, "Oh, Art, don't." I say, "This fuckin' guy!" He says, "Don't you cuss at me! I have you head shave!" This punky-assed street hype from Puerto Rico! Laurie says, "Art, please, please." She says to him, "What were we doing?" He says, "I saw you! You were almost doing it right here on the street!" I said, "Shut up, you asshole!" "Don't you talk to me! I shave you head!"

He wrote us up. A citation. This would go to our tribe leaders. He said, "Don't let me catch you again! You can keees, but that's all!" I'm forty-four years old. Laurie's nearly thirty.

I always wanted to go for walks, but Laurie didn't think it was good for me. I wasn't into the house enough: I should try to involve myself in the community. So one day I'm walking around the community and I can't find her. I go to her dorm: "No, we haven't seen her." I wait. I go down to the club and look around. I walk all over the beach. I come back to the Clump. Nobody's seen her. Then, here she comes with some other girl and a guy and a tall, gangly, gawky-looking rumpkin. She sees me. This tall asshole gives me one of those looks, "Yeah, sucker." She says, "Oh, Art, this is So-and-so." I say, "I know who he is." I say, "Can I talk to you?" He says, "I'll see you later, Laurie." "Goodbye, have a nice trip." "Be sure and come and visit."

I got her alone. "What is this shit?" She said, "Well, we went for a ride." "What do you mean you went for a ride? I thought we were going together! What's all this stuff—'we should stay in the house' and all that?" "Well, we've known each other for a long time. He's going to Tomales Bay. There were four of us. We went for a little ride to say goodbye." I told her, If you want that fuckin' asshole, go get him!" "You don't own me!" "Alright, fuck you!" I walked away.

Later on I started feeling bad so I walked to her dorm. I saw a bunch of people up in her tribe room, which was in an apartment near the dorms. She comes down the stairs. She sees me. "Art, I want to talk to you." Her new tribe leader comes to the door, Frankie Lago, some sage of the place. Laurie says, "I want to play a game with you." "What do you mean a game? I don't want no fuckin' game! If you want to make it with me, great. I'm not going in no game with you!" Frankie talked to me: "This is the Synanon way. It's a good way. Why don't you just try it once?" Against my better judgment, I was goaded into going upstairs. I walked into the room and here were all these people, all Laurie's tribe, all totally hostile toward me. She runs down this story—how unreasonable I was. I'm acting just like I'm in the streets. She's had enough of that bullshit. I tell her what I think, one thing leads to another, and all of sudden she shouts out, "Shut up, you motherfucker!" I looked at her. I looked into her face. I couldn't believe she had said that. I said, "That's it. It's over. What did I do to cause you . . . You must really despise me. What did you even start to get in a relationship with me for?" Everybody started talking: "That's the game." "You're *supposed* to get your feelings out." "You use those words. You don't really mean 'motherfucker' per se."

I had to get away from there. It was so humiliating to have a little chick, like, sitting there calling me a motherfucker in front of all these people and have these dumb little broads glaring at me, putting in their two cents' worth, and the madder you get the more they jump on you and the more you lose. No matter how loud you scream they can scream louder. And no matter how long you talk, when you run out of breath they're there to start raving again at you. And laughing.

I didn't let Laurie forget that incident for a long time, and whenever we got into a game together I'd rave at her about it. She apologized after. She didn't mean it in that way: "The only way you can make it here is playing games. It's worked for other people." She'd decided she wanted to do something for herself and had gone into Synanon wholly accepting whatever they said. I guess she was right. I guess that's the way. With my background and at my age I wasn't able to go along with anything or anybody that much, but I finally forgave her.

The day we got permission to be in a relationship Laurie and I had lunch together in the club. In order to get down you had to make an appointment through the woman who was in charge of the guestrooms. The guestrooms were in the club. We ran into this woman. I asked her, "Do you have anything right away?" She said, "Well, usually you have to hand in your request on Sunday night. You get two times a week to start out, just two-hour sessions. Later you can get four hours and when you have seniority you'll get overnights. You give me the times and days you prefer and then list alternate choices. You can't always get the times you want." I told her, "I'm just wigging out. I've gotta make it." She looked at her book: "Well, I've got some time this afternoon." I called my boss. I had a new one, a guy. I asked him if I could get off work an hour early to make this appointment. He said, "Oh, yeah, man, definitely. I tell you what you do. Take two hours so you'll have time to shower and all that."

Now we needed sheets. You take your own double bed sheets to the place. I told Laurie, "It doesn't matter. We don't need no sheets. We'll just lie on the floor." This guestroom chick asked Laurie, "What happened to the sheets you had before?" "I gave them away." I said, "Thank God!" The chick said, "I've got some brand-new sheets across the street in my place." She gave us two sheets and two new pillowcases. She was an older chick, and she liked us both. She was a real romantic.

I went back to work all excited. Just the idea of balling like that, by appointment, and doing it in the daytime! But I started worrying. "Will she like me? Will I be good? Will I like her?" And I couldn't remember the last time I'd balled without liquor or pills or dope.

I met Laurie back at the club. There she was with the sheets in a big straw purse; she was so embarrassed. News there travels fast; everyone in the club knew what was going on and they were all staring and the girls were giggling. I said, "Let's go up to the room." She said, "Why don't you go up and I'll follow. Or I'll go up. Please, you go get some coffee and bring it up. I'll have the bed made by the time you get there." I went for coffee. Everybody was saying, "Yeah! Work out, Art!" And, "Boy, I know you're going to enjoy *that*!" It was really far-out. I liked it. But all the attention got me nervous again. What if I couldn't get a hard-on being sober? I carried the coffee up the stairs, trying not to spill it. Six floors. No elevator. By the time I got there I was just panting. She's got the bed made and the shades pulled. She said, "Look what I got." She'd lit some candles, really pretty. I put the coffee down. We looked at each other for a moment. There was no strangeness at all. All of a sudden we had our clothes off and we were laying on the bed making love, and it was the most beautiful thing in the world. And it was so vivid. There was no numbness from juice or stuff. After we finally separated, we lay there looking at each other and I tried to cover up my stomach. At first I'd had a shirt on, but Laurie'd made me take it off; now I reached for it, but she said, "Oh, please don't. I think it's beautiful. That's you. You look real. I like the marks around your eyes, everything about you. I don't like a pretty man without wrinkles or scars." She stroked my stomach, and she kissed it.

23 | Synanon: Games, Raids, the Trip

1969 - 1971

THE GAMES were like group therapy. I'd been through that in Fort Worth, San Quentin, Chino; I figured this would be the same. But, whereas in prison a psychiatrist or a psychologist was in charge of the group, in Synanon actually nobody ran the games. In prison the therapy sessions were designed to find out problems and help people: they tried to build you up, very polite. In Synanon you put the game on a person and the way he sat, the clothes he wore, the expression on his face, the way he talked—those were the things you picked apart. And you got him so angry he lost his inhibitions. You got him so frustrated and humiliated he'd flip out and let his real feelings come forth. The game was a place to cathart. It was a verbal vomiting. In prison in group, I knew I could only say certain things. If I said other things it would put me in a bad light with the psychiatrist and might hurt my chances for release. I found out in Synanon I had nothing to lose. Well, if you drank or got loaded or balled some chick without permission (and later on if you smoked), those were things you could get a bald head for or get thrown out for. But you could talk about everything else. You could rave and rave.

At first I didn't want to expose myself. I was afraid it would be impossible to live in a place where I'd let people know my feelings. But it got to the point where people were so rank to me in the games I couldn't contain myself anymore. They called me an old man and said it was a wonder I could even make it up

431

the stairs. I got madder and madder. They said I was a has-been player playing old-time jazz. They got me so fuckin' upset! I started raving like a maniac. I started telling people what I thought of them, and the hate just poured out. Even I was surprised at the hatred I had.

But I wasn't an effective game player. All I was, was full of hate and anger, and after a while I noticed that people would say something to get me started and then just sit back and laugh. You weren't supposed to commit physical violence or threaten physical violence even in the game. Several times I threatened to kill somebody or throw them out the window, and they would just laugh until some old-timer who was the weight in the game would tell me to shut up or he'd have to call downstairs and have me locked up. When you put the game on someone else you run an indictment, but it has to make some sense so the game will follow you and back you in your indictment. The people were all against me and wouldn't follow me in my indictments, so I wasn't really getting anything out of the game and it was driving me crazy. I wasn't playing music at that time; I didn't have my horn to talk for me. But I did have my voice, and I *knew* I could express myself in these games if I could get the people on my side.

One time I remember I was sitting in a game with this guy, Bill Coates, a friend of mine, a black cat who'd grown a big natural. The black people had finally gotten away from conking their hair. They'd gotten on the black is beautiful trip, and now they were growing huge naturals that made them look like headhunters from the upper Amazon. Well, this cat grew one of these things. He was a groovy cat. We'd put each other on, but we really dug each other. So somebody was talking to someone in the game and all of a sudden I interrupted and said, real polite, "Oh, uh, pardon me, just a minute, excuse me. Before we go on I have to say something." Everybody looked at me and they said, "Aw, no!" They thought I was going to come up with my usual thing, but I finally got them to quiet down and then I said, "Pardon me, boy." And I looked at Bill Coates. He said, "Are you talking to me?" I said, "That's right, boy." He said, "Alright, honkie, whataya want?" And I said, "Lookit. Alright. I know you people are trying to get your thing together and that black is beautiful; that's great, you know, if you want to do that, and 'let the white people do the dirty jobs,' and 'we want free money from the government,' and 'we don't want to be sent to jail because we're black and prejudiced against,' but, well, I'll forget all that. There's just one thing now. There's women in this room, right?'' And he said, "Yeah . . ." And I said, "Well, would you please . . . before we go on . . . would you *please* remove your hat?'' Everybody just cracked up.

From that moment on I played a great game. And I remembered when I was with Kenton's band on the bus, I used to be the life of the party because I was so funny. I realized if I could put this humor into my game playing I'd get the people on my side and they'd follow me in my indictments. I could still get rid of my anger, but the comedy would make me popular. So I'd run long indictments on people, make them as funny as I could, and have the whole game behind me, laughing like crazy. Little by little I began to be looked upon as a great game player. It got to the point where when I'd go into the "Stew" . . .

The Stew was the only game that allowed spectators. There was a room set aside for it with twenty chairs for the participants and bleachers so people could watch. It ran twenty-four hours a day, every day, and everyone was scheduled for a stint in the Stew every month or so, which lasted up to seventy-two hours with two short breaks for sleep. Downstairs there was a stew schedule listing who was going to be in the Stew when. If you saw the name of someone you wanted to talk to in a game setting you could go up and join the stew for a little while. Everybody looked into the stew at least once a day. That was the center of the house. You picked up all the information about whatever was happening there, and it was the major entertainment of the place. Jack Hurst, the director and one of the sharpest, funniest game players, would drop into the Stew a lot to play, and you could pick up a lot of pointers from him. I began to get hooked on the game, and I started studying it, but I wanted to be original and have my own style, which I gradually developed. And then I started noticing that when I was scheduled into the Stew all the kids would come up to watch me and laugh. I was like an actor. It was beautiful. And I'll have to admit that nothing I've ever done has been more beneficial to me than the game playing.

By the time I got to Synanon I'd reached the point where I no longer enjoyed playing music, and because of my physical con-

dition I was afraid I wouldn't be able to play again. I was thinking when I left I'd find something else to do. I really enjoyed the
office work. But people kept after me all the time asking me to
play, and so when Christine contacted Synanon after I'd been
there for three months, I left word asking her to drop off my
tenor.

I started woodshedding down in the basement of the club. It
felt good to play again. I decided to blow just for my own enjoyment and to play hooplas when I felt like it. They had hooplas
after games, sometimes two or three in an evening. We'd play
"Ode to Billy Joe," "Watermelon Man." And there were some
excellent professional musicians in Synanon. We had Wendell,
a black tenor player, really played well; Marty Meade, "the
Troll," a crazy little guy who played good piano and wrote
music; Lew Malin, a very exciting drummer; and Lou Loranger,
who played bass. We had a Puerto Rican, Jaime Camberlin,
who played congas; other people sat in and played the shakers,
the maracas. Later on we got Frank Rehak on trombone; he was
on some of Miles's albums. And the people got the same thing
out of dancing to our hoopla's as we got out of playing them, a
complete release. It was very exciting.

I found myself getting stronger and stronger. My tone
developed. My mind cleared. I was sober and playing better
than ever. I ran into Stymie again in Synanon. He had orga-
nized a choral group. I started writing arrangements for it and
playing with them, and someone got a rock group together to
play upstairs for the kids, so I was playing with them, too. Then
Tom Reeves, an old-timer in Synanon, began organizing the
musicians and even instituted musical games.

We had our first musical game in the Stew. Instead of talking we blew our horns at each other. It was recorded and
sounded very far-out. Then we decided to have another game
alternating words with the blowing. We went down to the
weight room in the gym and set up the instruments. There were
about eight of us. We played for a while and then stopped, and
things just naturally took their course. From the playing
someone would emerge that we wanted to talk to. We were supposed to be playing together, but Wendell played longer and
louder than anybody. We couldn't shut him up. I told him,
"Boy, you sound just like you are—ugly and brutal and full of

hate." Everyone jumped on him, and he wigged out: "Fuck you assholes, fuckin' Uncle Toms and honkies! Fuck you, Art Pepper, fuckin' Colonel!" He ran out of the game while we hollered, "Yeah, yeah, baby! Cry, cry, baby!" Then all of a sudden he was back, "Fuck you honkies!" And he ran out again carrying his horn. Then we put the game on this chick, Karolyn, a lesbian. She played the flute. She was a great whipping post for me. I called her a double-ugly old whore and told her, "I wouldn't touch you with *Wendell's* dick!" She flipped out and started crying, grabbed her flute, and ran out of the room screaming. Then Lew Malin, the drummer, got mad and started throwing his sticks.

I've always been a perfectionist. I'd get mad at groups I was playing with and, thinking only of the music, if somebody goofed I'd turn around and look at them or say something to them on the stand right in front of the audience, and they'd get angry at me because it's not professional to do that, but I couldn't help it. By playing these games and ridding myself of these feelings I found I became much more tolerant and less quick to rank somebody on the stand. And the more games we played, the better the music was that we played together—those that were left. Hahahaha! No. They all came back, and it was a marvelous experience.

Tom Reeves was responsible for organizing the musicians and setting up these games. Tom was one of the gurus. He was very talented in a lot of things and really in nothing. He was a writer, a great game player, he had a real command of the language, and he played a little drums. He was a good tribe leader, too. He was a heavyset guy and wore a beard—I'm sure to make him look wise so the kids would look up to him. He was pretty far-out, and I used to think he was a real outsider until I discovered that he was more hooked on the Synanon system than the weakest woman.

We'd made some tapes of the musical games and of some really wonderful performances we'd done, and Tom kept these tapes. Then we had a glut raid, and afterwards the regents called a whole bunch of old-timers together and hauled them up in the dead of night to Synanon City at Tomales Bay, to Chuck, the old master. He wanted to play some games with them. While they were there, Chuck decided he'd have them all shave their heads to stop the decadence, to tighten their morales. But he did give them a choice, and I think there were a few people that had some balls and declined. Most of them went for it. Tom was one of the sheep. And later on, when Jack Hurst and Chuck Dederich began talking about jazz, saying it was decadent and evil, as was rock, Tom Reeves, all on his own, took these beautiful tapes we had made and destroyed them.

————————

(Karolyn April)   I went to Synanon, well, to be perfectly honest, I was trying to pursue my lover, Sherry. She had broken up with me. We had lived together and used for about two and a half years, and she had decided to quit being a call girl to support her habit. I ran out of government loans from the university to support my habit and there I was, in a very numbed state of mind, unable to think of anything else to do. I couldn't conceive of going back to the life that I'd led, even though the woman I'd lived with before was willing to have me stay with her. I could not do it. And I was in a state of true insanity, I think, and I was almost paralyzed. I was very unhappy. I was ripe for a mental institution, which is what, essentially, Synanon was. The only thing I knew to do was to follow Sherry, which is what I did. I don't think she actually minded it. She's a person who only has relationships for a couple of years at a time, but she doesn't really want to break off with people that she cares for, so she was kind of glad to see me.

The Synanon of that time was bad and good . . . and bad . . . and good. In some ways it was really good because you could be really crazy in Synanon without having to be in a mental institution. I personally had a real breakdown there after I had a serious bout with Hong Kong flu. I was very weak, and I came out of it having active hallucinations. All kinds of peculiar psychic and emotional experiences. So I was crazy in that environment, and in spite of the impossible rules everybody around you loves you. They all hate somebody—that presence that is so tyrannical—but they all love each other.

There's another thing that you know there, that nothing's

going to stay the same. You can't depend upon the status quo, no matter how good you think you are. You can never do it *all* right. There's always that vindictive spirit that goes about that environment, ready to point a finger. And in Synanon it's like something out of Salem, Massachusetts. You're accused as a witch; you are a witch; now all they have to do is burn you. And they do burn you. You know, that happened again and again. And the human engineering—I always used to note that I was like an android, that people were like androids, in that environment.

It was so atomized in Synanon. Most of the patterns of life are much too large for you to have any perspective on them, so you can never see them, but patterns do exist. In an enclosed environment like Synanon, everything becomes magical because everything is resolved. You are not too far away to see the pattern. You can always see how it comes out. There's no anonymity there. There's no chance meeting that has no meaning. There's nothing that has no meaning in an environment that's so enclosed. Everything was always interacting. I now work in a place of business, and I know nothing about the personal lives of the people I work with except for a couple of individuals, and they pick and choose very carefully what they tell me. I've worked there for two and a half years, which is almost as long as I was in Synanon, three years and three months, and I've found out nothing. I can only speculate. I know that this slob is an insane megalomaniac, but he does not supply me with any details and I do not have the Synanon game, where I can pry it out of him or where I can insult him for being seventy-five pounds overweight and a snob. So Synanon is really very educational

There was no privacy in Synanon. The only way you could be private, unless you were married or there a long time, was to lock the bathroom door. Even if you had a private room in a dormitory, people could enter without knocking. That's just the way it was. I was not interested in any men, though there was once a possibility that I would relate to Art. I was so hungry for affection and attention, because I'm a very sexual person, that I really considered Art, who, I felt, was a kindred soul somehow.

I can't remember all the details of our friendship because Art practically became a public person to me, but there were a number of times we played music together, for the dining room, and he. . . He helped me. He was prompting me in this silly music we were playing, so that I would come in right, because I was very frightened for some reason or other. And he was very supportive. But he used to always complain to me. He was a friend to me, and it was possible to empathize with how awful it was around there. And when we worked over in the Industries office, we really carried on at great length. The black humor in that office! It was unreal. And Art had a great sense of humor. He had this radio he kept at work; he had it set to the jazz station. Usually we worked the day shift, but sometimes we worked odd shifts, and Art had a note on the radio that said something like "How can you touch this radio without feeling terrible pangs of guilt?" And he had such a reputation for being able to hold his shit and never cop out to anything and such contempt for those people who did. But he liked to play that game, using the Synanon jargon for his own ends.

Art was funny, but he has a sadistic streak in him that apparently only comes out in how he treats himself and what he says about other people. Like, during the Puerto Rican episode in Synanon, when we had two or three hundred Puerto Ricans in Santa Monica, none of whom spoke English, he used to say things like "I'd like to get a grenade and pull the pin and just roll it down the bus aisle." That's a terrifying thing to say, and he said it with such relish. He expressed so much prejudice all the time that it was really shocking. I know he used to object to me because I'm gay, but one thing I've always known about him, which always knocks me out, is that he can learn from anybody. He really has respect for other musicians or for anybody who has any kind of skill. It's unbelievable that somebody who can express such chauvinistic, racist ideas and violent thoughts and jealousy and envy can suddenly become like a lamb when he's in the presence of someone he thinks is a real musician or who he thinks he can learn something from. I play the flute and although I've never been a professional musician Art always showed that kind of respect for the things I could do. I've seen him express the same kind of attention and interest and humility—I guess that's where you really see the humility operating in Art—for other musicians.

But in the games . . . Art is a person, to me, who is very unique in that you could never predict what he was going to say. He's always coming from left field or, you know, off the wall. His approach is so oblique that you don't ever expect it. And then he likes to get onto a theme, a leitmotif, and he just likes to beat it to death. He starts at a fairly slow tempo and intensifies it very slowly. Actually, he never really shouts but towards the end he's, like, bludgeoning; he's not hysterical. I remember a game that I was in with him because he nearly killed me. I can't remember why he did it, but he has done it to other people. It turned out one day that I was just ripe for it.

There was a certain tension between Art and Frank Rehak that kept them from being friends. You know, Frank was bankrupt when he came into Synanon, but he *had* been very successful. I never heard Art speak badly of Frank, but I think there was some competition between them. According to the experts in the place, Art had much greater improvisational ability than Frank. I was fond of Frank. He used to give me a back rub now and then. Frank was very affectionate. You see, Art isn't really affectionate. Art is standoffish, and he has an image to keep. He doesn't allow himself to be outgoing and to get the strokes that he actually wants. He wants to be the tough guy all the time.

I think what brought Art to Synanon was complete and total debilitation and, frankly, not another option at the time. And I think the reason he stayed there was that he could operate there. I mean, it was like jail except that there were women and clothes and adulation from fans and considerably more freedom and really nothing to worry about. And he *loves* gossip and intrigue. He likes to hear the dirt: that's his cup of tea. And what better place? He loved those games because they offered him so much. And as far as music, I don't think he ever played better.

One thing that was really very apparent about his playing in Synanon was the health that exuded from it. He played with a wonderful, buoyant tone, and since he felt, probably, pretty secure, it certainly showed. He played with wonderful crispness and clarity. I've never heard him play better than in Synanon. We had some bands come in, and he was featured with them—Phil Woods, Frank Rosolino. Art was truly a star. Of course, he's such a pro. He plays all this stuff, he plays it in spite of himself: he can't not play it. I don't know how that works. He couldn't do wrong.

Frankly, I've heard Art since then, and sometimes I've heard a deterioration. Because you have to be healthy. You can't play a wind instrument . . . It's an athletic feat. When you have to fill up an alto saxophone with air and make it sound and do all the things you have to do muscularly and somatically with your gut, you have to be in really good shape.

Art is a hypochondriac. And, in Synanon, he always had a pained expression on his face. Now I know that he arrived with some serious problems, spleen and so on, and he was always complaining about stomach trouble, problems with digestion, and I always felt he was an invalid. I felt like a lot of special care should be taken of him. I always had the impression that they weren't doing right by him in the environment and then I'd think, "Oh, this asshole, demanding all this!" But actually he *looked* quite handsome. He has beautiful hands. They always seem to be tan, and his nails are usually manicured, and since he has a lot of vanity, you know, he dresses nicely whenever he can. I had the impression that he was a kind of handsome hypochondriac who had something wrong, but of course he wants to make you feel that it's *really* bad. Maybe he thought he was going to get some morphine! Ahahaha! Or sympathy. I always gave him sympathy. Every now and then, I'd give him some special food. I'd bring back some yoghurt, and it would make his stomach feel just perfect!

As for Laurie, she was working in the school. She was completely overshadowed by Art. I had the impression that she had to confer about her relationship with Art with a lot of people because it was so difficult. It was very obvious that this was a great love affair, and Art quickly became obsessed by it.

I have a bad attitude about straight women. You know, I assume they can't read and write, that there's no other thought in their minds than this man they're in love with. I don't know how I can be so patronizing because as soon as I fall in love with a woman, I can think of nothing else but that woman. In love is in love.

I know that Art thought Laurie was the most wonderful thing in the world. He just thought she was so defenseless. Well, she's so small physically. She's the kind of person, she opens doors for herself. Wherever she goes, I'm sure people like her and love her and want to help her. And I know that's the way Art felt about her. He idolized her. He thought she was the most wonderful lover he'd ever had. Not only did she afford him a great deal of tenderness and love, but she was one of those people that are extremely lovable.

And I have a theory about men. Particularly macho men. And that is that they absolutely must have a woman because they have no one to be a baby around. You can't keep that act up twenty-four hours a day. Art needed to have a ma. In love, you can recapture that moment of infancy. That's what everyone wants back. That's what Art wanted.

I would describe Art as egotistical. He makes great demands on himself. He doesn't recognize the importance of cooperative effort, for instance, and, well, one night, long after Synanon, I was talking to him about AA. He came over to my house. He was in great stress: he would never have come otherwise. And I told him that the only thing that would help him would be belief in a higher power. It didn't have to be some sentimental figure out of the Presbyterian or the Methodist or the Catholic church. It could just be a higher power. After all, you know, *somebody's keeping it all going*. He said, "No. I'm it." That's what he said. Well, that's a lot to take on yourself, to be *it*. I believe people are fractional realities of God. But that's *all* people. Not one person. So he feels responsible for everything. And, of course, he has that naive belief in substances, which is the paradox of it all. "I will not believe in God, but I will believe in heroin or cocaine" or whatever it is. That's a great handicap, too. He's truly astounded me. I don't understand how he became a musician. How did he acquire the skills? Obviously, God and Art are playing when they play, and it's too bad that Art can't realize it. He'd be able to do so much more if he didn't have to feel this tremendous responsibility.

———————

THEY called them glut raids. I'd been in Synanon for about eight months. I was living in the Clump in an apartment with three bedrooms. I shared one of them with another guy. It was about

2 A.M. We were sleeping. All of a sudden somebody just grabs the door, flings it open, smashing it against the wall; at the same moment the lights go on, and here are two or three of these elders charging into the room screaming, "Get up! Get out of there! Don't touch anything! Get in the other room!"

They went through our closets, opened our dressers, took everything and threw it on the floor. Then they called us in. "Where'd you get this? How many of these you got?" Razors, underwear, socks, record albums, books, pictures. They looked through the mattresses and pillows just like narcs. "What's that? Only old-timers are supposed to have those!" These were guys I worked with! Alan Connors—I'd laughed with him about Synanon policies, but here he was caught up in this thing. Playacting. And here was this punk I'd seen in jail, just a little sissy guy; here he was hollering, "Get up against the wall! I'll have your hair! Bastards!" We were at the mercy of these animals, who suddenly had power over all these people and could exercise that power by treating them like dirt. Suddenly they'd received word from Jack Hurst or whoever was running the house at that time: "Alright, we're gonna disrupt the rabble! We're gonna have some fun!" They *planned* it. "Synchronize your watches! Let's go!" And they descended upon the Clump and came in screaming.

This was going on in every dorm. After they went through all our stuff somebody got the bright idea of taking the entire population of the Clump out to the swimming pool. They gathered us around the pool at three in the morning. It was cold. I saw these young girls—they'd never been into anything, maybe they'd run away from home—they were standing around in their nightclothes shivering, scared to death. The elders were standing around the edges of the crowd or on this L-shaped stairway that led to offices above the coffee shop. They were using the angle of this stairway as a podium or a stage. Joe Gianelli, an animal dopefiend from New York, got up there and started screaming insults at us, raving and shaking his fists. They took turns berating us and threatening us: "Alright! Who has done what? I know you've been out there shooting dope! I know you've been stealing!" And they wanted to know who had too much—too many things. They didn't want you to get pleasure out of owning anything. We were supposed to live on a more spiritual plane. Everybody knew that the elders owned all kinds of stuff: silk underwear, color TVs, cameras, stereos. But they demanded that people cop out on each other and on themselves, and these terrified young girls would raise their hands, "I saw So-and-so take two soaps from the Store instead of one!" "So-and-so has a record player and he's only been here ten months."

After a whole night of this they made us go back to the club in buses and jitneys and cars, and they divided us into groups to play games. In each game, they put one or two of these elders to get us to cop out on each other. "I saw him take two mouthwashes!" In the warehouse where I worked they had hundreds of thousands of cases of mouthwash which had been donated. After one of these glut raids I saw them fill several huge trucks with TV sets, beautiful stereo equipment, cameras, lamps, chairs, clothes, an upright piano—I had been trying to get access to a piano to write music on and they'd told me, "You can't have that"—they took this piano and thousands and thousands of dollars' worth of stuff, loaded it onto these trucks, and, I was told, took it to the city dump, and threw it away. And this happened more than once.

After the games they brought us down to the ballroom, where they had all these people sitting on the stage: guys with their heads shaved, girls in stocking caps. They berated us some more, and then they took us back to the Clump and paraded us around. One of the main attractions was right upstairs from where I lived. They had these five girls in stocking caps stand around while we all marched through their dorm. Each girl had a TV and a record player; shelves full of perfume, jewelry; closets stuffed with clothes from I. Magnin and Saks Fifth Avenue; hats; silk bedspreads, curtains; books, pictures. There wasn't a bare spot in the place. It looked like a Persian harem. After we finished with the tour we went to work, and then that night, when we thought it was all over, we were yanked from our beds again and taken to the club for a "general meeting" and more games.

In the end they drew up a list of allowable items. Each girl could have two dresses, three pairs of pants. Each guy was allowed two pairs of shoes. That was Synanon. That was really the way it was.

Everyone in Synanon would get a chance to go on a "trip," and I was thinking that if someone outside advertised, you know, "Take a trip! It only costs . . ." There would be no way to set a price on it.

First they would select a "trip conductor" and a group of "trip guides." Then they picked a hundred people or so to go on it. They divided the people up into "trip game groups" and tried to get a cross-section in each one: black, white, Puerto Rican, male, female, square, dopefiend, old, young. Before you went on the actual trip you played a game with your group to get to know everyone, and this game—all the trip games, unlike the other games in Synanon—was directed by the trip guide. In the pre-trip game his function was to really pick you apart and get you angry and mad so you were completely fucked up when you went into the trip. I was so mad I wanted to kill this guy, Frankie Lago, who was my guide. He was an old-time dope-fiend, someone I could relate to, and an excellent game player.

The trip would last for seventy-two hours. You went to the club in the late afternoon and took off your clothes. You put on a white cotton robe with pockets in the front. You weren't allowed any adornments, no jewelry. The women couldn't wear makeup. They wanted you just as you were. You could wear sandals or go barefoot; no shoes. You got one four-hour nap in the seventy-two-hour session. You went through game situations, you went for walks, you played charades, always together with your little game group or with the trip group as a whole.

There was a large room upstairs in the club where we all met after we'd put on our robes. The Woodshed was used for dances, rock-and-roll for the kids, but for the trip it was completely transformed with Oriental carpets on the floor and hangings covering the walls and the windows. The guides were dressed just like we were, but they had orange sashes around their necks and medallions. Tom Reeves, our trip conductor, wore a purple sash. Tom talked to us and to the guides. They played some music to get us into the right frame of mind, and then we went to our separate game rooms, where we would spend the greater part of the next three days.

The first game went on and on and on. I think there were ten or twelve people in my group. Some were very closed off.

Some were very open. The game was played gently at first, then more and more forcefully. Tom went from one game to another. He and the guide would pick a certain person and work on him, rank him something awful, beat him to death.

On the second day, without any sleep, people got kind of dingy. Things started to happen. The first guy that "broke" was this Puerto Rican from New York. He told how as a kid he and the other kids would find cats and dogs and torture them and throw them off the roofs. He felt so bad about this. He cried. That was the thing that most bugged him in his life, and the idea was to get these things out of people. There was a girl, Valerie, a square who'd moved into Synanon with her husband. When the game got on her she said she was afraid of people and thought that no one cared for her. She said she was unable to give of herself, to give love, because she was afraid of being rejected. I identified so strongly with her and felt such compassion, I couldn't find it in my heart to berate her. Frankie finally asked her, "Of all the people in this room, who is the one you're most afraid of but would want to have love you and be your friend?" She looked around the room. She said, "Art Pepper." And she turned her head away. She couldn't look me in the eye. Frank asked me what I thought of her. I said I thought she was a very sweet girl, and I would love to be her friend. I said, "I don't understand why you're afraid of me." She said, "You're so different from me. Your background . . . you've had such a hard life. I just feel that you hate people like me."

Frankie made us stand up in the middle of the room. He said to her, "Go to him. Put your arms around him." She couldn't do it. She cried and cried. I walked over to her and put my arms around her, and all of a sudden she completely broke down. She threw her arms around me and cried hysterically, and everybody in the room got up, and they surrounded us, and they were all crying, and they were all hugging us, and this lasted for ages, and it was such a release. And that's the way it went. One person would break, another person would break.

By the third day there were only a few that hadn't broke yet. I was one. During this time we went for walks together, we gathered in the ballroom and played charades, we performed skits, we went to meals, we went to the Woodshed and watched lightshows and movies. We had a Ouija session, and the Ouija talked to some of the people on the trip. It talked to me: "There's someone who's trying to hide the fact that he's desperately in need of love. He has to give in and accept people into his life. He has to give of himself. That person's name is Art Pepper."

During the last game they worked on the people who hadn't broken. Tom came in and ranked me and put me down some more, and everybody in the game group joined in, and finally I just stood up and started screaming, "Fuck the world! Fuck all you people! No one cares! Everyone's phony. Nobody cares about me! I've spent ten years in prison because of a fuckin' rat, supposed to be a friend of mine! My mother never wanted me! My wife left me as soon as I went to jail!" I went on and on. "Because I was white I was never really accepted in jazz! I've suffered all my life, and I've never done anything wrong!" Frankie said, "We *know* that's a lie. No one is that perfect. No one is that perfect. What have you done?" I tried to think. I started to tell him about the girl I'd raped in England but I said, "She led me on!" Frank just laughed at me. He said, "You don't feel bad about that. What have you done?" I told about slapping my daughter's hand when she wouldn't eat her dinner, and then I remembered that my father had done the same thing to me. That was wrong. I said, "But I never ratted on anybody! I never burned anybody!" He said, "You *must* have done something. Everybody's done something wrong. Isn't there anything that you'd like to tell us about to ease your conscience, something that's bothering you?" And all of a sudden it hit me about Wally:

I had gotten out of Tehachapi with a five-year tail. Diane was working at a TV station as a receptionist and telephone operator, and we were living in an apartment behind Otto's Barbershop on Sunset toward the Strip. I was on the Nalline program. I lasted for about three months, and then I couldn't make the tests anymore so I went to stay at Ann's house down in Manhattan Beach, to hide, because I was afraid my parole officer was going to pick me up and send me back to the joint with a violation.

One day Diane called me up in Manhattan Beach. A friend

of mine had called and wanted to score an ounce. Diane was going to do it for him, and we would get a portion of the stuff for scoring. Ann and I decided to go up to town to make a taste. We drove to Hollywood to my place. Diane wasn't there. On the door was a note from my parole officer saying that if I would call him he'd give me a break. The note was dated that day so I figured he'd gone home. I figured it was probably cool to go into the pad. I opened the door with my key. We waited and waited. Finally we hear a noise, we hide, the door opens, and it's Diane. I hadn't seen her for several days, and she's supposed to be my wife, you know, but there's no thought of hello or a kiss. It's just, "Have you got anything?" "Yeah, let me go first." "Ohhhh, man!"

We went into the bathroom and cooked up the heroin, and I hit her. Ann says, "Why don't you let me go next?" "*I'm* next." After I'd fixed and fixed Ann, Diane said, "Something awful just happened." And she told us this story.

"I copped from Wally. This friend of yours came by, left the bread, and I called Wally. I went over and laid the bread on him." They went to East L.A. and scored and came back and gave the guy his ounce. He'd given them four hundred fifty dollars and Wally had gotten two ounces for a hundred ninety each. Then they'd taken the other guy's ounce and cut it with milk sugar; so he got about two-thirds of an ounce for four hundred fifty dollars and Diane and Wally split the bread and the dope that was left.

Wally was a heavy set, kind of a Buddha-looking guy, a Mexican guy, a good friend. He had a little beat pad in a court. He and Diane went to this place and into his breakfast nook to divide the stuff and fix. Wally was drunk. That was his failing. He liked the kick of drinking and fixing. He fixed and then, as Diane looked on, the sweat started pouring out of him and his eyes went back in his head. She said, "Wally, Wally, are you cool?" He fell and his head hit the table right in the pile of heroin. She tried to raise his head and brush the heroin off his hair and face so she wouldn't lose any of it. She slapped him. She went and got some water and put it on him. She just goofed around. One time when *she* had gone out, I'd filled three droppers with milk and shot them into her vein and saved her life. All she did was slap him and holler at him and rub his wrists.

Then she panicked. She picked up our portion of the stuff, turned out the lights, and came back to the pad. And she hadn't said a thing to us until we'd all fixed.

I said, "We've gotta do something! Let's go!" Ann said, "You can't go, Art. He lives right in Hollywood in a court. There's people all around." Diane said, "I know he's dead! I'm sure he's dead! That's why I came back. There's no use you going. Why should you go to prison if he's already dead? It wasn't your fault. He's the one that got drunk. I *told* him not to drink!" I still felt bad because I liked the guy. I said, "Go back. If you can't revive him be sure you wipe your fingerprints off the place."

They went to Wally's. He hadn't moved. Ann, who's pretty hep, checked his pulse, took a mirror, and held it up to his mouth. He was dead. Diane grabbed up the remaining heroin and went through his pockets. She got all his money and found out he hadn't paid as much as he'd said. He'd got the stuff for a hundred fifty dollars an ounce. She said, "That bastard! He overcharged me!" Ann is wiping the doorknobs. She looks around and sees Diane—evidently Wally had been boosting and he had a lot of clothes in the pad—Diane was going through the stuff, grabbing this and that. Not only does she have his money and his dope, she's going to take the clothes, anything that'll fit. Ann says, "Are you kidding? Let's get outta here!" They come back. Diane says, "Well, look what we got!" And she threw down the money and the rest of the dope. She was all happy, and she had new clothes. We went into the bathroom and fixed again.

A couple of weeks later I'm in the county jail waiting to go to Chino for a six-month dryout, and I get a visit from my parole officer. We talk. He says, "By the way, I thought you might be interested in this." He knew that Wally and I were friends. He hands me a clipping about this guy who was discovered in a little court in Hollywood all bloated and turned blue. They found him by the smell.

I said, "But what could I have done? What could I have done? He was already dead!" But, "Oh, God," I said, "What really bothers me is the fact that I left him there in the house to rot, that I drove by the place and knew he was there, but I was afraid to call the police." And I felt Wally knew. I said, "But he's dead. If he was alive I could seek him out and ask him to forgive me!" Frankie said, "Look around the room. Is there anybody here who reminds you of Wally?" I looked at Frankie. I said, "God! *You* do!" He said, "Alright. Are you really serious? If you're not being real, it won't do any good."

Frankie lay down on the floor in the middle of the room. He crossed his hands on his chest. He said, "I'm Wally and I'm dead." You could hear a pin drop. I got down on my knees and stayed there looking at him, and he *was* Wally and he *was* dead. He said, "Art, I thought you were my friend. I thought we were tight. All the good times we had. All the favors we did for one another. I *know* you couldn't have saved my life, but why, why did you leave me sitting there, rotting away? Why didn't you call someone and have them take me and embalm me and put me in the ground? You know I wouldn't have left *you* like that." I said, "Oh God, Wally, I'm so sorry! I was afraid. I was afraid that they'd catch me and put me in jail. I was afraid they'd recognize my voice if I called on the telephone or that they'd trace the call. I was just afraid, and I felt so guilty about taking your dope and spending your money. I had nightmares about it. Wally, please forgive me!" And I started crying. I threw my arms around Frankie and hugged him. I said, "Wally, please forgive me! Please forgive me!" And Wally said, "I forgive you, Art. I understand. I can rest now, and I want you to be at peace, too." Everybody cried and gathered around us, and I felt such a warmth for Frankie and for everybody in the room. I went to them and kissed them and held them. I kissed this Puerto Rican who I'd hated because he'd tortured animals. It had been haunting him all his life. I forgave everybody. I felt that I'd been cleansed. I felt that I was floating on air.

At the end of the trip, we gathered in the Woodshed again. The ballroom downstairs was packed with people waiting for us. Somebody went down and gave word to the house that the trip was breaking. I had seen it happen. I had played for it with the band, but this was different. We came down in our robes, all of us kind of funky, all the faces swollen from crying and from not sleeping, and we looked really angelic, really beautiful, so pure and real. Everybody was touched by love, even the guides, and we walked down into the house, and the band started playing, and everyone rushed onto the floor and grabbed us and held us, and everybody was crying, and there was such a closeness. And it wasn't a sexual thing. It was just a real honest thing of love.

In Synanon your mind was completely free of the fears people outside use up their energy worrying about. You didn't have to think about food or rent or doctor bills. You didn't have to worry about what you were going to do when you got old, if you got ugly, if you lost a leg. The first tribe leader I had, Bob Holmes, had kidney trouble. He'd had an operation and the only way he could live was through a dialysis machine. Those machines are hard for people to get the use of, but because he was in Synanon and because of the money and power and influence Synanon has, Bob had access to a dialysis machine each week, as he needed it. If he'd been on the streets, living in some beat shack in Cleveland or Watts, he would have died. So all you had to do was accept these changes and periodic humiliations and you had nothing to worry about.

As far as sex went—Laurie and I went to the guestroom two or three times a week, and it was great. When we went we'd really be ready to make love; it was a place of love. Every now and then we'd get an extra day or an extra night—somebody had canceled—and we'd just have a ball. There was never once that we didn't enjoy it and didn't make love. Oh, a couple of times we had an argument for some ridiculous reason or other and didn't go, but the rest of the time—and this was for two and a half years, twice a week, every week—never once was there a failure. Never once was I unable to get an erection. Never once did I not come. Never once did she not come. It was perfect.

Sometimes I wonder if I had been able to go to Synanon as a seventeen- or eighteen-year-old, I wonder what might have happened with my life. Well, everything was going fine. I was blowing. Every now and then somebody would come in from the outside to play. Phil Woods dropped by, one of the greatest alto saxophone players living. He's a fan of Charlie Parker's. He's such a fan that when Bird died, Phil Woods got ahold of Chan, Charlie Parker's old lady, and he wooed her and wooed her and finally he married her. And he got Bird's horn when he married her. I don't know if he married her because he loved her or because she was Bird's old lady or to get the horn or what.

Hahahaha! They were together for a long, long time. He's a great player. I loved blowing with him, and I played beautifully, and I realized then than that was what I had to do. I had to play. But, as the people asked me in games, would I be playing like that if I was on the streets? They told me, "You'd be dead." I figured I'd better stay where I was.

Then something happened that turned everything around. There was an old guy in Synanon, Reid Kimball, a close friend of Chuck's, and he was dying of emphysema. He had to stop smoking. The doctors told Chuck that he should stop, too, but he couldn't. So all the kids in Tomales Bay, the fanatical followers, they got together with Chuck and said, "To help you stop we're going to stop smoking."

At first it was a voluntary thing. Then rumors started going around. Finally, one night a general meeting was called in the ballroom. I remember it was mobbed. I had a hard time finding a place for Laurie to sit. She sat down on a little rampway; I stood next to her, watching Jack, who was about to speak, and I had a strange premonition. I hadn't been so scared for a long time. Jack started talking about Reid and Chuck: "The founder has to stop smoking because he is also developing a lung condition." He went on to talk about how much things cost us, how we could get everything donated *except* cigarettes. Cigarettes was our biggest expense. "The kids in Tomales Bay have already stopped smoking. What do you say?"

It didn't stay voluntary long. Soon another general meeting was called and Chuck appeared in person and told us that smoking cigarettes would henceforth be as forbidden as the use of drugs and physical violence. After that meeting I went back to my dorm and took all my cigarettes and stashed them—in trash cans, under plants, all over. For a while it was an honor thing. People were supposed to turn in all their cigarettes, but you could still smell smoke in the air. Then they went through one of those crash-break-'em-down searches. Pretty soon almost everybody had stopped.

There were two bathrooms in my dorm. Next to my room was a little toilet and sink, and there was a fan over the toilet in the roof. You could turn the fan on, stand on the toilet, and the fan would suck the smoke out. I went in there every morning. I could hardly wait to get in there. We were put on restriction at that time, containment they called it, no walking, but I'd sneak away from the Clump and smoke at Santa Monica City College. In Santa Monica they have police helicopters that fly around. I got so panicked after sneaking around for a while that I was sure that the police helicopter was watching me at Santa Monica City College or wherever I was. I thought sure they knew I was in Synanon and that I was smoking and they were going to land and grab me. One of my duties on my job was to take the mail by car to the post office. I'd wrap two cigarettes in cellophane with a rubber band around them and stash them in my sock. I'd have a book of matches in my pocket. I carried gum and mouthwash and cologne. I smoked in the bathroom of the guestroom, and one time I was kissing Laurie and she started sniffing. She stuck her nose into my mouth. She said, "You've been smoking! You've been smoking!" She had her whole nose and half her head in my mouth: "You've been smoking!"

I couldn't stop smoking. People were turning in their husbands and wives. Guys were getting bald heads, losing their positions. I smoked like this for over a year and a half, every day. That's why I finally had to leave.

After I'd been in Synanon for about three years I knew I was as healthy as I was ever going to get, and I had to make a decision about what I was going to do next. I couldn't stay in Synanon and become a lifetime member. It was just a stopping-off place to straighten myself out before trying the world again. I wanted to play. The main thing was, I wanted to be free. I wanted to walk when I wanted to walk, smoke when I wanted to smoke; if I wanted to get loaded occasionally, I wanted to be able to do that. I'd stayed as long as I had because of Laurie. The thought of leaving her ... it was terrible. I couldn't imagine being without her, and I knew she'd never leave with me.

It was getting toward Christmas. That's always a hard time. I was at work, and a call came through on my telephone. It was Blackie Levinson. He'd been in Synanon two or three times while I'd been there, but I knew him from before, from jail. He'd split this last time about eight months ago. He asked me how I was doing. He said, "So-and-so is here, and So-and-so's here." They were all laughing. It seemed like they were having a ball. He said, "When are you leaving? Anytime you want to leave, you can stay at my place, you know. I can probably get you a job." His father owned a business. They sold electronic equipment.

I started thinking seriously about leaving then. And I thought that if Laurie really loved me, she would follow me. After I was gone she wouldn't be able to stand being without me. Blackie called a few more times and gave me a number where I could reach him.

Laurie and I were friends with a couple, life-stylers, who had an apartment in the Clump. They were going back east to visit their families for the holidays and told us we could stay at their place for a whole week while they were gone. Laurie sensed that I was leaving, even though I couldn't tell her. We had a wonderful week together in that apartment, and when it was over I gave Blackie a call and told him to come pick me up.

24 | The Return of Art Pepper

1971-1978

BLACKIE was a great big cat, about six, six; he looked like he weighed four hundred pounds. He looked like Murder Incorporated. He came to get me the next evening. I got the stuff I was going to take and put it in Blackie's car. One of the guys looked out a window, and he shook his head and waved good-bye. Blackie backed out of the driveway of the Clump, and my first thought was of Laurie down at the main club getting ready for a game. I had a feeling that was half elation and half sadness. Blackie said, "Oh, man, it must be great to get out of that fuckin' place, fuckin' assholes!" The only thing I wanted now was to get loaded. I'd saved about twenty-five dollars from my WAM. I told him to stop at the first liquor store we came to, and I bought a pint of brandy. As soon as it hit me, I felt better.

Blackie lived in Inglewood in one of these nondescript apartment houses with a pool in the middle. There's a million of them in Southern California. We got to his pad and sat down, and I asked him, "Man, did you save me any methadone?" I knew he was on the program. He said, "Oh, man, I'm sorry. I can't. I need every bit that I get." I said, "Well, I thought you'd save me some." He said, "Don't worry. I knew you'd have eyes to score. How much money have you got?" He called up a guy we both knew, Fred, that used to be in Synanon. He talks and gives me a kind of a smile. "Ok. We'll see you." He hangs up the phone. "I told you I wouldn't let you down. Everything's straight. Fred's dealing."

Fred came over. I got loaded. I forgot about Laurie, about my problems. It was a great night. I woke up the next morning, and I thought, "What am I going to do now?" I had no money. Blackie had a day job. He'd get up real early in the morning and drink his methadone; he'd go to work—"I'll see you about four o'clock"—and leave me sitting there thinking about Laurie and wondering what I was going to do.

Blackie tried to talk me into getting on the methadone program. He got a friend of his, Carl, to drive me to the Veteran's Hospital at Brentwood. I had an interview with a secretary. She asked about my health. I mentioned that I had cirrhosis. She said, "That ends that. You won't be able to get on the program, because methadone is very bad for your liver." This girl just confirmed my fears. I'd already had it in my mind, that I'd die if I got on the methadone program.

I went on like this for a while, hustling Blackie, trying to get money from him so I could score a couple more times. That was all I could do, drink and score. Blackie was getting drug. He was mad at me because he felt I didn't really try to get on the program. He said I could have got on if I'd really forced it. Nothing was happening for Blackie. His father owned a big factory, but Blackie had blown all that. He was driving a truck for the Salvation Army.

One day I got a phone call from someone who'd been in Synanon with me, inviting me to a party. A group of people who'd left Synanon and hung out together had heard that I was out and staying with Blackie, and they wanted to help me. They looked down on Blackie; they felt he wasn't really trying to help himself. He was trying as hard as he could. They invited me to a party at an apartment in Hollywood. Blackie drove me. I said, "Why don't you come in?" He said, "No, no. I don't like those people."

There were fifteen or twenty "splittees" at this party. We ate and drank and reminisced about things that had happened at Synanon. They asked me how I felt about being away from Synanon. Did I miss Laurie? What was I going to do? I said I wasn't sure. I was afraid to get back into music for a lot of reasons. I didn't know whether I could make it, playing, after all this time, whether I could get back into a field which is very difficult and competitive, whether people would give me the opportunity, whether I was physically able. I realized that the only times I'd been really happy were when I was working, like in the Paymaster's Office in San Quentin or in bookkeeping in Synanon, so I was thinking about getting a job where I wasn't playing music all the time, just playing for kicks and holding a job where I could make a living in another type of endeavor.

Bob and Nikki Deal had a proposition to make me. Bob had recently opened a health food bakery in Venice, Good Stuff Bread. They lived next door to the bakery; they had an extra room, and they told me if I'd like, I could stay with them and work with Bob, helping around the bakery, keeping the books. I told Bob I'd think about it. He told me he had a car, a little Honda that I could use. That was what finally made me decide to stay with them.

Carl drove me to Bob's house. Bob showed me my little room in the back of the house. It was a large house. In front was Nikki's studio; she was a commercial artist. My room was off the enormous kitchen and dining area. There was a desk and a bunch of windows, a bed in the corner, a chair, a big closet and a little bathroom with a shower, a toilet and sink. It was a nice room and very convenient. I could go in there and close the door and feel safe.

Bob made a heavy dark brown bread, supposed to be very good for you, and a carrot cake, a banana cake, and an apple cake all out of whole wheat. I took care of ordering the labels, ordering supplies, checking the big freezer making sure the bakers had enough to work with—nuts, honey, flour. I'd straighten the place up and get it ready for the day's work. I'd slice the bread and cakes and wrap them, put labels on them and price them. I'd set up the window display. I'd fill the orders and sometimes make deliveries. There were several delivery guys. Each had a sales book; he'd be billed for whatever he took out, and all that had to be watched, so they didn't cheat us. Sometimes I'd put on big rubber gloves and wash trays or sweep and mop the place. Then Bob would come in and say, "I'm going to take over for a little while so you can go do the books." I'd walk back to my room. I made out all the paychecks, took out the taxes, did the accounts payable and accounts receivable. I had to make everything match out. That was hard, hard, hard. Faye, my old boss in the Synanon bookkeeping department, was a splittee now, too. She'd come around once a month and help me when we made out a sheet that had to be sent in to the government. Every day I'd go to the bank and deposit all the money. Sometimes I'd have as much as twelve or fifteen thousand dollars. Then I'd go to the post office and pick up the mail. I'd take all the mail that had to do with the business and go through it.

The truck drivers came in at about three or four. I'd check them in. I'd take all the spoilage and throw it away and do an inventory on what they'd brought back. After they left, the people that worked in the bakery would want to talk to me—there wasn't enough of this left, or somebody had an argument with someone and I'd have to straighten them out. The phone would ring. Somebody didn't get their apple cake. The honey place would say they couldn't make their delivery. Bob would be in and out asking for things and giving orders. At five, I'd check out the register, take the cash to the house, put everything away.

At five thirty, we'd have supper. Nikki would come in with some Hamburger Helper or a salad. We had to eat at that particular time, and if we weren't on time, she'd flip out. We'd eat in the little living room in front of the TV, and then the dishes were put in the sink for Bob to wash. Sometimes I did it. After dinner, it was time for me to do the daily report. Bob usually went back to the bakery to fill last minute orders or experiment with new recipes.

At first the daily report took me two or three hours; it was very complicated. I used an adding machine and made everything jibe. I'd enter all this into the books and put all the slips into the files. I wrote to Laurie, telling her how well I was doing and asking her to join me. She called Bob and Nikki to make sure. Then she left Synanon and got a little apartment nearby in Venice. She got a job at the bakery.

I was happy being in something legitimate. Bob told me I'd get a percentage of the business. I was only getting my room and food and ten dollars a week, but it seemed as if I'd have a good future, financially, and not have to play in clubs anymore.

Bob's house was a visiting place for people who'd left Synanon. This drummer, Lew Malin, came down, and he had a thing going with a musical office; they booked bands for parties. He had a lot of say-so as to who did the gigs, and he said that if I would learn the Jewish tunes for the weddings and bar mitzvahs, he could get me some gigs. He loaned me some money.

While I'd been in Synanon, a guy had written me a letter from the University of Denver. He asked if I'd be interested in doing a "clarinet clinic." He explained that I would go to the school and lecture and play a concert for the kids who would pay to attend this thing and to associate with me and learn from me. He'd heard me on clarinet on *Plus Eleven* and on an album I'd done with Henry Mancini called, *Combo*. I'd told him, "I can't travel while I'm in Synanon, but I've been thinking of leaving." He said, "Well, if you do leave, let me know right away. Call me collect." I borrowed a clarinet from Les Koenig and gave this guy a call. He was really happy. He told me he'd pay me a lot of money and my expenses. I decided to go.

At these clinics, representatives of musical instrument companies—Selmer, Conn, Buffet, and so on—sometimes set up displays of their horns, trying to sell horns to the students. In Denver, I struck up a friendship with a guy named Ken Yohe who was working for Chicago Musical Instrument Company at that time, handling Buffet. He'd been a fan of mine for years. He asked what kind of clarinet I was using. It was some obscure French model; he'd never heard of it. Nobody had. He said, "Why don't you use one of ours?" A Buffet clarinet is one of the best made. I used it and played very well, even though I was playing with classical players from all over the world. When the clinic ended, Ken told me his company might be interested in having me work for them, play their horns, do clinics for them. He said he could probably arrange for me to get some Buffet horns. About this same time, Lew Malin was talking to me about playing these casuals. I told him, "If I get these horns, maybe I can do it."

I didn't think anything would really happen with this because of my past. I couldn't see them sending instruments like that, that cost so much money, to a person like me, but a couple of weeks after the clinic in Denver, a United Parcel truck pulls up in front of Laurie's apartment and a guy comes and knocks on the door. He's got several big packages addressed to me. I open them. There's a brand-new Buffet alto sax, a tenor sax, a clarinet, and an Armstrong flute. A couple of days later, here's a letter from Ken:

August 29, 1972

Dear Art:

I am most pleased that you have received the instruments I sent you and that they got there without any damage, and I am very happy that you like the instruments. . . .

Art, believe me when I tell you that I am extremely happy that you have decided to accept the Veteran's Hospital offer of getting you on their methadone program. The most important thing for either you or me to consider at this point in your life, is for you to gain complete health and freedom from this disease. Regardless of what either your future plans or my future plans might hold for you, it is absolutely necessary for you to regain your health and well being.

Even though there may be a few additional months involved, this period of time would also give you the opportunity to do lots of practicing, perhaps develop some new ideas musically speaking, and really explore the instruments on which you will be playing . . . .

I needed the methadone program. A friend, Tom, had been bringing me codeine tablets at the bakery; I was using them every day; I was getting hooked; I didn't realize how strong they were. Another friend was chippying with heroin, so, before I realized what was happening, I was getting a heroin habit again. My old friend, Ann Christos and her husband, John were living in Hollywood; they were on the methadone program. I ran into them, and they sold me some of their methadone; I'd drink one hundred, two hundred milligrams of methadone several times a week, and I was drinking a six-pack a night of malt liquor.

They were getting suspicious at the bakery. I quit. I wanted to move in with Laurie, but she wouldn't let me unless I straightened out. She wanted me to get on the methadone program. I went down to the Veterans Hospital but didn't say anything about my liver. I passed. I got on the program, and to my amazement, the methadone got me loaded, and I had no desire to use heroin. I had found a cure for heroin addiction.

Methadone is a drug that's given to you every day, in a liquid, by mouth, and once you have the methadone in you, you can fix and you don't feel the heroin, unless you fix such a huge amount that you're almost ready to die—I did try it several times. The program itself is just wonderful. I saw friends of mine that had been armed robbers and burglars, hustling and stealing to support their habits. They got on the methadone program and started leading regular lives, working. And those were people I never would have dreamed could be straight and hold down a regular day job. For me, it was a panacea. I couldn't believe that they were actually giving me a drug that got me loaded and killed my desire to shoot heroin. I moved in with Laurie. A few months earlier, we had started taping this book.

Everything was fine. I went to work for Lew Malin, playing casuals, and going out to colleges all over the country for Buffet, doing clinics. The clinics started really rolling in, and I liked them. The kids looked up to me. They called me "sir" and "Mr. Pepper." The highschool and college bands, instead of playing all rock and roll, were getting into jazz, learning about swing and bebop. I collected big band arrangements from writers I knew—Don Piestrup, Don Menza, and from the Kenton organization, and I built up a library. When I'd get called for a clinic, Laurie would send three or four arrangements to the college, so the kids could learn their parts, and then, when I got there, I'd rehearse them, polish them up, and we'd give a concert. I'd play the solo part. I'd talk to them and tell them how they were doing as section players, as soloists, and I told them how I'd learned to play jazz, learned chords. It was very gratifying. I gave them a long talk, each time. It was beneficial to them, and even more so to me, because it made me feel that my life was worthwhile.

The kids were usually awestruck, especially after I showed them what I could do. If they hadn't really heard of me, before I even started talking, I'd take out my horn and play and beat them down with my playing. Once I had shown off, technique-wise and chord-wise and soul-wise, they *had* to look up to me. I talked about dope sometimes, what they'd be headed for. And usually I'd stay a couple of days, and I'd talk to the kids in the hallways or over breakfast, they'd ask me questions. For that I got the horns, my airfare, expenses, and a fee for doing the clinic. That did a lot for my self esteem.

Moving in with Laurie was a great help to me too. I still wasn't completely honest with her, and we had some hassles, but I was doing the best I could except for drinking. That really became a problem. Finally, one day, Laurie moved out. She said she wouldn't come back until I stopped. I realized what the drinking was doing to my health. I consented to take antabuse. If you drink while you're taking antabuse, you get terribly sick. It looked like all I'd be able to do was take methadone and smoke—cigarettes. I don't like marijuana anymore. It makes me nervous. I was buying extra methadone from Ann and John twice a week. I stopped drinking to excess. Every now and then, I'd stop taking the antabuse and goof. I always felt awful afterwards.

(Ann Christos) Art was working at the bakery in Venice. Someone told us he was there so John and I drove out to see him. A few days later he called and asked us if we could score for him. He came to Hollywood in that little tiny car. John and I were both on the state methadone program, but we did score for him—and for ourselves. That was the only time, and the stuff had no effect on us; we thought we'd been burned. But Art fell out. The methadone was just blocking the heroin; it was doing its job. Not long after that we drove out to the bakery again to give Art some methadone. Laurie was there. That's the first time we met her and she was very cold. I told John I understood why. She thought we were leading Art astray, but actually we thought that meth would be good for him. John was trying to convince him to get on the program. We thought it would be his salvation.

Art was quiet—like I've always known him to be when he's not working in music and hasn't anything in sight. Lethargic. No goals. No pleasure in anything. We would talk to him at times, though, and get laughs out of him. When you get Art goin', you know, he's funny. Even after he got on the program he'd come to buy meth a couple of times a week, and we used to look forward to his coming down. It was time to talk and crack up. We saw a lot of him, and our relationship with Laurie grew. We saw the way she was handling him. He was stagnating, playing those Jewish weddings. Actually I think Laurie's the one that pulled him to the fore. I think it was all her energy that got it together. Laurie's very feminine. She's very petite, pretty, with china doll features. She has a bright, bright smile and a keen mind. She wouldn't cater to Art or indulge his depressive attitude. She just soared right on ahead, kept on cookin'. She sort of turned it around and laughed at all his little woe-isms.

———————————

LAURIE pushed me, in music, and she took care of a lot of things I couldn't deal with—arranging the clinics, writing to the colleges, answering the phone. When the phone rings I get terrified. I never know what it's going to be. She shielded me from a lot of people from my past . . . so that I wouldn't get involved with them.

We had lived in Venice, which we loved very much, but the place was tiny, and our rent kept going up, and I was getting so much work. We decided to move to the valley. That's where all the musicians are stationed. The valley is a great point of departure. We found a little frame house, very reasonable rent, and we've been there ever since.

In 1975, Les and I got together again, and we made a new album, *Living Legend*. I was very proud of that. In 1976, Don Ellis, the trumpeter and bandleader, called me and asked me if I'd like to join his band. It was an extremely modern band with a lot of amplified and electronic instruments. And instead of just four beats to the bar, like all jazz music, except for 3/4 waltz time, his arrangements would be in 5/4, 7/4, 9/8. It was difficult to read the parts; it was very hard to feel the beat and to play jazz solos. I figured it would be good for my name, to get that experience. People would look up to me because a lot of the real good players in my age group were afraid to go with that band, afraid they might not be able to cut it and word would get around. I wanted to be thought of . . . I could do anything. There was a guy in the saxophone section, we'll call him Phil, a very nice guy, he gave me a lot of help. I had to play piccolo, flute, clarinet, alto. We played at a big place on the strip, a rock and roll place, and we played an arrangement I was featured on, all the way through, "Invincible." It opened up with just myself and an amplified cello. I went through all the changes and time patterns. I got a standing ovation. I stayed with Don as long as I could, but the band was going to Europe and the money was nothing to what I could get on my own, so I left. I had a lot of great moments with Don Ellis.

ART PEPPER
"I'M HERE TO STAY!" *by Charles Marra*

When jazz enthusiasts, musicians, critics and historians hear the name Art Pepper, the universal reaction is that here is a musician who has done much with his alto saxophone, a champion of the cause of inventiveness, lyricism, and vigorous emotional warmth.

Arthur Edward Pepper, then, is recognized as a brilliant musician, yet little has been heard of—or from—him in recent years. His career has not exactly been a bed of roses.

But here is some welcome and happy news: Art Pepper is alive and well, living in California and a participant in what he terms "a life-saving methadone program administered by the Veterans Association. The program has been the biggest factor in my re-awakened interest in life and in music.

"I feel absolutely certain that the past that—past! I have no fear whatsoever of any future hangups. I'm here to stay . . . ." down beat, *March 1, 1973. Copyright 1973 by* down beat. *Reprinted by special permission.*

ART PEPPER LIVING LEGEND *by Doug Ramsey*

. . . He has overcome the monster and emerged from the struggle a strengthened person and deeper artist.

. . . Aside from the free aspects of Pepper's playing today, the listener will hear an emotional concentration, a cry, sometimes a sob and sometimes a joyous shout- that come from the wisdom of experience. In that sense, this is autobiographical music, a testatment of the artist's life.

...On the blues called Mr. Yohe, the section builds such a powerful swing, that by the 13th of his 15 choruses, Pepper has been propelled to an intensity that for a few bars becomes nearly unbearable. It is a cathartic listening experience .... He is a virtuoso but not an exhibitionist.

...Art Pepper was never really away in the minds of serious listeners, but it is satisfying to know he is well, happy, and again creating important music. *Radio Free Jazz, September, 1976.*

I'D ONLY tried cocaine a couple of times in my life, when I'd shot it; it made me very nervous. One night we were playing some club with Don Ellis' band, and this guy, Phil, said there was an old friend of mine from San Quentin in the audience. I hadn't seen the guy in years. Phil says, "Come on , we'll meet him." This guy was Phil's coke connection. He asked me, "Would you like to have a little toot?" I enjoyed it, sniffing it. The guy came around again and again. I found myself really liking it, not realizing how expensive it was. That was my start into coke. I liked it better and better, and, of course, I started paying for it—more and more. But I felt I deserved it. Ann and John had moved away. I'd fallen into the habit of buying a "treat" from them, extra methadone, once or twice a week. They wouldn't let me overdo it. It gave me a little buzz. It was something to look forward to. It kept me out of trouble. Now they were gone. I started using cocaine the same way.

Coke is sort of an upper. But it gives you a feeling that's very hard to describe. You're animated, interested in things, and, as withdrawn a person as I am, it made me very gregarious. And it made me really love music again, as I had when I was a kid. But it was just the pattern of my past, using heroin, using Cosanyl, using codeine, using alcohol. Coke was the most insidious of all. It wreaks such havoc on your body and your mind. You stay up day and night. You don't eat. And the more you use it, the more you like it. I got to the point where, when I didn't have it, I had no energy at all and I'd become very depressed. I felt I couldn't play without it. I couldn't live without it. It was controlling me. Maybe it isn't addictive as a physical thing, but it really gets you messed up. And it's against the law.

My records were really selling in Japan. I was considered the number one jazz alto player over there. I couldn't believe it. I was asked to go to Japan, but we weren't sure, because of my past, whether I could get into the country or whether I could take my methadone with me. It worked out, and I went with Cal Tjader and did three concerts. It was very hard, even for that short time, to do without coke. I took enough to last me on the plane trip. Just before we landed in Tokyo, I went to the bathroom and did the last of it. I couldn't take the chance. If they decided to shake me down it would have been suicide.

Friday, April 8, 1977

Dear John and Ann:

Our trip to Japan was beautiful. Both Laurie and I thought maybe the reported popularity and record sales I was supposed to have in Japan might be just another shuck; neither of us related that feeling to the other as we didn't want to rank the other's trip. Even Les Koenig, who owns my record company had his doubts about my getting into the country. So you can imagine the pressure we felt before my first appearance on stage. To make these feelings worse was the fact that the promoter didn't know I would even be admitted into the country until I actually got through customs and was waiting for the car to take us to the hotel. So no advertising was done on me. Everything, stories, tickets, programs, ads, marquees, etc., had only Cal Tjader Sextet on them. He's not very well known there, so the first concert in Tokyo had a very poor advance sale and it was in a gigantic theater with two balconies. As soon as the word was out that I was actually there, they added a one page flyer to the program and added my name, where possible, to the posters, but the time was just too short to reach the people in a city the size of Tokyo. It at least made a terribly small crowd a respectable one. Naturally, I wasn't aware of all this at the time, so I got angry, and my ego took a beating. I couldn't figure out why all the written material said THE CAL TJADER TOUR instead of the ART PEPPER—Cal Tjader TOUR. I wouldn't ask anyone because I was too hurt and angry. To add to my bad feelings, my contract stated that Cal's rhythm section would be required to learn all the arrangements. I had given the arrangements to Jimmy Lyons a month before we left for Japan. I spent several days and nights writing out all the parts in ink, putting them in plastic sheets with complete beginnings and endings, solo orders, etc. in individual folders, one for each instrument—plus Laurie recorded on cassettes each tune, one cassette for each instrument. We gave all that to Jimmy Lyons, and we were promised he would give them to Cal who would give them to his rhythm section with the word that they must each learn all the charts so that when we arrived in Japan a short rehearsal would be all that would be required. We made sure this was in writing. Cal showed each guy his packet for a few minutes. They said there wouldn't be any problem, so he collected them, put them in his briefcase and carried them to Japan with him. I learned this while waiting for the Japan Airlines 747 in San Francisco. Before the first concert, my also-promised long rehearsal lasted about eight minutes. So you can see I was pretty drug when I was about to go on stage after the intermission, allowed only four tunes which had to be all standards. Laurie went out into the audience. The intermission ended. I was called to the wings and introduced by Cal Tjader. Then I started a slow walk to the microphone. The minute my body became visible, the audience started clapping and cheering. It continued, getting louder and louder, until I reached the mike. I stood there for at least 5 minutes, bowing and waiting for them to stop and feeling the most beautiful feeling I think I've ever felt in my life. Laurie later told me that the feelings of warmth and love were so strong that she just started crying like a baby. I knew then that it wasn't another shuck, another injustice, another disappointment. It was real. Retribution? Maybe—whatever it was, it justified my whole existance, my whole past, my whole life!

In '76, I'd made another album for Contemporary. *The Trip.* The '75 album, *Living Legend,* was excellent, and I thought, after that, the next album couldn't possibly be as good. It was even better. It got a lot of praise. It's one of my favorite albums of all time, and it pushed me into the limelight a little bit. I got an offer to tour the east coast. I'd never toured before as an individual. Here I was in my fifties, and I'd finally made it. I was invited to perform at the Newport Festival. I was scared, so I didn't carry any coke with me. I played in Toronto for a week, then New York. On the last day of my appearance at the Village Vanguard, a friend, to my surprise, offered me a taste of coke. I had the money, so I decided I'd use a little bit during the tour.

Pretty soon I was staying up all night long, writing music in the toilets of our hotel rooms, sitting on the tile floor, sniffing coke.

By the time I got to Chicago, I was really strung out on coke. I asked around at the methadone program there if anyone knew a connection. We had rented a car, so I drove all over the city looking for some way to score. I wound up in an industrial area near a methadone clinic, and I saw a black guy and his old lady in an old, beat car. They were stalled or something. I drove over and introduced myself. I asked them if I could help them out. I said, "You wouldn't know where I could get any coke?" The guy said, "Yeah." They took me to an old boarded-up building in the black ghetto of Chicago. It was filthy, no running water. We shot the coke instead of sniffing it. I got an outfit.

We went to Boston and Dayton and back to New York. Les Koenig came out from L.A. to record me, three nights, live, at the Village Vanguard. On the third night I had a fight with Laurie. On top of the coke I'd been buying huge quantities of extra methadone from another friend in New York. Laurie had stolen some of my money to pay the hotel bill, and I hit her, and she left the room. I knelt down to snort some coke off the little bedside table. It had a glass top. I hadn't slept in days so I passed out with my head on this table and the glass cut my cheek and made an indentation in my face. Laurie came back and woke me up. I looked in the mirror. My eyes were all puffy and I had this mark across my face. I'd had no sleep in days, hadn't been eating. I'd lost about twenty pounds on this trip. None of my clothes fit me. I shot the rest of my coke, and they practically carried me to the Village Vanguard for the final night of recording.

(Hersh Hamel) Art got out of Synanon, and he came around to my house while I was out on the road. He was working at a bakery or something. He had just broken up with Laurie and he was really moanin' the blues to my old lady. My old lady said that he stayed there that night and after the second day it was just too much for her. She started to get real depressed. It was just too heavy for her, because he was moanin' the blues so bad.

Laurie is the most positive woman that he's had. The most able to help, to really help. The others tried with very little success. She's the firmest and also she doesn't mess around with any dope which is good for him. He's got to have somebody that's removed from that. And also she's been able to make him look at himself as no one else has been able to do. That's good for him. Sometimes, I feel, you know, I've thought she seemed a little overprotective. Regardless, my main impression is that she's helped him more than any other woman. I was a little taken aback when I met her. I didn't expect him to have an old lady like that. She was really enthusiastic about the music. She wasn't super cool. More extroverted. More honest, able to show her feelings and not playing the "I'm a jazz musician's wife" scene. I was very happy for him.

I have to say that there was one time that amazed me. Art went to New York or something. Came back. And he looked like he was gonna die. He played at Donte's one night, and he looked like he was sixty years old. Then he played at Donte's about three weeks, a month later, and he looked fifteen years younger than he was. His skin was beautiful. I was amazed. Amazed. I asked him, I says, "What did you do?" "Awwww," he says, "Laurie wouldn't let me out of the house."

I think Art still has the same main problem in his life. He can't accept success. Everytime success starts comin' his way, he starts his destructive behaviour. He just cannot seem to function with things going his way. Things start getting good he puts it in the toilet. I don't think he consciously wants to do that. It's just that he feels a lot of pressure under those circumstances, whatever it is in his psyche that makes him go crazy. He'll start doing well, and people'll start respecting him, and he'll start almost living down this terrible reputation he's had for, what, thirty-five years: big monstrous doper, outta control. He starts to get some success, and then he'll be going around Donte's and the other clubs that he's working asking people if they've got any coke to sell, any dope. He starts doing that number and man, the next thing I hear is, "Art's up to his old stuff again, isn't he?" Or, "That poor guy, man, can't ever get himself straightened out." And that's what I hear. From the other guys.

WE CAME back to L. A. Laurie did what she could, but I was completely out of control. She gave up on me. I was hanging out with the guy I knew from Quentin and with some other guys who lived out in Venice who dealt coke and played music. I'd jam with them, and they'd give me coke. Every minute of the day was spent in getting money, driving to score, and getting loaded. I pawned my horns. I'd sworn I would never do that again.

One day—I don't even know what happened—I'd been up all night, playing out of town, and I drove into town to get my methadone. Then I went to a friend's house and shot some coke and fixed some heroin, and the methadone on top of that, and the no sleep . . . I was driving my beautiful new car. In 1976, Les advanced us the money to buy this brand-new red Olds Cutlass Supreme Brougham with all the extras. I decided to turn left. To this day, I have no idea where I was going. I pulled into the left turn lane going too fast, and by the time I saw the cars stopped in front of me, waiting to turn, it was too late. I crashed into them. My head almost went through the windshield. The other people were injured slightly. I got out of the car and looked at this wreck. I was having memory lapses. I thought, "Boy, somebody sure got wiped out." I was walking around among all this glass. An ambulance came and the police, and the next thing I knew I was in a car going to jail.

I spent a week in jail. As it worked out, it cost us fifteen hundred dollars for the lawyer, a fine of about four hundred dollars and three more weekends in jail. One of the things that saved me was a contract I had for another tour of Japan. I think that impressed the judge or the D.A. Since I was on the methadone program, there was no point in putting me on probation. The methadone program can be very strict. I got thirty-six months summary probation.

In April of 1978, I toured Japan for nineteen days with my own group. We did eighteen concerts. It was really hard, and I had very little energy, because I wasn't using coke anymore. I was depressed and tired, but the audiences were wonderful. We played to packed houses. After the concerts, the fans would line up; they had all my albums, and they wanted my autograph.

I did do some heavy drinking in Japan after the concerts. I

came back to the U.S. and did a tour of Oregon. I was unbelievably tired, and my memory was failing me. I couldn't remember the words for things. I couldn't remember what tunes we were playing or how long we'd been playing. My fingers were stiff and hard to move. Laurie kept begging me to give it up and go home. I wouldn't do it. I didn't play the last night of the tour. I didn't even know if it was day or night anymore.

Laurie had called the V.A. from Oregon. When we got back to L.A., my counselor from the methadone program came to the house and took me to the hospital. I was fighting against it. I thought Laurie had ratted on me. When I checked in, the head psychiatrist asked me what month it was. I said it was March. It was June. I couldn't remember the name of the President of the United States.

They kept me in the hospital for about two months. I underwent a million tests. They found some brain damage, and they diagnosed anemia, in addition to the Thalassemia Minor I was born with. They gave me lots of food and vitamins and put me on an anti-depressant. By the time they let me go, I was more or less back to normal. Later, Laurie took me to her doctor who looked over my records and said my problems might be a result of my liver disease. I'd wanted to have another operation on my hernia. It's a blow to my ego to have my stomach stick out like that. The doctor at Kaiser said an operation could be fatal. My liver might not be able to handle the anesthetic.

My mother is dead. My father is dead. My daughter's grown up; she's a stranger. I've set up a barrier between us that I'm afraid to cross. I have very few friends, and one of the best of them, Les Koenig, died not long ago.

When my contract with Contemporary expired, several people asked me to do one-shot recordings. I was scared but I did one, *Among Friends*, and that helped restore my confidence, and then I signed with another company. I did my first album for them a few weeks ago. On it I played "Patricia" again, the ballad I wrote so many years ago. It came out very well. It might be the best thing I've ever recorded.

As for the future—physically, emotionally, I can't work very much. I can't take much pressure, but I do have to survive, and I do still want to play. I do still need to be accepted as an artist. But I want to be more than just a "jazz player" playing. I want to make the people forget the categories and hear what's really happening. I want to make them feel the joy or sadness. I want to make them open up and listen. That's what I've always wanted. I'll do the best I can.

JAZZ: PEPPER RETURNS WITH STYLE by *John S. Wilson*

. . . he has developed a clear, full-toned style, glistening with bright, glancing lines and bubbling, dancing phrases that flow easily. There is no suggestion of pushing or frenzy, and yet he projects a fiery intensity that becomes overt only occasionally, when he seizes a phrase and shakes it like a terrier.

Mr. Pepper shows an unusual sensitivity in his use of colors and textures, particularly in a slow, atmospheric piece ("Lost Life"), which carries a brooding air of sorrow that avoids obvious sentimentality. *The New York Times, June 23, 1977.*

NEWPORT JAZZ: ART PEPPER by *Robert Palmer*

. . . Art Pepper's appearance was an unqualified triumph. . . .the celebrated alto saxophonist . . . brought a lively and cohesive group and a precarious but riveting balance of technique and emotional intensity to his set. . . . *The New York Times, June 29, 1977.*

IN PRAISE OF ART PEPPER
ART PEPPER: THE WHITENESS OF THE WAIL by *Gary Giddins*

. . . His present work is alive with splintered tones, modal arpeggios, furious double timing, and acerbic wit. He continues to play from deep inside.

. . . He plays like a knowing athlete, trained and poised. *The Village Voice, July 4, 1977.*

SUDDENLY, ART PEPPER IS RED HOT by *John B. Litweiler*

. . . At no time was the extent of Pepper's total mastery clearer than in a particular version of "Straight Life." Pepper had been bummed out by some customers who'd talked through his preceding ballad; he unloaded by choosing an incredibly fast tempo, and then, as his solo progressed, *speeding it*. He managed to lose each of his accompanists, however briefly, to the absolutely vicious solo, and its most stunning feature was the perfect clarity of every note, even the smallest-valued passing ones. The theme of "Straight Life" is made up of broken phrases, and these served as the model for asymmetric, angular lines in a cathartic fury. Beyond the wealth of invention here, the demarcations of note values, lines, and space was surely an ultimate answer to any possible questions about Pepper's powers.

... Pepper, above all, is an architect of emotion .... [He] has proved the best show of 1977 in jazz .... *The Chicago Reader, July 29, 1977*.

(Marty Paich)   You know, there's honest musicians and there's dishonest musicians. Let me clarify that: An honest musician, to me, plays with his heart and soul and gives you his all, all the time. And then there's the dishonest musician who plays, and he gives you his all, but not all of the time. It's like a race horse. When Art plays, it's all, all the time. I never heard him lay back at any time, and that, to me, is an honest musician. And there aren't too many of them in the entire world.

(Don Menza)   There are a lot of pressures on an honest player like Art, pressures of having to create and perform. Some musicians ... Dizzy Gillespie can be a clown, make it look as if it's really easy and fun. However a lot of people don't have that outlet, and when things really get bad on the stage, they don't know how to grab a handle on it, how to hold it together. Dizzy can just loosen up immediately. And then there are people that do the total opposite; there are the Charlie Minguses ... take the bass and break it over the piano player's back, you know? You know what I'm talking about? But Art, I've seen him get super tense and not be able to really say what he wants to say, or say what he means, and I could see his knuckles turning white and see his color drain. And still not be able to cope with it. Maybe that's got something to do with his other problems. He's a super sensitive cat, and that shows in his playing. It's obvious. You listen to him play a ballad or a pretty lyrical song. A certain style is involved in that kind of playing. You can't be a cold-hearted bastard and be able to play that way. It's very obvious the kind of person he is underneath, regardless of what he may have been doing at one time or another. And I don't have on record, I don't know of anybody saying, "He turned around and beat me for this; he beat me for that." Anybody. Everybody feels bad that it hasn't worked out better than it already has for him.

(Shelly Manne)   Musicians should really sit down by themselves and realize what a great life they have. They're doing something they want to do. They're being creative. Very few people have an outlet for their creativity. They're getting paid for it, and, when gifted, get paid very well for it. They can travel all over the world, expenses paid. They eat the best food in the world. They have it made, especially when they have talent and are available and working. To destroy that by being irresponsible, unreliable, which are the main reasons that guys end up down the tubes . . .

What the hell. Art's playing because he wants to play. Hopefully, to make a great living. Hopefully, to be accepted by his peers. But he gets to that point, and when he's at that point it destroys him. He's got to turn his head around. He's got to realize that all those people write about him and there's a resurgence of Art Pepper because they love him. That's not a hate relationship. That's a love relationship. They dig what he's doing. They dig what he's been through. They understand what he's been through. And to see him come back and play great, that's what they want. That's why they're paying money at the door to come in. That's why they go to the concerts, write an article in the New Yorker, whatever the hell, about Art. Those are love things. People aren't trying to put pressure on him to destroy him again. He's got to get some psychiatric help if he thinks that. He's got to get his head turned around where he becomes selfconfident about those things. He's Art Pepper.

Everybody has inner doubts. You've got to realize that. But what can they do to you? Who's gonna do what to you? I want to play. I want to have fun. And you've got to realize that those great moments, when you're playing, when it's almost like self-hypnosis, when you're almost outside your body watching yourself play, and when everything you play turns to gold; nothing goes wrong; the group is swinging, and you can do anything you want, even things you thought you could never do . . . those moments don't happen everytime you pick up your horn. That's not possible. It's not possible.

———————

Conclusion

I WAS GIVEN a gift. I was given a gift in a lot of ways. I was given a gift of being able to endure things, to accept certain things, to be able to accept punishment for things that I did wrong against society, the things that society feels were wrong. And I was able to go to prison. I never informed on anyone. As for music, anything I've done has been something that I've done "off the top." I've never studied, never practiced. I'm one of those people, I knew it was there. All I had to do was reach for it, just do it.

I remember one time when I was playing at the Black Hawk in San Francisco. I forget the date, but Sonny Stitt was touring with Jazz At The Philharmonic. He came in, and he wanted to jam with me. He came in, and he says, "Can I blow?" I said, "Yeah, great" We *both* play alto, which is . . . It really makes it a contest. But Sonny is one of those guys, that's the *thing* with him. It's a communion. It's a battle. It's an ego trip. It's a testing ground. And that's the beautiful part of it. It's like two guys that play great pool wanting to play pool together or two great football teams or two magnificent basketball teams, and just the joy of playing with someone great, being with someone great . . . I guess it's like James Joyce when he was a kid, you know. He hung out with all the great writers of the day, and he was a little kid, like, with tennis shoes on, and they said, "Look at *this* lame!" They didn't use those words in those days. They said, "God, here comes this nut." And he told them, "I'm great!" And he sat with them, and he loved to be with them, and it ended up that he *was* great. That's the way Sonny felt; that's the way I've always felt.

I said, "What do you want to play?" Sonny says, "Let's play 'Cherokee.' " That's a song jazz musicians used to play. The bridge, which is the middle part, has all kinds of chord changes in it. It's very difficult. If you can play that . . . If some kid came around, and he wanted to play, you'd say "Let's play 'Cherokee,' " and you'd count it off real fast. I said, "Well, beat it off." He went, "One-two, one-two;" he was flying. We played the head, the melody, and then he took the first solo. He played, I don't know, about forty choruses. He played for an hour maybe, did everything that could be done on a saxophone, everything you could play, as much as Charlie Parker could have played if he'd been there. Then he stopped. And he looked at me. Gave me one of those looks, "All right, suckah, your turn." And it's *my* job; it's *my* gig. I was strung out. I was hooked. I was drunk. I was having a hassle with my wife, Diane, who'd threatened to kill herself in our hotel room next door. I had marks on my arm. I thought there were narcs in the club, and I all of a sudden realized that it was *me*. He'd done all those things, and now I had to put up or shut up or get off or forget it or quit or kill myself or do *something*.

I forgot everything, and everything came out. I played way over my head. I played completely different than he did. I searched and found my own way, and what I said reached the people. I played myself, and I knew I was right, and the people loved it, and they felt it. I blew and I blew, and when I finally finished I was shaking all over; my heart was pounding; I was soaked in sweat, and the people were screaming; the people were clapping, and I looked at Sonny, but I just kind of nodded, and he went, "All *right*." And that was it. That's what it's all about.

Afterword

THIS BOOK was begun in April, 1972, completed early in 1979, and first published in November of that year. Art died in June, 1982, but during the two and a half years between its publication and Art's death, STRAIGHT LIFE changed everything for him. It and the publicity around it revived and created interest in Art's career; there were television and radio interviews and articles in major newspapers and magazines worldwide. As a result, Art spent those last years performing almost continuously, all over the world, for the biggest and most receptive audiences he'd ever seen, and recording more albums (with more major jazz names) than he had during the whole rest of his life. All of that finally got him the critical and popular recognition he'd craved, and put him, finally, jazz-historically speaking, on the map. He confidently predicted that after he died he would at last be elected to the *down beat* Hall of Fame, and he was—beating out Sonny Stitt who died the same year. It would be easy to say, therefore, that Art died happy. But that isn't the whole story. Not the way Art would have told it.

STRAIGHT LIFE shows that Art valued honesty above fame, even above art. In the book, people refer to him as an "honest" musician. He believed that truth was beauty and vice versa, and, when he played, he felt he was expressing the beauty of his honest emotion—which he shaped into powerful music with his skill. He had to know—and say—what was really going on. He was obsessed with knowing and with being known and believed that a failure of honesty in his life would contaminate his soul and his music. I don't want to contaminate his story, so I'm going to try to finish telling it as truthfully as he would have. At least this is what the truth looks like to me—now.

Because the book played such a major role at the end, I'll say something first about how it was made.

When Art and I first became lovers and he began telling me his adventures, I thought, as did many other people who had heard them, that they should be in a book. I'd done some writing, but I knew I couldn't write this story. And I thought it would lose too much, it would lose Art, if it were *written* at all. One of my favorite books is Oscar Lewis's *The Children of Sanchez*. It's an oral history of a poor Mexican family. Lewis was a sociologist and the book was classified as sociology, but the statistical and political information it included were, it seemed to me, just a pretext for offering the true work—the most poetic, personal, revealing, and touching autobiography I'd ever read. I re-read it in Synanon. I thought Art and I might do a book with that kind of format and told him so. He liked the idea. After he left Synanon and then wrote to me, asking me to join him, I started thinking about it again. I'd studied cultural anthropology and folklore. Art could certainly talk. I was enamored of him, but I could be objective.

I left Synanon in 1972 in response to Art's letter—he was clean, he was working, and he loved me—though I didn't necessarily believe what he said. (Art could always lie, domestically, briefly and badly about whether or not he was using, but then he invariably eventually blurted out the truth, no matter what it cost him.) I told myself that I was joining him in order to do this book. I also suggested to myself that that was a rationalization; I loved him and wanted to be with him.

We got together in February. He wasn't clean, and I was far from sure we had a future, but I still wanted to try to do the book.

Art said he was willing to tell me his story, but he kept putting me off. He was awfully gloomy at that time. I finally cornered him one afternoon in April, turned on the tape recorder, and began by asking him if he believed he had genius. In answer to my question, he told me the story of his bandstand battle with Sonny Stitt which appears as the Conclusion to this book. When he finished talking, I said, "Wow!" and he started laughing happily at what was clearly a virtuoso piece of narrative. He told me to turn the machine off and began to talk enthusiastically about the possibilities of the book. I turned the machine back on and asked him why he wanted to do a book about his life. He said,

> Well, the reason I want to get the book started is because I feel a real sense of urgency, because I feel something pulling at me, and I've been wanting to withdraw and hide. Just miserably unhappy. I can feel this presence. And the presence is death. Before I started talking into the tape recorder, I had nothing to say. I did not exist. I do not exist. My life is lived. My life is finished. But in talking about the past I see that then my life has meaning. So I want to tell my story. I think that's the only way I can give any meaning to my life, for having lived the life I've lived, is by having people know it. And get something out of it. *Feel* something from it.

During the next months we began to tape every few days. I became compulsive about it. Art started resisting again. At first I thought it was laziness or maybe unwillingness to go into certain aspects of his life, and that must have been part of it. But the real reason, I figured out in time, was that in this storytelling, too, he was an artist, and he demanded *so* much of himself when the tape started rolling, he might as well have been playing a solo in a recording studio. So, it was challenging, exhausting work with no payoff (but my approbation) and he tried to avoid it. Sometimes he'd get so loaded beforehand, he'd nod out in mid-sentence. I'd kick his foot and he'd start up again just like the Dormouse in *Alice*. Sometimes I bribed him with candy and ice cream (he *was* a lazy person, and I was willing to walk to the store). I'd beg him to talk for 15 minutes and sometimes keep him going for an hour.

I had an old electric typewriter. After a month or so I transcribed what I'd recorded. I read the transcript and realized that as he'd told the stories, he'd described nobody and nothing. I instituted truly brief sessions (which he came to a little more willingly) that were "fill-ins." I'd ask, "What was your mother like?" He'd give me a few minutes of telling description. "What about Patti?" A few more minutes. "Just one more: 'Dicky Boy.'" I'd go down a list of people and things and also try to clear up any confusions about events he'd already narrated. We continued that way from then on with both chronological narrative (which I hesitated to interrupt with requests for details) and fill-ins for description and clarification.

Les Koenig at Contemporary knew what we were doing and suggested that someone he knew at a skin magazine (I think it was *Penthouse*) might be interested in excerpting and paying for some part of it. I thought that what they might be interested in would be sex, so I got Art started talking about his sexual career. And because there was a possibility of publication, I began to edit that material (most of it wound up in the HEROIN chapter). The magazine offered $200 or something like that and it didn't seem like enough, so we decided not to go for it, but editing had begun.

The telling of the story took about two years, the editing took four or five. Art tended to tell an anecdote a little differently every time he told it, with different flourishes, sometimes with a different emphasis. So I got him to tell me some of the same stories over and even over again. Then I'd take my transcriptions of his different versions plus the transcriptions of the applicable fill-ins, pick out the best parts, cut redundancies and excess, clarify ambiguities by changing words and/or syntax, make or ask Art to make transitional sentences and then read it all back into the tape recorder, making sure I could "talk" the changed material with ease and that it reflected Art's speech patterns and rhythms. I'd make him listen. I'd ask him, "Does this sound like you?" After I typed out the edited story—or philosophical observation—I would have to decide whether it really belonged in the book, and, if it did, where it belonged.

Many chapters fell together naturally. Others had to be built, with difficulty, out of lots of bits and pieces elicited over months. The chapter called STEALING chronicles a spiritual disintegration I had to work hard to understand and convey. It began to take shape when Art told me the tale of the armed robbery it ends with. That story troubled me terribly.

I made him tell it several times and then spent days and weeks nagging him about it, asking and rephrasing questions, explaining why I had to ask them. It was tortuous work for him to try to answer them, and it took time to really look at that day and then dredge up the ideas, influences, pressures, and acts that brought him to it. We both did our jobs so well that that remains my favorite chapter.

STRAIGHT LIFE was semi-complete by 1977, when Les Koenig called and said a fan was visiting in town and was really anxious to meet Art. Art was extremely reclusive; he said no, but Les told me the fan worked for the *New Yorker*. "Oh!" Says I, "Well! Send him right over!"

Todd Selbert sold advertising space at the *New Yorker*, and he was one of those fans who knew more about Art's career than Art did. Not surprisingly, Art warmed to him. Especially after Todd brought out of his briefcase a careful little grey paperback that he himself had published, a discography of all recordings Art had made. Art's Virgo-bookkeeper sensibilities were touched by the meticulous work that had gone into it. "Why did you do this?" he asked. "For the hell of it," Todd said.

We told Todd about our book, and he asked if he could take it back to New York with him. He took it to an editor at one publishing house who sent him to Ken Stuart at Schirmer/Macmillan. Ken is a funny, wise, smart guy. He loved the book for all the right reasons and was ready to publish it. Why did I *do* what I next did? I don't remember. I sent it to every other publisher in New York. They didn't want it. We signed with Schirmer in August, 1978, and I asked for two years in which to complete the manuscript. We had to bring it up to date. I had to do the interviews.

I had shown the manuscript to a number of people while I was trying to sell it to someone other than Schirmer, and one woman friend suggested I interview some of the characters in the book. It had completely slipped my mind that this was supposed to be *The Children of Sanchez*. The oral histories of some of the characters in it were essential. And it became clear, too, that because Art's point of view was frequently so extreme, I needed other people's voices to balance him—or just to bear witness. During the next year, I searched for the people, interviewed them, and edited the interviews. I interviewed all of them in person except for Alan Dean who turned up in Australia. He was kind enough to send spoken answers to my questions on a cassette.

As we neared publication, I got concerned with accuracy and started doing (sometimes purposeless, obsessive) research. I found out that Art was right about the kinds of rifles the San Quentin guards were issued during his stays there; I learned the spellings of some arcane and/or obsolete pharmaceuticals, and picked up a lot of Chicano slang. I dug through all the old *down beats* at UCLA and copied articles having to do with Art. I managed to get a look at a copy of Art's rap sheet. That was invaluable. Using the rap sheet and Todd's discography, I was able to get very clear about when things must have happened and to put them in their right order.

Ken told me, years later, that after the book was finished, The Powers That Be at Schirmer wanted him to cut the book to half its length. He didn't do that. He sent it to an outside editor who cut almost nothing of Art's part. She cut most of the other people's interviews down a bit. I agreed with most of her changes; I was editing, myself, right down to the wire. Ken never touched the book except, once, to restore something I had cut.

The book came out a year early. Art was, by then, with Fantasy Records, and their PR person, Terri Hinte, persuaded Macmillan to hire a New York PR guy who put us on the road. At the end of 1979 we were doing radio talk shows, TV morning shows, and being interviewed by press people all over the country.

Art was as happy and as focussed as I had ever known him to be. He was hell to travel with. Complaining constantly about any discomfort, he could be as droopily unhappy and unhelpful as a small child. But almost every interview reenergized him—because he was talking about real things that went on in his world and in his soul. He hated most social interaction, with its cold-hearted small talk. He loved the Synanon game because it was a truth game. He played his own game with these journalists. Most were willing participants, the rest could be manipulated into intimacy (or else into being an audience—a close thing, for Art, to intimacy). Sometimes they'd be moved to confess to *him*. He loved to talk about himself, but he could be all ears for your secrets. And of course he was unshockable.

Instead of picking up his daily methadone at local clinics (where he'd run into other addicts and lead them or be led astray—as on the '77 East Coast tour) we carried it with us, and I doled it out, a daily bottle at a time, from a handsome, costly, locked leather case I'd bought in New York. We both adored pretty, expensive things, and I guessed correctly that Art wouldn't risk damaging the case by trying to pick the lock unless he was desperate, and there was no reason for him to get desperate. He was getting coke mailed to him at our hotels from a connection in L.A.

I was handling the money and the drugs. After Art's last hospitalization, I decided that that was the way it would have to be. Art, on the prowl, got into too much trouble. He'd been scratching around with ex-cons in bad neighborhoods, disappearing for days, buying grams and half grams, and ingesting any unpredictable get-high substances these people had handy. And he wasn't going to stop. He was sure he hadn't long to live, and he was determined to spend what time he had left loaded. It seemed likely, the way he was operating, that he'd soon be busted again—and go to prison. *I* had no criminal record. And I had old friends who knew upscale dealers. One day I went out and came back with an ounce of the best cocaine he'd ever had. Art made an immediate and joyous commitment to the new program. Inevitably, it wasn't long before I was snorting cocaine too.

I'd gone into Synanon in '68 because my life was chaos and I was suicidal as a result of using pills, pot, and alcohol. In 1979, I'd been clean for eleven years. Then one day, while I was repainting the bathroom, Art suggested that a sniff of coke would make the work go faster. I'd never tried it before. Within the next week or so I'd not only repainted the bathroom, I'd put new linoleum on the floor, built shelves, made window curtains, repainted my office and the kitchen, wallpapered Art's room, and recarpeted the whole house. By myself. With probably half an ounce of coke. And built a trellis around the front porch and planted bougainvillea to climb it—in front of this dilapidated shack we were renting in Van Nuys.

Over the next months and years I continued to use cocaine. It wasn't always fun. Frequently it was nerve-wrackingly, teeth-gnashingly just awful, but whenever it was around, I still had to use it, and it was around most of the time because it was Art's fuel. I started drinking in order to come down. I gained weight, lost health, lost dignity. Many people we knew during the next few years used coke, too, and I believe I was sufficiently sneaky to make most of the ones who didn't use it think *I* didn't use it either. No one, except Art, seemed to notice that I was an addict. And Art liked me getting high with him, especially since, when we only had a little, or we were traveling and had to make it last, all the coke was his. Not long after Art died I cleaned up for good.

So I was using coke on the book tour. I was energetic and efficient, keeping us moving, confirmed, and on time. Right around then *Straight Life*, the album, was released.

The record company Art refers to in the last chapter of the book was Fantasy Records (Art recorded on their Galaxy label). The album he talks about was *Art Pepper Today*. It was a wonderful album and very successful, voted the best jazz album of the year in France, really popular in Japan, it even sold well here. They had recorded and released a second album, *Straight Life*, to coincide with the book tour. That album is one of my very favorites, and it did well, too.

When Fantasy signed Art early in '79, it seemed like a miracle to me. Since Les's death, I'd been trying, with no luck, to find Art a label. And he desperately longed for the security of a recording contract and the sense that some company would be his home. He needed a Daddy. He found one in Ralph Kaffel, the President of Fantasy. Ralph was actually seven years younger than Art. That didn't matter. Ralph was perfect. He's calm and enigmatic, has a beard and just a trace of an accent (he's Russian). He's witty and very, very smart, softspoken, unpretentious, a little eccentric. He was everything

Art admired in a man: He was a gentleman. And he obviously liked Art or why would he sign him?

This is how it happened: In June of '78, I had brought Art back from the Oregon tour during which he'd suffered some kind of a physical "episode." He was aphasic. He was confused, frightened, resentful, incredibly lethargic. I put him in the V.A. Hospital. I was working as a temp, and during weekends and evenings I was doing all the interviews I used in STRAIGHT LIFE—which had been bought by Macmillan. I visited Art every day. I brought him his clarinet but he wouldn't even try to play it. It was at this time that I first heard from Fantasy. Their main office was and is in Berkeley, but at that time they had a small L.A. office, and they employed a fellow named Bob Kirstein. Bob called me in the middle of this and asked if Art would be interested in signing with Galaxy, Fantasy's jazz label. I'd never heard of them. I told Bob the truth. I said that Art was hospitalized and didn't even know his own name. I didn't know whether he'd get better or how much better he'd get or whether he'd ever play again. A C.A.T. scan had turned up some brain damage, but they weren't sure of the nature of it.

Bob was very laid back. "Well," he said, "just please keep in touch with us and let us know how he's doing; we'd really like to sign him." A week later Bob called again. How is he? A week later, ditto. I mean, these people wouldn't leave us alone. And Art slowly got better. In July Art and I went to see Bob in Fantasy's L.A. office. Art was still kind of out of it, but we'd carefully discussed the terms of the contract before we went, mostly standard stuff. We'd been warned Ralph Kaffel would have to approve everything. We sat down, and I told Bob what we wanted. He listened. When I finished Art spoke up for the first time. He said, "And a non-recoupable bonus of $10,000 for signing." I nearly fell off my chair.

I like to think I kept a straight face. Bob nodded. That night he called us and said that Ralph had agreed. In August we flew up to Berkeley. Art said they wanted to make sure that he could walk and talk. We chatted with Ralph who took us on a tour of the studios. He informed us that Ed Michel, working freelance under Orrin Keepnews, head of A&R, would be Art's producer. I objected.

During the summer of 1959, when I was in my teens, I worked at an L.A. coffee house called The Ash Grove. I sold records in a shop in the club. Ed Michel was the house rhythm section. He played the bass for the folkies who didn't bring their own bands. Ed was dating one of the waitresses, and he and I became good pals. When he wasn't working we'd spend hours talking and philosophizing. He was wise and old. I think he was 21. I went off to college and Ed went to work for Pacific Jazz and then for Verve in L.A. He worked for an American based company in Europe. So Ed and I never saw each other again. For eighteen years. Until one Saturday in 1976 or '77, Les Koenig called to say that he would be coming by Donte's, an L.A. jazz club, to hear Art play. That was rare. He was bringing two friends, both record producers. John Snyder and Ed Michel. Ed Michel! Does he play the bass? Same guy. The evening was fine; Art played wonderfully. He played some ballad, and Les, not given much to praise let alone hyperbole, remarked that Art was probably the greatest ballad player living. John agreed. Ed said, "Oh, I don't know...."

Once, during the book tour, when I asked Art after an interview why he seemed to have taken such an obvious dislike to the interviewer, he gave me this classic reply: "He wasn't reverent enough." Well, Ed Michel has never been reverent enough—toward anyone, about anything. Even though I still had warm feelings for him from the past, I didn't think he deserved to produce Art's albums. I told Ralph I didn't think he was the best person for the job.

Ralph smiled. He said, "Well, let's go and talk to him. I think you'll like him." We talked to him. Ed can be really charming when he feels like it. He felt like it. Art liked him well enough. I was reconciled. Ed became Art's producer and was the shrewd and patient guiding force behind some of the best work Art ever did.

(Ed told me later that when Ralph informed him he was signing Art, Ed said, "What do you want to do that for? He's a great player, but he's nuts. Why do you want all that trouble?" I asked Ed what Ralph said to that. Ed said Ralph smiled.)

These were some of the key creative relationships of Art's last years. John Snyder promoted and sponsored the '77 East Coast tour which put Art back on the scene. And the magnificent Contemporary recordings of Art at the Village Vanguard were made possible largely through his efforts. He also produced what turned out to be four of Art's great late recordings (*So In Love*, *Artworks*, *The New York Album* and *Stardust*). Ed Michel produced most (but not all) of the rest of them. Ralph Kaffel gave Art the support and security he required. Another creative relationship was the one Art had with George Cables.

Les had brought George in to play piano for Art's *The Trip* album and for the one that followed it, *No Limit*, in 1977. After that Art worked with George, locally, whenever he could, and in 1979, I managed to hire George away from Freddie Hubbard for our third and so-far biggest tour of Japan. (Three terrific albums eventually came out of that tour, *Landscape*, *Besame Mucho*, and *Tokyo Encore*). Art loved the way George played and compared him to his all-time favorite pianist, Wynton Kelly. I have a series of snapshots of Art listening to George solo in a nightclub. First, listening raptly, eyes closed. Then staring with amazed delight. Then, gesturing to the audience, "Did you hear that? Isn't he incredible?" George is probably also one of the sweetest people on earth. He's a decorous man, but he's an affectionate man. Art was always afraid to touch people, but he loved to be hugged, patted, and pushed by those open and generous people, like George, who are able to do that sort of thing. George has an empathetic, tender heart, and it comes out in his music, and Art responded to him on every level. In those years George was irresponsible and late, late all the time. It didn't matter. Art was overjoyed to see him when he showed. One of my nicknames for George was "Monsignor," and George told me that, in fact, when he was young he'd planned to be a preacher. George is just good. And George is black, and that was really important to Art.

The scrap of poetry at the beginning of STRAIGHT LIFE comes from one of Ezra Pound's translations—of a poem called "Exile's Letter." The whole poem seemed apropos to me, because in Art's view he had been exiled, by color, from his own world, the world of jazz.

He was hanging out, actually working on Central Avenue from age fourteen. He was accepted and admired in a world he loved. Then he was suddenly rejected by that world. That's how he saw it, at age 18, when he experienced racism for the first time in North Carolina. He spent most of the rest of his life in a state of chronic paranoia, only it wasn't always paranoia (as I first believed) because the bad vibes he got from many black musicians—sarcasms, slights, willful incomprehension, onstage shenanigans—were not usually imaginary (and were not a response to anything he, personally, had done). And he was incredibly sensitive to that stuff. Always expecting it. As he said in STRAIGHT LIFE, "people don't like you, pretty soon you don't like them." Pretty soon he got bitter, suspicious, and nasty. And then prison just exacerbated everything.

But I believe Art's last years were a period of reconciliation for him. The tension never ended, but during those years it seemed a lot of black musicians became kinder, more tolerant, and Art was always exceedingly grateful—and my tongue is not in my cheek. He was cynical, but when he found genuine acceptance he was so *grateful*. A typical example of the kind of bad/good thing that happened: In 1980 Art was playing a prestigious European concert in a major concert hall as part of an all-star lineup. Each soloist got one featured performance piece. Art chose to do "Over the Rainbow." He was accompanied by an all black rhythm section, a very well known pianist, and a bassist and a drummer who were fairly famous. Art, during that time, always played "Rainbow" with a long *a capella* intro, a kind of wild, passionate, personal statement, and then, unlike most jazz players, he explored not just the song's melody and structure but its emotional content as well, so he kept the tempo slow, never sped it for variety or pyrotechnics. He loved ballads so much. He revered and envied the great singers who sang them. He couldn't make his voice hum an identifiable phrase, so he used his horn to speak and sing these beautiful songs. And he played each one, each time, as if his life depended on it. On this important evening, he carefully told the band what he wanted. He told the pianist, "Don't play an introduction. I'll start out alone and signal when I start the melody." He told the drummer, "No double-time, just brushes." They preceded him to the stage and sat down. Art was introduced and walked on. But before he could reach the mike, the pianist lifted his hands and dived into an introduction. Maybe he forgot the instructions. Maybe he resented them. Art's previous experience told him that it was sabotage and racially motivated. In the middle of the song, the drummer, very obviously bored with just brushes, got up and left the stage during Art's solo. Just walked off. After a few minutes, he wandered back on with a glass of water in his hand, casually sat down and picked up his brushes. It wasn't a long song. How thirsty could he have been? Art got mad. He always played great mad. He played great that night. He got a long, long, standing ovation. At the end of the show, all the stars were lined up on stage, and each took a bow. Art got an absolute roar of love from the crowd, and as the guys came walking off (I saw and heard this), Freddie Hubbard put his arm around Art's shoulder and said, "Man, you got the biggest hand of all of us." The drummer overheard and said, "Yeah, why *was* that?" Freddie said, "Because he's the greatest alto saxophone player in the world, that's why."

When we were at the Nice festival the second time, in '81, one of the booths at the festival had jazz photographs for sale. Art stopped to look at the pictures. He asked the girl in the booth, "No white jazz musicians? You don't have pictures of any white musicians?" She giggled and stared at him. I said, "Art, she's French. She doesn't understand you." He said, "She understands. No white guys?" The girl blushed, shook her head, and said, clearly, no, they had only black musicians. She giggled again, and Art laughed with her, resigned, but not bitter. The band we were touring with then was *the* Art Pepper Quartet, George Cables, David Williams, and Carl Burnett: three black guys with whom Art had found accord. With George, especially, there was intimacy and love. Although it wasn't exactly Central Avenue. One time, when Art was explaining to George how he wanted a tune to sound he kept using a phrase he often used—it meant funky—he said, "down home." George got irritated, and he finally said, "What do you mean, 'down home,' man? I'm from *Brooklyn!*"

George, Carl, David, Ed Michel, the greatly talented Bulgarian, Milcho Leviev, Art's alternative pianist during those years—these were good friends. But there were bad friends, too. As far as I was concerned, the bad friends were the fans who wanted to be near Art no matter what, and who gave Art bad drugs—in order to spend time with him. They couldn't be reasoned with, wouldn't be discouraged or driven away. They messed him up. And then they got to tell people that they knew Art Pepper, and, "Boy, he's really messed up." Bad drugs were alcohol (he had very little liver left that wasn't cirrhotic), powerful downers, uppers that burned up his body and his brain, and Valium. Valium: First it made him dopey and forgetful, then, as an afterthought, it rendered him psychotic. Maybe it was just a coincidence, but it seemed to happen the same way every time. He'd take some Valium and then, six to eight hours later, he'd decide that he'd lost a gram of coke and that he *had* to find it. He'd ransack the house, turning out every single drawer and closet, every container, taking things apart, dismantling the beds, all the furniture, pulling up the carpeting (he did that once in a motel when we were on the road). I could promise, I could deliver, more coke. It didn't matter—he had to find that particular gram. I never touched Valium. Years earlier I'd learned that its hangover depression made me want to kill myself. Art never learned, and these people always gave it to him. "It was only Valium," they'd say. The not-so-bad drugs were small amounts of cocaine, which he was using anyway, and marijuana (which affected his sightreading ability. He stopped being able to read music, even his own charts, when he smoked).

Don't get me wrong, Art liked these people who wanted to turn him on. He looked for them, manipulated them, got annoyed at me when I insulted them, said, "Awwww, baby you shouldn't say that. You'll hurt his *feelings.* He *means* well."

One of the worst of these bad friends was a woman whose apartment was a drug salon for stars. She didn't sell, she bestowed—and surrounded herself with talent. At her house Art got flattery, bad drugs, and too much pharmaceutical cocaine. Art thought it was a shame to waste such good stuff, so he got a needle from one of her friends and took it home and shot the coke, and shot it and shot it. He wound up in the hospital with an infected arm. She went to see him there and brought him more cocaine. She brought some to the house when he came home (she arrived in a Cadillac with a driver and a bodyguard), and I wouldn't let her in, and she wouldn't leave our front yard. I finally called Art's best friend who came over and threw her, bodily, out. He's a little guy, but he tossed her over our four foot fence with such energy and menace he scared the bodyguard. The woman never came back.

Chris Fisherman was the little guy. He was plumpish, curly haired, about Art's age, and he was probably Art's oldest friend. Chris had been a teenager dealing drugs on Central Avenue while Art had been playing in the clubs and after-hours spots. Chris had had a long, interesting career, in and out of prison (on his bookshelf I found a copy of Mickey Cohen's autobiography inscribed, "To my brother, Chris"), and he and Art had had infrequent friendly contact. He had cleaned up and he came into our lives. He'd settled in West L.A., and, though Art preferred to hole up at home when he wasn't working, he was willing to go out from time to time—to Chris's house where they talked and talked about the people they'd known and the adventures they'd had. Chris locked up his liquor cabinet and doled out, Art complained, a stingy little line of coke an hour. If that. Art would try to manipulate more cocaine. He'd try to manipulate Chris into scoring some heroin for him. It's likely that Chris hinted that maybe he would actually get some heroin for him sometime, but Chris was unmanipulatable. It was a game Chris played that kept Art hopeful and harmlessly engaged.

Chris is a man of many parts. On another occasion Art got stopped for a traffic violation. The police searched the car. They found something. Art was jailed, arraigned, and sent home with a court date. Our lawyer was out of town. Chris told Art to go to court, and, if "things" didn't work out, he said, "Ask for a postponement." Chris said, "I'll meet you there." Art went to court and found Chris dressed in a suit and tie and carrying a briefcase. Chris got Art's case number from the bailiff and read the paperwork.

Chris told me, "It said something about 'paraphernalia.' I read further and it said, 'a straw containing cocaine residue.' I went to the D.A.'s office. She was a gorgeous woman—tall, blonde, with the face of an angel. I said, 'Don't make me make you look ridiculous.' She said, 'What do you mean?' I asked her, 'Have you read this thing on Pepper?' She said, 'No, not really.' She was very nice. I told her what she had was a case that was built on a *straw*. She laughed. She read the paperwork. She said, 'There's got to be more to it than this.' I said, 'Mr. Pepper's a famous musician. He's got obligations. He's got two big tours coming up. Don't make him wait around for something this stupid.' She read the report again. She said, 'You're right. Okay. It's off the docket.' I hurried back into the courtroom, grabbed Art's arm and said, 'Let's go.' Art said, 'What's happening?' I said, 'I'll tell you later, man. Let's just *go*!'"

Chris told me, "I never actually said I was a lawyer."

We did have a couple of tours coming up, and Chris came along for the ride. After STRAIGHT LIFE, we were able to get a booking agent and in May of 1980, we went to Boston, D.C., Atlanta, Houston, and some other places that I can't remember. The band was Milcho Leviev, Bob Magnusson on bass, and Carl Burnett. In June, Chris came with us on our first real European tour. Art and I had been to London and Birmingham for a few days for a festival a year earlier; Art had been a last-minute replacement for Phil Woods. This time we went for about a month with Milcho, Tony Dumas, and Carl. We did two weeks at Ronnie Scott's in London where Art recorded a fine album for Mole Jazz under Milcho's name. (For that date Art wrote and recorded a slow blues we named for

Chris, "Blues For the Fisherman." It was saluted by a British critic as "The twelve bars of the decade.") The band did festivals and clubs all over the Continent. Chris's function seemed to be to show us how much fun we could have. He managed to meet and introduce us to the most interesting people, and he found and took us *all* out to the best and most interesting restaurants.

Chris got busted three days after we returned home from Europe. The charge was "conspiracy to distribute narcotics." He was held on 1.5 million dollars bail. When the bail was reduced he was able to get out while he fought his case, but he spent the last year of Art's life (and seven years after that) in prison—where we visited him as often as we could. He swore he was innocent, and Art never reproached him with failing to give him a taste.

During the rest of 1980, and during '81 and '82, we toured almost nonstop. We covered the U.S., Canada, Japan, Europe, and Australia. Art loved the look of Europe. The baroque-er the better. And he shared with me a deep appreciation of decay. A journalist once asked him what was his favorite city. He named Paris. And when the journalist asked why, Art said, "Because you can get anything you want there." He got a little bit of heroin there. Just a little. He sniffed it, wrote a song, and then took me for a walk on the *Champs Elysees* at 5 AM. Of course the next night when he had to perform in Holland after an all-day trip spent sniffing that same stuff, it wasn't so romantic. I was pouring coffee down his throat and throwing cold water on his face right up to stage time. Once in front of an audience, though, he came to life and performed beautifully. He never missed a gig and was late only once during the whole time we were touring.

Art, onstage, during those years, was a riot. He'd gotten used to talking; after STRAIGHT LIFE it was even expected. Sometimes, when he was low, his verbal riffs were harsh and bitter, but mostly they were comical. He'd always admired good comics. He was very conscious of things like timing and delivery. He had a great ear for intonation. He didn't tell jokes, he told stories; he described people and things. When we were touring with Milcho (who'd defected from Bulgaria under in-

teresting but ultimately boring circumstances), Art would tell
the audience how Milcho escaped from behind the Iron Curtain. He told the story night after night, and it got wilder and
more fantastic with each telling until he had Milcho tunneling
under the English channel with a knife in his teeth, killing
and eating old women and little children. So he could be Free.
To play Jazz. The crowds loved it. Milcho took it well, only
begging Art to leave out the part about the children. One night
in Boston, Art's ankles were so swollen, he had to go onstage
in his socks. That night he talked about his ankles. He talked
about his grandmother's ankles. It was hilarious. (I have it on
tape, but its essence can't be reproduced on paper, because it
isn't just the words that crack you up and touch you, it's the
pauses and the the edges on the words. Also, Art gave you
the feeling that he didn't know what he was going to say next.
Usually, he didn't. So when the words came out, *and* came
out funny, you shared the surprise with him, and that was
part of the kick.) When he finished talking that night, he'd
described his grandmother's knees, and he had the audience
in hysterics. And when he turned to the band to kick off the
next tune, he found Milcho collapsed on the piano, and Bob
on the floor weeping with laughter.

Art didn't get into too much trouble on the road. He
didn't have the time or the energy. But if we were at home
for a few weeks, he did. He tossed the house a number of
times, and he wound up in the hospital, for a short stay, after
shooting cocaine, at least once more. But he also wrote new
charts and rehearsed them.

When we travelled in the U.S. and Canada, I worked
hard. I did all the negotiations with band members, and,
through the booking agent, with the promoters. I made the
travel arrangements; I devised itineraries which took full advantage of excursion rates—much to the dismay of Art and
the guys, who got sick of changing planes in Denver so that
we could save money. I rented vans, when necessary, and I
drove us. I dealt, as well as I could, with local promoters,
with bad sound systems and bad pianos. Trips in Europe and
Japan were easier. The promoter supplied a roadie or two and
made most of the arrangements. My main responsibility

abroad became just Art, keeping him rested, fairly sober, and fed. He rarely went out to eat, found it too exhausting. He was content to live on candy bars and airport sweets. I toted a boy-scout mess kit, and brought hot meals to him in our hotel rooms which had no room-service, from nearby restaurants which had no facilities for preparing food "to go."

Art gave me complete autonomy, and, though he always complained, he never criticized anything I did. And all the work and hassle were so patently worth it at the moment when he made his music—in a concert hall or club or recording studio. Because what Art was doing was important. I'm not alone in what I feel about what he did. I've read reviews and letters from fans that said pretty much the same thing. Real art is important. When he played what he felt, Art played what we all feel, and because he was an artist, he showed us that was beautiful. The artist dignifies himself and us and makes us think that, maybe, all that lives *is* holy. When Art played, it was a sacrament. It felt like church to me. I've heard musicians who worked with him say, "He made me play way over my head." He made them better than they were. He made me better than I was. He also adored me, respected and praised me, awed me, fascinated and educated me, and kept me entertained. He was the wittiest and most perceptive person I've ever known. He gave me himself, as completely as he could, to love and care for. And he gave me a very interesting job.

I learned how to do my job from experience and from two terrific women. During the hellish '77 New York experience, Keiko Jones (Mrs. Elvin) lectured me nightly in the kitchen of the Village Vanguard. She told me how to act, how to dress, and how much power to take: All of it. She told me to take control of the money. Later, Jill Goodwin, Phil Woods's partner, gave me practical tips on touring: If it's costing you *this* much, you have to make *this* much. Carl Burnett, our drummer, a seasoned traveller with many bands, was always a source of calm and of good advice and information. And I learned about the business of music from two marvelous men, both lawyers, Jimmy Tolbert (who kept Art from going to jail in Chapter 24), and Al Schlesinger, who did us countless kindnesses. Before he died, Les Koenig showed me how to affiliate Art with BMI as a writer, so that he could finally collect performance royalties on all the songs he'd written. By the time Art signed with Fantasy, Art and I were publishing the songs he wrote, and he was collecting 100% of mechanical royalties on them.

In July of 1980, we met young Don McGlynn, just out of U.S.C. film school. He wanted to make a documentary about Art, and we agreed. He raised $30,000 and made a 48-minute film. *Art Pepper: Notes from a Jazz Survivor* seems to me a good, intelligently (and cleverly) made, honest film. It won some awards and gave Art great satisfaction.

But the biggest event, for Art, of his last years, after STRAIGHT LIFE, was the ballad album, *Winter Moon*.

Our contract with Fantasy was *supposed* to guarantee Art a ballad album with strings. As it turned out, the contract didn't include that stipulation, but Ralph Kaffel, with some urging from his Japanese licensee, decided to underwrite a ballad album anyway.

Ed Michel was living in an idyllic little country town in Northern California. Art and I drove up and stayed there for a week in the only motel. Every day we drove to Ed's house and listened to successive installments of a great big compilation of good ballads—almost all performed by vocalists—which Ed had put together for Art to listen to and choose from.

For the first couple of days, during the listening sessions, Art kept nodding out. I don't know why. He swore he wasn't taking anything besides his methadone and coke. Maybe he was just staying up too late sniffing while I slept. Ed got annoyed. He'd done all this work and here was Art, on the nod. Ed finally made some too tactful remark about what drugs Art was or wasn't using. Art took offense. There was a quarrel. I tried to make peace. Back at the motel, Art sat down and drafted a contract for Ed to sign. He wanted Ed to guarantee that he wouldn't say a word to Ralph about Art using drugs. As he prepared it, he asked me to help him with the wording of it: "Is Ed the 'defendant' and am I the 'plaintiff,' or is it vice versa?"

Art went out to the roadside phone booth, called Ed, and read the contract to him. Ed said he wouldn't say anything to Ralph, but he refused to sign any formal agreement without first consulting his attorney. "Art bought that," Ed told me, laughing, years later. "That made sense to him." Art was impressed by Ed's caution and reassured on the subject of Ed's silence, and the next day they solemnly shook hands. Art, mysteriously, woke up and selected the tunes he wanted to play.

Ed chose Bill Holman, whom Art knew and admired, and Jimmy Bond, with whom Art was acquainted, to write the arrangements. Art wanted to do the record date live. Common practice these days is to overdub. The strings come in on Monday and lay down their written tracks. On Tuesday or next year the soloist comes in and plays his part or improvises over what the strings have recorded. Art wanted to feel the living presence of the string players. He knew they'd inspire him. He was sure he'd inspire them.

Ed agreed to a live date but warned that the maximum studio time we could afford with the strings was two days. So Art would have to do it quickly and right because, live, there'd be too much leakage all over the place to do any editing. Ed wanted to use the rhythm section he'd put together for the *Art Pepper Today* album. Art agreed to Stanley Cowell on piano and Cecil McBee on bass, but he asked especially for Carl Burnett on drums. We had hoped to have maybe a flute, maybe an oboe, but we couldn't afford it. Ed said he thought it might be good to have Howard Roberts play guitar.

This was in August. We left Ed to go on a short tour up the coast to Seattle. At the end of the month Art had a weeklong gig at a hotel in Phoenix—with a house band. We would fly directly from Phoenix to Berkeley to do the string album. I strongly suggested to Art that we take Milcho Leviev with us to Phoenix. I reasoned that with Milcho, Art would have a chance to practice playing "Our Song," the ballad he'd just written for the album, and he could also practice "Winter Moon," which he hadn't played in years. Milcho came along, and they did play the tunes. And there was a bonus. One morning Milcho came to our room with a chart. He said he'd

been taping some of the sets, and he'd taped a little blues riff
Art had played last night, and he liked it so much he'd transcribed it. That was the tune that became "Melolev" on *One
September Afternoon*, the quintet album which was made in
one day, the day after the strings went home. Art was not
drinking or smoking or arguing with anybody. He wasn't talking much. He wrote a few tunes.

We flew to Berkeley on September 2nd, and on September 3rd and 4th they taped the album. I don't remember which
was the first tune, but I do remember Art standing in front
of the mike, ready to rehearse it. The strings played an introduction, and Art was supposed to come in, but he didn't. Bill
Holman turned to Art—who just grinned at him and apologized. Art said that he was listening to the strings, and they
sounded so beautiful, he just forgot to play.

Winter Moon got great reviews. (Art rarely got bad reviews. The critics, worldwide, either liked or loved him. Remarks on his performances and recordings ranged from
"darkly lyrical" and "brilliantly crisp" to "demon jazz god"
and "celestial.") Artie Shaw called to say how much he liked
it. He was one of Art's heros. Art had never met him. Art
said, in Don's movie, that *Winter Moon* was the best album
he'd ever made, that "Our Song" was the most beautiful song
he'd ever written, and that his solo on that tune was the best
solo he'd ever recorded.

But he hadn't yet recorded the Maiden Voyage albums.

On August 13th, 14th, and 15th of 1981, Art was recorded
live at an L.A. club called the Maiden Voyage with George,
David, and Carl. Four albums have been released from that
session, *Roadgame*, *Art Lives*, *APQ*, and *Arthur's Blues*. I think
they're phenomenal.

Well, it was Art's band. George grew more graceful and
perfect every day, Carl, consistent and serene, was our anchor,
and then there was our bassist, David Williams, a slender, elegant Trinidadian with perfect manners who was capable of
daring leaps of precarious invention at the most critical moments. Art was inspired by his musicianship and admiringly
deplored his personal, social style, which was both cagey and
reckless.

Art was well aware, while he was doing the date, how wonderful it was. John Overton owned the sound truck which housed the recording equipment for the date. It was parked in the club lot. He wrote me, after Art died, that he'd always treasure the memory of the night Art climbed up into the truck during a break one evening and listened to a playback of "But Beautiful." "And then," John wrote, "he was so delighted, he began to dance to it."

So much was recorded that Ed asked Art to listen to all of it and make careful notes on each selection. Art did that, twice. He knew it would take years to release so much material. He told me slyly, "Ed won't say it, but he wants these notes so he'll know what to release after I'm dead." While we'd been at Ed's house, making the ballad album selections, Ed's partner at that time, Francesca, had read Art's fortune from a Tarot deck. Art was unsurprised when he drew the death card.

The notes Art wrote for the performances he liked are full of praise for the band and for himself; they're decorated with joyful little cartoon characters kicking up their heels. Of his original "Arthur's Blues," he wrote, "My whole life went into this."

His whole life also went into "Everything Happens to Me" which should have been Art's theme song. To the best of my knowledge, he did play the tune fairly frequently during his early years. But he never really recorded it, and he could never have played it—or in my opinion anything else—the way he plays "Everything Happens To Me" here. (In my opinion, though, which is worth very little at this point because it's so subjective, nobody ever played anything quite as wonderful as this "Everything Happens To Me.")

I'll tell you Art's opinion. One afternoon he sat down and listened to it seriously. When it was over he looked up at me and shook his head. He was absolutely dazzled. He said, "I don't know... Am I *crazy*?"

I knew exactly what he meant. He meant that he didn't think anybody had ever before played anything quite as wonderful as this "Everything Happens To Me." But, obviously, he must be crazy because the world was not beating a path to his door or crowning him with lilies or electing him emperor—or even putting his picture on the cover of *down beat*.

We went back on the road after recording ended, returning to Berkeley in April of '82 to record a duo album—just Art and George. Art was eager to be recorded playing clarinet. He considered it a lovely but intractable instrument, practiced on it, just a little, nearly every day, and never believed that he could really master it (many serious critics disagreed), though he sometimes felt he came close. This would be the perfect setting for it.

The tunes were chosen by Art and George and Ed. I suggested "Goin' Home." When we'd been in Japan the previous November, I'd heard George fooling around on the piano before a soundcheck. It was the last concert of the tour. We'd been away a month, and the following morning we'd be flying back to Narita to change planes for L.A. George was playing, appropriately enough, "Goin' Home." Since Art was always hungry for clarinet-appropriate tunes, I brought it to his attention. Art brought a cassette of Ray Charles singing "Don't Let The Sun Catch You Cryin'" to the studio for George to listen to. It was a favorite of Art's, something he'd always wanted to play. He played saxophone on that one. George suggested "Isn't She Lovely," which Art never stopped calling "that weird Stevie Wonder tune," and he played it on both alto sax and clarinet. He had a hard time with it for some reason. But George had a hard time with "Billie's Bounce," an Ed suggestion and another alto tune. Most of the rest of the tunes were Art's choices.

Unfortunately, there were some technical problems. The plan had been to do that date direct-to-digital. Ed and his engineer were inexperienced with the technology. The sound they'd recorded was much too dry. It could be transferred to analogue and remixed (as was done later for an album titled *Tête à Tête*), but that wasn't true digital. George said we ought to try again. We all went back to Berkeley. Art and George played some of the same tunes, including "Goin' Home," and some new ones.

I've been to a lot of record dates but none to equal those for sweetness and light and dedicated hard work.

Immediately after this, we left for a short tour of the U.S. George was unavailable. He was working with Sarah Vaughan. We brought Roger Kellaway along with David and Carl. We went to Chicago, Milwaukee, and then to a big KOOL jazz festival in D.C. where Art got to see one of his oldest friends, Zoot Sims, and where he played like an angel.

We went straight home from D.C. on May 30th. On the morning of June 9th Art told me he had a headache. He never had headaches. He asked me if I thought his face looked weird. The left side of his mouth was drooping. I told him we had to go to the hospital. He refused to go. I said we'd better go see his doctor.

We were on a health plan, courtesy of the Musicians' Union. We belonged to Kaiser Permanente, an HMO. His doctor looked him over, and *she* said he'd better go to the hospital. Art said he didn't want to go. He told her that he was supposed to play in Carnegie Hall in two weeks with Phil Woods. He said, "People die in hospitals." She laughed. She said not everybody does. She wanted to call an ambulance, but Art refused it. I said I'd drive him. It wasn't far.

Art sat beside me as I drove and calmly told me that he loved me. He said if this was "it" he wanted me to know that he was grateful for all I'd done. I told him that this wasn't it. He said that I'd made it possible for him to do the book, the documentary, the ballad album, all the music. If this was it he was satisfied, and he wanted me to know that. He was quiet for a while. Then he said, proudly, "I'm leaving you well provided for." Finally he said, "No matter what happens, promise me there won't be any surgery. I can't take any more of that. Don't let them cut me." I promised.

We were put into a cubicle in the emergency area. Art jumped up on the examining table and told me he was starving. He asked me to buy him a candy bar. I left, found one for him, and returned to find him sniffing a line of coke. He said, jokingly, "I want to be high when I die." I took the coke away from him. Suddenly he cried out. He said he couldn't see out of his left eye and he couldn't move his left side.

I called a doctor who made him lie down and started questioning him. He confessed to the doctor, a kindly, grey-haired man, that yesterday he'd acquired a needle from a friend and last night he'd shot some coke. I hadn't known. He asked the doctor if that could have caused this. The doctor told him maybe. By this time Art's headache was giving him terrible pain, and he begged for a painkiller. The doctor said not yet.

The doctor left. Art said to me, "You have no idea how scared I am." I told Art, I told myself, "They can fix it. These days they can do all kinds of things. They'll fix it. Remember my father's heart. He's an old man, but they fixed his heart." Art said, "Oh, man, I don't want to hear about your father." He despised my father. It seemed like a good sign to me that he could remember to hate my father. I said, "I was just saying they can fix it. I don't care about my father (I didn't)." I told him that I loved him more than anyone in the whole world (I did). I kissed and stroked him and called him every outlandish pet name we'd ever invented. He relaxed. He said, "That's what I need. I need love." He passed out.

He was C.A.T. scanned. There was a bleed in his brain. He had to be rushed to another Kaiser hospital to be seen and possibly operated on by a neurologist. I told the doctor that I'd promised Art there'd be no cutting. The doctor told me there was a chance that Art could be restored to normal health. I let an ambulance take us to the other hospital where, after horrible hassles, a supercilious neurologist tried to tell me, standing over Art's body, what the scan showed. I made him follow me out of the room. He said, "He's unconscious. He can't hear." He told me that without surgery Art would die. He told me that with surgery he might die, too, given the state of his liver and his run-down condition. He said surgery could also save him, but, as a direct result of the surgery, he probably wouldn't be able to move his left side, speak, or see. I understood that I'd be able to keep my promise. I told him surgery was out. I asked, "If Art stayed in this hospital would you be his doctor?" He said that he would. I asked if we could return to the other hospital. He said we could. I asked if Art could have a painkiller now. He said he'd send some Demerol.

I went back into the examining room where Art was lying, eyes closed, grimacing in agony. I whispered in his ear,

"They're going to give you something for the pain." Art was conscious enough to say his last words. He said, "It's about time."

Back at the original hospital he was put in intensive care. I called his regular doctor, who would now be the one to care for him, and explained that Art absolutely had to have his daily methadone. She understood. It was nighttime. I went home to bed.

The next morning I arrived to find Art still unconscious but dripping with sweat and writhing in pain. I asked the nurse in charge if Art had had his methadone. She said, "Methadone! That's the last thing he needs!" Out of Art's earshot, I told her he was dying and he wasn't going to do it painfully. He was an addict and he needed his methadone. I'd used a word she couldn't tolerate, and it wasn't "addict" and it wasn't "methadone." She threw a fit. She screamed at me. "Dying! Who told you he was dying!" I yelled back at her. I was angry, then, but I can see, now, that she'd been driven crazy by her job. I called our doctor who had Art moved to a regular room away from that peculiar environment. Art got his methadone. I sat by his bed and watched him relax. I stroked his hair. I sang to him, and when I finished, I saw a tear roll down his cheek. That's when it finally hit me. I was going to lose him. I cried and cried and cried.

I sat by his bedside for six days. I wept and talked to him and sang to him and joked to him and wept and kissed and touched him. The hospital issued a no visitors edict, but we let a few friends come. The band came all at once. George gave him a kiss goodbye. Journalists were calling the hospital. People were calling the house. I got our answering service to refer calls to a good friend of mine, a compassionate and convivial woman who was willing to deal with everyone. Our doctor and all the regular Kaiser nurses and technicians were absolutely wonderful. On the morning of June 15th I watched Art die.

My mother helped me with the funeral arrangements, and my friend, Joy, handled the newspapers and callers. I asked Ed Michel to put together a tape from the duo sessions to play for the crowd. I asked Ed to leave in the in-between-take

talk. I wanted to hear Art's voice. I said we'd call the album
"Goin' Home." "Goin' home" is also a bandstand phrase. It
was what Art said to the band when he'd finished improvising
and wanted to return to the original melody and end the song.

The funeral played to a packed house. It looked like the
funeral of a celebrity, and it was. Art's friends talked about
him with affection and respect and humor. The biggest and
most beautiful wreath—gardenias and white orchids—was
sent by our coke connection. The best was sent by the band.
Art always complained, "I tell them when they play well, but
they never tell me when I play well." The banner on the
wreath said, "To the Greatest Saxophone Player in the World."

Art and I had talked about his death hundreds of times.
He told me he was afraid to be buried in the ground; he was
afraid of the worms. But he was terrified of fire. So I had him
interred in a crypt at the Hollywood Cemetery, like Rudolph
Valentino. He would have enjoyed the location, the company,
and that creepy word, crypt.

He's come to me many times in dreams. Sometimes I'm
overwhelmed with joy to see him. Sometimes the dreams are
nightmares which are simply realistic recreations of the worst
times we had, and I'm glad, and feel guilty to be glad, to wake
up.

But I remember the best times, too. When Art was having
fun, the world was a miracle. I wish I could explain it. Art's
joy was like some heavenly gift he somehow shared with you,
and when you had a good time in company with Art, it was
the best good time you could possibly have.

I remember a day. The band was working at a pleasant
club called Parnell's in Seattle. A local friend, a man who'd
been in San Quentin with Art and was now rehabilitated and
successful, rented a seaplane and flew us to an island off the
coast, to a restaurant there for lunch. Art was thrilled with
the hipness of the adventure and the loveliness of the day.
I've lost all the negatives and all the photographs I shot that
day but one. I have a snapshot of Art on the island. He's wearing his usual neat, not too casual clothes and borrowed rose-
colored glasses. In the picture, his head's back and he's
looking upward with an open-mouthed, attentive smile, as if

he's looking right at God. On the way home, the fellow landed us on the water so I could take some photos of Seattle. It was evening. The sun was sinking, bright on the ocean, gold and pink on the city. We climbed out onto the pontoons. I have a memory of that that's sharper than a snapshot. I can still feel how joyous and perilous it was and how blessed I felt to be there, out on the rocking, lapping, sparkling, monstrous sea, there with my camera, clicking away, catching the sunset, catching Seattle, catching Art laughing, Art walking on the water, stumbling in his Florsheims, steadied by his friend, happy.

LAURIE PEPPER
Los Angeles, California
October 11, 1993

Art Pepper Discography

by Todd Selbert

This is a comprehensive discography delineating all known commercial recordings on which Art Pepper plays. Titles by Stan Kenton and His Orchestra are limited to those containing Pepper solos. The discography was aided by the pioneer work of the late Ernest Edwards, Jr., but was exhausting nonetheless and undertaken out of admiration for an awesome musician and the greatest alto saxophonist I ever heard.

Abbreviations of Foreign Recordings

(*D*)utch
(*Dan*)ish
(*E*)nglish
(*F*)rench

(*G*)erman
(*It*)alian
(*J*)apanese
(*S*)wedish
(*Sp*)anish

Other Abbreviations

a   arranger
acc by   accompanied by
afl   alto flute
as   alto saxophone
b   bass
bar   baritone saxophone
bg   bass guitar
blitz-b   blitz bass
btb   bass trombone
btp   bass trumpet
cl   clarinet
comp   composer
cond   conductor
d   drums

el-b   electric bass
F-hn   French horn
fender-b   fender bass
fl   flute
flh   flugelhorn
g   guitar
p   piano
perc   percussion
tb   trombone
tp   trumpet
ts   tenor saxophone
vo   vocal
vtb   valve trombone
vbs   vibraharp/vibraphone

STAN KENTON AND HIS ORCHESTRA
Ray Borden, John Carroll, Buddy Childers, Karl George, Dick Morse (tp); Harry Forbes, George Faye, Bart Varsalona (tb); Ed Meyers, Art Pepper (as); Red Dorris, Morey Beeson (ts); Bob Gioga (bar); Stan Kenton (p/a); Bob Ahern (g); Clyde Singleton (b); Joe Vernon (d).   *Hollywood, Nov. 19, 1943.*

113	**Harlem Folk Dance** aSK	Capitol 145, Creative World of Stan Kenton 1062
113	**Harlem Folk Dance** aSK (alternate)	Capitol 15192, 903

JUST JAZZ ALL STARS
Art Pepper (as); Teddy Edwards (ts); unknown rhythm.   *Los Angeles, Apr. 27, 1947.*

Scratch (Donna Lee) (solo)	Crown CLP 5008

STAN KENTON AND HIS ORCHESTRA
Al Porcino, Buddy Childers, Ray Wetzel, Ken Hanna, Chico Alvarez (tp); Eddie
Bert, Harry Betts, Milt Bernhart, Harry Forbes (tb); Bart Varsalona (btb); George
Weidler, Art Pepper (as); Bob Cooper, Warner Weidler (ts); Bob Gioga (bar); Stan
Kenton (p); Laurindo Almeida (g); Eddie Safranski (b); Shelly Manne (d); Jack
Costanzo (bongo/conga); June Christy (vo); Pete Rugolo, Neal Hefti (a). *Holly-
wood, Oct. 22, 1947.*

2361 **Unison Riff** aPR	Capitol 15018, 2416/F2416, 907/
	F907, 15928, H/T358, DT2327,
	Creative World of Stan Kenton
	1062

Add Carlos Vidal Bolando, Jose Luis Manguel (Latin-perc). *New York, Dec. 6,
1947.*

2667 **Cuban Carnival** aPR	Capitol 10124, 661/F661, H/T172,
	(E) CL13613, LC6546, (G)
	LCA172, World Record Club
	(E) TP-87, Creative World of
	Stan Kenton 1037

Frank "Machito" Grillo replaces Manguel (Latin-perc).* *New York, Dec. 21,
1947.*

2936 *Journey to Brazil aPR	Capitol 57-631, 631, EAP1-508,
	T155, (E) CL13152, (G) C80014,
	Creative World of Stan Kenton
	1034
2937 **How High The Moon** voJC, aNH	Capitol 15117, 911/F911, T358, (E)
	CL13224, (G) C80010, Creative
	World of Stan Kenton 1035,
	Capitol CDP 7 97350 2

Omit Bolando and Grillo. *New York, Dec. 22, 1947.*

2942 **Harlem Holiday** aSK	Capitol 15248, 906/F906, 2418/
	F2418, T358, (E) CL13347, (G)
	C80132, Creative World of
	Stan Kenton 1036, 1078

EDDIE SAFRANSKI AND THE POLL CATS (EP512)
THE POLL CATS DIRECTED BY EDDIE SAFRANSKI (851/864)
Ray Wetzel (tp); Eddie Bert (tb); Art Pepper (as); Bob Cooper (ts); Pete Rugolo
(p/a); Eddie Safranski (b); Shelly Manne (d). *New York, Dec. 20, 1947.*

A 91 **Sa-Frantic**	Atlantic 851, EP512, Esquire (E)
	10-143, Blue Star (F) 111
A 92 **Bass Mood**	Same issues
A 93 **Turmoil**	Atlantic 864, EP512, Esquire (E)
	10-113, Blue Star (F) 117
A 94 **Jumpin' For Jane**	Same issues as "Turmoil"

STAN KENTON AND HIS ORCHESTRA
Buddy Childers, Ray Wetzel, Al Porcino, Chico Alvarez, Ken Hanna (tp); Milt
Bernhart, Eddie Bert, Harry Betts, Harry Forbes (tb); Bart Varsalona (btb);
George Weidler, Art Pepper (as); Bob Cooper, Warner Weidler (ts); Bob Gioga
(bar); Laurindo Almeida (g); Stan Kenton (p); Eddie Safranski (b); Jack Costanzo
(bongo); Shelly Manne (d). *Click Ballroom, Philadelphia, Feb. 5, 1948.*

Message To Harlem aSK	Joyce LP-1040

Same personnel. *Click Ballroom, Philadelphia, Feb. 7, 1948.*
　　Pepperpot aPR　　　　　　　　　Joyce LP-1040

EARLE SPENCER AND HIS ORCHESTRA
John Check, Buddy Childers, Jake Gerheim, Jerry Munson (tp); Jimmy Knepper, Harry Betts, Harry Forbes (tb); Bob Lively, Art Pepper (as); Tommy Makagon, Anthony Ortega (ts); Howard Phillips (bar); Shannon Fletcher (p); Laurindo Almeida (g); Willie Stater (b); Roy Hall (d); Toni Aubin (vo); Paul Nelson (a). *Hollywood, February 1949.*

BW730-3 **Oh! You Beautiful Doll** voEnsemble	Black&White 871-A, Tops LP1532, LP929, EP529
BW731-1 **Jazzbo**	Black&White 871-B
BW732-1 **Sunday Afternoon** voTA	Black&White 875-B
BW733-2 **Box Lunch (At The Factory)**	Black&White 875-A

BABS GONZALES AND HIS ORCHESTRA
J. J. Johnson (tb); Art Pepper (as); Herbie Steward (ts); Wynton Kelly (p); Bill "Pee Wee" Tinney (g); Bruce Lawrence (b); Jackie Mills (d); Babs Gonzales (vo). *Hollywood, Mar. 15, 1949.*

4099 **The Continental**	Capitol unissued
4100 **Prelude To A Nightmare** (solo)	Capitol 57-60012, (E) T20578, M-11059, (D) 5C 052-80852

JUNE CHRISTY (VO) WITH BOB COOPER'S ORCHESTRA
Buddy Childers (tp); Johnny Mandel (btp); Billy Byers (tb); Art Pepper (as); Bob Cooper (ts); Irving Roth (bar); Jasper Hornyak (violin); Cesare Pascarella (cello); Hal Shaeffer (p); Joe Mondragon (b); Don Lamond (d); Louis Martinez (conga); Bob Graettinger, Pete Rugolo (a). *Hollywood, Mar. 25, 1949.*

4118 **The Way You Look Tonight** aPR	Capitol 57-578
4119 **Everything Happens To Me** aBG	—

THE KENTON ALL-STARS "JAZZ OFF THE AIR, Vol. 2"
Art Farmer (tp); Art Pepper (as); Bob Cooper, Teddy Edwards (ts); Hampton Hawes (p); John Simmons (b); Chuck Thompson (d). *Shrine Auditorium, Los Angeles, mid-April 1949.*

Perdido	Spotlite SPJ145
The Great Lie	—

DAVE PELL AND HIS ORCHESTRA
Frank Beach (tp); Ray Sims (tb); Art Pepper (as); Dave Pell (ts); Geoff "Jeff" Clarkson (p); "Iggy" Shevack (b); Roy Harte (d); Eileen Wilson ("Kay Karma"), Ray Kellogg, "Stumpy Brown (vo); Frank Comstock, Wes Hensel (a). *Hollywood, 1949.*

CRC-5 **Boptized** aWH	Checker 702-A
CRC-6 (No takes used on this master)	
CRC-7 **You Made Me Cry Once Too Often** voSB	Checker 703
CRC-8 **I Said It Before** voSB	—
CRC-9 **Close Your Eyes** voEW	Checker 704

CRC-10 **It Was Lovely While It**   —
   Lasted voRK
CRC-11 **Pell Mell** aFC   Checker 702-B

STAN KENTON AND HIS ORCHESTRA

Maynard Ferguson, Don Paladino, Buddy Childers, Chico Alvarez, Shorty Rogers (tp); Harry Betts, Milt Bernhart, Bob Fitzpatrick, Bill Russo (tb); Bart Varsalona (btb) John Graas, Lloyd Otto (F-hn); Gene Englund (tuba); Bud Shank (fl/as); Art Pepper (as); Bob Cooper, Bart Calderall (ts); Bob Gioga (bar); Stan Kenton (p); Laurindo Almeida (g); Don Bagley (b); Shelly Manne (d); Shorty Rogers, Pete Rugolo (a). *Hollywood, Feb. 5, 1950.*

    5491 **Jolly Rogers** aSR   Capitol 1043/F1043, T667, (E)
                                      CL13334, T20841, (J) 2LP142,
                                      Creative World of Stan Kenton
                                      1036, Capitol CDP 7 97350 2
    5492 **Blues In Riff** aPR   Capitol 888/F888, (E) CL13283,
                                      (G) C80051, (D) 5C052–80799,
                                      Creative World of Stan Kenton
                                      1036

Clyde "Stumpy" Brown (btb), John Cave and Sinclair Lott (F-hn) replace Varsalona, Graas, Otto. Sixteen strings added for next title. *Hollywood, May 18, 1950.*

    6045 **Art Pepper** aSR   Capitol 28008/F28008, H/T248, (E)
                                      11010, LC6548, Creative World
                                      of Stan Kenton, 1023, Capitol
                                      CDP 97350 2

Note: Above 3 titles also on Book-of-the-Month 81-7572.

JOHNNY PARKER (VO) ACC BY KING SISTERS VOCAL GROUP AND PETE RUGOLO AND HIS ORCHESTRA

Maynard Ferguson, Don Paladino, Buddy Childers, Chico Alvarez, Shorty Rogers (tp); Kai Winding, Bill Russo, Harry Betts, Milt Bernhart, Bob Fitzpatrick (tb); Bart Varsalona (btb); Bud Shank, Art Pepper (as); Bob Cooper, Bart Calderall (ts); Bob Gioga (bar); Pete Rugolo (p); Laurindo Almeida (g); Don Bagley (b); Shelly Manne (d). *MGM Studios, New York, May 26, 1950.*

    5760 **Our Little Ranch House**   Capitol 1108/F1108
    5761 **Can't Seem To Laugh**   Capitol 1162/F1162
        Anymore
    5762 **Two Weeks With Pay**   Capital 1108/F1108
    5763 **Never Again** (no vocal   Capitol 1162/F1162
        group)

JUNE CHRISTY (VO), ORCHESTRA CONDUCTED BY SHORTY ROGERS

John Graas (F-hn); Gene Englund (tuba); Art Pepper (as); Bob Cooper, Bud Shank (ts); Bob Gioga (bar); Claude Williamson (p); Don Bagley (b); Shelly Manne (d); Shorty Rogers (a). *Hollywood, Sept. 11, 1950.*

    6563 **A Mile Down The Highway**   Capitol 1207/F1207
        There's A Toll Bridge
    6564 **He Can Come Back Anytime**   —
        He Wants To (solo)

STAN KENTON AND HIS ORCHESTRA
Maynard Ferguson, John Howell, Al Porcino, Chico Alvarez, Shorty Rogers (tp);
Eddie Bert, Milt Bernhart, Harry Betts, Bob Fitzpatrick (tb); Bart Varsalona (btb);
Bud Shank, Art Pepper (as); Bob Cooper, Bart Calderall (ts); Bob Gioga (bar);
Stan Kenton (p); Ralph Blaze (g); Don Bagley (b); Shelly Manne (d); Miguel
Rivera (conga). *Hollywood, Sept. 12, 1950.*

6579 **Viva Prado** aSR	Capitol 1279/F1279, (E) CL13453, World Record Club (E) T109, Creative World of Stan Kenton 1027, Capitol CDP 7 97350 2
6581 **Round Robin** aSR	Capitol F15848, H325, T796, (J) 2LP62, (E) LC6561, T20841, Creative World of Stan Kenton 1036, Book-of-the-Month 81-7572

MAYNARD FERGUSON AND HIS ORCHESTRA
Maynard Ferguson (tp/vo); Chico Alvarez, Al Porcino, Shorty Rogers (tp); Milt
Bernhart, Harry Betts, Bob Fitzpatrick (tb), John Graas (F-hn); Gene Englund
(tuba); Bud Shank, Art Pepper (as); Bob Cooper, Jimmy Giuffre (ts); Bob Gioga
(bar); Joe Rotundi (p); Don Bagley (b); Shelly Manne (d); Shorty Rogers, Paul
Villepigue (a). *Hollywood, Sept. 13, 1950.*

6577 **Take The "A" Train** aSR	Capitol F15851, H326, (E) LC6579
6582 **Short Wave** aSR (solo)	Capitol H325, (E) LC6561, (J) 2LP62
6583 **Love Locked Out** aPV	Capitol 1269/F1269, (E) CLI3426
6584 **Band Ain't Draggin'** voMF, aSR	Same issues as "Love Locked Out"

STAN KENTON AND HIS ORCHESTRA
Al Porcino, Maynard Ferguson, John Howell, Shorty Rogers, Chico Alvarez (tp);
Milt Bernhart, Harry Betts, Bob Fitzpatrick, Eddie Bert or Dick Kenney (tb); Bart
Varsalona (btb); Bud Shank, Art Pepper (as); Bob Cooper, Bart Calderall (ts); Bob
Gioga (bar); Stan Kenton (p); Ralph Blaze (g); Don Bagley (b); Shelly Manne
(d). *Rustic Cabin, Englewood Gulf, N.J., Dec. 9, 1950.*

Jolly Rogers aSR	Moonlite KH 1–2
Viva Prado aSR	—

STAN KENTON AND HIS ORCHESTRA
Ray Wetzel, Maynard Ferguson, John Howell, Shorty Rogers, Chico Alvarez
(tp); Milt Bernhart, Harry Betts, Bob Fitzpatrick, Dick Kenney (tb); Bart Varsalona (btb); Bud Shank, Art Pepper (as); Bob Cooper, Bart Calderall (ts); Bob
Gioga (bar); Stan Kenton (p); Ralph Blaze (g); Don Bagley (b); Shelly Manne
(d); Jay Johnson (vo). *Palladium Ballroom, Hollywood, February-March 1951*

Minor Riff aPR	First Heard (E) FH 1004
Gone with the Wind aNH, voJJ	—
Viva Prado aSR	—
I Only Have Eyes for You	Rendezvous CD-1001
Intermission Riff aRW	—
Round Robin aSR	—
Blues in Riff aPR	—
Viva Prado aSR	—

Autumn Leaves aSR   Joyce LP-1070
Viva Prado aSR   —
I'll Remember April aPR   —
Blues in Riff aPR   —

STAN KENTON AND HIS ORCHESTRA
Maynard Ferguson, John Howell, Ray Wetzel, Chico Alvarez, Shorty Rogers (tp);
Dick Kenney, Milt Bernhart, Harry Betts, Bob Fitzpatrick (tb); Bart Varsalona
(btb); Bud Shank, Art Pepper (as); Bob Cooper, Bart Calderall (ts); Bob Gioga
(bar); Stan Kenton (p); Ralph Blaze (g); Don Bagley (b); Shelly Manne
(d). *Hollywood, Mar. 28, 1951.*

7344 **Dynaflow** aSK   Capitol 1535/F1535, T421, (E)
                                        CL13561, World Record Club
                                        (E) T109, Creative World of
                                        Stan Kenton 1062, Book-of-the-
                                        Month 81-7572, Capitol CDP
                                        797350 2

Jimmy Salco (tp), Paul Weigand (btb), Jimmy Giuffre (ts) replace Wetzel, Varsalona, Cooper. Gene Roland (a). *Hollywood, May 31, 1951.*

7605 **Jump For Joe** aGR   Capitol 1704/F1704, T421, (E)
                                        CL13577, (G) C80160, Creative
                                        World of Stan Kenton 1064

Buddy Childers (tp), John Halliburton (tb), Bob Cooper (ts) replace Salco,
Weigand, Giuffre. Jack Costanzo (conga) added; Pete Rugolo (a). *Hollywood,
June 29, 1951.*

7824 **Francesca** aPR   Capitol 1774/F1774, T421, (E)
                                        CL13608, World Record Club
                                        (E) T109, Creative World of
                                        Stan Kenton 1064

George Roberts (btb) replaces Halliburton. Omit Costanzo. *Casino Ballroom,
Catalina Island, Cal., July 8, 1951.*

Pepperpot aPR   Moonlite KH 1–2

same   *Marine Ballroom, Steel Pier, Atlantic City, NJ, July 1951*
I Only Have Eyes for You   Joyce-1113
Jolly Rogers aSR   —

Conte Candoli (tp) replaces Alvarez. *Marine Ballroom, Steel Pier, Atlantic
City, N.J., late July 1951.*

Jump For Joe aGR   Joyce LP-1016
Dynaflow aSK   —
Intermission Riff aRW   —
Round Robin aSR   —
Viva Prado aSR   —

John Coppola and Stu Williamson (tp), Bill Russo (tb) replace Childers, Rogers,
Bernhart. Shorty Rogers (a). *Hollywood, Sept. 19, 1951.*

9038 **Sambo** aSR   Capitol (E) T20244, Creative
                                        World of Stan Kenton 1028

Add Stan Fletcher (tuba). *Hollywood, Sept. 20, 1951.*

9052 **Street Of Dreams** aSK   Capitol 1823/F1823, T462,
                                        RHB2029, (E) CL13792, World
                                        Record Club (E) TP-87, Creative
                                        World of Stan Kenton 1042,
                                        Book-of-the-Month 81-7572

Add John Graas, Lloyd Otto, and George Price (F-hn), 16 strings; Manny Albam and Bill Russo (a). *Cornell University, Ithaca, N.Y., Oct. 14, 1951.*

| 13299 **Samana** aMA | Capitol WDX569–6, (E) LCT6159, Cornell Rhythm Club, Creative World of Stan Kenton 1030 |
| **Improvisation** aBR | Cornell Rhythm Club |

Omit French horns and strings, Neil Hefti (a). *Unknown location, probably fall 1951.*

| **In Veradero** aNH | Laserlight 15 770 |

Readmit French horns and strings.

| **Art Pepper** aSR | — |
| **Improvisation** aBR | — |

Omit French horns and strings.   Carnegie Hall, NYC, October 19, 1951

| **Sambo** aSR | Joyce 1080 |

Readmit French horns and strings.

Art Pepper aSR	—
Improvisation aBR	—
Samana aMA	—

same   Seattle, November 25, 1951

| **Samana** aMA | Mark56 860 |

Omit French horns and strings.

| **Sambo** aSR | — |

Readmit French horns and strings.

| **Art Pepper** aSR | — |
| **Improvisation** aBR | — |

SHORTY ROGERS AND HIS GIANTS

Shorty Rogers (tp); John Graas (F-hn); Gene Englund (tuba); Art Pepper (as); Jimmy Giuffre (ts); Hampton Hawes (p); Don Bagley (b); Shelly Manne (d). *Hollywood, Oct. 8, 1951.*

9117 **Popo** aSR	Capitol 6F-15763/7-15763, H294/ EAP2-294/KCF-294
9118 **Didi** aSR	Capitol 6F-15765/7-15765, H294/ EAP2-294/KCF-294, (E) CL13678
9119 **Four Mothers** aJG	Same issues
9120 **Over the Rainbow** aSR	Capitol 6F-15764/7-15764, H294/ EAP2-294/KCF-294
9121 **Apropos** aSR	Same issues as "Popo"
9122 **Sam And The Lady** aSR	Same issues as "Over The Rainbow"

Note: Above 6 titles also issued on Capitol T691, DT2025, (E) LC6549, Mosaic MR6-125.

SHELLY MANNE SEPTET

Conte Candoli (tp); Bill Russo (tb/a); Art Pepper (as); Bob Cooper (ts); Gene Esposito (p); Don Bagley (b); Shelly Manne (d/vo); Shelby Davis (vo). *Chicago, Nov. 12, 1951.*

DG3600	**Pooch McGooch**	Dee Gee 3802, Savoy MG12045
DG3601–4	**All Of Me** voSM	Dee Gee 3801A, Savoy MG12045
DG3602	**Back In Your Own Backyard** voSD	Dee Gee 3802, Regent MG6031

DG3603–4 **The Count On Rush**   Dee Gee 3801B, Savoy MG12045
Street

Note: All 4 titles also issued on Dee Gee EP4006, LP1003, London (E)
LTZ-C14019.

SHORTY ROGERS AND HIS GIANTS
Shorty Rogers (tp); Art Pepper (as); Frank Patchen (p); Howard Rumsey (b);
Shelly Manne (d). *Lighthouse, Hermosa Beach, Cal., Dec. 27, 1951.*

Popo	Xanadu 148
Lullaby In Rhythm	—
Omit Rogers.	
All The Things You Are	—
Add Rogers.	
Robbins Nest	—
Scrapple From The Apple	—
Omit Rogers.	
Body And Soul	—
Add Rogers.	
Jive At Five	—
Cherokee	—

Note: Art Pepper not present on other titles on this recording.

ART PEPPER QUARTET
Art Pepper (as, cl-1); Hampton Hawes (p); Joe Mondragon (b); Larry Bunker
(d/vibes). *Surf Club, Los Angeles, Feb. 12, 1952.*

How High The Moon	Xanadu 108
Suzy The Poodle	—
Easy Steppin'	—
Tickle Toe	Xanadu 108, 5001
Patty Cake	Xanadu 108
Move	—
All The Things You Are	—
Don't Blame Me	—
Surf Ride	—
Rose Room (1)	—
Suzy The Poodle	—

ART PEPPER QUARTET
Art Pepper (as); Hampton Hawes (p); Joe Mondragon (b); Larry Bunker
(d/vibes). *Surf Club, Los Angeles, February 12, 1952.*

A Night in Tunisia	Xanadu 117
Spiked Punch	—
The Way You Look Tonight	—
Minor Yours	—
Suzy the Poodle	—
Easy Steppin'	—
Chili Pepper	—
LAMJHP	—
Everything Happens To Me	—
Move	—

Note: *Minor Yours* is not the same *Minor Yours* recorded subsequently.

ART PEPPER QUARTET

Art Pepper (as); Hampton Hawes (p); Joe Mondragon (b); Larry Bunker (d).
Los Angeles, Mar. 4, 1952.

D-6001–7	**Brown Gold**	Discovery 157, Savoy MG12089, Vogue (E) V2237, Swing (F) 391, Jazz Selection (S) 4021, Savoy SV-0115
D-6002–4	**These Foolish Things**	Discovery 157, Regent MG6069, Vogue (E) V2237, Swing (F) 391, Jazz Selection (S) 4021, Savoy CD-DENSV-0161
D-6003–5	**Surf Ride**	Discovery 158, Savoy MG12089, MG12125, Swing (F) 392, Jazz Selection (S) 4022, Savoy SV-0115
D-6004–4	**Holiday Flight**	Discovery 158, Savoy MG12089, Swing (F) 392, Jazz Selection (S) 4022, Savoy SV-0115

Note: All 4 titles also issued on Discovery LP3019, EP19, Vogue (E) LDE-067,
   Jazz Selection (S) JEP4550, JSLP50005, CBS (J) SOPL 78-SY, Savoy SJL 2215,
   Toshiba (J) WAJ-70099.

ART PEPPER QUARTET

Art Pepper (as); Russ Freeman (p); Bob Whitlock (b); Bobby White
(d). *Hollywood, Oct. 8, 1952.*

D-6058-2	**Chili Pepper**	Discovery 171, Savoy MG12089, Vogue (E) V2291, Swing (F) 417, Savoy SV-0115
D-6058-2	**Chili Pepper**	Savoy SJL 2217
D-6058-3	**Chili Pepper**	Savoy SJL 1170
D-6058-5	**Chili Pepper**	Savoy SJL 1170
D-6059-1	**Suzy The Poodle**	Discovery 170, Savoy MG12089, Vogue (E) V2291, Swing (F) 418, Savoy SV-0115
D-6059-6	**Suzy the Poodle**	Savoy SJL 2217
D-6059-3	**Suzy the Poodle**	Savoy SJL 1170
D-6059-5	**Suzy the Poodle**	Savoy SJL 1170
D-6060-4	**Everything Happens To Me**	Discovery 171, Regent MG6069, Swing (F) 417, Savoy CD-DENSV-0161
D-6060-1	**Everything Happens To Me**	Savoy SJL 2217
D-6060-2	**Everything Happens To Me**	Savoy SJL 1170
D-6060-3	**Everything Happens To Me**	Savoy SJL 1170
D-6060-6	**Everything Happens To Me**	Savoy SJL 1170
D-6061–4	**Tickle Toe**	Discovery 170, Savoy MG12089, Swing (F) 418, Savoy SV-0115
D-6061–9	**Tickle Toe**	Savoy SJL 2217

Note: Four masters orginally issued on Discovery also issued on Discovery
   LP3019, Vogue (E) LDE-067, Jazz Selection (S) JSLP50005, CBS (J) SOPL 78-SY,
   Savoy SJL 2217, Toshiba (J) WAJ-70099.

SHORTY ROGERS AND HIS GIANTS

Shorty Rogers (tp); Milt Bernhart (tb); John Graas (F-hn); Gene Englund (tuba); Art Pepper ("Art Salt") (as); Jimmy Giuffre (ts); Hampton Hawes (p); Joe Mondragon (b); Shelly Manne (d). *Hollywood, Jan. 12, 1953.*

E3VB0007	**Powder Puff**	Victor 47-5397, LPM3137
E3VB0008	**The Pesky Serpent**	Victor LPM3137
E3VB0009	**Bunny**	Victor EPA731, LPM3137, (F) 430,665
E3VB0010	**Pirouette**	Victor EPA731, LPM3137

Same personnel. *Hollywood, Jan. 15, 1953.*

E3VB0011	**Morpo**	Victor 47-5397, LPM3137, EPA731, (F) 430,665
E3VB0012	**Diablo's Dance**	Victor LPM3137, EPA731
E3VB0013	**Mambo Del Crow**	Victor LPM3137
E3VB0014	**Indian Club**	—

Note: All 8 titles also issued on Victor LPM1195, HMV (E) DLP1058, RCA (F) A130122, Bluebird 5917-1-RB.

SHORTY ROGERS AND HIS ORCHESTRA

Shorty Rogers, Maynard Ferguson, Conrad Gozzo, John Howell, Tom Reeves (tp); Milt Bernhart, Harry Betts, John Halliburton (tb); John Graas (F-hn); Gene Englund (tuba); Art Pepper ("Art Salt") (as/ts); Bud Shank (as/bar); Bob Cooper, Jimmy Giuffre (ts/bar); Marty Paich (p); Curtis Counce (b); Shelly Manne (d). *Hollywood, Mar. 26, 1953.*

E3VB0059	**Coop De Graas**	Victor LPM3138, LPM1350
E3VB0060	**Infinity Promenade** (ts solo)	Victor LPM3138, 47-5503
E3VB0061	**Short Stop** (as solo)	Victor LPM3138, LPM1350, RCA (F) 75357
E3VB0062	**Boar-Jibu** (ts solo)	Same issues as "Short Stop"

Same personnel. *Hollywood, Apr. 2, 1953.*

E3VB0064	**Contours**	Victor LPM3138, LPM1350
E3VB0065	**Tale Of An African Lobster** (as solo)	Victor 47-5503, LPM3138, LPM1350, HMV (E) B10781, 7M267
E3VB0066	**Chiquito Loco** (as solo)	Same issues as "Contours"
E3VB0067	**Sweetheart Of Sigmund Freud** (ts solo)	Victor LPM3138, LPM1350, HMV (E) B10781, 7M267, RCA (F) 75357

Note: All 8 titles also issued on HMV (E) DLP1030, Electrola (G) WD1030, RCA (F) FXL1 7234, Bluebird 5917-1-RB.

SHELLY MANNE AND HIS MEN

Bob Enevoldson (vtb); Art Pepper ("Art Salt" on C353, C354) (as); Bob Cooper (ts); Jimmy Giuffre (bar); Marty Paich (p); Curtis Counce (b); Shelly Manne (d); Shorty Rogers, Bill Russo (a). *Hollywood, Apr. 6, 1953.*

LK 339	**Mallets** aSR	Contemporary C354, EP4001, C2503
LK 340	**You And The Night And The Music** aBR	Contemporary C353, EP4001, C2503

LK 341 **La Mucura** aSR   Same issues as "Mallets"
LK 342 **Gazelle** aBR   Same issues as "You And The
                                    Night And The Music"

Note: All 4 titles also issued on Contemporary C3507, Vogue (E) LDE-072,
   LAC12138, Jazz Selection (S) JSLP50003.

ART PEPPER QUARTET

Art Pepper (as); Sonny Clark (p); Harry Babasin (b); Bobby White (d). *Lighthouse, Hermosa Beach, Cal., March 30 & April 1, 1953.*

Deep Purple	Straight-Ahead SAJ-1004
Bluebird	—
S'Wonderful	—
Pennies from Heaven	—

ART PEPPER WITH THE SONNY CLARK TRIO

Art Pepper (as); Sonny Clark (p); Harry Babasin (b); Bobby White (d).   *Lighthouse, Hermosa Beach, Cal., May 31, 1953.*

Brown Gold	Straight-Ahead SAJ-1001
These Foolish Things	—
Tickle Toe	—
Tenderly	—
Strike Up The Band	—
Night And Day	—

ART PEPPER QUINTET

Art Pepper (as); Jack Montrose (ts); Claude Williamson (p); Monte Budwig
(b); Paul Ballerina (d). *Hollywood, Aug. 25, 1954.*

D-6301-3	**Nutmeg**	Discovery DL3023, Savoy MG12089, SV-0115
D-6301-1	**Nutmeg**	Savoy SJL 2217
D-6301-6	**Nutmeg**	Savoy SJL 1170
D-6301-7	**Nutmeg**	Savoy SJL 1170
D-6303-2	**Deep Purple**	Discovery DL3023, Regent MG6069, Savoy CD-DENSV-0161
D-6304-5	**Cinnamon**	Discovery DL3023, Savoy MG12089, SV-0115
D-6304-3	**Cinnamon**	Savoy SJL 2217
D-6304-2	**Cinnamon**	Savoy SJL 1170
D-6305-3	**What's New**	Discovery DL3023, Regent MG6069, Savoy CD-DENSV-0161
D-6305-2	**What's New**	Savoy SJL 2217
D-6305-1	**What's New**	Savoy SJL 1170

same except Larry Bunker replaces Paul Ballerina.

D-6306-2	**Thyme Time**	Discovery DL3023, Savoy MG12089, SV-0115
D-6306-3	**Thyme Time**	Savoy SJL 2217
D-6306-1	**Thyme Time**	Savoy SJL 1170
D-6307-2	**Straight Life**	Discovery DL3023, Savoy 4518, MG12089, MG12126, SV-0115
D-6307-3	**Straight Life**	Savoy SJL 2217
D-6307-1	**Straight Life**	Savoy SJL 1170

D-6308-5 **Art's Oregano**	Discovery DL3023, Savoy MG12089, SV-0115
D-6308-2 **Art's Oregano**	Savoy SJL 2217
D-6308-1 **Art's Oregano**	Savoy SJL 1170
D-6309–5 **The Way You Look Tonight**	Discovery DL3023, Savoy MG12089, Savoy SV-0115
D-6309–2 **The Way You Look Tonight**	Savoy SJL 2217

Note: All titles issued on Discovery also issued on CBS (J) SOPL 78-SY, Savoy SJL 2217.

SHORTY ROGERS AND HIS ORCHESTRA

Shorty Rogers, Conte Candoli, Pete Candoli, Maynard Ferguson, Harry Edison (tp); Bob Enevoldson (vtb); Milt Bernhart, Frank Rosolino (tb); George Roberts (btb); John Graas (F-hn); Paul Sarmento (tuba); Charlie Mariano, Art Pepper (as); Bill Holman, Jack Montrose (ts); Jimmy Giuffre (cl/bar); Lou Levy (p); Ralph Pena (b); Stan Levey (d). *Hollywood, July 5, 1956.*

G2JB4752 **Pay The Piper** (solo)	Victor LPM1350
G2JB4753 **Home With Sweets** (solo)	Victor LPM1350, EPA910, HMV (E) 7EG8250
G2JB4754 **Pink Squirrel**	Same issues as "Home With Sweets"
G2JB4755 **Blues Express** (That's Right) (solo)	Victor LPM1350, EPA910, HMV (E) 7EG8250, RCA (It) LPM10044

Note: All 4 titles also issued on RCA (F) FXL1 7234.

CHET BAKER (1)
CHET BAKER-ART PEPPER SEXTET (2) (on album cover)
CHET BAKER-ART PEPPER-RICHIE KAMUCA SEXTET (2) (on record label)
CHET BAKER QUINTET (3)
ART PEPPER-RICHIE KAMUCA QUINTET (4)

Chet Baker (tp); Art Pepper (as); Richie Kamuca (ts); Pete Jolly (p); Leroy Vinnegar (b); Stan Levey (d); Johnny Mandel (a). *Hollywood, July 26, 1956.*

Sonny Boy a/M (3:55) (1)	Playboy PB# 1958
Minor Yours (7:11) (2)	Pacific Jazz PJ-LA896-H
Tynan Time (6:14) (2)	—
The Route (5:04) (2)	Pacific Jazz JWC509, Vogue (E) LAE12156
The Route (4:49) (3)	Crown CLP5317/CST317
The Route (3:21) (4)	World Pacific ST1021, JWC/ST513

Note: On 4, Chet Baker is edited out.

CHET BAKER SEXTET (5)

Full group as above. *Hollywood, July 26, 1956.*

Little Girl a/M (4:15) (5)	Pacific Jazz JWC507, EP4–48, PJ-LA896-H, Jazztone J1274, Vogue (E) LAE12115, Swing (F) LPM30078

ART PEPPER QUARTET (6)
ART PEPPER WITH LEROY VINNEGAR AND STAN LEVEY (7)

Art Pepper (as); Pete Jolly (p-6); Leroy Vinnegar (b); Stan Levey (d). *Hollywood, July 26, 1956.*

Old Croix (4:25) (6)	Pacific Jazz JWC507, Jazztone J1274, Vogue (E) LAE12115, Swing (F) LPM30078, Music (It) LPM2043, Pacific Jazz PJ-LA896-H, PJ60 (3:23), PJ (J) JR-8113 (3:23)
I Can't Give You Anything But Love (4:00) (7)	Pacific Jazz JWC505, Vogue (E) LAE12106, Swing (F) LPM30078, Music (It) LPM2027, Pacific Jazz PJ60 (3:14), PJ (J) JR-8113 (3:14)
The Great Lie	Mosaic MR3-105

Note: All 8 titles issues on Mosaic MR3-105, Pacific Jazz CDP7 92931 2.

ART PEPPER QUINTET

Jack Sheldon (tp); Art Pepper (as); Russ Freeman (p); Leroy Vinnegar (b); Shelly Manne (d). *Hollywood, Aug. 6, 1956.*

Angel Wings	JazzWest JLP10, Score SLP4032, Sonet (Dan) SLP31, Imperial LP9238
Broadway	JazzWest JLP10, Score SLP4032, Sonet (Dan) SLP31
Five More	Same issues as "Broadway"
Funny Blues	Same issues as "Angel Wings"
Mambo De La Pinta	Same issues as "Broadway"
Minority	Same issues as "Broadway"
Patricia (omit tp)	Same issues as "Broadway"
Pepper Returns	Same issues as "Angel Wings"
Walkin' Out Blues	Same issues as "Broadway"
You Go To My Head (omit tp)	Same issues as "Broadway"

Note: All 10 titles issued on Liberty (J) LR-8036, Blue Note BN-LA591-H2, Toshiba (J) LLJ-70057, Blue Note CDP7 46863 2.

MARTY PAICH QUARTET FEATURING ART PEPPER
ART PEPPER QUARTET (Interlude)

Art Pepper (as); Marty Paich (p); Walter "Buddy" Clark (b); Frank Capp (d). *Hollywood, August 1956.*

Abstract Art	Tampa TP28, Interlude MO512, London (E) LZU14040, Charlie Parker PLP829, AJ 510, Iris MO 512
All The Things You Are	Tampa TP28, Interlude MO514, London (E) LZU14040, Sonet (Dan) SXP2812, Charlie Parker PLP 829, AJ 510, Iris MO 512
Marty's Blues	Tampa TP28, Interlude MO514, London (E) LZU14040, Charlie Parker PLP 829, AJ 510, Iris MO 512

Melancholy Madeline	Tampa 45–149, TP11, TP28, RS1000, SA100, Interlude MO512, Charlie Parker PLP831, London (E) LZU14040, Sonet (Dan) SXP2812, Charlie Parker PLP 829, AJ 510, Iris MO 512
Over The Rainbow	Same issues as "Abstract Art"
Pitfall	Same issues as "Marty's Blues"
Sidewinder	Same issues as "Abstract Art"
What's Right For You?	Same issues as "All The Things You Are"
You And The Night And The Music	Tampa TP28, Interlude MO512, London (E) LZU14040, Sonet (Dan) SXP2812, Charlie Parker PLP 829, AJ 510, Iris MO 512

Note: All 9 titles also issued on JVC (J) SMJX 10138.

HOAGY CARMICHAEL WITH THE PACIFIC JAZZMEN, ARRANGED AND CONDUCTED BY JOHNNY MANDEL

Harry Edison, Conrad Gozzo (tp); Jimmy Zito (btp); Harry Klee (fl/as); Art Pepper (as); Mort Friedman (ts); Marty Berman (bar/reeds); Jimmy Rowles (p/celeste); Al Hendrickson (g); Joe Mondragon (b); Irv Cottler (d); Hoagy Carmichael (vo/comp). *Hollywood, Sept. 10, 1956.*

Baltimore Oriole	Pacific Jazz PJ1223, Jazztone J1266, Kimberly LP2023/S11023, Vogue (E) VA160112
New Orleans (solo)	Same issues
Georgia On My Mind (solo)	Same issues

JOHNNY MANDEL BAND-SOLOIST ART PEPPER*
JOHNNY MANDEL ORCHESTRA FEATURING ART PEPPER**

Same personnel as above, except omit Hoagy Carmichael (vo). Same date.

Georgia On My Mind (PJ 731–1)	World Pacific WP1257,* ST1015,** ST1291,** HFS2/SS2,** Vogue (E) LAE12211

HOAGY CARMICHAEL WITH THE PACIFIC JAZZMEN

Same personnel as before, except add Hoagy Carmichael (vo), and Ralph Pena (b) replaces Mondragon. *Hollywood, Sept. 11, 1956.*

Memphis In June	Pacific Jazz PJ1223, Jazztone J1266, Kimberly LP2023/ S11023, Vogue (E) VA160112
Two Sleepy People (solo)	Pacific Jazz PJ1223, Jazztone J1266, Kimberly LP2023/ S11023, Vogue (E) VA160112, VE170113

Lazy River (solo)   Pacific Jazz PJ1223, Jazztone
                                            J1266, Kimberly LP2023/
                                            S11023, LP2026/S11026, Vogue
                                            (E) VA160112, VE170113

JOHNNY MANDEL ORCHESTRA
Same personnel as above except omit Hoagy Carmichael (vo). Bill Holman (ts
solo) dubbed in in 1958. Same date.

Lazy River (2:45) (solo)   Pacific Jazz PJM-410

HOAGY CARMICHAEL WITH THE PACIFIC JAZZMEN
Don Fagerquist, Ray Linn* (tp); Jimmy Zito (btp)*; Art Pepper (as); Harry Klee
(fl)*; Mort Friedman (ts)*; Marty Berman (bar)*; Jimmy Rowles (p); Al Hendrickson (g); Joe Mondragon (b); Nick Fatool (d); Hoagy Carmichael (vo); Johnny
Mandel (a/cond). *Hollywood, Sept. 13, 1956.*

Winter Moon (solo)   Pacific Jazz PJ1223, Jazztone
                                            J1266, Kimberly LP2023/
                                            S11023, Vogue (E) VA160112
*Skylark (solo)   Same issues
Rockin' Chair (solo)   Pacific Jazz PJ1223, Jazztone
                                            J1266, Kimberly LP2023/
                                            S11023, Vogue (E) VA160112,
                                            VE170113
*Ballad In Blue (solo)   Same issues as "Rockin' Chair"

CHET BAKER BIG BAND
Chet Baker, Conte Candoli, Norman Faye (tp); Frank Rosolino (tb); Art Pepper
(as); Bill Perkins, Phil Urso (ts); Bud Shank (bar); Bobby Timmons (p); Jimmy
Bond (b); Lawrence Marable (d); Jimmy Heath (a). *Hollywood, Oct. 26, 1956.*

Tenderly (solo)   Pacific Jazz 45x636, PJ1229,
                                            World Pacific WP1257/ST1015,
                                            JWC514, Vogue (E) LAE12109,
                                            LAE12211, Swing (F)
                                            LDM30079, Mosaic MR 3-105
Darn That Dream   Pacific Jazz PJ1229, Vogue (E)
                                            LAE12109, Swing (F)
                                            LDM30079.
A Foggy Day   Same issues as "Darn That
                                            Dream"

CHET BAKER-ART PEPPER-PHIL URSO
Chet Baker (tp); Art Pepper (as/a); Phil Urso (ts); Carl Perkins (p); Curtis Counce
(b); Lawrence Marable (d); Jimmy Heath (a). *Hollywood, Oct. 31, 1956.*

For Miles And Miles aJH   Pacific Jazz PJ1234, PJ18, EP4-51
Picture Of Heath aJH   Same issues
Minor-Yours aAP   Pacific Jazz PJ1234, PJ18, EP4-65
C.T.A. aJH   Pacific Jazz PJ60 (see note),
                                            PJ1234, PJ18, EP4-65, PJ (J)
                                            JR-8113 (2:58)

Resonant Emotions aJH   Pacific Jazz PJ1234, PJ18, EP4–66
Tynan Tyme aAP   Same issues
For Minors Only aJH   Pacific Jazz PJ1234, PJ18
Note: Above 7 titles also issued on Vogue (E) LAE12183, Mosaic MR3-105, and Pacific Jazz CDP7 94474 2. The PJ60 issue of "C.T.A." is edited with solos by Urso and Counce omitted. Chorus and half of "8's" also cut.

RUSSELL GARCIA ORCHESTRA

Buddy Childers, Don Fagerquist, Maynard Ferguson, Ray Linn (tp); Milt Bernhart, Lloyd Elliot, Tommy Pederson, Frank Rosolino (tb); Art Pepper, Bud Shank (as); Ted Nash (ts); Chuck Gentry (bar); Gerald Wiggins (p); Howard Roberts (g); Max Bennett (b); Alvin Stoller (d). *Hollywood, Nov. 2, 1956.*

Music City (2nd as solo)   Kapp KXL5001, London (E)
     LTZ-R15083, Kapp (Sp) KXL 5001

Fish Tail (1st as solo)   Same issues
Smoggy Day (2nd as solo)   Kapp KXL5001, London (E)
     LTZ-R15084, Kapp (Sp) KXL 5001

Los Angeles River (2nd as solo)   Same issues as "Smoggy Day"
Number Four (solo)   Kapp (Sp) KXL 5001

ART PEPPER QUARTET

Art Pepper (as); Russ Freeman (p); Ben Tucker (b); Gary Frommer (d). *Hollywood, November 23, 1956.*

Art's Opus   Tampa RS1001, TP20, Interlude
     MO514, Sonet (Dan) SXP2810,
     London (E) LZU14038

Besame Mucho   Tampa 45–149, RS1001, TP20,
     TP38, Interlude MO512,
     Charlie Parker CP836, Sonet
     (Dan) SXP2807, London (E)
     LZU14038

Blues At Twilight   Tampa RS1001, TP20, Sonet (Dan)
     SXP2807, London (E)
     LZU14038

Blues At Twilight (alt)   V.S.O.P. 61
Diane   Tampa RS1001, TP20, Interlude
     MO512, Charlie Parker CP836,
     London (E) LZU14038

I Surrender Dear   Tampa RS1001, TP20, Interlude
     MO512, Charlie Parker CP836,
     Sonet (Dan) SXP2810, London
     (E) LZU14038

Pepper Pot   Same issues as "Diane"
Val's Pal   Tampa RS1001, TP20, Interlude
     MO514, Sonet (Dan) SXP2807,
     London (E) LZU14038

Note: All 7 titles issued on Tampa (J) JVC SMJ 6022, Overseas (J) 1861-V, V.S.O.P. 61.

ART PEPPER WITH THE WARNE MARSH QUARTET

Art Pepper (as); Warne Marsh (ts); Ronnie Ball (p); Ben Tucker (b); Gary Frommer (d). *Los Angeles, Nov. 26, 1956.*

I Can't Believe That You're In   Contemporary S7630, (J) LAX
Love With Me   3131, Contemporary OJC-389
All The Things You Are   Same issues

What's New	Same issues
Tickle Toe	Same issues
I Can't Believe That You're In Love With Me (alt)	Contemporary OJC-389
All The Things You Are	—
Avalon	unissued
Warnin'	unissued
Warnin' (alt)	unissued
Stompin' at the Savoy	unissued

BILL PERKINS-ART PEPPER-RICHIE KAMUCA (401)
ART PEPPER FEATURING BILL PERKINS (60)
Art Pepper (as); Bill Perkins (ts); Jimmy Rowles (p); Ben Tucker (b); Mel Lewis (d). *Hollywood, Dec. 11, 1956.*

A Foggy Day	Pacific Jazz PJM401 (3:52), PJ60 (3:53), PJ (J) JR-8113
Diane-A-Flow (401)/Diana Flow (60)	Pacific Jazz PJM401 (4:02), PJ60 (3:06), PJ (J) JR-8113
What Is This Thing Called Love?	Pacific Jazz PJM401 (5:27), PJ60 (5:18), PJ (J) JR-8113
Zenobia	Pacific Jazz PJM401 (5:15), PJ60 (3:43), PJ (J) JR-8113

Note: All 4 titles as issued on PJM401 also on Vogue (E) LAE12088, Mosaic MR3-105, Pacific Jazz CDP7 97194 2.

TED BROWN SEXTET
Art Pepper (as); Ted Brown, Warne Marsh (ts); Ronnie Ball (p); Ben Tucker (b); Jeff Morton (d). *Hollywood, Dec. 21, 1956.*

Aretha	Vanguard VRS8515, (J) SR(M)3146
Arrivals	Same issues
Avalon	Same issues
Broadway	Same issues
Foolin' Myself	Same issues
Long Gone	Same issues

Note: Art Pepper not present on other titles from this session.

ART PEPPER QUARTET
Art Pepper (as); Russ Freeman (p); Ben Tucker (b); Chuck Flores (d). *Hollywood, Dec. 28, 1956.*

Bewitched	Intro ILP606, Score SLP4030, Blue Note BN-LA591-H2
Blues In (as and b only)	Same issues
When You're Smiling	Same issues
Cool Bunny	Same issues

Note: All 4 titles also issued on Toshiba (J) LLJ-70080, Blue Note CDP7 46848 2.

JOE MORELLO (Intro)
PEPPER-NORVO (Score)
Art Pepper (as-1, ts-2); Red Norvo (vibes-3); Gerald Wiggins (p); Ben Tucker (b); Joe Morello (d). *Hollywood, Jan. 3, 1957.*

Pepper Steak (1, 3)	Intro ILP608, Score SLP4031, Blue Note BN-LA591-H2, Blue Note CDP7 46863 2

Straight Life (1)	Same issues
Tenor Blooz (2, 3)	Same issues
Yardbird Suite (1)	Same issues
You're Driving Me Crazy (1, 3)	Same issues

ART PEPPER QUARTET
Same personnel as Dec. 28, 1956. *Hollywood, Jan. 14, 1957.*

What Is This Thing Called Love?	Intro ILP606, Score SLP4030, Blue Note BN-LA591-H2
Stompin' At The Savoy	Same issues
Diane's Dilemma	Same issues
Diane's Dilemma (alternate)	Blue Note BN-LA591-H2
Blues Out (as and b only)	Intro ILP606, Score SLP4030

Note: Four titles on Intro also issued on Toshiba (J) LLJ-70080. All titles on Blue Note CDP7 46848 2.

ART PEPPER QUARTET
Art Pepper (as); Red Garland (p); Paul Chambers (b); Philly Joe Jones (d). *Hollywood, Jan. 19, 1957.*

Birk's Works	Contemporary C3532, S7018, (J) GXC 3101, S7532, Vogue (E) LAC12066
Imagination	Same issues
Jazz Me Blues	Same issues
Red Pepper Blues	Same issues
Straight Life	Same issues
Tin Tin Deo	Same issues
Waltz Me Blues	Same issues
Star Eyes	Contemporary C3532, S7018, S7532, Vogue (E) LAC12066, EPC1232
You'd Be So Nice To Come Home To	Contemporary C3532, S7018, S7532, EPC1232
The Man I Love	Contemporary S7630, (J) LAX 3131, OJC-389

QUINCY JONES AND HIS ORCHESTRA
Art Pepper, Benny Carter, Herb Geller, Charlie Mariano (as); Lou Levy (p); Red Mitchell (b); Shelly Manne (d); Jimmy Giuffre, Lennie Niehaus (a). *Hollywood, Feb. 25, 1957.*

Dancin' Pants aJG (1st solo)	ABC LP186, HMV (E) CLP1157
Be My Guest aLN (3rd solo)	Same issues
King's Road Blues aLN (4th solo)	Same issues

ART PEPPER QUARTET
Art Pepper (as, cl-1); Larry Bunker (p); Don Payne (b); Chuck Flores (d). *Los Angeles, Mar. 31, 1957.*

All The Things You Are	Calliope CAL 3015
Everything Happens To Me	—
St. Louis Blues (1)	—

Add Pam Rusell (vo); Victor Feldman (p) replaces Bunker.

Stormy Weather (intro and obbligato)	—

ART PEPPER QUARTET
Art Pepper (as); Carl Perkins (p); Ben Tucker (b); Chuck Flores (d). *Hollywood, April 1, 1957.*

Holiday Flight (5:10)	Omegatape OMT 7020, Baccarola (G) 80 116 ZT, Onyx ORI 219, Nadja (J) PA-3140, Blue Note CDP7 46853 2
Too Close For Comfort (6:08)	Omegatape OMT 7020, Baccarola (G) 80 116 ZT, Onyx ORI 219, Nadja (J) PA-3140, Blue Note LT-1064, Blue Note CDP7 46853 2
Webb City (4:35)	Nadja (J) PA-3141, Blue Note CDP7 46848 2
Webb City (4:56)	same issues as "Too Close For Comfort"
Surf Ride (3:39)	same issues as "Too Close For Comfort"
Body and Soul (4:20)	same issues as "Too Close For Comfort"
Begin the Beguine (6:17)	Nadja (J) PA-3141, Blue Note CDP7 46848 2
Begin the Beguine (7:22)	same issues as "Too Close For Comfort"
The Breeze and I (3:30)	Omegatape ST-2030, Overseas (J) ULS-1534-V, Onyx ORI 219, Nadja (J) PA-3141, Blue Note CDP7 46853 2
Fascinatin' Rhythm (4:23)	Omegatape ST-2030, Overseas (J) ULS-1534-V, Onyx ORI 219, Nadja (J) PA-3141, Blue Note LT-1064, Blue Note CPD7 46853 2
Fascinatin' Rhythm (4:02)	Nadja (J) PA-3140, Blue Note CDP7 46848 2
Long Ago and Far Away (4:10)	same issues as "The Breeze and I"

I Can't Believe That You're In Love With Me (5:41)	
	same issues as "The Breeze and I"
Summertime (7:26)	Blue Note CDP7 46848 2
Summertime (6:32)	Nadja (J) PA-3140, Blue Note LT-1064, Blue Note CDP7 46853 2
Blues Rock (2:34)	unissued
Rock Blues (2:38)	unissued

Note: Onyx issued in monaural; all other issues stereo.

SHOWCASE FOR MODERN JAZZ
Howard Lucraft (leader/a); Art Pepper (as-1, ts-2); Bob Cooper (ts-3, oboe-4); Claude Williamson (p); Monte Budwig (b); Stan Levey (d). *Hollywood, c. June 1957.*

California Zephyr (1, 3, 4)	Decca DL8679, Brunswick (G) LP86055

| Midnight Sun (1, 2, 3, 4) | Same issues |
| Two-Part Contention (1, 3) | Same issues |

JOHN GRAAS NONETET
John Graas (F-hn); Conte Candoli (tp); Red Callender (tuba); Art Pepper (as); Bob Cooper (ts); Buddy Collette (bar); Paul Moer (p); Red Mitchell (b); Shelly Manne (d). *Hollywood, July 22, 1957.*

L10376 Midnight Sun	Decca DL8677
L10377 Jazz Overture	—
L10378 Petite Poem	—

Buddy Clark (b) replaces Mitchell. *Hollywood, Aug. 13, 1957.*

L10458 Id	Decca DL8677
L10459 Will Success Spoil Rock And Roll?	—
L10461 Jazz Chorale	—

ART PEPPER BAND
ART PEPPER NINE*
Don Fagerquist (tp); Stu Williamson (vtb); Red Callender (tuba); Art Pepper (as); Bill Holman (ts); Bud Shank (bar); Russ Freeman (p); Monte Budwig (b); Shelly Manne (d); Shorty Rogers (a). *Hollywood, Aug. 12, 1957.*

*Bunny	World Pacific Jazz WP1257, ST1015, PJ-LA894-H, JWC(ST)514, PJ60, Vogue (E) LAE12211, PJ (J) JR-8113, Mosaic MR3-105
Popo	World Pacific Jazz ST1009, JWC(ST)510, PJ60, PJ-LA894-H, PJ-LA896-H, Vogue (E) LAE12177, SEA5008, PJ (J) JR-8113 Mosaic MR3-105
Popo (alt)	Mosaic MR3-105
Powder Puff	World Pacific ST1031, JWC(ST)511, Pacific Jazz PJ-LA896-H, Vogue (E) LAE12235, Music (It) LPM2093, Mosaic MR3-105
* Didi	Pacific Jazz PJ-LA896-H, Mosaic MR3-105
*Diablo's Dance	—
* Diablo's Dance (alt)	Pacific Jazz CDP7 97194 2

Note: All titles released on Pacific Jazz CDP7 97194 2

JOHN GRAAS NONETET
John Graas (F-hn); Conte Candoli (tp); Red Callender (tuba); Art Pepper (as); Bob Cooper (ts, oboe-1); Buddy Collette (fl or bar); Paul Moer (p); Buddy Clark (b); Larry Bunker (d/perc). *Hollywood, Aug. 15, 1957.*

15631 Block Sounds	Mercury MG36117/SR80020, MG20533/SR60210
15632 Blues Street	Same issues
15633 Van Nuys Indeed	Same issues

Pete Candoli (tp) replaces Conte Candoli. On 2, omit Collette; on 3, omit Pete
Candoli. Same date.

15634 **Development**	Same issues
15635 **Land Of Broken Toys** (2)	Same issues
15636 **Swing Nicely** (1, 3)	Same issues

JOHN GRAAS QUINTET
John Graas (F-hn); Art Pepper (ts); Paul Moer (p); Buddy Clark (b); Larry Bunker
(d). Same date.

15638 **Rogeresque**	Same issues
15639 **Walkin' Shoes**	Same issues

JACK SHELDON BIG BAND
Jack Sheldon, Chet Baker (tp); Stu Williamson (vtb); Art Pepper, Herb Geller (as);
Harold Land (ts); Paul Moer (p/a); Buddy Clark (b); Mel Lewis (d). *Hollywood,
August 1957.*

Anyhow (solo)	Gene Norman GNP(S)60
Aplomb (solo)	—
J.S. (solo)	—
Julie Is Her Name	—
Sunset Eyes	—

ALL STAR LATIN JAZZ—"MUCHO CALOR"
Conte Candoli (tp/a); Art Pepper (as/a); Bill Perkins (ts); Russ Freeman (p); Ben
Tucker (b); Chuck Flores (d); Jack Costanzo, Mike Pachecco (Latin-perc); Benny
Carter, Bill Holman, Johnny Mandel (a). *Forum Theatre, Los Angeles, October
1957.*

Autumn Leaves aBC (solo)	Andex A(S)3002
I Love You aBH (solo)	—
I'll Remember April aAP	—
Mambo De La Pinta aAP (solo)	—
Mambo Jumbo aCC	
Old Devil Moon aBH (solo)	—
Pernod aJM (solo)	—
That Old Black Magic aBH (solo)	—
Voya Hombre Voya aBH (solo)	—
Mucho Calor aBH (solo)	—

JOHN GRAAS AND HIS ORCHESTRA
Jack Sheldon (tp); Bob Enevoldson (vtb); John Graas (F-hn); Red Callender (tuba);
Art Pepper (cl/as); Bill Perkins (ts); Buddy Collette (bar/fl); Paul Moer (p); Red
Mitchell (b); Larry Bunker (d/vibes/timpani). *Hollywood, August 1958.*

Jazz-Chaconne Number One	Andex A(S)3003

DAVE PELL OCTET
Frank Beach, Jack Sheldon (tp); Bob Enevoldson (vtb); Arthur Maebe (F-hn); Phil
Stephens (tuba); Art Pepper (as); Dave Pell (ts-1; bar-2); Marty Berman (bar);
Marty Paich (p); Buddy Clark (b); Mel Lewis (d); Jimmy Priddy (a). *Hollywood,
February 1959.*

31342 **Walkin' Shoes** (2)	Capitol ST1309
Beach and Berman out.	
31343 **Boplicity** (2)	—
Omit Enevoldson.	
31344 **Popo** (1) (solo)	—

MARTY PAICH AND HIS ORCHESTRA

Frank Beach (tp); Stu Williamson (tp); George Roberts (btb); Bob Enevoldson (vtb/ts); Art Pepper (as); Jimmy Giuffre (cl/bar); Marty Paich (p/a); Scott LaFaro (b); Mel Lewis (d); Victor Feldman (vibes). *Hollywood, Feb. 23, 1959.*

B10339 **Too Close For Comfort** (solo)	Warner Brothers WB/WS1296, (J) 7539W, (E) WSEP6032/2032
B10340 **Younger Than Springtime** (solo)/**The Surrey With The Fringe On Top**	Warner Brothers WB/WS1296, (J) 7539W
B10341 **I've Grown Accustomed To Her Face** (solo)	Same issues

Same personnel. *Feb. 25, 1959.*

B10342 **It's All Right With Me**	Same issues as "Too Close For Comfort"
B10343 **I Love Paris**	Warner Brothers WB/WS1296, WB/WS1328, (E) WM4005, (J) 7539W

Note: The above title was remade Feb. 27, 1959.

B10344 **Lazy Afternoon** (solo)	Same issues as "Younger Than Springtime"/"The Surrey With The Fringe On Top"

Same personnel. *Feb. 27, 1959.*

B10345 **Just In Time** (solo)	Same issues as "Younger Than Springtime"/"The Surrey With The Fringe On Top"
B10346 **If I Were A Bell** (solo)	Same issues
B10347 **I've Never Been In Love Before** (solo)	Same issues

ART PEPPER PLUS ELEVEN

Pete Candoli, Jack Sheldon (tp); Dick Nash (tb); Bob Enevoldson (vtb); Vince DeRosa (F-hn); Art Pepper, Herb Geller (as); Bill Perkins (ts); Med Flory (bar); Russ Freeman (p); Joe Mondragon (b); Mel Lewis (d); Marty Paich (a/cond). *Hollywood, Mar. 14, 1959.*

Opus De Funk	Contemporary M3568/87568, (J) GXC 3102. Vogue (E) LAC12229, Contemporary OJC-341
'Round Midnight	Same issues
Walkin' Shoes	Same issues
Airegin	Same issues

HERB ELLIS AND JIMMY GIUFFRE

Art Pepper, Bud Shank (as); Richie Kamuca (ts); Jimmy Giuffre (ts/a); Lou Levy (p); Herb Ellis (g); Jim Hall (rhythm g); Joe Mondragon (b); Stan Levey (d). *Hollywood, Mar. 26, 1959.*

Goose Grease	Verve MGV8311/MGVS6045, HMV (E) CLP1337
When Your Lover Has Gone	Same issues
Remember (2nd as solo)	Same issues
A Country Boy	Same issues

You Know	Same issues
My Old Flame	Same issues
People Will Say We're In Love	Same issues

Note: Pepper not present on 8th title from this date. "Patricia."

ART PEPPER PLUS ELEVEN

Al Porcino, Jack Sheldon (tp); Dick Nash (tb); Bob Enevoldson (vtb); Vince DeRosa (F-hn); Art Pepper (cl*/as); Bud Shank (as); Bill Perkins (ts); Med Flory (bar); Russ Freeman (p); Joe Mondragon (b); Mel Lewis (d); Marty Paich (a/cond). *Hollywood, Mar. 28, 1959.*

Groovin' High	Contemporary M3568/S7568,
	(J) GXC 3102 Vogue (E)
	LAC12229, Contemporary OJC-341
Shaw Nuff	Same issues
Donna Lee	Same issues
*Anthropology	Same issues
Donna Lee (alt)	Contemporary OJC-341

BARNEY KESSEL SEPTET

Joe Gordon (tp); Art Pepper (cl-1, as-2, ts-3); Jimmy Rowles (p); Barney Kessel (g/bg); Jack Marshall (g); Monte Budwig (b); Shelly Manne (d). *Hollywood, Mar. 30–31, 1959.*

Some Like It Hot (3)	Contemporary M3565/S7565, (G)
	M503565, Contemporary OJC-168
I Wanna Be Loved By You (1)	Same issues
Sweet Sue (1)	Same issues
Runnin' Wild (2)	Same issues
Sweet Georgia Brown (2)	Same issues
Down Among The Sheltering Palms (3)	Same issues
Sugar Blues (1)	Same issues
By The Beautiful Sea (2)	Same issues
Sweet Sue (alt) (1)	Contemporary OJC-168
Runnin' Wild (alt) (2)	—

ART PEPPER PLUS ELEVEN

Al Porcino, Jack Sheldon (tp); Dick Nash (tb); Bob Enevoldson (vtb, ts-2); Vince DeRosa (F-hn); Art Pepper (ts, as-1); Charlie Kennedy (as, ts–2); Richie Kamuca (ts); Med Flory (bar); Russ Freeman (p); Joe Mondragon (b); Mel Lewis (d); Marty Paich (a/cond). *Hollywood, May 13, 1959.*

Bernie's Tune (1)	Contemporary M3568/S7568, (J)
	GXC 3102, Vogue (E) LAC12229,
	Contemporary OJC-341
Four Brothers (2)	Same issues
Move	Same issues
Walkin'	Same issues
Walkin' (alt A)	Contemporary OJC-341
Walkin' (alt B)	—

JOANIE SOMMERS (VO) WITH MARTY PAICH AND HIS ORCHESTRA

Personnel includes Conte Candoli (tp), Frank Rosolino (tb), Art Pepper (cl/as),

Buddy Collette (bar), Marty Paich (p), and possibly musicians from the previous recording sessions.   *Hollywood, June 1959.*

Heart And Soul (as solo)	Warner Brothers WB/WS1346
My Heart Belongs To Daddy (as solo)	—
Something I Dreamed Last Night	—
So In Love (as solo)	—
Oh, But I Do	—
Squeeze Me (cl solo)	—

Note: Art Pepper not present on other titles in this album.

MARTY PAICH AND HIS ORCHESTRA

Conte Candoli, Al Porcino, Jack Sheldon (tp); Bob Enevoldson (vtb); George Roberts (btb); Vince DeRosa (F-hn); Art Pepper (as); Bill Perkins (ts); Bill Hood (bar); Russ Freeman (p); Joe Mondragon (b); Mel Lewis (d); Victor Feldman (vibes); Marty Paich (a/cond).   *Hollywood, June 30, 1959.*

B10810	**It Don't Mean A Thing** (solo)	Warner Brothers WB/WS1349, (E) WSEP6018/2018
B10811	**No More**	—
B10812	**Love For Sale** (solo)	Warner Brothers WB/WS1349

Same personnel.   *Hollywood, July 2, 1959.*

B10813	**Moanin'** (solo)	Warner Brothers WB/WS1349
B10814	**Violets For Your Furs** (solo)	Warner Brothers WB/WS1349, (E) WSEP6018/2018
B10815	**Warm Valley**	Warner Brothers WB/WS1349

Same personnel.   *Hollywood, July 7, 1959.*

B10816	**What Am I Here For?** (solo)/**Cottontail** (solo)	Warner Brothers WB/WS1349, (E) WSEP6018/2018
B10817	**Things Ain't What They Used To Be** (solo)	Same issues

ANDRE PREVIN (AND THE MGM STUDIO ORCHESTRA)

Jazz soloists: Jack Sheldon (tp); Bob Enevoldson (vtb); Art Pepper (as); Gerry Mulligan (bar); Andre Previn (p); Red Mitchell (b); Shelly Manne (d). On 1, omit Enevoldson and Mulligan.   *Hollywood, c. November 1959.*

A Rose And The End	MGM SE3812, (E) C864/CS6038
Analyst	MGM SE3812, (E) C864/CS6038, Verve VSP 38
Look Ma, No Clothes	Sames issues as "A Rose And The End"
Two By Two	Same issues as "A Rose And The End"
Why Are We Afraid?	MGM SE3812, SE4186, (E) C864/CS6038
Raising Caen (1) (solo)	Same issues as "A Rose And The End"

Art Farmer (tp); Bob Enevoldson (vtb); Art Pepper (as); Bill Perkins (ts); Gerry Mulligan (bar); Russ Freeman (p); Buddy Clark (b); Dave Bailey (d).   *Similar dates.*

Bread And Wine (solo)	MGM SE3812, (E) C864, Verve VSP-6
Things Are Looking Down (solo)	Same issues

JESSE BELVIN (VO) WITH MARTY PAICH AND HIS ORCHESTRA
Art Pepper (as); Larry Bunker (vibes); Bill Pittman (g); Russ Freeman (p); Joe Mondragon (b); Red Callender (tuba); Mel Lewis (d); Jesse Belvin (vo); Marty Paich (a). *Hollywood, Dec. 8, 1959.*

It's All Right With Me (solo)	Victor LPM/LSP-2105, APL1-0966
Something Happens To Me (obbligato)	Victor LPM/LSP-2105
Let There Be Love (solo)	—
The Best Is Yet To Come (obbligato)	—

JESSE BELVIN (VO) WITH MARTY PAICH AND HIS ORCHESTRA
Al Porcino, Conte Candoli, Stu Williamson, Dick Collins (tp); Dick Nash, Harry Betts, Pete Carpenter, Marshall Cram (tb); Art Pepper (as, cl-1); Al Hendrickson (g); Milt Holland (vibes); Russ Freeman (p); Joe Mondragon (b); Mel Lewis (d); Jesse Belvin (vo); Marty Paich (a); strings. *Hollywood, Dec. 16, 1959.*

In The Still Of The Night (obbligato)	Victor LPM/LSP-2105, APL1-0966
Blues In The Night (1) (solo)	Same issues
Makin' Whoopee! (obbligato and coda)	Victor LPM/LSP-2105
I'll Buy You A Star	—
My Last Goodbye	Camden CAL/CAS-960

ETHEL AZAMA (VO) WITH ORCHESTRA ARRANGED AND CONDUCTED BY MARTY PAICH
Art Pepper (as); remaining personnel unknown. *Los Angeles, Feb. 22, 1960.*

Johnny One Note	Liberty LRP 3142/LSP 7142
Like Someone In Love (solo)	—
Surrey With The Fringe On Top (obbligato and coda)	—
You Smell So Good (solo)	—
I'm Glad There Is You	—
My Ship (solo and obbligato)	—
Squeeze Me (solo)	—
Daybreak (solo)	—
All I Need Is You (solo and coda)	—
When The Sun Comes Out (obbligato)	—
You're So Bad For Me	—
Time After Time (obbligato and coda)	—

ART PEPPER QUINTET*
ART PEPPER QUARTET
Conte Candoli (tp-1); Art Pepper (as, ts-2); Wynton Kelly (p); Paul Chambers (b); Jimmie Cobb (d). *Hollywood, Feb. 29, 1960.*

***Whims Of Chambers** (1)	Contemporary M3573/S7573, (J) GXC 3103, Vogue (E) LAC12262/SCA5019, Contemporary OJC-169
***Bijou The Poodle** (1, 2)	Same issues
Why Are We Afraid	Same issues

Softly As In A Morning Sunrise	Same issues
*****Rhythm-A-Ning** (1)	Same issues
Gettin' Together (2)	Same issues
Diane	Same issues
The Way You Look Tonight	Contemporary S7630 (J) LAX 3131, OJC-389
Gettin' Together (2) (alt)	Contemporary OJC-169

THE HI-LO'S (VO) WITH ORCHESTRA CONDUCTED BY MARTY PAICH

Al Porcino, Jack Sheldon (tp); Frank Rosolino, Dave Wells (tb); Red Callender (tuba); Art Pepper (as); Bill Perkins (ts); Bill Hood (bar); Bill Pittman, Al Hendrickson (g); Douglas Fisher (p); Buddy Clark (b); Mel Lewis (d); the Hi-Lo's (vo). *Hollywood, Mar. 24, 1960.*

Isle Of Capri (solo)	Columbia CL 1509/CS8300.
My Little Grass Shack In Kealakekua, Hawaii	Same issues
A Lot Of Living To Do	Columbia 4–41647
Cindy's Prayer	—

Note: The following 3 sessions are listed because Art Pepper is thought to be present on them. The 11 titles are stereo background remakes, with the vocal tapes of the original recordings dubbed over the remakes. Dates of the original recordings are given in parentheses.

JUNE CHRISTY (VO) WITH PETE RUGOLO AND HIS ORCHESTRA

Personnel unknown but may be similar to original but now including Art Pepper (as). See Jorgen Jepsen's *Jazz Records*, volume 2, for details on original recordings. *Hollywood Apr. 26, 1960.*

33683 **Softly As In A Morning Sunrise** (12–29–54)	Capitol ST-516
33684 **Midnight Sun** (12–27–53)	Capitol ST-516, ST1693
33685 **Something Cool** (8–14–53)	Same issues

Hollywood, Apr. 27, 1960.

33687 **It Could Happen To You** (1–18–54)	Capitol ST-516
33688 **I'll Take Romance** (1–19–54)	—
33689 **A Stranger Called The Blues** (1–19–54)	—
33690 **I'm Thrilled** (5–9–55)	—

Hollywood, Apr. 28, 1960.

33712 **I Should Care** (1–18–54)	Capitol ST-516
33713 **This Time The Dream's On Me** (5–9–55)	—
33714 **Lonely House** (1–18–54)	—
33715 **The Night We Called It A Day** (5–9–55)	—

SHORTY ROGERS AND THE BIG BAND

Shorty Rogers, John Audino, Conte Candoli, Ray Triscari, Jimmy Zito (tp); Harry Betts, Frank Rosolino (tb); George Roberts, Ken Shroyer (btb); Art Pepper (as); Bud Shank (fl/as); Bill Holman, Richie Kamuca, Bill Perkins (ts); Chuck Gentry (bar); Pete Jolly (p); Joe Mondragon (b); Mel Lewis (d); Shorty Rogers (a).   *Hollywood, May 17, 1960.*

L2PB0603	Flowers For The Cats	Victor LPM/LSP2110, RCA (E) RD27199/SF5084
L2PB0604	Blue Reeds	Same issues
L2PB0605	Pass The Duke	Same issues
L2PB0606	Six Pak	Same issues

Lou Levy (p) replaces Jolly. Jimmy Giuffre (cl-1).   *Hollywood, May 26, 1960.*

L2PB0607	Snowball (1)	Victor LPM/LSP2110, RCA (E) RD27199/SF5084
L2PB0608	China, Where?	Same issues
L2PB0609	Like Nutty Overture	Same issues

MARTY PAICH PIANO QUARTET

Stu Williamson (tp); Dave Wells (tb); Art Pepper, Bud Shank (saxes); Pete Jolly, Marty Paich, Jimmy Rowles, John Towner Williams (p); Bill Pittman (g); Joe Mondragon (b); Mel Lewis (d).   *Hollywood, June 2, 1960.*

L2PB0668	Little Rock Getaway (alto solo)	Victor LPM/LSP2259
L2PB0669	Boogie Woogie On Handy's St. Louis Blues	—
L2PB0670	One O'Clock Jump (tenor solo)	—
L2PB0671	Honky Tonk Train (tenor solo)	—

HENRY MANCINI AND HIS ORCHESTRA

Pete Candoli (tp); Dick Nash (tb); Art Pepper (cl); Ted Nash (fl/as); Ronny Lang (a fl/bar); John Towner Williams (p/harpsichord); Bob Bain (g/bg); Rollie Bundock (b); Shelly Manne (d); Ramon Riviera (perc); Larry Bunker (vibesmarimba).   *Hollywood, June 14, 1960.*

L2PB3101	Castle Rock (solo)	Victor LPM/LSP2258
L2PB3102	Sidewalks Of Cuba (solo)	—
L2PB3103	(No takes used on this master)	
L2PB3104	Charleston Alley (solo)	—

Same personnel.   *Hollywood, June 17, 1960.*

L2PB3105	Scandinavian Shuffle	Victor LPM/LSP2258
L2PB3106	Playboy's Theme	—
L2PB3107	Dream Of You	—
L2PB3108	Far East Blues	—

Same personnel.   *Hollywood, June 21, 1960.*

L2PB3109	Tequila	Victor LPM/LSP2258
L2PB3110	A Powdered Wig	—
L2PB3111	Everybody Blow! (solo)	—
L2PB3112	Swing Lightly (solo)	—
L2PB3118	Moanin' (solo)	—

MEL TORME (VO) WITH THE MARTY PAICH ORCHESTRA

Al Porcino (tp); Stu Williamson (tp/vtb); Frank Rosolino (tb); Vince DeRosa (F-hn); Red Callender (tuba); Art Pepper (as); Bill Perkins (ts); Bill Hood (bar); Marty Paich (p/a); Joe Mondragon (b); Mel Lewis (d). *Hollywood, June 1960.*

A Sleepin' Bee	Verve MGV6 2132, VSP (E) 17
All I Need Is A Girl	Same issues
Hello Young Lovers (solo)	Same issues
Just In Time	Verve MGV6 2132, MGV68505, MGV68593, VSP (E) 17
Lonely Town	Same issues as "A Sleepin' Bee"
Old Devil Moon	Same issues as "A Sleepin' Bee"
Once In Love With Amy	Same issues as "A Sleepin' Bee"
The Surrey With The Fringe On Top	Same issues as "A Sleepin' Bee"
Too Close For Comfort (solo)	Verve MGV6 2132, MGV68593, VSP (E) 17
Too Darn Hot (solo)	Same issues as "A Sleepin' Bee"
Whatever Lola Wants (solo)	Same issues as "A Sleepin' Bee"
On The Street Where You Live (solo)	Verve MGV6 2132, MGV68593, VSP (E) 17, MGM SE4243

MEL TORME (VO) WITH MARTY PAICH'S ORCHESTRA AND THE MEL TONES

Jack Sheldon (tp); Art Pepper (as/ts); Victor Feldman (vibes); Marty Paich (p, celeste-1); Joe Mondragon (b); Mel Lewis (d); Mel-Tones: Ginny O'Connor, Sue Allen, Bernie Parke, Tom Kenny, Mel Torme (vo group). *Hollywood, August 1960.*

A Smooth One (ts solo) (1)	Verve MGV2120/MGVS6083
A Bunch Of The Blues: Keester Parade/T.N.T./Tiny's Blues (ts solo)	— —
It Happened In Monterey (as)	Verve MGV2120/MGVS6083, Metro MS532
Makin' Whoopee (as solo)	Verve MGV2120/MGVS6083
Some Like It Hot (as solo)	Same issues as "It Happened In Monterey"
What Is This Thing Called Love (ts solo)	Verve MGMV2120/MGVS6083
Truckin' (as solo)	Same issues as "It Happened In Monterey"

Note: Pepper not present on other titles from these sessions.

HELEN HUMES (VO) WITH MARTY PAICH'S ORCHESTRA

Jack Sheldon, Al Porcino, Ray Triscari, Stu Williamson (tp); Harry Betts, Bob Fitzpatrick (tb); Art Pepper (cl/as); Teddy Edwards, Ben Webster (ts); Bill Hood (bar); Andre Previn (p); Barney Kessel (g); Leroy Vinnegar (b); Shelly Manne (d). *Hollywood, Sept. 6–7, 1960.*

Don't Worry 'Bout Me (as solo)	Contemporary M3582/S7582, Vogue (E) LAC12283, Contemporary OJC-171
Love Me Or Leave Me	Same issues
St. Louis Blues (as solo)	Same issues

I Want A Roof Over My Head	Same issues
Million Dollar Secret (cl coda. scored)	Same issues
You're Driving Me Crazy	Same issues
Please Don't Talk About Me When I'm Gone (as coda)	Same issues
Mean To Me	Same issues
Don't Worry 'Bout Me (alt) (as solo)	Contemporary OJC-171

ART PEPPER QUINTET

Jack Sheldon (tp); Art Pepper (as); Pete Jolly (p); Jimmy Bond (b); Frank Butler (d). *Hollywood, Oct. 24-25, 1960.*

Smack Up	Contemporary C385, M3602/ S7602, Vogue (E) LAC12316
Las Cuevas De Mario	Same issues
A Bit Of Basie	Contemporary M3602/S7602, Vogue (E) LAC12316
How Can You Lose?	Same issues as "A Bit Of Basie"
Maybe Next Year (no tp)	Same issues as "A Bit Of Basie"
Tears Inside	Same issues as "A Bit Of Basie"
Solid Citizens (take 33)	Contemporary OJC-176
Solid Citizens (take 37)	—

Note: First 2 titles on C385 are edited. All titles on Contemporary (J) LAX, 3035, OJC-176

ART PEPPER QUARTET

Art Pepper (as); Dolo Coker (p); Jimmy Bond (b); Frank Butler (d). *Hollywood, Nov. 23-25, 1960.*

Gone With The Wind	Contemporary M3607/S7607, Vogue (E) LAC/SCA553, Contemp. OJC-387
I Wished On The Moon	Same issues
Too Close For Comfort	Same issues
I Can't Believe That You're In Love With Me	Same issues
I Love You	Same issues
Come Rain Or Come Shine	Same issues
Long Ago And Far Away	Same issues
Autumn Leaves	Contemporary S7630, (J) LAX 3131, OJC-389
Fine Points	Contemporary OJC-387

HELYNE STEWART (VO) ACC BY TEDDY EDWARDS' SEPTET

Jack Sheldon (tp); Frank Rosolino (tb); Art Pepper (as); Teddy Edwards (ts/a); Pete Jolly (p); Jimmy Bond (b); Frank Butler (d). *Hollywood, Jan. 20, 1961.*

Love Is Here To Stay	Contemporary M3601/S7601, Vogue (E) LAC/SCA544
The Man I Love (solo)	Same issues
How Deep Is The Ocean?	Same issues
My Silent Love	Same issues

ART PEPPER QUARTET

Art Pepper (as); Frank Strazzeri (p); Hersh Hamel (b); Bill Goodwin (d). *San Francisco, May 8, 1964*

The Trip	Fresh Sound (Sp) FSR-402
Interview with Ralph Gleason	—
D Section	—
Groupin' (inc)	—

same   Jazz Workshop, San Francisco, June 1964

Summer Night	Fresh Sound (Sp) FSR-402
Sonnymoon for Two	—
Art Pepper talks	—

BUDDY RICH AND HIS ORCHESTRA

Bill Prince, Al Porcino, Dave Culp, Ken Faulk (tp); Rick Stepton, Jimmy Trimble (tb); Peter Greaves (btb); Art Pepper, Charlie Owens (as); Don Menza, Pat LaBarbera (ts); John Laws (bar); Joe Azarello (p); Walt Namath (g); Gary Walters (b/fender-b); Buddy Rich (d); Phil Wilson, Don Sebesky, Bill Reddie, Don Piestrup, Don Menza, Charlie Owens (a). *Caesars Palace, Las Vegas, July 7, 1968.*

Mercy, Mercy, Mercy aPW	Pacific Jazz 88145, ST20133, Liberty (E) LBL/LBS83168E
Big Mama Cass aDS	Same issues
Preach And Teach aDS (solo)	Pacific Jazz ST20133, Liberty (E) LBL/LBS83168E
Channel 1 Suite aBR (solo)	Same issues as "Preach And Teach"
Goodbye Yesterday aDP	Same issues as "Preach And Teach"
Acid Truth aDM	Same issues as "Preach And Teach"
Alfie aDP (solo)	Same issues as "Preach And Teach"
Ode To Billy Joe aCO	Same issues as "Preach And Teach"

ART PEPPER QUINTET

Art Pepper (as); Joe Romano (ts); Frank Strazzeri (p); Chuck Berghofer (b); Nick Ceroli (d). *Donte's, Los Angeles, November 24, 1968.*

Groupín'	Fresh Sound (Sp) FSR-5001
Lover Come Back To Me	—

MIKE VAX BIG BAND FEATURING ART PEPPER

Mike Vax, Jim Schlicht, Fred Berry, Bill Main, Dave Candia, Warren Gale (tp/flh); Bill Robinson, Dean Hubbard, Phil Zahorsky (tb); Jed Rodriguey, Nick TenBroek (btb); Art Pepper (as); Jim Rothermel, Kim Frizell (as/fl); Lloyd Rice, Gerry Gilmore (ts/fl); Dave Luell (bar); Si Perkoff (p); Mario Suraci (el-b); John Rae (d/perc/timbales); Gary Nash (d/timpani/perc). *San Francisco, July 3–4, 1973.*

Evil Eyes (solo)	Artco LPJ 117 (945) LD
If	—
Is Anything Still There	—

Passage West —
Joe's Inn —
The Shadow Of Your Smile (solo) —
Beginnings (solo) —
West Side Story —

ART PEPPER QUARTET

Art Pepper (as); Tommy Gumina (polychord); Fred Atwood (b); Jimmie Smith (d). *Foothill College, Los Altos, February 14, 1975.*

Foothill Blues   Trio (J) PAP-25041
I'll Remember April —
Here's That Rainy Day —
Cherokee —

ART PEPPER WITH SONGBOOK

Art Pepper (as); Pete Robinson (keyboards, synthesizer); Hersh Hamel (b); Steve Strazzeri (d); Linda McCrary, Judy Brown, Brenda Burns (vo). *Holly-wood, summer 1975.*

Mr. Yes   Fresh Sound (Sp) FSR-CD 150
The Image Before You —
If It Feels Good, Do It —
Song of Ecstasy —
Come to Me —
Dance Now —

ART PEPPER QUARTET

Art Pepper (as); unknown p,b,d. *Los Angeles, probably summer 1975.*

The Trip   Contemporary unissued
Daphne —
Mr. Dom —
That Crazy Blues —
So In Love —
I'll Remember April —

ART PEPPER QUARTET

Art Pepper (as); Hampton Hawes (p); Charlie Haden (b); Shelly Manne (d). *Los Angeles, Aug. 9, 1975.*

Ophelia   Contemporary S7633, (J) GXP
    6004, Contemporary OJC-408

Here's That Rainy Day   Same issues
What Laurie Likes   Same issues
Mr. Yohe   Same issues
Lost Life   Same issues
Samba Mom-Mom   Same issues
Samba Mom-Mom (alt)   Contemporary OJC-408

MELANIE (VO)

Art Pepper (as); unidentified rhythm; Melanie Safka (vo). *Los Angeles, July 12, 1976.*

I'm So Blue (obbligato and solo   Atlantic SD 18190
    overdub)

ART FARMER QUINTET
Art Farmer (flh); Art Pepper (as); Hampton Hawes (p); Ray Brown (b); Steve Ellington (d). *Los Angeles, July 26, 1976.*
Namely You   Contemporary S7636, OJC-478

Same personnel. *Los Angeles, July 28, 1976.*
Downwind   Contemporary S7636, OJC-478

Shelly Manne replaces Ellington. *Los Angeles, Aug. 16, 1976.*
What Am I Here For?   Contemporary S7636, OJC-478
Will You Still Be Mine?   —   —

ART PEPPER QUARTET
Art Pepper (as); George Cables (p); David Williams (b); Elvin Jones (d). *Los Angeles, Sept. 15–16, 1976.*
The Trip   Contemporary S7638, (J) GP 3113,
                                     OJC-410

A Song For Richard   Same issues
Sweet Love Of Mine   Same issues
Junior Cat [Groupin']   Same issues
The Summer Knows   Same issues
Red Car   Same issues
The Trip (alt)   Contemporary OJC-410

DOLO COKER QUINTET
Blue Mitchell (tp, flh-1); Art Pepper (as, ts-2); Dolo Coker (p); Leroy Vinnegar (b); Frank Butler (d). *Los Angeles, Dec. 27, 1976.*
Jumping Jacks (2)   Xanadu 142
Gone With The Wind (1)   —
Roots 4FB (2)   —
Mr. Yohe   —
Tale Of Two Cities (1)   —

ART PEPPER QUARTET
Art Pepper (as); Smith Dobson (p); Jim Nichols (b); Brad Bilhorn (d). *Half Moon Bay, Calif., January 23, 1977.*
Mr. Yohe   Trio (J) PAP-25044
The Trip   —
Lost Life   —
A Night in Tunisia   —

ART PEPPER QUARTET
Art Pepper (as, ts overdub-1); George Cables (p); Tony Dumas (blitz-b); Carl Burnett (d). *Los Angeles, Mar. 26, 1977.*
Rita-San   Contemporary (J) GP3153, S7639,
                                     OJC-411

Ballad Of The Sad Young Men   Same issues
My Laurie   Same issues
Mambo De La Pinta (1)   Same issues
No Limit   Contemporary OJC-411

ART PEPPER
Art Pepper (as); Clare Fischer (p); Rob Fischer (b); Pete Riso (d). *Tokyo, April 5, 1977*

Cherokee	Polydor (J) JOOJ 20390
The Spirit Is Here	—
Here's That Rainy Day	—
Straight Life	—

add Cal Tjader (vbs); Bob Redfield (g)

Manteca	—
Manha de Carnival	—
Felicidade	—

ART PEPPER QUARTET
Art Pepper (as, ts-1, cl-2); George Cables (p); George Mraz (b); Elvin Jones (d). *Village Vanguard, NYC, July 28-30, 1977.*

Valse Triste	Contemporary (J) GHX 3009-11,	7642,	OJC-694
Goodbye	—	—	—
Blues for Les	—	—	—
My Friend John	—	—	—
Las Cuevas de Mario	—	7643,	OJC-695
But Beautiful	—	—	—
Caravan-1	—	—	—
Labyrinth	—	—	—
You Go To My Head	—	7644,	OJC-696
The Trip	—	—	—
Cherokee	—	—	—
No Limit	Contemporary C-7650,	JC-697	
These Foolish Things-1	—	—	
More for Les-2	—	—	

omit p, b, d.

Over the Rainbow	—	—

readmit p, b, d.

Blues for Heard	Contemporary OJC-694
A Night in Tunisia	Contemporary OJC-695
For Freddie	Contemporary OJC-696
Scrapple from the Apple	Contemporary OJC-697

THE GAUNTLET/ORIGINAL SOUND TRACK
JERRY FIELDING (CONDUCTOR AND ARRANGER)
FEATURED SOLOISTS: ART PEPPER AND JON FADDIS
Art Pepper (as/bar); Jon Faddis (tp); remaining personnel unidentified. *Burbank, Cal., Sept. 13 and 15, 1977.*

Bleak Bad Big City Dawn	Warner Brothers BSK 3144, (J) P-10445W
The Pickup (as solo)	Same issues
Exit Tunnel, Roaring!	Same issues
The Gauntlet	Same issues
The Box Car Incident	Same issues
Closer Look At A Closer Walk	Same issues
The Black Sedan (bar solo)	Same issues
Manipulation On The Center Divider (as solo)	Same issues

The Delivery	Same issues
Postlude	Same issues

ART PEPPER QUARTET
Art Pepper (as); Milcho Leviev (p); Bob Magnusson (b); Carl Burnett (d).
Yamagata, Japan, March 14, 1978.

Ophelia	Trio (J) PAP-25037, Tofrec (J) TFC6-88901-2	
Besame Mucho	—	—
My Laurie	—	—
Caravan	PAP-25038	—
The Trip	—	—
The Summer Knows	—	—
Red Car	—	—

same   *Kobe, Japan, 1978*

Kobe Blues	Laserlight 17 012, Fresh Sound (Sp) FSR CD192

ART PEPPER QUARTET
Art Pepper (as); Russ Freeman (p); Bob Magnusson (b); Frank Butler (d).   *Holly-wood, Sept. 2, 1978.*

Among Friends	Interplay IP-7718, Trio (J)
	PAP-9129
'Round Midnight	Same issues
I'm Getting Sentimental Over You	Same issues
Blue Bossa	Same issues
What Is This Thing Called Love	Same issues
What's New	Same issues
Besame Mucho	Same issues
I'll Remember April	Same issues

ART PEPPER QUARTET
Art Pepper (as); Stanley Cowell (p); Cecil McBee (b); Roy Haynes (d).   *Berkeley, Cal., Dec. 1, 1978.*

I Love You	Galaxy GCD-1016-2
These Foolish Things	Galaxy GXY-5119, OJC-474
Chris's Blues	— —
Pepper Pot	Galaxy GCD-1016-2
Lover Come Back To Me	Unissued
Patricia	Galaxy GXY-5119, OJC-474

Same personnel. *Berkeley, Cal., Dec. 2, 1978.*

Miss Who?	Galaxy GXY-5119, OJC-474
Yardbird Suite	Galaxy (J) SMJ-9532-2, GXY-5133,
	Milestone MCD 9166-2

Add Kenneth Nash (conga/perc).

Mambo Koyama	Galaxy GXY-5119, OJC-474

Omit Nash.

Lover Come Back To Me	— —
Over The Rainbow	Galaxy GCD-1016-2
These Foolish Things (alt)	—, OJC-474
Over The Rainbow	Galaxy (J) SMJ-9532-3, GXY-5133,
	Milestone MCD 9166-2.
Over the Rainbow (alt)	Galaxy GCD-1016-2

ART PEPPER QUARTET
Art Pepper (as); Hank Jones (p); Ron Carter (b); Al Foster (d). *New York, February 23, 1979.*

Straight, No Chaser	Artists House AH 9412
Straight, No Chaser (alt)	Galaxy GXY-5154
Yesterdays	Galaxy GCD-1016-2
A Night In Tunisia	Galaxy GXY-5154
A Night In Tunisia (alt)	Galaxy GCD-1016-2
Diane	Artists Houses AH 9412
My Friend John	Galaxy GXY-5154

Omit Jones and Foster.

Duo Blues	Galaxy GXY-5154

BILL WATROUS QUINTET
Bill Watrous (tb); Art Pepper (as); Russ Freeman (p); Bob Magnusson (b); Carl Burnett (d). *Hollywood, Mar. 26 and 27, 1979.*

Funny Blues	Yupiteru (J) YJ25-7024
Funny Blues (alt)	Atlas (J) LA27-1023

Omit Watrous.

Angel Eyes	Yupiteru (J) YJ25-7024
Angel Eyes (alt)	Atlas (J) LA27-1023

Add Watrous.

For Art's Sake	—
Just Friends	—
P. Town	—
Begin The Beguine	—

Note: Pepper not present on 7th title. "When Your Lover Has Gone."

ART PEPPER QUARTET
Art Pepper (as, cl-1); George Cables (p); Charlie Haden (b); Billy Higgins (d). *Burbank, Cal., May 25 and 26, 1979.*

Blues For Blanche	Artists House AH 9412
Blues For Blanche (alt A)	Galaxy GXY-5148
Blues For Blanche (alt B)	Galaxy GCD-1016-2
Landscape	Galaxy GCD-1016-2
Stardust	Artists House AH 9412
Stardust (alt)	VJC (J) VIJ-6442
Donna Lee	Galaxy GXY-5148
Donna Lee (alt)	Galaxy GCD-1016-2
So In Love	Artists House AH 9412

Omit Cables, Haden and Higgins.

Lover Man	Galaxy GXY05154
Body and Soul	Galaxy GXY-5148
You Go To My Head	—

Add Cables, Haden and Higgins.

Tin Tin Deo	JVC (J) VIJ-6442
Desafinado	Galaxy GXY-5148
My Friend John	JVC (J) VIJ-6442
My Friend John (alt)	Galaxy GCD-1016-2

Omit Cables.

Anthropology (1)	Galaxy GXY-5148
In A Mellotone (1)	JVC (J) VIJ-6442

ELVIN JONES QUARTET
Art Pepper (as); Roland Hanna (p); Richard Davis (b); Elvin Jones (d). *Englewood, New Jersey, June 13, 1979.*

Sweet Mama	Trio (J) PAP-9173
Zange	—
Tin Tin Deo	—

Same personnel. *Englewood, New Jersey, June 14, 1979.*

The Witching Hour	Trio (J) PAP-9173

HEART BEAT/ORIGINAL SOUND TRACK
JACK NITZSCHE (composer)
FEATURED SOLOIST: ART PEPPER
Art Pepper (as); others unidentified *Los Angeles, 1979*

On the Road	Capitol 500-12029
Jack's Theme	
Jam	
Neal's Theme	
901	

Note: Art Pepper solos on above titles and is not present on additional titles.

ISHIGURO KEI
Art Pepper (as); Tsunehide Matsuki (g); Hiromasa Suzuki (keyboard); Akira Okazawa (b); Syuichi Murakami (d); Ishiguro Kei (vo). *Tokyo, July 1979.*

Love Song of the Darkness (solo, obbligato & coda)	Victor (J) SJX 20174
Are You Free Tonight? (solo, obbligato & coda)	—

ART PEPPER QUARTET
Art Pepper (as); George Cables (p); Tony Dumas (b); Billy Higgins (d). *Tokyo, 1979*

True Blues	Pingham (J) RPJ 1002, Disques Dreyfus (F) 005	
Avalon	—	—
Over the Rainbow	—	—
Landscape	—	—
Red Car	—	—
Straight Life	—	—
Besame Mucho	—	—

ART PEPPER QUARTET
Art Pepper (as, cl-l); George Cables (p); Tony Dumas (b); Billy Higgins (d). *Tokyo, July 16, 1979*

True Blues	JVC (J) VIJ-6310, Galaxy GXY-5128, OJC-676		
Avalon	—	—	—
The Trip	JVC (J) VIJ-6372		
Landscape	JVC (J) VIJ-6310, Galaxy GXY-5128, OJC-676		
Sometime-1	—	—	—
Mambo de la Pinta	Galaxy GCD-1016-2, OJC-676		
Red Car	JVC (J) VIJ-6372		
Over the Rainbow	Galaxy GCD-1016-2		
Mambo Koyama	—		
Straight Life	—		
Besame Mucho	JVC (J) VIJ-6372		

same   *Tokyo, July 23, 1979*

True Blues	Galaxy GCD-1016-2

Avalon	—
The Shadow of Your Smile	JVC (J) VIJ-6372
Landscape	Galaxy GCD-1016-2
Sometime-1	—
Mambo de la Pinta	JVC (J) VIJ-6372
Red Car	Galaxy GCD-1016-2
Over the Rainbow	JVC (J) VIJ-6310, Galaxy GXY-5128, OJC-676
Mambo Koyama	Galaxy GCD-1016-2
Straight Life	JVC (J) VIJ-6310, Galaxy GXY-5128, OJC-676
Besame Mucho	Galaxy GCD-1016-2

JACK SHELDON & HIS WEST COAST FRIENDS
Jack Sheldon (tp); Art Pepper (as); Milcho Leviev (p); Tomy Dumas (b); Carl Burnett (d). *Hollywood, February 21 & 22, 1980.*

Angel Wings	Atlas (J) LA27-1001
Softly As In A Morning Sunrise	—
You'd Be So Nice To Come Home To	—
Jack's Blues	—
Broadway	—
Historia de un Amor	—
Minority	—
You'd Be So Nice To Come Home To (alt)	Atlas (J) LA27-1023
Broadway (alt)	—

PETE JOLLY & HIS WEST COAST FRIENDS
Art Pepper (as); Pete Jolly (p); Bob Magnusson (b); Roy McCurdy (d). *Hollywood, February 26 & 27, 1980.*

Strike Up the Band	Atlas (J) LA 27-1003
You Go To My Head	—
I Surrender Dear	—
Y.I. Blues	—
Night and Day	—
Everything Happens to Me	—
Out of Nowhere	—
Y.I. Blues (alt)	Atlas (J) LA27-1023

THE MILCHO LEVIEV QUARTET
Art Pepper (as); Milcho Leviev (p); Tony Dumas (b); Carl Burnett (d). *Ronnie Scott's, London, June 1980.*

Make a List, Make a Wish	Mole (E) 1
Sad, A Little Bit	—
Ophelia	—
Blues for the Fisherman	—

same   *Ronnie Soctt's, London, June 28-29, 1980*

True Blues	(Mole (E) 5
Goodbye	—
Y.I. Blues	—
Straight Life	—

same   *June 27, unknown location and year*

A Song for Richard	Fresh Sound (Sp) FSR CD 192

ART PEPPER
Art Pepper (as).   *New York, August 21, 1979.*
    But Beautiful   Galaxy GCD-1016-2
    When You're Smiling   —

ART PEPPER QUARTET
Art Pepper (as); Tommy Flanagan (p); Fred Mitchell (b); Billy Higgins (d).
Berkeley, September 21, 1979
    Surf Ride   Galaxy GXY-5127, OJC-475
    Nature Boy   —   —
    Nature Boy (alt)   Galaxy GCD-1016-2
    Straight Life   Galaxy GXY-5127, OJC-475
    September Song   —   —
    Long Ago and Far Away   Galaxy GCD-1016-2,   —
add Kenneth Nash (cowbell)
    Make a List   Galaxy GXY-5127,   —

ART PEPPER QUARTET
Art Pepper (as); Milcho Leviev (p); Bob Magnusson (b); Carl Burnett (d). *At-lanta, May 1980.*
    Patricia   Laserlight 17 012, Fresh Sound (Sp)
                                      FSR CD 192.

SONNY STITT & HIS WEST COAST FRIENDS
Art Pepper, Sonny Stitt (as, ts-1); Lou Levy (p); Chuck DeMonico (b); Carl
Burnett (d). *Hollywood, July 28 & 29, 1980.*
    Scrapple from the Apple   Atlas (J) LA27-1004
    Wee   —
    Bernie's Tune   —
    How High the Moon   —
    Walkin'   —
    Groovin' High   —

Russ Freeman (p); and John Heard (b) replace DeMonico and Burnett. *Hol-lywood, July 30 & 31, 1980.*
    Atlas Blues   Atlas (J) LA27-1007
    Lester Leaps In-1   —
    Autumn in New York   —
    My Funny Valentine   —
    Lover Man   —
    Imagination   —

ART PEPPER
Art Pepper (as, cl-1); Stanley Cowell (p); Howard Roberts (g); Cecil McBee
(b); Carl Burnett (d) with strings arranged by Bill Holman and Jimmy Bond.
Berkeley, September 3-4, 1980.
    Our Song   Galaxy GXY-5140, OJC-677
    Our Song (alt)   Galaxy GCD-1016-2,   —
    Here's That Rainy Day   Galaxy GXY-5140,   —
    Here's That Rainy Day (alt) Galaxy GCD-1016-2
    That's Love   Galaxy GXY-5140, OJC-677
    Winter Moon   —   —
    Winter Moon (alt)   Galaxy GCD-1016-2

When the Sun Comes out	Galaxy GXY-5140, OJC-677
When the Sun Comes Out (alt)	Galaxy GCD-1016-2
Blues in the Night-1	Galaxy GXY-5140, OJC-677
The Prisoner	— —
The Prisoner (alt)	Galaxy GCD-1016-2 —
Ol' Man River	— —

ART PEPPER

Art Pepper (as); Stanley Cowell (p); Howard Roberts (g); Cecil McBee (b); Billy Higgins (d). *Berkeley, September 5, 1980.*

Mr. Big Falls His J.G. Hand	Galaxy GXY-5141, OJC-678

omit Roberts

Close to You Alone	— —
There Will Never Be Another You	— —
There Will Never Be Another You (alt)	Galaxy GCD-1016-2 —
Melolev	Galaxy GXY-5141 —
Melolev (alt)	Galaxy GCD-1016-2 —
Goodbye, Again!	Galaxy GXY-5141 —
Goodbye, Again! (alt)	Galaxy GCD-1016-2 —

Roberts returns with two guitar parts; omit Cowell.

Brazil	Galaxy GXY-5141 —

SHELLY MANNE & HIS HOLLYWOOD ALL STARS

Bill Watrous (tb); Art Pepper (as); Bob Cooper (ts); Pete Jolly (p); Monty Budwig (b); Shelly Manne (b). *Hollywood, May 4, 1981.*

Just Friends	Atlas (J) LA27-1012
These Foolish Things	—
Hollywood Jam Blues	—
Lover Come Back To Me	—
Limehouse Blues	—
I'm Getting Sentimental Over You	—
I'm Getting Sentimental Over You (alt)	Atlas (J) LA27-1023

LEE KONITZ & HIS WEST COAST FRIENDS

Lee Konitz (as); Art Pepper (as, cl-l); Mike Lang (p); Bob Magnusson (b); John Dentz (d). *Hollywood, January 18 & 19, 1982.*

S'Wonderful	Atlas (J) La27-1016
S'Wonderful (alt)	Atlas (J) LA27-1023
Whims of Chambers	Atlas (J) LA27-1016
A Minor Blues in F	—
This Can't Be Love	—
The Shadow of Your Smile	—
Anniversary Song	—
Cherokee	—

ART PEPPER QUARTET

Art Pepper (as); Duke Jordan (p); David Williams (b); Carl Burnett (d). *Club Monmartre, Copenhagen, July 3, 1981.*

Blues Monmartre	Tofrec (J) 88916-7
What Is This Thing Called Love	—
Over the Rainbow	—
Caravan	—

Rhythmning	—
You Go To My Head	—
Besame Mucho	—
Cherokee	—
Radio Blues	—
Good Bait	—
All the Things You Are	—

ART PEPPER QUARTET

Art Pepper (as, cl-l); George Cables (p); David Willams (b); Carl Burnett (d). *Maiden Voyage, Los Angeles, August 13, 1981.*

Donna Lee	Galaxy GCD-1016-2, Galaxy OJCCD-680-2
What's New	Galaxy GXY-5151
Landscape	—, GCD-1016-2 (unedited)
Valse Triste	—
Thank You Blues	
(listed as For Freddie)	Galaxy GXY-5145

same personnel and location   *August 14, 1982*

Road Waltz	Galaxy GCD-1016-2, Galaxy OJCCD-680-2
For Freddie	—
But Beautiful	—, Galaxy OJCCD-680-2
Mambo Koyama	—
Landscape	—

same personnel and location   *August 15, 1982*

Roadgame	Galaxy GCD-1016-2
Mambo Koyama	Galaxy GXY-5151
Everything Happens to Me	Galaxy GXY-5142
Allen's Alley (Wee)	Galaxy GXY-5145
Road Waltz	Galaxy GXY-5142
Samba Mom Mom	Galaxy GXY-5145
When You're Smiling-1	Galaxy GXY-5142
Roadgame	—
For Freddie	Galaxy GCD-1016-2, Galaxy OJCCD-680-2
Arthur's Blues	— —

omit Williams and Burnett.

But Beautiful	Galaxy GXY-5145

ART PEPPER & ZOOT SIMS ALL STARS

Art Pepper (as); Zoot Sims (ts); Victor Feldman (p); Ray Brown (b); Billy Higgins (d). *Royce Hall, UCLA, September 27, 1981.*

Wee	West Wind (G) 2071
Blues	—

omit Zoot Sims; Charlie Haden (b) replaces Ray Brown.

Over the Rainbow	West Wind (G) 2071

ART PEPPER QUARTET

Art Pepper (as); George Cables (p); David Williams (b); Carl Burnett (d). *Tokyo, November 22, 1981*

Straight Life	Laserlight 17 012, Fresh Sound (Sp) FSR CD 192

same   *Tokyo, November 24, 1981*

Allen's Alley (Wee)	Laserlight 17 012, Fresh Sound (Sp) FSR CD 192

RICHIE COLE
Richie Cole (as, ts, bars); Art Pepper (as, cl); Roger Kellaway (p); Bob Magnusson (b); Billy Higgins (d). *San Francisco, February 16, 1982.*

Return to Alto Acres	Palo Alto PA 8023
Art's Opus #2	—
A&R	—
Palo Alto Blues	—
Broadway	

Note: Art Pepper not present on remaining title from this session.

ART PEPPER-JOE FARRELL QUINTET
Art Pepper (as); Joe Farrell (ts); George Cables (p); Tony Dumas (b); John Dentz (d). *Hollywood, March 23, 1982*

Section-8 Blues	Realtime RT-309
Sweet Lorraine	—
Mode for Joe	—
Who Can I Turn To	—

omit Farrell

Darn That Dream	—

ART PEPPER QUARTET
Art Pepper (as, cl-l); Roger Kellaway (p); David Williams (b); Carl Burnett (d). *Kool Jazz Festival, Washington, D.C., May 30, 1982.*

Landscape	Tofrec(J) TFCL-88918
Ophelia	—
Mambo Koyama	—
Over the Rainbow	—
When You're Smiling-1	—

ART PEPPER AND GEORGE CABLES
Art Pepper (as-l, cl-2); George Cables (p). *Berkeley, April 13-14, 1982.*

Over the Rainbow	Galaxy GXY-5147
Tête à Tête	—
Darn That Dream	—
Body and Soul	—
The Way You Look Tonight	—
'Round Midnight	—
A Night in Tunisia	Galaxy GCD-1016-2
Samba Mom Mom	—
Last Thing Blues 1&2	—
Over the Rainbow (alt)	—
Body and Soul (alt)	—

same personnel and location   *May 11, 1982*

Goin' Home-2	Galaxy GXY-5143 , OJC-679	
Samba Mom Mom	—	—
In a Mellow Tone-2	—	—
Don't Let the Sun Catch You Cryin'	—	—
Isn't She Lovely 1&2	—	—
Billie's Bounce	—	—
Lover Man-2	—	—
The Sweetest Sounds	—	—
You Go To My Head	Galaxy GXY-5147	

You Go To My Head (alt)   Galaxy GCD-1016-2, OJC-679
Stardust   —
Don't Let the Sun Catch You Cryin' (alt A)   —   , OJC-679
Darn That Dream   —
Don't Let the Sun Catch You Cryin' (alt B)   —

Note: Every Galaxy, Artists House, and JVC title listed herein also on Galaxy
    GCD-1016-2 (16-CD boxed set).

Index

Other titles of interest

CHASIN' THE TRANE
The Music and Mystique
of John Coltrane
J. C. Thomas
256 pp., 16 pp. of photos
80043-8 $12.95

DEXTER GORDON
A Musical Biography
Stan Britt
192 pp., 32 photos
80361-5 $13.95

THE FREEDOM PRINCIPLE
Jazz After 1958
John Litweiler
324 pp., 11 photos
80377-1 $13.95

FORCES IN MOTION
The Music and Thoughts
of Anthony Braxton
Graham Lock
412 pp., 16 photos, numerous illus.
80342-9 $15.95

ASCENSION
John Coltrane and his Quest
Eric Nisenson
298 pp.
80644-4 $13.95

JOHN COLTRANE
Bill Cole
278 pp., 25 photos
80530-8 $14.95

ORNETTE COLEMAN
A Harmolodic Life
John Litweiler
266 pp., 9 photos
80580-4 $14.95

MILES DAVIS
The Early Years
Bill Cole
256 pp.
80554-5 $13.95

FREE JAZZ
Ekkehard Jost
214 pp., 70 musical examples
80556-1 $13.95

BIRD: The Legend
of Charlie Parker
Edited by Robert Reisner
256 pp., 50 photos
80069-1 $13.95

**JAZZ MASTERS IN
TRANSITION 1957–1969**
Martin Williams
288 pp., 10 photos
80175-2 $13.95

A CENTURY OF JAZZ
From Blues to Bop, Swing to
Hip-Hop: A Hundred Years
of Music, Musicians,
Singers and Styles
Roy Carr
256 pp., $9\frac{5}{8} \times 11\frac{1}{2}$
350 illus., 200 in color
80778-5 $28.95

BIRD LIVES!
The High Life and Hard Times
of Charlie (Yardbird) Parker
Ross Russell
431 pp., 32 photos
80679-7 $15.95

IMPROVISATION
Its Nature and Practice in Music
Derek Bailey
172 pp., 12 photos
80528-6 $13.95

JAZZ STYLE IN
KANSAS CITY
AND THE SOUTHWEST
Ross Russell
342 pp., 80 photos
80748-3 $14.95

'ROUND ABOUT MIDNIGHT
A Portrait of Miles Davis
Updated Edition
Eric Nisenson
336 pp., 27 photos
80684-3 $14.95

Available at your bookstore

OR ORDER DIRECTLY FROM 1-800-386-5656

VISIT OUR WEBSITE AT WWW.PERSEUSBOOKSGROUP.COM

Made in United States
North Haven, CT
16 March 2024

50095118R00342